T0200400

Object-Oriented Systems Analysis and Design

Using UML

FOURTH EDITION

Object-Oriented Systems Analysis and Design

Using UML

FOURTH EDITION

Simon Bennett, Steve McRobb and Ray Farmer

London Boston Burr Ridge, IL Dubuque, IA Madison, WI New York San Francisco
St. Louis Bangkok Bogotá Caracas Kuala Lumpur Lisbon Madrid Mexico City
Milan Montreal New Delhi Santiago Seoul Singapore Sydney Taipei Toronto

Published by

 Higher
Education

An imprint of each of:

McGraw-Hill International (U.K.) Limited
Shoppenhangers Road
Maidenhead
Berkshire
SL6 2QL
England
Telephone: 44 (0) 1628 502 500
Fax: 44 (0) 1628 770 224

The McGraw-Hill Companies, Inc
The McGraw-Hill Building
1221 Avenue of the Americas
New York
New York 10020-1095
USA

Website: www.mheducation.co.uk
www.mheducation.com

British Library Cataloguing in Publication Data
A catalogue record for this book is available from the British Library
ISBN-13 978-0-07-712536-3
ISBN-10 0-07-712536-3

Library of Congress Cataloguing in Publication Data
The Library of Congress data for this book has been applied for from the Library of
Congress

Acquisitions Editor: Catriona Hoyle
Development Editor: Tom Hill
Marketing Manager: Alice Duijser
Head of Production: Beverley Shields
Cover design by: Adam Renvoize
Printed and bound in Great Britain by: Ashford Colour Press

Dedication

To all our families and friends

Brief Table of Contents

Preface		xi
Guided Tour		xvi
Technology to enhance learning and teaching		xviii
Custom Publishing Solutions		xix
Make the grade!		xx
Acknowledgements		xxi
About the Authors		xxiii
	Introduction	1
A1	Agate Ltd Case Study—Introduction	4
B1	FoodCo Ltd Case Study—Introduction	8
1	Information Systems—What Are They?	16
2	Challenges in Information Systems Development	43
3	Meeting the Challenges	64
4	What is Object-Orientation?	90
5	Modelling Concepts	113
6	Requirements Capture	138
A2	Agate Ltd Case Study—Requirements Model	169
7	Requirement Analysis	180
A3	Agate Ltd Case Study—Requirements Analysis	225
8	Refining the Requirements Model	233
9	Object Interaction	259
10	Specifying Operations	292
11	Specifying Control	313
A4	Agate Ltd Case Study—Further Analysis	338
12	Moving into Design	347
13	Systems Design and Architecture	363
14	Detailed Design	395
15	Design Patterns	422
16	Human–Computer Interaction	446
17	Designing Boundary Classes	469
18	Data Management Design	500
A5	Agate Ltd Case Study—Design	544
19	Implementation	559
20	Software Reuse	584
21	Software Development Processes	610
	Appendix A: Notation Summary	634
	Appendix B: Selected Solutions and Answer Pointers	643
	Glossary	655
	Bibliography	665
	Index	675

Detailed Table of Contents

Preface   xi
Guided Tour   xvi
Technology to enhance learning and
teaching   xviii
Custom Publishing Solutions   xix
Make the grade!   xx
Acknowledgements   xxi
About the Authors   xxiii

Introduction   1

**A1 Agate Ltd Case Study—
Introduction**   4
A1.1 Introduction to Agate   4
A1.2 Existing Computer Systems   5
A1.3 Business Activities in the Current
     System   5
A1.4 Summary of Requirements   6

**B1 FoodCo Ltd Case Study—
Introduction**   8
B1.1 Introduction to FoodCo   8
B1.2 FoodCo Today   11
B1.3 The Proposal   15

**1   Information Systems—
    What Are They?**   16
1.1   Introduction   16
1.2   Information Systems
      in History   17
1.3   Information Systems Today   20
1.4   What is a System?   22
1.5   Information and Information
      Systems   33
1.6   Strategies for Success   38
1.7   Summary   41

**2   Challenges in Information
    Systems Development**   43
2.1   Introduction   43
2.2   What Are the Challenges?   44
2.3   Why Things Go Wrong   52
2.4   The Ethical Dimension   56
2.5   Costs of Failure   60
2.6   Summary   61

3   Meeting the Challenges   64
3.1   Introduction   64
3.2   Responding to the Problems   66
3.3   Project Lifecycles   70
3.4   Methodological Approaches   77
3.5   Managing Information Systems
      Development   81
3.6   User Involvement   82
3.7   Software Development Tools   83
3.8   Summary   87

4   What is Object-Orientation?   90
4.1   Introduction   90
4.2   Basic Concepts   91
4.3   The Origins of Object-
      Orientation   106
4.4   Object-Oriented Languages
      Today   109
4.5   Summary   111

5   Modelling Concepts   113
5.1   Introduction   113
5.2   Models and Diagrams   114
5.3   Drawing Activity Diagrams   122
5.4   A Development Process   128
5.5   Summary   135

6   Requirements Capture   138
6.1   Introduction   138
6.2   User Requirements   138
6.3   Fact-Finding Techniques   142
6.4   User Involvement   150
6.5   Documenting Requirements   152
6.6   Use Cases   154
6.7   Requirements Capture and
      Modelling   163
6.8   Summary   164

**A2 Agate Ltd Case Study—
Requirements Model**   169
A2.1 Introduction   169
A2.2 Requirements List   169
A2.3 Actors and Use Cases   171
A2.4 Glossary   176
A2.5 Initial Architecture   177
A2.6 Activities of Requirements
     Modelling   178

                                                     vii

7 Requirements Analysis 180
7.1 Introduction 180
7.2 The Analysis Model 181
7.3 Analysis Class Diagram:
Concepts and Notation 184
7.4 Use Case Realization 194
7.5 Drawing a Class Diagram 197
7.6 Class Responsibility
Collaboration Cards 215
7.7 Assembling the Analysis Class
Diagram 218
7.8 Summary 219

**A3 Agate Ltd Case Study—
Requirements Analysis** 225
A3.1 Introduction 225
A3.2 Use Case Realizations 225
A3.3 Assembling the Analysis Class
Diagram 231
A3.4 Activities of Requirement
Analysis 232

**8 Refining the Requirements
Model** 233
8.1 Introduction 233
8.2 Software and Specification Reuse 234
8.3 Adding Further Structure 237
8.4 Reusable Software Components 246
8.5 Software Development Patterns 252
8.6 Summary 256

9 Object Interaction 259
9.1 Introduction 259
9.2 Object Interaction and
Collaboration 260
9.3 Interaction Sequence Diagrams 262
9.4 Communication Diagrams 280
9.5 Interaction Overview Diagrams 284
9.6 Timing Diagrams 286
9.7 Model Consistency 289
9.8 Summary 289

10 Specifying Operations 292
10.1 Introduction 292
10.2 Role of Operation Specifications 293
10.3 Contracts 294
10.4 Describing Operation Logic 295
10.5 Object Constraint Language 304
10.6 Creating an Operation
Specification 308
10.7 Summary 310

11 Specifying Control 313
11.1 Introduction 313
11.2 States and Events 314
11.3 Basic Notation 316
11.4 Further Notation 321
11.5 Preparing a State Machine 328
11.6 Protocol and Behavioural State
Machines 333
11.7 Consistency Checking 334
11.8 Quality Guidelines 335
11.9 Summary 335

**A4 Agate Ltd Case Study—
Further Analysis** 338
A4.1 Introduction 338
A4.2 Sequence Diagrams 339
A4.3 State Machines 341
A4.4 Operation Specifications 342
A4.5 Further Refinement of the Class
Diagram 343
A4.6 Further Activities of
Requirements Analysis 344

12 Moving into Design 347
12.1 Introduction 347
12.2 How is Design Different from
Analysis? 348
12.3 Logical and Physical Design 350
12.4 System Design and Detailed
Design 352
12.5 Qualities and Objectives of
Design 354
12.6 Summary 360

13 System Design and Architecture 363
13.1 Introduction 363
13.2 What Do We Mean by
Architecture? 364
13.3 Why Produce Architectural
Models? 367
13.4 Influences on System
Architecture 369
13.5 Architectural Styles 372
13.6 Concurrency 387
13.7 Processor Allocation 389
13.8 System Design Standards 389
13.9 Agate Software Architecture 390
13.10 Summary 392

14 Detailed Design 395
14.1 Introduction 395
14.2 What Do We Add in Object-Oriented Detailed Design? 396
14.3 Attribute and Operation Specification 396
14.4 Grouping Attributes and Operations in Classes 403
14.5 Designing Associations 410
14.6 Integrity Constraints 416
14.7 Designing Operation Algorithms 419
14.8 Summary 420

15 Design Patterns 422
15.1 Introduction 422
15.2 Software Development Patterns 423
15.3 Documenting Patterns—Pattern Templates 424
15.4 Design Patterns 426
15.5 How to Use Design Patterns 441
15.6 Benefits and Dangers of Using Patterns 443
15.7 Summary 444

16 Human–Computer Interaction 446
16.l Introduction 446
16.2 User Interface 447
16.3 Approaches to User Interface Design 456
16.4 Standards and Legal Requirements 464
16.5 Summary 466

17 Designing Boundary Classes 469
17.1 Introduction 469
17.2 Architecture of the Presentation Layer 470
17.3 Prototyping the User Interface 471
17.4 Designing Classes 475
17.5 Designing Interaction with Sequence Diagrams 479
17.6 Class Diagram Revisited 487
17.7 User Interface Design Patterns 488
17.8 Modelling the Interface Using State Machines 489
17.9 Summary 497

18 Data Management Design 500
18.1 Introduction 500
18.2 Persistence 501

18.3 File Systems 504
18.4 Database Management Systems 511
18.5 Designing for Relational Database Management Systems 516
18.6 Designing for Object Database Management Systems 524
18.7 Distributed Databases 529
18.8 Designing Data Management Classes 532
18.9 Summary 541

A5 Agate Ltd Case Study—Design 544
A5.1 Introduction 544
A5.2 Architecture 544
A5.3 Sample Use Case 546
A5.4 Class Diagrams 546
A5.5 Sequence Diagrams 552
A5.6 Database Design 555
A5.7 State Machines 555
A5.8 Activities of Design 557

19 Implementation 559
19.1 Introduction 559
19.2 Software Implementation 560
19.3 Component Diagrams 564
19.4 Deployment Diagrams 566
19.5 Software Testing 569
19.6 Data Conversion 573
19.7 User Documentation and Training 574
19.8 Implementation Strategies 575
19.9 Review and Maintenance 577
19.10 Summary 582

20 Software Reuse 584
20.1 Introduction 584
20.2 Why Reuse? 585
20.3 Planning a Strategy for Reuse 592
20.4 Commercially Available Componentware 595
20.5 Case Study Example 597
20.6 Web Services 605
20.7 Summary 607

21 Software Development Processes 610
21.1 Introduction 610
21.2 Process, Method and Methodology 611
21.3 Unified Software Development Process 614
21.4 Dynamic Systems Development Method 618

21.5 Scrum   624
21.6 eXtreme Programming   625
21.7 Issues in Choosing a
     Methodology   627
21.8 Hard *v.* Soft Methodologies   629
21.9 Summary   631

Appendix A: Notation Summary   634
Use Case Diagram   634
Static Structure Diagrams   634
Behaviour Diagrams   636
Interaction Diagrams   638
Implementation Diagrams   642

**Appendix B: Selected Solutions
and Answer Pointers**   643
Answers to Selected Review Questions   643
Answer Pointers for Selected Case
Study Work, Exercises and Projects   650
Glossary   655
Bibliography   665
Index   675

Background to the Book

At the time that we wrote the first edition of this book, universities such as De Montfort University, where we all worked, were just beginning to teach object-oriented analysis and design on undergraduate courses. Now object-oriented approaches are widely used and taught. Back in 1997 we wanted a book to support our teaching, one that put the analysis and design activities in the context of the whole systems life cycle, and that included generic analysis and design issues, such as fact finding. Most books on object-oriented approaches to analysis and design concentrated on object-orientation and on the notation. We also wanted a textbook that used a consistent case study throughout.

When McGraw-Hill offered us the opportunity to write our own book, these two ideas influenced the structure and content of the book that we put together. This is now the fourth edition of the book.

Since the publication of the first edition in 1999, many things have changed. Two of us left De Montfort University, though one has now returned in a non-academic role, having used UML and trained people in UML over the last ten years in three different jobs in industry. As well as our careers, our ideas have developed, helped in large part by all the feedback and reviews that we have received. UML itself has also changed, with the introduction of Version 2.0, which prompted the third edition, and has also become more widely accepted as the common language for systems modelling. But we still believe in the value for teaching and learning of basing the book around a consistent thread of case study material, and have therefore retained this approach in this new edition.

Who Should Read this Book?

The three authors of this book believe that systems analysis and design are activities that should take place in the context of the organizations that will use the information systems that are the result. The examples we use are based on business organizations, but they could be any kind of organization in the public or voluntary (not-for-profit) sectors, and the approach we adopt is suitable for most kinds of information system including real-time systems. The book starts with three chapters that set the development of information systems in this context.

We expect most of our readers to be students undertaking a Diploma, Bachelor's or Master's course in a computing or information systems subject. It will also be of relevance to some students of other subjects, such as business studies, who want to understand how business information systems are developed without wanting to be programmers, analysts or designers.

The book is also suitable for professionals in computing and information systems, many of whom began their professional career before the advent of object-oriented development techniques and who want to upgrade their skills by learning about object-oriented analysis and design. We have used the Unified Modelling Language (UML), which is the de facto standard notation for object-oriented development.

Case Studies

In our teaching and training we use case studies as the basis of tutorials and practical work. We also use the same case studies to provide examples in taught material and in student assessments. We believe that it is important that students see analysis and design as a coherent process that goes from initial fact-finding through to implementation, and not as a series of disjointed exercises. This book uses two practical case studies. The first of these, Agate Ltd, is an advertising company. Agate is used for examples in most of the chapters of the book that explain techniques and for some exercises. The second case study, FoodCo Ltd, is a grower of fruit and vegetables and a manufacturer of packaged foods. FoodCo is used for most of the exercises that are included in chapters for the reader to complete.

The two case studies are introduced in short chapters (A1 and B1) that can be found after the Introduction. In these first two case study chapters, we provide background material about the two companies and explain some of their requirements for computerized information systems. Chapter A2 (between Chapters 6 and 7) presents examples of the requirements model, while Chapter A3 (between Chapters 7 and 8) brings together some examples from the first version of the analysis model for Agate's new system. Chapter A4 (between Chapters 11 and 12) presents examples from the analysis model after it has been further developed. Chapter A5 (between Chapters 18 and 19) brings together some examples from the design model for the new system. We do not provide models for the FoodCo case study, but FoodCo forms the basis of most of the practical exercises at the end of chapters. A few partial solutions are provided where they are required as the basis for later exercises.

If you are using this book as a teacher, you are welcome to use these materials and to develop them further as the basis of practical exercises and assessments. Some exercises that you may want to use are provided in each chapter. Further models, solutions and case studies are provided on the book's website, and this will continue to develop over time.

Exercises for Readers

Each chapter contains two kinds of exercises for readers. First we provide Review Questions. The aim of these is to allow you to check that you have understood the material in the chapter that you have just read. Most of these Review Questions should only take a few minutes at most to complete. Solutions to some of these questions are to be found at the back of the book. The answers to many of them are to be found in the text. Some require you to apply the techniques you have learned, and the answers to these are not always provided.

At the end of each chapter are Case Study Work, Exercises and Projects. These are exercises that will take longer to complete. Some are suitable to be used as tutorial exercises or homework, some could be used as assignments, and some are longer projects that could be developed over a matter of weeks. We have provided answer pointers to some of these exercises to help you.

Solutions to more of these exercises are available via the book's website to bona fide university and college teachers who adopt the book as the set text for their courses. Please visit www.mheducation.co.uk/textbooks/bennett4 for details of the support materials.

Structure of the Book

Although we have not formally divided the book into sections, there are four parts to the book, each of which has a different focus.

Part 1

The new Introduction explains the roles of systems analysts and designers. Chapters 1 to 4 provide the background to information systems analysis and design and to object-orientation. In the first three of these chapters we explain why analysis and design are important in the development of computerized systems and introduce fundamental concepts such as those of systems theory. Chapter 4 introduces some of the ideas of object-orientation that will be developed in the second part.

Part 2

The second part of the book includes Chapters 5 to 11. The focus of this part of the book is on the activities of requirements gathering and systems analysis and the basic notation of the Unified Modelling Language (UML). In it we introduce use cases, class diagrams, sequence diagrams, communication diagrams, activity diagrams, state-chart diagrams and the Object Constraint Language (OCL). Chapter 5, which was added for the second edition, discusses models and diagrams and presents one of the UML diagramming techniques—activity diagrams—as an example. In Chapter 5 we also provide an overview of the way the UML techniques fit together in the iterative development lifecycle. This part includes three case study chapters (A2, A3 and A4), which illustrate the development of the UML models as the analysis activities progress. The purpose of the case study chapters in the book is to show how the models develop as the analysis and design progress. We do not have the space in the book to provide all the analysis and design documentation.

Part 3

The third part of the book is about system design. It includes Chapters 12 to 18 and concludes with examples from the design model for the Agate case study (Chapter A5). In this part we develop the use of most of the diagramming techniques introduced in Part 2. We do this by enhancing the analysis models that we have produced to take design decisions into account. This part covers system architecture, system design, design patterns, and the design of objects, user interfaces and data storage. The design model at the end of this part serves the same purpose as the one at the end of the analysis chapters. Some of the material about architecture that was in Chapter 12 in the third edition has moved to the book's website.

Part 4

In the final part we cover the implementation of systems and the issues of how the systems lifecycle is organised and how reusable components can be developed. The chapter on implementation introduces the last of the UML diagram types, component diagrams and deployment diagrams. The chapter on project management that was in the first and second editions is available on the book's website as part of an attempt to keep the page count, and hence the price, at a reasonable level.

Pathways through the Book

Whatever the formal structure of the book, you the reader are welcome to work through it in whatever order you like. However, the book has been written to be read sequentially and not used as a reference, as one critical reviewer pointed out on Amazon. One of the authors has written another book on UML, also published by McGraw-Hill, that can more easily be used as a reference book.

We have taught several analysis and design modules at both undergraduate and postgraduate levels. These include a first-year module on analysis and design, with the emphasis on the lifecycle and on analysis; and a second-year module with an emphasis on design and the use of methodologies. We would expect to cover the following chapters in each module.

Analysis module–Chapters 1, 2, 3, 4, 5, 6, 7, 8, 9, 10. (State-chart diagrams are omitted from this so that students are not overloaded with different diagramming notations in the first year.)

Design module–Chapters 11, 12, 13, 14 15, 16, 17, 18, 19, 20, 21, 22 (available from the book website).

We have tried to group together techniques under the general headings of analysis and design, even though many of them are used throughout the lifecycle. This does not mean that we necessarily advocate following a lifecycle model that treats analysis and design as separate phases. We suggest an iterative lifecycle in which the models of the system are progressively elaborated and in which analysis and design are interwoven. However, we do believe that analysis and design are separate activities, even if they are not separate stages in a project's lifecycle. We also think that it is easier to learn analysis and design as separate activities rather than merged together.

If plan to use this book for a course that concentrates on UML, then you may want to use the following path through the book–Chapters 5, 6, 7, 8, 9, 10, 11, 17, 18, 19, and including the case study chapters. The other chapters can be read as background.

If you are familiar with the general aspects of information systems development and of object-orientation, and are reading this book in order to gain an understanding of how you can use UML in analysis and design, then you can start with the Introduction and case study chapters, and then go to Chapter 5. If you are not familiar with object-oriented approaches, then you should also include Chapter 4.

Transferable Skills

Some of the skills of the systems analyst and designer can be classified as transferable or professional skills. Most employers place a high value on these skills. Many colleges and universities provide special modules on these skills, embed them in other modules or provide self-study packages for students. We have included material on fact-finding skills, particularly interviewing and questionnaire design, within the text of the book. We have not included other skills explicitly, but there are opportunities for teachers to use the exercises to develop skills in problem solving, group work, research, report writing and oral presentation.

Website and Support Materials

This book is supported by materials that we have placed on the book's website. The website is accessible at www.mheducation.co.uk/textbooks/bennett4/. The website material has been revised for the fourth edition. It includes self-test exercises for students.

Materials for lecturers also include Microsoft PowerPoint slides to accompany each chapter, solutions to some of the exercises and copies of the figures from the book that can be used for teaching. If you use these resources in your teaching materials, we ask that you acknowledge our copyright on the material. With every new edition, reviewers ask us to include more, but rarely agree on what to add or what can be taken out. With this in mind, we have added new short sections to the website that supplement some of the chapters in the book.

We welcome feedback about the book. Some of the changes that we have made in writing the third and fourth editions have been based on feedback from lecturers and students around the world who have used our book. You can email us at authors@ OOADtext.info or write to us care of McGraw-Hill at the address at the beginning of the book.

Latest Version of UML
This edition is based on UML Version 2.2, finalized in February 2009.

Changes in the Fourth Edition
The fourth edition has some significant changes from the third. All chapters have been revised and updated to reflect developments in the worlds of object-oriented analysis and design and information systems development, the evolution of UML and changes in our own thinking. Chapters 12, 13 and 14 have been reorganized to reinstate a chapter on the difference between analysis and design. A summary of changes is available on the website. This is provided for lecturers who need to revise their teaching materials.

Notation
We have used certain notational conventions in the book. New terms are shown in *italics* at the point where they are introduced and explained. Terms from the case study and code examples are shown in Courier font. Where we explain UML notation we use a variant of the Backus-Naur Form (BNF) that is close to that used in the UML Specification itself. Notation definitions are in italics to distinguish them from examples.

All names of special UML terms are enclosed between angle brackets (e.g., *<message-name>*).

All keywords, strings, etc. are enclosed between single quotes (e.g., *'loop'* or *'['*).

Rules that define a special UML term are signified with *::=* between the term and its definition.

Repetition of an item is signified by an asterisk placed after that item: ***.

Alternative choices are separated by the *|* symbol (e.g., *<alternative-A>* | *<alternative-B>*).

Items that are optional are enclosed in square brackets (e.g., *[<item-x>]*).

Where items need to be grouped they are enclosed in simple parenthesis; for example: *(<item-1>|<item-2>) **

signifies a sequence of one or more items, each of which is *<item-1>* or *<item-2>*.

Simon Bennett, Steve McRobb, Ray Farmer
February 2010

Guided Tour

Learning Objectives

Each chapter opens with a set of Learning Objectives, introducing the reader to the topics they should have come to understand after having worked through the chapter.

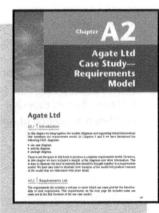

delivered?
n time to be useful?

n happen during the course of the proje
ts and ultimately whether a satisfactory s

ange over time, typically because users a
they learn more about the proposed syste
, it is called *requirements drift*. This can
fecting both the progress and the costs. In
ose sight of the original reason for the sys
nable to prevent all change requests, bec
example, staff at an insurance office ma
stem for recording details of vehicle accide
sessor at the scene of an accident could
not have been thought of when staff wer
stem. However, change requests can be
The longer a project proceeds, the more c

New Terms

New terms are highlighted as they are introduced in each chapter. UML terms are defined in the Glossary in the appendices.

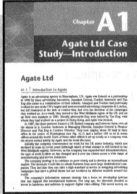

Case Studies

Two practical case studies are used: one to illustrate the approach and for worked examples; the other for exercises for the reader.

Case Study Development

One of the case studies is developed at four points in the book to reflect the way in which models and documents would evolve through the development lifecycle.

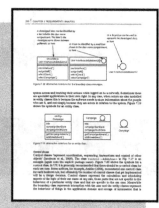

Practical Examples

Practical examples based on the case studies are developed throughout the book to show how the UML techniques are applied.

Chapter Summary

Each chapter closes with a summary of the key points covered in that chapter.

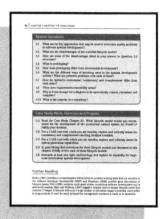

Review Questions and Exercises

At the end of each chapter, the reader will find questions to test their knowledge of the material covered and practical case study exercises and small projects to try. Solutions to some review questions and answer pointers for some exercises are provided in the appendices.

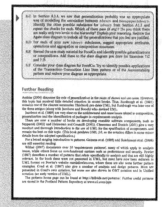

Further Reading

An annotated list of suggested further reading is provided at the end of each chapter. A full bibliography is included in the appendices.

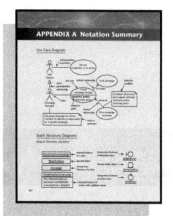

Notation Summary

A summary of the key UML notation for each type of diagram is provided in the appendices.

Technology to enhance learning and teaching

Visit www.mheducation.co.uk/textbooks/bennett4 today

Online Learning Centre (OLC)

After completing each chapter, log on to the supporting Online Learning Centre website. Take advantage of the study tools offered to reinforce the material you have read in the text. Resources include:

For lecturers:

- PowerPoint Slides
- Guide to new edition
- Solutions Manual

For students:

- Additional Chapters
- Multiple Choice Questions
- Web Links
- Glossary

Visit www.mheducation.co.uk/textbooks/bennett4 today

Custom Publishing Solutions: Let us help make our **content** your **solution**

At McGraw-Hill Education our aim is to help lecturers to find the most suitable content for their needs delivered to their students in the most appropriate way. Our **custom publishing solutions** offer the ideal combination of content delivered in the way which best suits lecturer and students.

Our custom publishing programme offers lecturers the opportunity to select just the chapters or sections of material they wish to deliver to their students from a database called CREATE™ at

http://create.mheducation.com/uk/

CREATE™ contains over two million pages of content from:

- textbooks
- professional books
- case books – Harvard Articles, Insead, Ivey, Darden, Thunderbird and BusinessWeek
- Taking Sides – debate materials

across the following imprints:

- McGraw-Hill Education
- Open University Press
- Harvard Business Publishing
- US and European material

There is also the option to include additional material authored by lecturers in the custom product – this does not necessarily have to be in English.

We will take care of everything from start to finish in the process of developing and delivering a custom product to ensure that lecturers and students receive exactly the material needed in the most suitable way.

With a Custom Publishing Solution, students enjoy the best selection of material deemed to be the most suitable for learning everything they need for their courses – something of real value to support their learning. Teachers are able to use exactly the material they want, in the way they want, to support their teaching on the course.

Please contact your local McGraw-Hill representative with any questions or alternatively contact Warren Eels e: warren.eels@mheducation.com.

Make the grade!

Acknowledgements

Our thanks go to the following reviewers for their comments at various stages in the text's development:

Klaas van den Berg	University of Twente
Huseyin Dagdeviren	University of Westminster
Mike Eccles	University of Cape Town
David Evans	Aston University
Charlie He	University of Ulster
Sam Lubbe	University of South Africa
Graham Mansfield	Staffordshire University
Farid Meziane	University of Salford
Simon Polovina	Sheffield Hallam University
Geoff Rubner	University of Manchester
Bob Solomon	University of Warwick
David Styles	City University, London

Our thanks also go to Jane Adams, Royal Literary Fund Fellow at De Montfort University, for her advice on our writing style and suggestions for improvements.

Extracts from OMG, *UML 2.2 Specification*, copyright © 1997–2009 Object Management Group. Reproduced with permission. Copyright © 2001–2003 Adaptive Ltd., Alcatel, Borland Software Corporation, Computer Associates International, Inc., Telefonaktiebolaget LM Ericsson, Fujitsu, Hewlett-Packard Company, I-Logix, Inc., International Business Machines Corporation, IONA Technologies, Kabira Technologies, Inc., MEGA International, Motorola, Inc., Oracle Corporation, SOFTEAM, Telelogic AB, Unisys, X-Change Technologies Group, LLC.

Extracts from Checkland/Scholes, SOFT SYSTEM METHODOLOGY IN ACTION. © 1990 John Wiley and Sons Ltd. Reproduced with permission.

Extract from Alexander et al., A PATTERN LANGUAGE: TOWNS, BUILDING, CONSTRUCTION. © 1977 Oxford University Press. Reproduced with permission.

Extract from Gabriel, PATTERNS OF SOFTWARE: TALES FROM THE SOFTWARE COMMUNITY. © 1996 Oxford University Press. Reproduced with permission.

Extracts from Garland/Anthony, *Large-Scale Software Architecture: A Practical Guide Using UML*, 2003. Copyright John Wiley and Sons Ltd. Reproduced with permission.

Definition of Architecture (page 365) reprinted with permission from IEEE *Standard 1471-2000*, 'IEEE Recommended Practice for Architectural Description of Software-Intensive Systems' by IEEE. The IEEE disclaims any responsibility or liability resulting from the placement and use in the described manner.

Figure from Allen/Frost, COMPONENT-BASED DEVELOPMENT FOR ENTERPRISE SYSTEMS. © 1998 by Cambridge University Press. Adapted with permission.

Extracts from Apperly/Hofman/Latchem/Maybank/McGibbon/Piper/Simons, SERVICE- AND COMPONENT-BASED DEVELOPMENT: USING THE SELECT PERSPECTIVE AND UML. © 2003 Pearson Education Ltd. Reprinted by permission of Pearson Education Ltd.

Screenshot from Enterprise Architect used by permission of Sparx Systems Pty Ltd.

About the Authors

The author team of Simon Bennett, Steve McRobb and Ray Farmer have worked together on editions of this text since 1999, when the first edition was published. Their collaboration combines a wealth of academic experience in teaching and researching in the Information Systems discipline. Their considerable industry experience also ensures a practical understanding of implementing UML in real organizations.

Simon Bennett is Training Consultant in the Faculty of Technology at De Montfort University, where he provides training in UML, analysis and design, and systems architecture. He is an associate member of the Centre for Computational Intelligence. He has previously held posts as an Enterprise Architect for Celesio AG and as Head of ICT for the Department of Regeneration and Culture at Leicester City Council, and taught as a Principal Lecturer at De Montfort University until 1999. Simon co-authored *Schaum's Outline of UML* (2nd edition), also published by McGraw-Hill.

Steve McRobb is a Principal Lecturer in the Department of Informatics at De Montfort University. He has taught object-oriented systems analysis and design for well over a decade and is currently course leader for popular MSc courses in Computing, Information Technology and Information Systems Management. His recent research is mainly in the areas of online privacy and the effects of ICT on power relationships. Steve was formerly Principal Administration Officer at the Yorkshire Dales National Park.

Ray Farmer is an Associate Dean in the Faculty of Engineering and Computing at Coventry University. His research interests include information systems analysis and design, service-oriented architecture and pedagogical developments in engineering and computing education. He regularly acts as a consultant on object-oriented analysis and design in the UK and internationally. Ray has previously held various posts in the Department of Information Systems at De Montfort University.

Introduction

to be made, from the very long specification to the detailed design… What will the users…

LEARNING OBJECTIVES

In this introductory chapter you will learn
☑ what is meant by systems analysis and design.

This book is about systems analysis and systems design, but what exactly do we mean by these terms?

Many people are familiar with the idea of computer programming. They understand that to get a computer to perform the kind of complex tasks involved in running a business, someone has to write a series of instructions that specify precisely what the computer should do. These instructions, written in programming languages such as C++, Java or C#, form what we are all familiar with as computer software.

However, fewer people are aware of the work that has to be done before the programmer can start writing the program code. The programmer cannot simply make up the rules that guide the operation of the business or guess at the kind of data that needs to be entered into the system, stored and later accessed to provide users with information on-screen or in reports. It is the work of the systems analyst to investigate the way the business works, to understand and document the existing system, whether it is manual or already computerized, and to record the type of data values the business needs to operate and the rules that determine how that data will be processed.

The *systems analyst* produces a specification of what the new system must do. This specification will define in clear and unambiguous terms most of the following aspects of the system:

- the characteristics of the data that needs to be held in the system;
- the rules to be used to ensure that the data that is entered is correct;
- the rules that describe how the data is to be processed;
- the layout and content of windows for data entry, enquiries and reports;
- the rules that ensure that only those people who are entitled to access the data can do so;
- expectations about the performance of the system, for example how much data it must handle and how quickly it must process requests for information.

1

Some of the early part of this work may be done by a specialist *business analyst*, whose expertise lies in understanding the way the organization wants the system to work and documenting those requirements in a way that the systems analyst can use. We include the work of the business analyst in the more general term systems analysis.

Given such a specification it is possible to build a computer system, but there are many ways that it could be built. If you give an engineer a specification that states the need for a river crossing, he or she can choose to build a ferry system, a tunnel or a bridge. If a bridge is the solution, there are many possible ways of supporting the roadway. The engineer designing the bridge can choose whether to make it a suspension bridge, how many pillars to use to support the roadway, how many lanes wide the roadway should be, whether to include a cycle path and footway. There are hundreds of design decisions to be made, from the very large scale down to the detailed design of hand rails for pedestrian users.

The *systems designer* performs a similar role in designing a new computerized information system. Given a specification of **what** the system must do, there will be many different possibilities for **how** the system will perform the required processes. The role of the system designer is to choose from that wide range of possibilities the design that will best meet the needs of the users and other people with an interest in the success of the system, such as the management of the organization where it will be used. In choosing that optimal design, the system designer will take into account not only the specification of what the system must do, but also all the expectations about how much data the system can handle, how fast it must respond, and so on.

Based on the specification produced by the systems analyst, the system designer produces a specification of how the new system will work. This specification will define in clear and unambiguous terms most of the following aspects of the system:

- how the system as a whole will be organized into modules and subsystems, how these will interact with each other and how they will be allocated to different processors and computers;
- the programming languages and ready-made software components that will be used to construct the software;
- in an object-oriented system, the specification of the classes that will deliver the system's functionality and hold its data when programs are running;
- the structures in the database where data will be stored and the characteristics of the data that needs to be held in the system;
- the detailed logic of the algorithms that will operate upon the data and meet the performance requirements of the system;
- the physical look and feel of the windows for data entry, enquiries and reports, including their colour schemes, fonts and the exact kinds of interface 'widgets' to be used–text boxes, radio buttons, etc.;
- the way in which a security subsystem will control access to the system;
- how the system will meet requirements for volumes of data and the rate at which that data can be processed and the users' requests can be responded to.

It is this design that the programmer then takes and converts into program code that will become the working information system.

Choosing to use an object-oriented programming language (see Chapter 4 for an explanation of object-orientation) is one of the decisions that has to be made early on in a project to develop a new system, and, if an object-oriented language is to be used, then it makes sense to carry out the analysis and design in a way that will easily translate into object-oriented program code.

The Unified Modelling Language (UML) is a way of documenting the outputs from the analysis and design activities in a way that makes it easy for the programmer to translate the design into code. UML is a standard notation for the models that are produced to document the analysis and design. Having a standard notation makes it easier to communicate between different teams.

Of course in the real world nothing is as clear cut as we have described above. You will find people with job titles like analyst/programmer, who talk to the users, analyse and document their requirements, design the solution and write the code. In some projects, management will want all the analysis completed before the design can begin. In others, as soon as a critical mass of analysis material is available, the designers will get to work, and the programmers may even begin producing initial versions of the software while the requirements are still being defined.

As you will read in Chapter 2, which describes some of the challenges that occur when developing information systems, this is not an easy process. There are many views on how to increase the likelihood that an organization going through the process of having a new system developed will get what it wants. Some see it as an engineering problem, arguing that the development of systems should be made more like the engineering of products such as bridges, cars or aircraft. Others argue that it is the human elements of systems (the people that use them) that make the job of developing systems so challenging, and systems analysis and design should take the socio-technical context of systems into account more than it does. Both views have some merit.

In this book, we explain what a system is and outline the challenges of developing information systems and some of the ways that people have proposed for addressing those challenges. We then work through the lifecycle of developing a system, from the business analysis to the design, and finish by explaining some of the points to be addressed in implementation and some methods that have been proposed for organizing this process.

Real information systems exist in businesses and other organizations in the real world. To illustrate the development of real systems we use case studies of two companies—one for examples in the book and the other for exercises for the reader. After introducing the two case studies we begin in Chapter 1 with an explanation of the theory of systems using some practical examples that should be familiar.

Agate Ltd Case Study—Introduction

Agate Ltd

A1.1 | Introduction to Agate

Agate is an advertising agency in Birmingham, UK. Agate was formed as a partnership in 1982 by three advertising executives, Amarjeet Grewal, Gordon Anderson and Tim Eng (the name is a combination of their initials). Amarjeet and Gordon had previously worked for one of the UK's largest and most successful advertising companies in London, but felt frustrated at the lack of control they had over the direction of the campaigns they worked on. As a result, they moved to the West Midlands region of the UK and set up their own business in 1981. Shortly afterwards they were joined by Tim Eng, with whom they had worked on a project in Hong Kong, and Agate was formed.

In 1987, the three partners formed a UK limited company and between them own all the shares in it. Gordon Anderson is Managing Director, Amarjeet Grewal is Finance Director and Tim Eng is Creative Director. They now employ about 50 staff at their office in the centre of Birmingham (see Fig. A1.1) and a further 100 or so at seven offices around the world. Each of these other offices is set up locally as a company with the shares owned jointly by Agate and the local directors.

Initially the company concentrated on work for the UK motor industry, which has declined in scale in recent years (although much of what remains is still located in the West Midlands region). However, as the company has expanded and internationalized, the type of work it takes on has changed and it now has clients across a wide range of manufacturing and service industries.

The company strategy is to continue to grow slowly and to develop an international market. The directors would like to obtain business from more large multinational companies. They feel that they can offer a high standard of service in designing advertising campaigns that have a global theme but are localized for different markets around the world.

The company's information systems strategy has a focus on developing systems that can support this international business. Not long ago, the directors decided to invest in hardware and software to support digital video editing. This saved money on

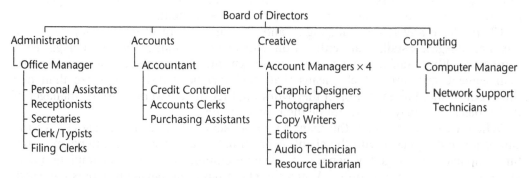

Figure A1.1 Staff at Agate Ltd UK office.

subcontracting the video-editing work, and with cheap broadband access they have the capability for fast file-transfer of digital video between offices. Now they are considering whether the company should also install its own video streaming servers for use in the growing market for online advertising.

A1.2 Existing Computer Systems

Agate already uses computers extensively. Like most companies in the world of design and creativity, Agate uses Apple Macintosh computers for its graphic designers and other design-oriented staff. The secretaries and personal assistants also use Apple Macs. However, the company also uses PCs to run accounts software in Microsoft Windows. Despite all this, Agate has been slow to install computer systems that support other business processes, such as tracking clients and managing campaigns. Last year, Agate had a basic business system for the UK office developed in Delphi for Windows. However, after the system was developed, the directors of Agate decided that it should have a system developed in Java, the object-oriented language originated by Sun Microsystems Inc. One of the reasons for the choice of Java was that it is portable across different hardware platforms and the company wants software that could run both on the PCs and on the Macs. Unfortunately, the person who developed the Delphi software for the company (and was going to rewrite it in Java) was headhunted by an American software house, because of her skills in Java, and has moved to the USA. Fortunately, this developer, Mandy Botnick, was methodical in her work and has left Agate with some object-oriented system documentation for the system she designed and developed.

This existing system is limited in its scope: it only covers core business information requirements within Agate. It was intended that it would be extended to cover most of Agate's activities and to deal with the international way in which the business operates.

A1.3 Business Activities in the Current System

Agate deals with other companies that it calls clients. A record is kept of each client company, and each client company has one person who is the main contact person within that company. His or her name and contact details are kept in the client record. Similarly, Agate nominates a member of staff–a director, an account manager or a member of the creative team–to be the contact for each client.

Clients have advertising campaigns, and a record is kept of every campaign. One member of Agate's staff, again either a director or an account manager, manages each campaign. Other staff may work on a campaign and Agate operates a project-based management structure, which means that staff may be working on more than one project at a time. For each project they work on, they are answerable to the manager of that project, who may or may not be their own line manager.

When a campaign starts, the manager responsible estimates the likely cost of the campaign, and agrees it with the client. A finish date may be set for a campaign at any time, and may be changed. When the campaign is completed, an actual completion date and the actual cost are recorded. When the client pays, the payment date is recorded. Each campaign includes one or more adverts. Adverts can be one of several types:

- newspaper advert–including written copy, graphics and photographs
- magazine advert–including written copy, graphics and photographs
- Internet advert–including written copy, graphics, photographs and animations
- TV advert–using video, library film, actors, voice-overs, music etc.
- radio advert–using audio, actors, voice-overs, music etc.
- poster advert–using graphics, photographs, actors
- leaflet–including written copy, graphics and photographs.

Purchasing assistants are responsible for buying space in newspapers and magazines, space on advertising hoardings, and TV or radio air-time. The actual cost of a campaign is calculated from a range of information. This includes:

- cost of staff time for graphics, copy-writing etc.
- cost of studio time and actors
- cost of copyright material–photographs, music, library film
- cost of space in newspapers, air-time and advertising hoardings
- Agate's margin on services and products bought in.

This information is held in a paper-based filing system, but the total estimated cost and the final actual cost of a campaign are held on the new computer system.

The new system also holds the salary grades and pay rates for the staff, so that the cost of staff time on projects can be calculated from the timesheets that they fill out. This functionality has been partially implemented and is not used in the existing system.

A1.4 Summary of Requirements

This section summarizes the requirements for the new system.

1. **To record details of Agate's clients and the advertising campaigns for those clients.**
   1.1 To record names, address and contact details for each client.
   1.2 To record the details of each campaign for each client. This will include the title of the campaign, planned start and finish dates, estimated costs, budgets, actual costs and dates, and the current state of completion.

1.3 To provide information that can be used in the separate accounts system for invoicing clients for campaigns.

1.4 To record payments for campaigns that are also recorded in the separate accounts system.

1.5 To record which staff are working on which campaigns, including the campaign manager for each campaign.

1.6 To record which staff are assigned as staff contacts to clients.

1.7 To check on the status of campaigns and whether they are within budget.

2. **To provide creative staff with a means for recording details of adverts and the products of the creative process that leads to the development of concepts for campaigns and adverts.**

2.1 To allow creative staff to record notes of ideas for campaigns and adverts.

2.2 To provide other staff with access to these concept notes.

2.3 To record details of adverts, including the progress on their production.

2.4 To schedule the dates when adverts will be run.

3. **To record details of all staff in the company.**

3.1 To maintain staff records for creative and administrative staff.

3.2 To maintain details of staff grades and the pay for those grades.

3.3 To record which staff are on which grade.

3.4 To calculate the annual bonus for all staff.

4. **Non-functional requirements.**

4.1 To enable data about clients, campaigns, adverts and staff to be shared between offices.

4.2 To allow the system to be modified to work in different languages.

FoodCo Ltd Case Study—Introduction

FoodCo Ltd

B1.1 Introduction to FoodCo

FoodCo produces a range of perishable foods for supermarkets and is based in the flat agricultural lands of the East Anglia region of the UK. John Evans, the present Chairman, started the company when he left the Royal Air Force. He borrowed money to buy 200 acres (81 hectares) of arable farmland, but his ambition was to be more than a farmer. As soon as Home Farm was running he opened a factory in a converted barn.

The first product was a pickle made to a traditional family recipe. It sold well, and success financed expansion. Soon John was able to acquire derelict land next to the farm and the company moved into a larger, purpose-built factory. The product range extended to pre-packed vegetables and salads, and later a wide range of sauces, pickles and sandwich toppings, in fact almost anything made of vegetables that can be sold in jars. FoodCo's traditional customers are major UK supermarket chains. Some lines (e.g. washed salads) sell to all customers, while others (most of the cooked products) are produced for a specific supermarket chain. Most are packaged under the supermarket's 'own brand' label.

The pickle started a company tradition that, as far as possible, ingredients are grown on the company's own farm. This now covers 1500 acres (607 hectares) and includes a market garden growing tomatoes, peppers, courgettes, chillies and other exotic vegetables under glass, and an extensive herb garden. Ingredients that do not grow well in the UK climate are sourced from carefully selected farms abroad, in Mediterranean Europe, East Africa, the USA and the Far East.

The company's annual turnover and employee numbers are summarized in Fig. B1.1.

There are now three factories on the site. Beechfield is the oldest, and this is where raw vegetables are prepared. This work is relatively unskilled. The newer Coppice and Watermead factories concentrate on the more complex cooking processes involved in making sauces, pickles and the like. These need more skilled and experienced staff. A bottling plant is also located in Watermead, and there are two warehouses in separate buildings. One is refrigerated and stores fresh vegetable and salad packs, while the other stores dry and bottled products. Figure B1.2 shows a recent organization structure chart.

The company is still privately owned and managed, with John's elder son Harold now the Managing Director and John keeping more in the background. When Harold

FoodCo Limited

Number of employees (actual)	347
Number of employees (full-time equivalent)	223
Annual turnover (current projection for 2009/2010)	£8.8m

Figure B1.1 FoodCo's staff complement and annual turnover.

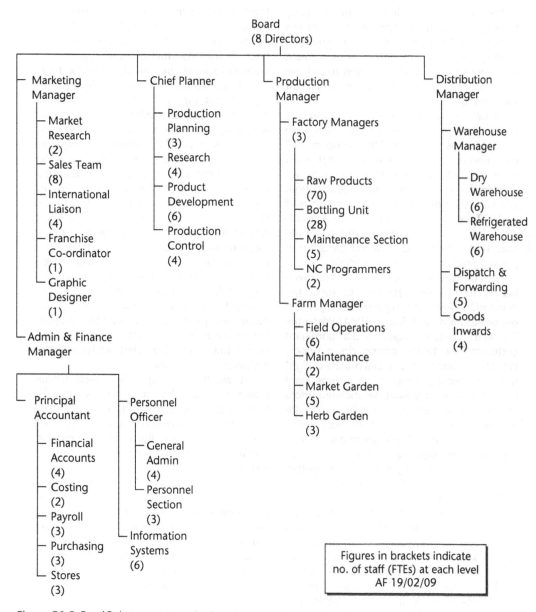

Figure B1.2 FoodCo's current organization structure, showing the distribution of staff.

took over, it was generally agreed by the Board that the company must improve profitability but there was no consensus on how to achieve this. John persuaded the Board that FoodCo must bypass its traditional supermarket customers and market directly to consumers. As a result of his analysis (Box B1.1 gives an edited version of his last speech

Box B1.1 Scene: the Board Room. John Evans speaks to the Directors about FoodCo's problems and a possible solution

'Fellow directors, we all know the company faces great difficulties. This year's profits will be the lowest ever. If we don't do something drastic, we'll be bankrupt in another year. But if we are to turn the situation round, we must understand why things are so difficult for us now.

'I believe the reason goes right back to our beginnings. Those of you who were with me in 1967, when I started this company, will remember having a degree of control that seems incredible now. Everything ran the way we wanted: farm, production, sales, distribution. We made consistently high quality goods, and by 1972 the new supermarkets were clamouring to buy. That was all a long time ago, but I think that early success is a direct cause of our present predicament. Let me explain.

'But remember 1978? When we borrowed heavily to finance expansion to meet the demand? Those loan repayments squeezed our profits hard. And then in 1984? When the TrustMart chain emerged as our dominant customer, and began driving down prices? We simply hadn't the financial muscle to fight them. We were still paying off a huge loan! Ever since then, TrustMart has dictated prices so low they have crippled us. We've been unable to do a thing about it, because we've simply been scared they'll go to our competitors for their supplies. Last year TrustMart bought 65% of our total production—altogether over £5m in sales—and we'll be lucky to clear £200,000 profit on it!

'That's also why TrustMart calls all the shots on new products. We don't have the cash to develop products for other customers. Now, I know we've grown in spite of that. It's not all been bad, but let's not kid ourselves it's been good. We haven't really run the game since 1990. We all know it! We've been

towed along behind TrustMart—and the supermarket sector—like a child dragged along by its father. We've only survived this long because TrustMart had no other suppliers big enough to meet their needs. But now that's changing. We have serious new rivals for the supermarket supply business, and TrustMart has driven our prices still lower, to the point where we may make no profit at all this year.

'We can beat off this attack, but only if we develop new products and sell in a wider market. There is no argument about that, but there is a problem. Our *real* customers are not the supermarkets, but *their* shoppers. And they don't know we exist, because our name is hidden behind all the TrustMart own-brand labels on all our packs and jars. The answer is to reach the consumers directly. Our market can only expand if they know our name, if they ask for our products. So here's what we will do. We're going to launch our own brand name, and promote it so well that everyone knows about us. Customers will begin to insist on our brand, and TrustMart will have to pay *our* price, for a change.

'It won't be cheap. We'll need serious market research. We'll need more staff in the Product Development team, and we'll need time. We'll need a new corporate image. We'll need TV advertising. But it will be worth it. There's a vast market out there, and I'm not just thinking of the UK.

'So can we finance it? Certainly! It means more heavy borrowing, but our profits on increased sales will repay the loan. It's a big risk, but we'll sink if we don't take it. There are many details to work out, but this plan can succeed. It *will* succeed! When I started out, we were the best in the business. I believe we can be the best again.

'Thank you. Are there any questions?'

to the Board as Managing Director), the 'World Tradition' range was launched. This now sells successfully at the quality end of the UK market. Helped by the growing respect for British food and cooking, the range has also begun to penetrate continental European and North American markets.

B1.2 FoodCo Today

B1.2.1 Current thinking

John Evans still believes that the company's major difficulty was over-reliance on one customer, and that this will be solved over time as the 'World Tradition' market expands. His son, Harold, feels that management procedures have become the main problem, particularly management information. He sees the systems as hopelessly inadequate and thinks the company has simply outgrown them. For him, this is an extremely serious issue since it will inevitably worsen as the company grows. But father and son are each as stubborn as the other, so they have never settled their differences on this vital point.

The company's Finance Director, Clare Smythe, is a relative newcomer. Less than a year after her appointment, she achieved a compromise that averted open war in the family. First, she championed the 'World Tradition' brand that successfully fulfilled John's vision. This is a range of international condiments and cook-in sauces, prepared to traditional recipes from many cultures and using only the finest ingredients. Growing numbers of people in the affluent world want to be able to prepare authentic dishes from world cuisine, ranging from aloo brinjal (Indian potato and eggplant curry) to Yucatan-style cod (Mexican fish cooked in orange, lime and coriander). The new range allowed the company to reposition itself in a new international market, where growth has been highly profitable. It also helps FoodCo to free itself from dependence on TrustMart, still by far their largest customer.

Second, Clare recently helped Harold to persuade the Board that the introduction of a new product range compelled the company to manage its information more effectively and efficiently. The Board agreed to undertake a major review and updating of all information systems, and a national firm of consultants was commissioned to recommend a strategy.

B1.2.2 Information systems

The current systems are a mixed set of applications, some dating back to the late 1960s, that run on diverse hardware platforms. An ageing mini-computer runs an inflexible suite of accounting programmes, a stock control system and a sales order processing system that is linked to Trustmart by electronic data interchange (this still uses a leased line connection, as the EDI software has not yet been adapted to connect over the web). The stock control system also generates product barcodes for the jar and bottle labels. The mini-computer is accessible from VT100 character-only terminals dotted throughout the factories and offices. Payroll is run off-site on a local computer bureau's server.

Managers and most administrative staff have networked PCs with standard office software, email and Internet access. A handful of proprietary packages includes the computer aided design program used to design production line layouts. The PC network is not linked to the mini-computer.

Some production is automated, including the washing and chopping operations in the Beechfield factory. The automated machines are of the numerical control type and are now obsolescent. Although they still do a reasonable job, by modern standards they are awkward to re-program, and maintaining them requires particular specialist skills.

The consultants' report

After some months of investigation the consultants submitted their report early in 2008. This identified serious weaknesses in a number of areas and recommended a phased approach to change. The top priority was to develop new product costing and production planning systems that would interface to a new in-house payroll package. The improved product costing and production information would give tighter control of production costs. Price negotiations with customers could be conducted on a more realistic basis, and better management information would help managers respond to the volatile international market for 'World Tradition' products.

The second main recommendation in the report was for a substantial investment in upgraded hardware. Many more PCs are to be installed, networked to each other and to the mini-computer. These need to be in place prior to phase 2 of the information systems plan, which calls for a rapid spread of automation through the production and distribution departments. Finally, all new software development was to fit in with a medium-term plan to make the most of new technology opportunities. For this reason, a move to an object-oriented development method was seen as a critical aspect. This would help later with building an integrated set of systems, ultimately to include factory automation, management information, more electronic links with suppliers and customers and an exploration of online Internet marketing. The Board accepted all the recommendations, and a detailed investigation into the requirements for the first systems was begun by FoodCo's in-house IS team, who had recently been trained in object-oriented development methods. Two staff were seconded from the consultants to act as mentors to the first two or three projects.

Product costing: current operations

This section describes the way that product costing activities are currently carried out at FoodCo. It concentrates particularly on the Beechfield factory, as this was an area identified by the consultants' report as a priority for action. Further information is given within chapters, where necessary, as part of case study exercises or review questions. Some information that is not strictly necessary for the completion of the exercises in this book has been included, in order to give a broader view of the overall operations.

Line operations. The nature of production control varies between the various factory and farm departments, depending on the operations undertaken and the nature of the product. At Beechfield, the main products are packs of washed salads and prepared raw vegetables, and some uncooked products such as coleslaw and Waldorf salad. There are three production lines. Each can be adapted to produce different products as the need arises, but only one at a time. Operatives' pay and the overall production costs for these lines are based on the entire batch produced during a single run, which often, although not always, equates to a single eight-hour shift. The line is switched on at the beginning of the run and temporarily halted for coffee breaks and lunch, or when a problem occurs. When a line is switched to a different product, this is treated as a separate run. If operatives are required to wait while the line is changed over to another product, or while a problem with the line is sorted out, they are paid a standing rate to compensate them for lost earnings.

Payroll and costing. For workers on the older lines at Beechfield, earnings are calculated using an algorithm that has as its input the following variables: the piecework rate for each item, the quantity of that item produced, the number of productive hours spent on the line by each employee and the employee's grade. For each run, the line supervisor completes a *daily production record sheet* (see Fig. B1.3). These are sent to the costing section for analysis before being passed on to the payroll section.

```
      ○                                    ○
           Daily Production Record Sheet No:
_____
 Line: .................   Supervisor: .....................   Date: ...............

 Product: ...............   Job No: ..............   Circle Day: M  T  W  T  F  S  S

 Run Start: ..............   Run Finish: ..............
_____
 Problem Report    When & where problem occurred: .................
 Brief Description:



 Fault Log No: ............  Downtime (H/m): ............ (Only if applicable)
_____|_____
                                | Production Control use only
 Signed: .....................  | Total Qty Produced: ..............
         (Supervisor)           |
                                | Checked by: .....................
                                |                          PR5/1.3
```

Figure B1.3 Daily production record sheet for Beechfield factory.

The supervisors also complete a *weekly timesheet* (see Fig. B1.4) for each employee. These are passed direct to the payroll section. Each Tuesday, the entire week's production record sheets and timesheets are batched up and sent to the computer bureau. Data from the production sheets and timesheets is input to a piecework system at the bureau to produce a weekly earnings figure for the payroll calculation. After the payroll has been run, all paperwork is returned to FoodCo's costing section for analysis. In practice, however, only a limited amount of analysis is carried out.

Some parts of the overall product costing function are outside the scope of this initial project and will be included either in a later increment or possibly in phase 2 of the plan. These are the Coppice and Watermead factories, where the problems with product costing are not as significant as at Beechfield, and Home Farm, where the operations are very different in nature.

Problems in product costing

The mini-computer accounting system includes a product costing module. This meets only some of the information needs of the Finance Director and very few of the requests of any other managers, least of all the factory and farm managers who have direct control of most operations. Since the existing product costing system cannot answer most

Weekly Timesheet

Name: .... ~~████████~~ .... W/E: ...22/3/09....

Factory: ....B.~~███~~........ Payroll number: ...~~████~~...

Date	Line	Job No	Prod Hrs		Downtime		Other		Code
16/3	2	2634	8						
17	-	2671	7	30		30			
18	-	2429	3	00	1	00	4	00	S
19	-	2528	8						
20	3	3714	8						
	Totals for weeks:		34	30	1	30	4	00	

Office use only

Hours	Grd	Rate

Signed (supervisor): ......~~████~~.........

Auth (manager): ....*H-P*...............

Date: ....24/3/09..........

Note: codes = (S)ick, (H)ol, (A)bsent   TS 2/97

Figure B1.4 The timesheet used in Beechfield factory (the employee's name and payroll number have been blacked out for reasons of confidentiality).

of the queries that are put to it, the costing clerks attempt to provide additional reports by using a spreadsheet application. But the sheer volume of data available for input each week is impossible to process accurately for all products. As a result of ongoing staff shortages in the office, it has only usually been possible to produce actual costs for one production line each week. Making the best of a bad job, each line is costed accurately every fifth week and estimates produced for the other four weeks in between. As a result, the 'actual' costs quoted in management reports are often really no more than estimates derived from samples of the data available.

Both Harold Evans and Clare Smythe are convinced that their inability to get accurate costs is a major contributory factor in the company's decline in profitability. In effect, it means that senior management cannot say with confidence which operations are profitable and which are not. Until they have better information, they cannot even tell where their real problems are.

B1.3 | The Proposal

The first system proposed for development is one to automate product costing. In Box B1.2, some staff from FoodCo's IS team are heard during a meeting early in the project. Louise Lee is the project manager, Ken Ong and Rosanne Martel are both analyst/developers on the team and Chris Pelagrini is a consultant in object-oriented development (he works for the consultancy firm that produced the IS report).

Box B1.2 Scene: FoodCo's IS Team Meeting Room

Louise Lee: I'll begin by welcoming Chris Pelagrini. Chris is a consultant on object-oriented development, and he will be working closely with us on this project.

Chris Pelagrini: Thank you, Louise. Yes, that's right, I've been seconded to you for the duration. Provided, that is, we complete in six months (laughs).

LL: Don't worry, we can hit that deadline. OK, let's get started. Today I mainly want to set the scope for the project. Rosanne, you had a meeting with the Beechfield factory manager, Hari Patel. What did you find out?

Rosanne Martel: Yes, I met Hari on Thursday. He's the principal client for this system, and he'll be a user too. He confirmed the reasons why we picked this as our first object-oriented project. It's strategically important, but not so critical that the whole company will fold if we mess up. It's tightly scoped, and only really affects operations in Beechfield and the costing office. But it does need access to a lot of data currently on the mini-computer and it's a feeder system for payroll and production planning. If we develop a system that integrates with these, we'll have a sound basis for re-engineering the entire IS provision.

LL: Good. This confirms the consultants' report too. Did you get any idea of the main functionality of the system? We'll need this to estimate timescales with any confidence.

RM: Ken, you've done some work on this. How far did you get?

Ken Ong: Well, it's too early to be precise, but I've sketched out some use cases and a rough class diagram. Users include Hari, his line supervisors, the sales team, production control and the costing office. The main system inputs are staff timesheets and production record sheets, and data we can import from payroll records and the existing costing system. The main system outputs will be production run costs. One obvious problem is that we don't hold any payroll data electronically, so we'll need access to the bureau's files at some point. I would say that as a whole it is not highly complex. My first class diagram has about a dozen classes. There are a few interactions that involve most classes—for example, producing the final cost for a production line run—but most are simpler.

LL: So this is a fairly small system with relatively few users, but lots of interfaces to other systems. Can you show us some of this on the whiteboard?

KO: Yes, of course. Just give me a few minutes (goes to whiteboard and starts to draw).

LL: (while Ken draws) What do you think so far, Chris? Perhaps you could say a little about how you see your role.

CP: My task is to help you apply to this project the object-oriented techniques that you have all learned on the training courses. You all know there is a big difference between knowing the techniques and understanding how they fit together. I'm here to help when you're unsure about anything. Rosanne's summary suggests this project is an ideal start and I'm confident we will make it a complete success.

LL: That's great, Chris, coming from the expert. OK Ken, now let's see your diagrams.

1

Information Systems—What Are They?

1.1 | Introduction

An information system is something that people create in order to capture, store, organize and display information. Information systems play a very important part in human affairs. They are used in all kinds of organization, whether a business, a government department or a private club. They help managers to manage their businesses. They enable customers to find out what they can buy, to place an order and to make a purchase. They help citizens to elect representatives and to pay their taxes. They help the police to detect criminals and to trace the owners of stolen cars. They enable search engines to find websites that match our interests. They make it possible for users of a social networking site to keep in touch with their online friends. They enable our emails to be delivered to the correct person's inbox. It is hard to think of any part of our social lives that could work at all without some use of information systems.

Any information system must have certain elements, without which it cannot fulfil a useful purpose. There must be a way of selecting relevant data, recording it on a reasonably permanent storage medium and retrieving it when it is needed. There must also be a method of processing the data to produce information that is useful for a task that the system's users wish to perform. At its simplest, the process may simply be a matter of retrieving a particular piece of data. More complex processes may involve a great deal of computation, such as the sophisticated mathematical modelling that produces a weather forecast. Most information systems today make use of information technology (IT), and especially of computers. But this is a recent innovation, and modern IT is not at all necessary to the existence of an information system.

This book as a whole shows you how to analyse and design information systems following an object-oriented approach. All of these terms will be explained in detail, but first we will focus on some examples from the history of information systems. This is so that we can identify more clearly the common features and concerns of all information systems. These are essentially the same whether or not the system uses IT for its operation. Then, since an information system is just one kind of system, it will be useful to examine what all systems have in common. Finally, we will apply this understanding to an analysis of businesses as systems. This will help you to appreciate the role of information systems in an organization.

1.2 | Information Systems in History

Information systems have probably existed in some form since our most distant ancestors first became capable of organized collective action. Palaeolithic cave paintings in Spain and France of hunters and animals from 30 000 years or more ago might even have been a simple sort of information system. Perhaps the aim of the cave artists was to record for future generations which animals they had seen and hunted near their homes, or the best techniques to use in hunting them, or even the prowess of individual hunters. We can never know this for sure, but certainly their paintings served some important purpose in stone-age society, and they show at least some signs of being an information system: the artists made some selection of what to paint, and they recorded information in an enduring form.

We do know that one of the earliest forms of writing—Sumerian cuneiform—was used in ancient Mesopotamia around 3500 BCE to keep accounts of agricultural commodities, such as grain brought by farmers to be placed in city storehouses. The storage medium for these records consisted of marks made in wet clay tablets, which were then dried hard to make a permanent record. Selection and processing of the data were carried out in the minds of the people who used these tablets, although it is possible that they also used an early form of abacus to help them with simple calculations. Certainly by the time of the Middle Kingdom in ancient Egypt (this began about 2000 BCE) record keeping was an important function in society, and this spread into Europe mainly through the Roman Empire. One impetus for this was because rulers wanted to know what their subjects owned so that they could tax them. But also citizens, especially producers—farmers, for example—and merchants, wanted to keep track of their land, other possessions and earnings.

A 19th-century railway signalman may seem to us just a manual worker of the early industrial age. But he was really an information worker, differing from many modern computer users only in that the technology available to him was much less sophisticated. The sociologist Frank Webster (1995) describes a signalman as someone who needs to know about track layouts, train timetables, safety rules and signalling procedures. He must keep in contact with other signalmen up and down the line, personnel at nearby stations and on trains, and he must carefully record all the trains that pass through the network. In other words, he operates an information system that comprises his ledgers,

Figure 1.1 Railway signal box.

the levers, signals and lamps and what he knows in his mind. On modern railways, the signalling systems are largely automated. However, the tasks are much the same, regardless of whether the work is done by networked computers linked electronically to electric motors that switch points and operate signal lights, or by a traditional signalman who pulls levers connected by steel cables to the points and signals and keeps careful records in a handwritten ledger. The technology may have changed, but the system is essentially similar.

In the 1940 Battle of Britain, the Royal Air Force (RAF) was responsible for defending Britain against bomber raids by Hitler's Luftwaffe. A complex information system at Fighter Command headquarters at Bentley Priory co-ordinated the defence. Checkland and Holwell (1998) describe it aptly as 'the information system that won the war'. This vital communications and control system monitored and controlled Spitfire and Hurricane fighter squadrons as they flew during the Battle of Britain. Almost exactly contemporary with the birth of the electronic digital computer, it contained nothing we would recognize today as information technology. The main 'hardware' was a large map the size of an enormous dining table. Coloured counters marked the position of various aircraft formations, and these were pushed around the map by hand as the situation changed. News about Luftwaffe raids was collected by radar and by observer posts throughout the country and sent in by telephone, teleprinter and radio. Information about RAF deployment was sent from a network of control rooms. A special filter room correlated and checked all reports before passing them through to the main control room for display. Other displays included a blackboard that showed at a glance the status of all current Luftwaffe raids, and a row of coloured lights flagged the readiness of

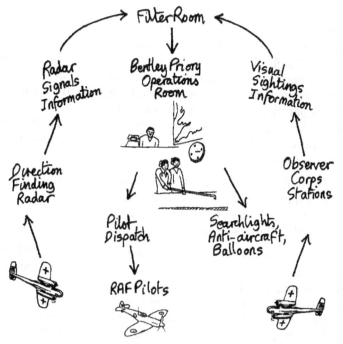

Figure 1.2 Simplified drawing of the Fighter Command system.

RAF fighter squadrons. Carefully co-ordinated duplicates of these displays were based at other control rooms, where controllers spoke directly by radio to the tense young pilots. Using this basic, but effective, technology, human operators performed communication, filtering, processing and display tasks that would today be carried out by computers. Historians still argue about what contributed most to winning the Battle of Britain. Radar technology, the aircraft and the bravery of the pilots all clearly played an important role. But it was only through Fighter Command's information system that human and technical resources were organized so effectively.

Despite the great age of some of its subject material, the academic study of information systems is young, even by the standards of the computer age, and owes its importance today mainly to the appearance of the digital computer. The earliest computer systems were developed with very little thought given to the analysis and design issues with which this book is primarily concerned. At first, computing was little more than a branch of mathematics. It received a great impetus during the Second World War, when emerging electronics technology was applied to military problems such as coding, code-breaking, naval gunnery calculations and similar mathematical tasks. The Colossus Computer allowed British code-breakers to decode German military signals, and some historians think it may have shortened the war by as much as two years. (You can see the rebuilt Colossus Computer working today at the National Museum of Computing at Bletchley Park.) The main focus of the engineers who built machines like the Colossus was on the technical difficulties of building the hardware, which used ideas from the cutting edge of research in electronics and control logic. But it was also necessary to invent efficient techniques for controlling the new machines, and in due course these evolved into today's computer programming.

As computer hardware became more powerful it also became more versatile. Once the world was again at peace, businesses began to be aware of the commercial potential that computers offered. The world's first business computer, LEO 1, was built for J. Lyons and Co. by a team at Cambridge University (Ferry, 2004). It was installed in 1951, and initially used for calculating the production requirements from daily orders. Later, its use was extended to payroll and inventory, which today are still bread-and-butter tasks for the computing departments of most organizations.

Computer technology quickly grew more sophisticated, and the tasks to which it was applied grew more complex. Computer scientists turned their attention to wider questions, such as the following.

- How do we establish the business requirements for a new system (often much subtler and more complex than the role of the earliest machines)?
- What effects will the new system have on the organization?
- How do we ensure that the system we build will meet its requirements?

From these concerns, the discipline of information systems emerged. These questions remain some of the main concerns of the field of information systems today, and they are also the principal subjects of this book.

Within the relatively new field of information systems, object-oriented analysis and design are even newer. They are derived from object-oriented programming, which dates from the 1970s, but object-oriented analysis and design were first conceived of only around 1990. Today the object-oriented approach is still by no means universal. However, we believe that, for most applications—although not quite all[1]—object-orientation is simply the best way yet found of carrying out the analysis, design and implementation of a computer-based information system.

1.3 Information Systems Today

The information systems we have described so far predated the digital electronic computer, and therefore naturally made no use of IT. To see how IT has changed—perhaps even revolutionized—the field of information systems, let us consider an online retailer. McGregor plc is an imaginary chain of retail stores that sells kitchen appliances, mobile phones and electronic home entertainment equipment. The company has an online shopping centre on its website. After registering with the site, shoppers can browse through products, select items and place them in a virtual trolley. At the end of the trip, shoppers can buy what is in their trolley, remove items or quit without making a purchase. Payment is made by submitting credit card details online, or by entering part of the card details and phoning to give the rest. Delivery times are usually within three working days for small items such as mobile phones, but up to three weeks for larger items such as cookers. Goods are dispatched direct to the customer's home. Credit cards are debited on the day of dispatch and, prior to delivery, customers can use the website to check on the progress of their order.

This is how an online shopper interacts with the system, but beneath the surface a great deal more is going on. A whole network of hardware connects the shopper's home PC and broadband modem, through a phone line to a telephone exchange, and then

---

1 We return to this question in Chapter 4.

through a fibre-optic cable to a computer that acts as a web server. This is connected to other networks at McGregor's head office and shops. Many software applications are also busy processing information captured through the web pages, and feeding various support activities. Some of these are computerized and others are carried out by people.

- Marketing staff keep prices and product details up to date on the electronic product catalogue system. This can also be accessed by touch-screen PCs in the shops.
- Credit card details are stored electronically for relay to the card processing centre when the goods are dispatched.
- Robot forklift trucks in the warehouse fetch items to the loading bay when they are due for dispatch, and warehouse staff load them onto delivery trucks.
- Delivery drivers follow a schedule linked to an electronic map in the vehicle cab. This is updated by radio every few minutes, helping to avoid traffic jams.
- Out-of-stock items are re-ordered from the supplier by electronic data interchange (EDI). When the goods arrive at the warehouse, arrangements for onward delivery and charging to the customer begin quite automatically.
- At each significant point in the sequence, a database entry is automatically updated, and this is displayed on the web page, allowing shoppers to discover what stage their order has reached.

There are many users besides the shopper, each with a different view of the overall system. A network manager monitors the number of hits on the web server and network traffic within McGregor, checking for hardware or software failure and breaches of network security (e.g. if hackers try to break in). Her concern is the efficient and secure flow of information; she is not interested in its content. A financial controller uses a linked accounting system to monitor sales transactions and cash flow. A dispatch clerk regularly checks forklift schedules on her PC, and compares them to delivery truck schedules faxed daily from the courier company. She smoothes the flow of goods through the loading bay, and spends long hours on the phone sorting out delays. A market researcher uses a specialized statistical package on a portable PC to analyse online sales, assessing the success of the web pages' presentation styles. Registration allows individual customers to be tracked as they browse the site; using information about their preferences, the design can be finely tuned to attract high-spending customers.

The use of modern IT has brought immense changes to the scope and nature of information systems. Some people even believe that we are living through an information revolution, on a scale that is comparable to the industrial revolution. This idea has been popular since the sociologist Daniel Bell coined the term 'post-industrial society' (1973) and it was an implicit undercurrent in Shoshana Zuboff's classic *In The Age Of The Smart Machine* (1988). But not everyone agrees that a direct comparison with the industrial revolution is valid. Another sociologist we mentioned earlier, Webster (1995), argues that contemporary changes in society, while significant, do not represent the radical break with the past implied by a 'revolution'. Information about transactions and operations has, as we saw in the previous section, been vital to governments and businesses for thousands of years. In any case, the picture is complicated by the fact that, in many countries, the introduction of modern IT is happening right alongside the process of industrialization. Still, it is clear that computers have had a dramatic and pervasive effect on our lives.

1.4 | What is a System?

In everyday speech, *system* can mean just about anything complex that shows some kind of organization. People refer to the legal system, a tropical storm system, the system of parliamentary democracy, an eco-system, a system for winning at roulette, a computer system in someone's office, a system for shelving books in a library, a system-built house, a hi-fi system and many more.

When information systems scholars refer to a system, they mean something more specific. This conception of a system traces its origins to a theoretical model called General Systems Theory (GST). GST defines a system as a complex set of interacting parts that act as if they were a single unified thing. Living organisms are good examples of this view of a system, and so are information systems. Systems, for GST, have the following characteristics.

- A system exists in an environment. This is everything relevant to the system that is outside it.
- A system is separated from its environment by some kind of boundary.
- A system receives inputs from its environment and sends outputs into its environment.
- A shared boundary between two systems (or subsystems), or between a system and its environment, used to pass information or physical flows from one system to the other, is known as an interface. Each flow is an output of one system and an input to the other.
- A system transforms its inputs in some way to produce its outputs. Typically, it combines simple ingredients to create a more complex product. Some systems, including information systems, have an explicit purpose, and this is achieved by the way that inputs are transformed into outputs.
- A system that exists for any prolonged period has a control mechanism. This alters the way that the system operates, in response to conditions in the environment or within the system itself.
- Control of a system relies on feedback (and sometimes feed-forward). Feedback means to sample the outputs of a system and literally feed them back to the control unit so that it can be used to make a decision about system operation. Feed-forward information samples the inputs rather than the outputs.
- A system has emergent properties. In other words, it is more than just the sum of its parts. As a whole, it has some property or characteristic that is more than the sum of the operations of its parts.
- A system may be made up of subsystems. Each subsystem can be considered as a system in its own right, and may even have further subsystems of its own.

Figure 1.3 illustrates the most important of these concepts.

1.4.1 Systems thinking

The activity of relating something to systems concepts is known as *systems thinking*. We can illustrate this by considering how each of these characteristics applies to McGregor plc.

Environment
McGregor's environment is made up of all the people, organizations, physical structures, etc. with which the business interacts. Customers, suppliers, sub-contractors, employment

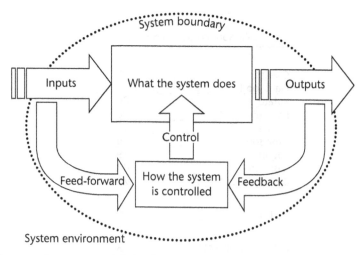

Figure 1.3 Main parts of a system and their relationships.

agencies and certain government departments all have some interaction with McGregor, and so would be considered as part of the company's environment. Employees would be regarded as part of the McGregor system, not part of its environment. The road and rail network used for deliveries and the public telephone network would be considered as part of its environment. The dedicated computer and phone network that connects together shops, offices and warehouses is part of the system, not of its environment. It can help to consider whether a system controls something or not; if it directly controls that thing (or person) then it (or they) are within the system. If the system does not have direct control, then that thing (or person) is outside the system.

Boundary

In some systems (such as a living organism) the boundary is clear because it is physical. Your skin is the boundary between your body and its environment. McGregor's boundary is more conceptual than this. The easiest way to define it is just to say that it separates what is inside the system from what is outside. The boundary here is an imaginary line around McGregor's staff, buildings, equipment, stock, IT systems, transport, and so on. It excludes everything in McGregor's environment. It is quite easy to draw in a diagram, but you could not actually see it in reality.

Inputs and outputs

McGregor receives many physical inputs, but the best example is deliveries of goods from suppliers. It also receives many informational inputs. Customers provide inputs to the website by placing orders, and to the shop by presenting their purchases to the checkout operator. Suppliers send inputs in the form of invoices and delivery notes. Market research companies provide inputs on sales trends and customer preferences. McGregor also produces both physical and informational outputs. A customer's trolley load of purchases is a physical output, while the till receipt is only physical in a trivial sense (because it is printed on paper), but more importantly it consists of information about the items purchased, their price, the date, etc. (see Fig. 1.4–it is instructive to consider all the systems involved in producing and using the information on something as simple as a commonplace till receipt).

```
                Lateco Minimarket
               Gt Sodden 01245 565381


       Cheese        *                4.00
       Plant food    *                2.00
       Potatoes      *                2.00
       Fruit juice   *                1.90
       Fresh milk                     0.95
       Lime squash   *                2.76
       Yogurt                         1.39
       Raspberry                      2.49
       Boxed chocs   *                1.79


       TOTAL                         19.28


       MAESTRO UK SALE               19.28


       AID           : B111114003
       NO            : ******1149      ICC
       PAN SEQ NO    : 00
       AUTH CODE     : 6532
       MERCHANT      : 0865234
       START: 02/09 EXPIRY : 03/12
       Cardholder PIN Verified
       CHANGE DUE                     0.00


       10/03/10                      15:43
```

Figure 1.4 A typical till receipt

Interfaces

McGregor uses a variety of interfaces to communicate with other entities in its environment. It communicates with customers via TV advertising, in-store display panels, signs on the side of delivery vans and via the website. The customer service desk in each store is an interface with customers; so is every checkout operator. Various employees of the company use the phone, email, fax, letters and forms such as invoices to communicate with suppliers, the bank, government departments, and so on. Each point of communication with each external person or organization is an example of an interface. The web page used by a customer to order a new refrigerator is her interface with the McGregor system. The data content and structure of the web page define and limit her interaction with the online shopping system. If there is no field on the web page where she can enter her address, it may not be possible for her new refrigerator to be delivered to her house. We shall see later in the book that the identification and understanding of interfaces is important in the development of information systems.

Transformation

McGregor does not physically manufacture any products. A retailer's main process is to sell things that are made by other businesses. It transforms its physical inputs (the products that it buys to sell in its stores) mainly by moving them, packaging them and presenting them to customers. This would be a fair description of McGregor's main process as a system. However, choosing what to sell and how to price, present and advertise it, and controlling the movement and display of products is also a very complex process. For this to run smoothly, many decisions must be made that rely on collecting, analysing and assessing a great deal of information. This is mainly the responsibility of McGregor's managers, or, in systems terms, its control unit.

Control

A Board of Directors under the overall leadership of the Managing Director has overall control of McGregor plc. Together, they make all the important decisions about the business as a whole, such as investment in new stores or product ranges and whether or not to try to take over a rival business. Each also has overall responsibility for running a division of the business, such as retail, marketing, IT, purchasing, finance, and so on. Below the directors are layers of other managers, each responsible for a department, activity or team within the company. The layers of management in an organization are often modelled as a pyramid, as shown in Fig. 1.5. According to this view a few strategic managers at the top make a relatively small number of major, long-term decisions for the business as a whole. An example of a strategic decision might be whether to build a new factory to produce a completely new product range. A larger number of tactical managers in the middle layer make medium-term decisions, usually for a smaller unit of the organization. For example, a department manager might decide to re-allocate some of his staffing budget to buy new equipment that he thinks will make the production process more efficient. At the 'lowest' level of the organization, an even larger number of operational managers or supervisors make short-term, routine decisions about day-to-day activities. Operational decisions include things like ordering more stock or asking an employee to work overtime. We could consider all managers together as McGregor's control unit, but it makes more sense to see different managers as controlling different subsystems. Together, when everything is working as intended, the various subsystems co-operate to achieve the overall aims of the company.

Feedback and feed-forward

McGregor's managers rely on a constant flow of information about the business and its environment to guide their decisions. Information from the environment is simply an input; for example, updates about the company's share price provide an input because

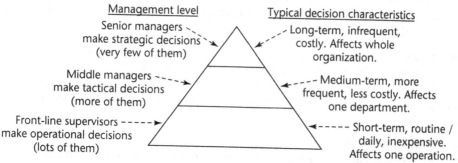

Figure 1.5 The pyramid model of management and decision-making in an organization.

they come from the stock exchange or from a news service, both of which are beyond McGregor's system boundary. Information from within the system is described as either feedback or feed-forward, depending on where it originates. Senior managers typically want to know how the business is performing as a whole, for example, by regular updates on sales and costs, productivity of the different departments or progress of major projects such as redeveloping the website or opening a new store. Most of this information is feedback, which reports on system outputs. Some may be feed-forward, which reports on system inputs. Sales information is feedback because it relates to an output. Information on deliveries from suppliers is feed-forward because it relates to an input.

Subsystems

The McGregor system is made up of many subsystems. Each separate department can itself be considered as a system and subjected to the same kind of analysis that we have applied here to the whole company. For example, consider the online retail division described earlier in this chapter. If we regard this as a system in its own right, then the rest of the company–its other subsystems–represent part of its environment. We can expect communication (and therefore interfaces) between the online retail division and the purchasing division, the finance division, senior management and many other parts of the company.

Emergent properties

McGregor has one obvious emergent property: as a commercial business it is capable of making a profit (at least, when times are good). This will only happen if all the parts of McGregor interact successfully with each other to achieve the goals of the business as a whole. Of course, this is a deliberate aim of the people who created McGregor, but it is emergent in the sense that only the organization as a whole can achieve the goal. While some departments may contribute more to the company profit than others do, that does not necessarily mean that departments that contribute less are actually contributing nothing. The various parts of an organization are designed to work together to fulfil the aims of the organization, but this is such a complex task that it is very difficult to get it right all the time. So managers may try to change a struggling department in some way to make it more successful. This is an example of control in systems.

1.4.2 The usefulness of systems thinking

Systems thinking helps us to understand how the world works. It does this by representing selected aspects of the world in an abstract way, as a system. For this to be helpful, it is not always necessary for the system to correspond exactly to the thing it represents. Checkland and Scholes (1990) explain:

> ...it is perfectly legitimate for an investigator to say 'I will treat education provision *as if it were* a system', but that is very different from saying that it *is* a system...Choosing to think about the world as if it were a system can be helpful. But this is a very different stance from arguing that the world *is* a system, a position that pretends to knowledge that no human being can have.

Figure 1.6 illustrates this point.

This does not mean that systems are never real. Many systems are made of real components. For example, all the parts of a central heating system are physical. But we

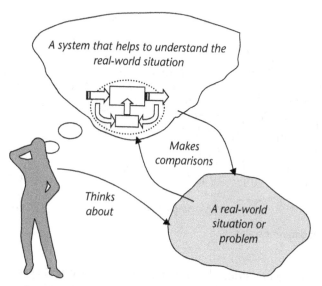

Figure 1.6 The relationship between system and reality (loosely adapted from Checkland and Scholes, 1990).

choose, based on our interest at a given moment, whether to *think* about it as a system. Any system that we think about exists only in our thoughts and not in the world, however closely it may correspond to the real system that it represents. Such a system located in our mind is a subjective view of reality, not the reality itself.

Boundary, environment and hierarchy in systems

The first step in analysing a system is to choose which system you wish to understand, and this largely means choosing its boundary. We can make different choices, depending on our interest. For example, a cell biologist may be interested in a single human cell as a system because she is trying to understand how a healthy skin cell becomes cancerous. Her system is bounded by a cell membrane. A specialist physician attempting to treat a skin cancer may consider a patient's whole skin as a system (although in everyday life we may think of our skin as a boundary, doctors see the skin as our body's largest organ, and quite a complex one, too). The boundary of this doctor's system might coincide with the skin itself, or it may be wider still, depending on how far the disease has spread. For a doctor in general practice, a person's whole body may be considered as a system bounded by its skin (but where the skin is also a component).

Each medical specialism has its own view of what is interesting or important, and these often overlap with other views. A neurologist may focus on the nervous system, consisting of brain, spinal cord and the network of nerves that spreads through the body to just beneath the surface of the skin. Its physical boundary is almost identical to that of the whole body, but the nervous system contains only specialized nerve cells. A haematologist focusing on the circulatory system, which consists of blood cells, blood vessels and the heart, has a similar physical boundary. Both these systems penetrate the other organs in the body, each of which may in turn be regarded as a system by another specialist.

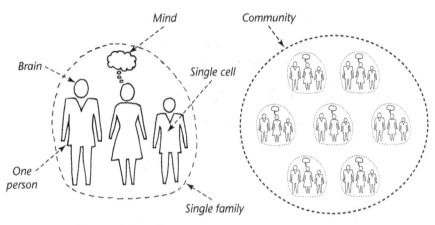

Figure 1.7 Systems at different scales.

A person can also be considered as a variety of non-physical systems. A psychologist may study an individual's cognitive system or emotional system, or may consider a child's intellect as a learning system. A social psychologist may think of a family as many overlapping systems: a child-rearing system, an economic system, a house-maintenance system, etc. These views of the family as a system have purely conceptual boundaries, since family members remain part of their system no matter how distant they are in space. We could continue zooming out in this way, perhaps until we reach a cosmologist (whose system of interest is bounded by the physical universe) or a theologian (whose interests arguably are even wider). Some of these different possible systems with their boundaries are illustrated in Fig. 1.7.

The existence of subsystems is a natural consequence of several aspects of systems discussed above. First, a system is a complex whole made of interacting parts. Second, our *idea* of a system is a matter of choice, so we can choose the scale at which we wish to apply systems ideas. The writer Arthur Koestler coined the term *holon* to describe something which is simultaneously both a complex whole, made of subordinate parts, and also a part of something still more complex. This clearly applies to any business organization, but Koestler thought that it is impossible to think of anything that is not also part of something else. It all depends on your focus. Subsystems are at once part of a larger system, and also coherent systems in their own right. Communication between subsystems is, by definition, through interfaces. Figure 1.8 shows some of the subsystems that can be found in the description of the Agate case study in Case Study Chapter A1. This kind of diagram is sometimes called a system map.

Another way of arranging systems and subsystems is as a hierarchy (this is how the Agate subsystems were shown earlier in Fig. A1.1). Hierarchies are a very important aspect of systems theory, and in Chapter 4 we shall also see the importance of hierarchy to understanding object-orientation.

Inputs, outputs, feedback and control

Most systems have interactions with their environment. They consume inputs and transform them to produce outputs. Human cells take in nutrients and oxygen and transform them into protein, energy, carbon dioxide and other waste. Figure 1.9 shows some inputs and outputs for three different systems.

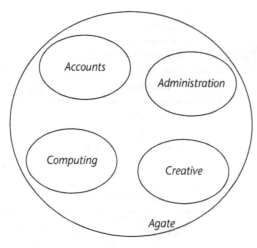

Figure 1.8 Subsystems of Agate.

System	Inputs	Outputs
A student	Information Exercises Guidance	New knowledge New ideas Solutions
A family	Money Social standards and norms (e.g. laws) Purchases Daily news	New citizens (i.e. children) Products of family members' work Social influence Votes in elections
A business	Raw materials and labour Investment Information (e.g. customer orders)	Profit and taxes Finished products Information (e.g. the company report)

Figure 1.9 System inputs and outputs (note that a single input does not necessarily correspond to a single output).

The transformation of inputs into outputs is an important characteristic of a system. It gives meaning to a purposeful system such as a business.

In any purposive system, it is possible to identify a specialist subsystem that controls the operation of the system as a whole. In fact, GST originates partly from the science of cybernetics, which studies control in natural and artificial systems. A common type of cybernetic control is the thermostatic device that controls a central heating, hot water or air conditioning system. These work on a simple feedback loop. Another familiar control unit, but a much more complex one, is the human brain.

Feedback control in very simple systems typically just compares two input values. For example, current temperature in a freezer is compared with the temperature set on the control dial. A logic mechanism of some kind (mechanical, electronic, digital or organic, depending on the type of system) is needed to do this. Depending on the similarity or difference of the input values, the control unit is responsible for deciding what action, if any, should be taken. This is illustrated in Fig. 1.10.

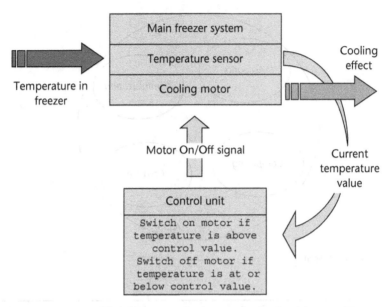

Figure 1.10 Thermostatic control in a freezer—a simple negative feedback loop.

Possible actions here are turning the cooling motor on and turning it off. Both are initiated by a signal from the motor by the control unit, thus closing the feedback loop. This is *negative* feedback, which aims to maintain equilibrium by opposing any deviations from some norm. It is used widely in physical systems, such as electronic devices and manufacturing systems.

By contrast, *positive* feedback reinforces deviations instead of opposing them. It therefore tends to increase movements away from equilibrium. Systems governed by positive feedback are inherently unstable, but that is not necessarily a bad thing. It is undesirable only when the deviation that is reinforced is itself undesirable. For example, the ear-splitting howl sometimes heard from public address systems is caused by a positive feedback loop. Sound output from a loudspeaker is caught by a microphone and re-input to the amplifier. The signal cycles repeatedly round the loop, growing quickly louder until the amplifier reaches its limit. However, positive feedback is beneficial when a steady state is undesirable. For example, in a competitive sport like football constant equilibrium would always result in a goal-less draw. It is the nature of competition that a team should exploit any legitimate edge that they can gain over their opponents. But since both teams continually strive to get the upper hand, it is rare to see the feedback cycle build to an extreme. Instead, the system (or game) usually continues in a state of dynamic disequilibrium. Negative feedback also plays a role in competition, as teams try to maintain any equilibrium that acts in their favour.

A complex mix of positive and negative feedback is seen in businesses such as McGregor. Competitive firms try to capitalize on any advantage they can gain over their rivals (positive feedback, aimed at disrupting an unhelpful equilibrium), while also trying to prevent their rivals from gaining an edge (negative feedback, aimed at maintaining a beneficial equilibrium). An example of negative feedback in business occurs when a firm adjusts its manufacturing output to maintain a constant inventory. When sales rise, so stock falls, and the rate of production needs to be increased. When sales fall, stock rises, and the rate of production needs to be reduced. Here the stock level is acting as a *buffer* between production and sales subsystems. (A buffer is a kind of interface that works to even out the flow of information or products by absorbing any irregularities.)

Positive feedback does not necessarily mean that every deviation from the norm is reinforced. Some may be allowed to die away through lack of encouragement. In audio amplifiers all frequencies are amplified, but only resonant frequencies are disastrously reinforced by the feedback cycle, while others fade naturally without ill effects. Often a sound engineer need only adjust the amplifier's tone control, reducing slightly the volume in the troublesome frequency band, to cure a feedback problem. A similar type of control can be discerned in businesses that directly link productive output to sales, perhaps because there is a very short-term seasonal market (say, toys at Christmas). In this case, when sales rise, production is increased as far as possible. But when sales fall below a critical level, a product may be dropped altogether.

The Christmas toy business may find that the use of feedback from sales (a measure of output) does not allow them to react quickly enough to changing market conditions. This would leave them with unsold stock, bought from manufacturers before they realized that demand had slumped. Ideally, they should adjust their manufacturing to suit the level of demand, and they may be able to use market research to forecast which toys will be popular among children this year. This would allow the firm to avoid buying products for which there is no market. Another way to use feed-forward would be to find out which toys are being manufactured in large numbers, and then advertise these aggressively in order to stimulate demand.

Effective feedback is an essential part of all learning. No one can develop a new skill without receiving appropriate feedback that highlights which aspects of their performance are satisfactory and which parts need improvement. On the other hand, feed-forward information about the changing job market may help you decide what to learn. This applies equally to the activity of software development. Most professionals continue to learn how to do the job throughout their careers. This is partly because techniques and technologies evolve continuously. But also, every project is unique, poses a new set of challenges and demands new approaches from the developers. Feedback on what worked in the past, and what did not, helps to guide the developer's choices in future. Feed-forward information about emerging technologies and techniques may help a software developer to be proactive in anticipating the future needs of her clients.

While feed-forward control information can help a system to be more responsive to environmental fluctuations, it is not always easy to implement or manage in a business organization. Difficulties still arise if the rate at which conditions change in the environment is faster than the rate at which the business can adapt. The effects of this are apparent to anyone who visits the kind of specialist book shop where remaindered titles are sold cheaply.

In the Agate case study used later in this book (see Case Study Chapter A1), the agency must employ and train sufficient staff to cope with the anticipated workload. If there is a serious slump in orders for new work, it may not be possible to reduce the number of staff quickly enough to avoid bankruptcy, because of the need to give staff a period of notice before they can be laid off. The company may also not be able to respond quickly enough to a sudden surge of orders, because of the lead time for recruiting and training new staff. Forecasting the level of demand for a service such as Agate's is an important role of information systems in business.

Emergent properties and the holistic view

An emergent property is a characteristic of a system that distinguishes it from being simply the sum of its parts. For example, a car is only a form of transport if there is enough of it to drive. It then has the property of being a vehicle, but the wheels, windscreen, motor, etc. do not have this property until they are correctly assembled. Of course, a car is meant to be a form of transport. There is nothing very mysterious about how it does this. Still, only a whole car is useful for the purpose. Many music and sports fans will be familiar with a stronger form of emergent property; a soccer team or a music group may have an outstanding star player, but winning a match or playing brilliant music often depends on a special magic that only happens when everyone in the team or group plays well together. If a key member of staff at McGregor were to leave, this could conceivably cause the business to fail, but that does not mean this person was doing all the work on their own. It is more likely that they just supplied some vital ingredient for the whole business to work together effectively.

For this reason, the systems approach is often described as *holistic*. In other words, we think about each system as a whole, not just as an assembly of components. Important aspects will be overlooked if we think only about its parts in isolation from each other.

The opposite approach is called *reductionism*. This begins with the assumption that complex phenomena can be fully explained by reducing them to their component parts. Reductionism is the basis of the technique of analysis, and has an important place in the methods of physical sciences such as physics and chemistry (although there are some dissenters even in those disciplines). It is also important in information systems development, but it cannot supply all of the answers when the object of analysis is a complicated human situation, such as a business organization.

1.4.3 Systems that are involved in information systems development

Any information system is meant to serve a useful purpose for an organization, or for a group of people such as the supporters of a cricket team or the citizens of a city. This business, or group of people, can also usefully be regarded as a system: a *human activity system* (Checkland, 1981). It is this that gives meaning to the construction or operation of an information system. Unless the purpose and operation of the human activity system is understood it is not possible to specify, still less to build, an information system that supports it. This means that the human activity system is important to developers, no less so than the information system that they are developing. One of the vital work-flows in a development project is to capture and understand the requirements. Unless this is done thoroughly and correctly, the information system will not perform as intended. A further difficulty is that participants in a human activity system often disagree widely about its purpose. This can be a significant problem for the analysis of information system requirements, and makes it even more important to understand the wider system in detail. Figure 1.11 shows how some of the people who work at Agate see the purpose of the business.

Developers are likely to belong to a project team, or an IT department or both, and these can also usefully be viewed as systems. This system transforms various inputs (money, skill, staff time, information from users about how they want the software to work, etc.) and aims to produce an effective software solution to a business problem. Its environment is typically the organization in which the developers work, including users of the software and their managers. We could regard it as being made up of subsystems that

System	Purpose of system	As seen from the perspective of . . .
Agate (a business system)	To become a successful advertising agency on the international stage, thus providing both wealth and prestige for its directors	A director
	To provide varied and interesting work with a good salary, and also to be a useful stepping stone towards the next career move	A copy-writer
	To provide a pleasant and comfortable life until retirement (5 years away), without the need to make too much effort	Another director

Figure 1.11 A human activity system with multiple purposes.

include different groups within the project team and the methodology they follow. The various analysis and design models that describe the software can be seen as information used in the operation of the system. A team leader or project manager exercises control, using regular feedback on progress and problems. Suitable feed-forward will help to alert the manager to anticipated problems, as well as those that have already happened.

Thus systems developers have to pay attention to a wide variety of systems. If their task is to develop an information system that supports online voting, they may need to take a professional interest in the system of parliamentary democracy. If it is to develop a system for a website that sells mp3 music downloads, they should take an interest in the system that comprises the music industry and its interactions with music fans. One advantage of taking a systems view of any activity is that it encourages those involved to think about the sorts of feedback and control that are needed for everything to run smoothly. This applies just as much to software development as to anything else.

1.5 Information and Information Systems

In order to design and build an information system, we must find out what information will be useful to the human actors who will use the system, and how they will use it. In the following sections, we will explain the relationship between information, information systems and the human activity systems they are intended to assist.

1.5.1 Information

Information is conveyed by messages and has a meaning that depends on the perspective of the person who receives it. We are always surrounded by a vast mass of potential information. Only some of it ever comes to our attention, and only some of that is actually meaningful in our present context. Finally, only some of what is meaningful is also useful. Many authors distinguish data from information by describing data as 'raw facts' while information is data that has been selected and given meaning. Checkland and Holwell (1998) show that the process of creating information from raw facts is actually a bit more complex than this. They describe a sequence of four stages by which raw facts become useful.

Consider four people watching the evening sky. A plume of smoke is rising in the middle distance. For Alex, the smoke is just part of the view, and she does not even consciously notice it. Ben sees it, and it evokes a memory of a camping trip long ago. But he is aware that the only connection between past and present smoke is a coincidence of shape and colour, so he moves on to look at something else. Chetan is thrown into consternation, because he sees that the smoke is rising from his house, which is on fire. Dipti runs to phone the fire service before doing whatever else she can to help Chetan save his house.

The sight of the smoke is, on the face of it, a single message available to be received by all, yet its meaning is different in each case. Alex does not even notice it. Checkland and Holwell call this *data* (from the Latin for 'given'), meaning a fact that has not been selected for any special attention. Ben notices the smoke but does not relate it to any present context. Checkland and Holwell call this *capta* (from the Latin for 'taken'), meaning a fact that has been selected but has no particular importance or meaning. Chetan gives the smoke a meaning derived from the context in which he sees it (recognizing his house, understanding the implications of the smoke, etc.). This is *information* because it has a meaning within Chetan's current context. The meaning of a fact is always dependent on its relevance to the observer.

There is a final step where information becomes *knowledge*, by being structured into more complex meanings related by a context. Dipti integrates information from several sources: the link between smoke and fire, the effect of fire on houses, the existence and purpose of a fire service and the location of nearby phones. She also links it to the context, and uses it to make a decision about appropriate actions. In a word, she *knows* what to do.

Most information systems are useful only when they select appropriate capta from the mass of background data and use it to create information that is useful to specific people in a specific context. Some information systems go further than this and aim to create knowledge.

1.5.2 What information systems do in organizations

Information systems today are often much more complex and more closely integrated with each other than they once were. As a result, the boundaries between categories of information system have become blurred. However, it is still helpful to give a brief overview of some of the general types of application in organizations. But note that this more often describes roles that an information system can play, rather than actual distinct types of system. Some authors identify clear relationships between different types of information system and the levels of management shown in Fig. 1.5. In practice, things are seldom clear-cut, and it is not unusual to find strategic managers who use operational or office systems while operational level workers may make use of management support systems. People naturally tend to use whatever systems are available to them if they find them to be useful.

Operational systems

Operational systems automate the routine, day-to-day record-keeping tasks in an organization. The earliest commercial information systems were operational ones, because routine, repetitive tasks involve little judgement in their execution, and are thus the easiest to automate. Accounting systems are a good example. All organizations need to keep track of money—the amount coming in, the amount going out, the cash available to be spent and the credit that is currently available. Few modern organizations could survive long without a computerized accounting system. Sensible organizations protect their ability to operate by having a 'disaster recovery plan' that details how they intend to cope with an emergency that destroys data or renders computer systems inoperable.

The flow of information through an accounting system is based on thousands, or even millions, of similar *transactions*, each of which represents an exchange of a quantity of something, usually a money value (this is why they are often called transaction processing systems). For example, when you buy a carton of milk in a supermarket, two separate records are made. One records that a carton of milk was sold, and the other records the money you paid in exchange for it. As this repeats day after day for each item, customer, checkout and branch, an overall picture is built up that allows the company's accountants to compare total income with total costs and to determine whether a profit has been made. Of course, many real accounting systems are more complicated than this, often with subsystems to handle wages, taxation, transport, budget planning and major investments. It should also be kept in mind that, important though numbers may be for the decision-making processes in an organization, the ways that staff interpret those numbers can be equally important, if not even more so (Claret, 1990). For instance, as we shall see in Chapter 2, the introduction of a new system that is intended to save money by improving the efficiency of an operation may also, if it is inappropriately designed, cause some disgruntled employees to quit their jobs. The costs arising from this (lost experience and knowledge, recruitment costs, the need to train replacement staff, and so on) are often very hard to attribute with any confidence to a single cause. For this reason, they are almost impossible to measure and are usually called *intangible*. The official accounts of a business seldom give a clear picture of intangible factors like these.

Other operational systems record orders received from customers, the number of items in stock, orders placed with suppliers, the number of hours worked by employees, time and cost of mobile telephone calls made by subscribers, and so on.

Management support systems

Management support systems (MSS) are information systems designed to support the work of managers. As the name suggests, these usually work at a higher level of the organization than operational systems. The information they present to their users is often more complex. This is principally because it involves information that has been combined from different sources. In addition, a manager is likely to be interested in more highly summarized information, such as the total quantity of milk sold last month, rather than an individual transaction, such as a sale to one customer. However, much of the information used by management to make decisions is derived directly from information stored at the operational level. In practice many management support systems are built on top of operational systems. In other words, the management support system works by retrieving and processing information that has already been stored by the operational system. In fact, the very first MSS (including some of those that ran on LEO 1, the first business computer) consisted simply of programs that extracted data from the files of an existing operational system. This was then analysed or combined to give managers information about their part of the organization. At the time, most business IT effort was spent on operational systems. These new systems were known as management information systems (MIS), and in many organizations this triggered a name change for the section that worked on information systems: from DP (for 'data processing') to MIS department.

We can easily see how the relationship between operational and management support systems would work for an accounting system. Once all routine sales transactions are stored on a computer it is a short step to a program that can analyse them, so that managers could tell at a glance which products were not selling well, which checkout operators took too long dealing with a customer, which store had the lowest volume of trade, and so on. This information is useful to a manager because she has responsibility for maximizing the performance of an organizational subsystem. An important part of this is identifying and resolving problems as they occur. Thus, one crucial aspect of a management support system is the feedback or feed-forward that it provides, alerting managers to problems and opportunities, and assisting them in the process of tuning the organization's performance. Operational and management support systems, then, fit into different parts of the diagram in Fig. 1.3. Operational systems are either located in the central box (labelled 'what the system does'), or they assist its work by supporting the flow of inputs or outputs. Management support systems are either located in the box in the lower part of the diagram (labelled 'how the system is controlled'), or they assist its work by supporting the flow of feedback to, or control information from, the control unit.

Office systems

Office systems automate or assist in the work of office workers, such as clerks, secretaries, typists and receptionists. They also support some aspects of the work of managers, for example, communication (word-processing, email, etc.), planning (personal information management, such as the diary facilities included in IBM Lotus Notes or Microsoft Outlook) and decision support (for example, using the built-in functions of any spreadsheet). This might suggest that they are a kind of MSS, and they can be seen as such, but they are used today by almost every kind of employee, not just by managers. This underlines the way in which the boundaries between different types of system have become blurred. It also highlights the way that the introduction of information systems has changed the way that people work–middle-ranking and senior staff often type their own letters and reports now using a word processor, when they might once have expected a secretary or typist to do this for them.

Real-time control systems

Real-time systems are concerned with the direct control of a system's operations, and have to respond quickly to external events. Typical examples are physical in nature, and include lift control systems, aircraft guidance systems and the robot forklifts at McGregor plc. They are best considered as a control subsystem of a physical processing system. Their role is thus very different from both business operational and management support systems. There are also control systems that do not need to react in real-time, for example the systems that control traffic lights. Real-time systems usually have human operators (to date, few are completely independent of human supervision, though this may become more common in the future), but they are generally insulated from the surrounding human activity system. In fact, many authors would not agree that real-time systems are information systems at all. We do not regard this as an important issue. The techniques used for the analysis, design and implementation of real-time systems are broadly similar to those used for other computer systems. However, when there is a safety-critical element to the system (for example, aircraft guidance), a more mathematical approach will be used for the analysis and design to ensure that the system is accurately specified to perform correctly under all operating conditions.

1.5.3 Information technology

Information technology (IT) is the machinery that makes an information system work. Today, this usually involves digital computers, but that is not necessarily the case. In many businesses, the department that looks after information systems is called the IT department, which is sometimes misleading. As we saw earlier in this chapter, information systems have been used throughout history, using whatever technology was available at the time. The decision of which IT to use for an information system should ideally be left until last in the cycle of development. Only when the human activity system has been understood, the need for an information system has been identified, the system's requirements have been defined, and a workable system has been designed—only then should the emphasis turn to the information technology that will implement it. This is not how things always happen in the real world. Indeed, it is partly for this reason that so many systems in the past have been unsuccessful. But it is how they *should* happen, wherever possible.

Information technology covers all the kinds of hardware familiarly known as, based upon, or that include within them, a computer or its peripheral devices. This includes obvious things like desktop PCs, pocket electronic organizers, modems, network cabling, file servers, printers and computer-controlled machinery in factories and airliners, and also less obvious things like digital mobile phones, the electronic circuits that calculate fuel consumption in some cars, the microchips in some cameras that set the aperture and shutter speed—in other words, everything inaccurately described in marketing literature as 'intelligent'.

The list of devices that can be described as IT increases almost daily, and the boundaries between them blur. As digital devices continue to advance in speed and processing power, manufacturers exploit these advances to develop and market new products. For example, many mobile phones combine a digital still and video camera, modem, email software, web browser, diary software, alarm clock, calculator and online gaming. Some have global positioning system (GPS) chips and even motion sensors. Interface technologies such as voice-activation may soon make it easy to interact with a computer with no need to press keys or click mouse buttons, while in many situations wireless networking makes cables unnecessary. Mobile commerce using handheld PDA devices or mobile phones is beginning to change the way that many people access information and communicate. For many, it has already removed the physical restriction that requires users to be in the same place as a bulky PC when they want to access the Internet. On the whole, it appears likely that computers will progressively disappear from view, while their effects will paradoxically be felt in more and more areas of everyday life.

All these examples of information technology are really just tools that, like any tool, can be used for many different tasks—and not only those for which they were intended. There is a saying that, if your only tool is a hammer, the whole world looks like a nail. The corollary is also true: if you can see only nails, you will use any tool that comes to hand as a hammer, whether it is actually a wrench, a book or a can of beans. It is how a tool will be *used* that matters, not so much how it is *meant* to be used. A modern word-processing package provides a skilled user with the facilities to automate many complex tasks by using macro programs, mailing lists and embedded objects like spreadsheets, sound clips and hyperlinks to the Web. Yet many users have no need of all this and would be happy with an electronic typewriter. The question is, then, if an electronic typewriter is all that is required, why install a powerful PC running all the latest software?

There is no point in installing IT unless it is needed by the information systems that will run on it. Nor is there any point in installing an information system that does not meet a defined need for its users.

1.6 Strategies for Success

In this section, we consider some ways that business needs can be identified, suggesting possible application areas for information systems and information technology.

1.6.1 Identifying a business strategy

It is important for a business to be clear about its goals. Unless these are known and agreed, it is not possible to decide which information systems the organization will need, or what exactly they should do. Once the goals are clear, it is usual to define the strategies that the business will use to achieve them. The development of a business strategy essentially begins with the question: 'Where would we like our organization to be in (say) ten years' time?' Logically, the next question is: 'How do we get from where we are now to where we want to be?' Answers to this question will consist of practical steps that can be taken towards achieving the strategic goals.

The contents of a strategy (i.e. the actual goals and steps it contains) depend on the characteristics of the organization, its environment, the skills of its workforce and many other factors. In the Agate case study (see Case Study Chapter A1), we see that the strategy is 'to continue to grow slowly and to develop an international market'. These are the goals. The directors also have a view about how to achieve them: they want to get more business from multinationals, and they hope to do this through the quality of their work and by developing 'campaigns that have a global theme but are localized for different markets around the world'. These are some of the steps in the business strategy. These elements have been included in the strategy because the directors are confident, for example, that the technical quality of Agate's work and the creativity of their staff are both strengths of the company, and will meet the demands placed on them. They probably also believe that their current client base and contact list is extensive enough for them to win the kind of work they are seeking.

1.6.2 The contribution of information systems

Information systems can contribute to the achievement of business goals in so many different ways that it can be difficult to decide which systems really matter. Many techniques can be used to help arrive at useful answers. One is the well-known strengths/weaknesses/opportunities/threats (SWOT) analysis. Usually created during a group brainstorming session, a SWOT analysis identifies and categorizes everything important about the organization's current circumstances. The resulting strategy is based on finding ways of exploiting the strengths and opportunities, while counteracting the weaknesses and threats. Another useful technique is Value Chain Analysis (VCA) (Porter, 1985). This presents a systemic view of an organization that is very useful for structuring a discussion about strategy and information systems. The metaphor of a chain in VCA is meant to reinforce the idea that any weak link in the series of activities undermines the value of the work done at other stages. For example, if a business is good at selling its

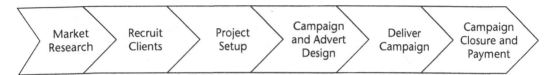

Figure 1.12 Value Chain Analysis adapted to the Agate case study.

products, but the products themselves are of poor quality, it is unlikely to be successful. Alternatively, a business that makes excellent products but has poor arrangements for obtaining its raw materials is also unlikely to be successful. In a successful organization, each primary activity (for simplicity the Agate example in Fig. 1.12 shows only primary activities) adds value to the products (i.e. it benefits the company more than it costs). Secondary activities (not shown in the Agate example) provide services, but do not directly add value to products. They are only worth doing at all if they make a contribution to the efficiency or effectiveness of primary activities. Their role must therefore be tuned to support the primary activities.

VCA is useful in information systems planning because it focuses attention on activities that are critical to a business, either because they are currently a problem, or because they represent a major source of profit or competitive edge. Development projects can then be targeted at assisting those operations that can make a difference to the success of the organization as a whole.

Porter's original model was based on analysis of typical manufacturing companies, and it does not apply well to a service sector business such as Agate. Many analysts have adapted the model to fit better with the activities of a particular organization. Figure 1.12 shows a value chain for Agate that takes account of its service nature. This analysis shows all the activities that contribute to the client's perception of the overall quality of service.

1.6.3 Information systems and information technology strategies

Many organizations explicitly separate their strategic plans into the three layers illustrated in Fig. 1.13. The idea is that development of a new information system should only be considered in the context of a well-thought-out business strategy, while the purchase of IT hardware should be specified on the basis of particular information systems that are planned for development. The business strategy drives the information system strategy, which in turn drives the IT strategy.

Information flows in the diagram go in both directions. When formulating a business strategy, managers need to know which business goals could be assisted by information systems. In the same way, those responsible for developing new information systems need to know the IT capabilities of the business. The planning cycle is iterative.

The relationships in Fig. 1.13 are important. For example, one objective of McGregor plc's current business strategy is to capture a share of the lucrative online market. Perhaps this is a business imperative because other online retailers have taken a growing share of the market and threaten McGregor's survival. In order to fulfil this business objective, McGregor's managers had to identify, define and then develop an appropriate set of software systems. This includes the online customer order system, the robot warehouse system, the stock control system, the purchase order system, and so on.

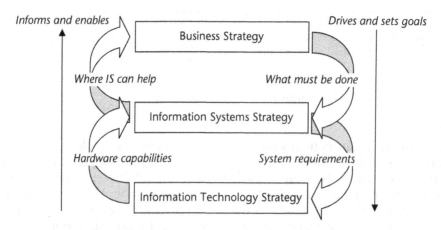

Figure 1.13 The relationship between business, IS and IT strategies.

It is the main purpose of the IS strategy correctly to identify which of many possible systems should be chosen for development, and also how these need to interface with other systems. Those chosen for development will then become projects. Selection of the wrong systems for development wastes time and resources, and can also distract attention from business priorities. In this context, 'wrong' may mean systems that are unimportant, but it can also mean systems that are not compatible with other vital systems. In this case, it could cause major business problems for McGregor if the online customer order system cannot correctly transfer details of the items ordered to the warehouse system, resulting in the wrong goods being delivered to the customer. This kind of difficulty could occur simply because a project team is not sufficiently aware that the software they are developing needs to interface with another system.

Another critical issue might be poor design of the online catalogue, resulting in frustrated customers leaving the McGregor website and buying instead from a competitor. While specific details of the website design would not be included in the IS strategy document, it is not unusual to spell out major business concerns, such as the need for clear navigation and interaction on a customer website.

The IT strategy is responsible for identifying the hardware components and configurations that will allow the software to operate effectively. In McGregor's case, this would include specifying the web servers to ensure that the response time is always fast enough to satisfy customers. Slow response times could frustrate customers and result in lost sales for the company. Here, too, the detailed specification of the servers (operating system, number of incoming phone lines, processors, RAM, etc.) will not be worked out until later, but the strategy will identify this as a business concern, and will also explicitly relate the various hardware components to the software systems they must run.

For many businesses, success depends on finding the best fit between overall business goals, the information systems that help to fulfil those goals and the IT on which the information systems run. This question of strategy alignment has even greater importance when the business is engaged in e-commerce, whether this is business-to-customer (B2C) or business-to-business (B2B). In either case, for customers, suppliers, partners, collaborators—indeed for any interaction that occurs electronically—the information systems *are* the company, since the website is really all that can be seen. Moreover, an Internet presence can be seen–and judged–by the whole world. An inappropriate strategy, at any of the three levels, or a poor implementation can bring swift business failure.

In Chapter 2, we will explore in more detail the problems that can occur during information systems development, and even *because of* information systems, while in Chapter 3 we introduce some ways that these problems can be resolved.

1.7 Summary

In this chapter we have introduced the key concepts of all information systems. These include: control, feedback, input, output and processing of information, communication via interfaces, the hierarchic organization of systems and their subsystems and the emergent properties of a system. We have also explained the relationship between information, meaning and context. For systems analysts and designers, an important part of the context is the human activity system of an organization within which the information system must work. This leads to a necessary set of relationships between the goals of an organization, the strategy it undertakes to fulfil them, the information that its staff need to do their work, the information systems that provide the information, and finally the IT that runs the information systems.

Information systems have been present throughout history. However, modern IT has increased their scope and changed the way they work almost beyond recognition. There are undoubtedly more changes to come, but however much information systems may change, valuable lessons may still be learned from historical information systems.

Review Questions

1.1 What is the difference between an information system and information technology?

1.2 Identify some things that a computerized information system can do, which are difficult or impossible for a non-computerized equivalent.

1.3 Why does it not matter whether a system is real, or exists only in someone's mind?

1.4 Why are boundary and environment important for understanding a system?

1.5 What is the difference between feedback and feed-forward?

1.6 Why has a human activity system more than one purpose?

1.7 What is the purpose of a management support system?

1.8 What is meant by disaster recovery? Why is it important for a business organization?

1.9 What are the relationships between business goals, information systems strategy and information technology strategy?

1.10 Define information. How does it differ from data?

1.11 Describe how knowledge differs from information.

1.12 Give an example of some knowledge that you possess. What is its purpose?

Case Study Work, Exercises and Projects

1.A Think of three or four information systems that are not computerized (either historical or contemporary). Identify (or imagine) a computerized equivalent. For each pair, write a brief description of the boundary and the main inputs and outputs. What are the main differences between the computerized and non-computerized versions?

1.B Reread the description of the McGregor online shopping system, and assume that everything described (computer software, hardware, human activities, etc.) is a single system. Identify its main subsystems and control mechanisms. What feedback and feed-forward information do you think they would use? Don't be constrained by the description given in this chapter—use your imagination too. And remember that some control may not be computerized.

1.C Read the first part of the FoodCo case study in Chapter B1, up to and including Section B1.2.1. What do you think are FoodCo's business goals for the next ten years? Make any assumptions that you feel are justified.

1.D Using your imagination as well as the information in Chapter B1, compile a SWOT analysis for FoodCo. Does your analysis suggest any information systems solutions to business problems?

1.E Carry out a Value Chain Analysis for FoodCo by working out a sequence of main activities the company must carry out in order to be successful. What flows through your value chain? Identify some of the people, activities, systems, etc. that fit in each compartment.

1.F Identify the value that you think is added by each activity to FoodCo's products. Which do you think are the weak links?

Further Reading

Checkland and Holwell (1998) is a very accessible account of the relationships between the subjects of systems, information and information systems.

Vidgen et al. (2002) describe approaches to the development of web-based information systems, like some of those described in the McGregor plc example. They also link business strategy with object-oriented analysis and UML (although not the current version).

Schneider (2009) is a useful source on e-business and e-commerce (although both are beyond the scope of this book).

Webster (1995) is a scholarly debunking of many of the more exaggerated claims about how the 'information revolution' is changing social relationships.

Turban, Aronson and Liang (2005) give an up-to-date and broad-ranging review of modern software technology for the support of managers at all levels.

Koestler (1967) is a classic text that applies systems concepts to many aspects of life. This book ranges widely over human history and society, and presents some early speculations on the systemic role of evolution in modern social behaviour.

Challenges in Information Systems Development

LEARNING OBJECTIVES

In this chapter you will learn
- ☑ who the main players are in an information systems project
- ☑ the challenges in information systems development
- ☑ the underlying causes of these problems
- ☑ how the concept of a stakeholder helps identify ethical issues in information systems development
- ☑ the costs of problems and ethical issues.

2.1 | Introduction

Many information systems are very successful, and failure is the exception rather than the rule. But the consequences of failure can sometimes be severe, ranging from unnecessary cost, through serious risk to the survival of an organization, to–in extreme cases–a threat to someone's personal safety. The types of failure are also various. In some cases, a project team has failed to deliver any working software at all. This usually means that a great deal of money is spent to no good purpose. Some systems are successfully installed but do not meet their users' requirements. Other systems appear to meet the stated requirements, but prove to be inefficient or difficult to use. These may not produce benefits that outweigh the costs of their development.

We can use the metaphor of a journey to describe the process of information systems development (Connor, 1985), as illustrated in Figure 2.1. This highlights the fact that there are many choices to make along the way, and we must try not to take the wrong turns. Some routes lead to the planned destination; in other words, the intended system is delivered to its clients. Other routes may reach a satisfactory conclusion by an unexpected

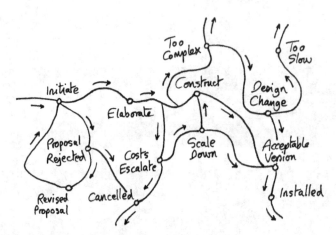

Figure 2.1 A possible map of the systems development 'journey'.

route. There are also routes that arrive at the wrong destination, while some are dead ends that lead nowhere. We must recognize and avoid these. Professional systems developers are naturally concerned to avoid the problems and to achieve a good result. They can do this only by understanding what goes wrong.

We will look at the question of project failure first from the perspective of each of the main players. Several different groups of people are associated with the project, and each has their own particular view on the things that can go wrong. The main groups we shall consider are the users, clients and the developers themselves. In the following section we will consider each in turn.

2.2 What Are the Challenges?

According to a survey of managers in 102 of the UK's top companies, almost half had recently encountered an IT project failure (Kelly, 2007). Poor specification was the most frequently cited cause, while poor understanding between business and IT departments was also a major factor. Another survey carried out by the Economist Intelligence Unit found that more than half of the IT projects in a majority of UK companies failed to meet expectations (Veitch, 2007).

This picture is not unique to the UK. For many years, the CHAOS reports have surveyed IS projects in the USA. The latest CHAOS report found a worsening situation, with only one-third of projects judged as successful, while one in four were either cancelled before completion or, if the software was delivered, it was never used (Standish Group, 2009).

Nor is there anything new about the scale of this problem. The bill for the London Stock Exchange Taurus system project (abandoned shortly before installation in 1993) was estimated at around £480m (Drummond, 1996). During the 1990s and early 2000s many UK public sector contracts for new information systems were cancelled or failed to deliver their intended benefits, but the true costs are often not known with any certainty. Significant problems occurred with systems for the UK Passport Agency, the

National Probation Service, the Immigration and Nationality Directorate, the Child Support Agency and the National Air Traffic Control Service. Poor project management and lack of financial control are blamed for many of the disasters (OGC, 2005).

All potential causes of failure are at least to some extent under the control of the developers. A professional must take the possibility of failure seriously and work hard to avoid it, even if this sometimes is limited to an awareness of the risks, followed by a damage-reduction exercise. But one difficulty is that the answer to the question 'What can go wrong?' depends partly on who gives it. Information systems development is a complex activity that always involves people. In any organization, people have varying perspectives that influence their view of a situation, and what, if anything, is to be done about it. It is useful to distinguish three categories of people with important relationships to a project. First, there is the group of employees who will become end-users of the information system when it is completed. Second, there are managers, here called 'clients', who have control (or at least influence) over the initiation, direction or progress of a project. Finally, there are the professionals responsible for the development of the information system, whom we refer to as the 'developers' here. For simplicity, we will ignore differences within each group.

2.2.1 An end-user's perspective

End-users come in many varieties, and can have varying relationships to an information system. The examples that follow concentrate on the experiences and frustrations of those who either consume the products of an information system (i.e. they use its outputs to help achieve a task, such as dispatching an ambulance to an emergency) or are responsible for entering raw data into an information system.

'What system? I haven't seen a new system'
One problem that can be experienced by an end-user is vividly expressed by a term that gained widespread usage in the 1980s. *Vapourware* describes a software product that is much talked about, but never released to its intended users. In other words, instead of arriving, it evaporates. Many businesses are naturally reluctant to talk about information system project failures in public, but vapourware may be common. In the commercial software field, it is very common indeed; the online magazine Wired gives an annual award for software and hardware products that are promised to the public but not delivered.

Some surveys have found that an astounding proportion of information systems development projects fail to deliver any product at the end. We mentioned above the CHAOS report finding that 24% of projects are never delivered or never used (Standish Group, 2009). In the UK, the total cost of a single system for the Wessex Regional Health Authority reached £63m, yet no system was ever delivered (Collins, 1998b). This indirectly affected patients, since the aim of the system was to help manage hospital resources more effectively, and thus to deliver a better, more responsive service. When a project is not completed, none of the expected benefits to users and other beneficiaries are achieved.

'It might work, but it's dreadful to use!'
This relates to systems that are unpleasant or difficult to use. Systems may fail to meet the criterion of usability in a number of ways, including: poor interface design, inappropriate

System characteristic	Example
Poor interface design	A web page with yellow text on a white background
Inappropriate data entry	A system where the backspace key sometimes deletes whole words
Incomprehensible error messages	A system message that 'explains' the problem in language that a user can neither understand nor act upon 
Unhelpful 'help'	A system message that says 'wrong date format—try again'
Poor response times	Nurses in an Intensive Care Unit complained that a new computerized patient chart system took longer to store and retrieve data, compared with the manual system. This took them away from patients for longer (Goss et al., 1995)
Unreliability in operation	A national insurance company lost most of its records of customers' policies due to a system error. Staff were unable to send renewal notices, but instead had to write to customers asking them to phone in with their policy details[1]

Figure 2.2 Aspects of poor system usability with examples.

or illogical sequence of data entry, incomprehensible error messages, unhelpful 'help', poor response times and unreliability in operation. Figure 2.2 gives some examples (what these mean, and how to avoid them, is explained more in later chapters).

When one of the authors bought a pair of shoes, shop staff struggled to register the sale correctly. There was a new cash register system and their difficulty arose because it was a promotional offer. A customer buying this style of shoe was also entitled to a free pair of socks. Since the socks were a normal stock item, correct records of stock had to be maintained. This meant that the socks had to be 'sold' through the till, even though they were actually being given away for free. A simple way to handle this would have been for the assistant to over-ride the price with zero at the time of sale. The assistant tried this, but the software specifically prevented the 'sale' of a stock item at a zero price. The assistant called the manager. After some experimentation, it appeared that the only way to deal with this transaction was to reduce the price of the shoes by 1p, and to sell the socks at a cost of 1p, thus giving the correct total for the sale. Now that the staff understand how to do this, it will not cause them difficulty in future. But it will always be an unnecessarily awkward way of handling a routine task. There are many examples of this sort of poor design, and they cause a great deal of frustration and lost time for users.

'It's very pretty—but does it do anything useful?'
A system may appear well designed and easy to use, but still not do the 'right' things. This may be a question of the tasks that should be carried out by the system. For example,

---

1 One of the authors was a customer at the time.

a library catalogue enquiry system would be of limited use if it could only retrieve shelving information about a book when provided with the title and the author's name, in full and spelt correctly. Readers often do not know the title of the book for which they are searching. Even if the author's name is known, it may be spelt incorrectly. Another way that a system may fail to meet its users' needs is through poor performance (this overlaps with the question of usability, discussed in the previous subsection).

A system may also be of doubtful value to its users because it requires them to work in a way that seems nonsensical. One example of this is now quite old, but still valuable because the author describes it so clearly. A warehouse management system was designed partly to increase managers' control over the use of scarce storage space in the warehouse. The workers found that the new system removed their discretion in the best ways to maximize the use of space:

> ...because they could see how improvements in these areas would save money for the company they found ways of working around the system.

> ...They were reproved by management for their bad attitude, and yet, it was their commitment to the company as a major employer in their local community which led to their frustration with what they regarded as unnecessarily wasteful rules and procedures.

> (Symons, 1990)

It is particularly worrying when software errors and failures present a hazard to life. An extreme example was the London Ambulance Service Computer Aided Dispatch (LASCAD) system, abandoned shortly after delivery in 1992. The total development cost was estimated at £43m. Designed to speed the process of sending an ambulance to an emergency, the system actually slowed response times down. The system was cancelled after several claims that it had caused patients to die while they waited for attention. Although these claims were never proven, the risk of continuing to operate the system was unacceptable (Barker, 1998).

Controversy continues to this day about whether software errors may have caused the Mull of Kintyre crash of a Royal Air Force Chinook helicopter in 1994. All 29 people on board were killed, including a number of high-ranking police and military intelligence officers. The official verdict, still accepted by the Government, was that the pilots were grossly negligent. However, an earlier Board of Enquiry had concluded that the crew might have been distracted by a major technical (i.e. software) malfunction. A series of reports in *Computer Weekly* and an item on British TV's Channel 4 News claimed that internal Ministry of Defence reports had raised concerns about the reliability under certain conditions of the engine control software in this type of helicopter. A House of Lords select committee report recommended that the Ministry of Defence view should be set aside (Collins, 2001). As recently as June 2007, there were claims that new evidence might change the official verdict (Collins, 2007), but to date the Government has refused to reopen the enquiry and continues to blame the pilots (Knapton, 2008).

2.2.2 A client's perspective

By *client* we mean that person, or group of people, responsible for paying for the development of a new information system. A client usually has influence over whether or not approval is given to a project before it starts. Some clients (but not all) also have the power to stop a project once it is under way. A client may also be a user. If so, we can assume that they share the user's perspective on the kind of things that can be a problem. They may make only indirect use of the system's outputs, which insulates them from the immediate experience of a badly designed interface, for example. While the concerns of a client may overlap with those of an end-user, they also include distinct matters relating to payment, ownership and value-for-money.

'If I'd known the real price, I'd never have agreed'

It is almost routine in many organizations for information systems projects to exceed their budget. We mentioned earlier a survey which found that half of all UK projects fail to meet expectations (Veitch, 2007). In many cases, this means running over budget or behind schedule (or both). Some projects reach a point where total costs already outweigh all the benefits that can be expected on completion. This point is not always recognized when it is reached, which may result in the expensive completion of a system that would have been better cancelled. Alternatively, a project may be cancelled because its managers do believe that its costs are escalating out of control, or because they can see that the benefits will not be as great as originally promised. The decision is summed up in the familiar saying: 'Don't throw good money after bad.' The London Stock Exchange Taurus system, also mentioned earlier in the chapter, was one of the most striking cases.

The rise of e-commerce has brought new ways for information systems to cost an organization money in unexpected ways, sometimes as a result of routine modifications to the software in use. Barclays Bank suffered some serious embarrassment in August 2000 when customers logged on to the online banking service and found that they could view other customers' accounts (BBC, 2000).

'It's no use delivering it now—we needed it last April!'

A project that is completed late may no longer be of any use. For example, a bricks-and-mortar retailer, threatened by rivals who sell at a lower price on the Internet, may have little use for an e-commerce site if it is not operational until all the customers have defected and the company has been declared bankrupt.

Many other kinds of project are time-critical. This can be due to new legislation that affects the organization's environment. An example of this was the deregulation of the UK electricity supply market in April 1998. This required electricity companies to make extensive modifications to their computer systems so that they would be able to handle customers' new freedom to switch between suppliers. A few years earlier, all local authorities in the UK faced a similar challenge twice in three years, when central government changed the basis for local tax calculations. Each change required hundreds of councils to specify, develop (or purchase) and successfully install new computer systems that allowed them to produce accurate invoices and record income collected from local tax-payers. Failure to implement the new systems in time risked a massive cashflow problem at the beginning of the new tax year.

Commercial pressures can also have an effect. This sometimes translates into whether a business succeeds in being the first to market a new product or service, although the advantage is not always permanent. For some time the continuing success of the Internet bookstore Amazon.com derived, at least in part, from the considerable competitive advantage of being the first of its kind. Some competitors (notably the established US bookseller Barnes and Noble) felt obliged to follow Amazon's lead. For the followers, there is not the same need to take risks with new technology. But attracting customers away from a leader may mean differentiating yourself in some way, perhaps offering new services, or perhaps by being even better at what the leader already does well. At the time of writing (summer 2009), Amazon seems to be doing well while some rival online booksellers struggle to survive the global recession. Recent profit announcements suggest that Amazon continues to grow strongly, with net profits for the first quarter of 2009 up 24% compared with the first quarter of 2008 (Stone, 2009).

'OK, so it works—but the installation was such a mess my staff will never trust it'

Once a new system gets a bad press it can be very difficult to overcome the resistance of the people who are expected to use it, particularly if there is an existing alternative available to them. The following scenario is based on a real situation, observed at first hand by one of the authors. While the technology involved is now a little dated and the system involved is IT rather than IS, the lesson still applies.

> A small company introduced a local area network (LAN) to connect the PCs in its office. Staff were encouraged to store files on the network disk drive, where other staff could also access them (previously, all data was stored on local hard drives, accessible only from one PC). Most saw the mutual benefit and complied. Management claimed that the routine daily back-up of the network drive was a further benefit, since there was no need to keep personal back-ups of data. Then a mechanical fault occurred. This erased all data on the network drive, and when the engineer tried to restore it from the tape, it emerged that the tape drive had not worked correctly for weeks. All tapes recorded over the previous six weeks were useless. Staff learned that all data stored in that time was permanently lost. Re-entering it took many person-days. The faulty disk and tape drives were replaced, and tapes are now checked after every back-up, but many staff reverted to keeping all important data on their local hard drives. Most keep personal back-ups too. Perhaps nothing will persuade them to trust the LAN again.

'I didn't want it in the first place'

Organizations are complex and political by nature. The politics with which we are concerned here are to do with conflicting ideals and ambitions, and the play of power within the organization. There can be disagreement between management and workers, as in the case of the warehouse management system mentioned earlier in this section. There can also be contention between individual managers, and between groups of managers. One result can be that a manager is sometimes an unwilling client in relation to a project. The following scenario is based on another real-life situation observed by one of the authors.

> The head office of a multinational company decided to standardize on a single sales order processing system in all its subsidiaries throughout the world. But the Hong Kong office already had information systems that linked electronically with customers in Singapore, Taiwan and other places in South East Asia. It became apparent that the existing links would not work with the new system. For the Hong Kong management, this meant extra costs to make the new system work, and disruption to established relationships which, in their view, already worked smoothly and did not need to be changed. They therefore had little desire to see the project succeed in their region, but felt they had no other choice. Had they been less scrupulous, they might have tried to find ways of sabotaging its progress, either in the hope that it would be abandoned altogether, or at least that they might be exempted from the global rule.

'Everything's changed now—we need a completely different system'

It is almost inevitable for any information system project that, by the time the system is completed, the requirements are no longer the same as they were thought to be at the beginning. Requirements can change for many reasons.

- Project timescales are sometimes very long (the Taurus project ran for three years) and business needs may change in the meantime.
- Users naturally tend to ask for more, as they learn more about what is available.
- External events can have a dramatic impact–for example, the global recession of 2008/2009 forced many organizations to cut their spending and IT projects have been scaled down to save money.

This does not apply only to new systems currently under development. Systems that have been in operation for some time may also be affected. This is part of the natural, ongoing process of maintenance, modification, upgrading and eventual replacement that all information systems undergo. From a client's perspective, the motivation is usually to make an information system fit better with the business, and thus to provide better support for business activities.

2.2.3 A developer's perspective

The perspective of the developer is quite different both from that of an end-user and from that of a client. This is because the developer adopts the role of 'supplier' to the 'customer' (i.e. client or end-user). For this reason, when problems occur the developer may feel forced into a defensive position of justifying the approach taken during the project. Since at this stage we are discussing only problems, many of the problems identified by a developer tend to centre on blame and its avoidance.

'We built what they said they wanted'

Changes to the requirements for a system, based on sound business reasons, always seem perfectly reasonable from a client's point of view. However, for a developer, given the responsibility for building a system to meet those requirements, they can be a real headache. If we were able to distil the essence of how many developers feel about this, it would read something like the following.

> No matter how skilled you are, you can't achieve anything until the users, clients, etc. tell you what they want, and at the start they don't even agree with each other. Eventually, with skill and perseverance, you produce a specification with which everyone is reasonably happy. You work for months to produce a system that meets the specification, and you install it. In no time at all, users complain that it doesn't do what they need it to do. You check the software against the specification, and you find that it does exactly what it was supposed to do. The problem is that the users have changed their minds. They just don't realize that it's not possible to change your mind late in a project. By then, everything you have done depends on everything else, and to change anything you would almost have to start all over again. Or it turns out that they didn't understand the specification when they accepted it. Or there is some ambiguity about what it meant, and you've interpreted it differently from them. Whatever the reason, it's always your fault, even though all you ever tried to do was to give them what they wanted.

In reality, of course, analysts, programmers, etc. often do understand why users and clients change their minds during a project, or after delivery. But this doesn't always make it less frustrating when it happens.

'There wasn't enough time (or money) to do it any better'

In every project, there are pressures from outside that limit the ability of the development team to achieve excellence. In the first place, projects almost invariably have a finite budget, which translates into a finite amount of time to do the work to a certain quality. There may also be an externally imposed deadline (for example, a project to develop a student enrolment system that must be ready by the start of the academic year). Another external pressure results from the impatience of users and clients to see tangible results. This, too, is often understandable, since they are not so much concerned with the information system itself, as with the benefits it can bring them—an easier way to do a tedious job, a quicker way to get vital information, and so on. But it can be very counter-productive if it becomes a pressure within the project team to cut short the analysis and get on with building something (anything!) quickly to keep the users happy. The result of haste in these circumstances is usually a poor product that meets few of the needs of its users. Developers know this, but they don't always have the power to resist the pressure when it is applied.

'Don't blame me—I've never done Linux networking before!'

In a successful information system development team, the members must possess a harmonious blend of skills that are appropriate to the needs of the project. These may include the use of techniques (such as object-oriented analysis), knowledge of methodologies (such as the Unified Software Development Process), skill in programming languages (such as VB.Net or Java), experience with the modelling software used to create analysis and design models or detailed knowledge of hardware performance (such as networking devices). There must be a complementary set of skills within the team for a project to succeed. Problems occur when the available staff do not have enough expertise in the skills required for a project.

In 2005, Birmingham City Council abandoned a project to migrate 1500 users from Windows XP to the open-source Linux operating system. The manager of the project said that one of his main problems was a skills shortage in the area of open-source networking. The total cost of the project was a little over £0.5m (Thurston, 2006).

The skills problem is not trivial. Even today, some highly skilled and experienced analyst/programmers in industry have little or no experience of object-oriented analysis and design. Some projects with highly skilled staff are still carried out rather poorly, because the staff are inexperienced with the particular techniques they must use.

'How can I fix it?—I don't know how it's supposed to work'

This complaint is often heard from programmers who have been asked to modify an existing program, and who have then discovered that there is no explanation of what it does or how it works. To modify or repair any artefact, whether a computer system or a bicycle, it is usually necessary to understand how it was intended to work, and thus what the consequences are of changing this or that feature. Anyone who has ever tried to repair anything electronic or mechanical, such as a motor vehicle, washing machine or mobile phone, will know that much of the time is spent trying to understand what the various parts do, and how they interact with each other. This is true even when a maintenance manual is to hand. The situation is no different for computer software. While software may be more intangible in form than a mobile phone, it is no less mechanistic in its operation.

'We said it was impossible, but no-one listened'
Just like client managers, systems developers can sometimes be overwhelmed by organizational politics. At times this means that a project is forced on an unwilling team, who do not believe that it is technically feasible to achieve the project's goals. Alternatively, the team may not believe the project can be completed within the time made available. But if opposing views prevail, the team may find itself committed to trying to achieve what it said could not be done. In these circumstances, it can be very hard for team members to become enthusiastic about the project.

'The system's fine—the users are the problem'
A few information systems professionals, especially those who understand least about the business or the organization, are prone to blame 'the stupid user' for everything. They believe that problems that occur in the use of software chiefly result from the fact that most users are too ignorant or too poorly trained to make proper use of the system. They generally believe that the design and execution of the software is not open to serious question. Many of these technocrats are undoubtedly very talented, but this view is patently absurd since it assumes that the answer to a problem is known before the situation has even been investigated. In a word, it is a prejudice. We will simply comment that anyone who hopes to learn the truth about a situation must also be prepared to examine critically their own preconceptions.

2.3 | Why Things Go Wrong

Flynn (1998) proposed an analytical framework to categorize project failures, and this is widely accepted as valid. A summary of the framework is shown in Figure 2.3.

Complete failure is the most extreme manifestation of a problem, but Flynn's framework can also be applied to less catastrophic problems. In Flynn's view, projects generally fail on grounds of either unacceptable quality or poor productivity. In either case, the proposed system may never be delivered, it may be rejected by its users or it may be accepted yet still fail to meet its requirements.

These categories are really what are known as 'ideal types'. In other words, they are meant to explain what is found in reality, but that does not imply that any real example will precisely, in all its details, match any one category. Real projects are complex, and their problems can seldom be reduced to one single cause. Many examples in the following sections show some characteristics of more than one cause.

2.3.1 Quality problems

One of the most widespread definitions of the quality of a product is in terms of its 'fitness for purpose' (see any standard text on software quality assurance, e.g. Galin, 2003). In order to apply this to the quality of a computer system, clearly it is necessary to know first for what purpose the system is intended and second, how to measure its fitness. Both parts of this can be problematic.

Type of failure	Reason for failure	Comment
Quality problems	The wrong problem is addressed	System conflicts with business strategy
	Wider influences are neglected	Organization culture may be ignored
	Analysis[2] is carried out incorrectly	Team is poorly skilled, or inadequately resourced
	The project is undertaken for the wrong reason	Technology pull or political push
Productivity problems	Users change their minds	
	External events change the environment	New legislation
	Implementation is not feasible	May not be known until the project has started
	Poor project control	Inexperienced project manager

Figure 2.3 Causes of IS project failure (adapted from Flynn, 1998).

The wrong problem

If an information system does not help to fulfil the aims of the organization, then it is a waste of resources. It may also be a distraction from the things that really matter. It may even do real harm if it works against the organization's business strategy. But it can be difficult to choose the right viewpoint when defining the aims of a project. The aims of the organization as a whole may be unclear, or those responsible for planning information system projects may not be aware of them. Then the developers and users of a system may regard it as a success, yet it appears a failure when seen in a wider frame of reference.

Sometimes projects are started with no clear idea of the nature or goals of the client organization. Then failure, or at least lack of success, is almost inevitable. If an organization itself is not understood, then it is very hard to identify, specify and develop information systems that support it in fulfilling its aims.

Neglect of the context

This emphasizes the fitness of an information system to fulfil its purpose. This can take the form of a system that is too difficult to use, since the designers have taken insufficient account of the environment in which its users work, or the way that they like to work. Some examples given earlier in this chapter can be interpreted in this way, depending on assumptions about the situation. For example, in one case cited earlier (Section 2.2.1) workers and managers held different views about the purpose of the warehouse management system. Managers believed they needed to control the activities of workers more closely. Yet the system designed to do this had also the side effect of obstructing the workers from carrying out their work in an efficient way, to the detriment of the whole company.

---

2   To this category, we would add design and implementation. Even when analysis is carried out correctly, this is still no guarantee that the software will be well designed, or that it will be correctly programmed.

Incorrect requirements analysis

We believe this category should include design and implementation, as well as analysis. The focus is still on a system's fitness to fulfil its purpose. Even if the aims are clear at the outset, the development team may not have the right skills, the right resources or enough time to do a good job. However, even when none of these present a difficulty, the project can still fail if the team members apply inappropriate techniques to the project.

This category of failure usually causes the most visible systems problems, because the user can see the results. These may include defects in the external design of the system (for example, the content or layout of its screens), or the selection of tasks that the system performs (for example, an essential function may not be included), or the operation of the software (the system may not be coded to work in the way that its analysts and designers intended).

Project carried out for the wrong reason

Here, the emphasis is once more on the intended purpose of the system. To give an example, during the late 1990s many organizations rushed into some sort of e-commerce activity. With the benefit of hindsight, this was clearly a great success for some, but others derived little or no benefit. At one point there were so many 'dot.com' crashes that the *Guardian* newspaper's website ran a column called 'Dot.com deathwatch', which featured stories about troubled and failing Internet companies.

The reasons for the crash were complex, but for many businesses they boil down to a simple failure to think carefully enough about some key questions posed by McBride (1997).

- What does the business aim to achieve by a presence on the Internet?
- How must the business reorganize to exploit the opportunities offered by the Internet?
- How can the business ensure that its presence on the Internet is effective?

It remains true today that any organization moving from offline to online operations should first be clear about their answers to these questions. There is a great deal more to successful trading on the Internet than just creating a website with a catalogue and payment facility and hoping it will work. Yet some organizations that moved to e-commerce were just following a trend. They did not understand what it could do for their business, but they feared the consequences of being left behind.

Two possible underlying reasons explain why this happens for established companies. First, there may be a political push within the organization. For example, a powerful group of managers may feel instinctively that the business must look more modern, even though no clear benefits have been identified. Major business decisions are often based on instinct rather than reason, so this scenario is not uncommon. Second, there is the pull of new technology. Managers who have little understanding of information technology can be very vulnerable to this. They have no rational basis for evaluating the exaggerated claims that some vendors make about their newest products. In practice these two reasons often combine into a single force that can be irresistible.

Some people who launched online businesses, typically Internet start-ups with no history of trading in the physical world, simply believed that the Internet was a 'new economy' where established business rules no longer applied. It is now generally accepted that some aspects of business on the Internet are clearly different—in particular, the speed at which things happen, including business failures. But few would now argue that the business fundamentals have really changed. It is still just as important as ever to plan and design with care, to pay attention to costs and income and to ensure that projects are properly controlled.

While much of the naïve, sloppy thinking that led to the dot.com crashes is no longer in evidence, the central point applies just as much now as it ever did in the past.

2.3.2 Productivity problems

Productivity problems relate to the rate of progress of a project, and the resources (including time and money) that it consumes along the way. If quality is the first concern of users and clients, then productivity is their other vital concern. The questions that are likely to be asked about productivity are as follows.

- Will the product be delivered?
- Will it be delivered in time to be useful?
- Will it be affordable?

A number of things can happen during the course of the project to affect adversely its rate of progress, its costs and ultimately whether a satisfactory system will be delivered.

Requirements drift

Requirements often change over time, typically because users ask for more, or they ask for different things, as they learn more about the proposed system. When this process of change is not managed, it is called *requirements drift*. This can cause the whole project to get out of control, affecting both the progress and the costs. In extreme cases a project team may completely lose sight of the original reason for the system.

It would be unreasonable to prevent all change requests, because many will be made for good reasons. For example, staff at an insurance office may request the facility to store video clips in a system for recording details of vehicle accident claims. Video records made by the claims assessor at the scene of an accident could be helpful in assessing claims, but this might not have been thought of when staff were first asked about their requirements for the system. However, change requests can bedevil a project and even prevent its completion. The longer a project proceeds, the more complex both its products and its documentation become. To compound this, each part of the final system probably depends on many others, and the interdependencies grow more numerous and complex. Thus it becomes progressively more difficult to make changes to a system under development, because a change to one part requires changes to many other parts so that they will continue to work together. The limit is reached when a project is stalled by an escalating workload of making all the changes required as a consequence of *other* changes requested by the users. At this point, management have only two choices. They can cancel the project and write off the money spent so far. This is what managers decided to do at the London Stock Exchange in 1993, and at Birmingham City Council in 2005 (although in those cases the causes of the cost escalation were different). Alternatively, an effort can be made to bring the project back on track. This is almost always both difficult and expensive, and requires highly skilled management, because by now there are many people who have unrealistic expectations.

External events

This cause of failure is normally beyond the control of both project team and higher management. Depending on the environment in which the organization operates, decisive external events can be impossible to anticipate. Still, it is prudent at least to assess the vulnerability of the project to external events, since some are more at risk than others. For example, a project to build a distributed information system for a business in a developing country that will operate on new, state-of-the-art computers communicating over public telephone circuits may be sensitive to external factors such as the reliability of the telephone network and call pricing. By contrast, a project to build an information system that will operate on existing, tried and tested hardware within one building can safely ignore such factors.

Poor project management

The manager of a project is ultimately responsible for its successful completion, and it could therefore be argued that any project failure is also a failure of the project management. To some extent this is true, but there are also some cases where the only identifiable cause of failure overall is a failure of management. This is usually due to poor planning at the start, or to a lack of care in monitoring progress. As a result, the manager allows the project to falter, or permits its costs to grow in an uncontrolled way.

Implementation not feasible

Some projects are over-ambitious in their technical aims, and this may not become evident until an attempt is made to implement the system. This is particularly the case when a system is intended to work together with other systems, whether or not these are already in use. The problems of testing and debugging a new system can grow steadily more complex as attention is focused on larger and larger subsystems. Sometimes the task of interfacing several large, complex software systems, written in different programming languages, installed at different sites and running on different makes of computer hardware, can turn out to be impossible to achieve.

Technical problems with the implementation do not always become evident until after the system is implemented. One example was the LASCAD ambulance dispatch system. Emergency operators who used this system found difficulties with the deliberately high-tech design that relied on an on-screen map display. This was a very early use of a digital map interface, and users found it difficult to pinpoint an ambulance with sufficient accuracy. They regarded it therefore as dangerous (Barker, 1998). This was one factor that led to the system's overall failure to send ambulances quickly to emergencies. A new technology had been applied to a critical task that was not sufficiently understood.

An implementation problem led to the crash of the online sportswear retailer Boo.com in May 2000. The software for their website was much delayed in development, but proved a disaster even when delivered. It turned out that very few home PCs were sufficiently advanced to run the sophisticated 3D visualizations without crashing. Even when the software ran without crashing, most images were very slow to download, adding to the users' frustration. As a result, too few customers bought from the website. The company called in the liquidators after reportedly spending £80m over six months, with no realistic prospect of sales increasing to the point where the business would become viable (Hyde, 2000). Problems of this kind can usually be avoided by sound design practices.

2.4 | The Ethical Dimension

Ethics is loosely defined as the branch of philosophy that is concerned with the rightness or wrongness of human behaviour, and the establishment of moral rules or principles to guide our behaviour. Thinking about ethics normally means that we are trying to work out how to judge the effects that one person's actions have on other people.

Given that all computer-based information systems have a direct effect on someone's life, it is hard to think of one that does not have a significant ethical dimension to its design, construction or use. A system meant to automate some activities of a business may result in job losses among the staff. A social networking site that aims to help people share personal information with their friends can become a means for bullying and harassment. A system with a poorly designed user interface may discriminate against disabled people by making it impossible for them to do their work. In a system designed to extract car registration numbers automatically from speed camera data, the algorithm that renders the car registrations into characters must be accurate and reliable, or else innocent drivers might be pursued by the authorities.

Any failure to consider the ethical consequences of an information system project may cause a problem for someone. Sometimes these problems are noticeable at the time and must be handled within the project; they can otherwise lead to a failure of the project overall. At other times there is hidden damage to a project, an organization, the information systems profession as a whole or even in extreme cases to society at large. However, this is often a contentious issue; there may be disagreement about what is harmful and what is not. A recent example is the debate about the images of city centre and ordinary residential streets posted on Google Street View. Some believe they constitute an infringement of personal privacy, while others can't understand what the fuss is all about. Residents in one UK village blocked access to a camera car because they thought that filming their homes would encourage crime (Moore, 2009). The Hellenic Data Protection Authority banned the filming of Greek streets for Street View until the privacy issues are clarified (BBC, 2009). Google agreed to reshoot its Tokyo images from a lower camera height after complaints from Japanese academics and lawyers (Reuters, 2009). Google believes that the privacy safeguards built into Street View–blurring of faces and removal of contentious images–are already sufficient (Google, 2009). The UK's Information Commissioner appears to agree, ruling that Street View causes only a relatively limited intrusion into people's privacy, and that it does not contravene any laws (ICO, 2009).

One of the difficulties in assessing the ethical issues in a project is that the person who may have a problem is not necessarily the developer of the system, its user, its client–or indeed anyone at all who is obviously connected with the project. In fact, one of the first problems that must be faced in this area is the identification of all the people who may be affected by the system. These are often called *stakeholders*, since, in their different ways, each has a stake in the outcome of the project.

To illustrate the diversity of stakeholders who may be associated with a project, consider the introduction of a network of bank ATM machines in the branches of a supermarket chain. Figure 2.4 shows a preliminary tracing out of the possible effects of this system, together with the groups of people affected.

Not every group identified in this analysis is equally affected by the project, and in some cases the effect is quite minor. However, until such an analysis has been carried out, it is not possible to speak with any confidence about the nature or the extent of impact that a new information system will have. One way of making a comprehensive identification of the ethical dimensions of a software project is to follow the Software Development Impact Statement process (SoDIS). This process is supported by the SoDIS Project Auditor software tool (Rogerson and Gotterbarn, 1998).

Stakeholder affected	Possible consequence of system	Nature of effect on stakeholder
Bank clerks	Automation of bank activities currently carried out manually	Reduced need for staff—redeployment or redundancies
Bank customers	More convenient access to bank services	Improved service
Supermarket customers	More people using supermarket car park	Reduction in service
Bank shareholders	More people attracted to use bank, so greater commercial success	Increased dividends
Supermarket shareholders	More people attracted to use supermarket, so greater commercial success	Increased dividends
Local citizens	More journeys to supermarket to use ATM	Increased pollution

Figure 2.4 Possible stakeholders in a bank ATM network.

2.4.1 Ethical issues within a project

The issue of professionalism is at the forefront of any discussion of ethics within information systems development. By their very nature, information systems projects have deep consequences for the lives and work of many people who either will use the software or will be affected in some way by its use. There are several reasons for this. First, information systems projects are often major investments for the client organization, and money spent on these is necessarily money that now cannot be spent on other worthwhile projects. Second, information systems projects are often concerned with the way that important business activities are carried out, and they can therefore have a direct effect on the overall success or failure of the organization. Third, the introduction or modification of information systems often causes radical changes in the way that employees carry out their work and how they relate to their managers, colleagues and customers. Given these responsibilities, it is important that project team members behave in a professional manner. To some extent this is just a matter of being aware of the rules for behaving in a professional way, and then following them.

Behaving ethically is usually not just a matter of applying a straightforward rule in a mechanical way. We often find ourselves confronting ethical dilemmas, where no single course of action seems entirely right, yet we must find some basis for making a decision. This is compounded when our actions affect different stakeholders in different ways.

Some ethical effects arise from aspects of a project that are not under the direct control of an individual developer. For example, Sachs (1995) describes a 'Trouble Ticketing System' that was intended to improve the work efficiency of testers (telephone repair staff) by tracking the progress of repairs and allocating the next step in a job to any tester that was available at the time. In practice, the system disrupted informal communication between employees, thus damaging their efficiency instead of improving it. According to Sachs, the fault lay in a failure to develop an adequate understanding of the testers' working practices, in particular the way that their informal communications helped in troubleshooting difficult problems. But individual developers are rarely free to choose which aspects of a situation should be analysed.

Legislation adds a further ethical dimension for the members of an information system project team. In the UK the relevant legislation includes the Data Protection Act 1998, the Computer Misuse Act 1990 and the Health and Safety (Display Screen) Regulations 1992. The increasing use of the Internet as a medium for information and exchange also brings cross-border complications. One example was the widely reported 'Internet adoption' case, which involved a British couple who adopted twin baby girls advertised on a website based in the USA. A British court later declared the adoption to be invalid and the twins were returned to the care of their natural father in the USA. In many cases it is far from clear which laws apply when information and services are provided via the Internet to residents of one country, but either the service provider or the information content are hosted within a different country.

2.4.2 Wider ethical issues

One of the longest-running debates associated with IT and IS focuses on the effect they may have on levels of unemployment throughout the world. Some authors have claimed that the spread of IT will cause a rise in global unemployment that will leave countless millions idle and impoverished (Rifkin, 1995). Others argue that, while IT has certainly destroyed some jobs (tens of thousands of jobs lost in the UK banking sector over the last decade), it has also created many new jobs to replace them, often bringing new opportunities to neglected backwaters in the world economy. There is no clear-cut evidence either way.

For many years, an ethical debate has raged between the proponents of freedom (some would say anarchy) on the Internet and the big business interests, who already own its infrastructure and may soon dominate most of its content. In its brief history, the Internet has been at the centre of many debates revolving around freedom of access, including the widespread concerns that have been expressed about the ready availability of pornography, political materials and other contentious content. Yet for many others, this chaotic situation has brought unprecedented opportunities to meet (in a virtual sense) and communicate with similarly minded people all over the world.

One issue that is likely to receive more attention in the next few years is the way that some companies use new applications of IT to gather and exploit unprecedented quantities of detailed personal information. For example, shortly before the first edition of this book was prepared, a South African bank had begun to issue its customers with mobile phones that displayed their current account balance each morning. The phones also enabled the bank to monitor all phone numbers dialled, and this added to the bank's profile of data about individual customers. Customers are categorized, and those that the bank feels are least profitable are 'encouraged' to leave the bank, e.g. by higher service charges. The bank was said to be considering plans to add a geographic information system capability, which would also allow customers' daily movements to be tracked, and a link with Internet providers, which would allow the bank to ascertain which websites are visited by their customers (Collins, 1998a).

Questions of access to computers and computerized information have wide implications. There have been arguments over the years about whether the use or the availability of computers has tended to favour men over women, the middle class over the working class, and those in the affluent north over those from the poor south of the globe. Some suggest that IT and the Internet have created a new 'digital divide' in the world's population, splitting people into the information-rich and the information-poor.

So many things are changing so fast at present that it is difficult to be sure how these questions will seem in a few years' time. It is clear that future generations will look back on our time as one of great change. Such an era inevitably raises profound ethical questions about the effects on our fellow citizens of the way that we design and apply technology.

2.5 Costs of Failure

Many projects discussed in this chapter, particularly the more famous ones (Taurus, the LASCAD system and Boo.com), had very large price tags attached. Private companies are widely thought to be reluctant to admit their failures, since this can reflect badly on the business as a whole, perhaps damaging customers' or investors' confidence. For this reason, it is thought that the known, high-profile failures represent only the visible tip of a much larger iceberg. But project failures are not the only costs associated with project problems. Projects that do not fail outright, but for a variety of reasons do not fully meet their requirements, may cost a great deal of money in other ways.

A system that is poorly designed or functionally limited has many consequences for its users. If we take interface design as an example, a screen layout that compels users to switch back and forth between two screens as they enter data could have effects that range from mild irritation to increased error rates, absence due to sickness, and greater staff turnover. Each has an associated cost, but it may be hard to measure this accurately. It may not be recognized at all. An employee who leaves for another job because of his or her frustration with a poorly designed computer system may not tell anyone their reason for leaving. Now that many businesses sell online, their customers are also users. Customers who dislike the interface of a web ordering or purchasing system may simply defect to another online retailer. A customer lost for this reason has probably been lost for good, but it is very unlikely the company will ever be able to calculate the cost.

System reliability can be important in determining overall costs. Recall the insurance company mentioned above in Figure 2.2, where customers were asked to resubmit personal details, as a computer system crash had caused most customer data to be lost. This is not a reassuring picture for any insurance company to give its customers, and it is a safe assumption that many switched to another insurer as a result. Some will also have told friends and colleagues, who in turn will be less likely to use this company in the future. It is very unlikely that anyone could accurately determine the full cost to this business in terms of lost customers. In the case of Boo.com, a technically inappropriate implementation resulted in the complete failure of the business.

Some of the more routine effects that can occur are summarized in Figure 2.5. This list is by no means exhaustive. But it underlines the importance of getting things right before problems have a chance to appear. This is true even if we ignore the ethical consequences of some information systems applications under development or already in use today. The full social cost of some ethical issues outlined in Section 2.4 is probably incalculable.

However, after so much concentrated attention on the many dead ends that our unluckier (or more careless) predecessors have encountered, it seems appropriate to end

Design aspect	Example	Immediate effects	Other consequences
User interface	Illogical screen layout	Wasted time	Loss of confidence in system
	Difficult to read screens Unhelpful help messages	Increased frustration Increased error-rate	Increased sickness Increased absenteeism Greater staff turnover
Program execution	System response is slow	As above	Increased operating costs
Data storage	Lost data	Extra work re-entering data	Reduced income
	Inaccurate outputs	Extra work checking outputs	Loss of customer confidence Lost sales

Figure 2.5 Some hidden costs of poor design.

the chapter on a final upbeat note. Two of the failures discussed earlier have since become success stories.

The London Stock Exchange went on to successfully install an online share trading system. The new system is much simpler than Taurus–and not all users are entirely happy with its functionality–but it does meet its basic requirements. It was introduced in April 1997, on time and within budget (Philips, 1997).

The London Ambulance Service successfully introduced its new ambulance dispatch system in 1997, too, five years after its disastrous predecessor was scrapped. This time, the project was so successful that it attracted attention from emergency services around the world, and it even won a coveted award (the Elite Group Information Systems Management Award) from the British Computing Society (Barker, 1998).

We can also remind ourselves of the many positive contributions that modern information systems make to our lives, enabling so many things that were not possible for earlier generations. It is difficult to imagine an aspect of life in modern society that is not facilitated in some way by a computerized information system. Our goal, then, should be to ensure that tomorrow's systems build on the successes of the past, while avoiding the problems and failures, as far as it is in our power so to do.

2.6 Summary

In this chapter we have looked at the issue of project failure from many different perspectives, including those of the people who use information systems, the people who purchase them and the people who build them. We have also outlined some of the deeper causes of project and system failure, and considered the costs and wider ethical issues.

The failures in information systems development can teach valuable lessons and, moreover, ignoring a difficulty does not make it go away. Rather, it increases the likelihood of repeating past mistakes. So it is important to understand as much as possible about what can go wrong with an information system development project, the better to be able to avoid it.

Review Questions

2.1 Why do users, clients and developers disagree on the nature and causes of the problems in information systems development?

2.2 What are the main underlying causes of problems in information systems development?

2.3 Define quality.

2.4 What are the main differences between quality problems and productivity problems?

2.5 Why do the requirements drift once a project is under way?

2.6 What can be the results of ignoring the organizational context of an information system?

2.7 Define stakeholder.

2.8 What ethical issues might be involved in setting up an online shopping system that has links to an organization's management information systems?

Case Study Work, Exercises and Projects

2.A Do some research in computing trade journals, and find examples of recent projects that failed or ran into difficulties. Draw up a table with four separate columns. Give these titles like: 'Nature of problem', 'Who sees it as a problem?', 'Probable cause' and 'Flynn category'. Enter the projects into your table, using your own intuition to complete column 3. Then complete the 4th column using Flynn's categories (summarized in Figure 2.3). How do your causes compare with Flynn's categories?

2.B The British Computer Society (BCS) publishes a Code of Conduct for its members, who include thousands of computing and information systems professionals in the UK. In the USA, similar codes are published by the Association for Computing Machinery (ACM) and the Institute of Electrical and Electronic Engineers (IEEE). In many other countries around the world, including India, Zimbabwe and Singapore, there is a national professional society with an equivalent code of professional ethics. Write down some ethical problems associated with the development of an information system to support staff who dispatch ambulances to medical emergencies, and use this to identify a list of issues you would expect to be covered in a professional code of conduct for information systems developers. Then obtain a copy of the BCS Code (BCS, 2009–or, if you are a reader in another country, your nearest local equivalent). Compare it to your list of issues. What are the main differences?

2.C Write down all the stakeholders who you think are associated with an emergency ambulance dispatch system. How are they affected?

2.D Review the ethical issues you identified in Exercise 2.B, and identify one or more issues that appear as a problem from the perspective of one stakeholder, but do not appear as a problem from the perspective of another stakeholder.

2.E Find out what legislation applies to information systems development activity in your country, and what implications it has for developers. Would the South African bank customer profiling system described in Section 2.4.2 be fully legal under these laws? Which particular aspects of the system make it ethically questionable, and from whose perspective?

Further Reading

Trade magazines such as *Computing* and *Computer Weekly* regularly publish articles that report on problems in current projects as they occur.

Sauer (1993) discusses reasons for project failures in terms of the project's organizational environment, and includes several practical case studies that illustrate the problems in practice.

Galin (2003) is one of many books that deal with software quality assurance (SQA), a discipline that endeavours to ensure that software systems fully meet their defined requirements. The latest edition of Pressman's standard software engineering text (2009) also has a good chapter on SQA.

De Montfort University's Centre for Computing and Social Responsibility runs a website that focuses on ethical issues in information systems development. This has many links to other sites, and also carries the full text of a number of academic papers in this field. It can be found at www.ccsr.cse.dmu.ac.uk.

Meeting the Challenges

3.1 | Introduction

For successful information systems development we need to adopt strategies and procedures that will address the challenges described in Chapter 2. The problems that give rise to these challenges can be categorized in various ways. We have chosen to divide them into: those that are concerned with productivity; those that relate to poor quality; and those concerned with installation and operation. These categories are not necessarily mutually exclusive and other broader categorizations could be adopted. For example, Poor Response Times could result from a quality problem in the design or construction of the software or it could be a consequence of poor installation. Figure 3.1 lists the problems and identifies some of the ways that they can be ameliorated. Some of the solutions are necessarily complex and involve the combination of several strategies or procedures. A common feature in many of the solutions discussed in this chapter is effective analysis and design.

The successful development and use of an information system is contingent upon many factors and these factors may vary between different types of development project. We believe that the object-oriented approach increases the chance of success in most information systems development projects. One major source of difficulty is the inherent complexity of software development. In an object-oriented approach, using object-oriented languages for implementation, complexity is managed in such a way as to help address this problem. This is not discussed in this chapter which considers more general issues but is considered from Chapter 4 onwards.

Type of problem	Problem	How to minimize risk
Quality	Wrong problem is addressed	Strategic Information Systems Planning, Business Modelling, Systematic Approach
	Project undertaken for wrong reason	Strategic Information Systems Planning, Business Modelling, Systematic Approach, Prototyping
	Wider influences are neglected	Systematic Approach, Requirements, Prototyping
	Missing or inappropriate functionality	
	Incorrect requirements analysis	Systematic Approach, RUP, AUP, EUP
	Users change their minds	Prototyping, User involvement, RUP, AUP
	External events change the environment	
	Poor interface design	Prototyping, User involvement
	Inappropriate data entry	
	Software causes inappropriate ways of working	Systematic Approach, User involvement
	Incomprehensible error messages	User involvement
	Unhelpful 'help'	
	Requirements changed before project delivery	Systematic Approach, RUP, Agile, AUP
Installation & Operation	Poor installation	Systematic Approach, Test, Deployment
	Unreliability in operation	
	Operational issues	Systematic Approach, Test
	Poor response times	
	Poor documentation inhibits maintenance	Systematic Approach, Software Development Tools
	Local resistance to new information system	User involvement
Productivity	Implementation is not feasible	Prototyping
	Impossible targets	Systematic Approach, Agile, AUP, DSDM
	Time constraints	
	Requirements drift	
	Poor project control	Manage IS development, Reuse
	Late delivery	
	Failure to deliver any system	
	Cost overrun	
	Developers not familiar with OO	Manage IS development, Training

Figure 3.1 Causes of IS project failure and indicative solutions.

3.2 | Responding to the Problems

The indicative solutions to the problems identified in Chapter 2 are introduced below. Where different problems share similar solutions they are discussed together. Later in the chapter the main themes that underpin these solutions are discussed in more detail.

3.2.1 Quality problems

Quality problems can mostly be managed by adopting a systematic approach to systems development. This is typically divided into a series of separate phases and activities to make it easier to manage. The waterfall lifecycle model is an example of a systematic approach that continues to be used after nearly 40 years, but it has various deficiencies that are discussed later in the chapter and organizations are moving to other approaches. Approaches have been developed to address the difficulties inherent in the waterfall lifecycle by involving users more and by making the development process more responsive to potential changes in requirements. Nowadays many of these approaches develop software using object-orientation. Examples of modern approaches to software development include the IBM Rational Unified Process (RUP) (IBM, 2009), the Agile Unified Process (AUP) (Ambler, 2009) and the Enterprise Unified Process (EUP) (Ambler et al., 2005). These approaches differ in the emphasis and scope. For example, EUP considers the retirement or decommissioning of an information system. AUP has a reduced number of activities. This makes it more responsive to changes in user requirements and working software can be delivered early in the development process. The different systematic approaches may be suited to different types of information systems development project. However, the appropriateness of particular approaches is hotly debated. Each of the problems is discussed in turn below.

Wrong problem. This sort of issue typically arises because the information system does not align with the organizational strategy or goals. One way to understand the organizational goals is to embark upon a *strategic information systems planning* exercise as a precursor to information systems development. As discussed in Chapter 1 the Business Strategy drives the IS Strategy which in turn drives the IT Strategy. Information systems work within the context of an organization and must satisfy its current requirements as well as provide a basis from which future needs can be addressed. This helps to ensure that wider influences, including the impact of organizational influences and culture, are not neglected. As a general example, in the Agate case study a strategic decision may be made to target multinational companies for international advertising campaigns. This has consequences for campaign management and its supporting information systems.

Strategic information systems planning does not address all the issues. Some form of *business modelling* needs to be undertaken to determine how an information system can support a particular business activity. It is important to understand how the activity is performed and how it contributes to the objectives of the organization. Campaign management is an important business function for Agate and it should be modelled in order to determine how it is carried out, thus providing some of the parameters for subsequent information systems development. To avoid addressing the wrong problem the objectives that the information system needs to meet must be carefully understood and analyzed. This can be achieved by ensuring requirements are captured effectively. These should be analyzed in the context of the organizational goals.

Project undertaken for the wrong reason. Organizational goals and strategy have to be understood and followed to ensure that the information systems development project is focused so that it will benefit the organization. Sometimes it is not obvious to potential users how a system is likely to operate and this can be addressed by adopting a prototyping approach. In software development a prototype is a system or a partially complete system that is built quickly to explore some aspect of the user requirements. A prototype will give the users the opportunity to experience how some aspects of the system operate earlier during the development so that they can determine if the original objectives are being addressed. A key feature of successful prototyping is user involvement in the evaluation of the prototype.

Wider influence neglected. The context within which an information system is going to operate should be considered during the requirements capture. However it is not always easy to anticipate how a system will operate in a particular work culture or environment and, as discussed earlier, a prototyping approach enables the users to experience and influence the development of the system.

Incorrect requirements analysis. This will produce incorrect or incomplete interpretation of the requirements leading to inappropriate design decisions resulting in a delivered system that does not satisfy the user needs. Requirements analysis is not the only activity in systems development that can have an adverse effect if performed incorrectly. Incorrect requirements capture, design, implementation and test should also be considered under this heading. A systematic approach that incorporates guidance on how these activities should be performed reduces the risk of them being performed incorrectly. (RUP or AUP are examples.)

Users change their minds. External events change in the environment. Users only change their minds because they have to–either external events have changed the requirements or the users have understood their needs more clearly and hence have to modify the requirements. It is not possible to avoid this happening but it is possible to minimize any adverse impact on the project. A key aspect is continuing user involvement throughout the project and this should include some early prototyping at least in terms of the way the system will operate. Although this might just be at the level of the non-functioning interface mock-ups it gives the users more insight into what will be offered by the completed system. Using an approach like RUP or AUP also gives the development team a better chance of responding to changing requirements effectively.

Poor interface design. This includes producing a system with *inappropriate data entry, incomprehensible error messages, unhelpful 'help'* and *inappropriate ways of working.* The importance of an appropriate human–computer interface cannot be overstated. If the interface does not support the users and the way they work, the success of the information system will be reduced significantly. Poor interface design can be addressed by adopting accepted good practice (discussed in Chapter 16) and ensuring that the users are involved in reviewing the proposed interface early on in the development cycle. This can be achieved by adopting a prototyping or an incremental development approach or both. An incremental approach aims to deliver the working system in parts (increments) thus giving the user part of the functioning system early in the development cycle.

Requirements changed before project delivery. Poor or incomplete requirements capture is one possible cause of this problem. As described earlier this can be remedied by adopting a systematic approach, the possible use of prototyping and incremental development, and effective user involvement. This particular problem has also been cited as a possible consequence of using the waterfall lifecycle model (Figure 3.3). In the waterfall lifecycle each particular stage has to be completed and agreed by the client before the next stage can begin. This tends to increase the time between requirements capture and system delivery, thus increasing the likelihood that requirements will have changed. This difficulty can be overcome by adopting a development approach that involves the users to a greater extent and delivers increments of the system early during the development. Agile development approaches like AUP help address this problem by focusing on producing working software as early as possible.

3.2.2 Installation and operation problems

The problems associated with *installation and operation* may be a consequence of quality problems during the development process. Many happen because installation or operational issues are not considered sufficiently (or at all). It may be that non-functional requirements such as response times or reliability targets are not captured, or the system that is constructed does not satisfy them.

Poor installation. Operational issues. Inefficient or incorrect installation results in poor system performance such as poor response time or other operational problems that can make the system completely unusable. Planning for the installation is an integral part of the systems development and should consider the hardware and operating system platform for deployment. A key factor for a successful installation is testing whether the system operating on the planned hardware and software platform can cope with the peaks of user activity and the maximum transaction throughput. This is known as stress testing and may be achieved by constructing a prototype installation so that the best installation parameters can be determined. A systematic approach to development will include a focus on deploying the new system and the transition from development to operation.

Poor response times. Unreliability in operation. These problems can be dealt with by ensuring that the system undergoes a thorough testing regime both during development and before full operation. It is important to test the system against all the requirements that have been elicited from the users. The approach to requirements capture and recording discussed in Chapter 6 helps in this respect.

Poor documentation inhibits maintenance. Many computer information systems need to be modified after they have been implemented (this is known as maintenance), either to correct problems or to add new functionality. If the system is not documented then modifying the system can be unnecessarily time consuming. If the system is appropriately documented it is much quicker to identify those parts of the system that need to be modified. An effective way of producing useful documentation is to follow a systematic approach (e.g. RUP) using a software development toolset. This makes it much easier to produce suitable documentation and to keep it up to date as the project progresses.

Local resistance to new information system. This can occur when a particular information system solution is being imposed by management without the agreement or support of the users. It can also occur when the information system is not seen as appropriate or relevant by the users. In all cases it is important to work with local management to reduce local hostility and this is likely to require user involvement in the project. This may allow alternative, more acceptable or more appropriate solutions to be found or at least a better demonstration of the value of the proposed information system.

3.2.3 Productivity problems

The problems associated with productivity are typically addressed by using a systematic approach to systems development. The reuse of existing software or other artefacts of development, in the form of components, is a feature of many approaches to systems development. This together with a move to service-oriented architectures where software components provides services for the application can help to reduce the time to development and cost. Productivity problems may also be addressed by applying project management techniques. Project management techniques are described in Chapter 22 on the book website.

Implementation is not feasible. On some projects it may become apparent that the implementation is not feasible only after a significant amount of time and money has been expended. Potential areas of difficulty should be identified early on in the project and prototypes constructed to determine the feasibility of implementation. Decisions can then be taken either to change the scope of the project so that it can be implemented or to cancel the project.

Impossible targets. Time constraints. The worst possible response to impossible targets is to continue with the project as if the targets do not matter. This will result in late delivery and user dissatisfaction. It is much better to have an open dialogue with the users and project sponsor about the difficulty of delivering the project within the time constraints given the objective of either increasing the time and resource available or reducing the requirements so that they can be delivered using the available resource and within the original time constraints. Frequently increasing the time or resource available is not a viable option because of increased cost or because the resource is not available or because the delivery deadline for the system is fixed by external factors. Omitting the least important requirements from a project needs careful negotiation with users and project sponsors. This should be done so that a useful product can be delivered on time. The management of the requirements to be delivered is a feature of several approaches and is very clearly described in the Dynamic Systems Development Method (DSDM) which is discussed in Chapter 21.

Requirements drift (*scope creep*). It is quite common for potential users to identify new requirements during systems development. If all additional requirements are included in the project it is quite likely that the delivery of the system will be delayed or even completely stalled. The addition of new requirements has to be controlled. The users and project sponsors need to understand when a new requirement is going to put the project back or cause an increase in cost or both. Agile approaches like DSDM or AUP offer greater flexibility in adding new requirements but the potential problems remain the same. A change control procedure should be put in place to manage changing requirements.

Poor project control. Late delivery. Failure to deliver any system. Cost overrun. These four issues are features of poor project control. The late delivery of computerized information systems can be attributed to various factors: possible poor requirements capture causing reworking of the system late in the project; poor project management or time control; a failure to identify over-ambitious delivery dates; encountering unanticipated technical problems and many others. Cost overruns can be caused by late delivery (developers have to be paid for longer), using additional developers on the project to address late running or to overcome a particular technical problem or perhaps most mundanely, underestimating the cost of software and hardware resources for the development of the information system or its operation. Poor project control is addressed by using appropriate project management techniques including risk identification and management. Alongside good project management an appropriate systematic approach to the development needs to be followed.

Developers not familiar with OO. Object-oriented methodologies and techniques are increasingly being used for software development. Many of the programming languages that are now used are object-oriented. However, there is still a significant proportion of development that uses non-object-oriented techniques and some developers may not be familiar with object-orientation. It is crucial that these developers are given the appropriate training before embarking upon a software development project that uses object-orientation. Failure to do this causes major problems as these developers inevitably will attempt to use O-O development environments and languages in a non-O-O manner which will not only negate any of the benefits of using an O-O approach but significantly reduce the likelihood of project success.

3.3 Project Lifecycles

A common theme in the indicative solutions discussed earlier is the need to use a systematic approach when developing information systems. There are many different approaches but most utilize, in some form or other, a general problem-solving approach. Figure 3.2 shows a general problem-solving model adapted from Hicks (1991) that has six phases or stages. The phases *Data gathering* and *Problem redefinition* are concerned with understanding what the problem is about; the *Finding ideas* phase attempts to identify ideas that help us to understand more about the nature of the problem and possible solutions. *Finding solutions* is concerned with providing a solution to the problem and *Implementation* puts the solution into practice. This approach to problem solving divides a task into subtasks, each with a particular focus and objective.

The information systems development process may be subdivided simply into three main tasks: understanding the problem, choosing and designing a solution, and finally building the solution. There are many other ways of subdividing an information systems

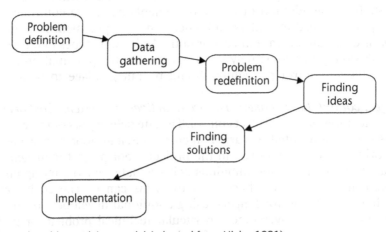

Figure 3.2 General problem-solving model (adapted from Hicks, 1991).

project but they all include an analysis activity that identifies what the system should do, a design activity that determines how best to do it and some construction activity that builds the system according to the design. The phases that contain these activities are given various names but the core activities remain the same.

Subdividing the development process produces smaller tasks that can be managed more easily. This helps achieve the appropriate quality standards and makes project management and budgetary control easier. We have already alluded to the benefits to be gained from managing the software development process effectively and have explicitly identified poor project management as a source of many of the problems. Building a software system is very different from building almost any other human artefact. Software is intangible, it cannot be weighed, its strength cannot be measured, its durability cannot be assessed, and its resistance to physical stress cannot be gauged. Of course we try to find (with some success) measures of a software system that enable us to make judgements about its size, its complexity, the resource required to build it, and so on. But these measures are much less well understood than their counterparts in the design and construction of tangible artefacts such as buildings.

3.3.1 Waterfall lifecycle model

Just as an animal goes through a series of developmental stages from its conception to its demise so, it is argued, does a computerized information system. Various lifecycle models can be applied to computerized information systems development. We will discuss some of the most commonly used.

Figure 3.3 shows one version of the waterfall lifecycle. Strictly speaking this does not cover the complete lifecycle as there is no stage concerned with the retirement or decommissioning of the information system. Some lifecycle models are more comprehensive than others. Earlier in Section 3.2 we identified strategic information systems planning and business modelling as important precursors to information systems development, and these could be viewed as two preliminary stages. The successful completion of these activities should ensure that the information system that is developed is appropriate to the organization. It can be argued that these are part of the information systems development lifecycle. However, their focus is not on computerization, per se, but rather the identification of organizational requirements. Their importance is almost universally accepted for commercially oriented computer systems development. There is a distinction to be made between systems development, where a system may incorporate human, software and hardware elements, and software development that focuses primarily on software construction, although it involves the human users and the hardware upon which it executes. It is perhaps a matter of perspective. Thus a software development project is, by definition, focused solely on producing a software system that will satisfy the user requirements, whereas strictly speaking a systems development project has a wider scope and may not even include software as part of the solution.

There are many variations of the waterfall lifecycle (e.g. Pressman, 2009; Sommerville, 2007), differing chiefly in the number and names of phases, and the activities allocated to them. One of the benefits of using lifecycle models is that their phases have explicitly defined products or deliverables. Sommerville (1992) suggests a series of deliverables produced by different phases of development, shown in Fig. 3.4.

These products can be used to monitor productivity and the quality of the activity performed. Several phases have more than one deliverable. If we need to show a finer

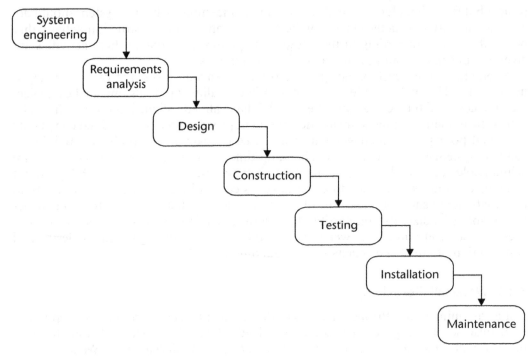

Figure 3.3 Waterfall lifecycle model.

Phase	Output deliverables
System engineering	High-level architectural specification
Requirements analysis	Requirements specification Functional specification Acceptance test specification
Design	Software architecture specification System test specification Design specification Subsystem test specification Unit test specification
Construction	Program code
Testing	Unit test report Subsystem test report System test report Acceptance test report Completed system
Installation	Installed system
Maintenance	Change requests Change request report

Figure 3.4 Lifecycle deliverables (adapted from Sommerville, 1992).

level of detail to assist in the monitoring and control of the project, phases can be split so that each sub-phase has only one deliverable. Alternatively, a phase may be viewed as comprising a series of activities, each of which has a single deliverable and can be managed individually. Different types of project and different styles of organization may suit different styles of project lifecycle. When an organization embarks upon a systems development project it should specify the stages in the systems development process, their associated deliverables and the type of lifecycle to be used in a way that is applicable to its organizational context and the nature of the systems being developed.

As mentioned earlier the waterfall lifecycle has been used for many years and is the subject of several criticisms.

- Real projects rarely follow such a simple sequential lifecycle. Project phases overlap and activities may have to be repeated.
- It is almost inevitable that some tasks will have to be repeated. For example inadequacies in the requirements analysis may become evident during design, construction or testing necessitating further requirements analysis, some potential reworking of design and further software construction and test. The cyclical repetition of tasks is termed iteration.
- A great deal of time may elapse between the initial systems engineering and the final installation. Requirements will almost inevitably have changed in the meantime and users find little use in a system that satisfies yesterday's requirements but hampers current operations.
- It tends to be unresponsive to changes in client requirements or technology during the project. For example, if architectural decisions have been made during systems engineering they can be difficult to change. A technological innovation that may make it feasible to automate different parts of the whole system may become available after the project has been running for some time. It may not be possible to incorporate the new technology without redoing much of the analysis and design work already completed.

The waterfall lifecycle, as an example of a systematic approach, does provide a structure for a systems development project which ameliorates some, but by no means all, of the problems discussed in Chapter 2. The effectiveness of an approach is dependent upon the type of project and the suitability of the techniques (e.g. analysis techniques such as data flow modelling which is briefly described on the book website). The waterfall approach is more suited to projects where requirements are stable and not likely to change during the development process, where there is less need for user involvement and where it is not necessary to see some parts of the information system (e.g. increments or prototypes) delivered during the development process. However, increasingly, these features are essential to successful development and consequently many development projects have moved away from the waterfall lifecycle. They are now adopting approaches that encourage greater user involvement, incremental delivery, iteration and possibly prototyping.

3.3.2 Prototyping

Users may find it difficult to imagine how their requirements will be translated into a working system. When the waterfall model is used, the final working system is produced at the end of the project. This approach has a significant difficulty, in that the user only actually experiences how the system operates once it is delivered. The prototyping approach overcomes many of the potential misunderstandings and ambiguities that may exist in the requirements.

In software development a prototype is a system or a partially complete system that is built quickly to explore some aspect of the system requirements and that is not intended as the final working system. A prototype system is differentiated from the final production system by incompleteness and perhaps by a less-resilient construction. If the prototype is to be discarded once it has fulfilled its objectives, the effort required to build a resilient prototype would be wasted. A prototype will typically lack full functionality. It may have limited data processing capacity, it may exhibit poor performance characteristics or it may have been developed with limited quality assurance. Prototype development commonly uses rapid development tools, though such tools are also used for the development of production systems.

Prototypes may be constructed with various objectives in mind. A prototype may be used to investigate user requirements as described in Chapter 5. For example, a prototype may be focused on the human–computer interface in order to determine what data should be presented to the user and what data should be captured from the user. A prototype might also be used to investigate the most suitable form of interface. A prototype may be constructed to determine whether a particular implementation platform can support certain processing requirements. A prototype might be concerned with determining the efficacy of a particular language or a database management system or the appropriateness of a technological choice (e.g. using hand-held devices for data capture in a factory). A lifecycle for prototyping is shown in Fig. 3.5.

The main stages required to prepare a prototype are as follows.

- Perform an initial analysis.
- Define prototype objectives.
- Specify prototype.
- Construct prototype.
- Evaluate prototype and recommend changes.
- If the prototype is not completed, repeat the process from the specify prototype stage.

These are described in more detail below.

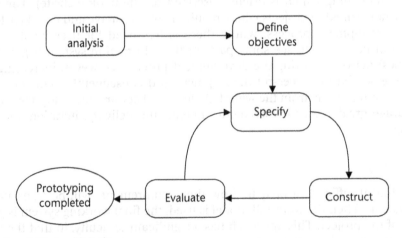

Figure 3.5 A prototyping lifecycle.

Perform an initial analysis
All software development activity utilizes valuable resources. A prototyping exercise that lacks some initial analysis is likely to be an ill-focused and unstructured activity that produces poorly designed software. The initial analysis should determine the general requirements of the information system so that the particular aspects that should be prototyped can be identified.

Define prototype objectives
Prototyping should have clearly stated objectives. A prototyping exercise may involve many iterations, each iteration resulting in some improvement to the prototype. This may make it difficult for the participants in a prototyping exercise to determine if there is sufficient value to continue the prototyping. However, with clearly defined objectives it should be possible to decide if they have been achieved. In most cases the objectives of the proto-typing activity should be agreed with the users so that there is no misunderstanding as to what will be achieved. For example, if the prototype is only intended to explore the human–computer interface requirements, the users should not be led to expect the delivery of a working part of the application. If a prototype is only built to test whether some technical aspect of the system will work, it may not be appropriate to involve the users at all.

Specify prototype
Although the prototype is not intended for extended operation it is important that it embodies the requisite behaviour. It is almost certainly the case that the prototype will be subject to modification and this will be easier if the software is built according to sound design principles. The approach to specification needs to be appropriate for the type of prototype. The techniques used to specify a prototype that focuses on testing the user interface (see Chapter 16) will be different from those to specify a prototype that aims to test some technical aspect of the system architecture and implementation (see Chapter 19).

Construct prototype
Since it is important that prototype development is rapid, the use of a rapid development environment is appropriate. For example, if an interactive system is being prototyped, environments such as Delphi or Visual Basic can be most effective.

Evaluate prototype and recommend changes
The purpose of the prototype is to test or explore some aspect of the proposed system. The prototype should be evaluated with respect to the objectives identified at the beginning of the exercise. If the objectives have not been met, then the evaluation should specify modifications to the prototype so that it may achieve its objectives. The last three stages are repeated until the prototyping objectives are achieved.

Prototyping has the following advantages:

- Early demonstrations of system functionality help identify any misunderstandings between developer and client.
- Client requirements that have been missed are identified.
- Difficulties in the interface can be identified.
- The feasibility and usefulness of the system can be tested, even though, by its very nature, the prototype is incomplete.

Prototyping also has several problems and their impact on a particular project should be estimated before engaging in prototyping:

- The client may perceive the prototype as part of the final system, may not understand the effort that will be required to produce a working production system and may expect delivery soon.
- The prototype may divert attention from functional to solely interface issues.
- Prototyping requires significant user involvement, which may not be available.
- Managing the prototyping lifecycle requires careful decision making.

Prototyping may be used as a part of the larger development lifecycle to avoid some of the problems identified in Chapter 2. For some projects it may be appropriate to use prototyping as the overall lifecycle approach. For example, if the requirements for the project are not clearly understood then repeated refinement of a prototype may be an effective way of producing the final system.

3.3.3 Iterative and incremental development

A common thread in many current approaches to software development is an iterative lifecycle. In an iterative approach the project is made up of a series of development activities that are repeated. Each of these repetitions is an iteration and each can be viewed as a mini-project in its own right producing new artifacts or successively better or more complete artifacts. Gilb (1988) suggests that successful large systems start out as successful small systems that grow incrementally. An incremental approach performs some initial analysis to scope the problem and identify major requirements. Those requirements that will deliver most benefit to the client are selected to be the focus of a first increment of development and delivery. The installation of each increment provides feedback to the development team and informs the development of subsequent increments. Boehm's (1988) spiral model can be viewed as supporting incremental delivery.

Figure 3.6 shows how Boehm's spiral model can be adapted to suit incremental delivery. Note that prototyping may be used either during the risk analysis or during the software development part of the development cycle.

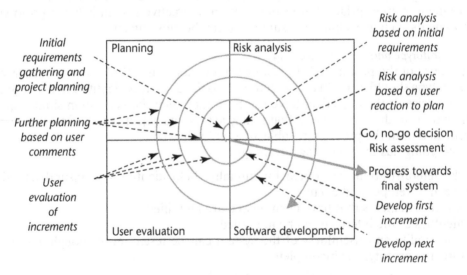

Figure 3.6 Spiral model for incremental delivery (adapted from Boehm, 1988).

Iterative development may result in incremental delivery, though some approaches produce the increments only for internal release to the development team and not for external release to the client. An increment is part of the final delivered system and could include any development artifacts (e.g. requirements documentation, some working software). Many current approaches are categorized as iterative and incremental to reflect the iterative nature of the development process and the incremental nature of the system delivery.

3.4 | Methodological Approaches

A methodology comprises an approach to software development, a set of techniques and notations that support the approach, a lifecycle model to structure the development process and a unifying set of procedures and philosophy. For example, RUP is an object-oriented methodology that uses UML and follows an iterative and incremental lifecycle. A methodological approach is a coherent and consistent systematic approach to development. Adopting an appropriate methodology for an information systems development project is one of the most important factors in minimizing the problems that we discussed in Chapter 2. In this text we do not espouse a particular named methodology but apply object-oriented techniques in a co-ordinated and methodical fashion using UML. Methodologies are discussed in more detail in Chapter 21 but we introduce some important examples here to illustrate how they address the problems from Chapter 2.

One of the major influences on the quality of the systems developed is the approach adopted. If the approach used is not appropriate for a particular type of application then it may limit the quality of the system being produced. We believe that the methodological approach adopted should be based upon object-orientation. Object-orientation provides a way of describing real-world problems in terms of abstractions from which software can be developed effectively. The increasing complexity of information systems makes the use of an object-oriented approach more important. Object-orientation provides conceptual structures that help to deal with the development of complex information systems by splitting the system into smaller, less complex parts that interact. It also aims to provide ways to support the reuse of program code, design and analysis models helping to improve quality and productivity.

3.4.1 Unified Software Development Process

The Unified Software Development Process (USDP) (Jacobson et al., 1999) arose from a desire to produce a single common methodological approach for object-oriented software development by bringing together best practice in the 1990s. The movement to produce a unified process resulted in the definition of the Unified Modelling Language (UML) which is considered in detail from Chapter 4 onwards. USDP reflected the emphasis in the 1990s on iterative and incremental lifecycles. It built upon previous approaches by Jacobson et al. (1992), Booch (1994) and Rumbaugh et al. (1991). USDP incorporates UML and comprises much good advice on software development. USDP will be discussed in more detail later (Chapter 21). The IBM Rational Unified Process (RUP) incorporates much of the practice embodied in USPD and has been developed significantly beyond the specification of USDP by Jacobson et al. in 1999.

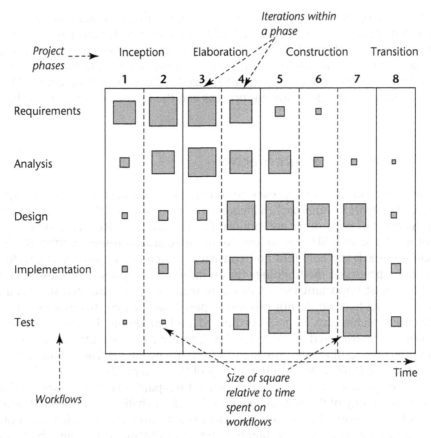

Figure 3.7 The Unified Software Development Process (adapted from Jacobson et al., 1999).

A development cycle for the USDP is illustrated in Fig. 3.7 and comprises four phases.

- *Inception* is concerned with determining the scope and purpose of the project.
- *Elaboration* focuses on requirements capture and determining the structure of the system.
- *Construction*'s main aim is to build the software system.
- *Transition* deals with product installation and rollout.

A development cycle may be made up of many iterations. In Fig. 3.7 there are two iterations in the inception phase and three in the construction phase. The actual number of iterations in each phase varies from project to project. At the end of each iteration an increment is delivered and its composition may range from elements of a requirements model to working program code for a portion of the system. In the USDP an increment is not necessarily additive; it may be a reworked version of a previous increment.

The diagram also illustrates that a phase may involve a series of different activities or workflows. This is different from the waterfall lifecycle, in which each phase largely comprises a single activity. The inception phase may include elements of all of the workflows, though it is likely that design, implementation (i.e. constructing the software) and test would be focused on any necessary exploratory prototyping. However, most commonly, inception would involve primarily the requirements and analysis workflows.

RUP has the same phases as USDP but has a more extensive series of workflows or activities (they are called disciplines in RUP). They are:

- *Business modelling* focuses on understanding the business, its current problems and areas for possible improvement.
- *Requirements* describes how to identify and document user requirements.
- *Analysis and design* is concerned with building analysis and design models from which the system can be constructed.
- *Implementation* deals with the coding and construction of the system.
- *Test* verifies that the products developed satisfy the requirements identified.
- *Deployment* deals with product releases and the delivery of the software to the end users.

These disciplines embody the procedures and techniques (using UML) that address many of the problems listed in Figure 3.1. For example, *business modelling* along with *strategic information systems planning* helps to ensure that the correct problem is addressed for the correct reasons. *Requirements* and *analysis and design* provide the detailed guidance needed to ensure that requirements capture is performed effectively, and that this is followed by detailed and thorough analysis and design.

The *test* discipline includes testing for reliability, functionality, application performance and system performance. All of these aspects contribute to the effective operation of a system. The *deployment* discipline provides guidance and techniques so that the software installation and the operation of the working system satisfy user requirements.

There are also three supporting disciplines: *configuration management*, *project management* and *environment*. These activities provide guidance and advice on controlling and managing the development project and are discussed in Section 3.5.

One extension to the RUP is the Enterprise Unified Process (EUP) (Ambler et al., 2005). This includes two additional phases after *transition*: *production* and *retirement*. *Production* is concerned with the operation of the information system during its working life. *Retirement* deals with decommissioning the system when it is no longer seen as useful.

3.4.2 Agile approaches

A group of software developers and methodology authors met in February 2001 and produced a manifesto for *Agile* software development. Their objective was to introduce approaches to software development that are less bureaucratic, less focused on documentation and more focused on user interaction and the early delivery of working software than current heavyweight methodologies. Their manifesto is shown in its entirety in Fig. 3.8. The preference for customer collaboration over contract negotiation in the manifesto suggests the need to adopt new forms of customer relationship that acknowledge that requirements change during software development. This in turn emphasizes the key importance of strong customer or user involvement.

Problems with some of the methodologies in the 1980s and 1990s that incorporated the waterfall lifecycle included unresponsiveness to change and a highly bureaucratic approach to analysis and design that was also heavy on documentation. USDP and RUP were also considered by some developers to be processes that required too much

---

Manifesto for Agile Software Development

We are uncovering better ways of developing software
by doing and helping others do it.
Through this work we have come to value:

Individuals and interactions over processes and tools
Working software over comprehensive documentation
Customer collaboration over contract negotiation
Responding to change over following a plan

That is, while there is value in the items on the right, we value the items on the left more.

Figure 3.8 The Manifesto for Agile Software Development.

documentation and were too bureaucratic. In order to overcome some of these problems, iterative lightweight approaches emerged that were typically used for small to medium business information systems where there was appreciable requirements change during the life of the project. XP (Extreme Programming) is an early example of such an approach (Beck, 2004). XP does not emphasize early analysis and design documentation and is an iterative and incremental approach. It is an example of a group of lightweight methodologies that are now termed 'Agile'. A fundamental feature of Agile approaches is the acceptance that user requirements will change during development and that this must be accommodated by the development process. DSDM (Dynamic System Development Method) is viewed by some as another example of an Agile approach (Fowler, 2004). Both XP and DSDM are described further in Chapter 21.

RUP can also be used in an Agile manner (Pollice, 2001). The Agile Unified Process (AUP) (Ambler, 2009) is one cut-down version of RUP and, as its name suggests, is considered to be an Agile approach. AUP has the same phases as RUP (and USDP) but incorporates business modelling, requirements, and analysis and design into a single discipline called *model*. The Essential Unified Process (EssUP) simplifies AUP even further. These Agile approaches aim to address the quality problems listed in Figure 3.1 and also many of the productivity problems by using a lightweight approach.

In many ways Agile approaches are the antithesis of methodologies based on the waterfall lifecycle model, which assume a belief that requirements are fixed. The degree to which requirements are subject to change during software development varies from project to project. The approach that is being used should be capable of coping with change in requirements. Nonetheless, the importance of effective requirements capture, documentation, analysis and design should not be underestimated irrespective of the size of project. Boehm (2002) draws a distinction between plan-based and Agile methods and suggests that both have their place. (As one might expect, the emphasis on planning early in the project varies from one Agile methodology to another.) The need for systems that dependably deliver agreed requirements suggests that planning and effective analysis and design with appropriate documentation have an important role in software development. One possible criticism of Agile approaches is that they rely heavily upon the experience and ability of the development team. Approaches like RUP (and possibly AUP) overcome this by providing much more detailed guidance on what artifacts to produce, what process to follow and what project roles are needed.

3.5 Managing Information Systems Development

Good management of an information systems development project can reduce the likelihood of many problems. These include requirements drift, late delivery and cost overrun. For example, the three supporting disciplines of RUP help to manage a development project:

- *Configuration management* is concerned with version control of the documents and artifacts produced and also with the management of change requests.
- *Project management* deals with project planning and control at the phase level describing the overall project and at more detailed level for each of the iterations.
- *Environment* is concerned with tailoring the development process, ensuring that it and its support tools are appropriate for the project.

Configuration management helps address the issues of requirement drift by including a process to manage and control change requests. This can ensure that potential changes to requirements during the development are examined to determine their impact on the delivery schedule and the project cost. It is then a matter of discussion with the project sponsors whether the benefits gained from the change outweigh any delay or cost overrun.

Effective project management is essential to ensure that the project runs to schedule and that costs are controlled. In RUP the project management discipline focuses on planning both at the phase level for the project as a whole and at iteration level within the phases. It also includes project monitoring to determine how the project is progressing and risk management to identify and take action to ameliorate any risks. This is a narrow view of project management. In addition it is necessary to manage the human resources in terms of employment and allocation to tasks, the budget in terms of resources allocated to different tasks and activities, and perhaps the contracts for the hardware and software to support the development. It is also important to manage the relationship with the customer. Some approaches include these aspects as part of the project management activity. No matter how they are categorized, human resource management, budget management and contract management are important to the success of a project.

3.5.1 Iterative lifecycle

The iterative lifecycle is fundamental to many of the modern approaches to systems development (e.g. RUP) and offers the following:

- risk mitigation
- change management
- team learning
- improved quality.

Risk mitigation

An iterative process enables the identification of potential risks and problems earlier in the life of a project. The early emphasis on architecture and the fact that construction, test and deployment activities are begun early on make it possible to identify technological problems and to take action to reduce their impact. Integration of subsystems is begun earlier and is less likely to throw up unpleasant surprises at the last minute.

Change management

Users' requirements do change during the course of a project, often because of the time that projects take, and often because until they see some results they may not be sure what they want. This last point is sometimes referred to as IKIWISI–'I'll Know It When I See It'. In a waterfall lifecycle changing requirements are a problem; in an iterative lifecycle there is an expectation that some requirements activities will still be going on late in the project and it is easier to cope with changes. It is also possible to revise decisions about technology during the project, as the hardware and software available to do the job will almost certainly change during the project.

Team learning

Members of the team, including those responsible for testing and deployment, are involved in the project from the start, and this makes it easier for them to learn about and understand the requirements and the solution. They are not suddenly presented with a new and unfamiliar system. It is also possible to identify training needs and provide the training while developers are still working on an aspect of the system.

Improved quality

Testing of deliverables begins early and continues throughout the project. This helps to prevent the situation where all testing is done in a final 'big bang' and there is little time to resolve bugs that are found.

The successful management of a software development project is important for its success.

3.6 User Involvement

Continued and effective user involvement throughout the project is an important factor in maximizing the chance of success. The traditional waterfall lifecycle is less amenable to user involvement during the whole project and hence is less likely to stay in line with the changing user requirements. A prototyping approach is normally dependent upon continuing user involvement and by its very nature encourages it. However, care has to be taken to ensure that the users have sufficient time to perform their roles effectively. In prototyping, the evaluation of the prototype requires significant time from the users.

Users can be involved in projects at various levels and can play many different roles. Some approaches to software development (e.g. DSDM) directly involve users in the development team, so that they then have a significant opportunity to influence the way the project proceeds, perhaps by identifying difficulties and suggesting more acceptable alternatives. It is important that users who have such a significant influence on the direction of the project should understand the organizational requirements and the needs of fellow users. Direct involvement of users is more likely to be successful if they are considered as full members of the project team and if they are genuinely empowered to represent the organization and make decisions within clearly defined operating parameters. There is always a danger that users who become members of a project team cease over time to represent the user perspective effectively, as they begin to view themselves more as a team member and less as a user representative. One way of overcoming this tendency is to rotate membership of the development team among a group of users. However, this can result in a loss of continuity. A more satisfactory approach is to scope each activity so that a user team member can see it through to completion in a reasonably short time, say within three months.

User involvement as participants only in fact gathering is at the other end of the spectrum. Such users may provide information about current working practice but they have little or no influence on the design of the new system. In this situation users are likely to be concerned about the project and may fear the effect it will have on their jobs. As a result, they may be less co-operative and will be less willing to take ownership of the new system when it is installed.

Even when users are not invited to join the project team, effective participation can still be encouraged through a consultative approach. Procedures are set up so that users are able to review certain aspects of the systems development, provide feedback, give their views of the system and then are able to see the response of the project team to their feedback. In some circumstances a large part of the task of requirements capture may be delegated to users. They are likely to feel a strong affinity to the delivered system, provided that it satisfies the requirements they specified.

Whatever form of involvement users have with the project, it is important that their role is carefully explained and that training is given as required. Some large organizations have gone to the trouble of training users so that they understand the terminology and models used by the systems developers. Users must also be given the time to participate. It is no good expecting users to review requirements documents effectively if the only time they have available is during their lunch break.

Users who participate in a systems development project can be selected in various ways. They can be designated by management as being the most appropriate representatives or they can be selected by their peers. In either circumstance they must be genuine representatives of the user perspective.

A responsibility assignment matrix (RAM) is a useful way of delineating roles and responsibilities for a project. The matrix normally has tasks or deliverables listed in the left-hand column and roles listed along the top row. Roles should be distinguished from individuals in the project team. A particular role can be performed by several people and one individual may occupy several roles. One form of RAM is a RACI matrix. RACI is an acronym for responsible, accountable, consulted and informed. A simple example of a RACI matrix is shown in Figure 3.9. The responsibilities that are normally assigned in the matrix are listed below with examples from Figure 3.9.

- *Responsible* – the role that does the work to perform the task or produce the deliverable. For example, the applications development role builds the software increments.
- *Accountable* – the role that is accountable for the completion of the task or production of the deliverable; only one *accountable* role is assigned to each task or deliverable. For example, the project sponsor is accountable for the Project Initiation Document and must ensure that it is produced by the project manager.
- *Consulted* – the role whose opinions are sought. For example, the user representative is consulted about the Use Case Model.
- *Informed* – the role that is kept up to date on progress. For example, the user representative is informed about the development of the software increments.

3.7 Software Development Tools

Computer Aided Software Engineering (CASE) tools have been widely available since the mid-1980s and now provide support for many of the tasks the software developer must undertake. The broadest definition of CASE includes the use of software tools for

Deliverable/Role	Project Sponsor	Project Manager	Applications Development	Analyst	User Representative	Development Manager
Project Initiation Document	A	R	I	C	C	C
Project Plan	C	A	C	C	C	C
Use Case Model	C	A	I	R	C	C
Priority Requirement List	A	I	I	R	C	C
Software Increments	I	I	R	C	I	A

Key: R – Responsible
        A – Accountable
        C – Consulted
        I – Informed

Figure 3.9 RACI matrix.

any technical, administrative or managerial aspects of software development. These software development tools range from modelling tools for the development of analysis and design models (frequently in the form of diagrams) and development environments for writing program code to project management tools. Modern software development tools provide an increasingly wide range of facilities and cover most lifecycle activities. Key features are discussed in turn below.

3.7.1 Model and technique support

Software development tools for modelling provide facilities to draw diagrams and prepare other models. Many tools provide specific support for standard notations like UML. These tools typically offer a range of features including:

- checks for syntactic correctness
- repository support
- checks for consistency and completeness
- navigation to linked diagrams or models
- layering
- traceability
- report generation
- system simulation
- performance analysis.

These features are described in turn below:

Syntactic correctness
The software development tool checks that the correct symbols are being used on the diagrams and that they are being linked in permissible ways but does not ensure that it is meaningful or relevant to client requirements.

Repository

A repository may contain diagrams, descriptions of diagrams and specifications of all the elements in the system. Some tool vendors use the term 'encyclopaedia' instead of repository.

Consistency and completeness

Most software development tools support various models that capture different aspects of the system. As all relate to the same system, it is important that any one element that appears on several diagrams or models (perhaps viewed from different perspectives) should be presented consistently. Most approaches to analysis and design stipulate that certain diagrams must be completed and that the elements referred to in those diagrams must all be documented in the repository. To manually check the consistency and completeness of a system of any significant size is a task that is very onerous, time-consuming and error-prone. A good software development tool may check the consistency and completeness of a large model in seconds and provide the developer with a comprehensive report on any inconsistencies found or omissions identified.

Navigation to linked diagrams

A complex system is likely to require many models to describe its requirements and its design. For a software development tool to be usable, easy navigation between linked diagrams is essential. For example, double-clicking on a component at one level of abstraction may automatically open up a diagram that describes it at a more detailed level. It is also helpful to be able to move directly from one view that contains a particular element to another view that contains the same element.

Layering

An information system of any significant size is by its nature complex and it is unlikely that all relationships between its components can be shown on a single diagram. Just as maps are drawn at different scales with different levels of detail, system models are produced at various levels of abstraction. A high-level diagram may represent the relationships between large components such as subsystems. A diagram drawn at a lower level of abstraction may describe the elements within a particular component in detail. In order to cope with complexity, we divide the system into manageable chunks and link them in layers. A good software development tool provides a capability to layer the models of the system at different levels of abstraction. The consistency and completeness checking discussed earlier should also check that the representations of one element at different levels of abstraction are consistent.

Traceability

Most of the elements created during the development of an information system are derived from other elements, and the connections between them should be maintained. It must be possible to trace through from the repository entries that describe a particular requirement to the program code that provides the functionality that satisfies the requirement. If a requirement changes, the maintenance activity is easier if all the code that implements that requirement can be readily identified. It should be possible to trace all requirements from the analysis documentation, through the design documentation to the implemented code. This feature is known as requirements traceability.

Report generation

Complex systems involve modelling many elements. Comprehensive reporting capabilities improve the usability of a software development tool by ensuring that the developer can easily obtain information about the models for a system in suitable formats. In fact, a software development tool would be of little use if the information it held about a project were not readily available, no matter how effective it was in other respects.

System simulation

When a software development tool has been populated with models of an application it should be possible to simulate some aspects of system behaviour. For example, how does the system respond to a particular event? Some software development tools provide capabilities that enable a software developer to examine the consequences of a design decision without the need to actually build the software.

Performance analysis

The performance of a system is an important ingredient in its success. For example, a system that supports staff who deal directly with customer enquiries should be able to respond quickly to a query about the availability of a certain product. If customers are kept waiting for too long, this will probably result in lost sales. The analysis of performance is particularly difficult for an application that runs on multiple processors and uses a complex communications infrastructure. Some software development tools provide the capability to perform a 'What if' analysis to examine the implications of alternative implementation architectures.

3.7.2 Software construction

Software development tools can offer a range of features to support software construction and maintenance. These include code generation and maintenance tools.

Code generators

The capability to generate code directly from a design model is a major benefit to the developer for several reasons. First, a working software system is likely to be produced more quickly. Second, one source of error is largely removed when the code is produced automatically and consistent with the design. Third, when requirements change, a consequent change to the design documentation can be followed by automatic code generation. If the application logic is defined completely and precisely in the design model, full code generation is possible. If a design model contains detailed operation specifications (these define how the system will function), then it is likely that a code framework can be generated to which further code can be added. In order to reduce the level of detail required for the design model, code generators may make certain assumptions concerning the implementation. Code generators are available for many different languages and development environments and are likely to include the capability to generate database schemas for the major proprietary database management systems.

Maintenance tools

Software maintenance is a major issue. All systems are subject to change as the enterprise changes, perhaps in response to legislative change. Various tools are available to help with systems maintenance. For some programming languages, reverse engineering tools are available that can generate design documentation directly from program code (although if the program code is poorly structured the resulting design documentation may be of little use). Tools are also available that can analyse program code and identify those parts that are most likely to be subject to change.

3.7.3 Benefits and difficulties of using software development tools

Software development tools can bring many benefits to the development activity. They help to standardize the notation and diagramming standards used within a project, and this aids communication among the team members. They can perform automatic checks on many aspects of the quality of the models produced by analysts and designers. The report generation capabilities of a software development tool reduce the time and effort that needs to be spent by analysts and designers in retrieving data about the system upon which they are working. Where a software development tool can carry out automatic code generation, this further reduces the time and effort that is required to produce a final system. Finally, the electronic storage of models is essential to the reuse of models, or components of them, on other projects that address similar analysis or design problems.

Like any other technology, software development tools also have their disadvantages. These include limitations in the flexibility of the documentation that they can provide. However, some software development tools include the capability to specify and tailor documentation templates to suit particular reporting requirements. The development approach may also be limited by the need to work in a particular way in order to fit in with the capabilities of the software development tool. The ability of a software development tool to check all models for their consistency, completeness and syntactic correctness can in itself give rise to a danger. Developers may make the erroneous assumption that, because their models are correct in those specific senses, they are therefore also necessarily relevant to user requirements. There are also certain costs attached to the installation of a software development tool. Aside from the cost of the software and manuals, there is also likely to be a significant cost in additional training for developers who will be expected to use the software development tools.

On balance software development tools can provide useful and effective support for the software development activity, but it requires appropriate management for this to be achieved without any adverse side-effects.

3.8 Summary

We have considered how to avoid the problems that typically arise during information systems development. Several strategies have been discussed. Lifecycle models are used to provide structure and management leverage for the development process itself. User involvement is crucial to ensure relevance and fitness for purpose of the delivered system. Furthermore, many of the difficulties that may occur during installation are reduced if ownership of the proposed system has been fostered by effective participation during development. An evolving range of methodological approaches to information systems development is available and a key factor for success is matching the most appropriate approach to project and organizational requirements. Finally, we discussed the importance of software development tool support for the software developer.

Review Questions

3.1 What are the key approaches that may be used to overcome quality problems in software systems development?

3.2 What are the disadvantages of the waterfall lifecycle model?

3.3 How are some of the disadvantages listed in your answer to Question 3.2 overcome?

3.4 What is prototyping?

3.5 How does prototyping differ from incremental development?

3.6 What are the different ways of involving users in the systems development activity? What are potential problems with each of these?

3.7 How do 'syntactic correctness', 'consistency' and 'completeness' differ from each other?

3.8 What does requirements traceability mean?

3.9 Why is it not enough for a diagram to be syntactically correct, consistent and complete?

3.10 What is the purpose of a repository?

Case Study Work, Exercises and Projects

3.A Read the Case Study Chapter B1. What lifecycle model would you recommend for the development of the production control system for FoodCo? Justify your decision.

3.B For a CASE tool with which you are familiar, explore and critically assess the consistency and completeness checking facilities available.

3.C For a CASE tool with which you are familiar, explore and critically assess its system generation capabilities.

3.D In your library find references for three lifecycle models not discussed in this chapter. Briefly review each of these lifecycle models.

3.E Research at least one Agile methodology and explore its capability for large-scale information systems development.

Further Reading

Hicks (1991) provides a comprehensive introduction to problem-solving skills that are valuable to the software developer. Sommerville (2007) and Pressman (2009) provide good discussions of lifecycle issues. Gilb (1988) contains much good advice concerning software development and is well worth reading. Texel and Williams (1997) suggest a detailed object-oriented lifecycle model that includes 17 stages. A lifecycle with such a large number of delineated stages is probably more suited to large projects. If used for small projects the management overhead is likely to be excessive.

Jacobson, Booch and Rumbaugh (1999) provide a description of the USDP and further information on the IBM-Rational variant of the USDP can be found at http://www-306.ibm.com/software/rational/index.html. Beck (2004) offers the seminal description of XP and Fowler (2004) provides a very readable review of Agile approaches at http://www.martinfowler.com/articles/newMethodology.html. Larman (2003) discusses Agile and iterative and development approaches. DeMarco and Boehm (2002) conduct an interesting dialogue about Agile approaches. More information regarding the Agile manifesto can be found at http://agilemanifesto.org/. A useful discussion concerning AUP can be found at http://www.ambysoft.com/unifiedprocess/agileUP.html and EUP is described in detail in Ambler et al. (2005).

Many software development tools are in widespread use and increasingly are providing support for the UML standard, though the styles of implementation do vary.

Chapter 4

What Is Object-Orientation?

LEARNING OBJECTIVES

In this chapter you will learn
- ☑ the fundamental concepts of object-orientation
- ☑ the justifications for an object-oriented approach
- ☑ how object-orientation is used in practice.

4.1 | Introduction

Object-orientation is an approach to systems development that helps to avoid many of the problems and pitfalls described in earlier chapters. In this chapter, we lay the foundations for understanding this approach by presenting an explanation of the main concepts. As the name suggests, the most important of these is the object. Using objects is a particular way of organizing a computer program. In an object-oriented program, data is encapsulated (or bundled together) with the functions that act upon it. This is fundamentally different from most of the earlier approaches to program organization. These typically stressed the separation of data and functions. An object is also a conceptual unit of both analysis and design. Thus the same conceptual unit links analysis to design and implementation. This, more than anything else, is what makes it possible for object-oriented projects to follow an iterative lifecycle.

Apart from the object itself, the most important concepts are class, instance, generalization and specialization, encapsulation, information hiding, message passing and polymorphism. In this chapter, we will explain what the parts of an object-oriented system are and how they use message passing to isolate one part of a system from the effects of changes to another. Mostly this boils down to controlling the complexity of the system as a whole by keeping the interfaces between subsystems as simple as they can be. Practical examples and analogies are used to illustrate the theoretical points wherever this is appropriate. Even experienced developers who are new to object-orientation sometimes find the transition difficult. You will need a sound grasp of the basic concepts before you can apply the techniques of object-orientation in an effective way.

4.2 Basic Concepts

The most important concept is the *object* itself, and it is to this that we first pay attention. The other concepts explained in this section are strongly dependent on each other, and all contribute to an adequate understanding of the way that objects interact, and thus to their significance for information systems.

4.2.1 Objects

In one of the very earliest books on object-oriented analysis and design, Coad and Yourdon (1990) define *object* as follows:

> An *abstraction* of something in a problem domain, reflecting the capabilities of the system to keep information about it, interact with it, or both.

Abstraction in this context means a form of representation that includes only what is important or interesting from a particular viewpoint. A map is a familiar example of an abstract representation. No map shows every detail of the territory it covers (impossible, in any case, unless it were as large as the territory, and made from similar materials!). The purpose of the map guides the choice of which details to show, and which to suppress. Road maps concentrate on roads and places, and often omit landscape features unless they help with navigation. Geological maps show rocks and other subsurface strata, but usually ignore towns and roads. Different projections and scales emphasize parts of the territory or features that have greater significance. Each map is an abstraction, partly because of the relevant features it reveals (or emphasizes), and also because of the irrelevant features it hides (or de-emphasizes). Objects are abstractions in much the same way. An object represents only those features of a thing that are deemed relevant to the purpose for which it is being analysed, and hides those features that are not relevant.

The system to which Coad and Yourdon refer is the proposed object-oriented software system, whose development is under consideration. However, we should note that other systems are also involved, in particular the human activity system. We must understand this before we can specify an appropriate software system. Objects are used in the requirements and analysis workflows to model an understanding of the application domain (essentially part of a human activity system). Objects are also understood in the design and implementation workflows to be models of, and indeed parts of, the resulting software system. These are distinct purposes and there will be some occasions when we need to be clear about which meaning is intended.

Rumbaugh et al. (1991) explicitly recognize this dual purpose.

> We define an *object* as a concept, abstraction, or thing with crisp boundaries and meaning for the problem at hand. Objects serve two purposes: They promote understanding of the real world and provide a practical basis for computer implementation.

In the Agate case study, one concept is the 'campaign'. Campaigns are clearly important, but they are intangible and difficult to define with precision. They really exist only as a relationship between a client (say Yellow Partridge, a jewellery company), the account manager, some other staff, some advertisements and various tasks and components that go into creating advertisements.

It is often necessary to model relationships between people, organizations and things such as contracts, sales or agreements. While intangible, some of these relationships are long lasting and can have a complex influence on how people and other things in the application domain are able to act.

Let us take a simple example. Imagine buying a tube of toothpaste in your local supermarket. On one level, this is just a sale, an exchange of money for goods. On a deeper level you may be entering into a complicated relationship with the shop and the manufacturer. This depends on other factors: e.g. the warranty may vary depending on the country that you are in at the time of the purchase, and perhaps the sale will earn points for you on a loyalty card. Perhaps the packaging includes a money-off coupon for your next purchase, or a contest entry form that must be accompanied by a valid proof of purchase. Now suppose you find something wrong with the toothpaste–you may be able to claim a refund or replacement. Maybe you can even sue the shop for damages. We cannot understand the business without understanding these possible consequences of the sale in some appropriate way. In this case, the real-world 'sale' will almost certainly be modelled as an object in the system.

At a fairly abstract level, when choosing the objects we wish to model–in fact, at the level that corresponds to a mapmaker–we need to ask: 'What sort of map is this, what details should it show, and what should it suppress?' All objects in a model of an information system have certain similarities to all other objects, summarized by Booch in the statement that an object 'has state, behaviour and identity' (Booch, 1994). Here, 'identity' means simply that every object is unique, while 'state' and 'behaviour' are closely related to each other. 'State' represents the condition that an object is in at a given moment, in the sense that an object's state determines which behaviours, or actions, an object can carry out in response to a given event. For a software object, 'state' is the sum total of the values of the object's data (interpreted broadly to include its links with other objects), while 'behaviour' stands for the ways that an object can act in response to events. The available actions are determined by an object's state, but generally speaking an object can 'act' only by changing its data or by sending a message to another object. Many 'behaviours' of a software object, but not all, will result in a change of its state.

Figure 4.1 lists some characteristics of a person, a shirt, a sale and a bottle of ketchup. Supposing that we wished to model these as objects, we can identify some possible identities, behaviours and states (these are for illustration only, and do not assume any particular system perspective).

Object	Identity	Behaviour	States
A person	'Hussain Pervez'	Speak, walk, read	Studying, resting, qualified
A shirt	'My favourite button-down white denim shirt'	Shrink, stain, rip	Pressed, dirty, worn
A sale	'Sale no. 0015, 15/02/10'	Earn loyalty points	Invoiced, cancelled
A bottle of ketchup	'*This* bottle of ketchup'	Spill in transit	Unsold, opened, empty

Figure 4.1 Characteristics of some objects.

The similarity between domain objects and software objects can be overstated. Although software objects are sometimes described as simulating the behaviour of objects in the real world domain that they represent, domain objects often do not behave in exactly the way that they are modelled. For example, a bottle of ketchup does not really 'store' data about its contents or its condition, nor does it 'update' this data when it is spilled. However, this is a useful way to model a domain when the goal is to understand it and, perhaps, develop an information system that will help people who work in that domain.

In some texts (e.g. Wirfs-Brock et al., 1990), objects are deliberately characterized as if they were people, each one with a role in the system that is based on its answers to three questions.

- Who am I?
- What can I do?
- What do I know?

This view of an object's responsibilities and its knowledge is the basis of the Class-Responsibility-Collaboration (CRC) technique, which we will describe in Chapter 7.

4.2.2 Class and object

Class is a concept that describes a set of objects that are specified in the same way. Here, we mean objects as abstractions within an information system–either a model or the resulting software–not the real-world objects that they represent.

All objects of a given class share a common specification for their features, their semantics and the constraints upon them. (In general use, *semantics* relates to the meaning of words or signs, but for computer scientists it usually means a formal mathematical description of the operations that can be carried out in a programming language. Here, it can be taken to mean very roughly the behaviour of the objects. Or to put it another way, the meaning that is assigned to the things they represent by people who work within the application domain.) This does not quite mean that all objects of a class are identical in every way, but it does mean that their specification is identical. Objects that are sufficiently similar to each other are said to belong to the same class. The class is an abstract descriptor for the specified logical similarities between those objects.

The idea of a class has its origins in object-oriented programming. For example, in a Java program a class acts as a kind of template from which individual objects are constructed when they are needed. (This is not the whole story, as software classes can also do other things that need not concern us here.)

A single object is also known as an *instance*. This carries a connotation of the class to which the object belongs. Every object is an instance of some class.

Figure 4.2 shows some classes that might be identified from the Agate case study (Chapter 7 describes a practical approach to identifying classes).

A class and its instances are related in the following manner. For staff at Agate, the idea of 'a campaign' is an abstraction that can represent any one of several specific campaigns. In an object-oriented software system, the class `Campaign` represents the relevant features that all campaigns have in common. For each real-world campaign, there is one instance of the class that represents it. Some examples of campaigns are: a series of adverts for various Yellow Partridge jewellery products broadcast on various

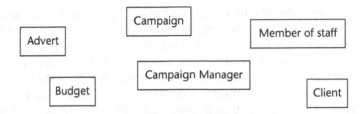

Figure 4.2 Some possible object classes in the Agate case study.

satellite and cable TV channels during Spring 2010; a national series of TV, cinema, magazine and Internet adverts for the launch of the Soong Motor Co's Helion hybrid-fuel car in August 2010.

Each instance of a class is unique, just as every living person is unique, however closely they resemble someone else. Instances are unique even when they share identical characteristics with another instance. For example, there could be two members of staff at Agate with the same name–say, 'Ashok Patel'. It is even possible (though unlikely) that both joined the company on the same date and work in the same section. Yet each remains a separate individual, and would therefore be represented by a separate instance of the class `StaffMember`.

4.2.3 Class membership

Membership of a class is based on logical similarity between the states and behaviour that the objects can exhibit. We have already noted that an object's state is defined by the data that describes it. More generally, all objects in a class share a common set of *properties*. A property is a descriptive characteristic; we will see shortly that for a class these include *attributes* that contain its data and *operations* that specify its behaviour.

When staff at Agate record a new client, they note the company name, address, telephone number, fax number, email address and so on. Each item in the list is useful in some way to the users of the system,[1] and the full list gives a complete description of a client. The value of each item (e.g. the actual company name) will vary from one client to another, but the information structure is the same for every client.

To take another example, some users of the Agate system need to know about the member of staff assigned as staff contact to a client. A staff member might be described by a name, staff number and start date. Again, the full list gives a complete description of a staff member (for the purpose at hand). Here, too, the value of each item (e.g. the staff name) will normally vary from one person to another, but again the structure is the same for all staff members.

Now compare the two descriptions, summarized in Figure 4.3.

Both staff members and clients have a name, but otherwise there is little in common. The information structure used to describe a client would not be capable of describing a member of staff, and vice versa. It is reasonable to consider all clients as members of

---

1 What appears in the list depends on the needs of the application. Another team may be developing a system to monitor whether client companies comply with environmental laws. Their list may share some characteristics with ours, but may also add others of no interest to our model.

Class	Characteristics	Class	Characteristics
Staff member	Name Staff number Start date	Client	Name Address Telephone number Fax number Email address

Figure 4.3 Information structures for two classes.

one class, and all staff as members of one class, but it would not be justified to consider them as members of the *same* class. When two objects cannot be described by a single set of features, they cannot belong to the same class.

All objects of a class also share a common set of valid behaviours. For example, clients may initiate a campaign, may be assigned a staff contact, may pay for a campaign, may terminate a current campaign, and so on. Perhaps no single client will actually do all this in reality, but that does not matter. Any client could do any of these things, and the information system must reflect this.

Staff members have a different set of valid behaviours. Staff can be assigned to work on a campaign, can be assigned to a campaign as staff contact, can change grade and maybe do other things we do not yet know about. It may be more likely for staff members than for clients that they will actually go through the same sequence of behaviours, but here this, too, does not matter. The point again is that a member of staff could do these things.

All clients, then, have a similar set of possible behaviours, and so do all staff members. But clients can do some things that a member of staff cannot do, and vice versa. Again, we can consider clients as a class, and staff as a class, but there is no case for considering clients and members of staff as instances of the same class. To summarize: Client is a valid class, and StaffMember is a valid class. This can also be expressed more informally, as described in Section 4.2.1, where we saw that all members of a class give the same answers to the questions: 'What do I know?' and 'What can I do?'

Sometimes the terminology for objects and classes is not completely clear. Some authors use 'object' and 'class' interchangeably to mean a group of similar objects. But, strictly speaking, 'object' means a single individual object, with 'class' reserved for the definition of a group of similar objects. Both object and class can refer to application domain things and concepts, as well as their representation in an object-oriented model. We should remember that the map is not the territory, even when the same words are used for both. Another possible confusion can occur when attention moves between the analysis and design activities. Then an analysis model of the application domain is transformed into a design model of software components.

A further distinction should be made between a class and its *type*. A type is similar to a class, but more abstract in the sense that it can contain neither physical implementations nor physical specifications of the operations. A type can be implemented by more than one class: for example in two different programming languages with different syntax and features. Some authors have suggested that an analysis model can contain only types and not classes (for example, Cook and Daniels, 1994). However, it has become standard usage for the term 'class' to have all of the following meanings: a collection of similar real-world objects; a collection of similarly specified objects in an analysis or design model; and a software construct in an object-oriented programming language (see, for example, Maciaszek, 2005). Meanwhile, 'object' is synonymous with 'instance', although the latter term is more generally used in the context of discussing the class to which an object belongs.

4.2.4 Generalization and specialization

Generalization and specialization are complementary concepts that are familiar to everyone through hierarchical classification schemes such as those we apply to plants and animals. For example, a cat is a kind of mammal and a mammal is a kind of animal. In this example, 'cat' is more specific while 'mammal' is more general and 'animal' is more general still. Generalization and specialization are very important to object-orientation. They help programmers, designers and analysts to reuse previous work instead of repeating it (there will be much more on the importance of reuse later, especially in Chapters 8 and 20). They also help to organize complex models and systems in a way that makes them more understandable.

In the UML Specification, the definition of generalization is written in such a way that it can apply to any *classifier*–a general concept that includes other modelling concepts such as interfaces, datatypes and components, as well as classes. For the moment, we will concentrate on classes. Generalization occurs where there is a taxonomic relationship between two classes. This means that the specification of one class is more general and applies also to the second class, while the specification of the second class is more specific and includes some details that do not apply to the first. Another way to put this is that any instance of the more specific class is also indirectly an instance of the more general class. The specific class 'inherits' all the features of the more general class, while also adding some features that are uniquely its own (OMG, 2009b).

Let's dismantle the definition into its main components, and examine each part on its own. We will highlight the general principles by looking first at an example of species classification (note that this is intended only to illustrate the concept of generalization and is not a technical presentation of modern biological taxonomy).

Taxonomic relationship

'Taxonomy' literally means a scheme of hierarchic classification–either an applied set of classifications or the principles by which that set is constructed. The word was originally used for the hierarchic system of classification of plant and animal species; hence the example shown in Fig. 4.4.

The taxonomic relationship between the two elements in this hierarchy labelled 'cat' and 'mammal' can be simply rephrased as 'a cat *is a kind of* mammal'. Many other relationships are also identified in the diagram. For example, a domestic cat is a kind of cat, as is a tiger, and both are also kinds of animals and kinds of living things. We can summarize this by saying that in each case the common relationship is that one element 'is a kind of' the other element. We should, however, be careful to avoid a common ambiguity. People often use the form 'a cat is an animal' as shorthand for 'a cat is a kind of animal.' But the statement 'a Persian is a kind of cat' means that Persians are a subclass of cats, while 'Fritz is a cat' conveys that Fritz is an individual member of the class of cats, not a subclass. Membership and subclassification are both types of abstraction, but they are not identical concepts.

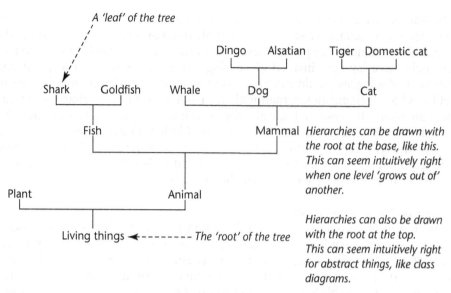

Figure 4.4 A simple, very incomplete, taxonomy of species.

A more general class

'Mammal' is a word we use to classify any animal with certain characteristics. For example, all mammals have warm blood, suckle their babies on milk, have hair on their bodies and so on. 'Cat' is a word that classifies a subgroup of mammals, usually with thick fur and retractable claws. Many also have an ability to purr. Mammal is a more general class than cat, which in turn is more general than the domestic cat or the tiger. Any description of a mammal must apply to many different animals: domestic cats, tigers, dogs, whales, etc. A description of a 'general' mammal really means just a description of the common characteristics shared by all mammals. This may be rather brief, perhaps consisting of only one or two characteristics: for example, that all mammals suckle their young and have hair on their bodies (even whales have some hair, although many people think they do not). In the tree diagram, the more general an element is, the nearer it is to the root of the tree.

A more specific class

'Cat' is more specific than 'mammal' and 'domestic cat' still more specific than 'cat'. The more specific word in any pair of related classes conveys more information. Knowing that an animal is a cat, we can guess something about its diet, general body shape, size (within certain limits), number of legs (barring accidents, etc.), and so on. If we know only that it is a mammal, we can guess little, if anything at all, of its physical description or diet. The more specialized elements of a hierarchy are those that are further from the root of the tree and closer to the leaves. The most specialized elements of all are those that actually form the leaves of the tree. In Fig. 4.4, the leaves are individual species.

Any instance of the specific class is also indirectly an instance of the more general class

Whatever is true for a mammal is also true for a domestic cat. If one defining characteristic of a mammal is that it suckles its young, then a domestic cat also suckles its young, and so does a tiger, a dog or a whale. This is an important feature of any hierarchic taxonomy.

As an illustration, we can think about what would happen if a zoologist discovers that a defining mammalian characteristic does not apply to an animal previously thought to be a mammal. For example, suppose a research project found conclusive evidence that common field mice lay eggs instead of bearing live young. Imagine the consternation and argument! Zoologists would have to decide whether to reclassify the field mouse or to redefine what distinguishes a mammal from other animals. Perhaps a brand new classification would be invented specifically to accommodate egg-laying mice. This is what occurred following the discovery of the duckbilled platypus and the echidnas in Australia in the 17th century. These animals are monotremes, which in most respects resemble mammals except that they lay eggs instead of bearing live young. Zoologists now regard monotremes as a separate subclass of mammals.

Specialization adds additional information
A full description of a domestic cat would contain a great deal more information than needed for a general member of the mammal class. For example, we might define a domestic cat by saying that, in addition to the general features of a mammal, it also has a certain skeletal structure, a particular arrangement of internal organs, carnivorous teeth and habit, thick fur, the ability to purr, and so on. Apart from the common mammalian features, none of these characteristics applies to *all* other mammals. No whales can purr, and baleen whales have no teeth; instead they have a kind of sieve in their upper jaw (called 'baleen'), which they use to filter their food from the water. A full zoological description of any species contains at least one characteristic (or a unique combination of characteristics) that differentiates it from all other species. Otherwise it would not make sense to consider it a species in the first place.

Practical uses of generalization
The main use of *generalization* in object-orientation is to describe relationships of similarity between classes. Object classes are arranged into hierarchies much the same as the species example. This has two main benefits.

The first results from the use of object classes to represent different aspects of a real-world situation that we wish to understand. Using generalization, we can build logical structures that make explicit the degree of similarity or difference between classes. This is an important aspect of the *semantics* of a model—in other words, it helps to convey its meaning. For example, to know what hourly-paid and monthly-salaried employees in a business have in common with each other may be just as important as to know how they differ. The former may help to understand that some types of information must be recorded in identical ways for both types of employee. Figure 4.5 illustrates this with an example that might be suitable for a payroll system.

In this model, every employee is represented by a date of appointment, date of birth, department, employee number, line manager and name. Some details, however, depend on whether their pay is calculated by months or by hours worked (the only significant differences shown). A hierarchically structured model allows the close similarity to be shown clearly, but also highlights the differences between a monthly paid and an hourly paid employee.

A second benefit comes from the relative ease with which a hierarchy can be extended to fit a changing picture. If this company were to decide that a new, weekly-paid type of employee is required, it is a simple matter to add a new subclass to the hierarchy to cater for it, as shown in Fig. 4.6.

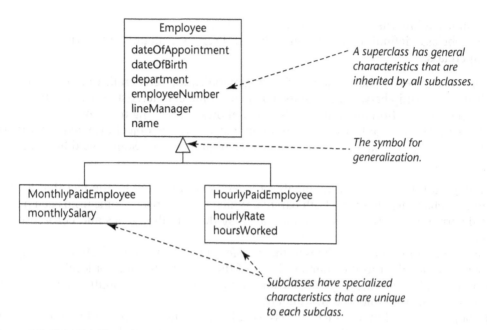

Figure 4.5 Hierarchy of employee types.

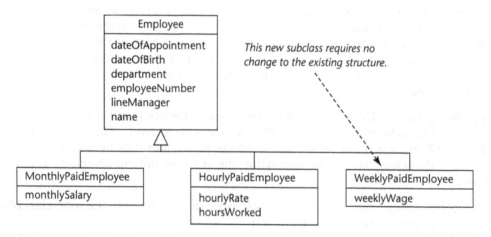

Figure 4.6 Hierarchies are easy to extend.

Other features of generalization

Some features of generalization that are not mentioned explicitly in the definition given earlier are sufficiently important to deserve some discussion at this point. These are: the mechanism of *inheritance*, the *transitive* operation of inheritance and the *disjoint* nature of generalization hierarchies.

Inheritance. This is a mechanism for implementing generalization and specialization in an object-oriented programming language. When two classes are related by the mechanism of inheritance, the more general class is called a *superclass* in relation to the other, and the more specialized is called its *subclass*. As a first approximation, the rules of object-oriented inheritance generally work as shown below:

1. A subclass inherits all the characteristics of its superclass.
2. A subclass definition always includes at least one detail not derived from its superclass.

Inheritance is very closely associated with generalization. Generalization describes the logical relationship between elements that share some characteristics, while inheritance describes an object-oriented mechanism that allows the sharing to occur.

Note that there is only a superficial resemblance between object-oriented inheritance and both the biological and the legal concepts of inheritance. Some key differences are listed below.

- Biological inheritance (in mammals, at least) is complicated by the fact that a child inherits characteristics from both parents. Which characteristics come from each parent is determined partly at random and partly by the way that genes and chromosomes work.
- Legal inheritance mainly relates to the transfer of property on the death of the original owner, rather than to the characteristics of the owner. The rules of legal inheritance vary from place to place, and are usually complex, but in most countries a legal heir is not necessarily a biological descendent.
- In object-oriented inheritance, a class usually has a single parent and it inherits all of that parent's characteristics. Two exceptions to this are *multiple inheritance* and the *overriding* of inherited characteristics. Multiple inheritance means that a subclass is at once a member of more than one hierarchy and inherits characteristics from its superclasses in each hierarchy. Overriding means that an inherited feature is redefined in a subclass. This is useful when an operation needs to be defined in a different way in different subclasses. In this case, the operation might be specified in an outline or default manner in the superclass, and then respecified in a detailed but different manner in each subclass.

Transitive operation. This means that the relationship between two elements at adjacent levels of a hierarchy 'carries over' to all more specialized levels. Thus, in Fig. 4.4, the definition of an animal applies in turn to all mammals, and thus by a series of logical steps to a domestic cat. So we can refine the rules of inheritance given above, as follows.

1. A subclass always inherits all the characteristics of its superclass, the superclass of its superclass, and so on as far as the hierarchy extends.
2. The definition of a subclass always includes at least one detail not derived from *any* of its superclasses.

Disjoint nature. In a hierarchic system, the branches of the tree diverge as they get further away from the root and closer to the leaves. They are not permitted to converge. This means, for example, that a cat cannot be both a mammal and a reptile. In other words, each element in a hierarchy can only be a member of one classification at any given level of the hierarchy (although, of course, it can be a member of other classifications at other levels of the hierarchy, due to the transitive nature of the relationship).

The disjoint aspect of generalization means that we sometimes need to be careful about the characteristics chosen to express a generalization. For example, we could not use 'Has four feet' as the only defining characteristic of a mammal, even supposing that it were true of all mammals–because many lizards also have four feet, and this would make it possible to classify a lizard as a mammal. A class must be defined in terms of a unique set of characteristics that differentiate it from all other classes at its level of the hierarchy.

The fact that generalization hierarchies are disjoint should not be taken to mean that a class can only belong to one hierarchy. Generalization structures are abstractions that we choose to apply, since they express our understanding of some aspects of an application domain. This means that we can choose to apply more than one generalization structure to the same domain, if it expresses a relevant aspect of the situation. Thus, for example, a person might be simultaneously classified as a creature (*Homo sapiens*), as a citizen (a voter in a city electoral division) and as an employee (an account manager in Agate's Creative Department). If each of these hierarchies were represented in an object-oriented model, the position of a person would be an example of multiple inheritance.

Real-world structures are not compelled to follow the logical rules we apply in object-oriented modelling. Sometimes they are not disjoint or transitive, and therefore not strictly hierarchic. This does not detract from the usefulness of hierarchic structures in object-oriented development.

4.2.5 Encapsulation, information hiding and message passing

These three concepts are closely related, so we will consider them together. Encapsulation is a feature of object-oriented programming, which is also applied in analysis modelling. It means the placing of data within an object together with the operations that apply to that data. An object really is little more than a bundle of data together with some processes that act on the data. The data is stored within the object's attributes; together these comprise the object's information structure that we discussed in Section 4.2.3. The processes are the object's operations and each has a specific *signature*. An operation signature defines the structure and content that a message must have in order to act as a valid call. This consists of the name of the operation together with any parameters (usually data values) that the operation needs in order to run. In order to *invoke* an operation, its signature must be given. Signatures are sometimes also called *message protocols*. The complete set of all an object's operation signatures is known as its interface. So each object provides an interface that allows other parts of the system to call its operations by sending it messages. The operations have access to the data stored within the object. The interface is separate from the implementation of both data and operations. The idea is that data should only be accessed or altered by operations of the same object (however most O-O programming languages provide ways of bypassing the encapsulation). Information hiding is the related but stronger design principle that states that no object or subsystem should expose the details of its implementation to other objects or subsystems. Both encapsulation and information hiding imply that, in order to work with each other, objects must exchange messages.

Objects often represent things in a real-world system that collaborate to carry out a collective task. Collaborating things and people send each other messages. For example, everything we say to our friends and family, the emails we read when we log on to the network, advertising posters on the bus, games shows and cartoons on TV, the colour of traffic light signals, the power-on indicator on a laptop, even the clothes we wear, our tone of voice and our posture—these are all messages of one sort or another. What makes all these messages useful is that they follow an understood protocol that lets us interpret their meaning. An obvious example is the international agreement that a red traffic light means 'stop' while a green light means 'go.' Software objects also need an agreed protocol so that they can communicate with each other.

Software was not constructed in this way until quite recently. Earlier approaches to systems development tended to separate data in a system from the processes that act on the data. This was done for sound analytical reasons and is still appropriate for some applications, but it can give rise to difficulties. Chief among these is the need for the person who designs a process to understand the organization of the data that it uses. For such a system, processes are said to be dependent on the structure of the data.

Dependency of process upon data structure can cause problems. A change to the data structure will often force a change to the processes that use it. This makes it harder to construct systems that are reliable, that can be upgraded or modified, and that can be repaired if they break down.

By contrast, a well-designed object-oriented system is modularized so that each subsystem is as independent as it can be of the way that other subsystems have been designed and implemented. Encapsulation contributes to this by locating each process with the data it uses.

In practice, processes usually cannot all be located with all the data that they must access, so data and processes are distributed among many different objects. Some operations are specifically written to give access to the data encapsulated within an object. For one object to use the operations of another, it must send it a message.

Information hiding goes one step further than encapsulation, and ideally makes it impossible for one object to access another object's data in any other way than through calls to its operations. This insulates each object from the need to 'know' any of the internal details of other objects.

Essentially, an object only needs to know its own data and its own operations. However, many processes are complex and require collaboration between objects. The 'knowledge' of some objects must therefore include knowing how to request *services* from other objects. A service is an action that one object or subsystem carries out on behalf of another, including, in this case, the retrieval of data stored by the other object. In this case, an object must 'know' which other object to ask and how to formulate the question. But it is not necessary for an object to 'know' anything about the way that another object will deliver the service. Such 'knowledge' would require the programmer responsible for implementing one object to have detailed knowledge of the way that the second object has been implemented.

We can think of an object as being wrapped in layers of protection like the skins of an onion. Encapsulation locates data with the operations that directly use it. Information hiding makes the internal details of an object inaccessible to other objects. For another object to access an object's data, it must send a message. When an object receives a message it can tell whether the message is relevant to it. If the message includes a valid signature to one of its operations, the object can respond. If it does not, the object cannot respond. An operation can only be invoked by a message that gives a valid operation signature. The object's data lies even deeper inside, and can only be accessed by an operation of that object. Thus, the way that an operation works and the organization of data inside an object can both be changed without affecting any collaborating objects. As long as no operation signatures are changed, the changes are not visible from the outside. Figure 4.7 illustrates encapsulation contrasted with information hiding.

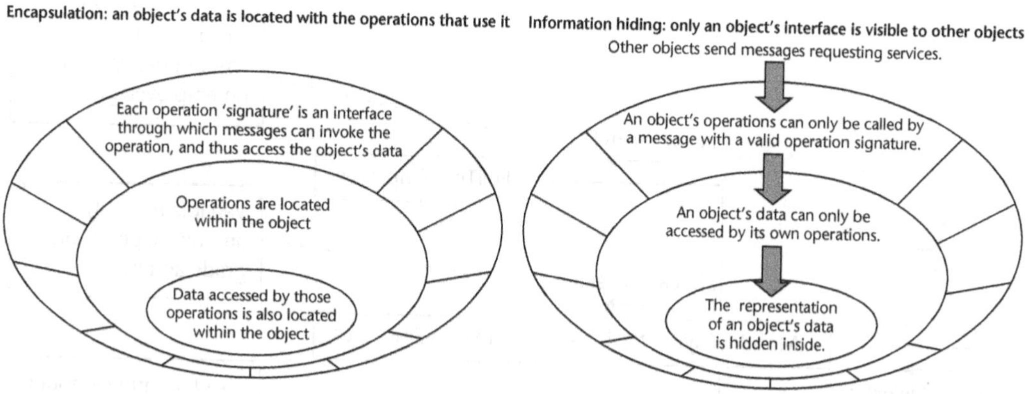

Encapsulation: an object's data is located with the operations that use it   Information hiding: only an object's interface is visible to other objects

Other objects send messages requesting services.

Each operation 'signature' is an interface through which messages can invoke the operation, and thus access the object's data

Operations are located within the object

Data accessed by those operations is also located within the object

An object's operations can only be called by a message with a valid operation signature.

An object's data can only be accessed by its own operations.

The representation of an object's data is hidden inside.

Figure 4.7 Encapsulation and information hiding: the layers of protection that surround an object.

This way of designing software has practical advantages. Consider a simple system to print pay cheques for employees in a business. Suppose that there is a class `Employee`, whose instances represent each person on the payroll. An `Employee` object is responsible for knowing about the salary earned by the real employee it represents. Suppose also that a `PaySlip` object is responsible for printing each employee's payslip each month. In order to print the payslip, each `PaySlip` object must know how much the corresponding employee has earned. One object-oriented approach to this is for each `PaySlip` object to send a message to the associated `Employee` object, asking how much salary should be paid. The `PaySlip` object need not know how the `Employee` object works out the salary, nor what data it stores. It only needs to know that it can ask an `Employee` object for a salary figure, and an appropriate response will be given. Message passing allows objects to hide their internal details from other parts of the system, thus minimizing the knock-on effects of any changes to the design or implementation.

4.2.6 Polymorphism

Polymorphism literally means 'an ability to appear as many forms' and it refers to the possibility of identical messages being sent to objects of different classes, each of which responds to the message in a different, yet still appropriate, way. This means the originating object does not need to know which class is going to receive the message on any particular occasion. The key to this is that each object knows how to respond to valid messages that it receives.

This is rather like the way people communicate. When one person sends a message to another, we often ignore the details of how the other person might respond. For example, a mother might use the same phrasing to tell her child to 'go to bed now!' But the precise tasks to be carried out by the child may be very different depending on his or her age and other characteristics. A five-year-old may set off towards bed by himself, but perhaps then requires help with washing his face, brushing his teeth and putting on his pyjamas; he may also expect to be read a bedtime story. A thirteen-year-old may not require any further help, once convinced that it really is bedtime.

Polymorphism is an important element in the way that object-oriented approaches encourage the decoupling of subsystems. Figure 4.8 uses a communication diagram to

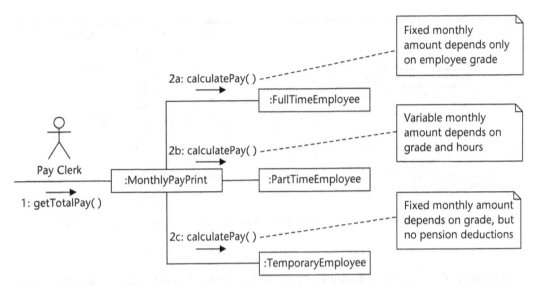

Figure 4.8 Polymorphism allows a message to achieve the same result even when the mechanism for achieving it differs between different objects.

illustrate how it works in a business scenario (communication diagrams appear again in Chapter 7 and their notation is described fully in Chapter 9). The diagram assumes that there are different ways of calculating an employee's pay. Full-time employees are paid a salary that depends only on their grade; part-time staff are paid a salary that depends in a similar way on grade, but must also take into account the number of hours worked; temporary staff differ in that no deductions are made for the company pension scheme, but the salary calculation is otherwise the same as for a full-time employee. An object-oriented system to calculate pay for these employees might include a separate class for each type of employee, each able to perform the appropriate pay calculation. However, following the principle of polymorphism, the message signature for all calculatePay operations could be the same. Suppose one output from this system is a print-out showing the total pay for the current month: to assemble the total, a message is sent to each employee object, asking it to calculate its pay. Since the message signature is the same in each case, the requesting class (here called MonthlyPayPrint) need not know the class of each receiving object, still less how each calculation is carried out.

Polymorphism is a powerful concept for the information systems developer. Working together with encapsulation and information hiding, it permits a clear separation between subsystems that handle superficially similar tasks in a different manner. This means that a system can easily be modified or extended to include extra features, since only the interfaces between classes need to be known by the person carrying out the modification. There is no need for a developer to know how any part of the system is implemented (its internal structure and behaviour) except for the part they are working on.

Program designers and programmers have struggled for many years to achieve such a high level of modularity in software. Object-orientation helps them to do this much more successfully than did any of its predecessors.

4.2.7 Object state

An object's *state* is defined as the totality of the current values of data within the object and its associations with other objects. All states are not equally important, but some differences of state imply significant differences in the behaviour that the object will display in response to the same message.

In the real world, people and objects do not always behave in the same way in response to similar stimuli. For example, if you have just eaten an enormous lunch you will probably refuse the offer of a large, sticky gateau. However, if you are very hungry this offer may be much more tempting. We could say that at any given time you can be in either of two states: well-fed or hungry. Each state is characterized by data that describes your condition–in this case your level of hunger. It is also characterized by a difference in behaviour. Your response to certain messages differs according to the current value of your internal data. When well-fed you refuse food, but when hungry you accept it. A stimulus can also change your state, resulting in a change of behaviour. After eating a large gateau, your state changes from hungry to well-fed and you will now refuse further food.

Objects also respond to messages according to their current state. Each state is represented by the current values of data within the object together with its associations with other objects. These can in turn be changed by the object's behaviour in response to messages. Thus a state is a steady or stable period in the life of the object, during which it carries out an activity, waits for some event to occur, or meets some specified condition (Booch et al., 1999). It is an object's state that determines what responses it can make to messages, under what circumstances it can make them, and also what responses it is unable to make. A good example of this is the behaviour of a computer printer. These typically have the states: ready, printing, off-line, out-of-paper, and so on. The printer's response to a 'print document' request will change according to its current state when the message is received. If ready, it prints the document; if already printing another document, it queues it; if out-of-paper, it returns an error message and waits for the paper to be replenished before printing the document; if off-line, it returns a different error message and stays off-line.

The importance of object state for controlling the behaviour of an object-oriented software system is perhaps most apparent for safety-critical real-time systems, such as the engine and flight controls in an airliner. For the greater part of the flight, an onboard computer flies the aircraft entirely automatically. During take-off and landing the pilot and flight crew take control, but even then it is still the software that directly operates the engine throttles, elevators, and so on. It could be disastrous if all the engines were shut down during the final approach to land, and the software is designed to prevent this occurring. However, it may sometimes be necessary for the pilot to override this constraint during an emergency. The software must also be designed to permit this to occur and to correctly discriminate between the different situations. In order to ensure safety, the control software must be designed so that only the appropriate control behaviours (shut down engine, full throttle, climb, descend, turn) can occur in each possible state of the aircraft (parked, climbing, flying level on auto-pilot, landing). This must also take account of all external events that could trigger a change in behaviour or state (pilot operates throttle, turbulence causes course deviation, sudden loss of cabin pressure, etc.).

The identification of object states can also be critical to the correct operation of business information systems. Here, the consequences of error are not usually life-threatening, but they can threaten the survival of the organization and thus have an impact on the lives and livelihoods of customers, workers, investors and others associated with the enterprise. For example, a DVD rental shop member with unpaid fines may not be permitted to borrow further DVDs until the debt has been cleared. If the shop's information systems fail to enforce this rule correctly, the shop may lose money that will be difficult to recover.

4.3 | The Origins of Object-Orientation

Object-orientation is the product of several converging developments in the history of computing. For a good understanding of how to carry out software development in a properly object-oriented manner, it is helpful to identify what these are.

Increasing abstraction

Throughout the history of computing, there has been a steady increase in the level of abstraction at which programmers can work. 'Abstraction' in this context means that the programmer is isolated from the physical details of the computer on which the program is to execute. He or she can write a single instruction, often a recognisable word with something close to its English meaning, which may be translated into a long sequence of 'machine code' instructions. At the same time, the purposes to which computers are applied have become enormously more complex and demanding, thus greatly increasing the complexity of the systems themselves. The usual way for programmers to give instructions to the earliest computers, such as the Colossus code-breaking machine, was to plug in wires and set switches that connected the thermionic valves of its processor. The physical configuration of the computer was effectively the program. This was the original machine code, and is regarded as the first generation of programming languages. There is not space here to cover the complex history of programming languages since those early days. Suffice it to say that object-oriented languages work at a higher level of abstraction than earlier languages, such as COBOL and C, which were themselves already much more abstract than machine code.

Event-driven programming

Research into computer simulation led directly to the object-oriented paradigm of independent, collaborating objects that communicate via messages. A typical simulation task is to model the loading of vehicles onto a large ferry ship, in order to determine the quickest safe way to do this. This simulation would be run many times under differing assumptions: for example, the sequence of loading, the arrangement of vehicles on the storage decks, the speed at which vehicles are driven onto the ship, the time separation between one vehicle and the next, and so on. The real-world situation that is being modelled is very complex and consists of a number of independent agents, each responding to events in ways that are easy to model at the level of individual agents, but very difficult to predict in the large, with many agents interacting with each other all at once. This kind of task is very difficult to program effectively in a procedural language (Pascal, for example, which several generations of university students learned as their first programming language). Program designs for procedural languages are based on the assumption that the program structure controls the flow of execution. Thus for a procedural program to tackle the simulation task described above, it must have separate routines that test for, and respond to, a vast number of alternative conditions.

One solution to this problem is to structure the program in a similar way to the problem situation itself, as a set of independent software agents, each of which represents an agent in the real-world system that is to be simulated. This insight evolved into early simulation languages such as Simula 67, and remains one of the key ideas in object-oriented software development: that the structure of the software should mirror the structure of the problem it is intended to solve. In this way, the tension between the model of the application domain and the model of the software (mentioned in Section 4.2.1) is resolved, turning a potential weakness into a strength.

The spread of GUIs

The rapid spread of graphical user interfaces (GUIs) in the 1980s and 1990s posed particular difficulties for contemporary development methods. GUIs brought some of the problems encountered earlier in simulation programming into the world of mainstream business applications. The reason for this is that users of a GUI are presented on their computer screen with a highly visual interface that offers many alternative actions all at once, each one a mouse-click away. Many other options can be reached in two or three more clicks via pull-down menus, list boxes and other dialogue techniques. Interface developers naturally responded by exploiting the opportunities offered by this new technology. As a result, it is now almost impossible for a system designer to anticipate every possible route that a user might take through a system's interface. This means that the majority of desktop applications are now very difficult to design or control in a procedural way. The object-oriented paradigm offers a natural way to design software, each component of which offers clear services that can be used by other parts of the system quite independently of the sequence of tasks or the flow of control.

Modular software

Information hiding in a well-designed object-oriented system means that classes have two kinds of definition. Externally, a class is defined in terms of its interface. Other objects (and their programmers) need only know the services that are offered by objects of that class and the signature used to request each service. Internally, a class is defined in terms of what it knows and what it can do–but only objects of that class (and its programmer) need to know anything about this internal definition. It follows that an object-oriented system can be constructed so that the implementation of each part is largely independent of the implementation of other parts. This is what modularity means, and it contributes to solving some of the most intractable problems in information systems development. In Chapter 2, we saw that these include the fact that requirements may change both during the development process and after implementation. A modular approach helps to address these problems in several ways.

- It is easier to maintain a system built in a modular way, as changes to a subsystem are much less likely to have unforeseen effects on the rest of the system.
- For the same reason, it is easier to upgrade a modular system. As long as replacement modules adhere to the interface specifications of their predecessors, other parts of the system are not affected.
- It is easier to build a system that is reliable in use. Subsystems can be tested more thoroughly in isolation, leaving fewer problems to be addressed later when the whole system is assembled.

- A modular system can be developed in small, manageable increments. Provided each increment is designed to provide a useful and coherent package of functionality, they can be deployed one at a time.

Lifecycle problems

Most systems development approaches until the early 1990s were based on the waterfall lifecycle model. This lifecycle model and its associated difficulties were discussed in Chapter 3. Object-orientation addresses these by encouraging an iterative lifecycle, also described in Chapter 3. In an iterative development process, the activities of analysis, design and so on are repeated as necessary until everyone is satisfied with the quality of the software—subject, of course, to time and budget constraints. Iteration is also based on the integration of user feedback into the development cycle. This only makes practical sense where there are tangible products (usually software) to which the users can respond. Thus even the very first iteration will normally result in some working software, and subsequent iterations will refine this product through user input, more detailed analysis and so on, until it is fit to be accepted.

This aspect is strongly linked to the highly modular character of an object-oriented system, described in the previous section, and also to the 'seamless' development of models throughout an object-oriented lifecycle, which is discussed in the next section.

Model transitions

Earlier approaches to information systems development created analysis models (e.g. data flow diagrams) that had a rather indirect relationship to the design models (e.g. structure charts and update process models) that followed them. This meant that designs for new systems, however good in their own right, were hard to trace back to the original requirements for the system. Yet what makes a design successful is that it meets the requirements in a way that is functional, efficient, economic and so on (see Chapter 12). This means that it is important to be able to trace the features of the final system back to the specific requirement (or requirements) that it is intended to fulfil.

Object-oriented analysis and design avoid these transition problems by creating a uniform set of models throughout analysis and design, adding more detail at each stage and avoiding the awkward discontinuities that arise when one model must be discarded to be replaced by another with a different, incompatible structure. In UML, the fundamental analysis models are the *use case* and the *class diagram* (described in Chapters 6 and 7, respectively) and these are the backbone of the design, too, with other design models derived directly or indirectly from them.

Reusable software

Information systems are very expensive, yet in the past their developers have tended to reinvent new solutions to old problems, many times over. This wastes time and money, and has led to the demand for reusable software components, which can eliminate the need to keep reinventing the wheel. Object-oriented development methods offer great potential, not yet fully realized, for developing software components that are reusable in other systems for which they were not originally designed. This is partly a result of the highly modular nature of object-oriented software, and also due to the way that object-oriented models are organized. Inheritance is of particular importance in this context and we will say more about this in Chapter 8, and about reuse in general in Chapter 20.

4.4 Object-Oriented Languages Today

A number of object-oriented programming languages are available today, with some significant differences between their capabilities and the extent to which they adhere to the object-oriented paradigm. Figure 4.9 lists some of the main characteristics of the most widely used of these languages. The 'popularity rating' is taken from an online index published by TIOBE Software BV (TIOBE, 2009). (TIOBE's rating is based on counting hits for each language when used as a search term on several widely used search engines. It gives an indication of the worldwide total number of programmers, training courses and vendors related to each language.) This is not a programming text-book, so we offer only a very brief description of each feature.

Strong typing refers to the degree of discipline that a language enforces on the programmer when declaring variables. In a strongly typed language (most modern languages are strongly typed), every data value and object that is used must belong to an appropriate type for its context. Static typed languages enforce this with type-checking at compile time. Dynamic typed languages check types at run-time, but some languages offer a hybrid approach that allows the flexibility of loading classes at run-time. Garbage collection is important for memory management in systems that create and delete many objects during their execution. If objects are not removed from memory when they are deleted, the system may run out of memory in which to execute. When this is provided automatically, it removes the responsibility for this task from the programmer. Multiple inheritance is important as it minimizes the amount of code duplication and hence reduces inconsistencies that can cause maintenance problems. In static typed languages, multiple inheritance can allow a new class to stand in for any of its superclasses,

Feature	Java	C++	PHP	VB.NET	C#	Python	Perl	Ruby
Popularity rating (July 2009)	20.5	10.4%	9.3%	7.8%	4.5%	4.4%	4.2%	2.6%
Strong typing	✓	optional	✗	✓	✓	✓	✗	✓
Static or dynamic typing (S D)	S	S	D	S	S + D	D	S + D	D
Garbage collection	✓	✗	✗	✓	✓	✓	✗	✓
Multiple inheritance	✗	✓	✗	✗	✗	✓	✓	✗
Pure objects	✗	✗	✗	✗	✗	✗	✗	✓
Dynamic loading	✓	✗	✓	✓	✓	✓	✓	✓
Standardized class libraries	✓	✗	✓	✓	✗	✓	✓	✓

Figure 4.9 Characteristics of some widely used object-oriented languages.

and this reduces the amount of special-case programming required elsewhere in the system.

Languages in which all constructs are implemented as classes or objects are said to be 'pure' object-oriented languages. Some languages permit data values that are not objects, but this introduces extra complexities for the programmer. Other languages allow unencapsulated types, but this gives the sloppy programmer opportunities to bypass the safer encapsulation of classes. Both of these circumstances can cause a system to be difficult to maintain and extend.

Dynamic loading refers to the ability of a language to load new classes at run-time. This can be used to allow software to reconfigure itself: for example, to cope with hardware or environment changes. It can help to propagate improvements and bug fixes, by concentrating maintenance efforts on the server side. It is also widely used to implement plug-ins such as those that allow a web browser to play video and audio content.

Standardized class libraries give the programmer access to classes that are known to run successfully on a variety of hardware platforms, and under a variety of operating systems. When these are not available, it can be difficult to modify an application so that it will run on another platform, or in conjunction with applications that have used a different library.

Finally, in earlier editions of this book we compared languages on the aspect of correctness constructs. However, only Eiffel provided these, and we have dropped this language from the comparison due its decline in popularity. This is a shame, as correctness constructs are a valuable feature in a programming language. They allow a programmer to define pre-conditions and post-conditions on methods, thus forming an enforced contract between two classes that participate in requesting and providing a service. Contracts are important to the development of robust software and are discussed in Chapter 10.

Limitations of object-orientation

Some applications are not ideally suited to object-oriented development and in this section we make a few comments about these. There are two main examples. The first kind is systems that are strongly database-oriented. These have a record-based structure of data that is appropriate to a relational database management system (RDBMS) and their main processing requirements centre on the storage and retrieval of the data (e.g. a management information system used mainly for querying data in the database). Such applications cannot easily be adapted to an object-oriented implementation without losing the many benefits of using a RDBMS for data storage. Commercial RDBMSs are a very mature form of technology and they organize their data according to sound mathematical principles. This ensures a good balance of efficiency of retrieval, resilience to change and flexibility in use. However, RDBMSs are limited in their capabilities for storing and retrieving certain kinds of complex data structure, such as those that represent multimedia data. The spatial (map-based) data that forms the basis of a geographic information system (GIS) is a particular example of data structures to which RDBMSs are not well suited, but which are ideally suited to object-oriented development. Multimedia data such as video and audio clips are also better suited to an object-oriented implementation. We return to the relative advantages and disadvantages of RDBMSs as compared to object-oriented database systems in Chapter 18.

Applications that are strongly algorithmic in their operation are less suited to an object-oriented development approach. For some scientific applications that involve large and complex calculations (for example, satellite orbit calculations) it may be neither feasible nor desirable to split the calculation down into smaller parts. Such a system, if developed in an object-oriented manner, might contain very few objects, but each would be extremely complex. This would not be sound object-oriented design, and so either a procedural or a functional approach (these are alternative styles of programming) is recommended instead.

4.5   Summary

In this chapter we have introduced the most important concepts in object-orientation, in particular, object and class, generalization and specialization, encapsulation, information hiding, message passing, object state and polymorphism. Understanding these gives an essential foundation for later chapters that deal with the practical application of object-oriented analysis and design techniques. We have also identified some of the main benefits of following an object-oriented approach, such as software and model reuse, modular systems that are easier to modify and maintain, and projects that deliver useful increments of software faster than other approaches. There is a great deal of synergy in the way that the different fundamental concepts contribute to the success of object-orientation. For example, message passing and polymorphism both play a significant role in achieving sound modularity in a system. But there is no clean break with the past; instead, the characteristics of object-orientation are best seen as the result of a gradual process of evolution that can be traced back to the earliest days of electronic digital computers. This evolutionary process is by no means finished yet. As applications and computing environments grow ever more complex, there is a continuing need for reliable, maintainable, modifiable information systems.

Review Questions

4.1   Define object, class and instance.

4.2   What do you think is meant by 'semantics'?

4.3   How does the object-oriented concept of message passing help to hide the implementation of an object, including its data?

4.4   What is polymorphism?

4.5   What is the difference between generalization and specialization?

4.6   What rules describe the relationship between a subclass and its superclass?

4.7   What does it mean to say that an object-oriented system is highly modular?

4.8   Why is it particularly hard for a designer to anticipate a user's sequence of tasks when using a GUI application?

4.9   What does 'object state' mean?

4.10   What is an operation signature?

4.11   Distinguish between 'encapsulation' and 'information hiding.'

Case Study Work, Exercises and Projects

4.A   Section 4.2.1 mentions the human activity system and the proposed software system as particularly important systems to consider, but these are not the only systems that an analyst will encounter or work with. Make a list of any other systems you can think of that might be involved in the process of software development. What interfaces exist between them?

4.B   Reread the description of generalization given in Section 4.2.4. How does object-oriented inheritance differ from inheritance between a parent and a child: (i) in biology and (ii) in law?

4.C   Arrange the following into a hierarchy that depends on their relative generalization or specialization: person, thing, green, shape, primary school teacher, cub, polar bear, square, law, child, colour, animal. Add more classifications as necessary so that it is clear what is generalized or specialized at each level.

4.D   Read the first section of the case study material for FoodCo (Section B1.1), and identify classes that represent FoodCo's whole business environment.

4.E   List all FoodCo's products that are identified in the case study material in Case Study B1 and arrange these into a hierarchy. Imagine some more products that make your hierarchy more interesting, and add these to your diagram.

Further Reading

Most standard texts on object-oriented analysis and design contain a section that introduces the fundamental concepts of object-orientation. Although predating the development of UML, Jacobson et al. (1992) and Rumbaugh et al. (1991) remain good general introductions.

Most recent books use UML notation, for example, Maciaszek (2005), McLaughlin et al. (2006), or, from a more technical, software engineering perspective, Lethbridge and Laganiere (2003).

Readers who are interested in learning more about object-oriented programming will find almost too many books on this subject to be able to count them all. In the Java field, McGrath (2007) is among the more readable.

Chapter 5

Modelling Concepts

LEARNING OBJECTIVES

In this chapter you will learn
- ☑ what is meant by a model
- ☑ the distinction between a model and a diagram
- ☑ the UML concept of a model
- ☑ how to draw *activity diagrams* to model processes
- ☑ the approach to system development that we have adopted in this book.

5.1 | Introduction

Systems analysts and designers produce models of systems. A business analyst will start by producing a model of how an organization works; a systems analyst will produce a more abstract model of the objects in that business and how they interact with one another; a designer will produce a model of how a new computerized system will work within the organization. In UML, the term 'model' has a specific meaning, and we explain the UML concept of a model and how it relates to other UML concepts, such as the idea of a package. Diagrams are often confused with models. A diagram is a graphical view of a part of a model for a particular purpose.

The best way to understand what we mean by a diagram is to look at an example. In the Unified Process (the method of developing systems that is promoted by the developers of UML) activity diagrams are used to model the development process itself. Activity diagrams are useful for modelling sequences of actions from business processes within an organization (or between organizations) down to the detail of how an operation works. Activity diagrams are one of the techniques that can be used to model the behavioural view of a system, and their use in systems analysis and design is explained in Chapter 10, where they are used as one way of specifying operations. We introduce them here as an example of a UML diagram and because, as in the Unified Process, we use them to model the development process that we use in the book.

A systems analysis and design project needs to follow some kind of process. We have adopted a relatively lightweight process based on the Unified Process.

5.2 | Models and Diagrams

In any development project that aims at producing useful artefacts, the main focus of both analysis and design activities is on models (although the ultimate objective is a working system). This is equally true for projects to build highways, space shuttles, television sets or software systems. Aircraft designers build wooden or metal scale models of new aircraft to test their characteristics in a wind tunnel. A skilled furniture designer may use a mental model, visualizing a new piece of furniture without drawing a single line.

In IS development, models are usually both abstract and visible. On the one hand, many of the products are themselves abstract in nature; most software is not tangible for the user. On the other hand, software is usually constructed by teams of people who need to see each other's models. However, even in the case of a single developer working alone, it is still advisable to construct visible models. Software development is a complex activity, and it is extremely difficult to carry all the necessary details in one person's memory.

5.2.1 What is a model?

A model is an abstract representation of something real or imaginary. Like maps, models represent something else. They are useful in several different ways, precisely because they differ from the things that they represent.

- A model is quicker and easier to build.
- A model can be used in simulations, to learn more about the thing it represents.
- A model can evolve as we learn more about a task or problem.
- We can choose which details to represent in a model, and which to ignore. A model is an abstraction.
- A model can represent real or imaginary things from any domain.

Many different kinds of thing can be modelled. Civil engineers model bridges, city planners model traffic flow, economists model the effects of government policy and composers model their music. This book is a model of the activity of object-oriented analysis and design.

A useful model has just the right amount of detail and structure, and represents only what is important for the task at hand. This point was not well understood by at least one character in *The Restaurant at the End of the Universe* by Douglas Adams (1980). A group of space colonists are trying to reinvent things they need after crash-landing on a strange planet, and are unable to proceed with a project to design the wheel, because they cannot come to an agreement on what colour it should be.

Real projects do get bogged down in this kind of unnecessary detail if insufficient care is taken to exclude irrelevant considerations (though this example is a little extreme). What IS developers must usually model is a complex situation, frequently within a human activity system. We may need to model what different stakeholders think about the situation, so our models need to be rich in meaning. We must represent functional and non-functional requirements (see Section 6.2.2). The whole requirements model must be accurate, complete and unambiguous. Without this, the work of analysts, designers and programmers later in the project would be much more difficult. At the same time, it must not include premature decisions about how the new system is going to fulfil its users' requests, otherwise analysts, designers and programmers may later find their freedom of action too restricted. Most systems development models today are held as data in modelling tools, and much of that data is represented visually in the form of diagrams, with supporting textual descriptions and logical or mathematical specifications of processes and data.[1]

5.2.2 What is a diagram?

A diagram is a visual representation of some part of a model. Analysts and designers use diagrams to illustrate models of systems in the same way as architects use drawings and diagrams to model buildings. Diagrammatic models are used extensively by systems analysts and designers in order to:

- communicate ideas
- generate new ideas and possibilities
- test ideas and make predictions
- understand structures and relationships.

The models may be of existing business systems or they may be of new computerized systems. If a system is very simple, it may be possible to model it with a single diagram and supporting textual descriptions. Most systems are more complex and may require many diagrams fully to capture that complexity.

Figure 5.1 shows an example of a diagram (a UML *activity diagram*) used to show part of the process of producing a book. This diagram alone is not a complete model. A model of book production would include other activity diagrams to show other parts of the overall system such as negotiating contracts and marketing the book. This diagram does not even show all the detail of the activities carried out by authors and the other participants in the process. Many of the activities, shown as rectangles with rounded corners in Fig. 5.1, could be expanded into more detail. For example, the activity Write Chapter could be broken down into other activities such as those shown in Fig. 5.2.

We might break some of the activities shown in Fig. 5.2 down into more detail, though it will be difficult to show the detail at a lower level, as activities like Write a Paragraph, Add a Figure, Revise a Paragraph and Move a Figure do not lend themselves to being represented in the flowchart notation of the activity diagram. There is also a limit to what we want to show in such a diagram. There are many activities such as Make Coffee, Change CD and Stare out of Window that are part of the process of writing, but like the colour of the wheel in the example from *The Restaurant at the End of the Universe*, they represent unnecessary detail.

---

1 Some approaches rely primarily on formal logic techniques and rigorous mathematical specification. These are most often applied to real-time and safety-critical systems, such as those that control aircraft in flight or manage nuclear power plants, and are not covered in this book.

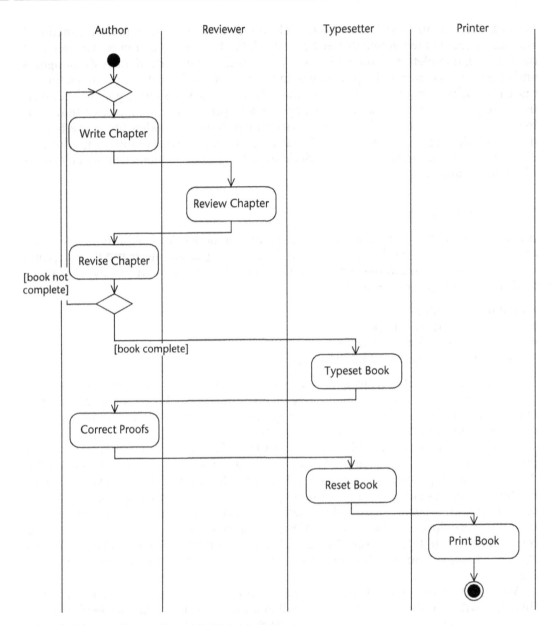

Figure 5.1 Activity diagram for producing a book.

The diagrams of Figs 5.1 and 5.2 are typical of the kind of diagrams used in systems analysis and design. Abstract shapes are used to represent things or actions from the real world. The choice of what shapes to use is determined by a set of rules that are laid down for the particular type of diagram. In UML, these rules are laid down in the *OMG Unified Modeling Language Specification 2.2* (OMG, 2009). It is important that we follow the rules about diagrams, otherwise the diagrams may not make sense, or other people may not understand them. Standards are important as they promote communication in the same way as a common language. They enable communication between

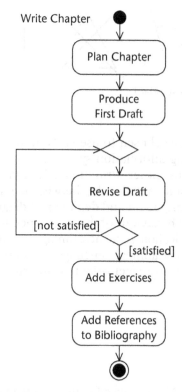

Figure 5.2 Activity diagram for the activity `Write Chapter`.

members of the development team if they all document the information in the same standard formats. They promote communication over time, as other people come to work on the system, even several years after it has been implemented, in order to carry out maintenance. They also promote communication of good practice, as experience of what should be recorded and how best to do that recording builds up over time and is reflected in the techniques that are used.

Modelling techniques are refined and evolve over time. The diagrams and how they map to things in the real world or in a new system change as users gain experience of how well they work. However, for the designers of modelling techniques, some general rules are that the techniques should aid (and enforce):

- simplicity of representation–only showing what needs to be shown
- internal consistency–within a set of diagrams
- completeness–showing all that needs to be shown
- hierarchical representation–breaking the system down and showing more detail at lower levels.

Figure 5.3 shows some symbols from a label in an item of clothing. These icons belong to a standard that allows a manufacturer of clothing in Argentina to convey to a purchaser in Sweden that the item should be washed at no more than 40°C, should not be bleached and can be tumble dried on a low setting.

While not following the UML standards will not cause your T-shirts to shrink, it will cause you problems in communicating with other analysts and designers–at least if they

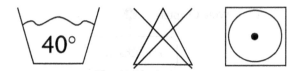

Figure 5.3 Example from a diagram standard.

are using UML as well. We have chosen to use UML in this book, as it has become the industry standard for modelling information systems.

UML classifies diagrams as either *structural diagrams* or *behavioural diagrams*. Structural diagrams show the static relationship between elements, and are package, class, object, composite structure, component and deployment diagrams. Behavioural diagrams show an aspect of the dynamic behaviour of the system being modelled, and are use case, activity, state machine, communication, sequence, timing and interaction overview diagrams.

UML consists mainly of a graphical language to represent the concepts that we require in the development of an object-oriented information system. UML diagrams are made up of four elements:

- icons
- two-dimensional symbols
- paths
- strings.

These terms were used in the UML 1.X specifications, and are no longer used in UML 2.2. However, they are useful to explain the graphical representation of UML diagrams.

UML diagrams are *graphs*–composed of various kinds of shapes, known as *nodes*, joined together by lines, known as *paths*. The activity diagrams in Figs 5.1 and 5.2 illustrate this. Both are made up of two-dimensional symbols that represent activities, linked by arrows that represent the control flows from one activity to another and the flow of control through the process that is being modelled. The start and finish of each activity graph is marked by special symbols–icons: the dot for the initial node and the dot in a circle for the final node. The activities are labelled with strings, and strings are also used at the decision nodes (the diamond shapes) to show the conditions that are being tested.

The UML Specification (OMG, 2009) provides the formal grammar of UML–the syntax–and the meaning of the elements and of the rules about how elements can be combined–the semantics. It also explains the different diagrams in more detail and provides examples of their construction and use (although with fewer examples than previous versions).

There is an example on the book's website of how the UML specification defines the syntax and semantics of UML. It may be difficult to follow at this stage in your understanding of UML, so feel free to skip it and come back to it when you know more about UML.

5.2.3 The difference between a model and a diagram

We have seen an example of a diagram in the previous section. A single diagram can illustrate or document some aspect of a system. However, a model provides a complete view of a system at a particular stage and from a particular perspective.

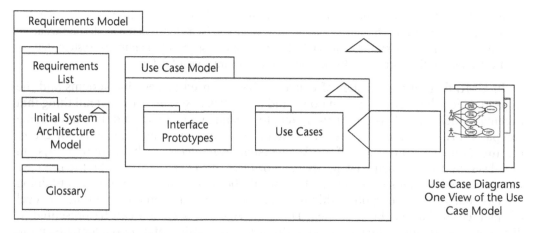

Figure 5.4 Illustration of a UML model and its relationship with one type of diagram.

For example, a requirements model of a system will give a complete view of the requirements for that system. It may use one or more types of diagram and will most likely contain sets of diagrams to cover all aspects of the requirements. These diagrams may be grouped together in models in their own right. In a project that uses UML, a requirements model would probably consist of a use case model, which comprises use cases and prototypes of some use cases (see Chapter 6) and an initial system architecture model which defines initial subsystems (see Section 5.2.4). Note that models can contain diagrams, data and textual information. Figure 5.4 shows this: on the left-hand side of the diagram is a UML diagram showing the contents of models and packages (see Section 5.2.4), while the right-hand side of the diagram illustrates schematically the fact that use case diagrams are one possible view of the contents of the use case model.

On the other hand a behavioural model of a system will show those aspects of a system that are concerned with its behaviour—how it responds to events in the outside world and to the passage of time. During the initial analysis activities of a project, the behavioural model may be quite simple, using communication diagrams to show which classes collaborate to respond to external events and with informally defined messages passing between them. As the project progresses and more design activities have taken place, the behavioural model will be considerably more detailed, using interaction sequence diagrams to show in detail the way that objects interact, and with every message defined as an event or an operation of a class.

A model may consist of a single diagram, if what is being modelled is simple enough to be modelled in that way, but most models consist of many diagrams—related to one another in some way—and supporting data and textual documentation. Most models consist of many diagrams because it is necessary to simplify complex systems to a level that people can understand and take in. For example, the class libraries for Java are made up of hundreds of classes, but books that present information about these classes rarely show more than about twenty on any one diagram, and each diagram groups together classes that are conceptually related.

5.2.4 Models in UML

The UML 2.2 Superstructure Specification (OMG, 2009b) defines a model as follows:

A model captures a view of a physical system. It is an abstraction of the physical system, with a certain purpose. This purpose determines what is to be included in the model and what is irrelevant. Thus the model completely describes those aspects of the physical system that are relevant to the purpose of the model, at the relevant level of detail.

In UML there are a number of concepts that are used to describe systems and the ways in which they can be broken down and modelled. A *system* is the overall thing that is being modelled, such as the Agate system for dealing with clients and their advertising campaigns. A *subsystem* is a part of a system, consisting of related elements: for example, the Campaigns subsystem of the Agate system. A *model* is an abstraction of a system or subsystem from a particular perspective or *view*. An example would be the use case view of the Campaigns subsystem, which would be represented by a model containing use case diagrams, among other things. A model is complete and consistent at the level of abstraction that has been chosen. Different views of a system can be presented in different models, and a *diagram* is a graphical representation of a set of elements in the model of the system.

Different models present different views of the system. Booch et al. (1999) suggest five views to be used with UML: the use case view, the design view, the process view, the implementation view and the deployment view. The choice of diagrams that are used to model each of these views will depend on the nature and complexity of the system that is being modelled. Indeed, you may not need all these views of a system. If the system that you are developing runs on a single machine, then the implementation and deployment views are unnecessary, as they are concerned with which components must be installed on which different machines.

UML provides a notation for modelling subsystems and models that uses an extension of the notation for *packages* in UML. Packages are a way of organizing model elements and grouping them together. They do not represent things in the system that is being modelled, but are a convenience for packaging together elements that do represent things in the system. They are used particularly in CASE tools as a way of managing the models that are produced. For example, the use cases can be grouped together into a Use Cases Package. Figure 5.5 shows the notation for packages, subsystems and models. In diagrams we can show how packages, subsystems and models contain other packages, subsystems and models. This can be done by containing model elements within larger ones. Figure 5.6 shows the notation for an example of a system containing two subsystems.

5.2.5 Developing models

The models that we produce during the development of a system change as the project progresses. They change along three main dimensions:

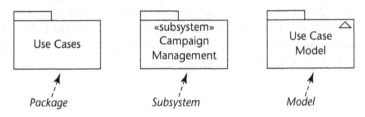

Figure 5.5 UML notation for packages, subsystems and models.

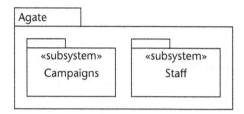

Figure 5.6 UML notation for a system containing subsystems, shown by containment.

- abstraction
- formality
- level of detail.

During a particular phase of a project we may extend and elaborate a model as we increase our understanding of the system that is to be built. At the end of each phase we hope to have a model that is complete and consistent, within the limitations of that phase of the project. That model represents a view of our understanding of the system at that point in the project.

In a system development project that uses an iterative lifecycle, different models that represent the same view may be developed at different levels of detail as the project progresses. For example, the first use case model of a system may show only the obvious use cases that are apparent from the first iteration of requirements capture. After a second iteration, the use case model may be elaborated with more detail and additional use cases that emerge from discussion of the requirements. Some prototypes may be added to try out ideas about how users will interact with the system. After a third iteration, the model will be extended to include more structured descriptions of how the users will interact with the use cases and with relationships among use cases. (Use cases are explained in Chapter 6.) Figure 5.7 illustrates this process of adding detail to a model through successive iterations. The number of iterations is not set at three. Any phase in a project will consist of a number of iterations, and that number will depend on the complexity of the system being developed.

It is also possible to produce a model that contains a lot of detail, but to hide or suppress some of that detail in order to get a simplified overview of some aspect of the system. For example, class diagrams (explained in Chapter 7) can be shown with the compartments that contain attributes and operations suppressed. This is often useful for showing the structural relationships between classes, using just the name of each class, without the distracting detail of all the attributes and operations. This is the case in the diagrams that show the classes in the Java class libraries (referred to in Section 5.2.3), where the intention is to show structural relationships between classes rather than the detail.

As we progress through analysis and design of a system, elements in the model will become less abstract and more concrete. For example, we may start off with classes that represent the kinds of objects that we find in the business, `Campaigns`, `Clients` etc., that are defined in terms of the responsibilities that they have. By the time that we get to the end of design and are ready to implement the classes, we will have a set of more concrete classes with attributes and operations, and the classes from the domain will have been supplemented by additional classes such as collection classes, caches, brokers and proxies that are required to implement mechanisms for storing the domain classes (see Chapter 18).

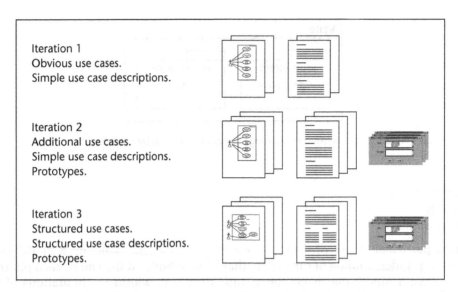

Iteration 1
Obvious use cases.
Simple use case descriptions.

Iteration 2
Additional use cases.
Simple use case descriptions.
Prototypes.

Iteration 3
Structured use cases.
Structured use case descriptions.
Prototypes.

Figure 5.7 Development of the use case model through successive iterations.

In the same way, the degree of formality with which operations, attributes and constraints are defined will increase as the project progresses. Initially, classes will have responsibilities that are loosely defined and named in English (or whatever language the project is being developed in). By the time we reach the end of design and are ready to implement the classes, they will have operations defined using activity diagrams, Object Constraint Language, structured English or pseudo-Code (see Chapter 10), with pre-conditions and post-conditions for each operation.

This iterative approach, in which models are successively elaborated as the project progresses, has advantages over the Waterfall model, but it also has shortcomings. First, it is sometimes difficult to know when to stop elaborating a model and, second, it raises the question of whether to go back and update earlier models with additional information that emerges in later stages of the project. Issues like these are addressed either as part of a methodology (Chapter 21) or as part of a project management approach (see supporting website). For now, we shall look at a first example of a UML diagram and see how it is developed.

5.3 Drawing Activity Diagrams

We have used activity diagrams earlier in this chapter to illustrate what is meant by a diagram. In this section we explain the basic notation of activity diagrams in UML and give examples of how they are used. We are introducing activity diagrams at this point, first to provide an illustration of a UML diagram type, and second, so that we can use them to illustrate the development process that we use in the book.

5.3.1 Purpose of activity diagrams

Activity diagrams can be used to model different aspects of a system. At a high level, they can be used to model business processes in an existing or potential system. For this purpose they may be used early in the system development lifecycle. They can be used to model a system function represented by a use case, possibly using object flows to show which objects are involved in each use case. This would be done during the phase of the lifecycle when requirements are being elaborated. They can also be used at a low level to model the detail of how a particular operation is carried out, and are likely to be used for this purpose in later analysis or system design activities. Activity diagrams are also used within the Unified Software Development Process (USDP) (Jacobson et al., 1999) to model the way in which the activities of USDP are organized and relate to one another in the software development lifecycle. We use them for a similar purpose in later chapters to show how the activities of the simplified process that we have adopted for this book fit together. (This process is described in Section 5.4.)

In summary, activity diagrams are used for the following purposes:

- to model a process or task (in business modelling for instance);
- to describe a system function that is represented by a use case;
- in operation specifications, to describe the logic of an operation;
- in USDP to model the activities that make up the lifecycle.

Fashions change in systems analysis and design–new approaches such as object-oriented analysis and design replace older approaches and introduce new diagrams and notation. One diagram type that is always dismissed by the inventors of new approaches but always creeps back in again is the flowchart.[2] Activity diagrams are essentially flowcharts in an object-oriented context.

UML 2.0 changed the underlying model for activity diagrams. In UML 1.X they were based on state machines (see Chapter 11), but are now distinct from state machines and based on Petri nets.

5.3.2 Notation of activity diagrams

Activity diagrams at their simplest consist of a set of *actions* linked together by flows from one action to the next, formally called `ActivityEdges`. Each action is shown as a rectangle with rounded corners. The name of the action is written inside this two-dimensional symbol. It should be meaningful and summarize the action. Figure 5.8 shows an example of two actions joined by a *control flow*.

Figure 5.8 Example of two activities joined by a control flow.

Actions exist to carry out some task. In the example of Fig. 5.9, the first action is to add a new client into the Agate system described in Chapter A1. The flow to the second

---

2   Flowcharts are useful because they model the way that people perform tasks as a sequence of actions with decision points where they take one of a set of alternative paths, in which some actions are repeated either a number of times or until some condition is true and some actions take place in parallel. In UML 2.2 activity diagrams have the semantics of Petri Nets.

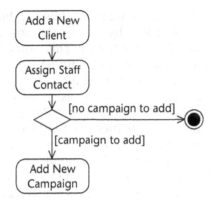

Figure 5.9 Activities with a decision node.

action implies that as soon as the first action is complete, the next action is started. Sometimes there is more than one possible flow from an action to the next.

In this example from the Agate system, the flow of work is summarized by this brief statement from an interview with one of the directors of Agate:

> When we add a new client, we always assign a member of staff as a contact for the client straightaway. If it's an important client, then that person is likely to be one of our directors or a senior member of staff. The normal reason for adding a new client is because we have agreed a campaign with them, so we then add details of the new campaign. But that's not always the case–sometimes we add a client before the details of the campaign have been firmed up, so in that case, once we have added the client the task is complete. If we are adding the campaign, then we would record its details, and if we know which members of staff will be working on the campaign, we would assign each of them to work on the campaign.

This transcript from an interview describes some choices that can be made, and these choices will affect the actions that are undertaken. We can show these in an activity diagram with an explicit *decision node*, represented by a diamond-shaped icon, as in Figure 5.9.

In UML 1.X, it was not necessary to use an explicit decision node like this. The diagram could just show the alternative flows out of the action `Assign Staff Contact`, as in Figure 5.10.

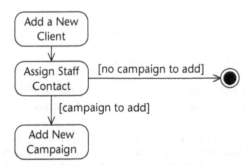

Figure 5.10 UML 1.X choice represented without an explicit decision point.

However, this is no longer possible since UML 2.0. In UML 1.X, if there was more than one flow out of an action, it was treated as an OR, i.e. only one flow would be taken. In UML 2.2, it is treated as an AND, i.e. all of the flows must be taken.

The alternative flows are each labelled with a *guard condition*. The guard condition is shown inside square brackets and must evaluate to either true or false. The flow of control will follow along the first control flow with a guard condition that evaluates to true. Alternative guard conditions from a single decision node do not have to be mutually exclusive, but if they are not, you should specify the order of evaluation in some way, otherwise the results will be unpredictable. We would recommend that they should be mutually exclusive.

Figures 5.9 and 5.10 illustrate another element of the notation of activity diagrams: when an activity has completed that ends the sequence of activities within a particular diagram, there must be a control flow to a *final node*, shown as a black circle within a white circle with a black border. Each activity diagram should also begin with another special icon, a black circle, which represents the start of the activity. Figure 5.11 shows the addition of the *initial node* into the diagram of Fig. 5.9. It also shows an additional action–to assign a member of staff to work on a campaign–and additional guarded flows.

Figure 5.11 also shows a feature of UML diagrams from version 2.0 onwards: every diagram can be drawn in a *frame*, a rectangle with the heading of the diagram in the top left hand corner. The heading consists of the kind of diagram (this is optional), in this

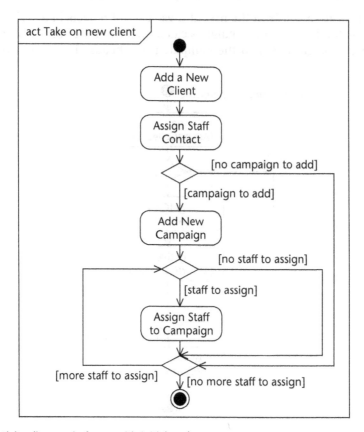

Figure 5.11 Activity diagram in frame with initial node.

case `activity` abbreviated as `act`, the name of the diagram and optional parameters. Frames are really only required for diagrams such as sequence diagrams where messages can enter the diagram from the boundary represented by the frame, as in Fig. 9.6.

Note that there is a loop or iteration created at the bottom of this diagram, where the activity `Assign Staff to Campaign` is repeated until there are no more staff to assign to this particular campaign.

Activity diagrams make it possible to represent the three structural components of all procedural programming languages: sequences, selections and iterations. This ability to model processes in this way is particularly useful for modelling business procedures, but can also be helpful in modelling the operations of classes. UML 2.0 added a large number of types of actions to the metamodel for activity diagrams. These actions are the kind of actions that take place in program code. These include actions such as *AddVariableValueAction* and *CreateObjectAction*. They are intended to make it easier to create activity diagrams that can model the implementation of operations and can be compiled into a programming language: *Executable UML*.

In an object-oriented system, however, the focus is on objects carrying out the processing necessary for the overall system to achieve its objectives. There are two ways in which objects can be shown in activity diagrams:

- the operation name and class name can be used as the name of an action;
- an object can be shown as providing the input to or output of an action.

Figure 5.12 shows an example of the first of these uses of objects in activity diagrams. In this example, the total cost of a campaign is calculated from the cost of all the individual adverts in the campaign added to the campaign overheads. The names of the classes

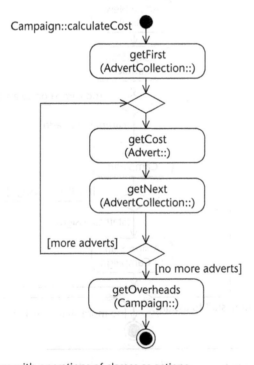

Figure 5.12 Activity diagram with operations of classes as actions.

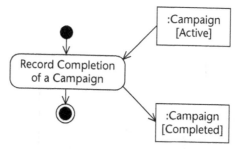

Figure 5.13 Activity diagram with object flows.

involved are shown followed by double colons in brackets beneath the names of the actions. If the name of the action is not the same as the name of an operation of the class, then the operation name can be shown after the colons. This is one of those specialized actions to support Executable UML: a *CallOperationAction*.

The second way that objects are shown in activity diagrams is by using *object flows*. An object flow is an arrow between an object and an action that may result in a change to the state of that object. The state of the object can be shown in square brackets within the symbol for the object. Figure 5.13 shows an example of this for the activity `Record Completion of a Campaign`, which changes the state of a `Campaign` object from `Active` to `Completed`. (Objects and classes are covered in much more detail in Chapters 7 and 8, and the idea of 'state' is covered in more detail in Chapter 11, where we explain state machine diagrams.)

A final element of the notation of activity diagrams that it is useful to understand at this stage is the idea of *activity partitions*, which were called *swimlanes* in UML 1.X and are generally known by this name. Activity partitions are particularly useful when modelling how things happen in an existing system and can be used to show where actions take place or who carries out the actions.

In the Agate system, when an advertising campaign is completed, the campaign manager for that advertising campaign records that it is completed. This triggers off the sending of a record of completion form to the company accountant. An invoice is then sent to the client and, when the client pays the invoice, the payment is recorded. (Some of these actions are documented as use cases in Fig. A2.2.)

In order to model the way that the system works at the moment, we might draw an activity diagram like the one in Fig. 5.14 in order to show these actions taking place. The brief for this project is to concern ourselves with the campaign management side of the business, as there is an existing accounts system in the company. However, the act of drawing this diagram raises the question of what happens to the payment from the client:

- Does the payment go to the accountant, and is there some way in which the campaign manager is notified?
- Does the payment go to the campaign manager, and does he or she record the payment and then pass it on to the accountant?

Clarifying points like these is part of the process of requirements capture, which is covered in detail in Chapter 6.

One of the reasons for introducing activity diagrams at this point is that they are used in the Unified Software Development Process to document the activities of the software development lifecycle. In USDP, the diagrams are *stereotyped*—the standard UML

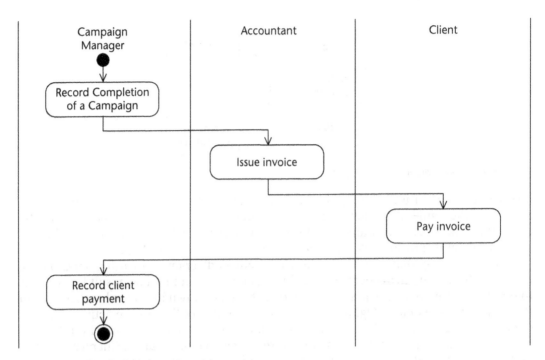

Figure 5.14 Activity diagram with activity partitions.

symbols are replaced with special icons to represent actions and the inputs and outputs of those actions. In the next section, we describe the simplified process model that we have adopted in this book. We use activity diagrams to summarize this process in the case study chapters later in the book.

5.4 A Development Process

A development process should specify what has to be done, when it has to be done, how it should be done and by whom in order to achieve the required goal. Project management techniques (see Chapter 22 on the supporting website) are used to manage and control the process for individual projects. One of the software development processes currently in wide use is the Rational Unified Process, a proprietary process now owned by IBM but based on the Unified Software Development Process (USDP) (Jacobson et al., 1999). USDP was originally developed by the team that created UML. It is claimed that USDP embodies much of the currently accepted best practices in information systems development. These include:

- iterative and incremental development
- component-based development
- requirements-driven development
- configurability
- architecture centrism
- visual modelling techniques.

USDP is explained in more detail in Chapter 21 on System Development Methodologies. USDP is often referred to as the *Unified Process*.

USDP does not follow the traditional Waterfall Lifecycle shown in Fig. 3.3 but adopts an iterative approach within four main *phases*. These phases reflect the different emphasis on tasks that are necessary as systems development proceeds (Fig. 5.15). These differences are captured in a series of *workflows* that run through the development process. Each workflow defines a series of activities that are to be carried out as part of the workflow and specifies the roles of the people who will carry out those activities. The important fact to bear in mind is that in the Waterfall Lifecycle, activities and phases are one and the same, while in iterative lifecycles like USDP the activities are independent of the phases and it is the mix of activities that changes as the project proceeds. Figure 5.16 illustrates how a simplified Waterfall Lifecycle would look using the same style of diagram as Fig. 5.15.

5.4.1 Underlying principles

In order to place the techniques and models described in this book in context we have assumed an underlying system development process. We are not attempting to invent yet another methodology. The main activities that we describe here appear in one form

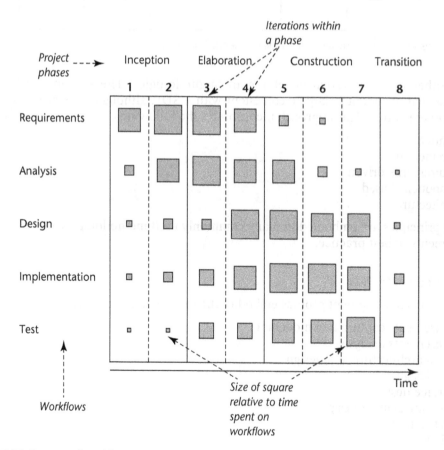

Figure 5.15 Phases and workflows in the Unified Software Development Process.

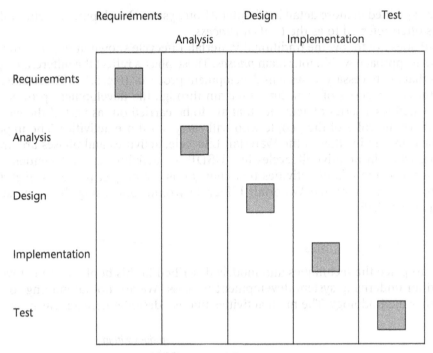

Figure 5.16 Phases and activities in a simplified waterfall process.

or another in most system development methodologies. The system development process that we adopt is largely consistent with USDP, although it incorporates ideas from other sources. This approach incorporates the following characteristics. It is:

- iterative
- incremental
- requirements-driven
- component-based
- architectural.

These principles are embodied in many commonly used methodologies and are viewed as elements of best practice.

5.4.2 Main activities

The systems development process embodies the following main activities:

- requirements capture and modelling
- requirements analysis
- system architecture and design
- class design
- interface design
- data management design
- construction
- testing
- implementation.

These activities are interrelated and dependent upon each other. In a waterfall development process they would be performed in a sequence (as in Fig. 5.16). This is not the case in an iterative development process, although some activities clearly precede others. For example, at least some requirements capture and modelling must take place before any requirements analysis can be undertaken. Various UML techniques and notations are used, as well as other techniques, and these are summarized in the table in Fig. 5.17.

Activity	Techniques	Key Deliverables	Diagrams Used
Requirements capture and modelling	Requirements elicitation Use case modelling Architectural modelling Prototyping	Use case model Requirements list Initial architecture Prototypes	Use case diagrams Package diagrams
Requirements analysis	Communication diagrams Class and object modelling Analysis modelling	Analysis models	Class diagrams Object diagrams Communication diagrams
System architecture and design	Deployment modelling Component modelling Package modelling Architectural modelling Design patterns	Overview design and implementation architecture	Package diagrams Component diagrams Deployment diagrams Class diagrams
Class design	Class and object modelling Interaction modelling State modelling Design patterns	Design models	Class diagrams Object diagrams Sequence diagrams State machine diagrams
Interface design	Class and object modelling Interaction modelling State modelling Package modelling Prototyping Design patterns	Design models with interface specification	Class diagrams Object diagrams Sequence diagrams State machine diagrams Package diagrams
Data management design	Class and object modelling Interaction modelling State modelling Package modelling Design patterns	Design models with database specification	Class diagrams Object diagrams Sequence diagrams State machine diagrams Package diagrams
Construction	Programming Component reuse Database DDL Programming idioms Manual writing	Constructed system Documentation	
Testing	Programming Test planning and design Testing	Test plans Test cases Tested system	
Implementation		Installed system	

Figure 5.17 Table of system development process activities.

Only the key deliverables are listed in the table and are likely to be produced in a series of iterations and delivered incrementally. A brief summary of each activity follows. The models that are produced and the activities necessary to produce them are explained in more detail in subsequent chapters.

Requirements capture and modelling

Various fact-finding techniques are used to identify requirements. These are discussed in Chapter 6. Requirements are documented in use cases and a requirements list. A use case captures an element of functionality and the requirements model may include many use cases. For example, in the Agate case study the requirement that the accountant should be able to record the details of a new member of staff on the system is an example of a use case. It would be described initially as follows:

Use Case: Add a new staff member
When a new member of staff joins Agate, his or her details are recorded. He or she is assigned a staff number, and the start date is recorded. Start date defaults to today's date. The starting grade is recorded.

The use cases can also be modelled graphically. The use case model is refined to identify common procedures and dependencies between use cases. The objective of this refinement is to produce a succinct but complete description of requirements. Not all requirements will be captured in use cases. Some requirements that apply to the whole system will be captured in a list of requirements. Requirements that are concerned with how well the system performs rather than what it does (non-functional requirements) are also captured separately. It is also common to capture rules that reflect how the business works (business rules) in a separate document and cross-reference them from use cases.

Prototypes of some key user interfaces may be produced in order to help to understand the requirements that the users have for the system.

An initial system architecture in terms of an outline package structure (see Fig. 5.18 for part of the Agate system) may be developed to help guide subsequent steps during the development process. This initial architecture will be refined and adjusted as the development proceeds.

Requirements analysis

This activity analyses the requirements. Essentially each use case describes one major user requirement. Each use case is analysed separately to identify the objects that are required to support it. The use case is also analysed to determine how these objects interact and what responsibilities each of the objects has in order to support the use case. Communication diagrams (Fig. 5.19) are used to model the object interaction. The

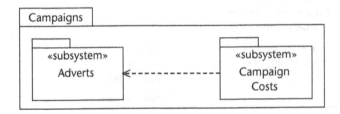

Figure 5.18 Part of the initial system architecture for the Agate system.

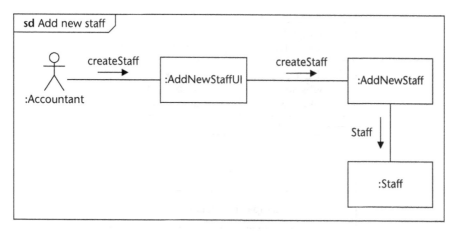

Figure 5.19 Part of a communication diagram for the use case Add New Staff.

Client
companyName companyAddress companyTelephone
«responsibilities» addClient updateClientDetails getClientDetails addNewCampaign getClientCampaigns

Figure 5.20 Partly completed sample analysis class.

models for each use case are then integrated to produce an analysis class diagram, as described in Chapters 7 and 8. Figure 5.20 shows an example of an analysis class. The initial system architecture may be refined as a result of these activities. Object diagrams may be used to analyse the links between objects in order to determine the associations between classes.

System architecture and design
In this activity various decisions concerning the design process are made, including the further specification of a suitable systems architecture. For example, a possible architecture for the system in the Agate case study is shown in Fig. 5.21. This architecture has four layers. The two bottom layers provide common functionality and database access for the campaign costing and advert planning subsystems. Part of the architectural specification may include the identification of particular technologies to be used. In this case it may be decided to use a client–server architecture with the subsystem interfaces operating through a web browser to give maximum operational flexibility.

As well as package diagrams, shown here, component diagrams are used to model logical components of the system, and deployment diagrams are used to show the physical architecture of processors and the software that will run on them.

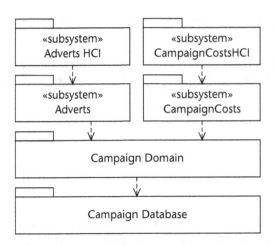

Figure 5.21 Possible architecture for part of the Agate system.

System architecture and design is also concerned with identifying and documenting suitable development standards (e.g. interface design standards, coding standards) for the remainder of the project. System architecture and design is explained in Chapter 13.

Class design
Each of the use case analysis models is now elaborated separately to include relevant design detail. Interaction sequence diagrams may be drawn to show detailed object communication (Chapter 9) and state machine diagrams may be prepared for objects with complex state behaviour (Chapter 11). The separate models are then integrated to produce a detailed design class diagram. Design classes have attributes and operations specified (Fig. 5.22) to replace the less specific responsibilities that may have been identified by the analysis activity (Fig. 5.20). The detailed design of the classes normally necessitates the addition of further classes to support, for example, the user interface and access to the data storage system (typically a database management system). Class design is explained in Chapter 14.

User interface design
The nature of the functionality offered via each use case has been defined in requirements analysis. User interface design produces a detailed specification as to how the required functionality can be realized. User interface design gives a system its look and feel and determines the style of interaction the user will have. It includes the positioning and colour of buttons and fields, the mode of navigation used between different parts of

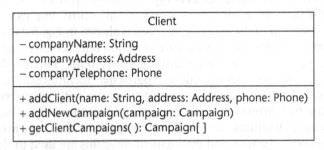

Figure 5.22 Partly completed sample design class.

the system and the nature of online help. Interface design is explained in Chapter 17 and is very dependent on class design. Sequence diagrams are used to model the interaction between instances of classes, and state machine diagrams are used to model the way in which the user interface responds to user events, such as mouse clicks and the entry of data. The class model is updated with new classes representing the user interface, and detail is added as the interaction becomes better understood.

Data management design

Data management design focuses on the specification of the mechanisms suitable for implementation of the database management system being used (see Chapter 18). Techniques such as normalization and entity–relationship modelling may be particularly useful if a relational database management system is being used. Data management design and class design are interdependent. Sequence diagrams are used to model the interaction between instances of classes, and state machine diagrams are used to model the way that objects change state over time in response to real world events. The class model is updated with new classes representing the way in which data will be stored, including data management frameworks.

Construction

Construction is concerned with building the application using appropriate development technologies. Different parts of the system may be built using different languages. Java may be used to construct the user interface, while a database management system such as Oracle would manage data storage and handle commonly used processing routines. Class, sequence, state machine, component and deployment diagrams provide the specification to the developers.

Testing

Before the system can be delivered to the client it must be thoroughly tested. Testing scripts should be derived from the use case descriptions that were previously agreed with the client. Testing should be performed as elements of the system are developed. Different kinds of tests are carried out as the construction work proceeds. Testing is not all left to the end.

Implementation

The final implementation of the system will include its installation on the various computers that will be used. It will also include managing the transition from the old systems to the new systems for the client. This will involve careful risk management and staff training.

5.5 Summary

As in many kinds of development projects, we use models to represent things and ideas that we want to document and to test out without having to actually build a system. Of course, our ultimate aim is to build a system and the models help us to achieve that. Models allow us to create different views of a system from different perspectives and, in an information system development project, most models are graphical representations of things in the real world and the software artefacts that will be used in the information system.

These graphical representations are diagrams, which can be used to model objects and processes. In UML a number of diagrams are defined and the rules for how they are to be drawn are documented. UML defines two types of diagram: structural and behavioural. Diagrams are also supported with textual material, some of which may be informal, for example in natural language, while some may be formal, for example written in Object Constraint Language.

As a project progresses a variety of models are produced in order to represent different aspects of the system that is being built. A model is a complete and consistent view of a system from a particular perspective, typically represented visually in diagrams. An example of a diagram notation that is used in UML is the activity diagram. Activity diagrams model activities that are carried out in a system and include sequences of actions, alternative paths and repeated actions. As well as being used in system development projects, activity diagrams are also used in the Unified Software Development Process to document the sequence of activities in a workflow.

The Unified Software Development Process provides a specification of a process that can be used to develop software systems. It is made up of phases, within which models of the system are elaborated through successive iterations in which additional detail is added to the models until the system can be constructed in software and implemented. For the purpose of this book, we have broken the software development process into a number of activities that must be undertaken in order to develop a system. These activities are described in more detail in subsequent chapters.

Review Questions

5.1 What is the difference between a diagram and a model?

5.2 What are the two types of UML diagram?

5.3 Why do we use models in developing computerized information systems and other artefacts?

5.4 Why do we need standards for the graphical elements of diagrams?

5.5 What is the UML notation for each of the following: package, subsystem and model?

5.6 In what way can we show in UML that something is contained within something else, for example a subsystem within another subsystem?

5.7 What is the notation used for an action in a UML activity diagram?

5.8 What links actions in an activity diagram?

5.9 In what way can a decision be represented in a UML activity diagram?

5.10 What is the notation for the two special nodes that start and finish an activity diagram?

5.11 What is meant by a guard condition?

5.12 What is an object flow?

5.13 What is the notation for an object flow?

5.14 What is the difference between USDP and the Waterfall Lifecycle in the relationship between activities and phases?

Case Study Work, Exercises and Projects

5.A Some people suggest that information systems are models or simulations of the real world. What are the advantages and disadvantages of thinking of information systems in this way?

5.B Think of other kinds of development project in which models are used. For each kind of project list the different kinds of models that you think are used.

5.C Choose a task that you carry out and that you understand, for example preparing an assignment at college or university, or a task at work. Draw an activity diagram to summarize the actions that make up this task. Use activity partitions if the task involves actions that are carried out by other people.

5.D Choose some of the actions in your activity diagram and break them down into more detail in separate diagrams.

5.E Read about the Rational Unified Process (RUP) (see references in the Further Reading section). Identify some of the differences between RUP and USDP.

Further Reading

Although activity diagrams are used in UML for a variety of purposes, including modelling business processes, there are other notations that are becoming more widely used specifically for business process modelling. These have their origins in workflow modelling notations and the growth of business process automation packages that use web services to carry out steps in a business process. The Business Process Modelling Notation (BPMN) is becoming the standard in this area, and is now managed by the OMG (http://www.bpmn.org/).

Booch et al. (1999) discuss the purpose of modelling and the differences between models and diagrams. They also describe the notation of activity diagrams. Jacobson et al. (1999) describe the Unified Software Development Process and explain the notation of the stereotyped activity diagrams that they use to model the workflows in USDP.

An alternative to USDP is the Rational Unified Process, see Kruchten (2004), Kroll and Kruchten (2003) or the IBM Corporation website (http://www.ibm.com/developerworks/rational/products/rup/).

Executable UML is explained in a book by Mellor and Balcer (2002).

Requirements Capture

6.1 | Introduction

Identifying what a new system should be able to do is one of the first steps in its development, whether you are developing some simple programs for your own use or embarking on the development of a large-scale system for a commercial client. The specification of what the system must do is based on the users' requirements, and gathering this information from users is a key role of the systems analyst or business analyst. Requirements will include what the existing system does, and what the new system has to do that the existing system doesn't do. To gather requirements, the analyst will read up on the organization, carry out interviews, observe people at work, collect samples of documents and possibly use questionnaires. The subjects of the investigation will include many stakeholders, not just users of the system, but all the people who have an interest in the new system and whose needs must be considered. UML provides a diagramming technique that can be used to document the stakeholders' requirements. This is the use case diagram, a relatively simple diagram that is supported by written information in the form of use case descriptions.

6.2 | User Requirements

The aim of developing a new information system must be to produce something that meets the needs of the people who will be using it. In order to do this, we must have a clear understanding both of the overall objectives of the business and of what it is that the individual users of the system are trying to achieve in their jobs. Unless you are in the rare position of developing a system for a new organization, you will need to understand how the business is operating at present and how people are working now. Many aspects of the current system will need to be carried forward into the new system, so it is important that information about what people are doing is gathered and documented. These are the requirements that are derived from the 'current system'. The motivation for the development of a new information system is usually problems with and inadequacies of the current system, so it is also essential to capture what it is that the users require of the new system that they cannot do with their existing system. These are the 'new requirements'. The requirements should identify benefits of buying or building the new system that can be included in the 'Business Case' or 'Cost-Benefit Analysis', which is used to justify the expense of the new system in terms of the benefits that it will bring.

6.2.1 Current system

The existing system may be a manual one, based on paper documents, forms and files; it may already be computerized; or it may be a combination of both manual and computerized elements. Whichever it is, it is reasonably certain that large parts of the existing system meet the needs of the people who use it, that it has to some extent evolved over time to meet business needs and that users are familiar and comfortable with it. It is almost equally certain that there are sections of the system that no longer meet the needs of the business, and that there are aspects of the business that are not dealt with in the existing system.

It is important that the analyst, gathering information as one of the first steps in developing a new system, gains a clear understanding of how the existing system works: parts of the existing system will be carried forward into the new one. It is also important because the existing system will have shortcomings and defects, which must be avoided or overcome in the new system. It is not always easy or possible to replace existing systems. So-called *legacy systems* may have been developed some time ago and may contain millions of lines of program code, which have been added to and amended over a period of time. One approach to dealing with such systems is to create new front-ends, typically using modern graphical user interfaces and object-oriented languages, and *wrap* the legacy systems up in new software. If this is the case, then it is also necessary to understand the interfaces to the legacy systems that the new *wrappers* will have to communicate with.

It is not always possible to leave legacy systems as they are and simply wrap them in new code. Sometimes the suppliers of legacy systems withdraw support for older versions of applications; sometimes the technology in which they were written becomes obsolete and unsupported. In these cases, the system may need to be replaced for IT reasons rather than because of business requirements for new functionality. It was not possible to ignore the problems that faced companies at the turn of the century, when it was realized that many systems were in danger of catastrophic collapse as a result of the decision to use two decimal digits to store the year. However, the process of changing the program code in such systems is a matter of understanding the internal working of existing systems rather than gathering information about the way the organization works and the way that people do their jobs.

Not everyone agrees that a detailed understanding of the current system is necessary. Advocates of Agile approaches to software development argue that the focus should be on understanding the users' requirements for the new system and not on the functionality of the old system.

We believe that a case can be made for investigating the existing system.

- Some of the functionality of the existing system will be required in the new system.
- Some of the data in the existing system is of value and must be migrated into the new system.
- Technical documentation of existing computer systems may provide details of processing algorithms that will be needed in the new system.
- The existing system may have defects that we should avoid in the new system.
- Studying the existing system will help us to understand the organization in general.
- Parts of the existing system may be retained. Information systems projects are now rarely 'green field' projects in which manual systems are replaced by new computerized systems; more often there will be existing systems with which interfaces must be established.
- We are seeking to understand how people do their jobs at present in order to characterize people who will be users of the new system.
- We may need to gather baseline information against which we can set and measure performance targets for the new system.

For all these reasons, an understanding of the current system should be part of the analysis process. However, the analyst should not lose sight of the objective of developing a new system. In the sections on functional, non-functional and usability requirements below, we shall explain what kind of information we are gathering.

6.2.2 New requirements

Most organizations now operate in an environment that is rapidly changing. The relative strength of national economies around the world can change dramatically and at short notice; the fortunes of large companies, which may be an organization's suppliers, customers or competitors, can be transformed overnight; new technologies are introduced that change production processes, distribution networks and the relationship with the consumer; governments and (particularly in Europe) supra-governmental organizations introduce legislation that has an impact on the way that business is conducted. Some authors make the case for developing business strategies to cope with this turmoil. Tom Peters in *Thriving on Chaos* (1988) argues that we must learn to love change and develop flexible and responsive organizations to cope with the dynamic business environment. A clear result of responding to a dynamic environment is that organizations change their products and services and change the way they do business. The effect of this is to change their need for information. Even in less responsive organizations, information systems become outdated and need enhancing and extending. Mergers and demergers create the need for systems to be replaced. The process of replacement offers an opportunity to extend the capabilities of systems to take advantage of new technological developments, or to enhance their usefulness to management and workforce. Many organizations are driven by internal factors to grow and change the ways in which they operate, and this too provides a motivation for the development of new information systems.

Whether you are investigating the working of the existing system or the requirements for the new system, the information you gather will fall into one of three categories:

'functional requirements', 'non-functional requirements' and 'usability requirements'. Functional and non-functional requirements are conventional categories in systems analysis and design, while usability is often ignored in systems development projects. In many university courses, issues surrounding the usability of systems are taught under the separate heading of human factors or human–computer interaction, or are only considered in the design stage of the development process. However, the lesson of human factors research is that usability considerations should be integral to the systems development lifecycle and so they are included here.

Functional requirements

Functional requirements describe what a system does or is expected to do, often referred to as its *functionality*. In the object-oriented approach, which we are taking here, we shall initially employ use cases to document the functionality of the system. As we progress into the analysis stage, the detail of the functionality will be recorded in the data that we hold about objects, their attributes and operations.

At this stage, we are setting out to establish what the system must do, and functional requirements include:

- descriptions of the processing that the system will be required to carry out;
- details of the inputs into the system from paper forms and documents, from interactions between people, such as telephone calls, and from other systems;
- details of the outputs that are expected from the system in the form of printed documents and reports, screen displays and transfers to other systems;
- details of data that must be held in the system.

Non-functional requirements

Non-functional requirements are those that describe aspects of the system that are concerned with how well it provides the functional requirements. These include:

- performance criteria such as desired response times for updating data in the system or retrieving data from the system;
- ability of the system to cope with a high level of simultaneous access by many users;
- availability of the system with the minimum of downtime;
- time taken to recover from a system failure;
- anticipated volumes of data, either in terms of transaction throughput or of what must be stored;
- security considerations such as resistance to attacks and the ability to detect attacks.

Usability requirements

Usability requirements are those that will enable us to ensure that there is a good match between the system that is developed and both the users of that system and the tasks that they will undertake when using it. The International Organization for Standardization (ISO) has defined the usability of a product as 'the extent to which specified users can achieve specified goals with effectiveness, efficiency and satisfaction in a specified context of use'. Usability can be specified in terms of measurable objectives, and these are covered in more detail in Chapter 16 on Human–Computer Interaction. In order to build usability into the system from the outset, we need to gather the following types of information:

- characteristics of the users who will use the system;
- the tasks that the users undertake, including the goals that they are trying to achieve;
- situational factors that describe the situations that could arise during system use;
- acceptance criteria by which the user will judge the delivered system.

Booth (1989) describes the issues surrounding system usability in more detail.

6.3 Fact-Finding Techniques

There are five main fact-finding techniques that are used by analysts to investigate requirements. Here we describe each of them in the order that they might be applied in a system development project, and for each one we explain the kind of information that you would expect to gain from its use, its advantages and disadvantages, and the situations in which it is appropriate to use it.

6.3.1 Background reading

If an analyst is employed within the organization that is the subject of the fact-gathering exercise, then it is likely that he or she will already have a good understanding of the organization and its business objectives. If, however, he or she is going in as an outside consultant, then one of the first tasks is to try to gain an understanding of the organization. Background reading or research is part of that process. The kind of documents that are suitable sources of information include the following:

- company reports
- organization charts
- policy manuals
- job descriptions
- reports
- documentation of existing systems.

Although reading company reports may provide the analyst with information about the organization's mission, and so possibly some indication of future requirements, this technique mainly provides information about the current system.

Advantages and disadvantages
+ Background reading helps the analyst to get an understanding of the organization before meeting the people who work there.
+ It also allows the analyst to prepare for other types of fact finding; for example, by being aware of the business objectives of the organization.
+ Documentation on the existing system may provide formally defined information requirements for the current system.
− Written documents often do not match up to reality; they may be out of date or they may reflect the official policy on matters that are dealt with differently in practice.

Appropriate situations
Background reading is appropriate for projects where the analyst is not familiar with the organization being investigated. It is useful in the initial stages of investigation.

6.3.2 Interviewing

Interviewing is probably the most widely used fact-finding technique; it is also the one that requires the most skill and sensitivity. Because of this, we have included a set of guidelines on interviewing that includes some suggestions about etiquette in Box 6.1.

A systems analysis interview is a structured meeting between the analyst and an interviewee who is usually a member of staff of the organization being investigated. The interview may be one of a series of interviews that range across different areas of the interviewee's work or that probe in progressively greater depth about the tasks under-taken by the interviewee. The degree of structure may vary: some interviews are planned with a fixed set of questions that the interviewer works through, while others are designed to cover certain topics but will be open-ended enough to allow the interviewer to pursue interesting facts as they emerge. The ability to respond flexibly to the interviewee's responses is one of the reasons why interviews are so widely used.

Interviews can be used to gather information from management about their objec-tives for the organization and for the new information system, from staff about their existing jobs and their information needs, and from customers and members of the public as possible users of systems. While conducting an interview, the analyst can also use the opportunity to gather documents that the interviewee uses in his or her work.

It is usually assumed that questionnaires are used as a substitute for interviews when potential interviewees are geographically dispersed in branches and offices around the world. The widespread use of desktop video conferencing may change this and make it possible to interview staff wherever they are. Even then, questionnaires can reach more people.

Interviewing different potential users of a system separately can mean that the analyst is given different information by different people. Resolving these differences later can be difficult and time-consuming. One alternative is to use group interviews or workshops in order to get the users to reach a consensus on issues. Dynamic Systems Development Method (DSDM) is a method of carrying out systems development in which group dis-cussions are used (DSDM Consortium, 2007). These discussions are run as facilitated workshops for knowledgeable users with a facilitator who aims to get the users to pool their knowledge and to reach a consensus on the priorities of the development project.

Advantages and disadvantages

+ Personal contact allows the analyst to be responsive and adapt to what the user says. Because of this, interviews produce high-quality information.
+ The analyst can probe in greater depth about the person's work than can be achieved with other methods.
+ If the interviewee has nothing to say, the interview can be terminated.
− Interviews are time-consuming and can be the most costly form of fact gathering.
− Interview results require the analyst to work on them after the interview: the transcrip-tion of tape recordings or writing up of notes.
− Interviews can be subject to bias if the interviewer has a closed mind about the problem.
− If different interviewees provide conflicting information, it can be difficult to resolve later.

Appropriate situations

Interviews are appropriate in most projects. They can provide information in depth about the existing system and about people's requirements from a new system.

Box 6.1 Guidelines on Interviewing

Conducting an interview requires good planning, good interpersonal skills and an alert and responsive frame of mind. These guidelines cover the points you should bear in mind when planning and conducting an interview.

Before the interview

You should always make appointments for interviews in advance. You should give the interviewee information about the likely duration of the interview and the subject of the interview.

Being interviewed takes people away from their normal work. Make sure that they feel that it is time well spent.

It is conventional to obtain permission from an interviewee's line manager before interviewing them. Often the analyst interviews the manager first and uses the opportunity to get this permission.

In large projects, an interview schedule should be drawn up showing who is to be interviewed, how often and for how long. Initially this will be in terms of the job roles of interviewees rather than named individuals. It may be the manager who decides which individual you interview in a particular role.

Have a clear set of objectives for the interview. Plan your questions and write them down. Some people write the questions with space between them for the replies.

Make sure your questions are relevant to the interviewee and his or her job.

At the start of the interview

Introduce yourself and the purpose of the interview.

Arrive on time for interviews and stick to the planned timetable—do not overrun.

Ask the interviewee if he or she minds you taking notes or tape-recording the interview. Even if you tape-record an interview, you are advised to take notes. Machines can fail! Your notes also allow you to refer back to what has been said during the course of the interview and follow up points of interest.

Remember that people can be suspicious of outside consultants who come in with clipboards and stopwatches. The cost–benefit analyses of many information systems justify the investment in terms of savings in jobs!

During the interview

Take responsibility for the agenda. You should control the direction of the interview. This should be done in a sensitive way. If the interviewee is getting away from the subject, bring them back to the point. If what they are telling you is important, then say that you will come back to it later and make a note to remind yourself to do so.

Use different kinds of question to get different types of information. Questions can be open-ended—'Can you explain how you complete a timesheet?'—or closed—'How many staff use this system?'. Do not, however, ask very open-ended questions such as 'Could you tell me what you do?'.

Listen to what the interviewee says and encourage him or her to expand on key points.

Keep the focus positive if possible. Make sure you have understood answers by summarizing them back to the interviewee. Avoid allowing the interview to degenerate into a session in which the interviewee complains about everyone and everything.

You may be aware of possible problems in the existing system, but you should avoid prejudging issues by asking questions that focus too much on problems. Gather facts.

Be sensitive about how you use information from other interviews that you or your colleagues have already conducted, particularly if comments were negative or critical.

Use the opportunity to collect examples of documents that people use in their work, ask if they mind you having samples of blank forms and photocopies of completed paperwork.

After the interview

Thank the interviewee for their time. Make an appointment for a further interview if it is necessary. Offer to provide them with a copy of your notes of the interview for them to check that you have accurately recorded what they told you.

Transcribe your tape or write up your notes as soon as possible after the interview while the content is still fresh in your mind.

If you said that you would provide a copy of your notes for checking then send it to the interviewee as soon as possible. Update your notes to reflect their comments.

6.3.3 Observation

Watching people carrying out their work in a natural setting can provide the analyst with a better understanding of the job than interviews, in which the interviewee will often concentrate on the normal aspects of the job and forget the exceptional situations and interruptions that occur and which the system will need to cope with. Observation also allows the analyst to see what information people use to carry out their jobs. This can tell you about the documents they refer to, whether they have to get up from their desks to get information, how well the existing system handles their needs. One of the authors has observed staff using a telesales system where there was no link between the enquiry screens for checking the availability of stock and the data entry screens for entering an order. These telesales staff kept a pad of scrap paper on the desk and wrote down the product codes for all the items they had looked up on the enquiry screens so that they could enter them into the order-processing screens. This kind of information does not always emerge from interviews.

People are not good at estimating quantitative data, such as how long they take to deal with certain tasks, and observation with a stopwatch can give the analyst plentiful quantitative data, not just about typical times to perform a task but also about the statistical distribution of those times.

In some cases where information or items are moving through a system and being dealt with by many people along the way, observation can allow the analyst to follow the entire process through from start to finish. This type of observation might be used in an organization where orders are taken over the telephone, passed to a warehouse for picking, packed and dispatched to the customer. The analyst may want to follow a series of transactions through the system to obtain an overview of the processes involved.

Observation can be an open-ended process in which the analyst simply sets out to observe what happens and to note it down, or it can be a closed process in which the analyst wishes to observe specific aspects of the job and draws up an observation schedule or form on which to record data. This can include the time it takes to carry out a task, the types of task the person is performing or factors such as the number of errors they make in using the existing system as a baseline for usability design.

Advantages and disadvantages
+ Observation of people at work provides first-hand experience of the way that the current system operates.
+ Data is collected in real time and can have a high level of validity if care is taken in how the technique is used.
+ Observation can be used to verify information from other sources or to look for exceptions to the standard procedure.
+ Baseline data about the performance of the existing system and of users can be collected.
- Most people do not like being observed and are likely to behave differently from the way in which they would normally behave. This can distort findings and affect the validity.
- Observation requires a trained and skilled observer for it to be most effective.
- There may be logistical problems for the analyst; for example, if the staff to be observed work shifts or travel long distances in order to do their job.
- There may also be ethical problems if the person being observed deals with sensitive private or personal data or directly with members of the public; for example in a doctor's surgery.

Appropriate situations

Observation is essential for gathering quantitative data about people's jobs. It can verify or disprove assertions made by interviewees, and is often useful in situations where different interviewees have provided conflicting information about the way the system works. Observation may be the best way to follow items through some kind of process from start to finish.

6.3.4 Document sampling

Document sampling can be used in two different ways. First, the analyst will collect copies of blank and completed documents during the course of interviews and observation sessions. These will be used to determine the information that is used by people in their work and the inputs to and outputs from processes which they carry out, either manually or using an existing computer system. Ideally, where there is an existing system, screen-shots should also be collected in order to understand the inputs and outputs of the existing system. Figure 6.1 shows a sample document collected from Agate, our case study company.

Second, the analyst may carry out a statistical analysis of documents in order to find out about patterns of data. For example, many documents such as order forms contain a header section and a number of lines of detail. (The sample document in Fig. 6.1 shows this kind of structure.) The analyst may want to know the distribution of the number of lines in an order. This will help later in estimating volumes of data to be held in the system and in deciding how many lines should be displayed on screen at one time. While this kind of statistical sampling can give a picture of data volumes, the analyst should be alert to seasonal patterns of activity, which may mean that there are peaks and troughs in the amount of data being processed.

Advantages and disadvantages

+ Can be used to gather quantitative data, such as the average number of lines on an invoice and the range of values.
+ Can be used to find out about error rates in paper documents.
− If the system is going to change dramatically, existing documents may not reflect how it will be in future.

Appropriate situations

The first type of document sampling is almost always appropriate. Paper-based documents give a good idea of what is happening in the current system. They also provide supporting evidence for the information gathered from interviews or observation.

The statistical approach is appropriate in situations where large volumes of data are being processed, and particularly where error rates are high and a reduction in errors is one of the criteria for usability.

6.3.5 Questionnaires

Questionnaires are a research instrument that can be applied to fact finding in system development projects. They consist of a series of written questions. The questionnaire designer usually limits the range of replies that respondents can make by giving them a choice of options. (Figure 6.2 shows some of the types of question.) YES/NO questions

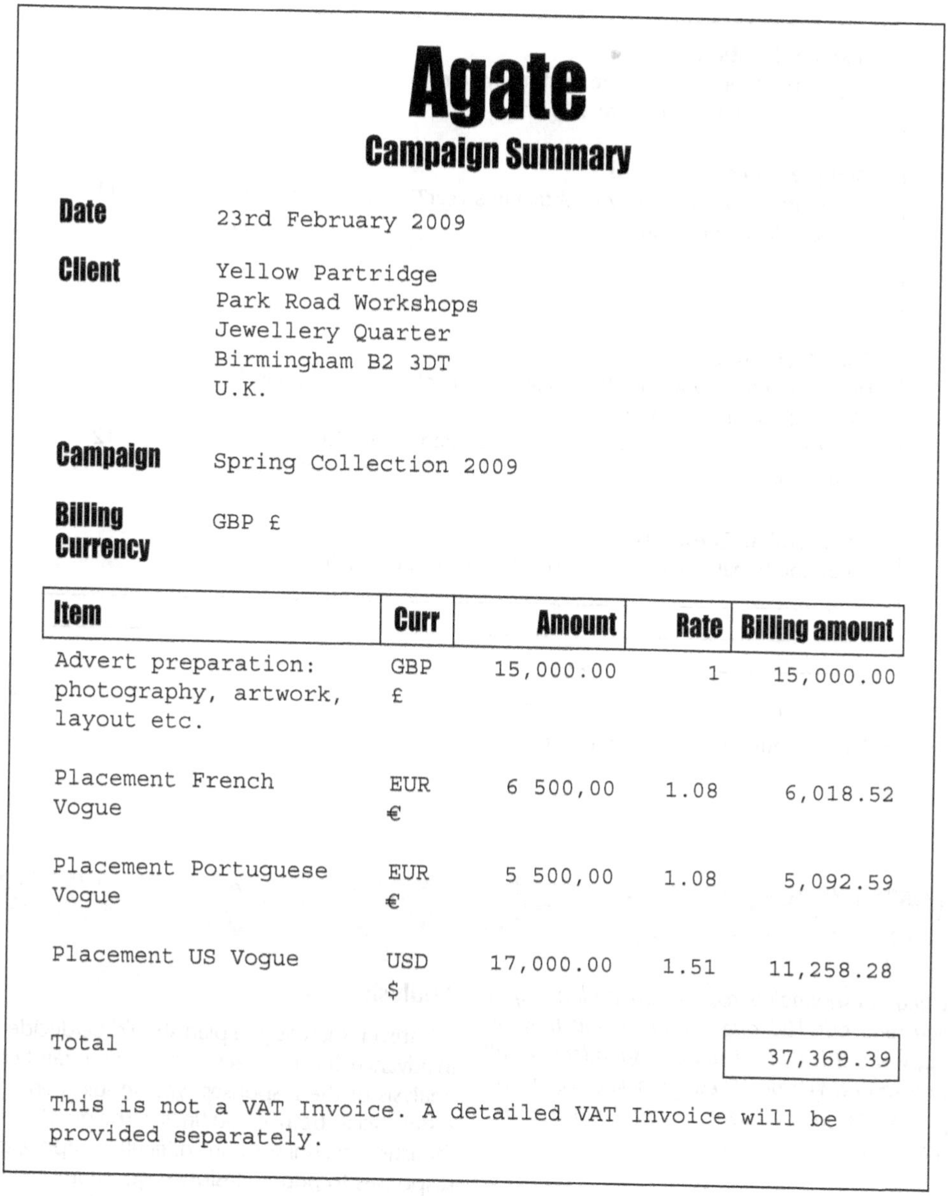

Agate
Campaign Summary

Date   23rd February 2009

Client   Yellow Partridge
Park Road Workshops
Jewellery Quarter
Birmingham B2 3DT
U.K.

Campaign   Spring Collection 2009

Billing Currency   GBP £

Item	Curr	Amount	Rate	Billing amount
Advert preparation: photography, artwork, layout etc.	GBP £	15,000.00	1	15,000.00
Placement French Vogue	EUR €	6 500,00	1.08	6,018.52
Placement Portuguese Vogue	EUR €	5 500,00	1.08	5,092.59
Placement US Vogue	USD $	17,000.00	1.51	11,258.28
Total				37,369.39

This is not a VAT Invoice. A detailed VAT Invoice will be provided separately.

Figure 6.1 Sample document from the AGATE case study.

only give the respondent two options. (Sometimes a DON'T KNOW option is needed as well.) If there are more options, the multiple choice type of question is often used when the answer is factual, whereas scaled questions are used if the answer involves an element of subjectivity. Some questions do not have a fixed number of responses, and must be left open-ended for the respondent to enter what they like. Where the respondent has a limited number of choices, these are usually coded with a number, which speeds up data entry if the responses are to be analysed by computer software. If you plan to use questionnaires for requirements gathering, they need very careful design. Box 6.2 lists some of the issues that need to be addressed if you are thinking of using questionnaires.

YES/NO Questions

Do you print reports from the existing system?   YES   NO   10
(Please circle the appropriate answer.)

Multiple Choice Questions

How many new clients do you obtain in a year?   a) 1–10   ☐   11
(Please tick one box only.)   b) 11–20 ☐
                                                 c) 21–30 ☐
                                                 d) 31+   ☐

Scaled Questions

How satisfied are you with the response time of the stock update?
(Please circle one option.)

1. Very   2. Satisfied   3. Dissatisfied   4. Very   12
   satisfied   dissatisfied

Open-ended Questions

What additional reports would you require from the system?

_____
_____
_____

Figure 6.2 Types of question used in questionnaires.

Box 6.2 Guidelines on Questionnaires

Using questionnaires requires good planning. If you send out 100 questionnaires and they do not work, it is difficult to get respondents to fill in a second version. These guidelines cover the points you should bear in mind when using questionnaires.

Coding

How will you code the results? If you plan to use an optical mark reader, then the response to every question must be capable of being coded as a mark in a box. If you expect the results to be keyed into a database for analysis, then you need to decide on the codes for each possible response. If the questions are open-ended, how will you collate and analyse different kinds of responses?

Analysis

Whatever analysis you plan should be decided in advance. If you expect to carry out a statistical analysis of the responses, you should consult a statistician **before** you finalize the questions. Statistical techniques are difficult to apply to responses to poorly designed questions.

You can use a special statistical software package, a database or even a spreadsheet to analyse the data.

Piloting

You should try out your questionnaire on a small pilot group or sample of your respondents. This enables you to find out if there are questions they do not understand, they misinterpret or they cannot answer.

Box 6.2 (continued)

If you plan to analyse the data using statistical software, a database or a spreadsheet, you can create a set of trial data to test your analysis technique.

Sample size and structure

If you plan to use serious statistical techniques, then those techniques may place lower limits on your sample size. If you want to be sure of getting a representative sample, by age, gender, department, geographical location, job grade or experience of existing systems, then that will help to determine how many people to include. Otherwise it may be down to you to choose a sensible percentage of all the possible respondents.

Delivery

How will you get the questionnaires to your respondents, and how will they get their replies back to you?

You can post them, or use internal mail in a large organization, fax them, email them or create a web-based form on the intranet and notify your target group by email. If you use the intranet, you may want to give each respondent a special code, so that only they can complete their own questionnaire.

Your respondents can then post, fax or email their responses back to you, or complete them on the intranet.

Respondent information

What information about the respondents do you want to gather at the same time as you collect their views and requirements? If you want to analyse responses by age, job type or location, then you need to include questions that ask for that information.

You can make questionnaires anonymous or you can ask respondents for their name. If the questionnaire is not anonymous, you need to think about confidentiality. People will be more honest in their replies if they can respond anonymously or in confidence.

If you ask for respondents' names and you store that information, then in the UK you should consider the provisions of the Data Protection Act (1998). (See also Chapter 12.) There are similar requirements in other countries.

Covering letter or email

In a covering letter you should explain the purpose and state that the questionnaire has management support. Give an estimate of the time required to fill in the questionnaire and a deadline for its return. Thank the respondents for taking part.

Structure

Structure the questionnaire carefully. Give it a title, and start with explanatory material and notes on how to complete it. Follow this with questions about the respondent (if required). Group questions together by subject. Avoid lots of instructions like: 'If you answered YES to Q. 7, now go to Q. 13'. Keep it reasonably short.

Return rate

Not everyone will necessarily respond. You need to plan for this and either use a larger sample than you need or follow up with reminders. If you use a form on the intranet, you should be able to identify who has not responded and email them reminders. Equally, you can email a thank you to those who do respond.

Feedback

This needs to be handled carefully—telling everyone that 90% of the company cannot use the existing system may not go down well—but people do like to know what use was made of the response they made. They may have spent half an hour filling in your questionnaire, and they will expect to be informed of the outcome. A summary of the report can be sent out to branches, distributed to departments, sent to named respondents or placed on the intranet.

Advantages and disadvantages

+ An economical way of gathering data from a large number of people.
+ If the questionnaire is well designed, then the results can be analysed easily, possibly by computer.
− Good questionnaires are difficult to construct.
− There is no automatic mechanism for follow-up or probing more deeply, although it is possible to follow up with an interview by telephone or in person if necessary.
− Postal questionnaires suffer from low response rates.

Appropriate situations

Questionnaires are most useful when the views or knowledge of a large number of people need to be obtained or when the people are geographically dispersed, for example in a company with many branches or offices around the country or around the world. Questionnaires are also appropriate for information systems that will be used by the general public, and where the analyst needs to get a picture of the types of user and usage that the system will need to handle.

6.3.6 Remembering the techniques

For those who like mnemonics, these techniques are sometimes referred to as SQIRO– sampling, questionnaires, interviewing, reading (or research) and observation. This order has been chosen to make it possible to pronounce the mnemonic. However, this is not the order in which they are most likely to be used. This will depend on the situation and the organization in which the techniques are being used.

6.3.7 Other techniques

Some kinds of system require special fact-finding techniques. *Expert systems* are computer systems that are designed to embody the expertise of a human expert in solving problems. Examples include systems for medical diagnosis, stock market trading and geological analysis for mineral prospecting. The process of capturing the knowledge of the expert is called *knowledge acquisition* and, as it differs from establishing the requirements for a conventional information system, a number of specific techniques are applied. Some of these are used in conjunction with computer-based tools.

6.4 User Involvement

The success of a systems development project depends not just on the skills of the team of analysts, designers and programmers who work on it, or on the project management skills of the project manager, but on the effective involvement of users in the project at various stages of the lifecycle. The term *stakeholders* was introduced in Chapter 2 to describe all those people who have an interest in the successful development of the system. Stakeholders include all people who stand to gain (or lose) from the implementation of the new system: users, managers and budget-holders. Analysts deal with people at all levels of the organization. In large projects it is likely that a steering committee with delegated powers will be set up to manage the project from the users' side. This will include the following categories of people:

- senior management—with overall responsibility for running the organization
- financial managers with budgetary control over the project
- managers of the user department(s)
- representatives of the IT department delivering the project
- representatives of users.

Users will be involved in different roles during the course of the project as:

- subjects of interviews to establish requirements
- representatives on project committees
- those involved in evaluating prototypes
- those involved in testing
- subjects of training courses
- end-users of the new system.

Case Study Example

The section that follows applies what has been covered in this chapter so far to the case study.

Objective	Technique	Subject(s)	Time commitment
To get background on the company and the advertising industry	Background reading	Company reports, trade journals	0.5 day
To establish business objectives. Agree likely scope of new system. Check out involvement of non-UK offices	Interview	Two directors	2 × 1 hour each
To gain understanding of roles of each department. Check out line management and team structure in the Creative department. Agree likely interviewees among staff	Interview	Department heads (only 1 account manager)	2 × 1 hour each
To find out how the core business operates	Interview	1 account manager 1 graphic designer 1 copy writer 1 editor	1.5 hours each
To follow up development of business understanding	Observation	2 creative staff	0.5 day each
To determine role of support admin staff and relationship to core business	Interview	2 admin staff (based on experience with the company)	1.5 hours each
To establish what records and resources are kept	Interview/ document sampling	Filing clerk Resource librarian	2 × 1 hour each
To determine what use is made of current computer system. To determine functionality of current system	Interview	Computer manager	2 × 1 hour

▶

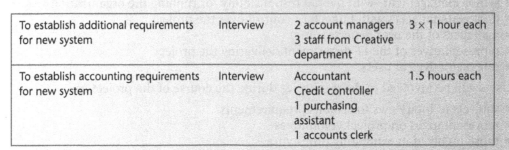

To establish additional requirements for new system	Interview	2 account managers 3 staff from Creative department	3 × 1 hour each
To establish accounting requirements for new system	Interview	Accountant Credit controller 1 purchasing assistant 1 accounts clerk	1.5 hours each

One of the first tasks in fact finding is to draw up a plan that outlines what information is being sought, which techniques will be used, who is involved and how long the fact finding will take. A draft plan for fact finding at Agate is shown above. The jobs of the subjects are those shown in the list in Figure A1.1 in the Agate case study.

6.5 Documenting Requirements

Information systems professionals need to record facts about the organization they are studying and its requirements. As soon as the analysts start gathering facts, they will need some means of documenting them. In the past the emphasis was on paper forms, but now it is rare for a large-scale project to depend on paper-based documentation. As we have explained in Chapter 5, systems analysts and designers model the new system in a mixture of diagrams, data and text. The important thing to bear in mind is that within a project some set of standards should be adhered to. These may be the agreed standards of the organization carrying out the analysis and design project or they may be a requirement of the organization that is having the work done. For example, government and military projects usually require that developers conform to a specific set of standards. We are using UML to produce models of the system from different perspectives. Computer Aided Software Engineering (CASE) tools are normally used to draw the diagrammatic models and to maintain in a repository the associated data about the various things that are shown in the diagrams.

However, there will also be other kinds of documents, not all of which fit into the UML framework. In large-scale projects a librarian or configuration manager may be required to keep track of these documents and ensure that they are stored safely and in a way that enables them to be retrieved when required. Such documents include:

- records of interviews and observations
- details of problems
- copies of existing documents and where they are used
- details of requirements
- details of users
- minutes of meetings.

Even in smaller projects that cannot justify a librarian, a filing system with an agreed set of conventions on how material is to be filed, and for recording who has taken items from the filing system, is good practice.

In many projects, these documents will be stored digitally, using a document management system or a version control system. Handwritten documents and sample documents can be scanned with an image scanner and held in digital form. In this case, many people can access the same document simultaneously. The system enforces control over whether a document can be updated, and ensures that no more than one person at a time is able to check out a document in order to amend it.

Not all of the documents listed above represent requirements, and it is necessary to maintain some kind of list or database of requirements. There are software tools available to hold requirements in a database and some can be linked to CASE tools and testing tools. This makes it possible to trace from an initial requirement through the analysis and design models to where it has been implemented and to the test cases that test whether the requirement has been met.

Use cases, which are explained in the next section, can be used to model requirements, but because they focus on the functionality of the system are not good for documenting non-functional requirements. Jacobson et al. (1999) suggest that the use case model should be used to document functional requirements and a separate list of 'supplementary requirements' (those not provided by a use case) should be kept. They say that, together, the use case model and the list of supplementary requirements constitute a traditional requirements specification. Rosenberg and Scott (1999) argue that use cases are not the same as requirements: use cases describe units of system behaviour, whereas requirements are rules that govern the behaviour of the system; one requirement may be met by more than one use case, and one use case may meet more than one requirement; some non-functional requirements are difficult to attribute to any particular use case.

Some people try to document requirements in use cases by writing long use case descriptions using templates that enable them to include non-functional requirements as well as functional requirements. This approach is explained in more detail, with examples in the on-line Chapter 6A on the book's website.

We favour the view that use cases can be used to model functional requirements, but a separate list of requirements should be kept, containing all requirements–functional and non-functional–for the system. Where there is a relationship between a particular use case and a particular requirement, this should be recorded. Moreover, some requirements describe very high-level units of behaviour and may need to be broken down into low-level requirements that describe more precisely what is to be done. Any database of requirements should make it possible to hold this kind of hierarchical structure of requirements.

There are software tools available to assist in the documentation of requirements. Essentially, they provide a database of requirements of different types with standard attributes of those requirements, and can usually be customized to allow the users to record other attributes of the requirements that are needed for a particular project or organization, such as priority or source. In some cases, these tools can be integrated with CASE tools or modelling tools in order to provide for 'traceability of requirements'. This means that model elements that deliver a requirement can be linked to the requirement in question. If a requirement subsequently changes, it is possible to trace the impact of that requirement change on all the model elements that it affects, such as use cases and classes.

Sometimes the process of requirement gathering throws up more requirements than can be met in a particular project. They may be outside the scope of the project,

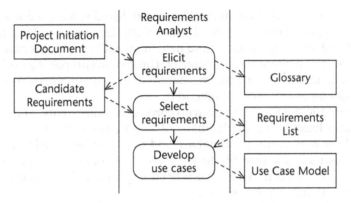

Figure 6.3 Activity diagram to show the activities involved in capturing requirements.

overambitious, too expensive to implement or just not really necessary at this stage. The process of building a requirements model for a system involves going through all the candidate requirements to produce a list of those that will be part of the current project. Figure 6.3 shows this as an activity diagram. (An approach such as the *MoSCoW rules* explained in Chapter 21 can be used to help prioritize requirements.)

6.6　Use Cases

Use cases are descriptions of the functionality of the system from the users' perspective. Use case diagrams are used to show the functionality that the system will provide and to show which users will communicate with the system in some way to use that functionality. Figure 6.4 shows an example of a use case diagram. This is a relatively simple diagramming technique, and its notation is explained below in Section 6.6.2.

　Use case diagrams were developed by Jacobson et al. (1992), and the subtitle of the book in which they are presented is *A Use Case Driven Approach*. Jacobson and his co-authors offer a complete approach to the development of object-oriented software systems, but use case diagrams are the starting point for much of what follows in their approach.

6.6.1 Purpose

The use case model is part of what Jacobson et al. (1992) call the requirements model; they also include a problem domain object model and user interface descriptions in this requirements model. Use cases specify the functionality that the system will offer from the users' perspective. They are used to document the scope of the system and the developer's understanding of what it is that the users require.

　Use cases are supported by *behaviour specifications*. These specify the behaviour of each use case either using UML diagrams, such as activity diagrams (see Chapter 5), *communication diagrams* or *sequence diagrams* (see Chapter 9), or in text form as *use case descriptions*.

　Textual use case descriptions provide a description of the interaction between the users of the system, termed *actors*, and the high-level functions within the system, the

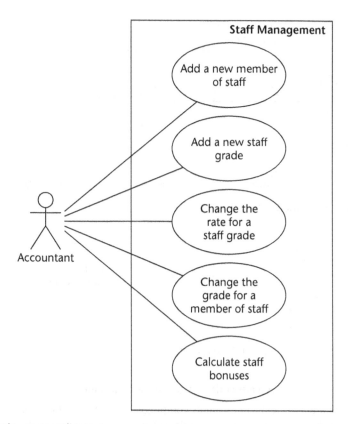

Figure 6.4 Example use case diagram.

use cases. These descriptions can be in summary form or in a more detailed form in which the interaction between actor and use case is described in a step-by-step way. Whichever approach is used, it should be remembered that the use case describes the interaction as the user sees it, and is not a definition of the internal processes within the system or some kind of program specification.

6.6.2 Notation

Use case diagrams show three aspects of the system: actors, use cases and the system or subsystem boundary. Figure 6.5 shows the elements of the notation.

Actors represent the roles that people, other systems or devices take on when communicating with the particular use cases in the system. Figure 6.5 shows the actor Staff Contact in a diagram for the Agate case study. In Agate, there is no job title Staff Contact: a director, an account manager or a member of the creative team can take on the role of being staff contact for a particular client company, so one actor can represent several people or job titles. Equally, a particular person or job title may be represented by more than one actor on use case diagrams. This is shown in Figs 6.5 and 6.6 together. A director or an account manager may be the Campaign Manager for a particular client campaign, as well as being the Staff Contact for one or more clients.

The use case description associated with each use case can be brief:

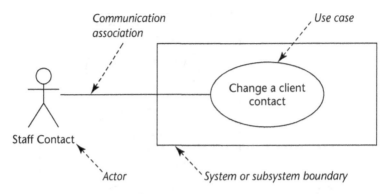

Figure 6.5 The notation of the use case diagram.

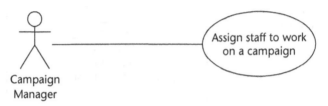

Figure 6.6 Use case showing Campaign Manager actor.

Assign staff to work on a campaign

The campaign manager selects a particular campaign. A list of staff not already working on that campaign is displayed, and he or she selects those to be assigned to this campaign.

Alternatively, it can provide a step-by-step breakdown of the interaction between the user and the system for the particular use case. An example of this extended approach is provided below.

Assign staff to work on a campaign

Actor Action	System Response
1. The actor enters the client name.	2. Lists all campaigns for that client.
3. Selects the relevant campaign.	4. Displays a list of all staff members not already allocated to this campaign.
5. Highlights the staff members to be assigned to this campaign.	6. Presents a message confirming that staff have been allocated.

Alternative Courses

Steps 1–3. The actor knows the campaign name and enters it directly.

Constantine (1997) makes the distinction between *essential* and *real* use cases. Essential use cases describe the 'essence' of the use case in terms that are free of any technological or implementation details, whereas real use cases describe the concrete detail of the use case in terms of its design. During the analysis stage, use cases are almost always essential, as the design has not yet been decided upon. In a real use case, Step 2 in the use case description for Assign staff to work on a campaign could be described as 'Lists all campaigns for the client in a list box, sorted into alphabetical order by campaign title'.

Each use case description represents the usual way in which the actor will go through the particular transaction or function from end to end. Possible major alternative routes that could be taken are listed as *alternative courses*. The term *scenario* is used to describe use cases in which an alternative course is worked through in detail, including possible responses to errors. The use case represents the generic case, while the scenarios represent specific paths through the use case.

As well as the description of the use case itself, the documentation should include the purpose or intent of the use case, that is to say details of the task that the user is trying to achieve through the means of this use case, for example:

> The campaign manager wishes to record which staff are working on a particular campaign. This information is used to validate timesheets and to calculate staff year-end bonuses.

One way of documenting use cases is to use a template (a blank form or wordprocessing document to be filled in). This might include the following sections:

- name of use case
- pre-conditions (things that must be true before the use case can take place)
- post-conditions (things that must be true after the use case has taken place)
- purpose (what the use case is intended to achieve)
- description (in summary or in the format above).

Cockburn (2000) provides examples of templates and guidance on how to write good use cases. More detail in his approach can be found on the book's website in on-line Chapter 6A.

Two further kinds of relationship can be shown on the use case diagram itself. These are the *Extend* and *Include* relationships. They are shown on the diagram using a piece of UML notation that you will come across in other diagrams: *stereotypes*.

A stereotype is a special use of a model element that is constrained to behave in a particular way. Stereotypes can be shown by using a keyword, such as 'extend' or 'include' in matched *guillemets*, like «extend». (Guillemets are used as quotation marks in French and some other languages. They are not the same as guillemots, which are seabirds found in the North Atlantic and North Pacific oceans!)

The extend and include relationships are easy to confuse. «extend» is used when you wish to show that a use case provides additional functionality that may be required in another use case. In Fig. 6.7, the use case `Print campaign summary` extends `Check campaign budget`. This means that at a particular point in `Check campaign budget` the user can optionally invoke the behaviour of `Print campaign summary`, which does something over and above what is done in `Check campaign budget` (print out the information in this case). There may be more than one way of extending a particular use case, and these possibilities may represent significant variations on the way the user uses the system. Rather than trying to capture all these variations in one use case, you would document the core functionality in one and then extend it in others. Extension points can be shown in the diagram, as in `Check campaign budget` in Fig. 6.7. They are shown in a separate compartment in the use case ellipse, headed `extension points`. The names of the extension points are listed in this compartment. If an extension point exists, it must have a name. A condition can be shown in a UML *comment* attached to the relationship. Comments are used to add to a diagram information that is not part of other graphical elements in the diagram. The condition must be true for the extension to take place in a particular instance of the use case.

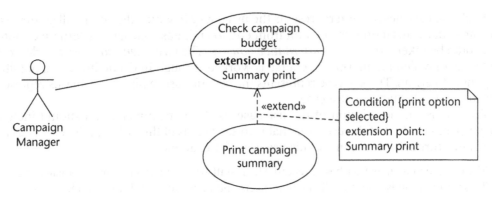

Figure 6.7 Use case diagram showing «extend».

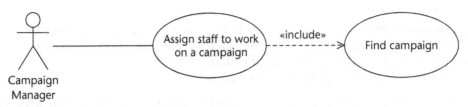

Figure 6.8 Use case diagram showing «include».

«include» applies when there is a sequence of behaviour that is used frequently in a number of use cases and you want to avoid copying the same description of it into each use case in which it is used. Figure 6.8 shows that the use case Assign staff to work on a campaign has an «include» relationship with Find campaign. This means that when an actor uses Assign staff to work on a campaign the behaviour of Find campaign will also be included in order to select the relevant campaign. Note the direction of the arrows in the examples of Include and Extend relationships. The arrow always points at the use case that is being included or extended.

It is important not to overuse include and extend relationships. Overuse can result in the decomposition of the functionality of use cases into many small use cases that deliver no real value to the users of the system.

As well as describing the use cases, it is worth describing who the actors are in terms of job titles or the way in which they interact with the system. Although at the moment we are concentrating on requirements, later we shall need to know who the actual users are for each high-level function that is represented by a use case. This may help in specifying the security for different functions or in assessing the usability of the functions.

Bear in mind that actors need not be human users of the system. They can also be other systems that communicate with the one that is the subject of the systems development project, for example other computers or automated machinery or equipment.

Figure 6.9 shows a use case diagram for the Campaign Management subsystem with both extend and include relationships. Note that you do not have to show all the detail of the extension points on a diagram: the extension points compartment in the use case can be suppressed. Of course, if you are using a CASE tool to draw and manage the diagrams, you may be able to toggle the display of this compartment on and off and,

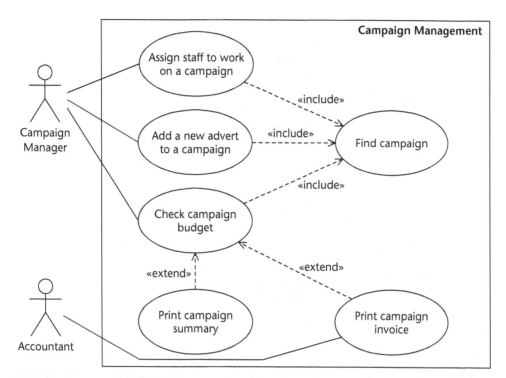

Figure 6.9 Use case diagram showing both «extend» and «include».

even if the information is not shown on a particular diagram, it will still be held in the CASE tool's repository.

In Chapter 4, the concepts of generalization, specialization and inheritance were introduced. They are explained in more detail in Chapter 8. Generalization and specialization can be applied to actors and use cases. For example, suppose that we have two actors, Staff Contact and Campaign Manager, and a Campaign Manager can do everything that a Staff Contact can do, and more. Rather than showing communication associations between Campaign Manager and all the use cases that Staff Contact can use, we can show Campaign Manager as a specialization of Staff Contact, as in Fig. 6.10. Similarly, there may be similar use cases where the common functionality is best represented by generalizing out that functionality into a 'super-use case' and showing it separately. For example, we may find that there are two use cases at Agate—Assign individual staff to work on a campaign and Assign team of staff to work on a campaign—which are similar in the functionality they offer. We might abstract out the commonality into a use case Assign staff to work on a campaign, but this will be an abstract use case. It helps us to define the functionality of the other two use cases, but no instance of this use case will ever exist in its own right. This is also shown in Fig. 6.10. The use of italics for the name of the use case shows that it is abstract.

6.6.3 Supporting use cases with prototyping

As the requirements for a system emerge in the form of use cases, it is sometimes helpful to build simple prototypes of how some of the use cases will work. A prototype is a working

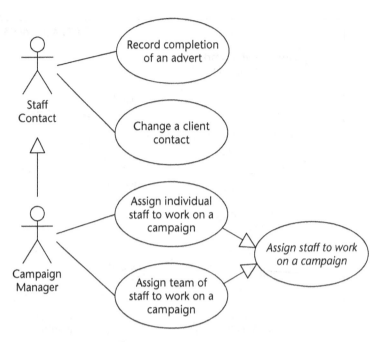

Figure 6.10 Generalization of actors and use cases.

model of part of the system–usually a program with limited functionality that is built to test out some aspect of how the system will work. (Prototypes were discussed in Section 3.3.2 and are explained in more detail in Chapter 17 on the design of the user interface.)

Prototypes can be used to help elicit requirements. Showing users how the system might provide some of the use cases often produces a stronger reaction than showing them a series of abstract diagrams. Their reaction may contain useful information about requirements.

For example, there are a number of use cases in the Campaign Management subsystem for Agate that require the user to select a campaign in order to carry out some business function. The use case diagram in Fig. 6.9 reflects this in the «include» relationships with the use case Find campaign. The use case Find campaign will clearly be used a great deal, and it is worth making sure that we have the requirements right. A prototype could be produced that provides a list of all the campaigns in the system. A possible version of this is shown in Fig. 6.11.

Showing this prototype interface design to the users may well produce the response that this way of finding a campaign will not work. There may be hundreds of campaigns in the system, and scrolling through them would be tedious. Different clients may have campaigns with similar names, and it would be easy to make a mistake and choose the wrong campaign if the user does not know which client it belongs to. For these reasons, the users might suggest that the first step is to find the right client and then display only the campaigns that belong to that client. This leads to a different user interface as shown in Fig. 6.12.

The information from this prototyping exercise forms part of the requirements for the system. This particular requirement is about usability, but it can also contribute to meeting other, non-functional requirements concerned with speed and the error rate: it might be quicker to select first the client and then the campaign from a short-list than

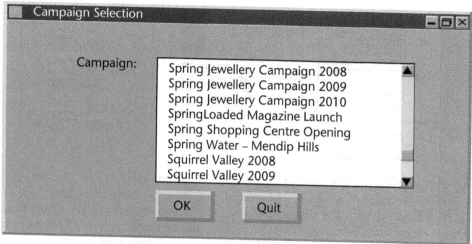

Figure 6.11 Prototype interface for the `Find campaign` use case.

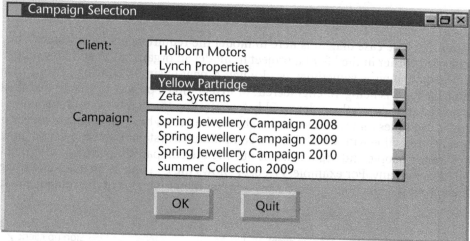

Figure 6.12 Revised prototype interface for the `Find campaign` use case.

search through hundreds of campaigns; and it might reduce the number of errors made by users in selecting the right campaign to carry out some function on.

Prototypes can be produced with visual programming tools, with scripting languages like TCL/TK, with a package like Microsoft PowerPoint or even as web pages using HTML.

Prototypes do not have to be developed as programs. Screen and window designs can be sketched out on paper and shown to the users, either formally or informally. A series of possible screen layouts showing the steps that the user would take to interact with a particular use case can be strung together in a storyboard, as in Fig. 6.13.

6.6.4 CASE tool support

Drawing any diagram and maintaining the associated documentation is made easier by a CASE tool, as described in Section 3.8.

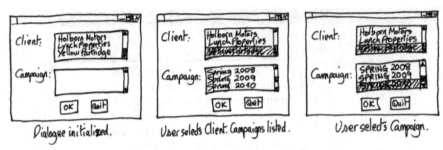

Figure 6.13 Prototype storyboard.

As well as allowing the analyst to produce diagrams showing all the use cases in appropriate subsystems, a CASE tool should also provide facilities to maintain the repository associated with the diagram elements and to produce reports. Automatically generated reports can be merged into documents that are produced for the client organization. The behaviour specification of each use case forms part of the requirements model or requirements specification, which it is necessary to get the client to agree to.

6.6.5 Business modelling with use case diagrams

We have used use case diagrams here to model the requirements for a system. They can also be used earlier in the life of a project to model an organization and how it operates. Business modelling is sometimes used when a new business is being set up, when an existing business is being 're-engineered', or in a complex project to ensure that the business operation is correctly understood before starting to elicit the requirements.

In the examples that we have shown above, the actors have all been employees of the company interacting with what will be a computerized system. In business modelling, the actors are the people and organizations outside the company, interacting with functions within the company. For example, Fig. 6.14 shows the `Client` as an actor and use cases that represent the functions of the business rather than functions of the computer system.

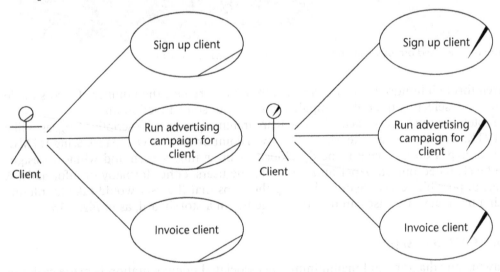

Figure 6.14 Example of business modelling with use cases.

Note the special symbols that are used for the business use cases and business actors in business use case diagrams. You may see these used, as they are part of a UML profile for business modelling, and are often shown as in the example on the left, although the original IBM paper on the subject (Johnston, 2004) shows them as in the example on the right.

A full business model of Agate would show all the functions of the company, and the actors would be the other people and organizations with which Agate interacts, for example the media companies (TV stations and magazine and newspaper publishers), from which Agate buys advertising time and space, and the subcontractors that Agate uses to do design work and printing. There are other approaches to business modelling, the most prominent of which use process charts, which are similar to activity diagrams. Although this kind of business process modelling has been around for a few decades, it has recently acquired a new significance with the development of web services and service-oriented architectures and the idea that it is possible to model business processes and then have them automated directly through the use of workflow tools and services. Notations such as Business Process Modelling Notation (BPMN) and XML-based languages such as Business Process Execution Language for Web Services (BPEL4WS) have been developed as a result of this interest in business process automation.

6.6.6 Testing and use cases

One of the benefits of developing use cases as part of the specification of the system that is to be implemented, is that they can form the basis of scenarios that can be used as test cases when the system has been developed. If you look at the more detailed use case description for the use case `Assign Staff to Work on a Campaign` in Section 6.6.2, you can see that if you were given a first delivery of the system to test, you could run through the steps in this use case with an agreed set of test data, and check that the system performed as required. Use cases alone are not the full specification of what needs testing but they provide a good basis for developing test cases, which are explained in more detail in Chapter 19.

6.7 Requirements Capture and Modelling

The first stage of most projects is one of capturing and modelling the requirements for the system. As we progress through the book, we shall include activity diagrams to illustrate the main activities in and products of each phase. These diagrams link back to the table in Fig. 5.17, which summarizes the approach that we are taking in this book. Figure 6.15 shows the first such diagram.

In this case we have not broken the activity `Requirements capture and model-ling` down into more detail, though it could potentially be broken down into separate activities for the capture of the requirements (interviewing, observation, etc.) and for the modelling of the requirements (use case modelling, prototyping, etc.).

We have used object flows to show the documents and models that are the inputs to and outputs from activities, and activity partitions to show the role that is responsible for the activities. In this case, one or more people in the role of `Requirements Team` will carry out this activity. In a small project, this may be one person, who carries out

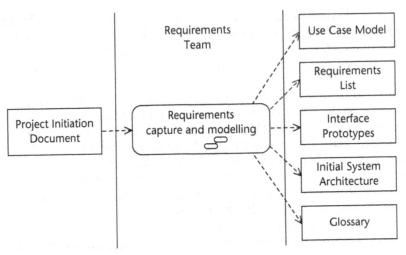

Figure 6.15 Activity diagram for `Requirements capture and modelling`.

many other analysis and design activities; in a large project or organization, this may be a team of requirements analysis specialists taking more specialist roles.

The Case Study Chapter A2, which follows this one, provides more extended examples of the outputs of the `Requirements capture and modelling` activity.

6.8 Summary

Analysts investigating an organization's requirements for a new information system may use five main fact-finding techniques–background reading, interviews, observation, document sampling and questionnaires. They use these to gain an understanding of the current system and its operation, of the enhancements the users require to the current system and of the new requirements that users have for the new system.

Using agreed standards to document requirements allows the analysts to communicate these requirements to other professionals and to the users. Use case diagrams are one diagramming technique that is used to summarize the users' functional requirements in a high-level overview of the way that the new system will be used.

Case Study Example

You have already seen several examples from the case study in this chapter. The use cases are determined by the analyst from the documentation that is gathered from the fact-finding process. What follows is a short excerpt from an interview transcript, which has been annotated to show the points that the analyst would pick up on and use to draw the use case diagrams and produce the associated documentation. The interview is between Dave Harris, a systems analyst, and Peter Bywater, an Account Manager at Agate. It is from one of the interviews with the objective: 'To establish additional requirements for new system' (in the fact-finding plan in the earlier case study section in this chapter). Commentary has been added in brackets.

Dave Harris: You were telling me about concept notes. What do you mean by this?

Peter Bywater: At present, when we come up with an idea for a campaign we use a word processor to create what we call a concept note. We keep all the note files in one directory for a particular campaign, but it's often difficult to go back and find a particular one.

DH: So is this something you'd want in the new system?

PB: Yes. We need some means to enter a concept note and to find it again. *(This sounds like two possible use cases. Who are the actors?)*

DH: So who would you want to be able to do this?

PB: I guess that the staff working on a campaign should be able to create a new note in the system.

DH: Only them? *(Any other actors?)*

PB: Yes, only the staff actually working on a campaign.

DH: What about finding them again? Is this just to view them or could people modify them?

PB: Well, we don't change them now. We just add to them. It's important to see how a concept has developed. So we would only want to view them. But we need some easy way of browsing through them until we find the right one. *(Who are the actors for this?)*

DH: Can anyone read the concept notes?

PB: Yes, any of the staff might need to have a look.

DH: Would you need any other information apart from the text of the concept itself? *(Thinking ahead to Chapter 7!)*

PB: Yes. It would be good to be able to give each one a title. Could we use the titles then when we browse through them? Oh, and the date, time and whoever created that concept note.

DH: Right, so you'd want to select a campaign and then see all the titles of notes that are associated with that campaign, so you could select one to view it? *(Thinking about the interaction between the user and the system.)*

PB: Yes, that sounds about right.

. . .

(From this information, Dave Harris is going to be able to develop the use case descriptions for two use cases:
> *Create concept note*
> *Browse concept notes*
The use case diagram is shown in Fig. 6.16. The use case descriptions will be as follows.)

Create concept note

A member of staff working on a campaign can create a concept note, which records ideas, concepts and themes that will be used in an advertising campaign. The note is in text form. Each note has a title. The person who created the note, the date and time are also recorded.

Browse concept notes

Any member of staff may view concept notes for a campaign. The campaign must be selected first. The titles of all notes associated with that campaign will be displayed.

▶ The user will be able to select a note and view the text on screen. Having viewed one note, others can be selected and viewed.

(The interaction here is quite straightforward, so we shall not need a more detailed breakdown of the interaction between user and system.

Note that in Fig. 6.16, because Campaign Staff *is a specialization of* Staff, *we do not need to show a communication association between the* Campaign Staff *actor and the* Browse concept notes *use case.)*

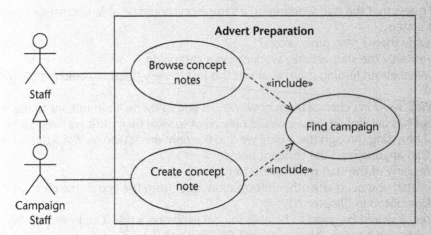

Figure 6.16 Use cases for Advert Preparation subsystem.

Review Questions

6.1 Read the following description of a requirement for FoodCo, and decide which parts of it are functional requirements and which are non-functional requirements.

The allocation of staff to production lines should be mostly automated. A process will be run once a week to carry out the allocation based on the skills and experience of operatives. Details of holidays and sick leave will also be taken into account. A first draft Allocation List will be printed off by 12.00 noon on Friday for the following week. Only staff in Production Planning will be able to amend the automatic allocation to fine-tune the list. Once the amendments have been made, the final Allocation List must be printed out by 5.00pm. The system must be able to handle allocation of 100 operatives at present, and should be capable of expansion to handle double that number.

6.2 Name the five main fact-finding techniques and list one advantage and one disadvantage of each.

6.3 Imagine that you will be interviewing one of the three staff in Production Planning at FoodCo. Draw up a list of ten questions that you would want to ask him or her.

6.4 What is the purpose of producing use cases?

6.5 Describe in your own words the difference between the «extend» and «include» relationships in use case diagrams.

6.6 What is the difference between an 'essential' and a 'real' use case?

6.7 Write a use case description in the extended form, used for the Assign staff to work on a campaign example in Section 6.6.2, for either Create concept note or Browse concept notes.

6.8 Think of the different possible uses you could make of a library computer system and draw a use case diagram to represent these use cases.

6.9 List some non-functional requirements of a library computer system (as in Question 6.8) that you would not model using use cases.

6.10 In what way are use case diagrams different when used for business modelling?

Case Study Work, Exercises and Projects

6.A Refer to the material for the second case study–FoodCo (introduced in Case Study Chapter B1). Draw up your initial fact-finding plan along the lines of the plan given in the Case Study Example on page 151.

6.B Read the following excerpt from a transcript of an interview with one of the production planners at FoodCo. Draw a use case diagram and create use case descriptions for the use cases that you can find in this information.

Ken Ong: So what happens when you start planning the next week's allocation?

Rik Sharma: Well, the first thing to do is to check which staff are unavailable.

KO: Would that be because they are on holiday?

RS: Yes, they could be on holiday or they could be off sick. Because staff are handling raw food, we have to be very careful with any illness. So factory staff often have to stay off work longer than they would if they were office workers.

KO: So how do you know who's off sick and who's on holiday?

RS: They have to complete a holiday form if they want a holiday. They send it to the Factory Manager, who authorizes it and sends it to us. We take a copy and enter the details into our system. We then return the form to the member of staff.

KO: What details do you enter?

RS: Who it is, the start date of the holiday and the first date they are available for work again.

KO: What about illness?

RS: The first day someone is off sick they have to ring in and notify us. We have to find someone to fill in for them for that day if we can.

KO: Right. Let's come back to that in a minute. How do you record the fact that they're off sick for your next week's production plan?

RS: We make an entry in the system. We record which member of staff it is, when they went off sick, the reason and an estimate of how many days they're likely to be off.

KO: Right, so how do you get at that information when you come to plan next week's allocation?

RS: Well, we run off three lists. We enter Monday's date, and it prints us off one list showing who is available all week, a second list showing who is not available all week, and a third list showing who is likely to be available for part of the week.

KO: Then what?

RS: Then we start with the people who are available all week and work round them. We pull each operative's record up on the screen and look at two main factors—first their skills and experience, and second, which line they're working on at the moment and how long they've been on that line. Then we allocate them to a line and a session in one of the three factories.

KO: So you can allocate them to any one of the three factories. Do you enter the same data for each one?

RS: No, there are slight variations in the allocation screen for each of the factories—mainly for historical reasons.

…

6.C Find out what you can about a software package to support requirements capture. Does it integrate with a modelling tool? What kind of traceability of requirements does it provide?

Further Reading

Booth (1989) Chapter 5 describes the issues surrounding the usability of systems in more detail than we can here, and explains the process of Task Analysis.

Oppenheim (2000) provides a very detailed coverage of questionnaire design for survey purposes. It is aimed mainly at social science and psychology students, but has some relevant chapters on how to formulate effective questions. Many books for students on how to carry out a research project cover fact-gathering techniques such as interviewing and questionnaire design. Allison et al. (1996) is an example, but most university libraries and bookshops will have a selection of similar books.

Hart (1997) gives a detailed explanation of the techniques that are specific to the development of expert systems.

Roberts (1989) addresses the role of users in a systems development project. This book is one of a series of guides written for civil servants in the UK government service, and is relatively bureaucratic in its outlook. However, it ranges widely over the issues that users may face. Yourdon (1989) discusses users and their roles in Chapter 3.

Jacobson et al. (1992) present the original ideas behind use cases as an analysis technique, and these are developed in Rosenberg and Scott (1999) or Cockburn (2000).

Agate Ltd Case Study— Requirements Model

Agate Ltd

A2.1 Introduction

In this chapter we bring together the models (diagrams and supporting textual information) that constitute the requirements model. In Chapters 5 and 6 we have introduced the following UML diagrams:

- use case diagram
- activity diagram
- package diagram.

There is not the space in this book to produce a complete requirements model. However, in this chapter we have included a sample of the diagrams and other information. This is done to illustrate the kind of material that should be brought together in a requirements model. We have also tried to illustrate how iteration of the model will produce versions of the model that are elaborated with more detail.

A2.2 Requirements List

The requirements list on the next page includes a column to show which use cases provide the functionality of each requirement. This requirements list includes some use cases not in the first iteration of the use case model.

No.	Requirement	Use Case(s)
1	To record names, address and contact details for each client	Add a new client
2	To record the details of each campaign for each client. This will include the title of the campaign, planned start and finish dates, estimated costs, budgets, actual costs and dates, and the current state of completion	Add a new campaign
3	To provide information that can be used in the separate accounts system for invoicing clients for campaigns	Record completion of a campaign
4	To record payments for campaigns that are also recorded in the separate accounts system	Record client payment
5	To record which staff are working on which campaigns, including the campaign manager for each campaign	Assign staff to work on a campaign
6	To record which staff are assigned as staff contacts to clients	Assign a staff contact
7	To check on the status of campaigns and whether they are within budget	Check campaign budget
8	To allow creative staff to record notes of ideas for campaigns and adverts (concept notes)	Create concept note
9	To provide other staff with access to these concept notes	Browse concept notes
10	To record details of adverts, including the progress on their production	Add a new advert to a campaign. Record completion of an advert
11	To schedule the dates when adverts will be run	Add a new advert to a campaign
12	To maintain staff records for creative and administrative staff	Add a new member of staff
13	To maintain details of staff grades and the pay for those grades	Add a new staff grade. Change the rate for a staff grade
14	To record which staff are on which grade	Change the grade for a member of staff
15	To calculate the annual bonus for all staff	Calculate staff bonuses
16	To enable data about clients, campaigns, adverts and staff to be shared between offices	Not applicable
17	To allow the system to be modified to work in different languages	Not applicable
18	To restrict the ability to create or update data to authorized users in the company.	All use cases that create or update data
19	To limit planned downtime to one hour a week during the night UK time.	Not applicable

A2.3 | Actors and Use Cases

Actor	Description
Accountant	The accountant works in the Accounts department and is responsible for the major resourcing issues for campaigns including staffing and related financial matters.
Campaign Manager	Either a Director or an Account Manager (job titles), who is responsible for estimating the campaign cost and agreeing it with the client. They are responsible for assigning staff to the team and supervising their work, managing the progress of the campaign, conducting any further budget negotiations and authorizing the final invoices.
Staff Contact	Member of staff who is the contact for a particular client. They provide a first point of contact for the client when the client wants to contact Agate.
Staff	Any member of staff in Agate.
Campaign Staff	Member of staff working on a particular campaign.

Figures A2.1 to A2.3 show the use cases from the first iteration, with use case descriptions in the tables. The use case diagram in Figure A2.1 has been drawn in a modelling tool, Enterprise Architect from SparxSystems, and is shown as a screenshot.

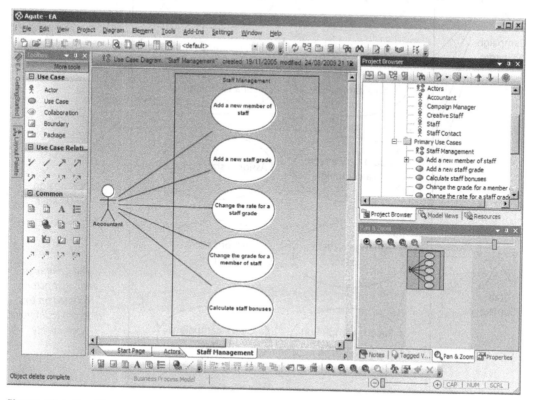

Figure A2.1 Staff Management use cases.

Use Case	Description
Add a new staff member	When a new member of staff joins Agate, his or her details are recorded. He or she is assigned a staff number, and the start date is entered. Start date defaults to today's date. The starting grade is entered.
Add a new staff grade	Occasionally a new grade for a member of staff must be added. The name of the grade is entered. At the same time, the rate for that grade and the rate start date are entered; the date defaults to today's date.
Change the rate for a staff grade	Annually the rates for grades are changed. The new rate for each grade is entered, and the rate start date set (no default). The old grade rate is retrieved and the rate finish date for that grade rate set to the day before the start of the new rate.
Change the grade for a staff member	When a member of staff is promoted, the new grade and the date on which they start on that grade are entered. The old staff grade is retrieved and the finish date set to the day before the start of the new grade.
Calculate staff bonuses	At the end of each month staff bonuses are calculated. This involves calculating the bonus due on each campaign a member of staff is working on. These are summed to give the total staff bonus.

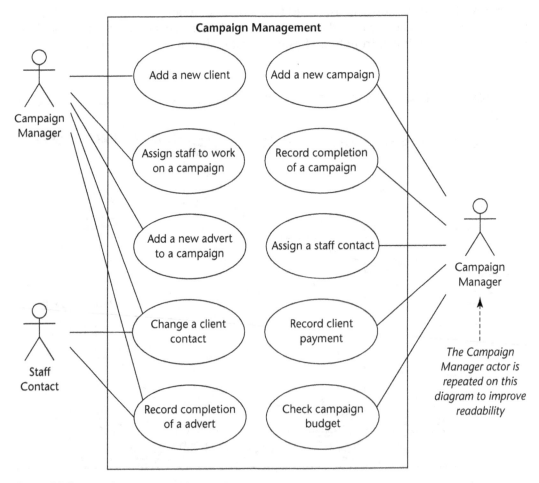

Figure A2.2 Campaign Management use cases.

Use Case	Description
Add a new client	When Agate obtains a new client, the full details of the client are entered. Typically this will be because of a new campaign, and therefore the new campaign will be added straight away.
Assign staff to work on a campaign	The campaign manager selects a particular campaign. A list of staff not already working on that campaign is displayed, and he or she selects those to be assigned to this campaign.
Add a new advert to a campaign	A campaign can consist of many adverts. Details of each advert are entered into the system with a target completion date and estimated cost.
Change a client contact	Records when the client's contact person with Agate is changed.
Record completion of an advert	The actor selects the relevant client, campaign and advert. The selected advert is then completed by setting its completion date.
Add a new campaign	When Agate gets the business for a new campaign, details of the campaign are entered, including the intended finish date and the estimated cost. The manager for that campaign is the person who enters it.
Record completion of a campaign	When a campaign is completed, the actual completion date and cost are entered. A record of completion form is printed out for the Accountant as the basis for invoicing the client.
Assign a staff contact	Clients have a member of staff assigned to them as their particular contact person.
Record client payment	When a client pays for a campaign, the payment amount is checked against the actual cost and the date paid is entered.
Check campaign budget	The campaign budget may be checked to ensure that it has not been exceeded. The current campaign cost is determined by the total cost of all the adverts and the campaign overheads.

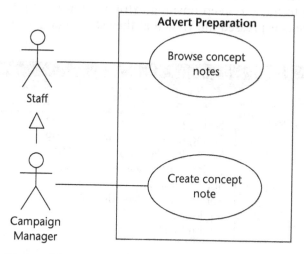

Figure A2.3 Advert Preparation use cases.

Use Case	Description
Browse concept notes	Any member of staff may view concept notes for a campaign. The campaign must be selected first. The titles of all notes associated with that campaign will be displayed. The user will be able to select a note and view the text on screen. Having viewed one note, others can be selected and viewed.
Create concept note	A member of staff working on a campaign can create a concept note, which records ideas, concepts and themes that will be used in an advertising campaign. The note is in text form. Each note has a title. The person who created the note, the date and time are also recorded.

As part of the second iteration of use case modelling, it is suggested that all the use cases that require the user to select a client, a campaign or an advert should have include relationships with use cases called Find client, Find campaign and Find advert. An example of this is shown in Fig. A2.4.

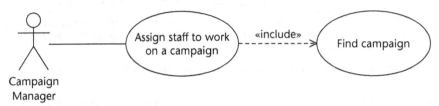

Figure A2.4 Inclusion of Find campaign use case.

In order to test out this idea, prototypes of the user interface were produced in the second iteration. The first prototypes used a separate user interface for these included use cases, as shown in Fig. A2.5.

However, feedback from the users indicated that this approach was not acceptable. They did not want to have to keep opening extra windows to find clients, campaigns and adverts. The users expressed the view that they should be able to select these from

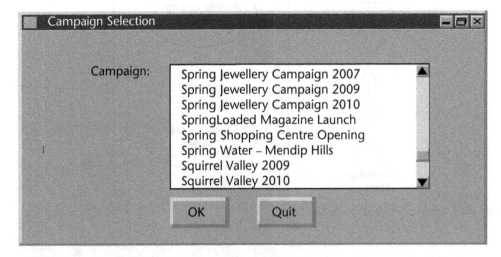

Figure A2.5 Prototype interface for the Find campaign use case.

listboxes or dropdown lists that were part of the interface for whatever use case they were in at the time.

In the third iteration of use case modelling, a set of prototypes was produced that uses listboxes. Figure A2.6 shows an example.

In the third iteration, some additional functionality was identified and added to the use case diagrams. As an example of this, Fig. A2.7 shows the use case Check campaign budget extended by the use case Print campaign summary and Print campaign invoice. This additional functionality will also require a change to the prototype interface in Fig. A2.6. Two additional buttons, Print Summary and Print Invoice, need to be added to the row of buttons at the bottom of the window.

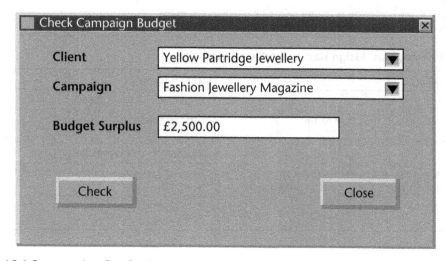

Figure A2.6 Prototype interface for the use case Check campaign budget.

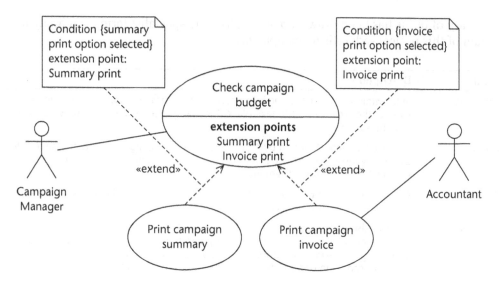

Figure A2.7 Modified use case Check campaign budget with extensions.

Also in the third iteration, the use case descriptions are elaborated to provide more detail about the interaction between the actors and the system. Two examples of these use case descriptions are provided below.

Use case description: Check campaign budget

Actor Action	System Response
1. None	2. Lists the names of all clients
3. The actor selects the client name	4. Lists the titles of all campaigns for that client
5. Selects the relevant campaign. Requests budget check	6. Displays the budget surplus for that campaign

Extensions
After step 6, the campaign manager prints a campaign summary.
After step 6, the campaign manager prints a campaign invoice.

Use case description: Assign staff to work on a campaign

Actor Action	System Response
1. None	2. Displays list of client names
3. The actor selects the client name	4. Lists the titles of all campaigns for that client
5. Selects the relevant campaign	6. Displays a list of all staff members not already allocated to this campaign
7. Highlights the staff members to be assigned to this campaign. Clicks Allocate button.	8. Presents a message confirming that staff have been allocated

Alternative Courses
None.

A2.4 Glossary

A glossary of terms has been drawn up, which lists the specialist terms that apply to the domain of this project—advertising campaigns.

Term	Description
Admin Staff	Staff within Agate whose role is to provide administrative support that enables the work of the creative staff to take place, for example secretaries, accounts clerks and the office manager
Advert	An advertisement designed by Agate as part of a campaign. Adverts can be for TV, cinema, websites, newspapers, magazines, advertising hoardings, brochures or leaflets. Synonym: Advertisement
Agate	An advertising agency based in Birmingham, UK, but with offices around the world. The customer for this project
Campaign	An advertising campaign. Adverts are organized into campaigns in order to achieve a particular objective, for example a campaign to launch a new product or service, a campaign to rebrand a company or product, or a campaign to promote an existing product in order to take market share from competitors
Campaign Staff	Member of staff working on a particular campaign

Term	Description
Client	A customer of Agate. A company or organization that wishes to obtain the services of Agate to develop and manage an advertising campaign, and design and produce adverts for the campaign
Concept Note	A textual note about an idea for a campaign or advert. This is where creative staff record their ideas during the process of deciding the themes of campaigns and adverts. Synonym: Note
Creative Staff	Staff with a creative role in the company, such as designers, editors and copy-writers; those who are engaged in the work of the company to develop and manage campaigns and design and produce adverts
Grade	A job grade. Each member of staff is on a particular grade, for example 'Graphic Artist 2' or 'Copywriter 1'
Grade Rate	The rate of pay for a particular grade, for example the Grade 'Graphic Artist 2' is paid £26 170 per year in the UK from 1/1/2010 to 31/12/2010
Staff	Any member of staff in Agate. Synonyms: Staff member, member of staff

A2.5 | Initial Architecture

The initial architecture of the system is based on the packages into which the use cases are grouped. These use cases have been grouped into three subsystem packages: `Campaign Management`, `Staff Management` and `Advert Preparation`.

Figure A2.8 shows the initial architecture of these three packages, and a package that will provide the mechanisms for the distribution of the application. At this early stage in the project, it is not clear what this will be, but something will be necessary to meet Requirement 16. At this stage the packages have names that reflect the business context rather than how they might be implemented in Java packages or C# namespaces or an equivalent structure. This will change later.

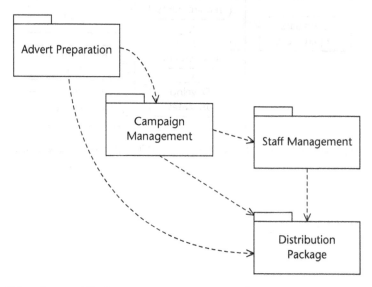

Figure A2.8 Initial package architecture.

A2.6 | Activities of Requirements Modelling

In Chapter 5, we outlined the phases and activities of the iterative lifecycle, and in Chapter 6 we included an activity diagram to show the activity `Requirements capture and modelling`. Figure A2.9 shows the same diagram. This activity can be broken down into other activities, and these are shown in Figs A2.10, A2.11 and A2.12.

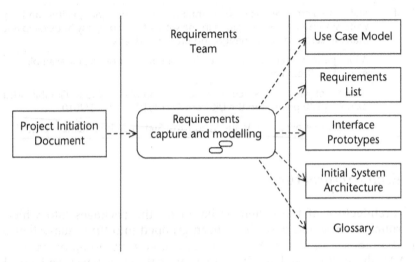

Figure A2.9 Activity diagram for `Requirements capture and modelling`.

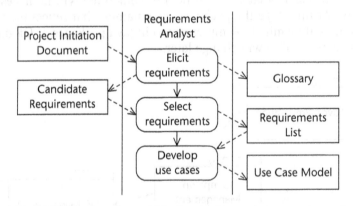

Figure A2.10 Activity diagram to show the activities involved in capturing requirements.

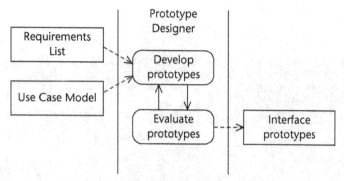

Figure A2.11 Activity diagram to show the activities involved in developing prototypes.

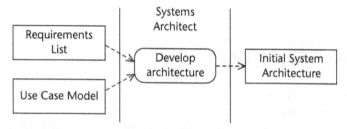

Figure A2.12 Activity diagram to show the activities in developing an initial architecture.

It is important to remember that in a project that adopts an iterative lifecycle, these activities may take place over a series of iterations. In the first iteration, the emphasis will be on requirements capture and modelling; in the second, it will shift to analysis, but some requirements capture and modelling activities may still take place. Refer back to Fig. 5.15. You may also want to look at Fig. 5.7, which illustrates the development of the use case model through successive iterations.

Requirements Analysis

7.1 | Introduction

The purpose of requirements analysis is to produce an analysis, or logical, model of the planned application. The analysis model can be seen as a necessary and important step between the requirements model, which was discussed in Chapter 6 and illustrated in Case Study Chapter A2, and the design model, which will be introduced in Chapter 12 and illustrated in Case Study Chapter A5. However, in an iterative lifecycle the three models represent different perspectives on the proposed system rather than distinct stages in its development. The analysis model focuses on the logical behaviour of the proposed system. It consists chiefly of a set of analysis classes contained in diagrams that collectively model the behaviour of the required application system in a way that is independent of any particular implementation approach. An analysis model helps to reduce errors and inconsistencies in software design and construction.

The analysis model is closely related to the domain model, if one exists. However, a domain model is a high-level view of the main concepts and logical elements related to the organization as a whole. An analysis model is specific to a single software system and its production forms part of the development of that system.

Some followers of Agile methods argue that it is rarely necessary to produce an analysis model. (Chapter 21 and the additional material on the book website give more information about Agile methods.) Indeed, some experienced developers follow familiar patterns and frameworks without building much in the way of tangible models at all. However, we believe that it is useful to produce an analysis model for all but the simplest of new software systems. This is particularly true for developers who are new to the profession.

We begin by considering how an analysis model differs from the other UML models mentioned above. Then we explain and illustrate the notation of the class diagram, which is the main artifact produced by the analysis workflow. We describe two approaches to creating an analysis class diagram for a use case (or for a set of use cases). One approach is called use case realization (it is also often called robustness analysis). The other is a non-UML technique called Class–Responsibility–Collaboration (CRC) cards, which predates UML by many years, but is still widely used in analysis. Finally, we explain how to derive an overall analysis class diagram from the various partial class diagrams that result from both CRC cards and the use case realization technique.

7.2 ┃ The Analysis Model

The analysis model is a product of the analysis workflow, which concentrates on achieving a detailed understanding of the problem domain, and of the logical behaviour of an application system that can meet the requirements specified in the requirements model.

7.2.1 How does an analysis model differ from other models?

The analysis model goes beyond the requirements model in its completeness, its level of detail and its analysis of the logical structure of the problem situation and the ways that its logical elements interact. For example, a use case in the requirements model may be represented in the analysis model by a set of collaborating classes, together with the attributes, operations and associations needed to fulfil the goals of the use case.

Meanwhile, the analysis model also stops short of the design model in that it ignores physical and implementation details of how the requirements are to be met. For example, an analysis class diagram might represent the user interface aspect of a use case (in other words, the windows, buttons, text boxes and other interface widgets which the user can see, can press, into which they can enter data, and so on) as a single class, while the corresponding design class diagram may contain a large number of classes that precisely represent the actual user interface in Java, or in whichever programming language has been chosen for the implementation.

The analysis model also differs from the domain model, although the two are closely related. A domain model is a high-level view of the main concepts and logical elements related to the organization as a whole. Not all organizations maintain a domain model, but in those that do it typically consists of a set of classes that represent important business concepts such as customers, orders, products, and so on. These are specified to the same level of detail as analysis classes, but will include only those attributes and operations that can be identified without reference to any given application system. The domain model acts as a reference model of 'the things of interest to the organization' that can be used as a way of eliminating duplication and as a basis for many different application systems. (Domain models are explained in more detail in the online material on the book website.)

The analysis model is important because it specifies the requirements. This means much more than just gathering and documenting facts and requests from users. The use case model gives a perspective on user requirements, and models them in terms of what the software system can do to help the user perform their work (or play). In order to design software that will deliver this help, we must analyse the logical structure of the problem situation and the ways that its logical elements interact. We must examine the way in which different, possibly conflicting, requirements affect each other. We must then communicate this understanding clearly and unambiguously as a basis for the design model, which in turn guides the implementation model.

It is one of the conceptual foundations of the object-oriented approach that the software developed to meet a need should be structured in a way that reflects the situation in which the need arises. The UML class diagram is designed to do just this. The structure of an analysis class diagram is a model of requirements that can be directly translated through design into software components. A successful analysis model must meet the following needs.

- It must contain an overall description of what the software should do.
- It must represent any people, physical things and concepts that are important to the analyst's understanding of what is going on in the application domain.
- It must show connections and interactions among these people, things and concepts.
- It must show the business situation in enough detail to evaluate possible designs.
- Ideally, it should also be organized in such a way that it makes a sound basis for the design model.

In the next section, we discuss what is involved in achieving these goals.

7.2.2 What makes for good analysis?

The cost of fixing faults in a system increases as the system progresses through the systems development lifecycle. If an error occurs in the analysis of a system, it is cheaper to fix it during an early phase than later when that error may have propagated through numerous aspects of the design and implementation. It is most expensive to fix it after the system has been deployed and the error may be reflected in many different parts of the system. The quality of the design is, therefore, dependent to a large extent on the quality of the analysis.

Some methodologies have explicit quality criteria that can be applied to the products of every stage of the lifecycle, but these quality criteria typically check syntactic aspects of the products, that is, whether the notation is correct in diagrams, rather than semantic aspects, that is, whether the diagrams correctly represent the organization's requirements. To provide a sound foundation for design, analysis should meet the following four criteria:

- correct scope
- completeness
- correct content
- consistency.

These are described in more detail below.

Correct scope

The scope of a system determines what is included in that system and what is excluded. It is important that the required scope of the system is clearly understood, documented and agreed with the clients from the start of the project. In many organizations, this will be defined in a formal document called a project initiation document (PID). (There is more about the role and content of a PID in the online chapter on project management on the book's website.) It is also important that everything that is in the analysis models *does* fall within the scope of the system. In the case of the Agate system, it is not a requirement to replace the existing accounting system that is used to invoice clients. It is, however, a requirement that the new system should interface with the accounting system to provide for the transfer of data relating to financial aspects of advertising campaigns. The scope of the system therefore excludes use cases for accounting but should include use cases both to handle the entry of data that will be transferred to the accounting system and to handle the transfer itself. Coad et al. (1997) include a *not this time* component with their other four components (problem domain, human interface, data management and system interaction). The not this time component is used to document classes and business services that emerge during the analysis but are not part of the requirements this time. This is a useful way of forcing consideration of the scope of the system.

Completeness

Just as there is a requirement that everything that is in the analysis models is within the scope of the system, so everything that is within the scope of the system should be documented in the analysis models. Everything that is known about the system from the requirements capture should be documented and included in appropriate diagrams. Often the completeness of the analysis is dependent on the skills and experience of the analyst. Knowing what questions to ask in order to elicit requirements comes with time and experience. However, analysis patterns and strategies, as proposed by Coad et al. (1997) and Fowler (1997), can help the less-experienced analyst to identify likely issues. (The use of patterns, which draw on past experience, can be a good way of ensuring that the analysis is effective.)

Non-functional requirements should be documented even though they may not affect the analysis models directly. Rumbaugh (1997) suggests that some of the requirements found during analysis are not analysis requirements but design requirements. These should be documented, but the development team may only have to consider them once the design phase has begun. An example in the Agate system is the requirement that the system should be usable in different offices around the world and should handle multiple currencies. This would be noted during analysis; during design, it will mean that the system must be designed to support localization (adaptation to local needs) and to display different national currency symbols (perhaps using the Unicode standard).

Correct content

The analysis documentation should be correct and accurate in what it describes. This applies not only to textual information, logic, business rules and diagrams but also to quantitative features of the non-functional requirements. Examples include correct descriptions of attributes and any operations that are known at this stage, correct representation of associations between classes, particularly the multiplicity of associations, and accurate information about volumes of data. Accuracy should not be confused with precision. FoodCo owns 1500 acres of land (to the nearest 100 acres). To state that the company owns 1700 is inaccurate. To state that it owns 1523 is more precise. To state that it owns 1253 is still inaccurate, although the precision gives a spurious impression of accuracy.

Consistency

Where the analysis documentation includes different models that refer to the same things (use cases, classes, attributes or operations), the same name should be used consistently for the same thing. Errors of consistency can result in errors being made by designers: for example, creating two attributes with different names that are used in different parts of the system but should be the same attribute. If the designers spot the inconsistency, they may try to resolve it themselves, but may get it wrong because the information they have about the system is all dependent on what they have received in the specification of the system from the analysts.

Errors of scope or completeness will typically be reflected in the finished product not doing what the users require; the product will either include features that are not required or lack features that are. Errors of correctness and consistency will typically be reflected in the finished product performing incorrectly. Errors of completeness and consistency will most often result in difficulties for the designers; in the face of incomplete or inconsistent specifications, they will have to try to decide what is required or refer back to the analysts.

One general way of ensuring that the analysis models reflect the requirements is to use walkthroughs. Walkthroughs are described by Yourdon (1985) (and also in an appendix to Yourdon, 1989). They provide a structured review with other developers. They may be used at various points in the systems development lifecycle as a way of ensuring the quality of products. For example, walkthroughs may also be used during program design and development to check the correctness of program code.

7.3 Analysis Class Diagram: Concepts and Notation

7.3.1 Classes and objects

The analysis class diagram contains classes that represent the more permanent aspects of the application domain, but specifically those that are relevant to the application under development. For example, as long as Agate continues to operate in the advertising business, its business activities are likely to involve offices, computers, clients, campaigns, budgets, invoices, payments, adverts, a variety of different operational staff (including those in the creative, accounts and IT departments), directors, several kinds of managers (looking after finance, marketing and campaigns) and various relationships between them. If Agate has a domain model, then it is likely to contain classes that represent all these people, things and concepts. Among these, some will be specifically related to the application of interest. For example, we can readily identify clients, campaigns, budgets, payments, adverts, creative staff and campaign managers as being particularly relevant to the requirements listed in Section A1.4. We can therefore expect that these will all appear as classes in the analysis model.

7.3.2 Attributes

Attributes are the essential description of the data that belongs to a class. They are the common structure of what a member of the class can 'know'. Each object will have its own, possibly unique, value for each attribute (or values, if the attribute is an array).

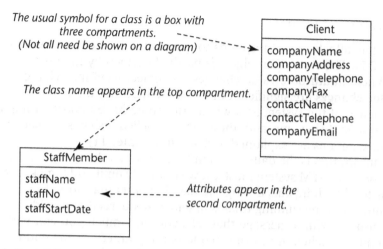

Figure 7.1 Including attributes on a class diagram.

Figure 7.1 shows some possible attributes of Client and StaffMember in the Agate case study.

Note that this symbol for a class is subdivided into three compartments. The top compartment contains the class name while the second contains the attribute names (which begin with a lower case letter). The third compartment will contain the operations, but it remains empty for the moment.

In the same way that a class is partly defined by its attributes, instances are described by the values of those attributes. For a particular client we give an appropriate value to each attribute. 'FoodCo' is the value given to the company name attribute for the instance of Client that represents the real-world client FoodCo. To describe an instance completely, we give a value to all its attributes, as in Fig. 7.2.

Some attribute values change during the life of an object. For example, FoodCo's managers may change their email address, their telephone number or their address. They may even decide to change the company's name. In each case, the corresponding attribute value should be updated in the object that represents FoodCo. Other attribute values may not change. For example, a client reference number may be assigned to each client. As long as this is correctly recorded in the first place, there is probably no need for its value ever to change.

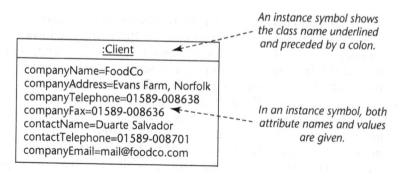

Figure 7.2 Including attribute values on an instance diagram.

7.3.3 Attributes and state

An object's state affects how it responds to events (the idea of state was first explained in Section 4.2.7). The state of an object is partly described by the instance values of its attributes. When an attribute value changes, the object itself may change state. Not all attribute value changes are significant in the sense that they affect the behaviour of the object, and hence of the system as a whole. But some have important implications for object and system behaviour and these are modelled using statemachine diagrams (statemachine diagrams are explained in detail in Chapter 11).

A simple illustration is the daily cash limit that most banks apply to ATM cash cards. For this to work, the ATM system must know your daily limit and it must keep a running total of your total withdrawals during the day. Requests that do not exceed your daily limit are granted and the running total is updated. Requests that would exceed the limit are refused, usually with a message that tells you how much you can withdraw. Once your daily limit is reached, no further requests are granted. At the end of the day, the total is reset to zero and the procedure starts again. (Note that this is greatly simplified–real bank systems are much more complex.)

To understand this in terms of object states, imagine an object yourCard with attributes dayTotal and dailyLimit. The values of these attributes at any given moment determine the object's state. At the start of each day's business, the value of dayTotal is set to zero. This places the object in its Active state. For as long as the value of dayTotal is less than the value of dailyLimit, yourCard stays in the Active state. If the value of dayTotal becomes equal to the value of dailyLimit, yourCard changes state to Barred. How yourCard responds to a withdraw(amount) message depends on which state it is in at the time. In the Active state, valid requests (those that do not cause the limit to be exceeded) are granted, while invalid requests (those that would cause the limit to be exceeded) result in a warning message instead of cash being issued. However, in the Barred state, all cash requests are refused and the message is different. Figure 7.3 shows this as a statechart diagram.

Although this example is not intended as a presentation of statemachine diagrams, the notation is useful to illustrate what can happen when an object changes its state. At the instance level this is merely an update of attribute values, yet the consequences can extend beyond the boundaries of the software system into the user's daily life–as some bank customers know from experience.

7.3.4 Links between instances

A link is a logical connection between two or more objects (in most modelling situations a link connects only two instances; a link can connect three or more instances, but this is rare and we do not consider it here). An example for Agate is the connection between FoodCo and the 'World Tradition' TV campaign, described by the sentence 'FoodCo is the client for the World Tradition campaign.' This is shown in Figure 7.4.

Linked instances may be from different classes, as in Fig. 7.4. A link can also connect instances of the same class: for example, the link supervises between a manager and another staff member who are both instances of Staff Member. Less commonly, a link can connect an instance to itself. An example might arise where the captain of a hockey team selects the players. Assuming that the captain is also a player, she might link to herself–for example 'the captain selects herself for the team'.

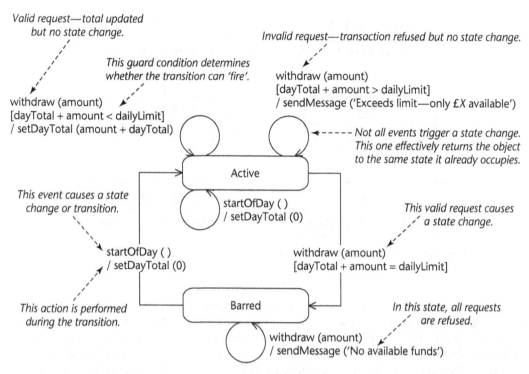

Valid request—total updated but no state change.

This guard condition determines whether the transition can 'fire'.

Invalid request—transaction refused but no state change.

withdraw (amount)
[dayTotal + amount < dailyLimit]
/ setDayTotal (amount + dayTotal)

withdraw (amount)
[dayTotal + amount > dailyLimit]
/ sendMessage ('Exceeds limit—only £X available')

Not all events trigger a state change. This one effectively returns the object to the same state it already occupies.

This event causes a state change or transition.

Active

startOfDay ( )
/ setDayTotal (0)

This valid request causes a state change.

startOfDay ( )
/ setDayTotal (0)

withdraw (amount)
[dayTotal + amount = dailyLimit]

This action is performed during the transition.

Barred

In this state, all requests are refused.

withdraw (amount)
/ sendMessage ('No available funds')

Figure 7.3 Simplified states and transitions for an ATM cash card.

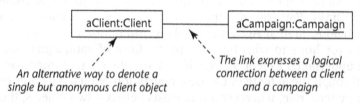

aClient:Client — aCampaign:Campaign

An alternative way to denote a single but anonymous client object

The link expresses a logical connection between a client and a campaign

Figure 7.4 A link between two instances.

Figure 7.5 shows some links between clients and campaigns, but this is not a very economic way of modelling them. To show every link would be unnecessarily complex. There may be many staff and hundreds of clients, not to mention many thousands of links between instances of other classes. In addition to this, links may change frequently and such a detailed model would soon be out of date.

7.3.5 Associations between classes

An association is an abstraction that connects two classes and represents the possibility of links between their instances. (An association may connect more than two classes, but–just as for links–this is rare and we do not consider it here.) For example, at Agate a member of staff is assigned to each client as a staff contact. This will be instantiated by a set of links, each connecting a specific `:Client` (the colon before the class name

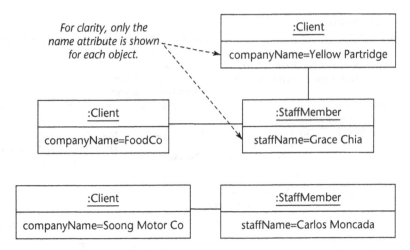

For clarity, only the name attribute is shown for each object.

Figure 7.5 Links between instances of StaffMember and Client.

indicates an anonymous instance of the class, in other words *any* client) to the corresponding :StaffMember. However, links are modelled only if this is necessary to show a specific requirement. We know from the use cases that campaign managers need to be able to assign and change a client contact. Therefore the model must permit these links to exist, otherwise it will not be possible to design software that meets these needs. In the same way that a class describes a set of similar objects, an association describes a set of similar links (links are called *association instances* by some authors).

Some associations can be recognized easily without any initial awareness that there are any specific links. For example, the association between a client and each of their campaigns is obvious. Staff at Agate need only record information about clients because they have won (or hope to win) business in the form of campaigns, and a campaign would not be undertaken except on behalf of a specific client. Other associations may be identified through the activity of use case realization (which we describe later in this chapter). As a general rule, wherever a link exists between two objects, there must be a corresponding association between their classes. Like object instances, links are not usually modelled explicitly on class diagrams.

Figure 7.6 shows an association that includes all possible liaises with links between clients and members of staff (although it does not tell us which instances are linked, if any–an association is abstract and general, not particular). The association is the line between the two class symbols. The text liaises with near the middle of the line is the *association name*. Every association must have a descriptive name (although it is not obligatory to show this on diagrams). The text at the association end gives a name to the role that the instances of the class at that end of the association play in relation to instances of the class at the other end of the association. The link acts as a constraint: only those instances of StaffMember that are linked to an instance of Client by the liaises with association will participate in collaborations that involve the role staffContact. At a later stage, we will see that this association end name represents a data value, not unlike an attribute; it just happens to hold a reference to an instance of another domain class rather than a value like an integer or a string. In design and implementation, the association end name will become an attribute.

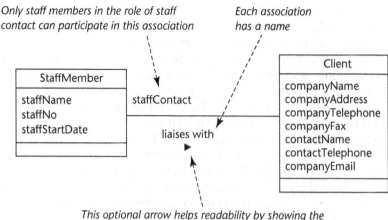

Figure 7.6 Liaises with association between StaffMember and Client.

7.3.6 Associations and state

As we saw in Section 7.3.3, an object's state is partly defined by its current attribute values. It is also partly defined by its current links. When a link to another object is created or destroyed, the object may change state. As with attribute value updates, some changes to links are significant and represent a state change. An example of link creation is when a campaign manager is assigned to a campaign. The creation of this link may be all that is needed for the campaign to be treated as commissioned, ready for work to start on advert preparation. This will affect the way that the :Campaign object should respond to certain messages and could be modelled as a transition to a Commissioned state.

The creation of other links is less significant and does not represent a state change. For example, when a campaign manager assigns a staff member to act as staff contact for a campaign this will not affect the behaviour of the :Campaign object, and thus need not be modelled as a state change.

7.3.7 Multiplicity

The *multiplicity* of an association is a description of the number of objects that can participate in the association. It reflects an *enterprise* (or *business*) *rule*; these are real-world constraints on the way that business activities are allowed to happen. Note that enterprise rules always come in pairs, because a full description of an association involves 'reading' it in both directions.

A familiar example is the relationship between a bank account and its designated accountholder(s). The enterprise rules that apply vary according to the type of account, as shown below.

- A sole account has *one and only one* accountholder. An accountholder has *one or more* accounts.
- A joint account has *exactly two* accountholders. An accountholder has *one or more* accounts.
- A business partnership account has *one or more* accountholders. An accountholder has *one or more* accounts.

In each case, we must specify both the number of accountholders that can be linked to an account, and also the number of accounts that can be linked to an accountholder. It is important to model these constraints correctly, as they may determine whether or not an operation will be permitted to execute in the software. A badly specified system might incorrectly allow an unauthorized second person to draw money from a sole account. Alternatively, it might prevent a legitimate customer from being able to draw money from a joint account. The multiplicity of an association defines upper and lower limits on the number of other instances to which any one object may be linked.

We already know that in the Agate case study, each client has one and only one member of staff assigned as `staffContact`, while each member of staff may be assigned to zero or more clients. This is shown in Fig. 7.7, where each end of the association is now qualified by its multiplicity. Thus the possible number of clients allocated to a staff member ranges from 'zero' to 'any number', while the possible number of staff members allocated to a client must be 'exactly one'.

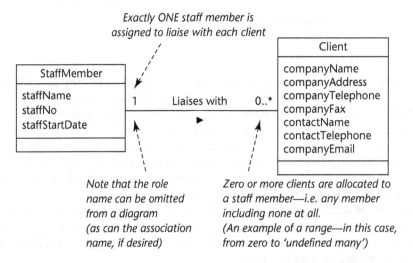

Figure 7.7 Multiplicity of the association between Client and StaffMember.

The statement of multiplicity at each end of an association is known as a *multiplicity string*. To be useful, the notation must cater for all possible multiplicities, not just 'exactly one' and 'zero or more'. There are many variations that allow any range of values to be specified, for example 0..3, 1..5, 2..10, 3..*, or discrete values, such as 3, 5 or 19, or combinations of the two, for example 1,3,7..*. Normally, however, it is best not to restrict the multiplicity unnecessarily. Multiplicity strings are formally defined in the BNF syntax of the UML spec as shown in Fig 7.8.

```
<multiplicity> ::= <multiplicity-range>

<multiplicity-range> ::= [<lower>'..'] <upper>

<lower> ::= <integer> | <value-specification>

<upper> ::= '*' | <value-specification>
```

Figure 7.8 BNF definition of the syntax for multiplicity strings.

(Note that for simplicity's sake, we have omitted from this definition the optional features for ordered sequences and unique values.) Figs 7.9–7.11 show some of the variations in practice (although these examples are not exhaustive).

Association multiplicity conveys important information about the structure of the problem domain. Different assumptions about multiplicity have significant effects on the software design. If association multiplicities are modelled incorrectly, this may later make it impossible for the software to do things that users want it to do.

Figure 7.9 A `Campaign` is conducted by zero or more `Adverts`, while each `Advert` belongs to exactly one `Campaign`.

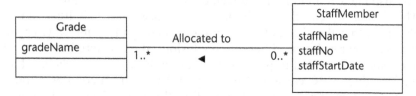

Figure 7.10 Every `StaffMember` is allocated to one or more `Grades`, while a `Grade` may have zero, one or more staff allocated to it.

Figure 7.11 A Poker `Hand` contains up to 7 `Cards`. Each `Card` dealt must be in only one `Hand` (although a card may still be undealt in the pack). This assumes no cheating!

7.3.8 Operations

Operations are the elements of common behaviour shared by all instances of a class. They are actions that can be carried out by, or on, an object. The classes modelled during requirements analysis represent real-world things and concepts, so their operations can be said to represent aspects of the behaviour of the same things and concepts. However, as the basic idea of an object-oriented system is that it should consist of independent, collaborating objects, it is probably better to understand operations as aspects of behaviour required to *simulate* the way that the application domain works. Another way of putting this is that operations are services that objects may be asked to perform by other objects.

For example, in the Agate case study, `StaffMember` needs an operation to calculate the amount of bonus pay due for a staff member, because other objects may request this information. And, since staff bonus is partly based on the profit of each campaign a member of staff has worked on, a `:StaffMember` object will ask the relevant `:Campaign` objects for this information. Therefore `Campaign` needs an operation to calculate the profit for each campaign.

The decision to model `StaffMember` with an operation to calculate its own bonus does not mean that we think a real member of staff has responsibility for calculating her own bonus. Nor are real (but abstract) campaigns capable of calculating their own profit–or anything else, for that matter. This is an appropriate way of simulating the real-world behaviour, but it does not imply that the model is identical to the reality. However, the ability to carry out these tasks is a requirement of the system and the behaviour must be located somewhere in the model.

From an analysis perspective, we do not need to be concerned with the details of how each operation will work. But we do need to make a good first guess at which operations to include. As a general rule, *primary* operations are excluded from the analysis model. These are: *constructor* operations, which create new instances of a class, *get* operations, which return attribute values in response to messages from other objects and *set* operations, which update attribute values.

We must also make a preliminary judgement about where to locate operations within classes. This is mainly based on thinking about class responsibilities, and does not necessarily mean that the classes will be implemented in the same way. From a design perspective, we may reach very different conclusions about where best to locate operations. Some may be delegated in part, or in full, to objects of other classes. Later in this chapter we introduce CRC cards and in Chapter 9 we introduce interaction diagrams, two techniques that can be used to help with the allocation of responsibilities to classes in a coherent manner.

Operations are defined for a class and are valid for every instance of the class. Figure 7.12 shows some examples of operations for the Agate case study.

Operation names are shown in the third compartment of the rectangular class symbol. As for attributes, operation names are written beginning with a lower-case letter. There is no separate notation for showing the operations of an object instance. In this respect, operations are unlike attributes and associations, in that they have exactly the same significance for instances as they do for classes.

The effects of an operation can include changing the characteristics of an object, for example, updating an attribute value. Another effect may be to change an object's links with other objects, for example assigning `:StaffMember` to work on `:Campaign`. (The creation of this link will be necessary for that member of staff to earn a bonus from the campaign profits.)

Some operations delegate part of their work to other objects. One example that we mentioned earlier is `StaffMember.calculateBonus()`. This operation needs data that is obtained by calling `Campaign.getCampaignContribution()` for each associated campaign in order to arrive at its result. Individual operations often represent only small parts of larger tasks that are distributed among many objects. A relatively even distribution of computational effort is desirable, and this is a big step on the way to building a modular system.

7.3.9 Operations and state

An object's operations and its state behaviour are related in two ways. First, it is only through the execution of an operation that an object can change its state. In fact, this is

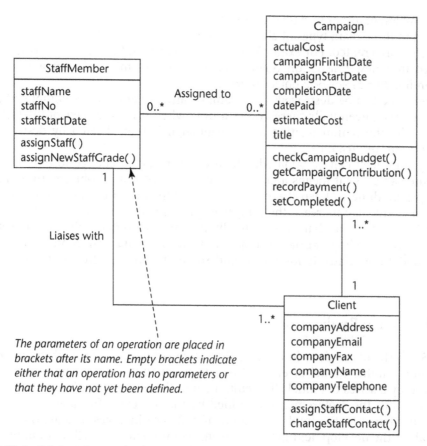

Figure 7.12 Partial class diagram for Agate, with some attributes and operations.

just another way of saying that an attribute cannot store or update its own values, nor can a link make or break itself. It also illustrates encapsulation in action, since it is only through invoking an object's operations that another object can get it to do anything at all–change its data, create or destroy links, or even respond to simple queries. Secondly, the way that an operation can respond when it is invoked by a message often depends on the object's current state. In the ATM cash card example described earlier, the behaviour of the withdraw() operation depends on whether yourCard is in the Active or the Barred state. In other words, it depends on the current value of the attributes dailyLimit and dayTotal.

Alternative courses of action, and the basis for choosing between them, are included in the detailed definition of an operation (we describe this in Chapter 10).

7.3.10 Stability of the analysis class diagram

The description of each class (its attributes, operations and associations–i.e. the specification of what it knows and what it can do) is likely to be relatively stable, and will probably only change as a result of major changes in the way that business itself operates. By contrast, object instances change frequently, reflecting the need for the system to maintain an up-to-date picture of a dynamic business environment. Instances are subject to three main types of change during system execution.

First, they are created. For example, when Agate undertakes a new campaign, details are stored in a new `Campaign` object. When a new member of staff is recruited, a corresponding `StaffMember` object is created.

Second, they can be destroyed. For example, after a campaign is completed and all invoices are paid, eventually there comes a time when it is no longer of interest to the company. All information relating to the campaign is then deleted by destroying the relevant `Campaign` instance.

Finally, an object can be updated, which either means a change to one or more of its attribute values, or it means a change to its links with other objects. In either case, this is typically done to keep the object in step with the thing that it represents. For example, a client may increase the budget for a campaign, in order to cover a longer run of a TV commercial than was originally planned. To reflect this, the budget value set in the corresponding `Campaign` object must also be changed. Many objects in the analysis model are relatively long-lived and some are updated frequently during their lifetime.

7.4 Use Case Realization

Realization is the name given in UML to the activity of developing an abstract model or element into another model or element that is closer to its implementation. Use cases are realized by a series of models that culminate in the implementation of software that adequately fulfils the requirements identified by the use case. To move from an initial use case ultimately to the implementation of software involves at least one iteration through all of the development activities, from requirements modelling to implementation. In this chapter, we are interested in producing an analysis model, and this consists mainly of the analysis class diagram. Initially, we will develop separate analysis class diagrams for each use case, based on the collaboration and using communication diagrams to refine our allocation of attributes and operations to classes. These separate use case class diagrams can then be combined into larger diagrams that together will comprise a class model for the application as a whole.

We will illustrate this with the use case `Add a new advert to a campaign`, introduced in Fig. 6.9. Figure 7.13 repeats the use case diagram, and the series of figures that follow show some of the alternative ways that the use case can be represented, viewing it both from different perspectives and at different levels of abstraction. Some of the notation used in the diagrams may not mean much yet, but do not worry about this. It will be explained step by step later in the chapter.

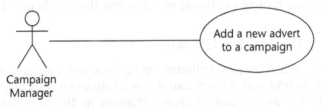

Figure 7.13 Use case diagram for `Add a new advert to a campaign`.

Among other things, use case realization involves the identification of a possible set of classes, together with an understanding of how those classes might interact to deliver the functionality of the use case. The set of classes is known as a *collaboration*. The simplest representation of a collaboration is shown in Fig. 7.14.

You can see immediately that this tells us little except that the collaboration has a relationship with a use case. However, this can be useful in itself. In particular, the *dependency* arrow signifies that the specification of the collaboration (together with the specifications of any classes or other components that it includes) must maintain a reference to the use case. Later, we will see many more examples of dependencies between one model element and another (this notation is particularly useful when the elements are in different packages).

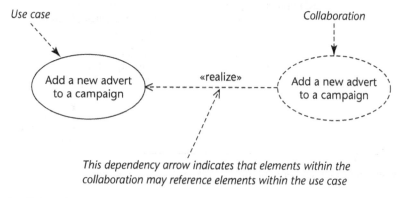

Figure 7.14 A collaboration can realize a specific use case.

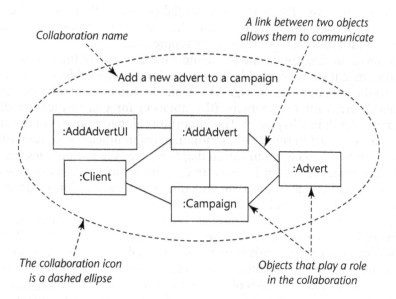

Figure 7.15 Collaboration for Add a new advert to a campaign.

Figure 7.15 gives a more detailed view of the collaboration, which shows the objects that participate in the collaboration and the links between them. These are the objects that will interact, when implemented as software, in such a way as to achieve the result

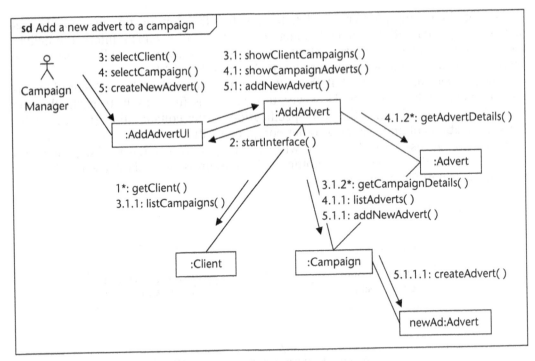

Figure 7.16 Communication diagram for `Add a new advert to a campaign`.

described by the use case. This view of the collaboration still doesn't tell us how they interact, nor does it show how they relate to other parts of the model. All details that are not directly relevant to the collaboration are suppressed.

A *communication diagram* is one of the most useful views of the internal details of a collaboration, since it shows explicitly the interaction between objects. Figure 7.16 adds interaction to the collaboration in Fig. 7.15. Don't be too concerned about making full sense of this diagram for the moment (the notation for communication diagrams is covered in more depth in Chapter 9). The important thing to notice is that it shows how the objects that take part in the collaboration may communicate with each other.

Interaction shown in a communication diagram takes the form of messages between objects, and the example shown here assumes quite a lot of understanding about the behaviour of the individual objects shown. Initial communication diagrams will not often be this detailed, as we will see later in this chapter.

Finally (for the time being, at any rate), a collaboration can be represented as a class diagram. Figure 7.17 shows a class diagram for this example (and, during a first iteration through requirements analysis, this is as far as we need to go). This has structural and notational similarities to the collaboration in Fig. 7.15 and the communication diagram in Fig. 7.16. There is a class for each object, some classes in the class diagram have associations that correspond to the links between objects in the communication diagram and the classes have operations that correspond to messages in the communication diagram.

In this example, however, even the obvious differences are perhaps more apparent than real. For example, this class diagram shows a lot of the internal detail of the classes.

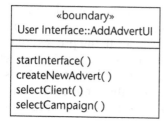

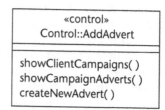

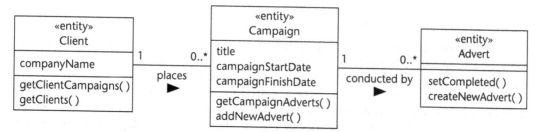

Figure 7.17 Analysis class diagram for `Add a new advert to a campaign`.

Collaborations and communication diagrams can show some (though not all) of these details if this is desired. Also, some links between objects in Fig. 7.15 have no corresponding association in the class diagram. The reason for this will be explained a little later in this chapter.

At this point, it is worth saying a little more about the purposes of all these diagrams. The collaboration icon in Fig. 7.14 is in itself simply a high-level abstraction that can stand for any of the other forms. The diagrams in Figs. 7.15–7.17 show some of the intermediate forms that realize a use case during the progressive and iterative development of the resulting software. Each form in this series is, in a sense, one step closer to executable code. Each also serves a particular modelling perspective. For instance, a collaboration identifies the participating objects and the links between them, but ignores messages and the internal details of objects. A communication diagram highlights interaction among a group of collaborating objects, although it can be hard to read the sequence of messages if the collaboration is complex. A class diagram ignores interaction, but shows the structure in more detail and usually shows a lot of the internal features of the classes. Collaborations can also be expressed in other ways that do not concern us so much from an analysis perspective–for example, interaction sequence diagrams hide most of the structure but display the sequence of messages with greater clarity (sequence diagrams are explained in Chapter 9). These other representations are useful for the design, test or implementation perspectives of the system model.

7.5 | Drawing a Class Diagram

7.5.1 Robustness analysis

There are several ways to produce an analysis class diagram for a use case, but we will mainly follow an approach known as robustness analysis, which was originally proposed by Rosenberg (1999). The essence of robustness analysis, and the reason for its name, is that the approach aims to define a set of classes that are robust enough to meet all the requirements of the use case. We will illustrate the process of developing an analysis class diagram in detail in Section 7.5.3. Later, in Section 7.6, we will introduce the Class–Responsibility–Collaboration (CRC) cards technique. CRC cards can be used either on their own or they can be used to complement the robustness analysis approach. Before going any further, however, it is necessary to explain the concept of analysis class stereotypes.

7.5.2 Analysis class stereotypes

These represent particular kinds of class that will be encountered again and again during analysis, and their use in modelling a use case is fundamental to the robustness analysis approach. (UML stereotypes were introduced in Chapter 5.)

Instances of a stereotyped class have a shared focus on certain kinds of task, which distinguishes them in a significant way from classes that are instances of another stereotype. It is often useful to identify this in our models. The everyday use of the word stereotype is not so very different. For example, if a friend says that the roles played by Arnold Schwarzenegger in his movies are quite stereotyped, you would probably understand that they think his characters are all similar to each other in certain ways, even though the plot and context may vary a lot from one film to another. Thus, if you know that Schwarzenegger is the star of a film that you are going to see, you already have some idea of what the film will be like, and also of some of the ways that it might differ from a Leonardo DiCaprio film.

UML is designed to be capable of extension, and developers can add new stereotypes where there is a clear need to do so. We need only concern ourselves at this point with three widely used analysis class stereotypes: *boundary*, *control* and *entity* classes. These date from the pre-UML work of Jacobson (Jacobson et al., 1992). Their use today in analysis modelling is recommended by a number of leading authors, including Rosenberg and Scott (2001), whose approach is based partly on these stereotypes, and Ambler (2004).

It is not always necessary to stereotype classes. Nor, if classes are stereotyped, is it always necessary to show the stereotype of a class on diagrams. Stereotypes are shown where they add useful meaning to a model, but their use is not obligatory. In many diagrams shown later in this book, the stereotype is omitted, either because it can be assumed from the context or because it has no specific relevance to the purpose of the diagram.

Boundary classes
Boundary classes 'model interaction between the system and its actors' (Jacobson et al., 1999). Since they are part of the requirements model, boundary classes are relatively abstract. They do not directly represent all the different sorts of interface widget that will be used in the implementation language. The design model may well do this later, but from an analysis perspective we are interested only in identifying the main logical interfaces with users and other systems. This may include interfaces with other software and also with physical devices such as printers, motors and sensors. Stereotyping these as boundary classes emphasizes that their main task is to manage the transfer of information across system boundaries. It also helps to partition the system, so that any changes to the interface or communication aspects of the system can be isolated from those parts of the system that provide the information storage or business logic.

The class `User Interface::AddAdvertUI` (shown in the communication diagram in Fig. 7.16 and in the class diagram in Fig. 7.17) is a typical boundary class. This style of writing the name shows that the class is `AddAdvertUI` (the `UI` is just an abbreviation for user interface) and it belongs to the `User Interface` package (the concept of packages was introduced in Chapter 5). When we write the package name in this way before the class name, it means that this class is imported from a different package from the one with which we are currently working. In this case, the current package is the `Agate Application` package, which contains the application requirements model, and thus consists only of domain objects and classes. As its name suggests, the `User Interface` package contains only user interface classes. While some of these may be developed specifically for the current application, they are placed in a separate package for ease of management.

If this is an early iteration of the analysis workflow, we are unlikely to know what the user interface will look like, how it will behave, or even the programming language or application package in which the software will be written. These are all design decisions. However, we know that some sort of interface is needed to manage communication with the user, and we can already identify its main responsibilities, modelled for now as operations. In effect, boundary classes shown in analysis models are little more than placeholders for the 'real' boundary classes that will be specified in much more detail in the design model.

On class diagrams and communication diagrams, the stereotype of a class can be shown in different ways. Figure 7.18 shows the different symbols for a boundary class.

Entity classes

Entity classes[1] model 'information and associated behaviour of some phenomenon or concept such as an individual, a real-life object or a real-life event' (Jacobson et al., 1999). The three classes `Client`, `Campaign` and `Advert` in Fig. 7.17 are all examples of entity classes (since these exist within the current package, their package name does not need to be made explicit). As a general rule, entity classes represent something from the application domain, external to the software system, about which the system must store some information. The thing they represent might be quite abstract, for example, a campaign, or it may be quite concrete, for example a member of staff.

Instances of an entity class usually require persistent storage of their information. This can sometimes help to decide whether an entity class is the appropriate modelling construct. For example, actors are not automatically represented as entity classes, although they can be when it is appropriate. Actors are within the application domain, external to the software system and important to its operation. But not all systems necessarily need to store information about their users, or need to model user behaviour. There are obvious exceptions to this, for example a system that monitors user access for security or audit purposes must store information about those users. In that case, the user would be modelled appropriately as an entity class as well as an actor, since the requirements for such a system would include storing information about users, monitoring their

---

1 Some readers may be tempted to confuse the concept of an entity class with the similarly named 'entity' in relational data modelling. There are similarities (e.g. entity classes may show the same kind of logical data structure that is revealed by relational data modelling), but there is also a crucial difference. Entity classes may have complex behaviour related to their information, whereas relational entities represent pure data structures with no behavioural aspect.

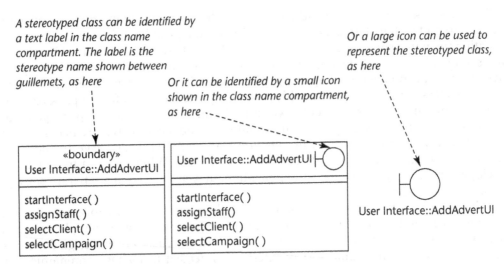

Figure 7.18 Alternative notations for the boundary class stereotype.

system access and tracking their actions while logged on to a network. Sometimes these are specialist applications in their own right. In any case, when actors are also modelled as entity classes this is because the software needs to store information about the people who use it, and not simply because they are actors in relation to the system. Figure 7.19 shows the symbols for an entity class.

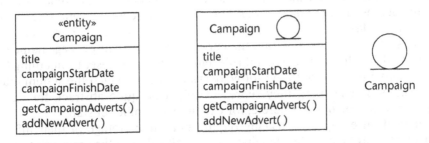

Figure 7.19 Alternative notations for an entity class.

Control classes

Control classes 'represent coordination, sequencing, transactions and control of other objects' (Jacobson et al., 1999). The class Control::AddAdvert in Fig. 7.17 is an example (again note the explicit package name). Figure 7.20 shows the symbols for a control class. In UP, it is generally recommended that there should be a control class for each use case. Some authors, for example, Ambler (2004), recommend one control class for each business rule, but ultimately the number of control classes that get implemented will be a design decision. Control classes represent the calculation and scheduling aspects of the logic of their use cases—at any rate, those parts that are not specific to the behaviour of a particular entity class and that are specific to the use case. Meanwhile the boundary class represents interaction with the user and the entity classes represent the behaviour of things in the application domain and storage of information that is

«control» Control::AddAdvert	Control::AddAdvert	
showClientCampaigns( ) showCampaignAdverts( ) createNewAdvert( )	showClientCampaigns( ) showCampaignAdverts( ) createNewAdvert( )	AddAdvert

Figure 7.20 Alternative notations for a control class.

directly associated with those things (possibly including some elements of calculation and scheduling).

In the next section we will examine the practical aspects of drawing a class diagram, in particular, where to look for the necessary information, and also a recommended sequence for carrying out the various tasks. However, neither the information sources nor the sequence of tasks are intended to be prescriptive. Nor do we try to cover every eventuality on every project. Experienced analysts will always use their own judgement on how to proceed in a given situation.

7.5.3 Identifying classes

The first practical step in use case realization is to identify potential classes that can provide the required functionality. In this section we illustrate how to do this by following a robustness analysis approach.

In parallel with analysing the static structure shown on class diagrams, we are also interested in the dynamic interaction among classes. This, too, can be derived from use cases and is shown on communication diagrams. Interaction is often further explored using sequence diagrams, especially where the interaction is complex. In practice, these are often developed side-by-side with the class diagrams. In this chapter, however, we will concentrate mainly on the notation and development of the class diagram. Object interaction is left for detailed consideration in Chapter 9.

Identifying the objects involved in a collaboration can be difficult at first, and takes some practice before the analyst can feel really comfortable with the process. Many texts, including the authoritative text on USDP (Jacobson et al., 1999), give little guidance for the novice on how to carry out the task. These authors suggest that a collaboration (i.e. the set of classes that it comprises) can be identified directly for a use case, and that, once the classes are known, the next step is to consider the interaction among the classes and so build a communication diagram. We believe that it is usually easier to identify classes through considering their interaction together with their static structure. But it is worth stressing again that first-cut models are often tentative, and may be refined and modified more than once during later iterations.

Since the starting point is the use case, an extended version of a use case description is repeated below (for simplicity, we ignore alternative courses).

The task is to find a set of classes that can interact to realize the use case. This means thinking about those things and concepts in the application domain that are important to the goals of the use case. We know from the use case diagram that the campaign manager is the actor. The use case description tells us how the system should respond to the actor's various inputs, such as selecting a client by name. The objective of this use case is to allow the manager to assign staff to a campaign.

Use case description: **Assign staff to work on a campaign**

Actor Action	System Response
1. None	2. Displays list of client names
3. The actor (a campaign manager) selects the client name	4. Lists the titles of all campaigns for that client
5. Selects the relevant campaign	6. Displays a list of all staff members not already allocated to this campaign
7. Highlights the staff members to be assigned to this campaign	8. Presents a message confirming that staff have been allocated

Let's begin by picking out the important things or concepts in the application domain. A first list might include: campaign manager, client name, campaigns, client, staff. But we are only interested in those about which the system must store some information or knowledge in order to achieve its objectives. The campaign manager will be modelled initially as an actor because we know that he or she is the user. It is possible that the system may need to encapsulate further knowledge about the campaign manager, for example, in order to ensure that only an authorized party can execute this use case, but we will leave that consideration to one side for the moment. We can also eliminate client name, since this is part of the description of a client. That leaves Client, Campaign and StaffMember in the collaboration.

Next, we begin work on a communication diagram using these classes. This will help us to see whether they are all needed, and whether any other, less obvious, classes are needed too. It will also help us to identify their structure. (Note that our use of communication diagrams in this chapter is limited to identifying classes for a use case. They are covered in greater depth in Chapter 9.)

Figure 7.21 shows an initial collaboration for this use case.[2] This is not yet a communication diagram (hence the differences in both detail and structure from the more highly developed diagram for Add a new advert to a campaign in Fig. 7.16. That, as we shall see over the next few pages, was the result of further analysis). So far, we have identified the main participating entity objects, their classes and some probable links that might carry suitable messages.

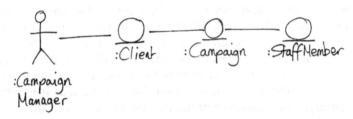

Figure 7.21 Initial collaboration for Assign staff to work on a campaign (not yet a communication diagram, as no messages are shown).

In Fig. 7.21, we have shown only entity object icons and links, because we have not yet thought about other details that will be added later. Once a class diagram has been derived from this relatively simple communication diagram, it will eventually grow quite

---

2   Hand-drawn diagrams are not necessarily rough-cut or transient, although it happens that this one is both. Most UML diagrams are drawn using a modelling tool, but this does not automatically lend authority. As long as a diagram adheres to the standard, any medium is as good as any other.

complex. Nevertheless it is a good start at abstracting some useful details from a description that may be cluttered with many irrelevant facts. As more detail is added to the class diagram, it will soon be much easier to absorb and less ambiguous than the corresponding text–subject, of course, to the modeller's skill and comprehension. In real life, of course, even first-cut models are often more complicated than this, and a great deal more effort may be needed to arrive at a preliminary understanding.

The diagram in Fig. 7.21 does not yet show any boundary or control objects, and these must be added. It is also based on certain assumptions about how the interaction between objects would take place, and we must make these assumptions explicit and question them. The diagram implies that there will be a linear flow of messages, along the following lines. An initial message could be directed to a Client, which is assumed to know its Campaigns. Each Campaign is also assumed to know which StaffMembers are currently assigned to it, and which are not.

Although we are primarily concerned with analysis questions at present, this scenario raises some serious design issues. In particular, it effectively locates control of the use case within the client object, which would give this class responsibility for tasks that are not directly relevant to the responsibilities of a Client. The introduction of a control object allows this responsibility to be encapsulated separately from the application domain knowledge that the entity classes represent. Figure 7.22 shows the collaboration after this refinement. Also, all links have now been routed centrally through the control object. This means that no entity class can directly request any information from any other entity class. Instead, each entity object must now ask the control object for any information it needs from an object of a different class, since the control object is the only one with a link that enables it to get the information. For example, the control object will need to keep track of which Client, Campaign and StaffMember objects participate in the current interaction. A boundary object has been added too. This will be responsible for the capture of input from the user and the presentation and display of results. In a limited sense, we have begun to design a software architecture that will allow a great deal of flexibility as to how the system will be implemented.

The collaboration in Fig. 7.22 is still drawn using the stereotype icon symbols for objects, but it could equally well be represented using rectangular object symbols, as shown in Fig. 7.23. This also adds the communication diagram frame, some messages and links

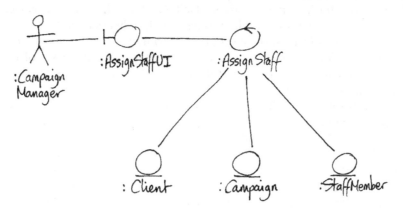

Figure 7.22 Boundary and control objects added to the collaboration, giving a different view on how the interaction might work.

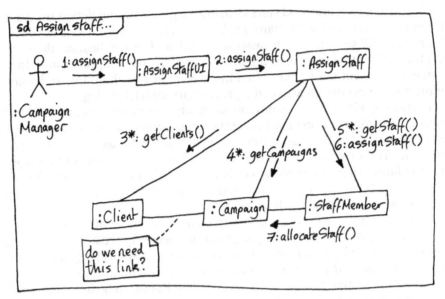

Figure 7.23 This communication diagram shows a more detailed version of the collaboration.

between :Client, :Campaign and :StaffMember. These links address the question of how a Client can be responsible for knowing its own Campaigns, or how a Campaign can know the StaffMembers who are assigned to it. Taken together, the sequence of messages in Fig. 7.23 shows how the interaction might work.

We can expand this as follows. First, the user interface starts and then the control object is instantiated. The control object then obtains a list of Clients, and we can assume that it asks the boundary object to display them, although this message is not yet shown. It then asks a Client for a list of its Campaigns. The link suggests that the Client may be able to obtain some information directly from the Campaign objects themselves (perhaps which ones are associated with the Client, along with their names or status), but this message, too, is not yet shown. The control object then directly asks a selected Campaign for information about itself. Next, it asks StaffMembers for some of their details (perhaps to find out which ones are already assigned to a Campaign). At each point, since much of the information flow is routed through the control object, we can assume that it asks the boundary object to display a chunk or set of information. Finally, the control object instructs each selected StaffMember to assign itself, which it does by sending messages to the Campaign.

Figure 7.23 illustrates a number of general notational points. The object symbols in a collaboration or communication diagram represent the lifelines of individual object instances, not classes. This is indicated by the colons before each class name; remember that these indicate anonymous instances rather than classes. Class names are always written in the singular, although we know there are many staff, campaigns, adverts, etc. This convention reinforces the view of a class as a descriptor for a collection of objects, rather than the collection itself. Another convention (derived from object-oriented programming style) is that most names are written in lower case, but classes are capitalized at the beginning of the name. Multiple words are run together, punctuated by upper case letters at the start of each new word to improve readability: for example, the control class `AssignStaff`. Note, however, that use case names, such as `Assign staff to work on a campaign`, are written in sentence case, while operation names, such as `getClients`, are run together with initial capitals after the first word. An asterisk (*) indicates that a message may be iterated. For example `3*:get clients()` refers to a request for the details of more than one client. Iteration in sequence and collaboration diagrams are explained further in Chapter 9.

Figure 7.24 shows almost the same collaboration using the stereotype icon notation. Other changes are minor. We have added messages between `Client` and `Campaign` and between `Campaign` and `StaffMember`. We have arrived at an initial judgement about how to distribute the responsibility for this use case among the various collaborating objects (this is shown by the sequence and labelling of the messages).

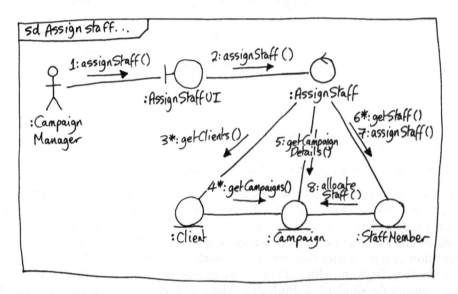

Figure 7.24 Alternative notation for a slightly refined version of the diagram.

The final diagram (for the moment) in this set is shown in Fig. 7.25. In this version, the first message is sent by the control object to request a list of clients. This allows the interface object to be populated with the client list immediately upon instantiation. The preliminary versions of the interaction shown in Figs 7.23 and 7.24 focused on how the entity classes might share responsibilities, but did not adequately address the flow of information to and from the actor. Several other changes to the sequence of messages follow from more careful analysis of the scenario. Even this is still a simplified version of the full interaction, with many details left to be determined by further analysis. For example, we will still need to think about the signatures of the operations that the messages will call. This will be important to understanding the interaction as a whole. But, while some issues remain to be clarified, this diagram approaches the level of understanding that we need in order to develop a robust class model capable of fully supporting the use case. But remember, too, that no decisions made at this stage are necessarily final, and we may well need to make several iterations through this activity before we achieve a full understanding.

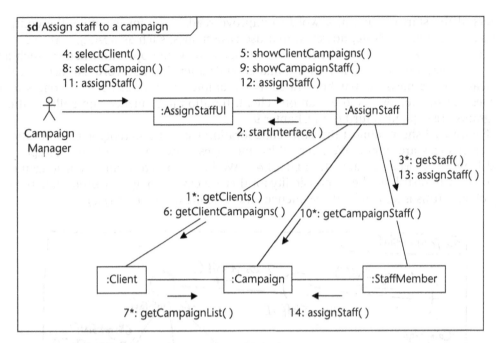

Figure 7.25 Near-final communication diagram for `Assign staff to work on a campaign`.

7.5.4 From communication diagram to class diagram

The next step is to produce a class diagram that corresponds to each communication diagram, which in turn is a realization of a use case. The class diagram that corresponds to the use case `Assign staff to work on a campaign` is shown in Fig. 7.26.

Provided that the communication diagrams are the result of reasonably careful analysis, the transition is not usually difficult. For a start, there are some obvious similarities between the two diagrams, although there are also some important differences.

First, consider the similarities. Both show class or object symbols joined by connecting lines. In general, a class diagram has more or less the same structure as the corresponding communication diagram. In particular, both should show classes or objects of the same types. Any of the three analysis stereotype notations for a class can be used on either diagram, and stereotype labels (if used) can also be omitted from individual classes, or from an entire diagram.

Next, we examine the differences, some of which are less obvious than others. Perhaps the most obvious difference is that an actor is often shown on a communication diagram, but rarely shown on a class diagram. This is because the communication diagram represents a particular interaction (for example, one that supports a specific path through a single use case) and the actor is an important part of this interaction. Actors *can* be shown on a class or object diagram when necessary, and they usually *are* if the actor is to be represented by a class—we mentioned this possibility earlier, in the discussion about entity classes in Section 7.5.2. However, a class diagram shows the more enduring structure of associations among the classes and frequently supports a number of different interactions that may represent several different use cases.

Some subtler details are associated with this change in conceptual emphasis. First, a communication diagram contains only object instances, while a class diagram (as its

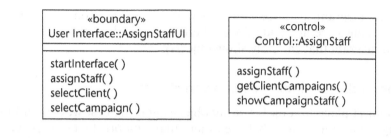

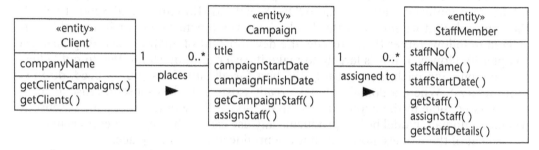

Figure 7.26 Class diagram for the use case Assign staff to work on a campaign.

name suggests) usually contains only classes. This is visible (but maybe not obvious) in the names given to the class and object symbols on each diagram. A class diagram can contain instances too, but this is relatively unusual in practice. Another difference is that connections between object symbols on a communication diagram symbolize links, while connections on a class diagram stand for associations between classes. This is why some links have not been shown on the class diagram—those between AssignStaffUI and AssignStaff and between AssignStaff and Client. Transient boundary and control objects like these are created only when needed during the execution of the software, while entity objects and their links normally endure beyond one cycle of execution, and probably therefore require persistent storage. But the classes that boundary and control objects instantiate are important aspects of the requirements, and so they are still included in the class diagram. As the model develops, we can anticipate that these classes will be located in separate packages. But, since the class diagram is essentially a model of static structure, we take the view that their transient links do not need to be modelled in an analysis class diagram; hence their omission here. By contrast, a communication diagram shows the dynamic interaction of a group of objects and thus every link needed for message passing is shown.

Next, the labelled arrows alongside links represent messages between objects. On a class diagram, associations are usually labelled, but messages are not shown.

Finally, there are differences in the class and object symbols. Although any stereotype symbol can be used on either diagram, there are differences in this notation. When the rectangular box variant of the notation is used in a communication diagram it represents the lifeline of an object instance rather than a class, is normally undivided and contains only the class name (optionally, together with the object name). On a class diagram, the symbol is usually divided into three compartments that contain in turn the class name (optionally, together with its stereotype), its attributes and its operations (but all except the class name can be omitted if desired). The style of instance names also differs slightly.

On a class or object diagram, instance names are underlined, while on a communication diagram instance names are not underlined (there is no need to distinguish an object from a class on a diagram that can only show objects).

7.5.5 Other approaches to finding objects and classes

Use cases are the best place to look for entity objects, and the best way to find them is through thinking about interactions between them that support the use case, but there are other approaches. One is to first develop a domain model. For example, the domain model is a significant feature of the ICONIX method (Rosenberg and Scott, 1999). In the approach that we follow in this book, the development of a domain model is considered to follow, rather than precede, the development of analysis class diagrams (see Chapter 8). However, this is largely to make it easier to understand. We do not believe that any one approach is necessarily the best for all situations (nor, indeed, do most other writers). Where a domain model already exists, it makes sense to reuse as many classes as possible in the application analysis model. Sometimes it may make sense to produce a domain model before producing any use cases. The key to success is iterative refinement of the models, however they are produced in the first place.

It is worth reviewing any background documentation gathered during the fact-finding stage. A second reading, after an initial attempt at class modelling, can discover more classes as a result of your clearer understanding of the problem.

Ideally, user representatives will be closely involved in discussing and developing the class diagram. Nowadays users often work alongside professional analysts as part of the project team. Most projects are a learning experience for everyone involved, so it is not unusual for users' understanding of their own business activity to grow and develop, and it is likely that users will identify a number of additional classes that were not apparent at first.

Your own intuition is another useful source, together with that of colleagues. And you can look for analysis patterns (an advanced technique that we will introduce in Chapter 8).

With experience these can all give guidance, but always check your intuitions with someone who knows the business well. Similarities to other projects can lead the developer to overlook important differences. As an analyst, you should remember at all times that users are the experts on the business and on what the software system should do. Your role is to make users aware of the possibilities offered by modern information systems, and to help translate their requests into a system that meets as many of their needs as possible.

However you approach the identification of classes, it helps to have a general idea of what you are looking for. Some pointers have been developed over the years that help to discriminate between likely classes and unlikely ones. Rumbaugh et al. (1991) usefully categorized the kinds of things and concepts that are more likely than others to need representation as an entity object or class.

The main categories shown in Fig. 7.27 are based on their categories. It is best to keep a list of potential classes, with a brief description for each. A rough list is fine; it will grow over time, but many items will also be crossed out and removed. When you enter your models into a CASE tool repository (CASE tools are discussed in Chapter 3), these textual descriptions and definitions will be an important supplement to the diagrams. Check your list carefully as it grows. Even the most experienced analyst will

Category	Examples
People	Mr Harmsworth (a campaign manager), Dilip (a copywriter)
Organizations	Jones & Co (a forklift truck distributor), the Soong Motor Company, Agate's Creative Department
Structures	Team, project, campaign, assembly
Physical things	Fork-lift truck, electric drill, tube of toothpaste
Abstractions of people	Employee, supervisor, customer, client
Abstractions of physical things	Wheeled vehicle, hand tool, retail goods
Conceptual things	Campaign, employee, rule, team, project, customer, qualification
Enduring relationships between members of other categories	Sale, purchase, contract, campaign, agreement, assembly, employment

Figure 7.27 Looking for objects.

probably include at first some potential classes that may cause confusion later if they are retained in the model.

Next, there are some guidelines to help you to prune out unsuitable candidate classes. For each item on the list, ask yourself the following questions.

Is it beyond the scope of the system?

You may have included people, things or concepts that are not strictly necessary to describe the application domain that you are investigating. Remove these from your list. They may become clear from use case descriptions or from collaborations, but do not worry if the odd one slips through. There will be lots of opportunities to catch them later on. Remember, too, that only the users can finally set the system boundary.

Beginners often include classes that represent the people who operate the current system, perhaps because their names or job titles appear in a use case description. It is frequently necessary to model the operators of the system as classes, but only when this is necessary to meet a requirement. An example might be an office worker handling a company's pension scheme, who is also a member of the scheme. In this case, you may need to model them as a member of the scheme (i.e. a potential object), as well as an operator of the system (i.e. an actor). Another example (which we will discuss further in Chapter 19) is when the system requirements include security restrictions on which users are permitted to carry out certain transactions. In this case we would model them as an operator (an entity class called `Operator`, that is, or something similar) in order to be able to assign access rights to certain parts of the system or to permit some users to be able to create, update or delete data that other users can only view. However, unless there is a clear system requirement for actors to be represented as objects, there is generally no need to do so.

Does it refer to the system as a whole?

You may include an item that refers to the system you are modelling, or to the department or organization that contains it. It is not usually necessary for a model to contain a class that represents the entire system.

Does it duplicate another class?

You may include two items that are really synonyms. If you are not sure, check with your users exactly what they understand by each item on the list. This should become clearer as you write the descriptions for each class.

Is it too vague?

Eliminate any potential classes for which you are unable to write a clear description, unless you are sure this is only because of a temporary lack of information.

Is it too specific?

Unless you are modelling a specific interaction (for example, when drawing an initial communication diagram), it is usually better to model classes, rather than instances. Think carefully about any items on your list that are unique. For example, a company may currently have only one supplier, tempting you to model the specific supplier. But a supplier might be replaced tomorrow for business reasons. A class named Supplier would be unaffected by this, whereas one modelled too closely on the specific company might require modification.

Is it too tied up with physical inputs and outputs?

Avoid modelling things that depend closely on the physical way that system inputs and outputs are currently handled. For example, the current system may involve telephone enquiries and printed order forms, but it is much too early to make a decision on whether they will play the same role in the new system. Try to think of names that express a logical meaning rather than a physical implementation: Enquiry and Order would be acceptable alternatives.

On the other hand, physical objects that are an essential part of the business activity should be included. This can depend a lot on context—Truck may be an acceptable class in a system to co-ordinate vehicles used for parcel deliveries, but irrelevant in another system that records customer payments for the deliveries, even though invoices and payments might travel on the same truck.

Is it really an attribute?

An attribute is a characteristic of a class. What makes this a problem is that an item that is an attribute in one domain may be a class in another, depending on the requirements. So some items on your potential class list may be better modelled as attributes. The primary test is this: does the item only have meaning as a description or qualification of another item? To illustrate this, we will look at examples that show how the significance of a date can vary between two different application domains.

In the Agate case study, the significance of a staff member's start date is to allow appropriate salary, bonus and grading calculations to be carried out. It would therefore be appropriate to model staffStartDate as a single attribute of StaffMember. But now consider a weather forecasting agency, keeping daily records of atmospheric conditions, and producing analyses for different weeks, months and years. Each date may be described by many other variables, e.g. maximum, minimum and average temperature, hours of sunshine, total precipitation, average windspeed, etc. These analyses might also require separate attributes for day of the week, month and year. We might then choose to model a Date class, with the other variables as its attributes.

Is it really an operation?

An operation is an action, a responsibility of a class. This can also be confusing, as some actions may be better modelled as classes. It is particularly easy to confuse the two if the use case descriptions are ambiguous. For an example of an action that can be considered as a class, consider a sale transaction. Whenever you buy something in a shop (a new CD, say), some sort of record is kept of the sale. The nature of this record depends on how the shop intends to use the information. This, in turn, determines whether we should model the sale as a class or as an operation. There are two considerations that might make a sale transaction a class rather than an operation.

- A sale may have characteristics of its own, which would be best modelled as attributes of a class, e.g. value, date, etc.
- There may be a requirement for the system to remember particular sales over a period of time, e.g. in order to respond to warranty claims or to audit the shop's accounts.

If there is no requirement to record a history made up of individual sales, or to describe sales in terms of their value, date, etc. it may make more sense to model them as an operation of another class, perhaps as `StockItem.sell()`. This would probably be quite adequate if the shopkeeper was only interested in knowing the total value or quantity sold for each item. For each action on your preliminary class list, consider whether these criteria apply. If they do not, it may be an operation rather than a class.

Is it really an association?

An association is a relationship of some kind between two classes. But this too can be confusing as we may prefer to represent some relationships as classes. The sales transaction can also be counted as an example of this (a sale is both an action and a relationship). How do we decide which relationships to represent as associations, and which as classes? This can sometimes be a difficult and complex problem. You can apply a similar test to those described above for attributes and operations. If an association is something we need to describe in terms of further characteristics–if it is apparent that it has attributes of its own–then it should be modelled as a class. If it only has meaning as a relationship between two classes, leave it as an association.

But the best answer at this stage is not to spend too long on making the distinction. The important thing during requirements analysis is to make sure all significant relationships are modelled, whether as classes or associations. We can review our judgements later when we understand more about the situation. Indeed, following the transition from requirements modelling to software design, it is often the case that certain types of association may be changed into classes, or further classes may be added to help implement the association effectively (this is covered in Chapter 14).

7.5.6 Adding and locating attributes

Many attributes will already appear in the use case descriptions. Others will become apparent as you think about your model in more detail. The simple rule is that attributes should be placed in the class they describe. This usually presents few problems. For example, the attributes `staffNo`, `staffName` and `staffStartDate` all clearly describe a member of staff, so should be placed in the `Staff` class.

Sometimes it is more difficult to identify the correct class for an attribute. The attribute may not properly belong to any of the classes you have already identified. An example will help to illustrate this. Consider this extract from an interview with Amarjeet Grewal (Agate Finance Director):

> **Amarjeet Grewal:** Agate's pay structure is based on distinct grades. Directors and managers negotiate their own salaries, but other staff are placed on a grade that determines their basic salary. You can only change grade as a result of an appraisal with your line manager.

> *(A member of staff has one grade at a time, but it sounds like they may have several previous grades, and several members of staff may be on the same grade at the same time. Staff and Grade are probably classes with an association between them.)*

> The basic salary for each grade is fixed, usually for a year at a time. Every year after the final accounts are closed, I review the grade rates with the Managing Director, and we increase them roughly in line with inflation.

> *(A grade has only one rate at a time, though it can change, and each rate has a money value. Grade may have a rate attribute.)*

> If the company has performed well, we increase the rates by more than the rate of inflation. In case there are any queries, either from an employee or from the Tax Office, it is most important that we keep accurate records of every employee's grades; that is, the rates for all present and all past grades, and the dates these came into force.

> *(There's quite a lot in this bit. A grade may have several previous rates, which suggests either that Grade has multiple rate attributes, or that Rate and Grade are distinct classes. If the latter, then Rate must have a date attribute, since we need to know when it took effect. We must also record when a member of staff changes to a grade, and possibly also when they change from a grade, which suggests one or two more date attributes. Each grade has a date it came into force – another attribute.)*

> It's actually quite complicated, because you can have an employee who changes to several different grades, one after the other, and then the rate for each grade also changes each year. So, for each employee, I have to be able to tell exactly what grade they were on for every day they have worked for the company, and also what the rate for each grade was when they were on it. This is all quite separate from bonus, which is calculated independently each year. For creative staff, bonus is based on the profits from each campaign they have worked on, and for other staff we use an average profit figure for all campaigns.

This is necessarily tentative, but a preliminary analysis yields the following list of classes and attributes:

- classes: `StaffMember`, `Grade`, `Rate`
- attributes: `gradeStartDate`, `gradeFinishDate`, `rateStartDate`, `rateFinish-Date`, `rateValue`.

In order to be reasonably lifelike, we can assume some other attributes not given above, such as `staffName` and `gradeDescription`, and also some other operations, such as `assignNewStaffGrade` and `assignLatestGradeRate`. An initial, though incomplete, class diagram might then look like the one in Fig. 7.28. One problem is where to put the attributes `gradeStartDate` and `gradeFinishDate`. These could be placed in `Grade`, but this would commit it to recording multiple start and finish dates. There may be also many members of staff associated with a grade. The computer system must be able to identify the member of staff to which each date applies, so the structure of dates

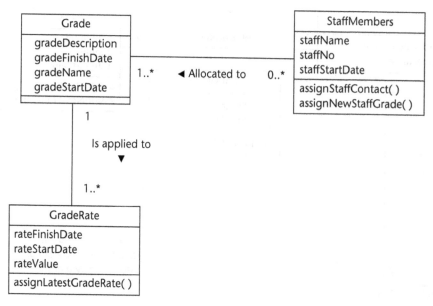

Figure 7.28 Partially completed Agate class diagram.

that might need to be stored could grow quite complex. A similar problem occurs if date attributes are placed in `Staff`. The explanation for this difficulty is that these attributes do not describe either a member of staff or a grade in isolation. They only have meaning as a description of the link between a specific member of staff and a specific grade. Thus, the clearest answer is to create an additional class (called an association class) specifically to provide these attributes with a home. This is shown in Fig. 7.29.

Some readers may be familiar with the relational database technique known as normalization, a technique that provides a rigorous guide to placing attributes in tables (or relations) and ensures minimum redundancy of data. The case illustrated is an example of normalization in practice, but a full treatment of the underlying theory is beyond the scope of this book. Normalization is used in object-oriented data design (this is discussed in Chapter 18) but on the whole, object-oriented approaches concentrate on capturing the structure of the world as perceived by the system's users. Unnormalized relations are therefore often acceptable in an object model, provided that they correspond accurately to users' intuitions about how their business activities are organized.

7.5.7 Adding associations

You can find some associations by considering logical relationships among the classes in the model. Associations may be found in use case descriptions and other text descriptions of the application domain, as stative verbs (which express a permanent or enduring relationship) or as actions that need to be remembered by the system. 'Customers *are responsible for* the conduct of their account' is an example of the first, while 'purchasers *place orders*' is an example of the second.

But this is not a very reliable way of finding associations. Some will not be mentioned at all, while others may be too easily confused with classes, attributes or operations. With practice, the most important ones will be found fairly easily, and for the moment it

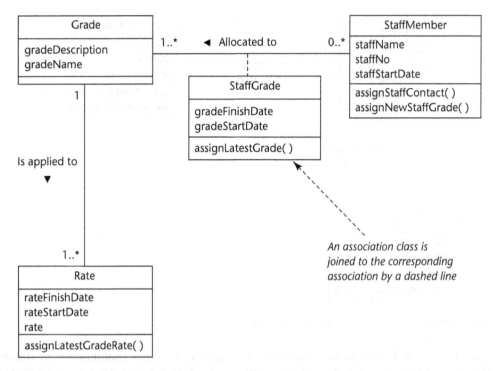

Figure 7.29 An association class gives a home to attributes that properly belong to a link between two objects.

is not important if some are missed. A full understanding of the associations in a class model can only be reached later by analysing the interaction between different classes. Chapter 9 describes how to model class interaction.

7.5.8 Determining multiplicity

Since association multiplicities represent constraints on the way users carry out their business activities, it is important to get these right, and the only way to do this is to question users about each association in turn. This is true even when the existence and character of the association have been inferred from user documents. An analyst should always check what is said in documents, in case it is ambiguous, erroneous or out of date.

> **Rosanne Martel:** So let me be clear about this. A client must have exactly one staff contact, but a member of staff can be contact for no clients, one client or several clients. Is there an upper limit on that? A campaign must have one client, but a client can have many campaigns. Can you have a client with no campaigns–say, a new client who hasn't given you any business yet?

7.5.9 Finding operations

Operations are really a more detailed breakdown of the high-level system responsibilities already modelled as use cases. An operation can be thought of as a small contribution of one class to achieving the larger task represented by a whole use case. They are sometimes found as action verbs in use case descriptions, but this picture is likely to be fairly incomplete until the interaction between classes has been understood in more depth. Chapter 9 describes how to model class interaction. So, as with associations, do not worry if your first attempt has gaps.

7.5.10 Preliminary allocation of operations

Before attempting to allocate operations to specific classes, it is worth remembering that each entity class is only a representation of something in the application domain. As an analyst, you are trying to build a logical model that helps to understand the domain, not necessarily a replica that is perfect in every detail. Two guidelines help in deciding which class to locate each operation in, but there is not a single answer—only a satisfactory fit:

1. Imagine each class as an independent actor, responsible for doing or knowing certain things. For example, we might ask: 'What does a staff member need to know or need to be able to do in this system?'
2. Locate each operation in the same class as the data it needs to update or access. However, this is often problematic, as you may not have identified all the attributes yet.

As a general comment on this stage, the most important thing is not to expect to get things right at the first attempt. You will always need to revise your assumptions and models as your understanding grows.

7.6 Class Responsibility Collaboration Cards

Class Responsibility Collaboration (*CRC*) cards provide an effective technique for exploring the possible ways of allocating responsibilities to classes and the collaborations that are necessary to fulfil the responsibilities. They were invented by Beck and Cunningham (1989) while they were working together on a Smalltalk development project. They found it helpful to think first in terms of the overall responsibilities of a class rather than its individual operations. A responsibility is a high-level description of something a class can do. It reflects the knowledge or information that is available to that class, either stored within its own attributes or requested via collaboration with other classes, and also the services that it can offer to other objects. A responsibility may correspond to one or more operations. It can be difficult to determine the most appropriate choice of responsibilities for each class as there may be many alternatives and all appear to be equally justified.

CRC cards can be used at several different stages of a project for different purposes. For example, they can be used early in a project to aid the production of an initial class diagram and to develop a shared understanding of user requirements among the members of the team. Here we concentrate on their use in modelling object interaction. The format of a typical CRC card is shown in Fig. 7.30.

CRC cards are an aid to a group role-playing activity that is often fun to do. A useful spin-off is that this can support team building and help a team identity to emerge. Index cards are used in preference to pieces of paper because of their robustness and the limitations that their size (approximately 15 cm × 8 cm) imposes on the number of responsibilities and collaborations that can be effectively allocated to each class. A class

Class Name:	
Responsibilities	Collaborations
Responsibilities of a class are listed in this section	*Collaborations with other classes are listed here, together with a brief description of the purpose of the collaboration*

Figure 7.30 Format of a CRC card.

name is entered at the top of each card and responsibilities and collaborations are listed underneath as they become apparent. For the sake of clarity, each collaboration is normally listed next to the corresponding responsibility.

Wirfs-Brock et al. (1990) and others recommend the use of CRC cards to enact a system's response to particular scenarios. From a UML perspective, this corresponds to the use of CRC cards in analysing the object interaction that is triggered by a particular use case scenario. The process of using CRC cards is usually structured as follows:

- Conduct a brainstorming session to identify which objects are involved in the use case.
- Allocate each object to a team member who will play the role of that object.
- Act out the use case. This involves a series of negotiations among the objects (played by team members) to explore how responsibility can be allocated and to identify how the objects can collaborate with each other.
- Identify and record any missing or redundant objects.

Before beginning a CRC session it is important that all team members are briefed on the organization of the session. Some authors (Bellin and Simone, 1997) recommend that a CRC session should be preceded by a separate exercise that identifies all the classes for that part of the application to be analysed. The team members to whom these classes are allocated can then prepare for the role-playing exercise by considering in advance a first-cut allocation of responsibilities and identification of collaborations. Others prefer to combine all four steps into a single session and perform them for each use case in turn. Whatever approach is adopted, it is important to ensure that the environment in which the sessions take place is free from interruptions and conducive to the free flow of ideas (Hicks, 1991).

During a CRC card session, there must be an explicit strategy that helps to achieve an appropriate distribution of responsibilities among the classes. One simple but effective approach is to apply the rule that each object (or role-playing team member) should be as lazy as possible, refusing to take on any additional responsibility unless persuaded to do so by its fellow objects (the other role-playing team members). During a session conducted according to this rule, each role-player identifies the object that they feel is the most appropriate to take on each responsibility and attempts to persuade that object to accept the responsibility. For each responsibility that must be allocated, one object (one of the role-players) is eventually persuaded by the weight of rational argument to accept it. This process can help to highlight missing objects that are not explicitly referred to by the use case description.

An alternative strategy is for each object to be equally keen to take on a responsibility, with the final choice determined by negotiation. Irrespective of the strategy chosen, it is important that all team members understand the need for an effective distribution of responsibilities. When responsibilities can be allocated in several different ways, it is useful to role-play each allocation separately to determine which is the most appropriate. The aim normally is to minimize the number of messages that must be passed and their complexity, while also producing class definitions that are cohesive and well focused.

We illustrate how a CRC exercise might proceed by considering the use case `Add a new advert to a campaign`. The use description is repeated below for ease of reference.

> The campaign manager selects the required campaign for the client concerned and adds a new advert to the existing list of adverts for that campaign. The details of the advert are completed by the campaign manager.

This use case involves instances of `Client`, `Campaign` and `Advert`, each role played by a team member.

The first issue is how to identify which client is involved. In order to find the correct `Client` the Campaign Manager (an actor and therefore outside the system boundary from the perspective of this use case) needs access to the client's name. Providing a client name and any other details for that client is clearly a responsibility of the `Client` object.

Next, the Campaign Manager needs a list of the campaigns that are being run for that client. This list should include the title, start date and finish date for each campaign. Although a `Campaign` object holds details of the campaign, it is not clear which object (and hence which class) should be responsible for providing a list of campaigns for a client. The team member playing the `Campaign` object argues that although it knows which `Client` object commissioned it, it does not know which other `Campaign` objects have been commissioned by the same `Client`.

After some discussion, the `Client` object is persuaded to accept responsibility for providing a list of its campaigns and the `Campaign` object is persuaded that it should provide the information for this list. Once the Campaign Manager has obtained details of the campaigns for that client, she requests that the `Campaign` object provide a list of its adverts, to which list the new advert will be added. Since the `Campaign` object already has responsibility for looking after the list of adverts, it is reasonable for it to add the new advert to its list. In order to do this it must collaborate with the `Advert` class which, by definition, has responsibility for creating a new `Advert` object. This completes the analysis of the use case interaction, and the new responsibilities and collaborations that have been identified are added to the cards, as shown in Fig. 7.31. We have already seen a preliminary communication diagram in Fig. 7.16 and a class diagram developed from this use case in Fig. 7.17. The reader is invited to refer back to these to see how CRC cards relate to the development of a requirements model.

During a CRC session, the team can keep track of the relationships between classes by sticking the index cards on a large board and attaching pieces of thread or string to represent collaborations. This is particularly useful when CRC cards are used early in the development cycle to help produce a class diagram. The cards and pieces of thread can be a very effective prototype of the class diagram. CRC cards can also be extended in various ways. For example, superclasses and subclasses can be shown beneath the class name and some users of the technique also like to list attributes on the back of each card.

Class Name Client	
Responsibilities	Collaborations
Provide client information.	
Provide list of campaigns.	Campaign provides campaign details.

Class Name Campaign	
Responsibilities	Collaborations
Provide campaign information.	
Provide list of adverts.	Advert provides advert details.
Add a new advert.	Advert constructs new object.

Class Name Advert	
Responsibilities	Collaborations
Provide advert details.	
Construct adverts.	

Figure 7.31 CRC cards for the use case `Add a new advert to a campaign`.

7.7 Assembling the Analysis Class Diagram

The final step that we look at in this chapter is to assemble the various class diagrams that result from use case realization into a single analysis class diagram. This may consist of a single package of entity classes (the domain model), with boundary and control classes typically located in separate packages. With large systems, the domain model alone may comprise several distinct packages, each representing a different functional subsystem of the overall system.

There is usually little conceptual or technical difficulty in this step. All we really have to do is to place the various entity classes into a single class diagram. Where we find that we have defined the same class in different ways to meet the needs of different use cases, we simply assemble all of the operations and attributes into a single class definition. For example, consider the `Campaign` class as seen in relation to `Add a new advert to a campaign` and `Assign staff to work on a campaign`. Different use cases have suggested different operations. Putting these together results in a class that is capable of meeting the needs of both use cases. When we consider other use cases too, a more complete picture of the class emerges. The stages are illustrated in Fig. 7.32.

Integrating the various associations derived from different use cases can seem a little more problematic, but it is actually quite straightforward. The general rule is that if *any* use case requires an association, it should be included. Where there is an apparent

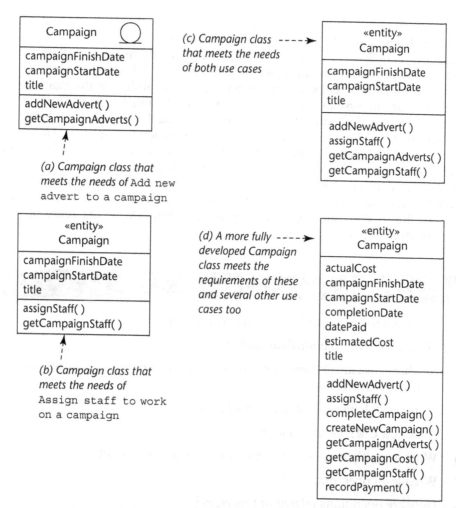

Figure 7.32 Putting together different partial definitions of a class.

conflict in the multiplicity values for an association, then clarification should be sought from users who understand the business rules of the organization.

Figure 7.32 illustrates the process of consolidation. A full analysis class diagram can be found in Case Study Chapter A3. This includes the requirements identified from many of the use cases modelled in Chapter 6.

7.8 Summary

In this chapter we have seen how to realize use cases, resulting in an initial version of the analysis class diagram. This is the main artefact of the analysis model. To do this, we followed the process known as robustness analysis to define boundary, control and entity classes that are closely based on the use cases in the requirements model. We have also seen how to use the CRC technique to help with the preliminary allocation of attributes and operations to classes. The important elements of the analysis model at this stage are analysis classes with attributes and operations, and associations that show the relationships between classes, together with any multiplicity constraints. Once it is complete, the analysis model will embody a good understanding of the main functional requirements for the system, in terms of its responsibilities for providing services to users and to other application systems. The analysis model also defines an initial logical architecture that will be a foundation for the design work that follows. However, the model is not yet complete. For detailed design to be undertaken successfully, we must next refine the analysis model. This is the subject of the next chapter, and will involve the identification of any latent generalization and aggregation associations and any opportunities for the application of analysis patterns. These can help to simplify the structure of the model, and may also suggest opportunities for the reuse of analysis components from previous models.

Review Questions

7.1 Explain what is meant by 'use case realization'.

7.2 Distinguish between attribute and value.

7.3 In what sense are classes generally more stable than their instances, and why is this usually the case?

7.4 Distinguish between link and association.

7.5 What is a UML analysis model?

7.6 What is multiplicity, and why can it be called a constraint?

7.7 What is an operation?

7.8 How are operations related to messages?

7.9 What is an attribute?

7.10 Section 7.4.6 discusses the creation and destruction of links but makes no mention of updating a link when it is changed. Why is this?

7.11 What is a collaboration?

7.12 How does a communication diagram differ from a class diagram?

7.13 Outline the main steps in developing a class diagram for a use case.

7.14 What are the advantages of team members acting the parts of objects when they are developing a set of CRC cards?

Case Study Work, Exercises and Projects

(The following transcript gives the first part of an interview that Rosanne Martel conducted with Hari Patel, the Factory Manager in charge of FoodCo's Beechfield factory. Read this through carefully, and then carry out the exercises that follow.)

Rosanne Martel: Hari, for the benefit of the tape, I'd be grateful if you could confirm that you're the manager responsible for all production at Beechfield.

Hari Patel: Yes, that's right.

RM: Good. Now the purpose of this interview is for me to find out about operations on the production lines. Can you tell me how this is organized?

HP: Sure. How much detail do you want?

RM: Can we start with those aspects that are common to all lines? That will give me a general feel, then if there are differences we can go into more detail later.

HP: OK, there are quite a few similarities. First, there are two main grades of shop-floor staff: operatives and supervisors. Different operatives have a range of skills, of course, but that doesn't affect the way the line works.

RM: How many operatives work on a line, and what do they actually do?

HP: There might be anything from around six operatives to over twenty, depending on the product. They really do all the actual work on the line, either by hand or operating a machine. This could be a semi-skilled labourer feeding in the different kinds of lettuce for salad packs, or a more skilled operator running one of the automatic mixing machines. In this factory, unlike Coppice and Watermead, the work is mostly quite unskilled.

RM: How many supervisors are there to each line?

HP: Just one. They are on full-time supervision duties, and they each look after one production line.

RM: Always the same line?

(Rosanne is trying to find out what possible classes there are. What else do you think her questions seek to discover?)

HP: Well, let's just say nobody has changed line in the last couple of years.

RM: How about the operatives—are they always on the same line too?

HP: No, we swap them around quite a bit. But it doesn't really matter what line an operative works on. They get paid piecework rates depending on the production run, and the rates are based on the job numbers that appear on their timesheets. There's a separate job number for each run.

RM: I'd like a copy of a timesheet please—preferably a real one with some data, if that's all right. We can blot out the name and staff number on the copy for confidentiality.

▶ *(A sensible request. Real documents with live data are an invaluable source of information. Figure B1.4 shows the timesheet that Rosanne collected.)*

HP: Sure. Remind me when we finish, and I'll get you one.

RM: Thanks. Now, does one line always produce the same product?

HP: No, that changes from one day to the next. The production planners produce a new schedule every Friday, and this lists all the production runs for each line for the following week.

RM: I'll take a copy of a production schedule too, please. So the supervisor finds out on Friday what their line is working on over the next week?

(Here Rosanne is checking where the inputs come from, as well as what they contain.)

HP: That's right.

RM: Good, I think I've got that clear. Now let's talk about what happens when people come in to work. Do all the lines start up first thing in the morning?

HP: Usually. Production runs generally last for a whole day if possible, or sometimes a half-day. Production Planning try to keep the change-overs simple, so they tend to schedule changes during breaks to avoid wasting productive time.

RM: The lines don't keep running all the time?

HP: No, they stop for coffee and meal breaks.

RM: What role does the line supervisor play in this?

HP: Well, they make sure the lines have enough raw materials, and they deal with minor emergencies. They also monitor output, liaise with production control, keep track of employee absences, and so on.

RM: Can we go through what a supervisor does on a typical run, please, step-by-step?

(Another sensible request. Asking someone to go over things again in more detail will often reveal aspects of the situation that are not obvious from a brief description.)

HP: First, they make sure everything is ready before the run starts. They check the storage area to see there is enough of each ingredient. If a long run is planned, you don't need all the ingredients ready at the beginning, but there has to be enough to keep the line running smoothly until the next supply drop. They also have to check if the staff allocated to that run have turned up. A line can usually run for a little while with one or two staff missing, but it's best to have everyone there from the start.

RM: How does a supervisor know what ingredients are required, and how many staff?

(A good analyst always probes to find out how, what, why, when, where and who.)

HP: Every run has a job card, with this information on it. The warehouse gets a copy of the job card too, so in theory they know what supplies to deliver, to which line and when they will be needed.

RM: Does that usually work?

HP: (Laughs) Sometimes!

RM: What if there aren't enough staff?

HP: Sometimes the supervisor can find a spare body on another line. Or they can run the line slower. You can manage with fewer staff if necessary, but productivity is a lot lower.

RM: Let's say the ingredients are all ready, and all the staff are there waiting to go. What next?

HP: The supervisor switches on the line, and then it's mostly troubleshooting and paperwork.

RM: What does the paperwork involve?

HP: Well, they start by taking the names of all the staff at the start of the run. They copy the job number from the job card to the production record sheet and all the timesheets. If it is the first time that operative has worked that week, then the supervisor makes out a new timesheet. When they start the line, they note the time on the production record sheet. Then they keep a rough note of anyone who leaves the line during a run, and how long they're absent.

RM: What kind of problems does the supervisor deal with?

HP: The main problem is if something goes wrong with the run. Say the line breaks down. They would have to call in maintenance, record the downtime while the line's not running, and try to find useful things for the staff to do while they're waiting for it to be repaired. If an ingredient runs out this could also halt the line, and might mean chasing the warehouse, or contacting the farm or an outside supplier. Sometimes people go missing, or leave early because they're sick. The supervisor has to find a replacement as quickly as possible.

RM: Right, now let's go to the end of a run. What information is formally recorded, and by whom?

HP: First the supervisor notes the finish time on the production record sheet.

RM: I'll have one of those too, please.

HP: OK, no problem.

(Figure B1.3 shows a blank production record sheet.)

HP: Next the supervisor phones for someone to come over from Production Control to verify the quantity produced and note this on the production record sheet. Then the supervisor totals all the absences, because if anyone has more than 15 minutes' absence, it's deducted from their total unless they have a good reason, say a medical certificate. Then they work out the total hours for each operative. If someone joined the line in mid-session they might not have a timesheet, so one is made out now and their hours are added in. By the time all that has been done, Production Control has usually checked out the total quantity produced, and this goes on the production record sheet. After that, it's just returning unused ingredients to the warehouse, tidying up the line ready for the next run, that kind of thing.

▶ **RM:** Thanks, that was really helpful. Now I'd like to ask about how the piecework formula works. Can you tell me what the calculation is?

HP: To be honest, I can never remember the exact formula. You'd do better asking a supervisor or someone from payroll . . .

Now carry out the following exercises, based on the information given in the interview transcript.

7.A Write descriptions for the following use cases:
- Start line run
- Record employee joining the line
- Record employee leaving the line
- Stop line
- Record line problem
- End line run

7.B From your use case descriptions, produce communication diagrams and then class diagrams.

7.C Produce a draft analysis class diagram, initially showing only classes and associations.

7.D Review your analysis class diagram together with the various intermediate models, and add any attributes and operations that you think are justified by your use cases. Make reasonable assumptions and add others that you think might be justified by other use cases not directly derived from the transcript.

Further Reading

The natural source for this subject, though now quite dated, is the 'Three Amigos' book on USDP (Jacobson et al., 1999). However this text, while authoritative, is not (in our view, at any rate) ideally suited to the novice requirements analyst.

Rosenberg and Scott (1999) and Rosenberg and Scott (2001) describe in a very accessible way a process that uses UML for object-oriented modelling. ICONIX, the development process described in these books, differs in many respects from the one followed in this book, but is very much in sympathy with our aim of producing a robust class model.

Larman (2005) also describes a process for using UML in object-oriented requirements modelling. Larman's approach is very different again from the one taken in this book, and also from that recommended by Rosenberg and Scott.

Agate Ltd

A3.1 | Introduction

In this chapter we analyse the Requirements Model described in Chapter A2 and produce a number of use case realizations. The activities involved in use case realization are described in Chapter 7 and involve the production of the following UML diagrams:

- communication diagrams
- class diagrams that realize individual use cases
- analysis class model.

Use cases are initially analysed as collaborations and as communication diagrams. This helps to identify classes involved in their realization. After individual use case realizations have been developed, a combined analysis class model is produced from them. A more detailed analysis class diagram is also included to indicate how the model develops as the use cases are analysed.

A3.2 | Use Case Realizations

The first use case analysed here is Add a new campaign (all the use cases are specified in Chapter A2). Figure A3.1 shows a collaboration that realizes the use case. Figure A3.2 shows the communication diagram, with boundary and control classes added.

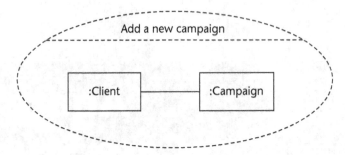

Figure A3.1 Collaboration for the use case `Add a new campaign`.

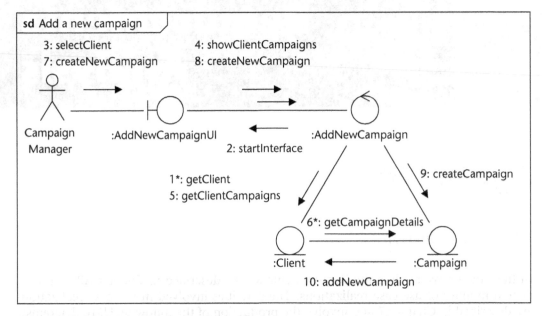

Figure A3.2 Communication diagram for the use case `Add a new campaign`.

Note that the initiation of the dialogue described by the use case is not modelled explicitly (apart from the inclusion of a `startInterface` message). Details such as this will be added later for this system, though in some projects it may be important to model them early on. The class diagram that supports this use case (and its collaboration) is shown in Fig. A3.3. Notice that the class `Campaign` includes only attributes that are required for the use case. The requirements analyst may identify the need for additional attributes (or functionality) while the use case is being analysed, but it is important to confirm any changes with the stakeholders. In these models we have named the constructor operation `createCampaign` to make it clear where in the interaction a new campaign object is created. If we were preparing a design model, the naming conventions used in object-oriented programming languages would be more appropriate.

Figures A3.4 to A3.12 show the development of the use case realizations for the use cases `Assign staff contact`, `Check campaign budget` and `Record completion of a campaign`. The use case `Record completion of a campaign` involves the production of a completion note. The boundary class `Completed CampaignPI` (we use the suffix PI to stand for printer interface) is responsible for printing the completion note.

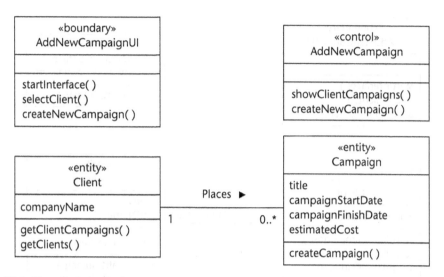

Figure A3.3 Class diagram for the use case `Add a new campaign`.

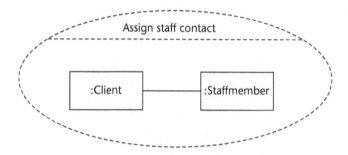

Figure A3.4 Collaboration for the use case `Assign staff contact`.

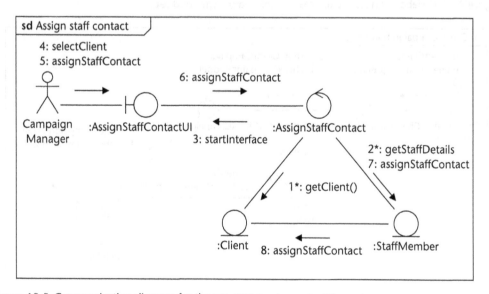

Figure A3.5 Communication diagram for the use case `Assign staff contact`.

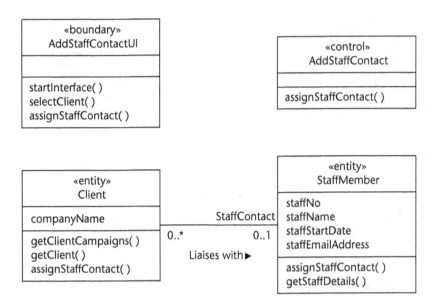

Figure A3.6 Class diagram for the use case `Assign staff contact`.

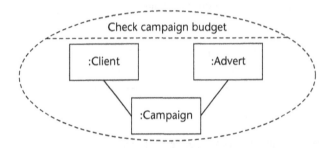

Figure A3.7 Collaboration for the use case `Check campaign budget`.

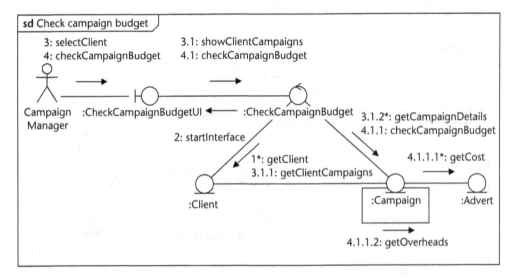

Figure A3.8 Communication diagram for the use case `Check campaign budget`.

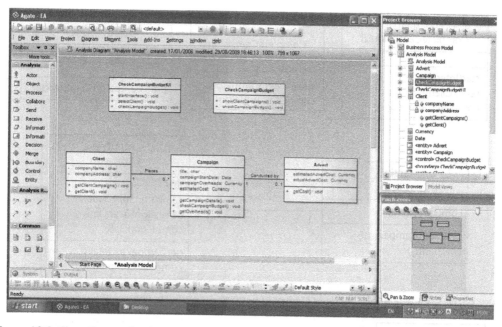

Figure A3.9 Class diagram for the use case Check campaign budget. This version has been drawn in the Enterprise Architect modelling tool.

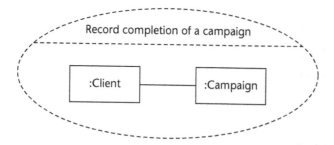

Figure A3.10 Collaboration for the use case Record completion of a campaign.

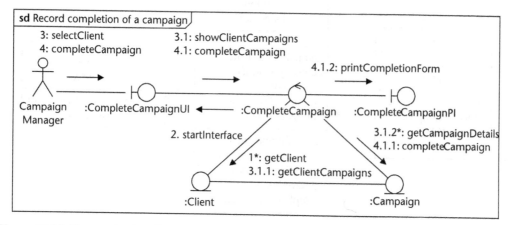

Figure A3.11 Communication diagram for the use case Record completion of campaign.

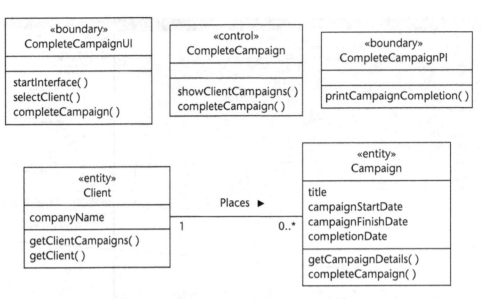

Figure A3.12 Class diagram for the use case `Record completion of campaign`.

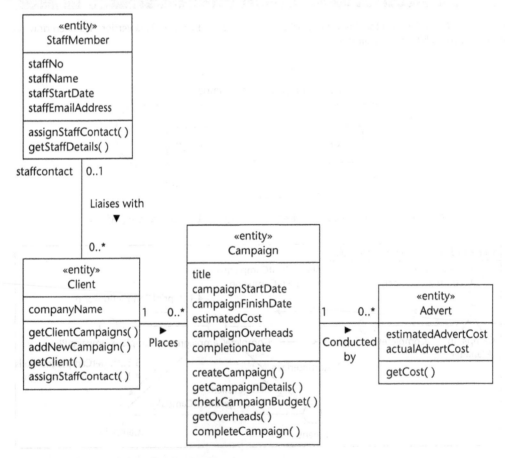

Figure A3.13 Combined class diagram for four use cases.

A3.3 | Assembling the Analysis Class Diagram

The class diagram in Fig. A3.13 has been assembled from the realizations for `Add a new campaign`, `Assign staff contact`, `Check campaign budget` and `Record completion of a campaign`.

Figure A3.14 shows a more fully developed class diagram that includes classes, attributes, operations and associations that have been identified from the other use cases in the `Campaign Management` package. This illustrates how a more detailed and complete picture of the analysis model is developed as the use cases are analysed. The use cases `Add a new advert to a campaign` and `Assign staff to work on a campaign` are analysed in Chapter 7. Their realizations are shown in Figs 7.17 and 7.26 respectively.

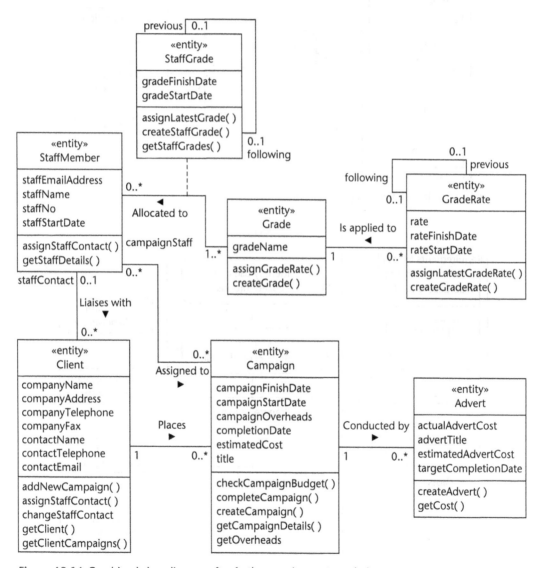

Figure A3.14 Combined class diagram after further requirements analysis.

A3.4 | Activities of Requirements Analysis

Figure A3.15 shows an activity diagram that illustrates the relationship between the requirements models and the products of requirements analysis. The activity diagram in Fig. A3.16 shows the main activities involved in use case realization.

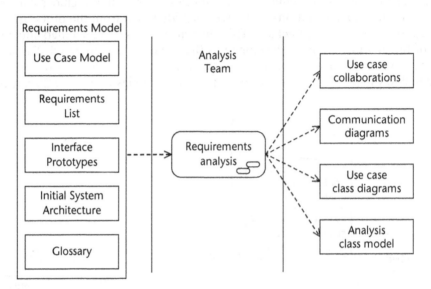

Figure A3.15 High-level activity diagram for `Requirements analysis`.

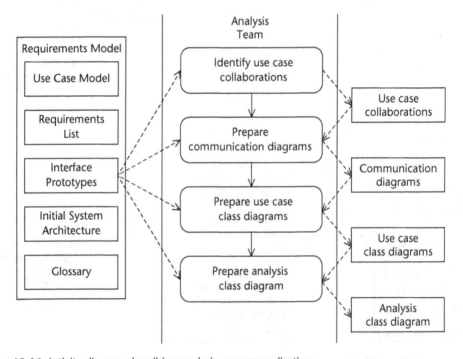

Figure A3.16 Activity diagram describing analysis use case realization.

Chapter 8

Refining the Requirements Model

LEARNING OBJECTIVES

In this chapter you will learn

☑ the significance of reuse in software development
☑ how object-oriented principles contribute to reuse
☑ how to identify and model generalization and composition
☑ one approach to modelling reusable components
☑ what the term *pattern* means in software development
☑ how analysis patterns can be used to help structure a model.

8.1 Introduction

The aim of refining and adding further structure to the analysis model is to create the conditions for reuse. This may mean the reuse of existing specifications or software originally written for an earlier system. Alternatively, the new specifications or software created for the current development project may be useful for other systems in the future. In either case, the model must be structured in such a way that reuse opportunities can be readily identified. While the practical benefits of reuse are more likely to be gained in the design and construction workflows, it is important to lay the groundwork in analysis since this is where the logical specification is created. Object-oriented analysis offers three main mechanisms for reuse:

- the fundamental abstraction mechanisms of generalization, composition, encapsulation and information hiding
- the specification of reusable software components
- the application of analysis patterns.

The key role of abstraction in object-orientation was explained in Chapter 4. Here we will consider how to introduce generalization and composition structures to the analysis class diagram introduced in Chapter 7.

Component-based development is based on the specification of composite structures that can function as reusable software components. Effective information hiding already requires that internal aspects of an object or structure should be hidden behind an interface. Components take this a step further, in that they are designed to be free standing. In this chapter we will introduce the UML notation for modelling components and their interfaces independently of their internal details. Components are also an important ingredient of the service-oriented architecture approach. (In Chapter 20, we will discuss web services, which are a common implementation of service-oriented architecture concepts.)

Since the late 1980s, the 'patterns' movement has offered a new way of capturing and communicating generalizable knowledge, particularly during analysis and design activities. In this chapter, we introduce the concept of patterns and show how to apply analysis patterns. (Later, in Chapters 12 and 15 respectively, we will discuss architecture and design patterns.)

Software and specification reuse requires careful management, since its application covers the entire lifecycle and is not restricted to a single workflow. We discuss this further in later chapters (particularly in Chapter 20).

8.2   Software and Specification Reuse

For several years now, a small revolution has been occurring in the software development world. Many people who work in the sector focus mainly on the assembly of systems, mainly from pre-existing components, rather than on the development of entire new software systems. Object-oriented development has always aimed to minimize the amount of new specification, design and programming work that must be done when a new system is built. In theory, the object-oriented approach made this possible through well-established principles of abstraction and information hiding, yet for many years large-scale reuse proved elusive. It is now at last becoming a reality. This is partly due to the familiar object-oriented principles mentioned above, but also due to newer ideas that have emerged from the patterns movement, and to the rise of component-based development and service-oriented architectures.

8.2.1 Why reuse?

Generally speaking, it is a waste of time and effort to produce from scratch anything that has already been produced elsewhere to a satisfactory standard. If you need a new light bulb for your room, it would not be very sensible to invent and build your own. Even if you have the knowledge, skill and equipment, the cost would be prohibitive.

This applies just as much to software development as to any other field of production. Good professionals have always learned as much as they could from their own experience, and from that of their colleagues. Programmers have built up extensive libraries that range from personal collections of useful subroutines to commercially distributed products that contain large numbers of industry-standard components. Examples of the latter include the DLL (Dynamic Link Library) files used in Microsoft Windows and the class libraries available to Java programmers. Designers have built up corresponding libraries that consist of fragments of designs, templates, patterns and frameworks. In most professional situations it makes very little sense to repeat work that others have done before.

8.2.2 Why has it been hard to achieve reuse?

Most authors agree that the promised benefits of software reuse were not fulfilled in practice until quite recently. Why was this so?

Reuse is not always appropriate
There are exceptions to the general rule that reuse is good. For example, students are frequently asked to solve, as if they were the very first person ever to do so, problems that have been completely solved by others before them. This makes good educational sense, since it is usually the process of enquiry that brings understanding, not just knowledge of the solution. This is one of the reasons that educators are deeply hostile to copying: a student who passes off another's work as his or her own has learned nothing from its creation.

It is also desirable to start a new project without preconceptions. For example, at first we probably know nothing about the requirements for a new system. Analysts should take account of the unique characteristics of a proposed system and its environment. Thus we should begin to investigate a new situation with as few preconceptions as possible. But it would be madness to assume that we know nothing about how to solve any of the problems encountered along the way. Wherever we can, we should capitalize on successful past work, provided that it is relevant to the current problem.

The 'not invented here' syndrome
Some software developers (even occasionally whole departments) seem to ignore the accumulated wisdom of their profession. Why? One reason is the NIH ('not invented here') syndrome, which is said mainly to afflict programmers. This describes the attitude of someone who thinks: 'I don't trust other people's widgets–even those that appear to work, suit my purpose and are affordable–I want to invent my own widgets anyway.' This may be understandable in someone who enjoys a technical challenge, or has reasons not to trust the work of others, but it usually does not make good commercial sense.

Reuse can be difficult to manage
One key to successful reuse is the management of the process. A developer who wishes to find artefacts for possible reuse (models, templates, program subroutines, entire programs, etc.) needs a catalogue. This must be comprehensive, up to date, and organized in such a way that it is easy to find artefacts that meet a present need. The artefacts themselves must be designed for reuse, and this often makes their construction more difficult and more costly. But any artefact that is too specific in its design is likely to need extensive adaption before it can be reused in another context. The adaptation may prove more trouble than the creation of a new artefact that precisely suits the context. The difficulties of managing this process well sometimes mean that reuse is difficult to achieve in practice, although few people doubt its benefits.

Analysis work is harder to reuse than either designs or software
At its simplest, software reuse can be very easy to achieve. For example, to use a library function within a program, you may need to import the library, call the function by name and pass to it any required parameters. Your program can then carry on to use the result. For the programmer, all that is required is a copy of the library, knowledge of its signature and some understanding of what the function does. These things are typically learned fairly early in any programming course.

Reuse of design artifacts can also be relatively straightforward. A familiar example in user interface design are the templates that give users some limited flexibility in the ways that they can customize a home page on a social networking site. Each template is essentially a design that can be reused many times by different users.

Analysis models, however, are still at a fairly high level of abstraction. Thus this is one of the least developed areas of reuse because it is complex by its nature and only parts of any model are likely to be reusable. It is also necessary to organize a model so that it abstracts out (hides) those features of a requirement that are not necessary for a valid comparison with a similar requirement on another project. Next, the whole point of reuse is to save work, so it should also not be necessary to develop a full model of a new requirement in order to make the comparison. Finally, any relevant differences between the two requirements being compared should be clearly visible–so it should also not be necessary to develop a full model of the new requirement in order to see these. We shall see later that patterns are one way of overcoming these difficulties.

8.2.3 How object-orientation contributes to reuse

Object-oriented software development relies on two main forms of abstraction that help to achieve reuse: first, generalization and second, encapsulation combined with information hiding. Not surprisingly, their use resembles the practice in many other industries.

Generalization

Generalization is a form of abstraction that (as we saw in Chapter 4) means concentrating on those aspects of a design or specification that are relevant to more than one situation, while ignoring those that are only relevant to a specific situation. It is often possible to identify some element of a design, or of a solution to a problem, that has general application to a variety of situations or problems. At the risk of labouring a metaphor, the wheel is a good example. Wheels can be made almost any size and of many different designs and materials, depending on their intended use. The little plastic wheels inside a mouse register its movement over the mousemat. The rubber-tyred wheels on a bicycle push and steer it along its track, and provide some cushioning to the rider. The huge iron balance wheel on an old-fashioned steam engine smooths the jerky motion of the pistons. Despite the obvious differences in their size, material and method of construction, all share the same general circular form and rotate around a central shaft.

The engineer who designs the wheels for a mouse must consider specific aspects of the situation, such as the need for them to be non-conducting, small, light and cheap to make. But the basic principle of circular movement around an axle requires no special thought, since this is a long-understood solution to a well-known family of engineering problems. The particular size, weight, etc. of a wheel are specific to its application. But the circular form is a general principle that has been abstracted from all the wheels made over the years, and can be applied again and again to the design of many other wheels to come.

Generalization in software is a lot like this. The aim is to identify features of a specification or design that are likely to be useful in systems, or for purposes, for which they were not specifically developed. In Chapter 4, we saw how the introduction of an abstract Employee superclass generalized the common aspects of the descriptions of different kinds of real employee (hourly, weekly and monthly-paid). In the next section, we explain how to find generalization using further examples from the Agate case study.

Encapsulation and information hiding

Encapsulation and information hiding together represent a kind of abstraction that, as we saw in Chapter 4, focuses on the external behaviour of something and ignores the internal details of how the behaviour is produced. This is necessary for successful modularization. The assembly of modern desktop computer systems provides many examples. For example, PC mice can use very different technologies, but still behave in a similar way from a user's perspective. On my desk as I write are three different mice: two are wired, but one of these is a wheel mouse while the other is optical; the third is optical and wireless. You can tell the difference if you look, since there are some external clues (presence or absence of wire or red light). But most of the time whether a mouse is wheeled or optical, wired or wireless, makes little practical difference. More important, modularization allows one component to be replaced by another with no need for an exact match. If a wired wheel mouse fails, it can be replaced with a wireless optical mouse. Regardless of how the mouse itself works, there is a standard definition of the interface between the mouse and the computer subsystem with which it interacts. This interface is defined by the plug type and pin connections (what type of signal each pin carries, and at what voltage). Modularization of software aims at the same ease of replacement, and software interfaces also need to be defined in a standard way for this to work. The definition of a software interface is usually in terms of services provided and the message signature required to call each service.

Composition involves encapsulating a group of classes that collectively have the capacity to be a reusable subassembly: in other words, an independent module. The idea is that a complex whole is made of simpler components. These, while less complex than the whole, may themselves be made of still less complex subassemblies, elementary components or a mixture of the two. In the next section, we consider the use of composition using examples from the Agate case study.

8.3 | Adding Further Structure

8.3.1 Finding and modelling generalization

Figure 8.1 shows a note of an interview carried out by an analyst in the Agate case study. Her main objective was to understand more about different types of staff. In her haste, the analyst gathered only a handful of facts, but these highlight some useful information that must be modelled appropriately.

- There are two types of staff.
- Bonuses are calculated differently.
- Different data should be recorded for each type of staff.

Figure 8.2 shows a partial class diagram that corresponds to this (for clarity, only the affected classes are shown).

Redefined operations

Why is there a `calculateBonus()` operation in all three classes in the hierarchy in Fig. 8.2? Has the analyst made a mistake? Or has she failed to take advantage of the economy of representation offered by the generalization notation?

The explanation is that the superclass operation is expected to be overridden in its subclasses (overriding of inherited characteristics was introduced in Chapter 4). While

17 March – brief interview with Amarjeet Grewal (Finance Director)
Purpose – clarification of points from last Thursday's interview

Asked about staff types
   – only two types seem relevant to system –
     creative staff (C) and admin staff (A)
How do they differ?
   – main difference is bonus payment . . .
     1. (C) bonus calculated on basis of campaign profits
       (only those campaigns they worked on)
     2. (A) paid rate based on average of all campaign profits
Any other diffs? Amarjeet says –
   – C qualifications need to be recorded
   – C can be assigned as contact for a client
   – A are not assigned to specific campaigns
No other significant differences.
     (NOTE – at next interview, get details of both algorithms)

Figure 8.1 Analyst's note of the differences between Agate staff types.

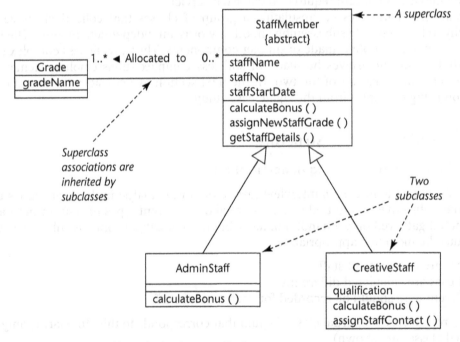

Figure 8.2 A generalization hierarchy for Agate staff roles.

both `AdminStaff` and `CreativeStaff` require an operation `calculateBonus()`, it works differently in each case. Since the precise logic for the calculation differs between these two groups of staff, the two operations need to be treated separately when each algorithm is designed, and also when code is written to implement them. This justifies the separate appearance of a superficially similar operation in both subclasses.

Why then include the operation in the superclass at all? The answer is that it is an attempt at 'future-proofing'. A superclass may later acquire other subclasses that are as yet unknown. Here, the analyst has recognized—or assumed—that objects belonging to *all* subclasses of StaffMember are likely to need an operation to calculate bonus. For this reason, at least a 'skeleton' of the operation is included in the superclass. This may consist of no more than the signature, but since the interface is all that matters to other classes, this alone justifies its inclusion in the superclass definition. Even if the superclass operation is defined in full, the programmers of some subclasses may choose not to use it because the logic for their version of the operation is different.

Abstract and concrete classes

StaffMember is *abstract* in the sense that it has no instances. This means that no staff exist at Agate who are 'general' members of staff, and not members of a particular subgroup, and is indicated by the {abstract} annotation below the class name in Fig. 8.2 (an alternative notation is to write the class name in italics.) Only a superclass in a generalization hierarchy can be abstract. All other classes can have one or more instances, and are said to be *concrete* or *instantiated*. All staff members encountered so far (among those that are relevant to the model) are defined as either AdminStaff or CreativeStaff. If we later discover another group of staff that is distinct in behaviour, data or associations, and if we need to model this new group, it will be represented in the diagram by a new subclass. The point of a superclass is that it sits at a higher level of abstraction than its subclasses. This generality allows it to be adapted for use in other systems. While this in itself is not always enough for it to be declared as an abstract class, this is usually the case, and for the moment we can safely ignore exceptions to the rule.

How generalization helps to achieve reuse

The reason for creating a generalization hierarchy is to enable the specifications of its superclasses to be reused in other contexts. Often this reuse is within the current application.

Imagine that the Agate system has been completed and is in regular use. Some time later, the directors reorganize the company, and as a result account managers are to be paid bonuses related to campaign profits. This bonus will be calculated in a different way from both administrative and other creative staff. For example, it may include an element from campaigns that they supervise and an element from the general profitability of the company. It is easy to add another subclass to cater for this new behaviour, as shown in Fig. 8.3.

Note also the alternative notation styles. In Fig. 8.2 each subclass is joined to the superclass by its own generalization association, while in Fig. 8.3 the three subclasses are organized into a tree structure with a single triangle joining this to the superclass. The single tree structure is known as the *shared target* form of the notation. Both forms are acceptable, but the shared target notation is used only where the generalization relationships belong to the same *generalization set*. In the example shown in Fig. 8.3 this is appropriate, since the types of employee shown represent a single coherent way of partitioning the superclass. However, suppose that for some reason we need also to specialize employees as Male and Female. The new generalization relationships for this belong to a different generalization set. The name of the applicable generalization set can optionally be shown on the diagram next to the relationship. This is illustrated in Fig. 8.4.

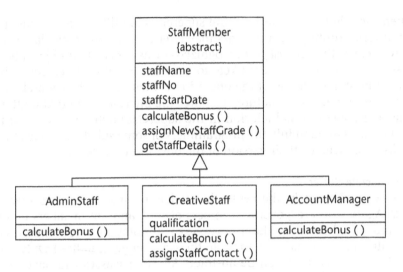

Figure 8.3 A new subclass is easy to add.

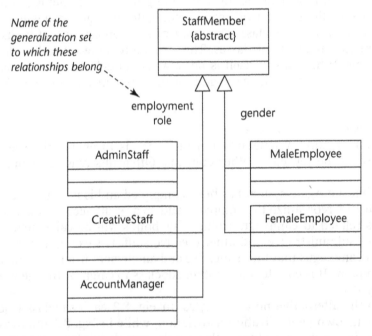

Figure 8.4 Generalization sets partition a superclass in different ways.

Adding a new AccountManager subclass has little or no impact on the rest of the class model. The reuse derives from basing AccountManager on the existing abstract class StaffMember. The new class inherits all attributes and operations that are not part of its own specialism—in this case roughly 85% of its specification. This is for only one class; over the many classes of a large system, the saving in design and coding effort can clearly be significant. But the opportunity is available because we have previously identified the generalized aspects of a staff member. This is the main benefit of generalization, that hierarchies can usually be extended without significant effects on existing structures.

Generalization can also provide possibilities of reuse within other applications. For example, the developers at Agate application may find that an abstract class StaffMember already exists in a catalogue that records the generalization hierarchies from previous projects. There is therefore no need to document it afresh, and analysis can focus on those characteristics that are specific to the current application. Of course, if this super-class were as simple as the one shown in Fig. 8.3 there would be little benefit. But in real projects, class hierarchies are sometimes complex, and inherited class definitions may be accompanied by complex structures of associations in addition to their attribute and operation specifications.

A top-down approach to finding generalization

It is relatively easy to discover generalization where both superclasses and subclasses have already been identified. If an association can be described by the expression *is a kind of*, then it can usually be modelled as generalization. Sometimes this is so obvious that you may wonder if that is all there is to it. For example, 'administrative staff are a kind of staff'. In just the same way 'a helicopter is a type of aircraft and so is a fixed-wing jet' and 'a truck is a type of vehicle and so is a buffalo cart' imply generalizations with similar structures.

It is not uncommon to find multiple levels of generalization. This simply means that a superclass in one relationship may be a subclass in another. For example, Aircraft is both a superclass of Helicopter and a subclass of Vehicle. In practice, more than about four or five levels of generalization in a class model is too many (Rumbaugh et al., 1991), but this is primarily for design reasons.

A bottom-up approach to finding generalization

An alternative approach is to look for similarities among classes in your model, and consider whether the model can be 'tidied up' or simplified by introducing superclasses that abstract out the similarities. This needs to be done with some care. The purpose of doing this is to increase the level of abstraction of the model, but any further abstraction introduced should still be 'useful'. The guiding principle is still that any new generaliza-tion must meet all the tests described in Chapter 4.

When not to use generalization

Generalization can be overused, so some judgement is needed to determine its likely future usefulness on each occasion. For example, at Agate, staff and (some) clients are people (for the sake of illustration we will ignore the fact that most clients are in fact companies and not individuals). An inexperienced analyst might feel that this justifies the creation of a Person superclass, to contain any common attributes and operations of Client and StaffMember. But it may quickly become apparent that the new class definition contains little but the attribute personName. This is really an attempt to force a generalization hierarchy to include subclasses that are too dissimilar.

Second, we should not anticipate subclasses that are not justified by currently known requirements. For example, at Agate AdminStaff and CreativeStaff are distinct classes based on differences in their attributes and operations. We also know about other kinds of staff in the organization, e.g. directors. But we should not automatically create another subclass of StaffMember called Director-Staff. Even if it were to turn out that directors have some relevance for the system, there is no reason yet to suppose they will be a distinct class. They may be adequately modelled by an existing class (say, AdminStaff) unless we find that their behaviour or information structure differs in some way.

There is a tension here. On the one hand, generalization is modelled to permit future subclassing in situations that the analyst cannot reasonably anticipate. The ability to take advantage of this is one of the main benefits of constructing a generalization hierarchy. On the other hand, if generalization is overdone, it adds to the complexity of the model for little or no return. There is no simple answer to this problem, except to use the judgement that comes with experience, and any guidance issued by the organization for whom you work.

Multiple inheritance

Multiple inheritance was introduced in Chapter 4. It is often appropriate for a class to inherit from more than one superclass. This is familiar in everyday classification. For example, if we classify household items according to their use, a coffee mug is a drinking vessel. If we classify the same items according to their value and aesthetic qualities, the mug might be 'everyday' rather than 'best'. If we classify the same items according to their health risk, the mug might be a hazard (because it is cracked). The mug can belong at one time to various categories derived from different classification schemes without any logical conflict.

In object-oriented modelling, especially during design, it can be useful to define classes that inherit features from more than one superclass. In each case, all features are inherited from every superclass.

8.3.2 Finding and modelling composition

Composition (or *composite aggregation*) is based on the concept of *aggregation*, which is a feature of many object-oriented programming languages. At its simplest, aggregation represents a whole–part relationship between classes, while composition shows a stronger form of ownership of the part by the whole.

One application of composition is familiar to users of any common computer drawing package. For example, many drawings in this text were prepared and edited with a widely used drawing package. This application allows the user to select and group several objects. Grouped objects behave as a single object, and can be sized, rotated, copied, moved or deleted with a single command. Figure 8.5 illustrates this, while Fig. 8.6 models the composition as a class diagram. Note that the composite structure is nested–a composition can itself contain a further composition. In the same way that a composite drawing object can only be handled as a single drawing component, the 'part' objects in a composition structure cannot be directly accessed, while the whole object presents a single interface to other parts of the system.

Composition and aggregation may both be identified during requirements analysis, but their main application is during design and implementation activities, where they can be used to encapsulate a structure of objects as a potentially reusable subassembly. This is more than just a matter of labelling the structure with a single name. Its encapsulation as a coherent, cohesive module is much more important. The external interface for a composition is the interface of the single object at the 'whole' end of the association. Details of the internal structure of the composition–that is, the other objects it contains, and to which it delegates some of its responsibilities–remain hidden from the client.

1. A collection of separate drawing objects ...

2. ... when grouped together, make a single composite:

3. When two composites are grouped together ...

4. ... they make a further composite ...

5. ... that can be scaled ...

6. ... or rotated ...

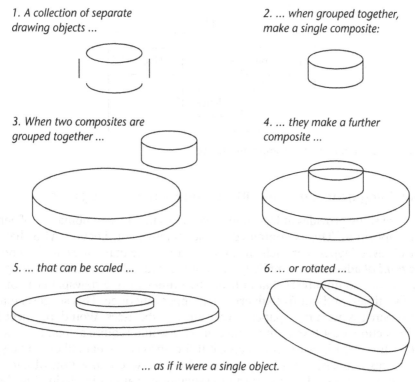

... as if it were a single object.

Figure 8.5 Composition of objects in a drawing package.

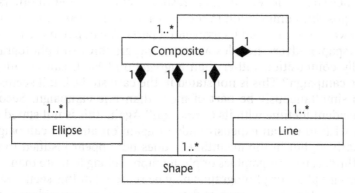

Figure 8.6 The same composite structure, expressed as UML classes.

The notation is similar to a simple association, but with a diamond at the 'whole' end. The diamond is filled with solid colour to indicate composition, and left unfilled for aggregation. An alternative notation for a composite structure is illustrated in Fig. 8.7. This explicitly shows the composite object as a container for its parts.

Use of composition and aggregation in business-oriented applications is more problematic than in the drawing package example, but it is still worth modelling where it conveys useful information about the structure of the business domain. An example from the Agate case study is used in the next section to illustrate how aggregation is identified.

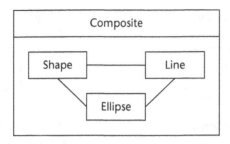

Figure 8.7 Alternative notation for a composite structure.

8.3.3 Combining generalization with composition or aggregation

The Agate case study provides at least one occasion to model a combination of generalization and composition. This is contained in the statement in Section A1.3 that 'adverts can be one of several types'. For each type, it is certainly true that, for example, a newspaper advert *is a kind of* advert. For simplicity, we assume that 'advert' refers to a *design*, rather than an *insertion*–so an advert that appears five times in one newspaper is one advert appearing five times, and not five adverts each appearing once. This suggests that advert could be a superclass, with newspaper advert, etc. as subclasses. Would this meet the tests described in Section 4.2.4? An authoritative answer would require a detailed examination of attributes and operations for each class, but the answer appears likely to be yes.

An advert also consists of a set of parts. The precise composition of each type of advert is different, and so this structure of associations cannot be defined at the superclass level (the attributes, operations and composition structure of television adverts may resemble newspaper adverts in some respects, but will differ in others).

We can see possible composition in the association between Campaign and Advert, and in turn between Advert and its associated parts. A campaign includes one or more adverts. A newspaper advert includes written copy, graphics and photographs.

Is this really composition rather than aggregation? First, can an advert belong to more than one campaign? This is not stated in the case study, but it seems unlikely that an advert can simultaneously be part of more than one campaign. Second, has each Advert a coincident lifetime with its Campaign? Again, this is not stated explicitly, but a client might wish to use an expensive advert again on another campaign. This point needs to be clarified, but in the meantime it does not appear justified to model this as composition. Third, can copy, graphics or photographs belong to more than one newspaper advert? Perhaps graphics or photographs may be reused, but this seems very unlikely to be the case for copy. Finally, has each of these components a coincident lifetime with the advert? Probably some do and some do not. This would all need further clarification, but in the meantime composition seems justified only in the case of NewspaperAdvertCopy, and aggregation has therefore been applied elsewhere. Figure 8.8 shows the partial class model that results from this analysis.

8.3.4 Organizing the analysis model—packages and dependencies

An analysis model may include completely free-standing components, which are discussed in the following section. Even if it does not, it must still be organized in such a way that it will remain robust in the face of changing requirements. This demands skill and judgement

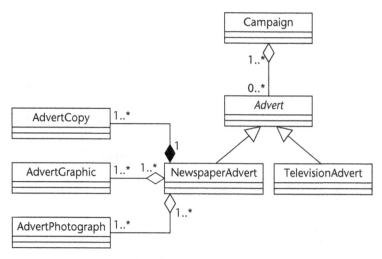

Figure 8.8 Aggregation, composition and generalization in the Agate model.

on the part of the analyst. Part of this task is the definition of analysis packages that are relatively independent of each other while still internally highly cohesive (cohesion is explained in detail in Chapter 14). We saw in Chapter 7 that packages (introduced in Chapter 5) are a means by which the developer can 'factor out' classes or structures that have potential use in a wider context than one project alone. But when a model is partitioned into packages (or when pre-existing components are used to support a current project) it is important to keep track of the dependencies between different classes and packages.

We saw in Chapter A2 that the Agate case study suggests three related but distinct application areas: advert preparation, campaign management and staff management. It probably makes sense to model these as separate packages, but it is likely that some entity objects will be used by more than one package. Based on our analysis so far, StaffMember plays a role in both the Campaign Management and the Staff Management packages. This leads to an architectural decision. Figure 8.9 illustrates some of the variations described below.

- We could place StaffMember in the Staff Management package. In this case, we need to model a dependency from Campaign Management to Staff Management, since the Client and Campaign classes need an association with StaffMember (diagram variation (i)).
- We could remove StaffMember to a separate package. This would be justified if it appeared to have more widespread use. For example, there may also be wages, personnel, welfare and pension applications that need this class. In this case, we need to model dependencies from all the corresponding packages to the package that contains StaffMember (diagram variation (ii)).
- Further analysis may yet reveal that in fact StaffMember is not a single class. In this case, the derivative classes may remain within their respective packages, but it is likely that there will be an association between them and the dependency must still be documented.

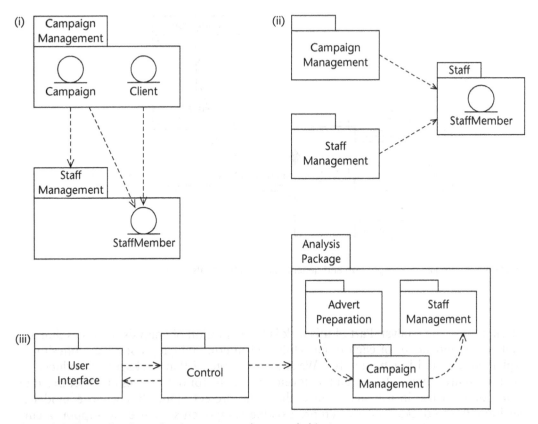

Figure 8.9 Alternative dependencies among packages and objects.

- In addition, we made a judgement in Chapter 7 to separate all boundary objects into a `User Interface` package and all control objects into a `Control` package. Objects in these specialized packages will certainly have dependencies on objects in other packages (diagram variation (iii)).

The significance of documenting package dependencies is perhaps not obvious when dealing, as we are here, with a relatively simple model. But it will become more important when the models are large, complex and, above all, when there is a substantial element of reuse involved, whether this occurs at the level of individual classes or at a component scale.

8.4   Reusable Software Components

A software component is a package or module that provides services to other components or systems. A reusable component is one that has been designed for use in more than one context. In one sense, a component is a special case of a composition structure, as described above. Indeed, in some circumstances, a single class can be a reusable component. However, the term is now generally reserved for relatively complex structures that operate independently of each other, are often developed separately at different times or in different organizations, and are then 'plugged together' to achieve the desired overall functionality. We will discuss reusable components in much more detail in Chapter 20; here, we will do no more than briefly introduce the concept and illustrate the UML notation.

The reasons for employing standardized components are familiar and obvious, and indeed it is hard to think of an industry that does not make widespread use of them. For example, houses are typically designed and assembled from bricks, roofing timbers, tiles, doors, window frames, electrical components, water pipes, floorboards, etc., that are all picked from a catalogue. An architect may use these components to design (and a builder to build) houses that differ widely in their overall appearance, floorplan and number of rooms. The difference is in the way that standard components have been assembled.

For anything to be treated as a component (a window, for example), it must be specified in a way that allows the architect, builder, etc. to work with it as a single, simple thing, even though really it is not. Elsewhere, specialist designers tackle the problems of window design (what materials, structure, etc. make a good window) and specialist constructors build them to the designers' specifications. Construction details of a standard window may change due to a design improvement, availability of materials or new manufacturing methods. However, as long as key features such as height, width and overall appearance—in effect, the window's interface—are not altered, a new window can be substituted for an old one of the same type should it need to be replaced in the future.

Similarly, the implementation of a software component is hidden from other components requesting its services. Different subsystems can thus be effectively isolated in operation. This greatly reduces the problems in getting them to interact with each other, even if they were developed at different times, or in different languages, or execute on different hardware platforms. It also allows one component to be substituted for another as long as both offer the same interface. Subsystems that have been specified in this way are said to be *decoupled* from each other.

The approach can be scaled up to any arbitrarily complex level. Any part of a software system—or model of one—can be considered for reuse in other contexts, provided the following criteria are met.

- A component meets a clear-cut but general need (in other words, it delivers a coherent service or set of services).
- A component has one or more simple, well-defined external interfaces.

Object-oriented development is particularly well suited to the task of designing reusable components. Well-chosen objects already meet both the above criteria. Object-oriented models, and hence also code, are also organized in a way that is helpful for reuse. For example, Coleman et al. (1994) point out that generalization hierarchies are a very practical way of organizing a catalogue of components. This is because they encourage the searcher to begin first with a general category, then progressively to refine their search to more and more specialized levels.

Inheritance permits a 'software architect' to spawn new classes from existing ones. Thus some parts of a new software component can often be built with minimal effort. Only the specialized details need to be added. There is nothing properly analogous to this in most other industries (although there may be a closer comparison between design activities). The manufacturing effort for a new window is similar to that for any previous window. Maintenance, too, can be easier—in a generalization hierarchy, characteristics that are specified at the superclass level are instantly available to any subclass upon instantiation.

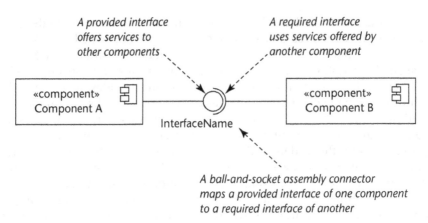

Figure 8.10 Basic notation in UML 2.0 for a component structure diagram.

8.4.1 UML notation for components

The basic notation for modelling components in UML is illustrated in Fig. 8.10. This shows two components whose interfaces are joined by a ball-and-socket assembly connector. Component A has a *provided interface*, which offers services to other components that know how to request those services. Meanwhile, component B has a *required interface*, which requests services from a provided interface on another component. The form of the protocol for requesting a service is the same as that for calling an object operation. The requesting component sends a message that contains an operation name and any necessary parameters.

Each interface may offer a range of services, and each service has its own specific protocol or signature. These are modelled independently of any decisions about the internal class structure of the component. The interface operations that result from this analysis imply what Cheesman and Daniels (2001) call 'an information model' of the interface, and this can give a good starting point for modelling the internal design of a component.

In this section we introduce some elements of the component notation and show how it can be used to model a component-based architecture and to specify important aspects of component interfaces. However, this is certainly not intended as a complete description of how to analyse software components for component-based development. Readers who are interested in learning more should consult a specialist work on the subject, such as Cheesman and Daniels (2001), which in our view is one of the clearest books on modelling components.

8.4.2 Component-based development

Many activities involved in component-based development (CBD) are much the same as they would be for the development of any other software. The classes that comprise an individual component must be identified, modelled, specified, designed and coded. These activities are carried out as described elsewhere in this book. CBD differs from 'simple' object-oriented analysis and design mainly in that it involves the specification of component architectures and component interactions. Much of this relates to interfaces and behaviour at a higher level of abstraction than single classes or the kind of small-scale composition structures that we have described up to this point.

Components can themselves be specified at different levels of abstraction. Cheesman and Daniels (2001) discuss the different forms that a single component can take. First, components must follow some sort of common standard if they are to work together with each other when they are assembled. An everyday example is the way that many electrical devices follow a standard that defines the operating voltage and the size and shape of the plug. Voltage and plug designs vary from one country to another; hence the need for the kind of travel adaptors sold at airports. The standard for software components is effectively realized as the environment within which a given component is designed to work.

Component function is also important. The speaker and headphone output sockets on most electric guitar amplifiers are designed to accept the same jack plug connectors. But if you plug a pair of headphones into the speaker output socket, you could end up blowing the headphones. Or, if it is a transistor amplifier, you might destroy the power transistors instead. Plugging in a speaker just allows you to hear the guitar. A component's behaviour is described by its specification, much of which will consist of definitions of its interfaces with other components.

Each specification may have many implementations. It should be possible to substitute one implementation of a specification for another, just as a guitarist can unplug one guitar and plug in another. That, after all, is the whole point of using components.

It is possible to imagine a component implementation that will be installed only once, but it is much more likely that there will be multiple installations of each implementation. Consider a web browser (Mozilla Firefox version 3.0, say) as an example. We can assume a single specification for the browser, but there are different implementations for each of the main operating systems (Windows, Mac and Linux). Each implementation is installed on millions of computers around the world. On each computer there is an installed copy of the implementation, and for this to work properly it needs to be registered with its operating system environment. Finally, each time that the software is launched, a new component 'object' starts. This brings us finally to the level where actual working components are realized—the level where data is stored and processes are executed.

Another way in which CBD differs from conventional systems development is that it involves not only the creation of new components, but also the reuse of existing ones. These may be components that have been developed in-house during earlier projects, or they may be supplied commercially by an external third party. In either case, there is a need for catalogues that describe components in a standardized way, so that developers can find components that will be useful, or—equally important—can determine that none yet exist. For this reason, CBD lifecycles typically have a pattern that differentiates between the development and the use of components, and that also recognize the need for life-long management of components from specification through to end use. We will return to the topic of managing components in Chapter 20. For now, we concentrate on describing how UML can be used in their specification.

8.4.3 Example of modelling components

An airline seat booking system provides a typical scenario for the use of software components. This is partly because legacy systems (see Section 6.2.1) are still in widespread use in the industry. These must interoperate with newer systems, themselves often developed using object-oriented methods and also (increasingly often) interacting over the web. New systems components developed for such an environment must be capable of integrating with components that are already in use—some quite antiquated in their design and implementation–and also with new components still to come, some of which have not yet been specified.

Let us assume that bookings are to be taken from various sources, including traditional travel agents, online travel agents and the company's own website. A component architecture makes sense, so that individual components can be replaced in a plug-and-play fashion without disrupting the operation of other systems. This will permit the upgrading of older components with minimum fuss. It will also allow the substitution of different booking processes and platforms while using a single component to manage all the transactions.

Figure 8.11 shows part of a possible component-based architecture for an airline. The main components in this simplified view are systems to handle bookings, to handle payments, to keep records of customers, to check in passengers at the airport, and to manage flight information (including the allocation of passengers to seats on the aircraft). A real airline would, of course, require many other systems to support its operations.

The Bookings component provides an interface called MakeBooking. This is available to any other system that understands how to use it, which really just means knowing the services that are provided by the interface and the protocol or signature for each service. Implementation details of a component are encapsulated in just the same way that the attributes and operations of an object are encapsulated.

In this case, other systems that might use the interface include those of travel agents and an e-commerce system on the airline's website. The interface decouples client systems that wish to make a seat booking from the actual operation of the booking system component, allowing bookings to be made remotely from other networks or over the Web. The architecture shown also permits new clients to be implemented for other platforms. For example, if the airline wishes to enable bookings from mobile devices, the booking system will need no modification. All that is required is for any new system using this interface to be designed so that it can send properly formed requests to the MakeBooking interface.

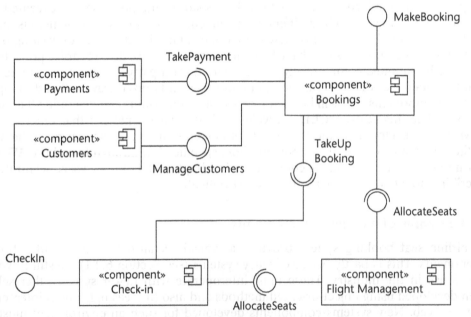

Figure 8.11 Component structure diagram for airline systems.

The `Bookings` component provides an interface to the `Check-in` component, which needs details of bookings to ensure that the correct customers are checked in. It uses an interface provided by the `Payments` component, which handles the processing of credit cards and any other types of payment. Both `Bookings` and `Check-in` components use an interface provided by the `Flight Management` component to obtain (and to update) details of seat availability on flights. Finally, the `Booking` component uses an interface provided by the `Customers` component to obtain and update details of the airline's customers.

A communication diagram can be used to model the interaction of these interfaces in more detail (communication diagrams are explained fully in Chapter 9). Figure 8.12 shows the interaction for checking in passengers for a booking. Note that individual messages are shown with their parameters, allowing the analyst to specify in some detail the operations and thus, by extension, the classes needed to implement each interface. Once a model has been built up that gives a complete picture of the interactions, the specification of a component can be represented as the totality of all operations on all its interfaces.

Figure 8.13 shows the `<realize>` dependency between the `Flight Management` component and its `AllocateSeats` interface. The component itself is realized by a package (or packages) of classes analysed as described elsewhere in this book.

Note that this diagram, even if it were complete and showed all interfaces offered by the `Flight Management` component, still represents the specification of a component, rather than its implementation. Component specifications concentrate on the external view of operations and attributes, in just the same way that a class specification does. A component implementation (in other words, the specification of classes and associations that exist within the component) would be much more detailed than we have shown here, but would also be beyond the scope of this chapter.

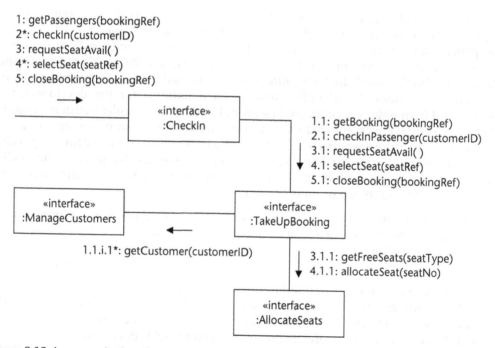

1: getPassengers(bookingRef)
2*: checkIn(customerID)
3: requestSeatAvail( )
4*: selectSeat(seatRef)
5: closeBooking(bookingRef)

«interface»
:CheckIn

1.1: getBooking(bookingRef)
2.1: checkInPassenger(customerID)
3.1: requestSeatAvail( )
4.1: selectSeat(seatRef)
5.1: closeBooking(bookingRef)

«interface»
:ManageCustomers

«interface»
:TakeUpBooking

1.1.i.1*: getCustomer(customerID)

3.1.1: getFreeSeats(seatType)
4.1.1: allocateSeat(seatNo)

«interface»
:AllocateSeats

Figure 8.12 A communication diagram can show interaction between instances of component interfaces.

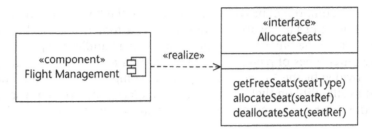

Figure 8.13 Dependency relationship between an interface and a package that implements it.

8.5 Software Development Patterns

A *software development pattern* (usually just called *pattern*) is an abstract solution to a recurring problem that can be applied in different ways depending upon the specific problem at issue. Patterns are applied widely in systems development, most of all in design, but also to requirements analysis, project management, business process design, testing and more. The boundary, control and entity object architecture introduced in Chapter 7 is in fact a pattern widely applied during requirements analysis and systems design. Other architectures that we will consider later are also examples of the application of patterns to the activities of analysis and design. A pattern is useful when it captures the essence of a problem and a possible solution, without being too prescriptive.

8.5.1 Origin of patterns

In everyday speech, a pattern refers to a kind of design that is used to reproduce images or products in a repetitive manner (on wallpaper or fabric, for example). This suggests that patterns are a sort of generalization, which is not too far removed from the use of the term in software development. The usage is traced back to the architect Christopher Alexander, who first used the term *pattern* to describe solutions to recurring problems in architecture. Alexander identified many related patterns for the development of effective and harmonious architectural forms in buildings. Alexander's patterns address many architectural issues–for example the best place to site a door in a room, or how to organize and structure a waiting area in a building so that waiting can become a positive experience. Alexander argued that his patterns became a design 'language' within which solutions to recurring architectural problems could be developed and described. Alexander's definition of a pattern is as follows.

> Each pattern describes a problem which occurs over and over again in our environment, and then describes the core of a solution to that problem, in such a way that you can use this solution a million times over, without ever doing it the same way twice.
>
> Alexander et al. (1977)

Alexander made no reference to buildings or architecture but only to 'our environment,' which he meant as the physical environment in which we live. There was clearly an analogy with software development, and some among the early object-oriented community took up his ideas. Beck and Cunningham (1989) documented some of the earliest software patterns in order to describe aspects of interface design in Smalltalk environments. Coplien (1992) catalogued a set of patterns specifically for use in C++ programming (patterns that relate to constructs in a specific programming language are now known as *idioms*).

The publication of *Design Patterns: Elements of Reusable Object-Oriented Software*[1] by Gamma et al. (1995) gave significant impetus to the use of patterns in software design, but other authors have identified patterns that are concerned with analysis (Coad et al., 1997; Fowler, 1997), organizational issues (Coplien, 1996) and systems architecture (Buschmann et al., 1996). Software patterns have also been applied to non-object-oriented development approaches. For example, Hay (1996) identified a series of analysis patterns for data modelling. These include patterns relating to concepts such as Party and Contract, which appear widely in information systems.

8.5.2 What is a software pattern?

Riehle and Zullighoven (1996) describe a pattern as a generalized abstraction from concrete forms that recur in certain situations. We can interpret 'concrete' as meaning 'specific' or 'particular'. Gabriel's (1996) definition is more detailed and expresses the structure of a pattern:

> Each pattern is a three-part rule, which expresses a relation between a certain context, a certain system of forces which occurs repeatedly in that context, and a certain software configuration which allows these forces to resolve themselves.

In this definition, *context* can be understood as a set of circumstances or preconditions and *forces* are issues that have to be addressed, while the software configuration addresses and resolves the forces. Coplien (1996) identifies the critical aspects of a pattern as follows.

- It solves a problem.
- It is a proven concept.
- The solution is not obvious.
- It describes a relationship.
- The pattern has a significant human component.

The human component is not simply a good user interface to a working application; it is concerned with the nature of the software constructs used to build the application. Software patterns should result in structures that are sympathetic to the human perspective. A good software pattern offers a solution that not only works, but that also has an aesthetic quality–that is in some way elegant. This aesthetic quality is sometimes called 'quality without a name' (QWAN). The exact nature of QWAN is naturally the subject of much controversy, and our discussion of patterns will not address issues of elegance. However, readers may judge for themselves whether the solutions developed from the patterns have a sense of elegance.

In the same way that a pattern captures and documents proven good practice, *antipatterns* capture practice that is demonstrably bad. It is sensible to do this. We should ensure not only that a software system embodies good practice but also that it avoids known pitfalls. Antipatterns are a way of documenting attempted solutions to recurring

---

1   The four authors of the book are known as the 'Gang of Four' (GOF) so the book is familiarly known as 'the GOF book'.

problems that proved unsuccessful. An antipattern can also include reworked solutions that proved effective (Brown et al., 1998). One example is 'mushroom management', which relates to the domain of software development organizations. It describes the adoption of an explicit policy to isolate systems developers from users in an attempt to limit requirements drift. In such an organization, requirements are passed through an intermediary such as the project manager or a requirements analyst. The negative consequence of this pattern is that inadequacies in the analysis documentation are both inevitable and not resolved. Furthermore, design decisions are made without user involvement and the delivered system may not address users' requirements. The reworked solution suggested by Brown et al. is to use a form of spiral process development model (see Chapter 3). Other reworked solutions include the involvement of domain experts in the development team, as recommended by the Dynamic Systems Development Method (DSDM) (we introduce DSDM in Chapter 21).

Coad et al. (1997) distinguish a strategy, which they describe as a plan of action intended to achieve some defined purpose, from a pattern, which they describe as a template that embodies an example worth emulating. This is slightly different from the views of a pattern described earlier as it does not emphasize contextual aspects to the same extent. One example of a Coad et al. strategy is 'organize and prioritize features', which relates to the need to prioritize requirements (discussed in Chapter 3).

8.5.3 Analysis patterns

An analysis pattern is essentially a structure of classes and associations that is found to occur over and over again in many different modelling situations. Each pattern can be used to communicate a general understanding about how to model a particular set of requirements, and therefore the model need not be invented from scratch every time a similar situation occurs. Since a pattern may consist of whole structures of classes, the abstraction takes place at a higher level than is normally possible using generalization alone. On the other hand, patterns stop a long way short of detailed specification, and so should not be confused with composition structures or components.

A simple example of an analysis pattern from Coad et al. (1997) is the Transaction–Transaction Line Item pattern shown in Fig. 8.14.

Figure 8.15 shows the pattern as it might be applied to a sales order processing system. Here the Transaction suggests a SalesOrder class and the Transaction Line Item suggests a SalesOrderLine class. Note that we have modelled the association as a composition. This differs from the published pattern, but appears to be justified here.

Very similar structures are used in a wide variety of circumstances (e.g. shipment and shipment line item, payment and payment line item). A novice software developer has

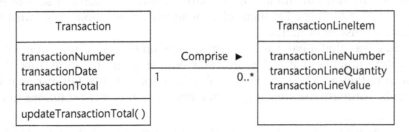

Figure 8.14 Transaction–Transaction Line Item pattern (adapted from Coad et al., 1997).

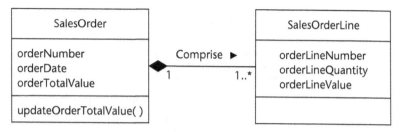

Figure 8.15 Simple application of the Transaction–Transaction Line Item pattern.

to learn this structure, or to reinvent it–but the latter is much less efficient. The act of describing it as a pattern highlights it as a useful piece of development expertise and makes it readily available to the novice. An example of a principle that makes this pattern advantageous is the desirability of low interaction coupling (see Chapter 14).

Fowler (1997) describes a number of patterns that recur in business modelling situations such as accounting, trading and organization structure. Figure 8.16 shows Fowler's Accountability pattern as an illustration of an analysis pattern in practice. For the sake of simplicity, we will discuss only the class structure, although patterns are normally documented in more detail than this (see Chapter 15). An accountability structure may be of many kinds, such as management or contract supervision. In the case of Agate, this pattern could apply to several different relationships: that between a manager and a member of staff they supervise, that between a client and a client contact, or that between a client and a campaign manager. Since the details of the relationship itself have been abstracted out as `AccountabilityType`, this one class structure is sufficiently general to be adapted to any of these relationships, given an appropriate set of attributes, operations and associations to other classes specific to the application model. The generalization of `Person` and `Organization` as `Party` similarly allows the pattern to represent relationships between individuals, organizations, or a mixture of the two.

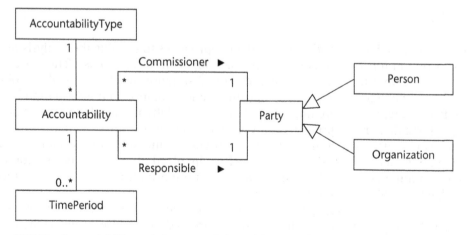

Figure 8.16 The Accountability analysis pattern (adapted from Fowler, 1997).

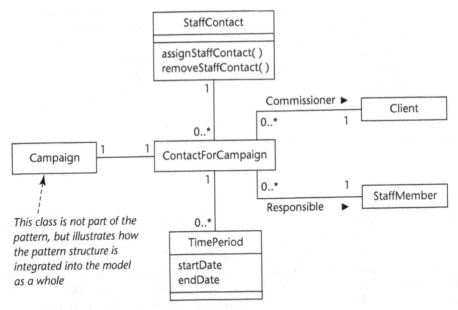

Figure 8.17 Accountability pattern applied to Agate's StaffContact relationship.

Figure 8.17 shows the pattern applied to the Staff-Contact relationship at Agate. In this context it seems unnecessary to model the generalization of the Commissioner and Responsible roles as Party. This illustrates that the structure suggested by a pattern can be adapted as appropriate to suit the circumstances.

Another pattern that might be useful in developing an analysis model for Agate is the Composite pattern (Gamma et al., 1995). However, since this pattern is useful from both analysis and design perspectives, we will defer its introduction until Chapter 15. The further use of analysis patterns is an advanced approach that is principally of use to experienced analysts, and we leave the interested reader to follow this up through further reading. They are closely related to design patterns, which we cover in some detail in Chapter 15.

8.6 Summary

In this chapter, we have introduced the main approaches to refining the analysis model. The main reason for doing this is to maximize opportunities for reuse. There are three particular ways that this can be achieved. The abstraction mechanisms of the object-oriented approach (generalization, composition, encapsulation and information hiding) are the first of these. They are important in their own right and can help significantly in making it possible to reuse previous analysis work. They also contribute to the other two approaches to reuse, which are reusable components and software development patterns. Components can greatly reduce the effort involved at all stages of development, although careful analysis and specification remain important. Patterns act as a store of knowledge that embodies best known practice.

Whatever form they take, opportunities for reuse occur in essentially only three ways. First, existing components or structures may be imported from sources outside the project boundaries. This requires careful evaluation of the degree of fit between the requirements of the current project and the features of the available components and structures. Second, new reusable components or structures may be developed for use on more than one part of the current project. This requires the analysis model to be at a high enough level of abstraction for common features between different aspects of the project to become evident. Finally, new reusable components or structures may be developed for export to other projects. Here, too, it is necessary for the requirements modelling to identify those aspects of the project that can be generalized for use in other contexts.

The explicit modelling of substitutable software components is a relatively new approach in software development and we expect that there will be more evolution in this area in the future. Patterns are now a more established approach to documenting, sharing and reusing useful insights into many aspects of the software development activity. This chapter has considered how components and patterns can be used in software development, in particular from an analysis perspective. Later chapters discuss in more detail the application of patterns and components to address issues of architecture and design.

Review Questions

8.1 What are the advantages of components?

8.2 Why does the NIH syndrome occur?

8.3 Which features of object-orientation help in the creation of reusable components?

8.4 Distinguish composition from aggregation.

8.5 Why are operations sometimes redefined in a subclass?

8.6 What is the purpose of an abstract class?

8.7 Why is encapsulation important to creating reusable components?

8.8 Why is generalization important to creating reusable components?

8.9 When should you not use generalization in a model?

8.10 What does the term pattern mean in the context of software development?

8.11 How do patterns help the software developer?

8.12 What is an antipattern?

Case Study Work, Exercises and Projects

8.A Find out from your library about the coding system that is used for classifying books, videos, etc. Draw part of the structure in UML notation as a generalization hierarchy. Think up some attributes for 'classes' in your model to show how the lower levels are progressively more specialized.

8.B Choose an area of commercial activity (business, industry, government agency, etc.) with which you are familiar. Identify some ways in which its products show the use of generalization, and some ways that components used as inputs show the use of generalization.

▶ **8.C** In Section 8.3.4, we saw that generalization probably was an appropriate way of modelling the association between `Advert` and `NewspaperAdvert`. Identify the other possible subclasses for `Advert` from Section A1.3 and repeat the checks for each. Which of them pass (if any)? Do you think there are really only two levels to the hierarchy? Explain your reasoning. Redraw the Agate class diagram to include all the generalizations that you feel are justified.

8.D For each of your new `Advert` subclasses, suggest appropriate attributes, operations and aggregation or composition structures.

8.E Reread the case study material for FoodCo and identify possible generalizations or compositions. Add these to the class diagram you drew for Exercises 7.C and 7.D.

8.F Consider your class diagram for FoodCo. Try to identify possible applications of the Transaction–Transaction Line Item pattern or of the Accountability pattern and redraw your diagram as appropriate.

Further Reading

Ambler (2004) discusses the role of generalization in the reuse of classes and use cases. However, this topic has received little detailed attention in recent books. Thus, Rumbaugh et al. (1991) remains one of the clearest summaries. This book pre-dates UML, but Rumbaugh was later one of the three amigos (along with Jacobson and Booch) who devised UML.

Jacobson et al. (1999) are very clear on the architectural and reuse issues related to composition, generalization and the identification of packages in requirements analysis.

There are now a number of books on developing reusable software components, such as Szyperski (2002) and Heineman and Councill (2001). Cheesman and Daniels (2001) give a very succinct and thorough introduction to the use of UML for the specification of components, and remain the best on this topic. (This book predates UML 2.0, so the notation differs in some minor details from the adopted specification.)

For a broad-ranging introduction to patterns, Gamma et al. (1995) and Buschmann et al. (1996) are still essential reading.

Withal (2007) documents over 30 'requirements patterns', many of which apply to analysis issues, while others focus on non-functional matters such as performance and security. Fowler (1997) describes a number of patterns that relate specifically to analysis and that are still highly relevant. In the book these were not presented in UML, but most have now been redrawn in UML format on Fowler's website martinfowler.com, where there are also some further pattern examples. Coad et al. (1997) also give a number of analysis and design patterns. Most are presented in Coad's own notation, but some are also shown in OMT notation and in Unified notation (an early version of UML).

The patterns home page can be found at http://hillside.net/patterns/. Further useful patterns are stored in the Portland Pattern Repository at www.c2.com/ppr.

Object Interaction

9.1 Introduction

Communication and collaboration between objects is fundamental to the operation of an object-oriented systsm. An object-oriented application comprises a set of autonomous objects, each responsible for a small part of the system's overall behaviour. These objects produce the required overall system behaviour through interaction: by exchanging messages that request information, that give information or that ask another object to perform some task. This mirrors the world in which we live, where most human endeavour involves communication, interaction and collaboration between individuals. For example, each employee in a manufacturing organization has specialized tasks. Different employees interact and work with each other in order to satisfy a customer request. This involves communicating to request information, to share information and to request help from each other.

We have already analysed use cases (in Chapter 7) to determine some aspects of the interaction and collaboration between objects leading to the identification of classes, their attributes and their associated responsibilities. As we move to design, these object interactions have to be specified more precisely. This involves deciding how to represent responsibilities as operations. CRC cards were suggested in Section 7.6 as a supporting technique to aid the analysis and the resulting identification and allocation of responsibilities. CRC cards can also be used effectively when designing object interaction in more detail to identify and allocate operations. UML 2.2 provides several diagram types and a rich syntax for modelling interaction between objects: interaction sequence diagrams, communication diagrams, interaction overview diagrams and timing diagrams. Communication diagrams were known as interaction collaboration diagrams in UML 1.X and have been introduced in Chapter 7.

9.2 Object Interaction and Collaboration

When an object sends a message to an object, an operation is invoked in the receiving object. For example, in the Agate case study there is a requirement to be able to determine the current cost of the advertisements for an advertising campaign. This responsibility is assigned to the Campaign class. For a particular campaign this might be achieved if the Campaign object sends a message to each of its Advert objects asking them for their current cost. In a programming language, sending the message getCost to an Advert object, might use the following syntax.

```
currentAdvertCost = anAdvert.getCost();
```

Note that in this example the Advert object is identified by the variable name anAdvert and the response to the message, known as the return value, is stored in the variable currentAdvertCost.

The cost of each advert returned by the operation getCost is totalled up in the attribute currentActualCost in the sending object, :Campaign (see Fig. A3.14 in Chapter A3 to see the attributes so far identified for the class). This attribute could be local to the operation in Campaign that calculates advertisement costs in the campaign. In order to calculate the sum of the costs for all adverts in a campaign, the statement above that gets the cost for each advert must be executed repeatedly. However, rather than think in terms of operation invocation we use the metaphor of message passing to describe object interaction, as this emphasizes that objects are encapsulated and essentially autonomous. Message passing can be represented on a class diagram, as in Fig. 9.1 where the message is shown as an arrow between two objects. This notation is like that of the communication diagram (Section 9.4) demonstrating that it is a natural extension of the class diagram.

It can be difficult to determine what messages should be sent by each object. In this case, it is clear that the getCost operation should be located in the Advert class. This operation uses data that is stored in the advertCost attribute, and this has been placed in Advert. We can also readily see that an operation that calculates the cost of a Campaign must be able to find out the cost of each Advert involved. But this is a simple interaction and the allocation of these operations is largely dictated by the presence of particular attributes in the classes. More complex requirements may involve the performance of complex tasks where an object receiving one message must itself send messages that initiate further interactions with other objects, but it may not be straightforward as to how these other objects should be involved in the interaction.

Figure 9.1 Object messaging.

It is an aim of object-oriented analysis and design to distribute system functionality appropriately among its classes. This does not mean that all classes have equal levels of responsibility but rather that each class should have relevant responsibilities. Where responsibilities are evenly distributed, each class tends not to be unduly complex and, as a result, is easier to develop, to test and to maintain. An appropriate distribution of responsibility among classes has the important side-effect of producing a system that is more resilient to changes in its requirements. When the users' requirements for a system change it is reasonable to expect that the application will need some modification, but ideally the change in the application should be of no greater magnitude than the change in the requirements. An application that is resilient in this sense costs less to maintain and to extend than one that is not. Fig. 9.2 illustrates this.

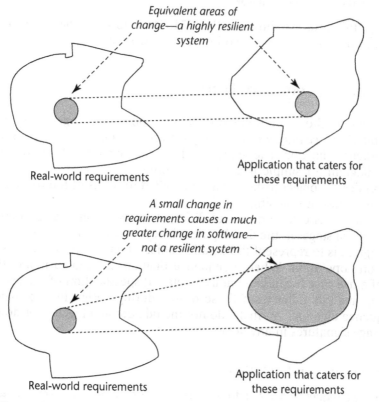

Figure 9.2 Resilience of a design.

The aim of modelling object interaction is to determine the most appropriate scheme of messaging between objects in order to support a particular user requirement. As we saw in Chapter 6, user requirements are first documented by use cases. Each use case can be seen as a dialogue between an actor and the system, that results in objects in the system performing tasks so that the system gives the required response. For this reason many interaction diagrams explicitly include objects to represent the user interface (boundary objects) and to manage the object interaction (control objects). When such objects are not shown explicitly, it can be assumed in most cases that they will need to be included at a later stage. The identification and specification of boundary objects is in part an analysis activity and in part a design activity. When we are analyzing requirements, our concern is to identify the nature of a dialogue in terms of the user's need for information and his or her access to the system's functionality. Deciding how an interaction should be realized in software will involve the detailed design of boundary objects that manage the dialogue and the introduction of other objects to enable the effective execution of the interaction. This is discussed in detail in Chapters 16 and 17.

In order to illustrate the preparation of interaction diagrams we build on the CRC card analysis of the use case Add a new advert to a campaign that was discussed in Section 7.6. The use case description used in Chapter 7 is repeated here:

> The campaign manager selects the required campaign for the client concerned and adds a new advert to the existing list of adverts for that campaign. The details of the advert are completed by the campaign manager.

The resulting CRC cards are shown in Fig. 7.31. These form the basis for the interaction sequence diagrams that are developed in the next two sections.

9.3 | Interaction Sequence Diagrams

A sequence diagram shows an interaction between objects arranged in a time sequence. An *interaction sequence diagram* (or simply a *sequence diagram*) is one of several kinds of UML interaction diagram. The sequence diagram is semantically equivalent to a communication diagram for simple interactions. Commonly, during requirements analysis or interaction design, object instances are modelled in terms of the roles they play and communicate by message passing.

Sequence diagrams can be drawn at different levels of detail and to meet different purposes at several stages in the development lifecycle. The commonest application of a sequence diagram is to represent the detailed object interaction that occurs for one use case or for one operation. When a sequence diagram is used to model the dynamic behaviour of a use case it can be seen as a detailed specification of the use case. Those drawn during analysis differ from those drawn during design in two major respects: analysis sequence diagrams normally do not include design objects; nor do they usually specify message signatures in any detail.

9.3.1 Basic concepts and notation

Figure 9.3 shows a sequence diagram for the use case Add a new advert to a campaign. The vertical dimension represents time and all objects[1] involved in the interaction are spread horizontally across the diagram. (The horizontal ordering of objects is arbitrary and has no modelling significance, though it improves readability if the interaction tends to proceed from left to right.) Time normally proceeds down the page. Each object (or element) in a sequence diagram is represented by a *lifeline*. This is a vertical dashed line with an object symbol at the top. The names of lifelines are not underlined even if the lifeline refers to an object. A message is shown by a solid horizontal arrow from one lifeline to another and is labelled with the message name. The only exception is an object creation message which is shown by a dashed line.

---

1   More generally an interaction may involve components, subsystems or other connectable elements.

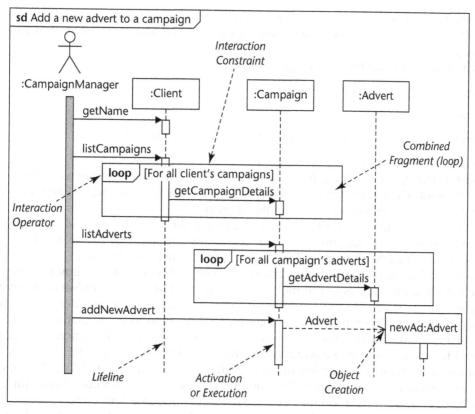

Figure 9.3 Sequence diagram for the use case Add a new advert to a campaign.

When a message is sent to an object, it invokes an operation[2] in that object. The message name is usually the same as the operation that is being invoked. Each message name may optionally be preceded by a sequence number that represents the sequence in which the messages are sent, but this is not usually necessary on a sequence diagram since the message sequence is already conveyed by its relative position along the time axis.[3]

Once a message is received, the operation that has been invoked begins to execute. The period of time during which an operation executes is known as an activation or an execution occurrence and is shown on the sequence diagram by a rectangular block laid along the lifeline. The activation period of an operation includes any delay while the operation waits for a response from another operation that it has itself invoked as part of its execution.

We have not included boundary or control objects on all the sequence diagrams in this chapter to simplify discussion. When preparing sequence diagrams during analysis, boundary and control objects are not considered in detail. Deciding how they should work and the number of these objects required for a use case is part of the detailed design process. Figure 9.3 shows a simple sequence diagram drawn without boundary or control

---

2 Though not explicitly specified in the UML specification, interaction sequence diagrams may be used to model interaction at the level of responsibilities as well.

3 The sequence of messages is partially ordered. Partially ordered means that the messages are placed in time sequence and two or more messages may be sent at the same time.

objects. The sequence diagram is drawn within a rectangle known as a *frame*. The sequence diagram has been given the same name as the use case whose interaction it models, namely Add a new advert to a campaign.

The general format for the heading of a frame is

```
[<kind>]<name>[<parameter-list>]
```

where

```
<parameter-list> ::= <parameter> [','<parameter>]*
```

Terms in square brackets [...] are optional.

In this example the kind of frame is a sequence diagram[4] and we are using the shortened form **sd**. The name field is the name of the use case that the interaction represents. There are no parameters for this sequence diagram.

The getName message is the first message received by the Client and is intended to correspond to the Campaign Manager requesting the name of the selected Client which is returned to the actor. The Client object then receives a listCampaigns message and a second period of operation activation begins. This is shown by the tall thin rectangle that begins at the message arrowhead. The Client object now sends a message getCampaignDetails to each Campaign object in turn in order to build up a list of campaigns. This repeated action is called an iteration. It is represented by enclosing the repeated messages inside a frame with the heading *loop*. The interaction in this type of frame is known as a *combined fragment*. The keyword loop is an example of an *interaction operator* that specifies the type of the combined fragment. We will introduce other interaction operators later. The conditions (known as guard conditions) for continuing or ending an iteration may be shown beside the frame's heading.

For the loop that retrieves all the campaign details for a client the guard condition is

```
[For all client's campaigns]
```

This is an example of an *interaction constraint*. A combined fragment with an interaction constraint will only execute if the constraint is evaluated as true.

The Campaign Manager next sends a message to a Campaign object asking it to list its advertisements. The Campaign object delegates responsibility for getting the advertisement title to each Advert object, although the Campaign object retains responsibility for the list as a whole (indicated by the continuation of the activation bar beyond the point where the message is sent).

When an advertisement is added to a campaign an Advert object is created. This is shown by the Advert *object creation* arrow (this invokes the constructor[5] operation) drawn with its arrowhead pointing directly to the object symbol at the top of the lifeline. Where an object already exists prior to the interaction the first message to that object points to the lifeline below the rectangle at the top of the lifeline. For example, this is the case for the Campaign object, which must exist before it can receive an addNewAdvert

---

4 A frame may be used for all UML diagram types. If the diagram has a naturally implied boundary then the frame may be omitted. Frames are used for interaction diagrams to make it clearer how they are combined.

5 A constructor operation creates an object instance. In the executable system a constructor typically allocates memory for the new object and intializes attribute values. It is conventional in object-oriented programming languages to name constructors with the class name; hence the constructor operation name begins with a capital letter as does the class name.

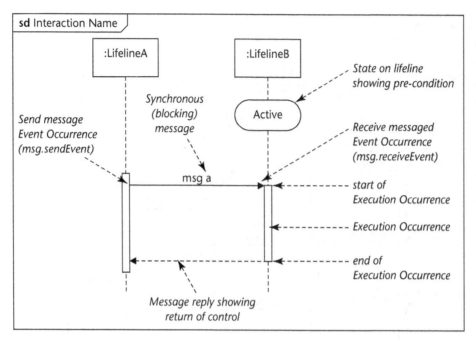

Figure 9.4 Sequence diagram showing message and execution events and states.

message. The sequence diagram in Fig. 9.3 corresponds directly to the interaction suggested by the CRC cards in Fig. 7.31. In effect, the sequence diagram is a more formal representation of the same interaction, but with the messages and the sequence of interaction both made explicit

Figure 9.4 shows the basic notation for sequence diagrams. The messages that we have been considering so far are synchronous messages or blocking calls. This means that the sending operation is suspended while the operation invoked by the message is executing. This is essentially a nested flow of control where the whole nested sequence of operations is completed before the calling operation resumes execution. This may be because the invoking operation requires data to be returned from the destination object before it can proceed. Formally sending the message is an example of a *send message event* and receiving the message is a *receive message event*. The execution occurrence starts with an *execution occurrence start event* and ceases with an *execution occurrence end event*. A reply message (with a dashed line) representing a return of control after the execution occurrence has ended is shown in the diagram. The reply message is optional in sequence diagrams.

This diagram also shows that the state of a lifeline can be shown on the lifeline in a sequence diagram. This is used to represent the constraint that the lifeline must be in the `Active` state before the message `msg a` can be accepted. Chapter 11 explains how states are used and represented in UML.

Most use cases imply at least one boundary object that manages the dialogue between the actor and the system. Figure 9.5 shows an alternative sequence diagram for the use case `Add a new advert to a campaign` but drawn this time with boundary and control objects. The boundary object representing the user interface is `:AddAdvertUI`. We have

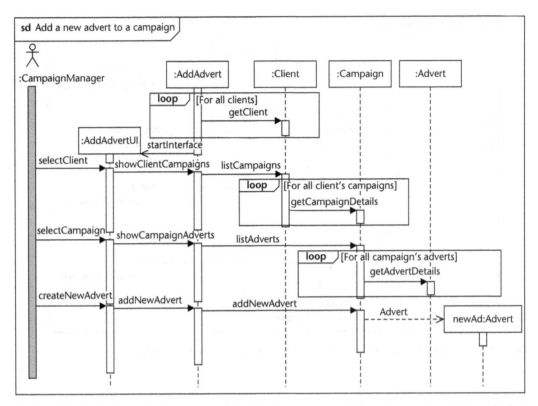

Figure 9.5 Sequence diagram for the use case Add a new advert to a campaign with boundary and control classes.

used the suffix UI to mean user interface. The control object is :AddAdvert and this manages the object interaction. Although not shown in Fig. 9.5, the interaction is initiated by the creation of the control object :AddAdvert. This then gets the client details before initiating the dialogue by creating the boundary class :AddAdvertUI.

Objects may be created or destroyed at different stages during an interaction.[6] On a sequence diagram the destruction of an object is indicated by a large X on the lifeline at the point in the interaction when the object is destroyed. An object may either be destroyed when it receives a message or it may self-destruct at the end of an execution occurrence if this is required by the operation that is being executed. This is shown in Fig. 9.6 where the lifeline representing the Advert class objects is named advert[i]:Advert to show explicitly that a set of Advert objects will be involved in the interaction one after the other.

An object can send a message to itself. This is known as a *reflexive message* and is shown by a message arrow that starts and finishes at the same object lifeline. The sequence diagram Check campaign budget includes an example of this. For ease of reference the use case description is repeated below.

---

6 Destructor operations are discussed in more detail in Chapter 14.

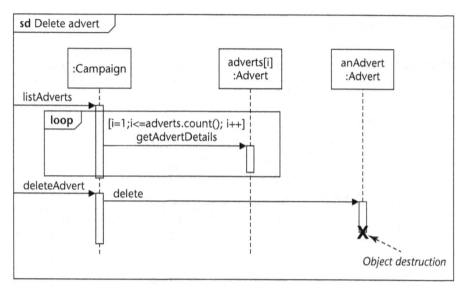

Figure 9.6 Object destruction.

The campaign budget may be checked to ensure that it has not been exceeded. The current campaign cost is determined by the total cost of all the adverts and the campaign overheads.

The corresponding sequence diagram is shown in Fig. 9.7 and this includes a reflexive message getOverheads sent from a Campaign object to itself.

In this case the reflexive message invokes a different operation from the operation that sent the message and a new activation symbol is stacked on the original execution occurrence. (This is the shorter second rectangle shown offset against the first execution occurrence.) In certain circumstances an operation invokes itself on the same object; this is known as *recursion* and can be similarly represented but is not illustrated here.[7] In Chapter 17, from Fig. 17.15 onwards, we show a number of sequence diagrams that are revisions to the sequence diagram Check campaign budget. These have been prepared from a design perspective and explicitly include boundary and control classes.

Until this point our discussion has centred on simple use cases and correspondingly simple interactions. These are typical of many modelling situations, but more complex interactions also occur in many systems. It is sometimes also necessary to represent in more detail the synchronization of messages. Figure 9.8 illustrates some variations in the UML notation, which are described as follows.

The *focus of control* indicates times during an execution occurrence when processing is taking place within that object. Parts of an execution occurrence that are not within the focus of control represent periods when, for example, an operation is waiting for a return from another object. The focus of control may be shown by shading those parts of the activation rectangle that correspond to active processing by an operation. In Fig. 9.8

---

7   If a limit has been set to the depth of recursion this can be recorded in a note on the diagram.

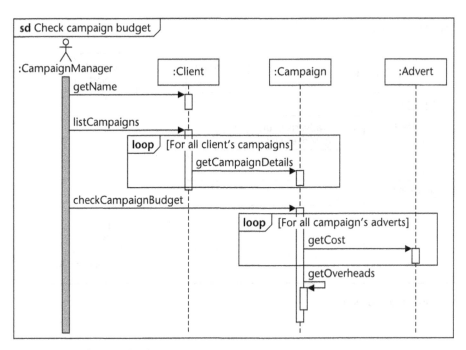

Figure 9.7 Sequence diagram for the use case `Check campaign budget`.

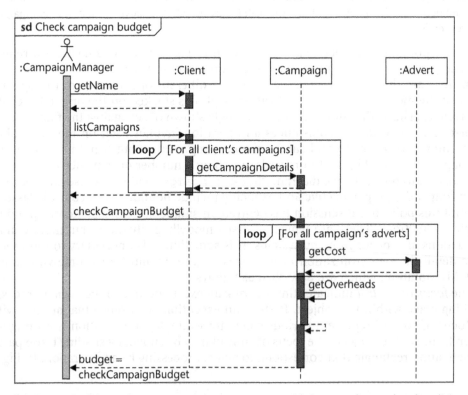

Figure 9.8 Sequence diagram for `Check campaign budget` with focuses of control and explicit replies shown.

the Check campaign budget sequence diagram of Fig. 9.7 is redrawn with foci of control shaded. The focus of control for the checkCampaignBudget operation is initially with the Campaign object, but is then transferred to the Advert object and the activation rectangle in the Campaign object is now unshaded while the Advert object has the focus of control. The checkCampaignBudget activation is also unshaded while the getOverheads operation is activated by the reflexive message getOverheads.

A *reply* is a return of control to the object that originated the message that began the activation. This is not a new message, but is only the conclusion of the invocation of an operation. Replies are shown with a dashed arrow, but it is optional to show them at all since it can be assumed that control is returned to the originating object at the end of the activation in a destination object (asynchronous messages–see Section 9.3.5–are exceptions). Replies are often omitted, as in Fig. 9.7. Figure 9.8 explicitly shows all replies for the same interaction.

A *return-value* is the value that an operation returns to the object that invoked it. These are rarely shown on an analysis sequence diagram, and are discussed further in Chapter 10. For example, in Fig. 9.8 the operation invoked by the message getName would have return-value of clientName and no parameters. In order to show the return-value the message could be shown as

```
clientName = getName
```

where clientName is a variable of type Name. The formal message label syntax is as follows:

```
[<attribute> '='] <signal-or-operation-name> ['('<argument-list>')']
[<return-value>] | '*'
```

where return-value and attribute assignment are only used on reply messages. The alternative message label of '*' is used to represent a message of any type being sent.

Lifelines in sequence diagrams may represent different types of UML element depending upon the scope and purpose of the sequence diagram; the choice of lifelines is very much up to the systems modeller. Although a lifeline may represent an object, the lifeline name is not underlined. In most of the examples used so far the lifeline name has represented an unnamed instance of a class, for example :Campaign in Fig. 9.8. In Fig. 9.5 the lifeline representing the newly created advertisement is named newAd:Advert. This could have been named simply newAd if we felt that it was not necessary to show explicitly that this was an object of the class Advert. In Fig. 9.9 the lifeline representing the Campaign class objects is named campaign[i]:Campaign to show explicitly that a set of Campaign objects will be involved in the interaction one after the other. In Fig. 9.14 the lifeline that is representing the subsystem ClientCampaignAds is named :ClientCampaigns ref ClientCampaignAds. Here the keyword ref is referring the reader to another sequence diagram ClientCampaignAds which describes what is happening within this lifeline.

Interaction constraints may be represented also in various formats. In Fig. 9.7 the first loop combined fragment has its interaction constraint specified as

```
[For all client's campaigns]
```

This is a straightforward statement of the condition that must be true for the combined fragment to execute. Alternatively, as in Fig. 9.9 the interaction constraint for the same combined fragment is more formally stated as

```
[i = 1;i <= campaigns.count();i++]
```

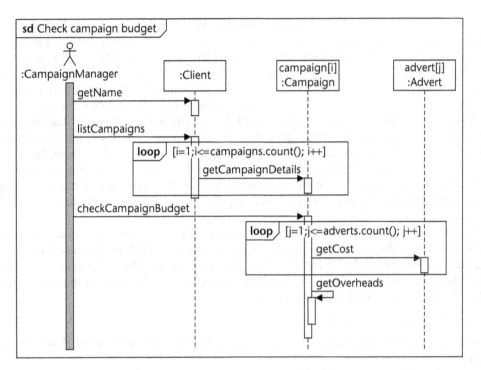

Figure 9.9 Sequence diagram for Check campaign budget with object selector notation shown.

This is stating that the loop will iterate from 1 to the value of campaigns.count(), which holds the number of campaigns associated with that particular client. This links in with the object selector naming for the lifeline campaigns[i]:Campaign, where the first iteration involves the first object and so on.

In Fig. 9.10 the loop interaction operator is shown with the parameters and to illustrate the notation we assume that :Client object will have at least one linked :Campaign object. The first parameter is the minimum number of iterations and the second is the maximum number of iterations. In this case the minimum number of interactions is 1. The '*' symbol indicates that a maximum is not set and is determined by the interaction constraint if present. The interaction constraint for the first combined fragment is stated as

    [i<=campaigns.count]

The loop operand will stop executing when the interaction constraint is not true and it has executed at least the minimum number of times. Of course, it is possible that the :Client object has no linked :Campaigns and consequently the loop operand should not execute even once and its parameters should be '0' and '*'. These are the default values and are normally not shown as in the case of the second combined fragment on the diagram.

A *synchronous message* or *procedural call* is shown with a full arrowhead (see Fig. 9.4) and is one that causes the invoking operation to suspend execution until the focus of control has been returned to it. In Fig. 9.8 the Check campaign budget interaction is shown with procedural calls and explicit returns. Procedural calls are appropriate for the interaction since each operation that invokes another does so in order to obtain data and cannot continue until that data is supplied.

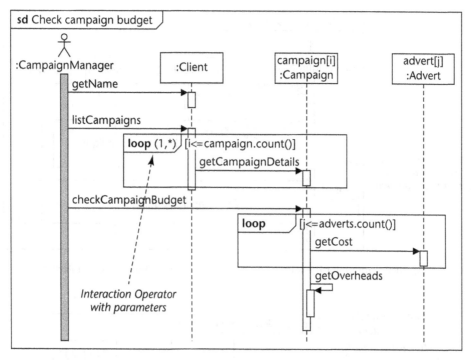

Figure 9.10 Sequence diagram for Check campaign budget with an interaction operator with parameters.

9.3.2 Managing sequence diagrams

Sometimes it is necessary to represent complex or large interactions using two or more sequence diagrams. This may be justified for several reasons. A single interaction may be too complex to represent in a single sequence diagram. It is possible that there are inter-action fragments common to several interactions and it is more effective to model these common interaction fragments only once. Also part of the interaction may involve complex messaging between members of a group of objects and this part of the interaction is best shown separately.

The first approach to modelling an interaction with more than one sequence diagram is to reference another interaction using an *interaction use* as shown in Fig. 9.11. Here there are two interactions, List client campaigns and Get campaign budget, being referenced. The keyword ref indicates that each is an interaction use and that they are referring to the sequence diagrams List client campaigns and Get campaign budget. These two sequence diagrams are shown in Figs 9.12 and 9.13 respectively. Each of these is an example of an *interaction fragment*. An interaction fragment is a piece of an interaction that can be used as part of one or more larger interactions. The inter-action fragment List client campaigns in Fig. 9.12 could clearly be reused in any interaction that requires a list of the campaigns for a specific client.

In Fig. 9.11 the message listCampaigns is being sent to the interaction use List client campaigns. This same message enters the corresponding interaction fragment in Fig. 9.12 and is shown coming from the edge of the frame.

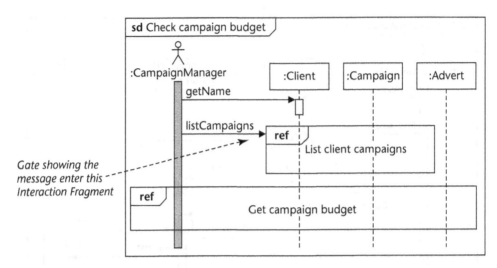

Figure 9.11 Sequence diagram for the interaction `Check campaign budget` with interaction use.

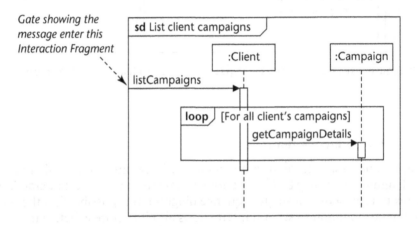

Figure 9.12 Sequence diagram for the interaction fragment `List client campaigns`.

The point where a message goes to an interaction use and from where a message enters an interaction fragment is known as a *gate*.

The interaction use `Get campaign budget` in Fig. 9.11 does not have any messages going to it so there are no gates shown on the interaction use or in the interaction fragment in Fig. 9.13. This interaction fragment has been chosen for illustrative purposes and has one clear disadvantage. It contains the actor *:CampaignManager* and consequently can only be used in interactions where the campaign manager is getting the campaign budget. If the interaction did not contain *:CampaignManager*, it could be used for interactions where, for example, the account manager wished to know the campaign budget.

Complex interactions can also be split up using lifelines to represent groups of objects and their interaction or to represent subsystems. Figure 9.14 shows the interaction `Add a new advert to a campaign` where the messaging between the :Client, :Campaign and :Advert lifelines is hidden within the :ClientCampaigns lifeline.

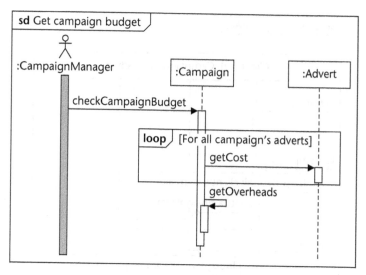

Figure 9.13 Sequence diagram for the interaction fragment `Get campaign budget`.

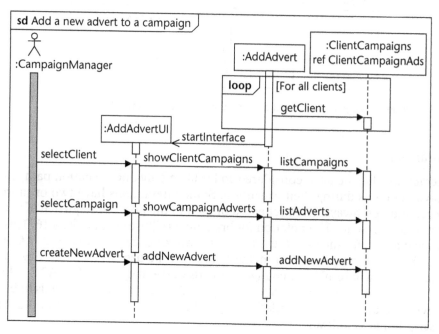

Figure 9.14 Sequence diagram with the detail of the interaction in `ClientCampaignAds` not showing.

The `:ClientCampaigns` lifeline references the sequence diagram `ClientCampaignAds` for the hidden detail. This is shown in Fig. 9.15. Note that the messages that are received by the lifeline `:ClientCampaigns` enter the interaction fragment `ClientCampaignAds` through gates.

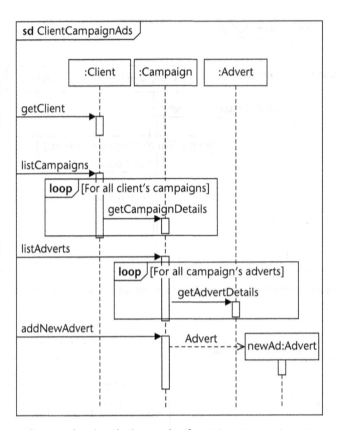

Figure 9.15 Sequence diagram showing the interaction for ClientCampaignAds.

9.3.3 Branching

The interactions that we have considered so far have only one execution path, although some have iterations during their execution. Some interactions have two or more alternative execution pathways. Each reflects a branch in the possible sequence of events for the use case it represents. The notation for branching is illustrated in Fig. 9.16. This shows a sequence diagram for the use case Add a new advert to a campaign if within budget. The relationship between this use case and the use case Add a new advert to a campaign will result in a change to the use case diagram in Fig. A2.2, where the use case Add a new advert to a campaign if within budget needs to be added and shown with an «include» relationship with Check campaign budget. The use case description is as follows.

> A new advertisement is added to a campaign by the campaign manager only if the campaign budget is not exceeded by adding the new advert. If adding the advertisement would cause the budget to be exceeded then a campaign budget extension request is generated. This will be recorded for later reference. The budget extension request is printed and sent to the client at the end of the day.

The first part of this sequence diagram uses the interaction use of two interaction fragments List client campaigns and Get campaign budget which have already

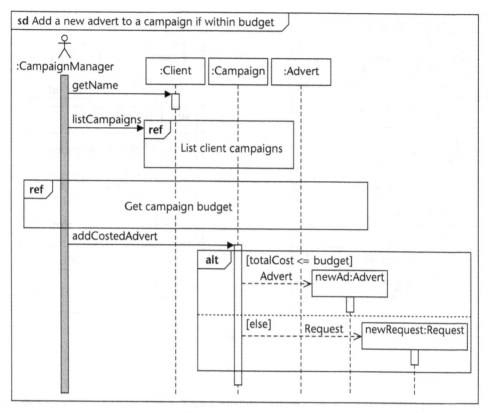

Figure 9.16 Sequence diagram for `Add a new advert to a campaign if within budget` showing branching.

be described in Figures 9.11 and 9.12. The branching is shown in the combined fragment named with the keyword *alt* which is a short form of *alternatives*. The combined fragment has two (or more) compartments known as *interaction operands*. Each operand corresponds to one of the alternatives in the combined fragment and each operand should have an interaction constraint to indicate under what conditions it executes. The sequence of the operands is not significant. In this example there are only two operands. The interaction constraint [else] can be used as the default in the last operand. The first operand deals with the case where the campaign is within budget and a new object of the class Advert is created by the message Advert. The second operand represents the case when the budget is spent or exceeded and a request to add a new advert has to be created. This is shown by the message Request creating the newRequest instance.

The branching notation can be used at a generic level to create a sequence diagram that represents all possible sequences of interaction for a use case. Such a generic diagram will typically be showing communication between anonymous objects or roles rather than particular instances. In general, looping and branching constructs correspond respectively to iteration and decision points in the use case. When drawn at an instance level a sequence diagram shows a specific interaction between specific objects. The two kinds of sequence diagram (generic and instance level) are equivalent to one another if the interactions implied by the use case contain no looping or branching constructs.

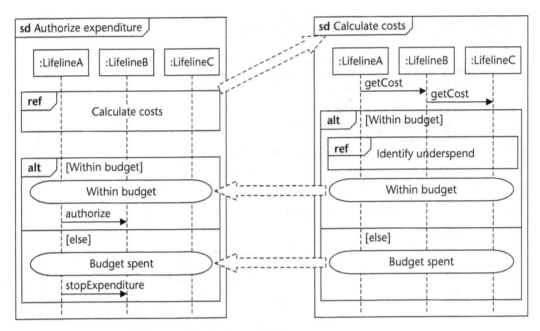

Figure 9.17 An example showing the use of continuations.

9.3.4 Continuations

Sequence diagrams can be linked using *continuations*. Continuations can be specified within an `alt` combined fragment to allow a link back to a referring sequence diagram. In Fig. 9.17 the continuations `Within budget` and `Budget spent` are used to link the two sequence diagrams. The sequence diagram `Authorize expenditure` includes the interaction use `Calculate costs`. At this point in `Authorize expenditure` the detail of the interaction is shown in `Calculate costs`. The interaction in `Calculate costs` proceeds with the two `getCost` messages. If the cost is within budget the interaction constraint in the first operand of the `alt` combined fragment is true and the interaction use `Identify underspend` is followed. (This interaction fragment is just illustrative and is not specified.) The flow of the interaction now comes to the continuation `Within budget`. The interaction now moves back to sequence diagram `Authorize expenditure`, continues from the point of the continuation with the same name and the message `authorize` is sent. In a similar way if the cost is not within budget the `[else]` operand within `Calculate costs` is satisfied and control is returned to `Authorize expenditure` at the `Budget spent` continuation. The dashed arrows between the two sequence diagrams are not part of UML and are only intended to illustrate the transfer of execution between the diagrams.

9.3.5 Asynchronous messages

So far we have been dealing only with synchronous messages. An *asynchronous message* or *signal*, drawn with an open arrowhead as in Fig. 9.18, does not cause the invoking operation to halt execution while it awaits a return. When an asynchronous message is sent, operations in both objects may carry out processing at the same time. Asynchronous

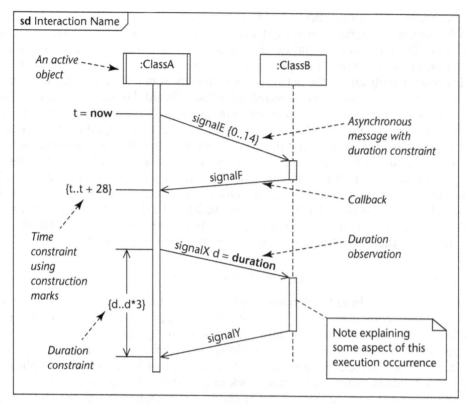

Figure 9.18 Sequence diagram showing different message types and time constraints.

messages are frequently used in real-time systems where operations in different objects must execute concurrently, either for reasons of efficiency or because the system simulates real-world activities that also take place concurrently. It may be necessary for an operation that has been invoked asynchronously to notify the object that invoked it when it has terminated. This is done by explicitly sending a message (known as a *callback*) to the originating object.

9.3.6 Time constraints

A sequence diagram can be labelled in various ways. Labels may be included using the note notation in UML with, for example, descriptions or explanations of aspects of the diagram or model. If time constraints apply to the execution of operations or other elements of interaction diagrams these may be shown. In Fig. 9.18 each of the messages is simply named with signalE, signalF and so on. Time expressions may be associated with the name of the message so that duration constraints can be specified for the execution of an operation or the transmission of a message. Construction marks may also be used to show a time interval with a constraint. This is illustrated in Fig. 9.18 to show the interval between the sending signalE and receiving signalF. Time constraints are frequently used in modelling real-time systems where the application must respond within a certain time, typically for reasons of safety or efficiency. For most other information systems the sequence of the messages is the most important issue.

So far we have only considered message arrows that have been drawn horizontally across the sequence diagram and at right angles to the object lifelines. Drawing a message arrow in this fashion indicates that the time taken to send a message is not significant in comparison to the time taken for operation execution. There is consequently no need to model another activity during the period while a message is in transit. In some applications the length of time taken to send a message is itself significant. For example, in distributed systems messages are sent over a network from an object on one computer to another object on a different computer. If the transit time for a message is significant, the message arrow is slanted downwards so that the arrowhead (the arrival of the message) is below (later than) the tail (the origination of the message). The asynchronous messages (e.g. signalE) shown in Fig. 9.18 illustrate this. The message signalE is constrained to take between 0 and 14 time units by the duration constraint shown in Fig. 9.18. The duration of signalX is shown as taking d time units and a duration constraint has been specified for the interval from sending signalX and receiving signalY. This duration constraint states that the interval must be between d and d*3 time units.

9.3.7 Modelling real-time systems and concurrency

Real-time systems are broadly characterized by the need to respond to external events within tight time constraints. Partly for this reason, they frequently exhibit concurrent behaviour in the form of simultaneous execution pathways or *threads of control*. An application that has concurrent execution always includes some objects that coordinate and initiate threads of control; these are *active objects*. In addition, real-time applications usually include many other objects that work only within a thread of control; these are known as *passive objects*. Active objects or classes are shown with a double line at each side of the head of the lifeline in an interaction diagram. The lifeline :ClassA in Fig. 9.18 is an example of an active object. Active objects can continue to operate without the invocation of operations from other objects. They have their own thread of control. Active objects are frequently composites with embedded parts (the interface or boundary class as a composite is discussed in Chapter 17).

It is important for a sequence diagram of a concurrent system to show clearly which threads of control are active at any time. Combined fragments to show parallel (keyword par), optional (keyword opt) and critical activity are useful when modelling real-time systems. Figure 9.19 shows a complete list of the interaction operators defined in UML with a short explanation of each. Timing diagrams provide a clear diagrammatic representation of the timing constraints, state changes and messaging between lifelines and are discussed later.

9.3.8 Guidelines for preparing sequence diagrams

Modelling interaction is an important activity during the information systems development process. The following are some general guidelines for the preparation of sequence diagrams in particular and are adapted from Bennett et al. (2005).

1. Decide at what level you are modelling the interaction. Is it describing an operation, a use case, the messaging between components or the interaction of subsystems or systems?
2. Identify the main elements involved in the interaction. If the interaction is at use case level the collaborating objects may already have been identified through the use

Interaction Operator	Explanation and use
alt	Alternative represents alternative behaviours, each choice of behaviour being shown in a separate operand. The operand whose interaction constraint is evaluated as true executes.
opt	Option describes a single choice of operand that will only execute if its interaction constraint evaluates as true.
break	Break indicates that the combined fragment is performed instead of the remainder of the enclosing interaction fragment.
par	Parallel indicates that the execution operands in the combined fragment may be merged in any sequence once the event sequence in each operand is preserved.
seq	Weak sequencing results in the ordering of each operand being maintained but event occurrence from different operands on different lifelines may occur in any order. The order of event occurrences on common operands is the same as the order of the operands.
strict	Strict sequencing imposes a strict sequence on execution of the operands but does not apply to nested fragments.
neg	Negative describes an operand that is invalid.
critical	Critical region imposes a constraint on the operand that none of its event occurrences on the lifelines in the region can be interleaved.
ignore	Ignore indicates the message types, specified as parameters, that should be ignored in the interaction.
consider	Consider states which messages should be considered in the interaction. This is equivalent to stating that all others should be ignored.
assert	Assertion states that the sequence of messaging in the operand is the only valid continuation.
loop	Loop is used to indicate an operand that is repeated a number of times until the interaction constraint for the loop is no longer true.

Figure 9.19 Interaction operators that may be used with combined fragments.

of CRC cards and their responsibilities partly allocated. Of course, CRC cards can be used at different levels of granularity to explore the behaviour of any group of lifelines.

3. Consider the alternative scenarios that may be needed. Again a CRC card exercise may be helpful in exploring these.
4. Identify any existing interactions that have already been modelled as sequence diagrams or that will be so that they can be included as interaction uses.
5. Draw the outline structure of the diagram.
   a. Create a frame with a suitable name.
   b. Add the appropriate lifelines starting with the lifeline that is first involved with the interaction and then placing the others from left to right. This can improve the layout of the sequence diagram. If an actor lifeline is being modelled, then this should be placed first followed by the boundary lifeline, if this being modelled.

6. Add the detailed interaction.
   a. Starting from the top of the frame add the first message. Lay out the subsequent messages from top to bottom, showing the appropriate level of detail in the message labels.
   b. Use combined fragments with appropriate interaction operators to describe, for example, looping, branching and optional paths. The full list of interaction operators is shown in Fig. 9.19. Add interaction constraints to these as necessary.
   c. Identify any interaction fragments that are or will be used in other interactions and place these in separate sequence diagrams. Prepare the sequence diagrams for these interaction fragments so that they are as reusable as possible. Place the corresponding interaction uses in the diagram being drawn.
   d. Annotate the diagram with comments where this is necessary, for example to include pre- and post-conditions or to improve readability.
   e. Add state invariants to the diagram as required (as shown in Fig. 9.4).
7. Check for consistency with linked sequence diagrams and modify as necessary. Sequence diagrams may be linked in various ways that have been described in Section 9.3.3. If the interaction is at the level of a use case it is useful to consider any other use cases that are linked by extend or include dependencies.
8. Check for consistency with other UML diagrams or models, in particular, with the relevant class diagrams (and state machine diagrams if they have been prepared at this point).

Once a first-cut sequence diagram has been produced, it is important to work through these steps again from step 2 to refine the model. For complex interactions it takes several iterations to produce a model that describes the required behaviour unambiguously and clearly.

9.4 | Communication Diagrams

Communication diagrams are the second kind of interaction diagram in the UML notation set. They have already been introduced in Chapter 7, where they have been used to represent the collaboration that realizes a use case. We will examine the notation for communication diagrams in more detail here.

9.4.1 Basic concepts and notation

Communication diagrams have many similarities to sequence diagrams. For straightforward interactions they express the same information in a different format and, like sequence diagrams, they can be drawn at various levels of detail and during different stages in the system development process. The most significant difference between the two types of interaction diagram is that a communication diagram explicitly shows the links between the lifelines that participate in a collaboration. (Collaborations have been discussed in Chapter 7.) Unlike sequence diagrams, there is no explicit time dimension and lifelines are represented only by rectangles. Figure 9.20 shows an example of a communication diagram.

In a communication diagram the interaction is drawn on what is essentially a fragment of a class or object diagram, as can be seen in Fig. 9.20. This example is drawn at quite

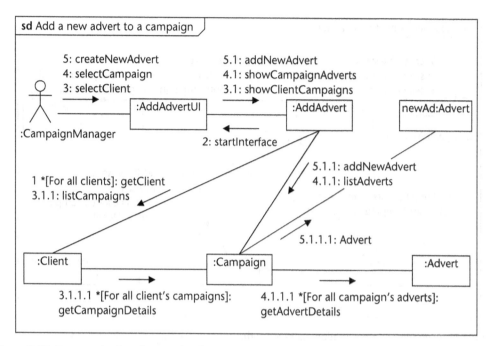

Figure 9.20 Communication diagram for the use case Add a new advert to a campaign.

a simple level of detail (but note that it includes a lifeline :AddAdvertUI representing a boundary object and the lifeline :AddAdvert representing a control object). This level of detail is often sufficient to capture the nature of an interaction. Since the diagram has no time dimension the order in which messages are sent is represented by sequence numbers. In this diagram the sequence numbers are written in a nested style (for example, 3.1 and 3.1.1) to indicate the nesting of control within the interaction that is being modelled. Thus the operation showCampaignAdverts passes control to the operation listAdverts, which has one deeper level of nesting. A similar style of numbering is used to indicate branching constructs.

The notation for iteration is different in communication diagrams and for message 3.1.1.1 is

    *[For all client's campaigns]

where the * indicates iteration. The message label syntax is discussed in more detail in the next section.

Typically, there is more than one possible way of designing the interaction for a particular use case and each of the alternative interactions will have different strengths and weaknesses. The alternatives arise because of the different possible allocations of responsibility. For example, although feasible, the interaction in Fig. 9.20 may have some undesirable features. The message getCampaignDetails from :Client to :Campaign requires the :Client lifeline to return these details to the :AddAdvert lifeline. If the campaign details only include the campaign names, then a relatively small amount of data is being passed from :Campaign to :Client and then on to :AddAdvert. This may be acceptable. On the other hand, if the campaign details also include the start and finish dates for each campaign and the campaign budget then much more data is

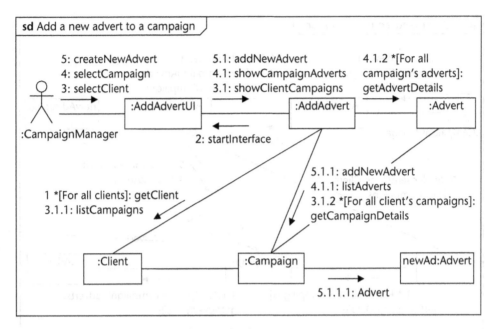

Figure 9.21 Alternative communication diagram for the use case `Add a new advert to a campaign`.

being passed through :Client. In these circumstances :Client is now responsible for providing significant amounts of data about the campaigns; arguably this should be the responsibility of the :Campaign lifelines themselves. An alternative interaction can pass data about campaigns directly from :Campaign to :AddAdvert. This alternative interaction is shown in Fig. 9.21, where :AddAdvert takes the responsibility for getting the campaign details directly from the :Campaign lifelines. In this interaction the :Client object is only responsible for providing :AddAdvert with a list of its campaigns.[8] This is an appropriate responsibility for :Client.

9.4.2 Message labels in communication diagrams

Messages on a communication diagram are represented by a set of symbols that are the same as those used in a sequence diagram, but with some additional elements to show sequencing and recurrence as these cannot be inferred from the structure of the diagram. Each message label includes the message signature and also a sequence number that reflects call nesting iteration, branching and concurrency within the interaction. The formal message label syntax is as follows:

```
<sequence-expression> [<attribute> '='] <signal-or-operation-name>
['('<argument-list>')'] [<return-value>]
```

Guard conditions may be written in Object Constraint Language (OCL) (see Chapter 10), and are only shown where the enabling of a message is subject to the defined condition.

---

8 This will be a list of object identifiers that is then used by :AddAdvert to navigate to each Campaign object in turn.

Type of message	Syntax example
Simple message	`4: addNewAdvert`
Nested call with return-value. *The return value is placed in the variable* `name`	`3.1.2: name = getName`
Conditional message. *This message is only sent if the condition* `[balance > 0]` *is true*	`5 [balance > 0]: debit(amount)`
Iteration	`4.1*[For all adverts]: getCost`

Figure 9.22 Examples of the syntax for various types of message label.

A *sequence-expression*[9] is a list of *sequence-terms* separated by dots ('.') and terminated by a colon:

`<sequence-term> '.' [<sequence-term>]* ':'`

A *sequence-term* has the following syntax:

`<integer> [<name>] [<recurrence>]`

In this expression *integer* represents the sequential order of the message. This may be nested within a loop or a branch construct, so that, for example, message 5.1.3 occurs after message 5.1.2 and both are contained within the activation of message 5.1. In Fig. 9.21 messages 4.1.1 and 4.1.2 are nested within the activation of message 4.1. The *name* of a sequence-expression is used to differentiate two concurrent messages since these are given the same sequence number. For example, messages 3.2.1a and 3.2.1b are concurrent within the activation of message 3.2. *Recurrence* reflects either iterative or conditional execution and its syntax is as follows:

Branching: `'['guard']'`
Iteration: `'*''['iteration-clause']'`

Some sample message labels are listed in Fig. 9.22.

Figure 9.23 illustrates the use of a communication diagram to show the interaction for a single operation, in this case `checkCampaignBudget`, which is one of the operations shown in the sequence diagrams in Fig. 9.7.

Communication diagrams are preferred to sequence diagrams by some developers as they offer a view of object interaction that is easy to relate to the underlying collaboration because of the visibility of links between the lifelines. However, they do not provide the same level of syntax as sequence diagrams and are not suitable for complex interaction. Generally, communication diagrams are probably useful during analysis activities while sequence diagrams are better at representing design detail. Communication diagrams are used to describe analysis use case realizations because typically the messages are not fully specified at this stage. However, when there are many messages between two objects in one interaction then a collaboration diagram is more difficult to read than the

---

9 *Sequence-expressions* are commonly omitted from interaction sequence diagrams as the sequence is normally implied by the relative position of the messages one after the other or by using combined fragments with interaction operators.

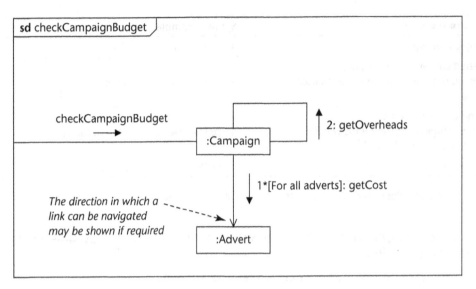

Figure 9.23 Communication diagram for the operation `checkCampaignBudget`.

equivalent sequence diagram. In particular, sequence diagrams also offer more explicit visual cues to the duration of each activation and show detailed design interactions more clearly. We believe that it is seldom useful to draw both kinds of interaction diagram for the same purpose. Some developers use sequence diagrams for the generic model of the interaction and collaboration diagrams for specific scenarios. The choice of which is the more appropriate usually depends on the nature of the interaction and the purpose of the diagram. Often neither offers a clear advantage and it should be a matter of organizational policy as to which is normally prepared.

9.5 | Interaction Overview Diagrams

Interaction overview diagrams are variants of activity diagrams (explained in Chapter 5) and incorporate interaction diagrams. An interaction overview diagram focuses on the overview of flow of control in an interaction where the nodes in the diagram are interactions or interaction uses. As a result the detailed messaging of the interaction is hidden in the diagram. The syntax for activity diagrams is used including decision and merge nodes.

In order to produce an interaction overview diagram the interaction needs to be broken down into its key elements. The interaction Add a new advert to a campaign if within budget (Fig. 9.16) is already broken down to some extent by referring to two interaction fragments. However, the alt combined fragment could be broken down further to show the flow of control. Two more interaction fragments, Create advert and Create request are introduced (Figs 9.25 and 9.26 respectively) and each is shown as an interaction use in Fig. 9.24.

The interaction overview diagram is shown in Fig. 9.27. As it is a variant of an activity diagram, it starts with an initial node leading to the interaction fragment List Campaigns for Client. The next node is an interaction use (the interaction fragment

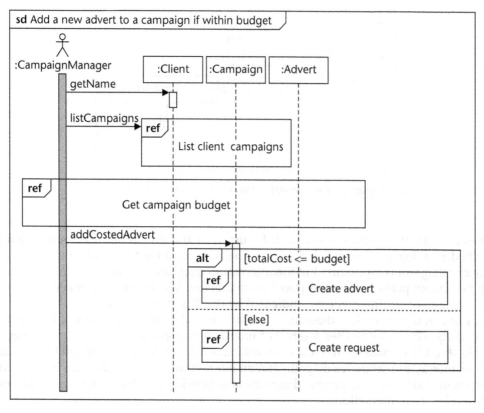

Figure 9.24 Alternative version of the sequence diagram for the interaction Add a new advert to a campaign if within budget.

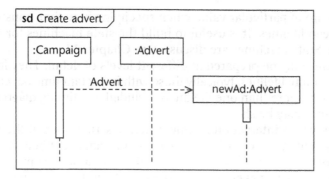

Figure 9.25 Sequence diagram for the interaction fragment Create advert.

referenced is shown in Fig. 9.12). This is followed by another in-line interaction fragment, Add Costed Advert. It is matter of judgement as to when it is best to have interaction fragments or interaction uses as nodes. It depends upon the level of detail that is most appropriate for the diagram. It is useful to reference interaction fragments where they have already been specified, but it does depend upon the purpose of the interaction overview diagram. In this case the interaction fragment could just as easily have been

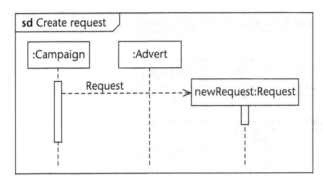

Figure 9.26 Sequence diagram for the interaction fragment `Create request`.

represented as an interaction use and the detail of the interaction fragment could be specified in a separate sequence diagram. The `alt` combined fragment in the original sequence diagram is represented in the interaction overview diagram as a decision node with two output paths, each with a guard condition, that lead to the appropriate interaction uses. The end of the interaction is indicated by the final node notation.

An interaction overview diagram is useful when describing a complex interaction, particularly when it comprises a series of interaction fragments, some of which may be used in several interactions. In most circumstances it is not going to be helpful to produce both an interaction sequence diagram and an interaction overview diagram for the same interaction. Interaction overview diagrams also provide a useful notation to describe high-level system interactions.

9.6 Timing Diagrams

Timing diagrams are of particular value when specifying how time constraints affect the interaction between lifelines. It is useful to build the state machines for the key lifelines at the same time. State machines are discussed in Chapter 11.

Timing diagrams may be prepared at different levels of detail. They include the state changes for one or more lifelines; typically those with important time dependent behaviour are modelled. Where more than one lifeline is included in a timing diagram the messages between the lifelines may be shown.

Figure 9.28 shows an interaction fragment that describes part of the interaction that occurs when a car enters a car park. It shows the messages sent between active objects, but does not show any activations. Access to the car park is controlled by a barrier which is only raised after a ticket has been requested and taken by the driver. There is a weight sensor just before the barrier that activates the ticket machine when a car is detected. When the car moves to go under the barrier the ticket machine is deactivated. There is another weight sensor after the barrier that detects when the car has passed under the barrier so that it can be lowered.

The timing diagram containing the lifelines `:TicketMachine` and `:Barrier` is shown in Fig. 9.29. The diagram is divided into two instances, one for each lifeline. The `:Barrier` lifeline starts off in the `Lowered` state and moves to the `Raised` state after the lifeline has received the signal `raiseBarrier`. The time `t` is set at the time the

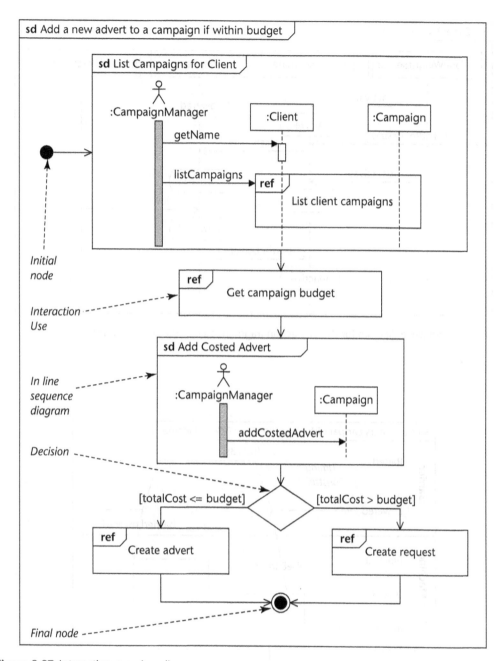

Figure 9.27 Interaction overview diagram.

raiseBarrier message is received by the lifeline :Barrier and the timing constraint specifies that :Barrier should change state within 3 seconds of time t. The sloped line between the two states models the duration of the state change. The Blocked state represents the ticket machine being unable to complete its cycle and issue another ticket until the car has gone through the weight sensor after the barrier and the barrier is lowered.

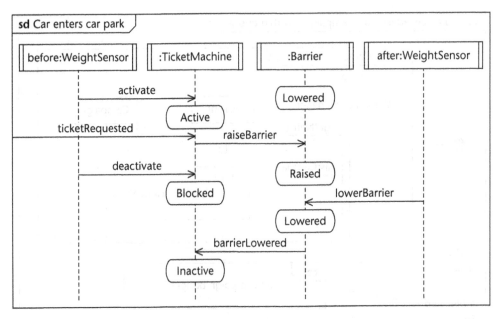

Figure 9.28 Sequence diagram for the interaction fragment `Car enters car park`.

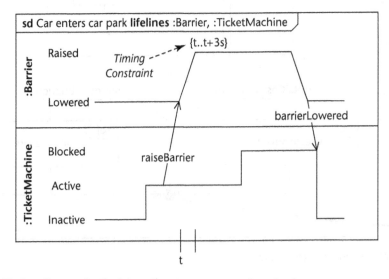

Figure 9.29 Timing diagram for the interaction `Car Enters Car Park`.

9.7 | Model Consistency

All the UML diagrams and documentation should be consistent with each other. The preparation of sequence and communication diagrams involves the allocation of operations to classes. These operations should be listed against the correct classes in the class diagram and, if operation signatures have been specified in full, these must be consistent. The sequence and communication diagrams and the class diagrams should be mutually consistent. A good CASE tool enforces this consistency at a syntactic level, usually by prompting the developer with a list of operations currently allocated to a class when he or she adds a message that is sent to an object of that class. If a corresponding operation has not been defined in the destination class, the appropriate operation should be added automatically to the class definition.

But to ensure full consistency between a class diagram and a set of related interaction diagrams requires more than the simple syntactic checking described above. Every sending object in an interaction diagram must have the ability to send its message to the destination object and this requires it to know the identity or *object reference* of the destination object. There are only two ways that a sending object can know the reference of a destination object. It may already be known by the sending object via a direct link, which really means that an association exists between the respective classes to which the objects belong. Alternatively, a sending object may obtain the reference it needs indirectly from another object (usually of a different class) that has a link with the destination object. The representation and placement of the object references that represent associations is a design issue that we discuss in detail in Chapter 14. At this stage it is sufficient to ensure that there is some possible pathway via object links (deduced from associations on the class diagram) that connects a sending object to a destination object. Any inconsistency between an interaction diagram and the corresponding class diagram indicates a flaw in one or the other. There may be a necessary association missing from the class diagram, for instance. Note that the existence of an association does not by itself guarantee the existence of any particular link. Where the minimum multiplicity of an association is zero there may not be any object that has a link for that association. If the multiplicity is one (or more), then each object must have at least one link. All message pathways should be analysed carefully.

When an interaction fragment is referenced within a more complex interaction (described in either a sequence diagram or an interaction overview diagram) it is important that this interaction use is consistent with the interaction fragment. Of course an interaction fragment may well be used in several other interactions.

State machines (described in Chapter 11) document information about messages from the perspective of an object rather than an interaction, and it is also important to check for consistency between the state machine diagram for a class and all interaction diagrams that involve objects of that class.

9.8 | Summary

Object interaction is a key feature of the object-oriented approach to systems development. When discussing object interaction we use the metaphor of message passing to describe the mode of collaboration between objects. Developing interaction diagrams requires a careful analysis of the use cases and may involve the use of CRC cards (see

Chapter 7). UML provides a range of modelling techniques to describe interactions–sequence, communication, interaction overview and timing diagrams–which provide a rich notation. Communication diagrams are more commonly used when analysing use cases to prepare analysis use case realizations. Sequence and interaction overview diagrams may be used effectively to represent detailed design specifications of interactions. Timing diagrams are particularly useful for real-time systems. When working with complex interactions it may be necessary to use several linked diagrams. UML provides various notational alternatives for this. It is common to have more than one possible interaction for a use case and it is a pragmatic judgement as to which is most appropriate. The design considerations that inform such judgements are discussed in detail in Chapter 14. An integral part of the process of developing interaction diagrams is ensuring that they and the class diagrams for an application are mutually consistent.

Review Questions

9.1   List two specific features of bad object-oriented modelling that are discouraged by the use of communication diagrams.

9.2   What are the benefits of keeping all classes reasonably small and self-contained?

9.3   What are the main differences between sequence diagrams and communication diagrams?

9.4   What are the essential parts of a message label (i) in a sequence diagram and (ii) in a communication diagram?

9.5   What is a lifeline?

9.6   What is meant by execution occurrence?

9.7   How are combined fragments used in sequence diagrams?

9.8   How do asynchronous messages differ from synchronous messages (i) in terms of the behaviour of the sending and receiving objects and (ii) in their notation?

9.9   In what circumstances are sequence numbers in a communication diagram written in nested style (e.g. 3.2.1)?

9.10 What consistency checks should be applied to interaction diagrams?

9.11 Describe three ways in which complex interactions may be represented using UML.

9.12 What is the difference between an interaction use and an interaction fragment?

9.13 What is the purpose of interaction overview diagrams?

9.14 What can be represented by the nodes in an interaction overview diagram?

9.15 How are timing diagrams used and when are they most useful?

Case Study Work, Exercises and Projects

Exercises 9.A–9.C are based on the use cases listed in Exercise 7.A and the use case realizations developed in Exercise 7.B.

9.A For each of the use cases prepare a sequence diagram.

9.B For the use case Start line run identify an alternative interaction and prepare a sequence diagram for this interaction.

9.C Critically compare the two interactions that you have identified for the use case Start line run and with suitable justification determine which is the more appropriate.

9.D Using a CASE tool with which you are familiar, enter several use case realizations including at least one communication and one sequence diagram (e.g. the FoodCo models).

9.E Critically evaluate the extent to which the CASE tool supports UML and the consistency check that is necessary between the different diagrams.

Further Reading

Rumbaugh et al. (1991) and Booch (1994) discuss their variants of message modelling in detail. Buschmann et al. (1996) provide interesting examples of system sequence diagrams using a notation from which the UML notation for sequence diagrams has developed. Douglass (2004) discusses the use of this notation for real-time systems.

Specifying Operations

10.1 Introduction

Operation specifications describe the detailed behaviour of the system. They support the graphical models in UML by adding detail and precision so that users can confirm the correctness of the model, and designers can use them as a basis for software development. But they are potentially the most complex of all entries in the repository given their level of detail. Before operations can be specified, object interaction (see Chapter 9) should be modelled as it helps to determine the distribution of behaviour among the various classes and results in the allocation of operations to classes.

Operation specifications provide the precision that is necessary for software construction and can be written at varying levels of detail. The 'contract' style is a kind of black box specification. If the behaviour of an operation is simple, a contract that describes only its external interface detailing its inputs and outputs may be all that is required. If its behaviour is not yet described in any detail, a black box specification may be all that is possible. Often, though, there is also a need to describe an operation's logic, or internal behaviour.

The two general ways of doing this are respectively called 'algorithmic' (or 'procedural') and 'non-algorithmic' (or 'declarative'). A non-algorithmic approach is generally preferred in object-oriented development, but in some situations only an algorithmic approach is sufficiently expressive. UML does not require any specific techniques or notations for specifying operations, but activity diagrams (first introduced in Chapter 5) can express the logic of an operation effectively in a graphical form. UML also has a formal language known as the Object Constraint Language (OCL), which was originally intended for specifying general constraints on a model. In its latest version (2.0), OCL also permits the writing of queries, business rules and other expressions that can apply to a model.

There are established non-UML techniques, in particular decision tables, pre- and post-condition pairs and Structured English that can be used for operation specification. None of these are specific to an object-oriented approach, but all can be used to specify operations in a UML model. A full description is beyond the scope of this book, so we introduce them at an overview level.

10.2 | Role of Operation Specifications

Each operation specification is a small but necessary step on a path that begins with a user's idea of a business activity and leads ultimately to a software system made up of collaborating objects with attributes and methods. From an analysis perspective, an operation specification is created at a point when the analyst's understanding of some aspect of an application domain can be fed back to users, ensuring that the proposals meet users' requirements. From a design perspective, an operation specification is a basis for a more detailed design specification, which later guides a programmer to a method that is an appropriate implementation of the operation in code. An operation specification can also be used to verify that the method does indeed meet its specification, which in turn describes what the users intended, thus checking that the requirements have been implemented.

Novice programmers often do not appreciate the need to design, still less specify, an operation before beginning to write it in program code. This is partly because beginners are given such simple tasks: e.g. to write a program that can calculate and display the area of a rectangle. More importantly, the student is shielded from the activity of requirements analysis. In effect, the teacher has already carried this out, and the student is presented with its results as a starting point: 'There is a need for a program to calculate the area of a rectangle.' Why? An answer given to a student will be put in educational terms, such as: 'This will help you to develop important basic skills in....'

Of course, the situation just described is quite artificial, and most students know this perfectly well. But it is only once the complexity or scale of a software system reaches a certain threshold that the production of code too early becomes extremely inefficient, and very possibly disastrous. To code a relatively small subtask in a large system requires some understanding of the ways in which that subtask will interact with other subtasks. If this understanding has not yet been achieved, assumptions must be made, and these may later turn out to be inappropriate, even catastrophic, for the system as a whole. Object-oriented programming is generally more immune to this kind of problem than other programming approaches, but it is still important to describe the logical operation of the planned software as early as possible.

There are differences of opinion on how much specification should be done. Many proponents of Extreme Programming (XP) argue that conversations among users and developers can effectively replace much of the documentation that has been traditionally created during systems development, including operation specifications (see Chapter 21 for more on XP). An alternative view is held by Rumbaugh et al. (1991), who suggest that only operations that are 'computationally interesting' or 'non-trivial' need be specified. 'Trivial' operations (e.g. those that create or destroy an instance, and those that get or set the value of an attribute) need not be specified at all. Further, operation specifications should be kept simple in form and should consist only of the operation signature and a description of its 'transformation' (i.e. its logic). On the other hand, Allen and Frost (1998), recommend the specification of all operations, although the level of detail may vary according to the anticipated needs of the designer. In practice the needs of a particular project and prevailing standards in the organization will determine the answer to this question.

Each operation has a number of characteristics, which should be specified at the analysis stage. Users must confirm the logic, or rules, of the behaviour. The designer and the programmer responsible for the class will be the main users of the specification, as they need to know what an operation is intended to do: does it perform a calculation, or transform data, or answer a query? Designers and programmers of other parts of the system also need to know about its effects on other classes. For example, if it provides a service to other classes, they need to know its signature. If it calls operations in other classes or updates the values of their attributes, this may establish dependencies that guide how these classes should be packaged during design or implementation.

Defining operations should be neither begun too early nor left too late. For Allen and Frost (1998), this task should be left until the class diagram has stabilized. In a project where the development activity has been broken down at an early stage to correspond to separate subsystems, this may refer only to that part of the class diagram that relates to a particular subsystem. But for any given part of the model, it is important to create all operation specifications before moving into the object design activity.

10.3   Contracts

The term 'contract' is a deliberate echo of legal or commercial contracts between people or organizations. Signing (or becoming a party to) a contract involves making a commitment to deliver a defined service to an agreed quality standard. For example, a small ground-care company has a contract to mow the grass on the lawn in front of the Agate headquarters building. The contract stipulates how often the grass must be cut (every two weeks from April to October), the maximum height of the grass immediately after it is cut (no more than 3 cm) and how much Agate will pay for the service (£80 per cut). The contract does *not* spell out how the work will be done—for example, what type of mower should be used (electric or petrol, cylinder or rotary), how many staff or mowers should be involved, or in which direction the lawn should be cut.

In the language of system theory, a contract is an interface between two systems. In this example, Agate is a business system and the ground-care company is a system for mowing Agate's grass. The contract defines inputs and outputs, and treats the grass-mowing system to some extent as a black box, with its irrelevant details hidden. Which details are deemed irrelevant is always a matter of choice, and any contract can specify that some details of the implementation should be visible to other systems. For example, Agate's directors might not wish to permit the ground-care contractor to use toxic pesticides or weedkillers. This can be included as a constraint in the contract.

Meyer (1988, 1991) was one of the first to draw an analogy between commercial contracts and service relationships between objects. The use of the term is now widespread in object-oriented development since it stresses the encapsulation of classes and subsystems in a model. Cook and Daniels (1994) used the concept extensively in the Syntropy methodology; it is applied in the SELECT Perspective methodology (Allen and Frost, 1998; Apperly et al., 2003); and design by contract is an important part of the thinking behind OCL (Warmer and Kleppe, 2003).

One of Meyer's principal arguments for using the analogy of a contract is that design by contract helps to achieve a software design that is correct in terms of its requirements. During requirements analysis, we do not yet need the full technical rigour that is required of a design specification, but there is still a clear advantage in adopting an approach that can later be extended seamlessly through design into implementation. Specification by contract means that operations are defined primarily in terms of the services they deliver, and the input they receive (usually just the operation signature).

Contracts can also be applied at a much higher level of abstraction than individual operations. Larman (2005) describes the use of contracts to define services provided by a system as a whole. Whether written for a single operation, for the behaviour of the system as a whole or for some intermediate packaged component, the structure of a contract is very similar. A commercial contract usually identifies the parties, the scope (i.e. the context in which it applies), the agreed service, and any performance standards that apply. In just the same way, in object-oriented modelling we identify the nature of the service provided by the server object, and what must be provided by the client object in order to obtain the service. These various aspects can be summarized as follows:

- the intent or purpose of the operation
- the operation signature including the return type (probably established during interaction modelling)
- an appropriate description of the logic (the following sections present some alternative ways of describing the logic of an operation)
- other operations called, whether in the same object or in other objects
- events transmitted to other objects
- attributes set during the operation's execution
- the response to exceptions (e.g. what should happen if a parameter is invalid)
- any non-functional requirements that apply.

This list of features is adapted from Larman (2005) and Allen and Frost (1998). Most of it is self-explanatory, but the critical part of an operation specification is the logic description, and it is to this that we turn in the next section.

10.4 Describing Operation Logic

Rumbaugh et al. (1991) suggest an informal classification of operations that is a useful starting point in considering the various ways of describing their logic. First, there are operations that have side-effects. Possible side-effects include the creation or destruction of object instances, setting attribute values, forming or breaking links with other objects, carrying out calculations, sending messages or events to other objects, or any combination of these. A complex operation may do several of these things, and, where the task is at all complex, an operation may also require the collaboration of several other objects. It is partly for this reason that we identify the pattern of object collaboration before specifying operations in detail. Second, there are operations that do not have side-effects. These are pure queries; they request data but do not change anything within the system.

Like classes, operations may also have the property of being either {abstract} or {concrete} (although this decision is often the result of design considerations, and is therefore not always made when an operation is first specified). Abstract operations have a form that consists of at least a signature, sometimes a full specification, but they will not be given an implementation (i.e. they will not have a method). Typically, abstract operations are located in the abstract superclasses of an inheritance hierarchy. They are always overridden by concrete methods in concrete subclasses.

A specification may be restricted to defining only external and visible effects of an operation, and we may choose either an algorithmic or a non-algorithmic technique for this. A specification may also define internal details, but this is effectively a design activity.

10.4.1 Non-algorithmic approaches

A non-algorithmic approach concentrates on describing the logic of an operation as a black box. In an object-oriented system this is generally preferred for two reasons. First, the implementation of a class should be hidden[1] from the rest of the system and thus only the designers and programmers responsible for a particular class need concern themselves with internal implementation details. Collaboration between different parts of the system is based on public interfaces between classes and subsystems implemented as operation signatures (or message protocols). As long as the signatures are not changed, a change in the implementation of a class, including the way its operations work, has no effect on other parts of the system. Second, the relatively even distribution of effort among the classes of an object-oriented system generally results in operations that are small and single-minded. Since the processing carried out by any one operation is simple, it does not require a complex specification.

Even in non object-oriented approaches, a declarative approach has long been recognized as particularly useful where, for example, a structured decision is made, and the conditions that determine the outcome are readily identified, but the actual sequence of steps in reaching the decision is unimportant. For situations like this, structured methods make use of non-algorithmic techniques such as decision tables and pre- and post-condition pairs (described in the following sections).

Decision tables

A decision table is a matrix that shows the *conditions* under which a decision is made, the *actions* that may result and how the two are related. They cater best for situations where there are multiple outcomes, or actions, each depending on a particular combination of input conditions. One common form shows conditions in the form of questions that can be answered with a simple yes or no. Actions are listed, and check-marks are used to show how they correspond to the conditions. The following is an example of a possible application in the Agate case study. Figure 10.1 shows a corresponding decision table.

> When a campaign budget is overspent, this normally requires prior approval from the client, otherwise Agate is unlikely to be able to recover the excess costs. A set of rules has been established to guide campaign managers when they identify a possible problem.

---

1   Applying the principles of information hiding (Parnas, 1972) to class design as discussed in Chapter 4.

Conditions and actions	Rule 1	Rule 2	Rule 3
Conditions			
Is budget likely to be overspent?	N	Y	Y
Is overspend likely to exceed 2%?	–	N	Y
Actions			
No action	X		
Send letter		X	X
Set up meeting			X

Figure 10.1 A decision table with two conditions and three actions, yielding three distinct rules.

If the budget is expected to be exceeded by up to 2%, a letter is sent notifying the client of this. If the budget is expected to be exceeded by more than 2%, a letter is sent and the staff contact also telephones the client to invite a representative to a budget review meeting. If the campaign is not thought likely to exceed its budget, no action is taken.

The vertical columns with Y, N and X entries are known as *rules*. Each rule is read vertically downwards, and the arrangement of Ys and Ns indicates which conditions are true for that rule. An X indicates that an action should occur when the corresponding condition is true (i.e. has a Y answer). We can paraphrase the table into text as follows:

- *Rule 1*. If the budget is not overspent (clearly in this case the scale of overspend is irrelevant, indicated by a dash against this condition), no action is required.
- *Rule 2*. If the budget is overspent and the overspend is not likely to exceed 2%, a letter should be sent.
- *Rule 3*. If the budget is overspent and the overspend is likely to exceed 2%, a letter should be sent and a meeting set up.

A single rule may have multiple outcomes that overlap with the outcomes of other rules. Decision tables are very useful for situations that require a non-algorithmic specification of logic, reflecting a range of alternative behaviours. But this is relatively unusual in an object-oriented system, where thorough analysis of object collaboration tends to minimize the complexity of single operations.

Pre- and post-conditions
As its name suggests, this technique concentrates on providing answers to the following questions:

- What conditions must be satisfied before an operation can take place?
- What conditions should apply (i.e. what states may the system be in) after an operation is completed?

Let us consider an example from Agate. The operation `Advert.getCost()`[2] was first discussed in Section 8.2. Let us suppose that it has the following signature.

```
Advert.getCost():Money
```

---

2   We have suffixed brackets to the names of operations to distinguish them from attributes. This does not mean that they are operations with no parameters, only that the parameters are not shown.

This operation has no pre-condition. (We may note that the object sending the message must know the identity of the object that contains the operation, but this is not in itself a pre-condition for the operation to execute correctly when invoked.) The post-conditions should express the valid results of the operation upon completion. In this case, a money value is returned (for simplicity, we ignore the question of valid values for an advert cost, but we should note that in reality this attribute may be able to take only a limited range of values, depending on business constraints).

Pre-condition: none
Post-condition: a valid money value is returned

More complex examples can easily be constructed from the use case descriptions, or by consulting users if existing descriptions are not sufficiently detailed. Consider the use case `Assign staff to work on a campaign`. This involves calling the operation `Campaign.assignStaff()` for each member of staff assigned. Let us assume that the signature of this operation is as follows:

```
Campaign.assignStaff(creativeStaffObject)
```

This example has one pre-condition: a calling message must supply a valid `CreativeStaff` object. There is one post-condition: a link must be created between the two objects:

Pre-condition: `creativeStaffObject` is valid
Post-condition: a link is created between `campaignObject` and `creativeStaffObject`

Let us look at one more example from Agate, with more complex conditions. This is taken from the use case `Change the grade for a member of staff` (we assume that the use case is being invoked for a member of creative staff). This use case involves several operations including:

```
CreativeStaff.changeGrade()
StaffGrade.setFinishDate()
StaffGrade()   (the constructor operation that creates a new instance of this class)
```

We examine only one of these in detail, `CreativeStaff.changeGrade()`, but our specification must still recognize calls made to other operations during execution. Let us assume that the operation signature is as follows:

```
CreativeStaff.changeGrade(gradeObject, gradeChangeDate)
```

The pre-conditions are straightforward, consisting only of a valid `gradeObject` and `gradeChangeDate`. The post-conditions are more involved, as once the operation is completed we should expect several effects to have taken place. A new instance of `StaffGrade` is created, and this is linked to the appropriate `creativeStaffObject` and `gradeObject` (by a `staffOnGrade` link). The new `staffGradeObject` is also linked to the previous `staffGradeObject` (by a `previousGrade` link). Attribute values in the new `staffGradeObject` are set by its constructor operation (including `gradeStartDate`, which is set equal to the supplied parameter `gradeChangeDate`). The attribute `StaffGrade.gradeFinishDate` in the previous instance is also set, through a message to invoke the operation `StaffGrade.setFinishDate`. A full logic description is thus as follows:

pre-conditions:	`creativeStaffObject` is valid
	`gradeObject` is valid
	`gradeChangeDate` is a valid date
	`gradeChangeDate` is greater than or equal to today's date
post-conditions:	a new `staffGradeObject` exists
	the new `staffGradeObject` is linked to the
	`creativeStaffObject`
	the new `staffGradeObject` is linked to the previous one
	the value of the previous `staffGradeObject.grade`
	`FinishDate` is set equal to `gradeChangeDate - 1 day`

For many operations in an object-oriented model, such a specification would be sufficiently detailed.

In general, any operation specification must pass the following two tests.

- A user should be able to check that it correctly expresses the business logic.
- A class designer should be able to produce a detailed design of the operation for a programmer to code.

However, while a declarative approach to operation specification usually meets all the needs of object-oriented development, there is still sometimes a case for using an algorithm. One example would be a requirement that involves carrying out a calculation where the sequence of steps is significant, and neither a designer nor a programmer could reasonably be expected to come up with a formula that produces the correct result.

10.4.2 Algorithmic approaches

An *algorithm* describes the internal logic of a process or decision by breaking it down into small steps (the word derives from al-Kwarazmi, an Arab mathematician of the ninth century). The level of detail to which this is done varies greatly, depending on the information available at the time and on the reason for defining it. An algorithm also specifies the sequence in which the steps are performed. In the field of computing and information systems, algorithms are used either as a *description* of the way in which a programmable task is currently carried out (this is their purpose in operation specification), or as a *prescription* for a program to automate the task. This dual meaning again reflects the differing perspectives of analysis (understanding a problem and determining what must be done to achieve a solution) and design (the creative act of imagining a system to implement a solution). An algorithmic technique is almost always used during method design, because a designer is concerned with the efficient implementation of requirements, and must therefore select the best algorithm available for the purpose. But algorithms can also be used with an analysis intention. A major difference here is that there is no need for the analyst to worry about efficiency, since the algorithm need only illustrate accurately the results of the operation.

Control structures in algorithms

Algorithms are generally organized procedurally, which is to say that they use the fundamental programming control structures of sequence, selection and iteration. We can illustrate this in the Agate case study by considering the operation that calculates the total cost of a campaign. This operation is invoked during the use case Check campaign budget. For ease of reference, the use case description is repeated below:

> The campaign budget may be checked to ensure that it has not been exceeded. The current campaign cost is determined by the total cost of all the adverts and the campaign overhead costs.

Let us suppose that there is a precise (though simple) formula for this calculation, based on summing the individual total costs of each advert and adding the campaign overhead costs. For further simplicity, let us assume that the overhead cost part of the calculation simply involves multiplying the total of all other costs by an overhead rate (this approximates to normal accounting practice). To convey an understanding of the calculation, we can begin by representing it as a mathematical formula:

Total_campaign_cost = (sum of all advert_costs) * overhead_rate

This does not explicitly identify all the steps, but a sequence can be deduced. In fact, several possible sequences can be deduced, but any sequence that always produces a correct result will do. One possible sequence, at a very coarse level of detail, would include the following three steps:

1. Add up all the individual advert costs.
2. Multiply the total by the overhead rate.
3. The resulting sum is the total campaign cost.

For such a relatively simple calculation as this one, the formula itself would almost certainly serve better as a specification, but some are a lot more complex. When it is necessary to specify the sequence of calculation in more detail, we can use Structured English for this.

Structured English

This is a 'dialect' of written English that is about halfway between everyday non-technical language and a formal programming language. When it is necessary to specify an operation procedurally, this is the most useful and versatile technique. Its advantages include the possibility, with a little care, of retaining much of the readability and understandability of everyday English. It also allows the construction of a formal logical structure that is easy to translate into program code. Structured English is very easy to write iteratively, at successively greater levels of detail, and it is easily dismantled into components that can be reassembled in different structures without a lot of reworking. The logical structure is made explicit through the use of keywords and indentation, while the vocabulary is kept as close as possible to everyday usage in the business context. Above all, expressions and keywords that are specific to a particular programming language are avoided. The result ideally is something that a non-technical user is able to understand, alter or approve, as necessary, while it should also be useful to the designer. This means it must be capable of further development into a detailed program design without undue difficulty.

The main principles of Structured English are as follows. A specification is made up of a number of simple sentences, each consisting of a simple imperative statement or equation. Statements may only be combined in restricted ways that correspond to the sequence, selection and iteration control structures of structured programming. The very simplest specifications contain only sequences and differ little from everyday English except in that they use a more restricted vocabulary and style (many organizations have their own Structured English house style). Here are some statements that illustrate a typical style of Structured English:

```
get client contact name
sale cost = item cost * ( 1 - discount rate )
calculate total bonus
description = new description
```

Selection structures show alternative courses of action, the choice between them depending on conditions that prevail at the time the selection is made. For example, an *if-then-else* construct, which has only two possible outcomes, is shown in the following fragment:

```
if client contact is 'Sushila'
  set discount rate to 5%
else
  set discount rate to 2%
end if
```

If the two alternatives are not really different actions, but are rather a choice between doing something and not doing it, the 'else' branch can be omitted. The following fragment shows this simpler form:

```
if client contact is 'Sushila'
  set discount rate to 5%
end if
```

Note that in each case the end of the structure is marked by end if. This important marker cannot be omitted. It allows the entire structure to be treated logically as an element, as if it were a single statement in a sequence.

Multiple outcomes are handled either by a *case* construct or by a *nested if*. This fragment illustrates the case structure:

```
begin case
  case client contact is 'Sushila'
    set discount rate to 5%
  case client contact is 'Wu'
    set discount rate to 10%
  case client contact is 'Luis'
    set discount rate to 15%
  otherwise
    set discount rate to 2%
end case
```

The 'otherwise' branch of a case construct can be omitted if it is not required, although it is generally good practice to include a catch-all to ensure completeness. The next fragment shows the same selection specified using a *nested-if* construct:

```
if client contact is 'Sushila'
  set discount rate to 5%
else
  if client contact is 'Wu'
    set discount rate to 10%
```

```
   else
     if client contact is 'Luis'
       set discount rate to 15%
     else
       set discount rate to 2%
     end if
   end if
 end if
```

This also illustrates how indentation can help the readability of a specification. For each corresponding set of control statements (lines beginning with 'if', 'else' and 'end if'), the indentation from the left margin is the same. This helps to show which sequence statements ('set discount rate to 10%', etc.) belong to each structure.

The third type of control structure is iteration. This is used when a statement, or group of statements, needs to be repeated. Typically this is a way of applying a single operation to a set of objects. Logically, once something has begun to occur repeatedly, there must be a condition for stopping the repetition (unless the repetition is to continue indefinitely). There are two main forms of control of iteration. These differ in whether the condition for ending the repetition is tested before or after the first loop. The next two examples show typical applications of each kind of structure; in the first, the test is applied before the loop is entered, so that if the list is empty no bonus is calculated:

```
do while there are more staff in the list
  calculate staff bonus
  store bonus amount
end do
```

In the second iteration example below, the test is applied after the loop is exited. This ensures that the action will be processed (or attempted) at least once. Note that the line at the end beginning until acts as an end-of-structure marker, just like the end do above:

```
repeat
  allocate member of staff to campaign
  increment count of allocated staff
until count of allocated staff = 10
```

Complex structures in Structured English. Different types of structure can be nested inside each other, as in the next fragment:

```
do while there are more staff in the list
  calculate bonus for this staff member
  begin case
    case bonus > £250
      add name to 'star of the month' list
    case bonus < £25
      create warning letter
  end case
  store bonus amount
end do
format bonus list
```

The operation mentioned near the beginning of this section (`Check campaign budget`) also illustrates the use of all three control structures, although in this case there is no nesting:

```
do while there are more adverts for campaign
  get next advert
  get cost for this advert
  add to cumulative cost for campaign
end do
set total advert cost = final cumulative cost
set total campaign cost =
      total advert cost + (total advert cost × overhead rate)
get campaign budget
if total campaign cost > campaign budget
  generate warning
end if
```

A Structured English specification can be made as complex as it needs to be, and it can also be written in an iterative, top-down manner. For example, an initial version of an algorithm is defined at a high level of granularity. Then, provided the overall structure is sound, more detail is easily added progressively. In refining the level of detail, structures can be nested within each other to any degree of complexity, although in practice it is unlikely that even the most complex operation would need more than two to three levels of nesting at most. It is in any case sensible to limit the complexity. One often-quoted guideline is that a Structured English specification should not be longer than one page of typed A4, or one screen if it is likely to be read within a CASE tool environment–although in practice the acceptable length of a section of text depends on the context.

The style in all the examples given above is based on that of Yourdon (1989), but this should not be taken as necessarily prescriptive. What passes for acceptable style varies widely from one organization to another, and in practice an analyst should follow the house style, whatever that happens to be.

Pseudo-code

Pseudo-code differs from Structured English in that it is closer to the vocabulary and syntax of a specific programming language. There are thus many different dialects of pseudo-code, each corresponding to a particular programming language. They differ from each other in vocabulary, in syntax and in style. Structured English avoids language specificity primarily to avoid reaching conclusions about design questions too early. Sometimes there seems no good reason to hold back, for example because the final implementation language has been decided early in the project. This can be misleading, as it may be desirable at a later stage to redevelop the system in a different programming language. If the operations have been specified in a language-specific pseudo-code, it would then be necessary to rewrite them.

However language-specific it may be, pseudo-code remains only a skeleton of a program, intended only to illustrate its logical structure without including full design and implementation detail. In other words, it is not so much a fully developed program as an outline that can later be developed into program code. The following pseudo-code for `Check campaign budget` can be compared with the Structured English version above:

```
{
  { while more adverts:
    next advert;
    get advertcost;
    cumulativecost = cumulativecost + advertcost;
  endwhile;
  }
  { campaigncost = cumulativecost + (cumulativecost × ohrate)
  get campaignbudget;
  case campaigncost > campaignbudget
    return warningflag;
  endcase
  }
}
```

Note that, while this pseudo-code resembles C in its syntax, it is not actually written in C. Pseudo-code requires further work to turn it into program code.

Activity diagrams

Activity diagrams can be used to specify the logic of procedurally complex operations. The notation of activity diagrams was introduced in Chapter 5; in this section we illustrate their role in operation specification. When used for this purpose, actions in the diagram usually represent steps in the logic of the operation. This can be done at any level of abstraction, so that, if appropriate, an initial high-level view of the operation can later be decomposed to a lower level of detail.

Activity diagrams are inherently very flexible in their use, and therefore a little care should be exercised when they are employed in operation specification. An activity diagram can be drawn to represent a single operation on an object, but this is less common than using an activity diagram to represent a collaboration between several objects (for example, one that realizes a use case). Figure 10.2 illustrates this for the use case Check campaign budget (compare with the corresponding sequence diagram later in Fig. 10.4).

An activity diagram can also be drawn for a more abstract collaboration between larger components of a system, or between entire systems. A single diagram does not necessarily translate into a single operation; whether or not it does is essentially a design decision.

10.5 Object Constraint Language

In drawing any class diagram, much of the time and effort is spent in working out what constraints apply. For example, the multiplicity of an association represents a constraint on how many objects of one class can be linked to any object of the other class. This particular example can be adequately expressed in the graphical language of the class diagram, but this is not equally so for all constraints. Among those for which it is not true are many of the constraints within operation specifications. For example, many pre- and post-conditions in a contract are constraints on the behaviour of objects that are party to the contract. Sometimes the definition of such constraints can be written in a relatively informal manner (as in the examples in Section 10.4), but where greater precision is required, OCL provides a formal language.

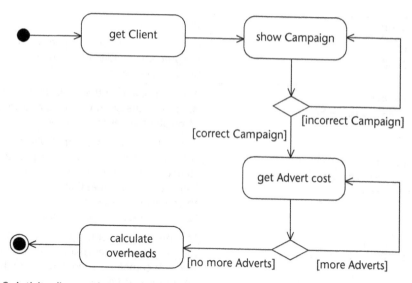

Figure 10.2 Activity diagram for the use case `Check campaign budget`.

OCL expressions are constructed from a collection of pre-defined elements and types, and the language has a precise grammar that enables the construction of unambiguous statements about the properties of model components and their relationships to each other. The latest version of OCL (2.0) (OMG, 2006) has been extended so that it can also be used to define queries, to reference values and to state business rules (Warmer and Kleppe, 2003). It is beyond the scope of this book to give a detailed treatment, and this section is intended only to illustrate some of the ways that OCL can be used to support a model, in particular for operation specification.

Most OCL statements consist of the following structural elements.

- A *context* that defines a domain within which the expression is valid. This is often an instance of a specific type, for example an object in a class diagram. A link (i.e. an instance of an association) may also be the context for an OCL expression.
- A *property* of that instance which is the context for the expression. Properties may include attributes, association roles and query operations.
- An OCL *operation* that is applied to the property. Operations include (but are not restricted to) the arithmetical operators *, +, - and /, set operators such as `size`, `isEmpty` and `select` and type operators such as `oclIsTypeOf`.

OCL statements can also include *keywords*, such as the logical operators **and**, **or**, **implies**, **if**, **then**, **else** and **not** and the set operator **in**, printed in bold to distinguish them from other OCL terms and operations. Together with the nonkeyword operations mentioned above, these can be used to define quite complex pre- and post-conditions for an operation. OCL expressions can specify both initial and derived values of attributes, and can be used to check various operation results, such as whether an object has been created or a message sent during the execution of the operation.

Figure 10.3 gives some examples of expressions in OCL, some of which are adapted from the OCL 2.0 Specification (OMG, 2006). All have an object of some class as their context.

OCL expression	Interpretation
`context Person` `self.gender`	In the context of a specific person, the value of the property 'gender' of that person, i.e. a person's gender.
`context Person` `inv: self.savings >= 500`	It is an invariant[3] of the model that the property 'savings' of the person under consideration must be greater than or equal to 500.

`context Person`
   `self.husband->notEmpty()`
   `implies self.husband.gender`
   `= Gender::male`
	If the set 'husband' associated with a person is not empty, then the value of the property 'gender' of the husband must be male. (This example assumes that `Gender::male` is an enumerated value in a `Gender «enumeration»` type)

`context Company` `inv: self.CEO->size() <= 1`	The size of the set of the property 'CEO' of a company must be less than or equal to 1. That is, a company cannot have more than one Chief Executive Officer.

`context Company`
   `self.employee->`
   `select(age < 60)`
	The set of employees of a company whose age is less than 60.

Figure 10.3 Examples of some expressions in OCL.

Since OCL can specify constraints that cannot be expressed directly in diagrammatic notation, it is useful as a precise language for pre- and post-conditions of operations. An OCL expression can also specify the result of a query operation. This differs from a post-condition, which specifies a side-effect of an operation. However, queries have no side-effects–that is, they do not change anything in the model or the system. The general syntax for operation specification is as follows:

```
context Type::operation(parameter1:type,parameter2:type):
        return type
pre:    parameter1 operation
        parameter2 operation
body:   -- an OCL expression that defines the query output
post:   result = /* some OCL expression that defines the
                effect of the operation, for example in
                terms of attribute values, objects created
                or destroyed, and so on */
```

Note that the contextual `type` is the type (for our purposes, normally a class) that owns the operation as a feature. The **pre:** expressions are functions of operation parameters, while the **body:** and **post:** expressions are functions of self, of operation parameters, or of both. OCL expressions must be written with an explicit **context** declaration.

---

3 An invariant is something that cannot be changed.

Note also the different styles of comment in the preceding example. A single-line comment is introduced with a double hyphen, thus: `--`, while a comment that spans more than one line is opened and closed thus: `/* comment text */`.

The following example illustrates the use of an **inv:** label to denote an invariant:

```
context Person
inv: self.age>=0
```

The invariant here is merely that a person's age must always be greater than or equal to zero–arguably, this should not need specification, but poorly specified computer systems often get the really obvious things wrong! For a complete list of keywords, see Section 8 of the OCL Specification (OMG, 2006).

This example shows an OCL expression that defines the initial value of an attribute in the Agate case study:

```
context Advert::actualAdvertCost
init: 0
```

Another useful feature of OCL is that you can define two values for a single property using the postfix @pre. As you might expect, this refers to the previous value of a property, and is only permitted in post-condition clauses. Thus it is possible to constrain the relationship between the values of an attribute before and after an operation has taken place. For example, the decision specified in Fig. 10.1 defines different actions depending on changes in the estimated cost of a campaign in comparison with its budget. If the new estimated cost is greater than the old estimated cost, but exceeds the budget by no more than 2%, the value of this attribute is set to `true`, flagging a need to generate a warning letter to the client.[4] We could model this in a very simple way by adding an attribute `Campaign.clientLetterRequired`. We could then write part of the logic in OCL as follows:

```
context Campaign
post: self.clientLetterRequired = 'false'
      if self.estimatedCost > estimatedCost@pre and
         self.estimatedCost > budget and
         self.estimatedCost <= budget * 1.02 then
         self.clientLetterRequired = 'true'
      endif
```

This expression will help to define tests that check if the system displays the correct behaviour when a campaign budget has changed. (However, note that this example is intended only to illustrate the notation. In practice, it is unlikely that this is really how we would model this requirement.)

Operation specifications frequently include invariants. An invariant that is associated with an operation specification describes a condition that always remains true for an object, and which must therefore not be altered by an operation side-effect. Formal definition of invariants is valuable because they provide rigorous tests for execution of the software.

---

4 If the budget is exceeded but the estimated cost has not increased, then we assume that a letter has already been sent and so the flag does not need to be set.

For example, the value of `Campaign.estimatedCost` should always equal the sum of all associated `Advert.estimatedCost` values multiplied by the current overhead rate. In OCL, this might be written as follows:[5]

```
context Campaign
inv:     self.estimatedCost = self.adverts.estimatedCost->
         sum() + (self.adverts.estimatedCost->sum() * ohRate)
```

In this example, the context is the `Campaign` class. To use an invariant within an operation specification, it can be written simply as an additional **inv:** clause:

```
context Class::operation(parameter1: type, parameter2:
         type):return type
pre:     parameter1...
         parameter2...
post:    result1...
         result2...
inv:     invariant1...
         invariant2...
```

For an example from the Agate case study, we revisit the operation `Creative Staff.changeGrade()`, for which we specified the logic in Section 10.4.1. To help make sense of this specification, it is also worth referring back to the analysis class diagram in Fig. A3.14. In particular, note the recursive association from `StaffGrade` to itself. However, remember also that, as we saw in Chapter 8, `CreativeStaff` is a subclass of `StaffMember` and therefore inherits the same associations and roles (Chapter A4 includes a revised analysis class diagram that shows this specialization). Here is the main part of the operation specification rewritten in OCL:

```
context CreativeStaff::changeGrade(grade:Grade,
         gradeChangeDate:Date)
pre:     grade oclIsTypeOf(Grade)
         gradeChangeDate >= today
post:    self.staffGrade->exists() and
         self.staffGrade[previous]->notEmpty() and
         self.staffGrade.gradeStartDate = gradeChangeDate and
         self.staffGrade.previous.gradeFinishDate =
         gradeChangeDate - 1 day
```

10.6 Creating an Operation Specification

Figure 10.4 shows the sequence diagram for the use case `Check campaign budget` first introduced in Chapter 9 (the use case description is repeated above in Section 10.4.2 and an activity diagram is shown in Fig. 10.2). In this particular example the message `checkCampaignBudget` invokes the operation `Campaign.checkCampaignBudget()`.

A specification for `Campaign.checkCampaignBudget()` is given below. We have used different fonts to signpost the specification as follows. This font (Arial) labels the

---

5 Note that this makes some assumptions about the way that the classes are designed and is really intended only to illustrate the style of this kind of statement when written in OCL.

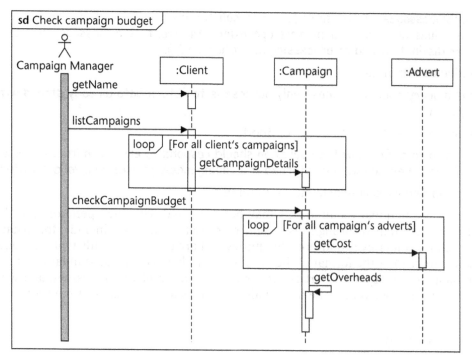

Figure 10.4 Sequence diagram for the use case `Check campaign budget`.

specification structure, `while this` (Courier) `highlights its content.` Comments on the reasoning behind the specification are formatted like this (in Comic Sans).

   Operation specification: `checkCampaignBudget`
   Operation intent: `return difference between campaign budget and`
            `actual costs.`

The invocation appears not to require any parameters, but does have a return type that we can expect to contain a numerical value. Let us assume that there is a Money type available. The signature is shown below, followed by the pre- and post-conditions:

   Operation signature: `Campaign::checkCampaignBudget()`
               `budgetCostDifference:Money`
   Logic description (pre- and post-conditions):
     context `Campaign`
     pre: `self->exists()`
     post: `result = self.originalBudget - self.estimatedCost` **and**
            `self.estimatedCost = self.adverts.estimated Cost->sum()`

As can be seen from the sequence diagram, this operation calls two other operations and these must be listed. In a full specification, full signatures would be recorded, but we omit this detail here.

   Other operations called: `Advert.getCost(), self.getOverheads()`
   Events transmitted to other objects: `none`

The only messages are those required to call the operations just mentioned, whose return values are required by this operation. An 'event' is a message that starts another distinct thread of processing (see Chapter 11).

Attributes set: none

This is a query operation whose only purpose is to return data already stored within the system.

Response to exceptions: none defined

Here we could define how the operation should respond to error conditions, e.g. what kind of error message will be returned if a calling message uses an invalid signature.

Non-functional requirements: none defined

Several non-functional requirements may be associated with the operation, but these need to be determined through discussion with users. They may include, for instance, response time under live conditions (enquiries that are made frequently typically require a faster response) or the format of the output (e.g. if there is a house standard that over-spent budgets are displayed in red). However, these are really design issues, and would be noted at this stage only if the information happens to be available at the time.

10.7 Summary

Operation specifications are the most detailed description of the behaviour of a system model. As such, they are also one of the more significant elements in the project repository. They provide an important link between the system's users, who typically possess a detailed understanding of the required system behaviour, and the designers and programmers who must implement this in software. Accurate specification of operations is essential if the software is to be coded correctly.

In this chapter we introduced the 'contract' as a framework for specifying operations, in terms of the service relationship between classes. Contracts are a particularly useful element of operation specification since they concentrate on the correctness of each object's behaviour.

We also described several techniques for describing operation logic. Non-algorithmic techniques, such as decision tables and pre- and post-condition pairs, take a black box approach and concentrate on specifying only the inputs to an operation (its pre-conditions) and the intended results of an operation (its post-conditions). In many cases, particularly where the operations themselves are simple, this is all the specification that a programmer needs to code the operation correctly.

Algorithmic techniques, such as Structured English, pseudo-code and activity diagrams, take a white box approach, and this means that they concentrate on defining the internal logic of operations. These techniques are particularly useful when an operation is computationally complex. They are also useful when we need to model some larger element of system behaviour, such as a use case, that has not yet been decomposed to the level of individual operations that can be assigned to specific classes.

Many elements of an operation specification can be written in OCL (UML's Object Constraint Language). OCL is intended for use as a formal language for specifying constraints and queries on an object model, and this includes operation pre- and post-conditions and invariants.

Review Questions

10.1   What are the two main purposes of an operation specification?

10.2   To what kinds of situation are decision tables particularly suited?

10.3   Why is it important to specify both pre- and post-conditions for an operation?

10.4   What are the main differences between algorithmic and non-algorithmic approaches to operation specification?

10.5   Why are non-algorithmic (or declarative) approaches generally preferred in object-oriented development?

10.6   Why are operation specifications in an object-oriented project likely to be small?

10.7   What are the three kinds of control structure in Structured English?

10.8   What is a sensible limit on the size of a Structured English specification?

10.9   What are the three components of most OCL expressions?

10.10 What is an invariant?

Case Study Work, Exercises and Projects

10.A   Consider the first sequence diagram you drew for the use case `Start line run` from the FoodCo case study (in Exercise 9.A). Choose an operation in one of the classes involved in this ISD and write a contract for it. Make reasonable assumptions where necessary, and use a pre- and post-conditions approach for describing its logic.

10.B   Consider the decision table in Fig. 10.1. Suppose you have learned that an extra condition must be taken into account: the rules in the current table actually apply only to campaigns with a total budget of £5000 or over, but for smaller campaigns the thresholds for each action are different. Thresholds for smaller campaigns are as follows. For an expected overspend of less than 10%, no action is taken. For expected overspends of 10–19%, a letter is sent. For an expected overspend of 20% or more a letter is sent and a meeting is arranged. Draw a new version of the table that caters for small campaigns.

10.C   Redraw the original decision table in Fig. 10.1 as an activity diagram. Do the same for your new decision table from Exercise 10.B.

10.D   Consider the decision table in Fig. 10.1. Which of the three control structures are required to convert this into a Structured English specification? Rewrite the decision table in Structured English format.

10.E   Find out how a decision tree differs from a decision table (e.g. from one of the books listed in Further Reading). Produce a decision tree that corresponds to the decision table in Fig. 10.1. What are the relative advantages and disadvantages of decision trees, decision tables and Structured English?

Further Reading

Decision tables and decision trees are both covered well in Kendall and Kendall (2005), while Avison and Fitzgerald (2006) and Hoffer et al. (2005) are both good sources on Structured English.

Larman (2005) describes a contract-based approach to object-oriented analysis and design, with examples taken through to Java code.

Meyer (1997) is perhaps the definitive text on design-by-contract in object-oriented software engineering. This book is very comprehensive, and quite technical in tone.

For a thorough introduction to OCL, Warmer and Kleppe (2003) have at the time of writing no real rivals.

For a statement of the school of thought (expressed chiefly by proponents of XP and other Agile Methods) that documentation, including operation specifications, is often unnecessary, see Jeffries (2001).

Further examples of operation specifications for Agate can be found in Case Study Chapter A4.

Chapter 11

Specifying Control

LEARNING OBJECTIVES

In this chapter you will learn
- ☑ how to identify requirements for control in an application
- ☑ how to model object lifecycles using state machines
- ☑ how to develop state machine diagrams from interaction diagrams
- ☑ how to model concurrent behaviour in an object
- ☑ how to ensure consistency with other UML models.

11.1 Introduction

Specifying the control aspects of a system deals with how the system should respond to events. For some systems this can be complex as the response to events can vary depending upon the passage of time and the events that have occurred already.

For a real-time system it is easy to understand that its response to an event depends upon its state. For example, an aircraft flight control system should respond differently to events (for example, engine failure) when the aircraft is in flight and when it is taxiing along a runway. A more mundane example is that of a vending machine, which does not normally dispense goods until an appropriate amount of money has been inserted. The state of the vending machine depends on whether or not sufficient money has been inserted to pay for the item selected and this determines its behaviour. In reality, of course, the situation is more complicated than this. For example, even when the correct amount of money has been inserted, the machine cannot dispense an item that is not in stock. It is important to model state-dependent variations in behaviour such as these since they represent constraints on the way that a system should act.

Objects in all kinds of systems—not only real-time ones—can have similar variations in their behaviour dependent upon their state. UML uses state machines to model states

313

and state dependent behaviour for objects[1] and for interactions. The notation used in UML is based upon work by Harel (1987) and was adopted by OMT (Rumbaugh et al., 1991) and also in the second version of the Booch approach (Booch, 1994). UML 2.2 draws a distinction between behavioural state machines and protocol state machines. Behavioural state machines may be used to specify the behaviour of individual entities, for example class instances. Protocol state machines may be used to describe usage protocols for classes, interfaces and ports.

There is an important link between interaction diagrams and state machines. A model of state behaviour in a state machine captures all the possible responses of a single object to all the use cases in which it is involved. By contrast, a sequence or a communication diagram captures the responses of all the objects that are involved in a single use case or other interaction. A state machine can be seen as a description of all the possible lifecycles that an object of a class may follow. It can also be seen as a more detailed view of a class.

The state machine is a versatile model and can be used within an object-oriented approach to describe the behaviour of other model entities. In Chapter 17 we show how to use state machines to build models of human–computer dialogues.

11.2　States and Events

All objects have a *state*. We introduced the concept of state in Chapter 4 (Section 4.2.7) and discussed how state relates to attributes in Chapter 7 (Section 7.3.3). The current state of an object is a result of the events that have occurred to the object and is determined by the current value of the object's attributes and the links that it has with other objects. Some attributes and links of an object are related to its state while others are not. For example, in the Agate case study the values of the staffName and staffNo attributes of a StaffMember object have no impact upon its state, whereas the date that a staff member started his or her employment at Agate determines when the probationary period of employment ends (after six months, say). A StaffMember object is in the Probationary state for the first six months of employment. While in this state, a staff member has different employment rights and is not eligible for redundancy pay in the event that they are dismissed by the company.

A state describes a particular condition that a modelled element (e.g. object) may occupy for a period of time while it awaits some event or *trigger*. The possible states that an object can occupy are limited by its class. Objects of some classes have only one possible state. For example, in the Agate case study a Grade object either exists or it does not. If it exists it is available to be used, and if it does not exist it is not available. Objects of this class have only one state, which we might name Available. Objects of other classes have more than one possible state. For example, an object of the class GradeRate may be in one of several states. It may be Pending, if the current date is earlier than its start date, Active, if the current date is equal to or later than the start date but earlier than the finish date (we assume that the finish date is later than the start date), or Lapsed, if the current date is later than the finish date for the grade. If the current date is at least a year later than the finish date then the object is removed from

---

1　State machines, previously known as statecharts, may be used to show state changes for various UML elements including systems, subsystems, interfaces and ports.

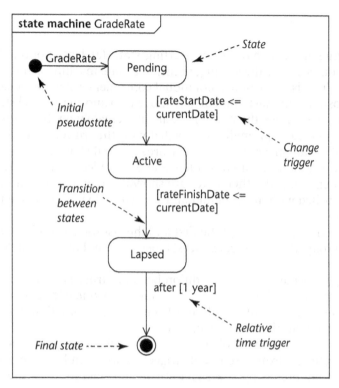

Figure 11.1 State machine for the class GradeRate.

the system. The current state of a GradeRate object can be determined by examining the values of its two date attributes. Alternatively, the GradeRate class might have a single attribute (an enumerated type–that has an integer value for each possible state) with values that indicate the current state of an object. An attribute that holds the value of the current state of an object is sometimes known as a *state variable*. It is important to note that movement from one state to another for a GradeRate object is dependent upon events that occur with the passage of time. Figure 11.1 shows a state machine for GradeRate. This state machine is presented in a frame of the kind state machine (sm could be used as shortened form). UML 2.2 is quite flexible about the use of frames, and states that they need not be used when the diagram boundary is clear.[2]

Movement from one state to another is called a *transition*, and is initiated by a *trigger*. A trigger is an event that can cause a state change and that is relevant to the object (or to the modelled element). When its triggering event occurs a transition is said to *fire*. A transition is shown as an open arrow from the source state to the target state. For example, the cancellation of an advert at Agate is a trigger that will change the state of the Advert object being cancelled. Just as a set of objects is defined by the class of which they are all instances, events are defined by an *event type* of which each event is an instance. For example, the cancellation of an advert in the CheapClothes jeans campaign is one instance of an event, and the cancellation of an advert in the Soong Motor Co Helion campaign is another instance. Both are defined by the event type cancellationOfAdvert. This event is a trigger as it causes a state change.

---

2   Except for interaction diagrams, where frames must be used.

11.3 | Basic Notation

All state machines need to have some starting state (at least notionally). The *initial pseudostate* (in other words the starting point) of a state machine is indicated by a small solid filled circle. This is really only a notational convenience. An object cannot remain in its initial pseudostate, but must immediately move into another named state. In Fig. 11.1 the GradeRate object enters the Pending state immediately on its creation. A transition from the initial state can optionally be labelled with the trigger that creates the object. The end point of a state machine (in other words its final state) is shown by a bull's-eye symbol. This too is a notational convenience and an object cannot leave its final state once it has been entered. All other states are shown as rectangles with rounded corners and should be labelled with meaningful names. Each node in a state machine diagram is known as a vertex.

In Fig. 11.1 all transitions except the first and the last transitions have *change triggers*. Triggers can be grouped into several general types and can have parameters and a return value.

A *change trigger* occurs when a condition becomes true. This is usually described as a Boolean expression, which means that it can take only one of two values: true or false. This form of conditional event is different from a guard condition, which is normally evaluated at the moment that its associated event fires.

A *call trigger* occurs when an object receives a call for one of its operations, either from another object or from itself. Call triggers correspond to the receipt of a call message and are annotated by the signature of the operation as the trigger for the transition.

A *signal trigger* occurs when an object receives a signal.[3] As with call triggers the event is annotated with the signature of the operation invoked. There is no syntactic difference between call triggers and signal triggers. It is assumed that a naming convention is used to distinguish between them.

A *relative time trigger* is caused by the passage of a designated period of time after a specified event (frequently the entry to the current state). Relative time triggers are shown by time expressions near the transitions. The time expression is placed in parentheses and should evaluate to a period of time. It is preceded by the keyword *after* and if no starting time is indicated it reflects the passage of time since the most recent entry to the current state. In Fig. 11.1 the transition from the state Lapsed to the final state is a relative time trigger.

The state machine for a GradeRate object is very simple, since it enters each state only once. Some classes have much more complex lifecycles than this. For example, a BookCopy object in a library system may move many times between the states OnLoan and Available.

Figure 11.2 shows an alternative notation for a state, which may be used for composite states. Figure 11.3 illustrates the basic notation for a state machine with two states for the class Campaign and one transition between them. A transition should be annotated with a *transition string* to indicate the event that triggers it.

---

3 An asynchronous message.

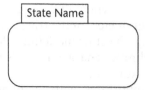

Figure 11.2 Alternative notation for a state.

For call and signal events the format of the transition string is as follows:

```
trigger-signature '[' constraint ']' '/' activity-expression
```

The trigger signature takes the following form:

```
event-name '(' parameter-list ')'
```

where the event-name may be the call or signal name and the parameter-list contains parameters of the form:

```
parameter-name ':' type-expression
```

separated by commas. (Characters in single quotes, such as ` ( `, are *literals* that appear as part of the event.) Note that empty brackets ` () ` have not been used when no parameters are listed.

A constraint is a Boolean expression that is evaluated at the time the trigger fires. It is known as *guard condition* or just a *guard* ('it guards the transition'). The transition only takes place if the guard condition evaluates to true. A guard condition is a constraint that may involve parameters of the trigger, attributes or links of the object that owns the state machine. A guard is shown in square brackets–` [ ` ... ` ] `.

In Fig. 11.3 the guard condition is a test on the contractSigned attribute in the class Campaign and since the attribute is Boolean it may be written as follows:

```
[contractSigned]
```

This expression evaluates to true only if contractSigned is true. A guard condition can also be used to test concurrent states of the current object or the state of some other reachable object. Concurrent states are explained later in Section 11.4.2.

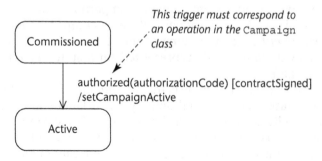

Figure 11.3 Fragment of the state machine for the class Campaign.

An *activity-expression* is executed when a trigger causes the transition to fire. Like a guard condition, it may involve parameters of the trigger and may also involve operations, attributes and links of the owning object or modelling element. In Fig. 11.3 the activity-expression begins with the '/' delimiter character and is the execution of the `Campaign` object's operation `setCampaignActive`.

An activity-expression may comprise a sequence of actions and include actions that may generate events such as sending signals or invoking operations. Each action in an action string is separated from its preceding action by a semi-colon.

An example of an activity-expression with multiple actions is shown in the transition string below:

```
left-mouse-down(location) [validItemSelected] / menuChoice =
pickMenuItem(location); menuChoice.highlight
```

The sequence of actions in an activity-expression is significant since it determines the order in which they are executed. In the example above, if the actions were in the reverse order, the value of `menuChoice` would be likely to be different when the `highlight` message is sent and the effect of the event would be different. Actions are considered to be atomic (that is, they cannot be subdivided) and cannot be interrupted once they have been started. Once initiated this action must execute fully before any other action is considered. This is known as *'run-to-completion'* semantics. An action will actually take time to execute in a live application but this is dependent only upon internal factors such as the complexity of the program code and the speed of the processor. The duration of a state is normally dependent upon external events in the application environment.

The effect of a trigger can be deferred to another state. This *deferred event* is shown by listing the trigger in the state symbol with postfix `/defer`. For example, if a person going through a semi-automatic door presses the close door button, it should not close until the person is no longer obstructing the doorway. This means that the door would only respond to the event, `closeDoorButtonPressed`, after it had moved from the state `OpenObstructed` to the state `OpenClear`. Its response to the event is deferred from the `OpenObstructed` state to the `OpenClear` state where it causes a transition to the state `Closed`.

So far we have considered only action-expressions that are associated with a transition. It can also be useful to model internal activities associated with a state. These activities may be triggered by events that do not change the state, by an event that causes the state to be entered or by an event that results in exiting the state. A state vertex may be subdivided into separate compartments: name compartment, internal activities compartment and internal transitions compartment. In Fig. 11.4 a state symbol is shown with two compartments, a name compartment and an internal activities compartment, and in Fig. 11.5 one is shown with three compartments.

The *name compartment* holds the name of the state. States may be unnamed and anonymous. Normally a state is only represented on a state machine diagram once (except for the final state).

The *internal activities compartment* lists the *internal activities* or *state activities* that are executed in that state. Each internal activity has a label stipulating under which circumstances the activity expression will be invoked. Three kinds of internal event have a special notation. Two of these are the *entry activities* and the *exit activities*, respectively indicated by the keywords *entry* and *exit*. These cannot have guard conditions as they are invoked implicitly on entry to the state and exit from the state respectively.

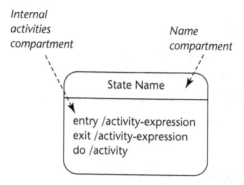

Figure 11.4 Internal activities for a state.

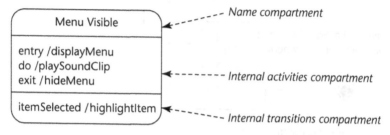

Figure 11.5 `Menu Visible` state for a `DropDownMenu` object.

Entry or exit *activity-expressions* may also involve parameters of incoming transitions (provided that these appear on all incoming transitions) and attributes and links of the owning object. It is important to emphasize that any transition into a state causes the entry activity to fire and all transitions out of a state cause the exit activity to fire.

```
'entry' '/' activity-name '(' parameter-list ')'
'exit' '/' activity-name '(' parameter-list ')'
```

State activities are preceded by the keyword *do* and have the following syntax:

```
'do' '/' activity-name '(' parameter-list ')'
```

State activities may 'persist' for a period of time, perhaps the duration of the state. For example in Fig. 11.5 the state activity `playSoundClip` will last as long as the sound clip or as long as the object remains in the state `Menu Visible`, whichever is the shorter.

The *internal transitions compartment* lists internal transitions. Each of these transitions is described in the same way as a trigger. Internal transitions do not cause a state change and do not invoke the exit or entry activities.

Figure 11.5 shows the `Menu Visible` state for a `DropDownMenu` object with three compartments. On occasions the internal transitions and the internal activities are placed in a single compartment within a state. This is a matter of notational style. In this example, the entry activity causes the menu to be displayed. The entry activity runs to completion before the state do activity is invoked. While the object remains in the `Menu Visible` state, the state do activity causes a sound clip to be played and, if the event `itemSelected` occurs, the action `highlightItem` is invoked. It is important to note

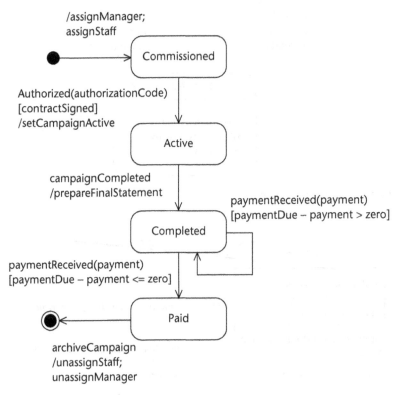

Figure 11.6 State machine for the class `Campaign`.

that, when the event `itemSelected` occurs, the `Menu Visible` state is not exited and entered and as a result the exit and entry activities are not invoked. When the state is actually exited the menu is hidden.

Figure 11.6 shows a state machine for the class `Campaign`. The transition from the initial pseudostate to the `Commissioned` state has been labelled only with an activity-expression that comprises the operations `assignManager` and `assignStaff`. Execution of these operations ensures that when a campaign is created a manager and at least one member of staff are assigned to it.[4] The operations are triggered by the event that creates a `Campaign` object. The transition from the `Completed` state to the `Paid` state has a guard condition that only allows the transition to fire if total amount due (`paymentDue`) for the `Campaign` has been completely paid (note that this guard condition allows a `Campaign` to enter the `Paid` state when the client overpays).

The reflexive transition from the `Completed` state models any payment event that does not reduce the amount due to zero or less. Only one of the two transitions from the `Completed` state (one of which is recursive) can be triggered by the `paymentReceived` event since the guard conditions are mutually exclusive. It would be bad practice to construct a state machine where one event can trigger two different transitions from the same state. A state machine is only unambiguous when all the transitions from each state are mutually exclusive.

---

4 Unless the specifications for these operations permit a null option.

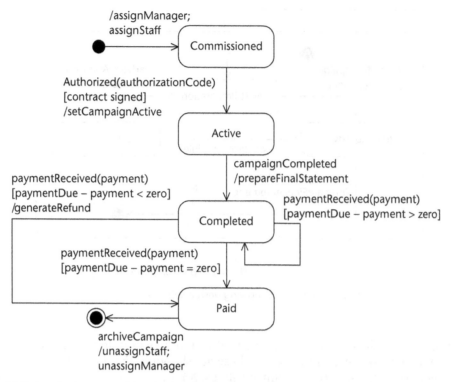

Figure 11.7 A revised state machine for the class `Campaign`.

If the user requirements were to change, so that an overpayment is now to result in the automatic generation of a refund, the state machine could be changed. Since the action that results from an overpayment is different from the action that results from a payment that reduces `paymentDue` to zero, a new transition is needed from the `Completed` state to the `Paid` state. The guard conditions from the `Completed` state must also be modified. Figure 11.7 shows a state machine that captures this requirement. It is important to appreciate that the state machines in Figs 11.6 and 11.7 are not equivalent to each other, but capture different versions of the users' requirements.

11.4 ▌ Further Notation

The state machine notation can be used to describe highly complex time-dependent behaviour. If a single state machine diagram becomes too complex to understand or to draw, state hierarchies can be nested, thus modelling different levels of detail on separate diagrams. The notation can also be used to represent concurrent behaviour.

11.4.1 Composite states

When the state behaviour for an object or an interaction is complex, it may be appropriate to represent it at different levels of detail and to reflect any hierarchy of states that is

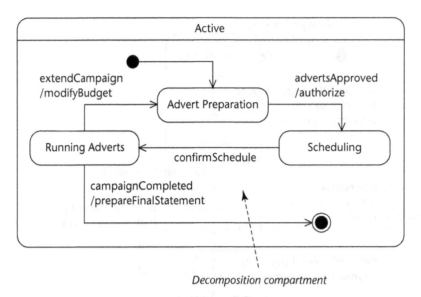

Figure 11.8 The Active state of Campaign showing nested substates.

present in the application. For example, in the state machine for Campaign the state Active encompasses several *substates*. These are shown in Fig. 11.8 where the Active state is seen to comprise three disjoint substates: Advert Preparation, Scheduling and Running Adverts, which are placed in the *decomposition compartment* of the state. This decomposition compartment has one region. This diagram now shows a single state that contains a nested state diagram within it known as *submachine*. In the nested state machine within the Active state, there is an initial pseudostate with a transition to the first substate that a Campaign object enters when it becomes active. The transition from the initial pseudostate to the first substate (Advert Preparation) should not be labelled with event but it may be labelled with an action, though this is not required in this example. It is implicitly fired by any transition to the Active state.[5] A final pseudostate symbol may also be shown on a nested state diagram. A transition to the final pseudostate symbol represents the completion of the activity in the enclosing state (i.e. Active) and a transition out of this state triggered by the completion event unless overridden by a specific trigger. This transition may be unlabelled (as long as this does not cause any ambiguity) since the event that triggers it is implied by the completion event (see Fig. 11.11).

When a campaign enters the Active state in Fig. 11.8 it first enters the Advert Preparation substate, then if the adverts are approved it enters the Scheduling substate and finally enters the Running Adverts substate when the schedule is approved. If the campaign is deemed completed, the object leaves the Running Adverts substate and also leaves the Active enclosing state, moving now to the Completed state (see Fig. 11.7). If the campaign is extended while in the Running Adverts substate, the Advert Preparation substate is re-entered (Fig. 11.8). A high-level state machine for

---

5 Except transitions to entry or history pseudostates. These are explained in Sections 11.4.3 and 11.4.5 respectively.

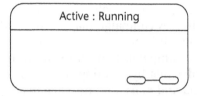

Figure 11.9 The Active submachine state of Campaign with detail hidden.

the class Campaign can be drawn to show within the main diagram the detail of the nested state machine for the Active state. If the detail of the submachine is not required on the higher-level state machine or is just too much to show on one diagram, the higher-level state machine can be annotated with the hidden decomposition indicator icon (two small state symbols linked together) as shown in Fig. 11.9. The submachine Running is referenced in the state name compartment using the syntax:

    state name ':' reference-state-machine-diagram-name

The state Active is known as a *submachine state* because it contains a submachine.

11.4.2 Concurrent states

Objects can have *concurrent* states. This means that the behaviour of the object can best be explained by regarding it as a product of two (or more) distinct sets of substates, each state of which can be entered and exited independently of substates in the other set. Figure 11.10 illustrates this form with two submachines, Running and Monitoring of the state Active.

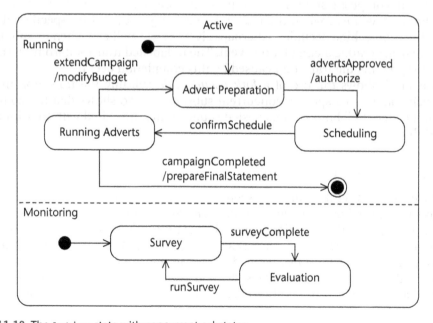

Figure 11.10 The Active state with concurrent substates.

Suppose that further investigation reveals that at Agate a campaign is surveyed and evaluated while it is also active. A campaign may occupy either the Survey substate or the Evaluation substate when it is in the Active state. Transitions between these two states are not affected by the campaign's current state in relation to the preparing and running of adverts. We model this by splitting the Active state into two concurrent nested submachines, Running and Monitoring, each in a separate region of the Active state machine decomposition compartment. This is shown in Fig. 11.10 by dividing the decomposition compartment with a dashed line. The concurrent states are described as orthogonal,[6] meaning that they are independent of each other.

A transition to a complex state such as this one is equivalent to a simultaneous transition to the initial states of each concurrent submachine. An initial state must be specified in both nested submachines in order to avoid ambiguity about which substate should first be entered in each concurrent region. A transition to the Active state means that the Campaign object simultaneously enters the Advert Preparation and Survey substates after any entry activities defined for the Active state itself have been invoked. A transition may now occur within either concurrent region without having any effect on the substate in the other concurrent region. However, a transition out of the Active state applies to all its substates (no matter how deeply nested). In a sense, we can say that the substates inherit the campaignCompleted transition from the Active state (shown in Fig. 11.7) since the transition applies implicitly to them all. This is equivalent to saying that an event that triggers a transition out of the Active state also triggers a transition out of any substates that are currently occupied. The submachine Monitoring does not have a final state. When the Active state is exited, whichever of the two states Survey or Evaluation is currently occupied at that time will also be exited. Inherited transitions can be masked if a transition with the same trigger is present in one of the nested state machines (as is the case for the campaignCompleted transition from the Running Adverts state in Fig. 11.10).

In general, composite states may exit in several ways. Figure 11.11 illustrates two of these. State 1 will exit when the trigger someTrigger occurs irrespective of which substate the submachine occupies. Alternatively State 1 will exit when its submachine is completed, generating a completion event. The unlabelled transition from State 1 to State 2 represents the transition caused by this completion event.

Figure 11.12 shows the use of a *fork pseudostate* splitting the transition into two paths, each leading to a specific concurrent substate. It also shows that the containing state is not exited until both parallel nested submachines are exited with transitions that merge at the *join pseudostate*.

11.4.3 Entry and exit pseudostates

On occasions it is useful to model exceptional entry to and exit from a submachine state. This is achieved using an *entry pseudostate* and an *exit pseudostate*. Figure 11.13 shows an example of this notation in use. The state machine Advert has three states StoryBoard, AdvertPrep and AdvertRunning. AdvertPrep is a submachine state with entry and exit pseudostates defined. The state machine AdvertPrepSM also has the same entry and exit pseudostates defined (they have the same names—Advert Reworked and Advert Aborted respectively). In AdvertPrepSM these pseudostates

---

6 Orthogonal literally means at right angles.

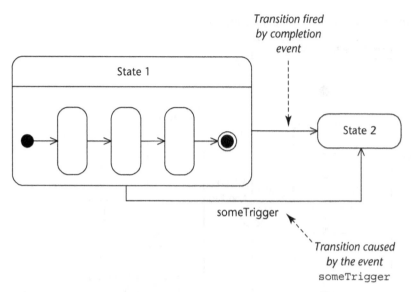

Figure 11.11 Completion event.

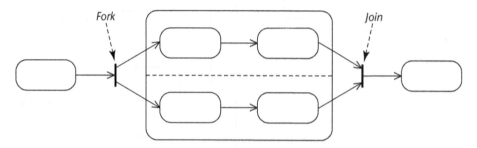

Figure 11.12 Parallel states using fork and join.

are shown on the frame boundary. Alternatively they could have been placed inside the frame. The trigger abort causes the state machine AdvertPrepSM to exit via Advert Aborted and this then follows the transition to the final state in the state machine Advert. The transition from AdvertRunning to Advert Reworked causes the sub-machine to start from the state linked to that entry pseudostate.

11.4.4 Junction and choice pseudostates

UML offers notation to show decision points on state machine diagrams. Junction and choice pseudostates may both be used for this purpose, although they have subtly different semantics. Figure 11.14 illustrates the notation. The diagram shows transitions from StateA to StateB and from StateA to StateC, which illustrate a compound transition. In general a compound transition may have more than one source state and more than one target state and will use junction, choice, fork or join pseudostates.

A *junction pseudodate* (the notation is the same as that for the initial pseudostate) has one or more entry transitions and will have one or more exit transitions. When there are many entry transitions and one exit transition this is known as a *merge*. When there are several exit transitions and only one entry transition this is known as a *static*

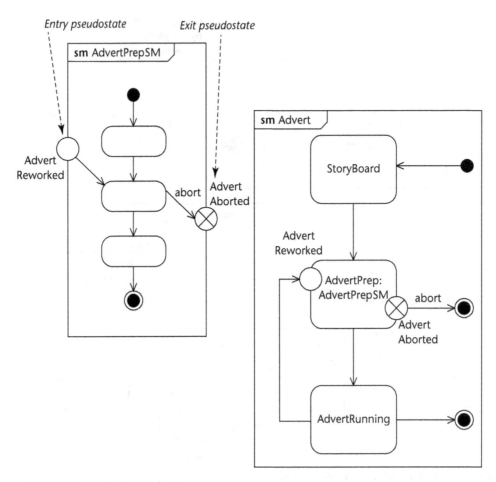

Figure 11.13 Entry and exit pseudostates.

conditional branch. Each exit transition will have a guard condition and the one whose guard condition evaluates as true fires. These guards are evaluated before the compound transition fires. If several guard conditions evaluate as true the transition that fires will be one of these.

Choice pseudostates allow the splitting of transitions into multiple exit transitions. Each exit transition will have a guard condition and, as can be seen in Fig. 11.14, if they all share a common argument it may be placed in the diamond-shaped choice symbol. The difference between choice and junction pseudostates is that for choice pseudostates the guard conditions are evaluated at the time the choice point is reached. Any actions associated with the first transitions in the compound transition (before the choice state) will have been executed and may affect which of the guard conditions evaluates to true.

11.4.5 History pseudostates

Composite states can be entered in various ways. We have already discussed the use of an entry pseudostate, which allows the submachine of composite state to be entered at

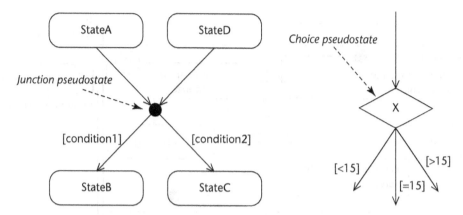

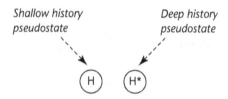

Figure 11.14 Junction and choice pseudostates.

Figure 11.15 History pseudostates.

a pre-determined substate. If a composite state has been entered and then exited prematurely before its submachine has completed, it may be useful to resume the composite state at the substate that was last active. The *shallow history pseudostate* and *deep history pseudostate* in Figure 11.15 are used to represent this.

For example, in Figure 11.16, a `Campaign` in the `Active` state may be suspended by the `suspendCampaign` trigger and move into the `Suspended` state. At some point the issue that resulted in the suspension is resolved and the campaign resumes where it left off. In this example the state `Active` has two parallel submachines, both of which need to be resumed from their last active substate. This is shown by the transition `resume-Campaign` from `Suspended`. This goes to the fork pseudostate and splits into two pathways, one going to the shallow history pseudostate in `Running` and the other going to the shallow history pseudostate in `Monitoring`. (A region may have no more than one history pseudostate.) Each of these history pseudostates then activates the last substate that was active in its region. The unlabelled transition from the shallow history pseudostate indicates the default shallow history substate. This state is activated if the last active substate was the final state or if the composite state had not been previously active. For `Running` the default shallow history substate is *Advert Preparation* and for *Monitoring* it is *Survey*.

Composite states may have substates that are in turn composite and so on. Thus, there may be an arbitrarily deep nesting of substates. The deep history pseudostate works in a similar way to the shallow history pseudostate but causes the composite state to resume at the last active state in each of the nested submachines within that region, no matter how deeply nested they are. In Fig. 11.16 shallow history and deep history pseudostates would have the same effect as there is only one level of nesting.

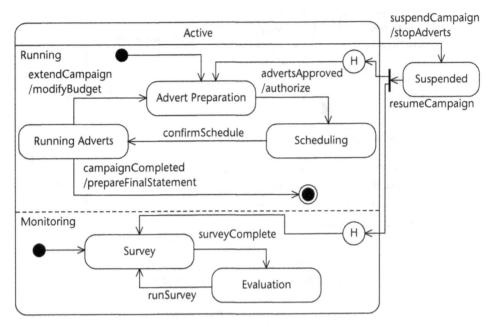

Figure 11.16 The `Active` state with history pseudostates.

11.4.6 State machine specialization

State machines model the behaviour of objects of a class. Classes can be extended to produce specialized sub-classes and consequently state machines can also be extended. States can be specified as {*final*} meaning that they cannot be extended in specializations. Transitions can be extended too, but the source state and the trigger must not be changed. For example, a new class `International Campaign` might be identified for Agate. The state machine for objects of this new class would be a specialization of the `Campaign` state machine and may add new states and transitions.

11.5 Preparing a State Machine

State machines can be prepared from various perspectives. The state machine for a class can be seen as a description of the ways that use cases can affect objects of that class. Use cases give rise to interaction diagrams (sequence diagrams or communication diagrams) and these can be used as a starting point for the preparation of a state machine.

Interaction diagrams show the messages that an object receives during the execution of a use case. The receipt of a message by an object does not necessarily correspond to an event that causes a state change. For example, simple 'get' messages (e.g. `getTitle`) and query messages (e.g. `listAdverts`) are not events in this sense. This is because they do not change the values of any of the object's attributes, nor do they alter any of its links with other objects. Some messages change attribute values without changing the state of an object. For example, a message `receivePayment` to a `Campaign` object will only cause a change of state to `Paid` if it represents payment of at least the full amount due.

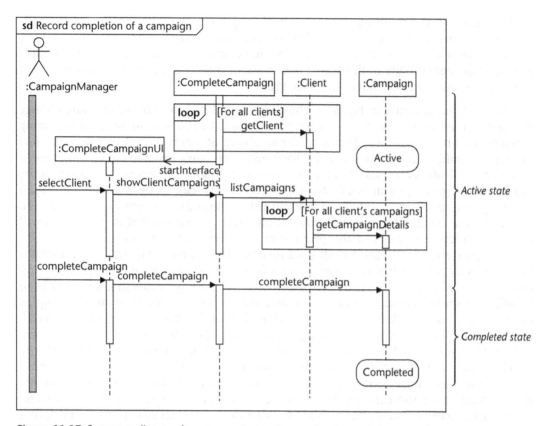

Figure 11.17 Sequence diagram for use case `Record completion of a campaign`.

11.5.1 A behavioural approach

Figure 11.17 shows a sequence diagram for the use case `Record completion of a campaign`. The receipt of the message `campaignCompleted` by a `Campaign` object is an event from the perspective of the `Campaign` object. In this example this event is a call trigger and causes the `campaignCompleted()` operation to be invoked, triggering a transition from the `Active` state to the `Completed` state. Incoming messages to an object generally correspond to a trigger causing a transition to fire. Allen and Frost (1998) describe the use of interaction diagrams to develop a state machine as a behavioural approach.

The preparation of a state machine from a set of interaction diagrams using this behavioural approach has the following sequence of steps:

1. Examine all interaction diagrams that involve each class that has heavy messaging.
2. For each class for which a state machine is being built follow steps 3 to 9.
3. On each interaction diagram identify the incoming messages that may correspond to events for the class being considered. Also identify the possible resulting states.
4. Document these events and states on a state machine.
5. Elaborate the state machine as necessary to cater for additional interactions as these become evident, and add any exceptions.
6. Develop any nested state machines (unless this has already been done in an earlier step).

7. Review the state machine to ensure consistency with use cases. In particular, check that any constraints that are implied by the state machine are appropriate.
8. Iterate steps 4, 5 and 6 until the state machine captures the necessary level of detail.
9. Check the consistency of the state machine with the class diagram, with interaction diagrams and with any other state machines.[7]

The sequence diagram in Fig. 11.17 has been annotated to indicate the state change that is triggered by the event campaignCompleted. In order to identify all incoming messages that may trigger a state change for an object, all interaction diagrams that affect the object should be examined (sequence diagrams are probably easier to use for this purpose than communication diagrams, but this is a matter of personal preference). Analysis of the interaction diagrams produces a first-cut list of all events (caused by incoming messages) that trigger state changes, and also a first-cut list of states that the object may enter as a result of these events. If only major interactions have been modelled then the lists will not be complete, but they can still provide an effective starting point.

The next step is to prepare a draft state machine for the class. Figure 11.18 illustrates the level of detail that might be shown in a first-cut state machine for the Campaign class. This would need to be expanded in order to reflect any events that have not been identified from the interaction diagrams, and also to include any exceptions. Complex nested states can be refined at this stage. A review of the state machine in Fig. 11.18 results in the addition of the Active state to encompass the states Advert Preparation, Scheduling and Running Adverts (shown in the revised state machine in Fig. 11.19).

The state machine is then compared to use cases in order to check that the constraints on class behaviour shown in the state machine satisfy the requirements documented in the use case. In this example the states Surveying and Evaluating have not yet been included. These might be identified in a final sweep-up to check that the state machine is complete, and could then be added as concurrent states within the Active state.

Let us suppose that further investigation of behaviour that can affect a campaign reveals that in some circumstances a campaign can be cancelled. This is not permitted after a campaign has been completed but a campaign can be cancelled while it is in the Commissioned state or in the Active state. In either case cancellation costs are calculated for billing to the client. If the campaign is active then advertisement schedules are also cancelled. A final state machine that includes this additional requirement is shown in Fig. 11.20. In this version the transition campaignCompleted is shown explicitly from the nested concurrent substate Running Adverts to the state Completed. When a transition like this fires, any exit activities for the other concurrent substates that are occupied are performed.

11.5.2 A lifecycle approach

An alternative approach to the preparation of state machines is based on the consideration of lifecycles for objects of each class. This approach does not use interaction diagrams as an initial source of possible events and states. Instead, they are identified directly from

---

7 This step should also include checking for consistency with any class diagram or operation specification constraints. Operation specification constraints are typically defined in pre- and post-conditions and invariants.

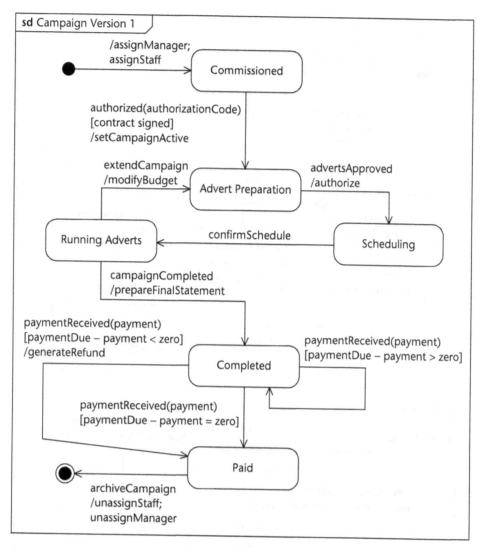

Figure 11.18 Initial state machine for the `Campaign` class—a behavioural approach.

use cases and from any other requirements documentation that happens to be available. First, the main system events are listed (at Agate '*A client commissions a new campaign*' might be one of the first to consider). Each event is then examined in order to determine which objects are likely to have a state dependent response to it.

The steps involved in the lifecycle approach to state modelling are as follows.

1. Identify major system events.
2. Identify each class that is likely to have a state dependent response to these events.
3. For each of these classes produce a first-cut state machine by considering the typical lifecycle of an instance of the class.
4. Examine the state machine and elaborate to encompass more detailed event behaviour.

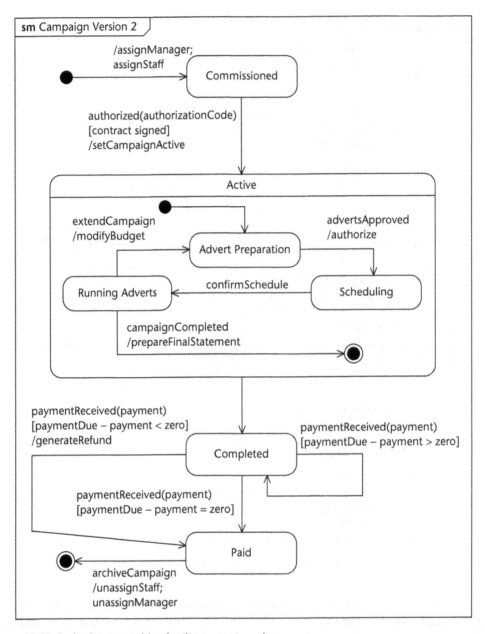

Figure 11.19 Revised state machine for the Campaign class.

5. Enhance the state machine to include alternative scenarios.
6. Review the state machine to ensure that it is consistent with the use cases. In particular, check that the constraints that the state machine implies are appropriate.
7. Iterate through steps 4, 5 and 6 until the state machine captures the necessary level of detail.
8. Ensure consistency with class diagram and interaction diagrams and other state machines.

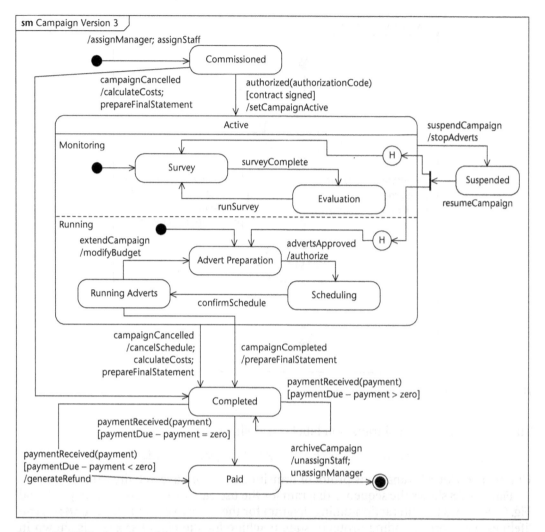

Figure 11.20 Final version of the Campaign state machine.

The lifecycle approach is less formal than the behavioural approach in its initial identification of events and relevant classes. It is often helpful to use a combination of the two, since each provides checks on the other. A lifecycle approach might produce Fig. 11.6 as an initial first-cut state machine for the Campaign class, but further elaboration should still result in the state machine shown in Fig. 11.20.

11.6 Protocol and Behavioural State Machines

So far in this chapter we have been developing behavioural state machines. Protocol state machines differ in that they only show all the legal transitions with their pre- and post-conditions. The states of a protocol state machine cannot have entry, exit or do activity sections, they cannot have deep or shallow history states and all transitions must be protocol transitions.

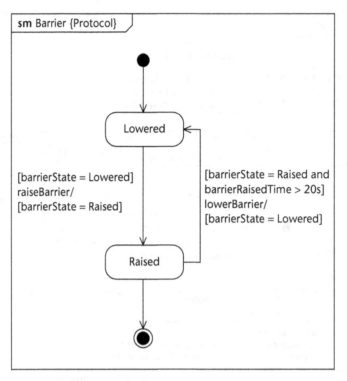

Figure 11.21 Protocol state machine for `Barrier`.

The syntax for a protocol transition label is as follows:

```
'[' pre-condition ']' trigger '/' '[' post-condition ']'
```

Unlike behavioural transitions protocol transitions do not have activity expressions.

Figure 9.28 shows the sequence diagram for the use case `Car enters car park` and Fig. 9.29 shows the interaction timing diagram for the `:Barrier` and `:TicketMachine` lifelines. The corresponding protocol state machine for the class `Barrier` is shown in Fig. 11.21. This provides a description of all the transitions that are permitted for the `Barrier` class and the circumstances under which they are valid. For example, the barrier can be lowered only if the pre-condition

```
[barrierState = Raised and barrierRaisedTime > 20s]
```

is true. This states that before the barrier can be lowered it must be raised and that it has been raised for at least 20 seconds.

11.7　Consistency Checking

The need for consistency between different models was discussed in Chapter 9 in relation to interaction diagrams. State machines must also be consistent with other models:

■ Every trigger should appear as an incoming message for the appropriate object on an interaction diagram.

- Every trigger should correspond to an operation on the appropriate class (but note that not all operations correspond to triggers).
- Every action should correspond to the execution of an operation on the appropriate class, and perhaps also to the dispatch of a message to another object.
- Every outgoing message sent from a state machine must correspond to an operation on another class.

Consistency checks are an important task in the preparation of a complete set of models. This process highlights omissions and errors, and encourages the clarification of any ambiguity or incompleteness in the requirements.

11.8   Quality Guidelines

Preparing state machines is an iterative process that involves refining the model until it captures the semantics of the object or model element behaviour. A series of general guidelines that aid the production of good quality state machines is listed below:

- Name each state uniquely to reflect what is happening for the duration of the state or what the state is waiting for.
- Do not use composite states unless the state behaviour is genuinely complex.
- Do not show too much complexity on a single state machine. If there are more than seven states consider using substates. Even with a small number of states, a state machine may be too complex if there are a large number of transitions between them. Arguably the state machine in Fig. 11.20 would be better represented on three diagrams: one for the high-level state machine with the detail of the `Active` state hidden and one diagram for each of the two submachines, `Running` and `Monitoring`.
- Use guard conditions carefully to ensure that the state machine describes possible behaviour unambiguously.

State machines should not be used to model procedural behavior. Activity diagrams (see Chapters 6 and 10) are used for this. Typical symptoms of a state machine that is procedural include the following:

- Most transitions are fired by state completion.
- Many messages are sent to `self`, reflecting code reuse rather than actions triggered by events.
- States do not capture state dependent behaviour associated with the class.

Of course, a model that was intended to be a state machine but turns out to be an activity diagram describing procedural flow may be a valuable model; it just is not a state machine.

11.9   Summary

The specification of the dynamic and behavioural aspects of an application is an important aspect of both analysis and design. They are described in part by interaction diagrams but these focus only on a use case or an operation. In order to capture fully the behavioural constraints for each class it is necessary to model the impact of events on that class and to model the resulting state changes with their attendant limitations on behaviour. It is only necessary to prepare state machines for classes that have state dependent variations in behaviour. UML's state machine notation permits the construction of detailed models that may include the nesting of states and the use of concurrent states to capture complex behaviour.

State machines must be checked for consistency with their associated class and interaction diagrams and this may highlight the need to make modifications to these other models.

The notations provided by UML are very detailed and should be used with some care. There is no advantage in producing a state machine that utilizes every UML feature unless this is really necessary for the application that is being modelled. Ideally, state models should be kept as simple as possible but should have sufficient detail to make them unambiguous and informative. The use of multiple nested states does not aid clarity unless the behaviour being described is itself complex.

Review Questions

11.1 Define event, state and transition.

11.2 What is the effect of a guard condition?

11.3 Why should all the guard conditions from a state be mutually exclusive?

11.4 What is a composite state?

11.5 What does it mean to say that an object can be in concurrent states?

11.6 How do nested states differ from concurrent states?

11.7 When are entry and exit pseudostates used?

11.8 What is the difference between shallow history and deep history pseudostates?

11.9 Which UML modelling elements can have their behaviour described by a state machine?

11.10 What is a trigger?

11.11 What indications would suggest that a state machine has not been drawn to model state changes?

11.12 Describe the difference between behavioural and protocol state machines.

11.13 Against which other UML diagrams should a state machine be cross-checked?

11.14 What cross-checks should be carried out?

Case Study Work, Exercises and Projects

11.A Using the interaction sequence diagrams that you prepared for Exercises 9.A–9.C, list events that affect a `ProductionLine` object and identify appropriate states for this class.

11.B Prepare a state machine for the class `ProductionLine`.

11.C List any changes that may have to be made to the class diagram for the FoodCo case study in the light of preparing this state machine.

Further Reading

State machines have been used widely to model complex control behaviour. Various non-object-oriented approaches have used state machines very effectively. In particular, the texts by Ward and Mellor (1985, 1986) and Hatley and Pirbhai (1987) provide detailed descriptions of their application in real-time applications. From an object-oriented perspective both Rumbaugh et al. (1991) and Booch (1994) provide useful descriptions of the Harel (1987) notation used in UML. Object-oriented real-time development approaches are well discussed by Douglass (2004) and also by Selic et al. (1994). The latter text is based on the ROOM (Real-time Object-Oriented Modelling) approach. Cook and Daniels (1994) give an interesting alternative perspective on the modelling of events and states. Useful advice on preparing state machines can also be found in the IBM-Rational Unified Process (IBM, 2009). For a more recent view of state machines from Harel, see Harel and Politi (1998), which presents the STATEMATE approach.

Agate Ltd Case Study—Further Analysis

Agate Ltd

A4.1 | Introduction

In this chapter we show how the analysis model presented in Chapter A3 has been refined in a further iteration. The refinement has been carried out with two particular aims in mind.

First we aim to improve our understanding of the domain and thereby increase the general usefulness of the model in a wider context. This essentially means identifying opportunities for reuse through the elaboration of generalization, composition and aggregation structures in the class model, as described in Chapter 8.

Second, we aim to improve the level of detail of the model and also the accuracy with which it reflects user requirements. This is addressed partly through appropriate allocation of behaviour to classes, derived from the analysis of class interaction using sequence diagrams and state machines. We also seek to specify the behavioural aspects of the model in more detail through the specification of operations. The related techniques are described in Chapters 9, 10 and 11.

As a result of these activities, the analysis class model is revised to reflect our greater understanding of the domain and of the requirements.

The following sections include:

- samples of the sequence diagrams and state machines that help us to understand the behavioural aspects of the model;
- specifications for some operations that capture this behaviour and communicate it to the designers;
- a revised analysis class diagram that shows the effects of further analysis on the static structure of the model.

Together, the class diagram and operation specifications comprise an analysis class model.

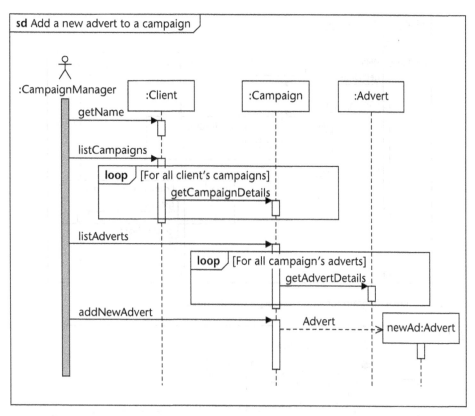

Figure A4.1 Sequence diagram for Add a new advert to a campaign.

A4.2 Sequence Diagrams

The first sequence diagram, shown in Fig. A4.1, is for the use case Add a new advert to a campaign. The second sequence diagram, shown in Fig. A4.2, is for the use case Check campaign budget. Both these sequence diagrams are discussed in some detail in Chapter 9; note that for simplicity we show here the version of Add a new advert to a campaign that does not include boundary and control classes.

Sequence diagrams help the requirements analyst to identify at a detailed level the operations that are necessary to implement the functionality of a use case. It is worth mentioning that, although at this point we are still primarily engaged in analysis–in other words, an attempt to understand the demands that this information system will fulfil–there is already a significant element of design in our models. There is no one correct sequence diagram for a given use case. Instead, there are a variety of possible sequence diagrams, each of which is relatively more or less satisfactory in terms of how well it meets the needs of the use case. The sequence diagrams illustrated here are the product of experimentation, judgement and several iterations of modelling carried out by analysts and users together.

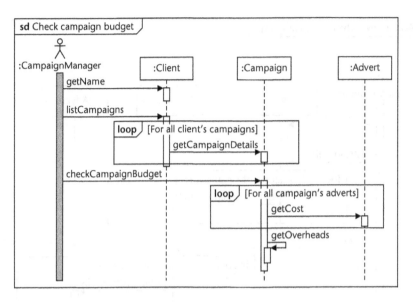

Figure A4.2 Sequence diagram for Check campaign budget.

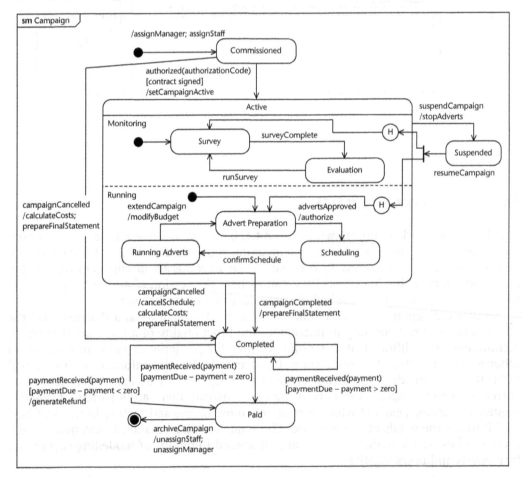

Figure A4.3 State machine for Campaign.

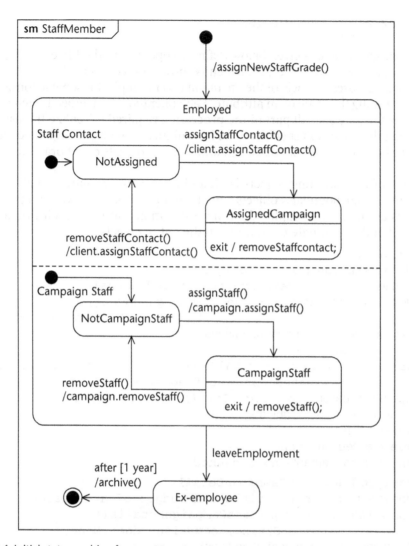

Figure A4.4 Initial state machine for StaffMember.

A4.3 State Machines

In this section we present the final state machine for Campaign (Fig. A4.3), which has already been discussed at some length in Chapter 11, and an initial state machine for StaffMember (Fig. A4.4), which is presented here for the first time. These represent the behaviour of objects of significant classes in the Campaign Management and Staff Management analysis packages, respectively.

In conjunction with sequence diagrams, state machines help to identify the operations that are required and to allocate those operations to appropriate classes. All operations shown on sequence diagrams and state machines are added to the relevant class definitions. Each operation must also in due course be specified, and it is to this that we turn in the next section.

A4.4 | Operation Specifications

The operation specifications given below define all operations identified for the sequence diagram Check campaign budget, which is shown above in Fig. A4.2.

Note that in all cases the logic of the operation is very simple; for some it consists of little more than returning the value of an attribute. Each operation, and, indeed, each object, has responsibility for only a small part of the processing required to realize the use case.

By reading the operation specifications in conjunction with the sequence diagram, it is easy to see how the Client, Campaign and Advert objects collaborate to realize this use case.

This view of collaborating objects is simplified to some extent, in that it does not include control and boundary objects and their operations. However, operations in these objects are no more complex than those shown below, since their primary role is simply to call and co-ordinate operations on the entity objects.

Context: Campaign

    Operation specification: checkCampaignBudget()
    Operation intent: return campaign budget and actual costs.
    Operation signature: Campaign::checkCampaignBudget()
                                budgetCostDifference:Money
    Logic description (pre- and post-conditions):
      pre: self->exists()
      post: result = self.originalBudget-self.estimatedCost **and**
           self.estimatedCost = self.adverts.estimatedCost->sum()
    Other operations called: Advert.getCost(), self.getOverheads()
    Events transmitted to other objects: none
    Attributes set: none
    Response to exceptions: none defined
    Non-functional requirements: none defined

    Operation specification: getCampaignDetails()
    Operation intent: return the title and budget of a campaign.
    Operation signature: Campaign::getCampaignDetails()
                 title:String, campaignBudget:Money
    Logic description (pre- and post-conditions):
      pre: self->exists()
      post: result = self.title, self.estimatedCost
    Other operations called: none
    Events transmitted to other objects: none
    Attributes set: none
    Response to exceptions: none defined
    Non-functional requirements: none defined

    Operation specification: getOverheads()
    Operation intent: calculate the total overhead cost for a campaign.
    Operation signature: Campaign::getOverheads()
                 campaignOverheads:Money
    Logic description (pre- and post-conditions):
      pre: self->exists()
      post: result = self.campaignOverheads

Other operations called: none
Events transmitted to other objects: none
Attributes set: none
Response to exceptions: none defined
Non-functional requirements: none defined

Context: Client
Operation specification: getName()
Operation intent: return the client name.
Operation signature: Client::getName()name:String
Logic description (pre- and post-conditions):
   pre: self->exists
   post: result = self.name
Other operations called: none
Events transmitted to other objects: none
Attributes set: none
Response to exceptions: none defined
Non-functional requirements: none defined

Operation specification: listCampaigns()
Operation intent: return a list of campaigns for a client.
Operation signature: Client::listCampaigns()titles:String[]
Logic description (pre- and post-conditions):
   pre: self->exists
   post: result = self.campaign->collect(campaign.title)
Other operations called: Campaign.getCampaignDetails
Events transmitted to other objects: none
Attributes set: none
Response to exceptions: none defined
Non-functional requirements: none defined

Context: Advert
Operation specification: getCost()
Operation intent: return the actual cost for an advert.
Operation signature: Advert::getCost()
                   actualAdvertCost:Money
Logic description (pre- and post-conditions):
   pre: self->exists()
   post: result = self.actualAdvertCost
Other operations called: none
Events transmitted to other objects: none
Attributes set: none
Response to exceptions: none defined
Non-functional requirements: none defined

A4.5　Further Refinement of the Class Diagram

Figure A4.5 shows the revised analysis class diagram, after inheritance and aggregation structures have been added. For reasons of space, all attributes and operations have been suppressed from this view.

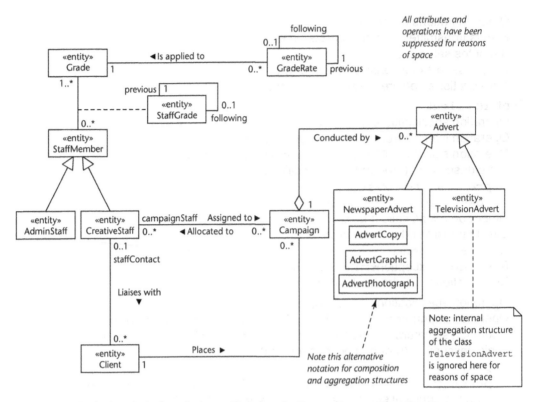

Figure A4.5 Revised analysis class diagram with generalization and aggregation structures.

Figure A4.6 shows an excerpt from the analysis class diagram, detailing the generalization and aggregation structure for `Advert` with attributes and operations visible. This partial diagram reflects a further iteration of investigation and requirements modelling, which revealed that there is a requirement to keep track of the various elements used to create an advertisement. This is because photographs, music clips and so on can often be used for more than one advertisement in a campaign, and it has been a problem to identify and retrieve these elements when they are needed.

A4.6   Further Activities of Requirements Analysis

Figure A4.7 shows an activity diagram that illustrates the relationship between the products of the analysis model before and after this iteration of analysis. Some details are worth highlighting.

- The analysis class model now includes some detailed class definition. In particular, all operations should be specified at least in outline.
- Some parts of the analysis model may be substantially unchanged during this iteration, for example the communication diagrams and the glossary. Although this is not necessarily the case, we have shown these as unaffected in Fig. A4.7.
- As a result of the operation specification activity, many attributes may also have been specified in more detail. Some, particularly those that are required to provide

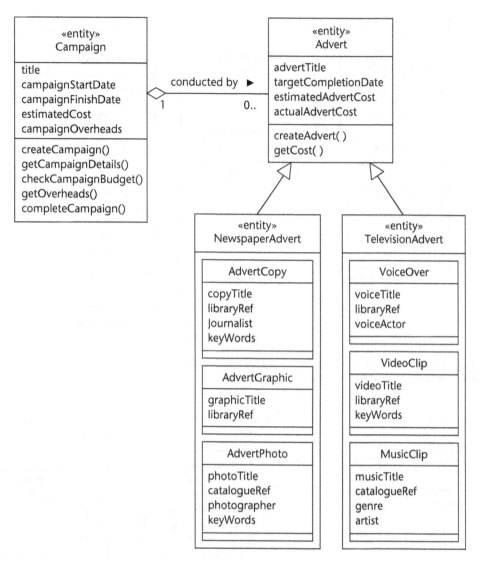

Figure A4.6 Generalization and aggregation structure for `Advert`.

parameters to operations in other classes, will certainly now be typed. We have not shown this yet, since the typing of attributes is essentially a design activity. But in practice, some design decisions are made in parallel with the more detailed analysis that we describe in this chapter.

Figure A4.8 shows a more detailed view of the activities that are carried out and the products directly used or affected during this iteration. In this diagram, we have tried to suggest a sensible outline sequence for carrying out the various activities. However, it should be noted that this is no more than a guide, and is certainly not meant to be prescriptive. An iterative approach should always be followed that is sensitive to the needs of the project, to the skill of the developers and to the often haphazard manner in which understanding grows during the modelling and analysis of requirements.

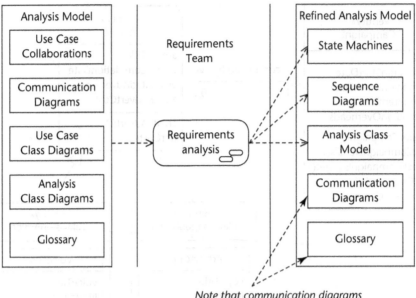

Figure A4.7 High-level activity diagram showing how elements of the analysis model are created or updated during this iteration of analysis.

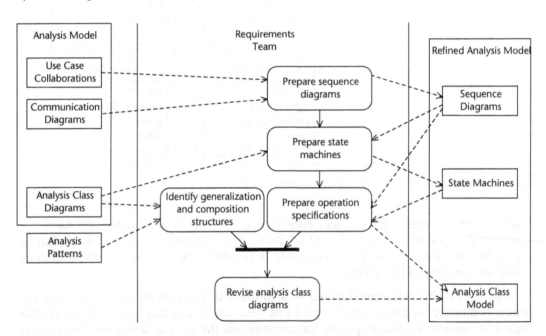

For clarity, we have detailed only those activities and products that are most directly involved in this iteration. Note also that the flow of activities is indicative and is not intended to be prescriptive.

Figure A4.8 The activities that are carried out and the products directly used or affected during this iteration of analysis.

Moving into Design

12.1 Introduction

Two questions that may be asked by those who are new to systems analysis and design are: 'What is the difference between analysis and design?' and 'Why treat analysis and design as separate activities?' In the development of information systems, as in the development of many kinds of system, the process of analysis is distinguished from the process of design. Analysis is often said to be about the 'What?' of a system, and design is described as being about the 'How?'. Design can start before or after the decision has been made about the hardware and software to be used in implementing the system. Implementation-independent or logical design is distinguished from implementation-dependent or physical design. Design takes place within the context of the architecture of the enterprise and its information systems. Design also takes place at more than one level: system design or architectural design, which addresses structural aspects and standards that affect the overall system, and detailed design, which addresses the design of classes and the detailed working of the system.

In producing a design for a system, a designer will be working within a framework of general quality criteria and will also be trying to achieve measurable objectives for the design that are specific to the particular system.

12.2 | How is Design Different from Analysis?

Design has been described by Rumbaugh (1997) as stating 'how the system will be constructed without actually building it'. The models that are produced by design activities show how the various parts of the system will work together; the models produced by analysis activities show what is in the system and how those parts are related to one another.

12.2.1 Moving to design

The word *analysis* comes from a Greek word meaning to break down into component parts. When we analyse an organization and its need for a new system, the analysis activity is characterized as asking *what* happens in the current system and *what* is required in the new system. It is a process of seeking to understand the organization, investigating its requirements and modelling them. The result of this analysis activity is a specification of what the proposed system will do based on the requirements.

Design is about producing a solution that meets the requirements that have been analysed. The parts that have been broken down are assembled into one of a number of possible solutions. The design activity is concerned with specifying *how* the new system will meet the requirements. There may be many possible design solutions, but the intention is to produce the best possible solution in the circumstances. Those circumstances may reflect constraints such as limits on how much can be spent on the new system or the need for the new system to work with an existing system. Jacobson et al. (1992) regard design as part of the construction process (together with implementation). The systems designer has his or her attention focused on the implementation of the new system, while the systems analyst is focused on the way the business is organized and a possible better organization; the focuses of these two activities are very different.

A simple example of this can be seen in the Agate case study. Analysis identifies the fact that each `Campaign` has a `title` attribute, and this fact is documented in the class model. Design determines how this will be entered into the system, displayed on screen and stored in some kind of database together with all the other attributes of `Campaign` and other classes. This is shown schematically in Fig. 12.1.

Design can be seen either as a stage in the systems development lifecycle or as an activity that takes place within the development of a system. In projects that follow the waterfall lifecycle model (Fig. 3.3), the analysis stage will be complete before the design stage begins. However, in projects that follow an iterative lifecycle, design is not such a clear-cut stage, but is rather an activity that will be carried out on the evolving model of the system. Rumbaugh (1997) distinguishes between the idea of design as a stage in the waterfall lifecycle and design as a process that different parts of the model of the system will go through at different times.

In the Unified Process (Jacobson et al., 1999), design is organized as a workflow—a series of activities with inputs and outputs—that is independent of the project phase. In the Rational Unified Process (Kruchten, 2004), analysis and design are combined into a single workflow—the analysis activities produce an overview model, if it is required, but the emphasis is on design—and the workflow is similarly independent of the project phase. We have adopted a similar approach to the Unified Process in the process outlined in Chapter 5. A project consists of major phases (inception, elaboration, construction and transition); each phase requires one or more iterations and, within the iterations, the amount of effort dedicated to the activities in each workflow gradually increases and

Requirements   Analysis   Design

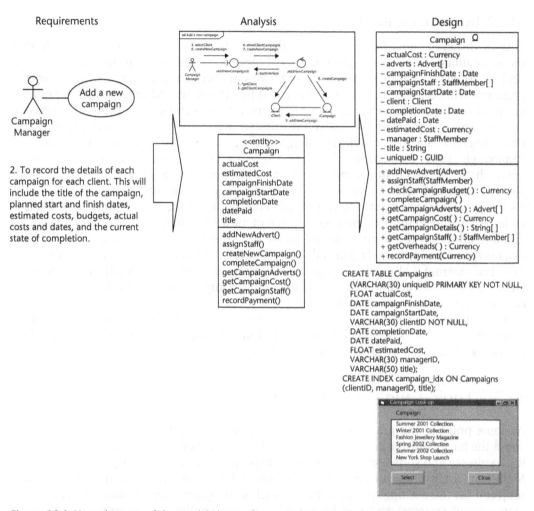

Figure 12.1 How elements of the model change from requirements through analysis to design.

then declines as the project progresses. The difference between this kind of approach and the traditional waterfall model is that in the traditional approach analysis, design, construction and other stages in the waterfall are both activities and stages: during the analysis stage, for example, all the analysis activity is meant to take place. Real projects are not like this: during the early part of the project, which may be called 'analysis', some design activity may take place; during the later part of the project, which may be called 'design', some analysis activity may take place. Process models such as the Unified Process recognise this and give the phases different names to decouple them from the activities. As long as less and less analysis and more and more design (and then implementation) take place as the project develops, the project is making progress. Despite this, many projects still treat analysis and design as separate stages rather than activities that gradually elaborate the model as the project progresses. This has some benefits for project management, as the full scope of the system is analysed and agreed before any design begins, so it is easier to plan and estimate costs. However, the requirements often change, and it is better to recognize this and adopt an iterative approach.

12.2.2 Design in the iterative lifecycle

One of the arguments put forward for the use of object-oriented approaches is that the same model (the class diagram or object model) is used right through the life of the project. Analysis identifies classes, those classes are refined in design, and the eventual programs will be written in terms of classes. While this so-called *seamlessness* of object-oriented methods may seem like an argument for weakening the distinction between analysis and design, when we move into design, different information is added to the class diagram, and other different diagrams are used to support the class diagram. Rumbaugh (1997) distinguishes between analysis and design in terms of the amount of detail that is included in the model. On a continuum, the analysis stage provides an abstract model of 'what to do' while the design stage documents 'exactly how to do it'. As the project moves from one end of this continuum to the other, additional detail is added to the model until a clear specification of 'how to do it' is provided. This additional detail is added in the form of diagrams such as interaction diagrams, state machine diagrams and deployment diagrams that supplement the information in the class diagram. The class diagram is also enhanced during design by the addition of detail about attributes and operations and additional classes to handle the implementation of the user interface, communication between subsystems and data storage.

In an iterative project the whole system does not go through this evolution together; different parts of the system will be prioritized in successive iterations. In each iteration, a set of use cases can be taken forward for development.

12.3 | Logical and Physical Design

At some point in the life of a systems development project a decision must be made about the hardware and software that are to be used to develop and deliver the system—the hardware and software platform. In some projects this is known right from the start. Many companies have an existing investment in hardware and software, and any new project must use existing system software (such as programming languages and database management systems) and will be expected to run on the same hardware. However, service-oriented architectures (see Chapter 13) and open system standards, which allow for different hardware and software to operate together, have meant that even for such companies, the choice of platform is more open. For many new projects the choice of platform is relatively unconstrained and so at some point in the life of the project a decision must be made about the platform to be used.

Some aspects of the design of systems are dependent on the choice of platform. These will affect the system architecture, the design of objects and the interfaces with various components of the system. Examples include the following.

- The decision to create a distributed system with elements of the system running on different machines will require the use of some *middleware*, to allow objects to communicate with one another across the network. This will affect the design of objects and the messages used to communicate.
- The decision to write programs in Java and to use a relational database that supports ODBC (Object Data Base Connectivity) will require the use of JDBC (Java Data Base Connectivity) and optionally a framework, such as the Java Persistence API, to map between the objects and the relational database.

- The choice of Java as a software development language will mean that the developer has the choice of using the standard Java AWT (Abstract Windowing Toolkit), the Java Swing classes, the Standard Widget Toolkit (SWT) or proprietary interface classes for designing the interface.
- Java does not support multiple inheritance; other object-oriented languages such as C++ do. If the system being developed appears to require multiple inheritance then in Java this will have to be implemented using Java's interface mechanism.
- If the system has to communicate with special hardware, for example bar-code scanners, then it may be necessary to design the interface so that it can be written in C as a *native method* and encapsulated in a Java class, as Java cannot directly access low-level features of hardware.

Java has been used here as an example. The same kinds of issues will arise whatever platform is chosen.

It is also the case that there are many design decisions that can be made without knowledge of the hardware and software platform.

- The interaction between objects to provide the functionality of particular use cases can be designed using interaction diagrams or communication diagrams.
- The layout of data entry screens can be designed in terms of the fields that will be required to provide the data for the objects that are to be created or updated, and the order in which they will appear on the screen can be determined. However, the exact nature of a textbox and whether it is a Borland C++ `TEdit`, a Java `TextField`, a C# `TextBox`, a Visual Basic `TextBox` or something else can be left until later.
- The nature of commands and data to be sent to and received from special hardware or other systems can be determined without needing to design the exact physical format of messages.

Because of this, design is sometimes divided into two stages. The first is *implementation-independent* or *logical* design and the second is *implementation-dependent* or *physical* design. Logical design is concerned with those aspects of the system that can be designed without knowledge of the implementation platform; physical design deals with those aspects of the system that are dependent on the implementation platform that will be used.

Having an implementation-independent design may be useful if you expect a system to have to be re-implemented with little change to the overall design but on a different platform: for example, a Windows program that is to be ported to MacOS and Linux, or a program that must run on different types of handheld and smartphone using Windows Mobile, Symbian and Android.

In many projects, design begins after hardware and software decisions have been made. However, if this is not the case, then the project manager must ensure that the plan of work for the project takes account of this and that logical design activities are tackled first. In an iterative project lifecycle, logical design may take place in the early design iterations or, if the system is partitioned into subsystems, the logical design of each subsystem will take place before its physical design.

The OMG promotes an initiative called Model-Driven Architecture (MDA). This approach is based on the idea that a system can be modelled in UML to create a platform-independent model (PIM), and that this PIM can then be transformed using automated modelling and programming tools into a platform-dependent model (PDM) for a specific platform. The same PIM can be translated into many different PDMs for different platforms.

12.4 | System Design and Detailed Design

Design of systems takes place at two levels: system design and detailed design. These design activities take place in the context of the architecture of the enterprise as a whole and the architecture of the system. Figure 12.2 shows the relationship between enterprise architecture, system architecture, system design and detailed design in schematic form.

Enterprise architecture deals with the way the organization operates, its people, its locations, its strategy and how the information technology and information systems support the organization. The enterprise architect ensures that all IT projects across the organization conform to this high-level architecture.

System architecture deals with the architecture of single systems or groups of related systems within the framework provided by the enterprise architecture. The structure of

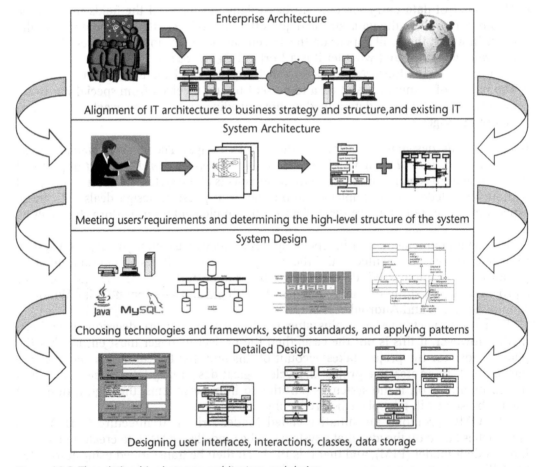

Figure 12.2 The relationships between architecture and design.

and relationships between subsystems are the domain of the system architect. Within a project, the system architect acts as an advocate of the users' interests, making sure that the architectural features of the system meet both their functional and non-functional requirements.

System design is concerned with the design of the components of the system and the setting of standards: for example, for the design of the human–computer interface. Within the constraints of the enterprise architecture and the system architecture, the system designer chooses appropriate technologies and sets standards that will be used across the system. Design patterns can be used in system architecture, system design and detailed design, but the choice of patterns that will be used in the implementation is most relevant to system design.

Detailed design is concerned with designing individual elements to fit the architecture, to conform to the standards and to provide the basis for an effective and efficient implementation. In an object-oriented system, the detailed design is mainly concerned with the design of objects and classes. Detailed design also addresses the user interface and database design.

The reality is that most organizations do not have the luxury of employing people in all these roles. Few businesses, even large ones, employ enterprise architects, and most blur the distinction between system architecture and system design. Detailed design may even be left to developers. We cover system design and system architecture together in Chapter 13, with a short discussion of how enterprise architecture frameworks influence the system level work. Detailed class design is covered in Chapter 14, while Chapters 15 to 18 deal with the use of design patterns, the user interface design and the database design.

12.4.1 System design

During system design the designers make decisions that will affect the system as a whole. The most important aspect of this is the overall architecture of the system (Chapter 13). Many systems use a client–server architecture in which the work of the system is divided between the clients (typically PCs on the users' desks) and a server (usually a Unix, Linux or Windows machine that provides services to a number of users). This raises questions about how processes and objects will be distributed on different machines, and it is the role of the system designer or system architect to decide on this. The design will have to be broken down into subsystems and these subsystems may be allocated to different processors. This introduces a requirement for communication between processors, and the systems designer will need to determine the mechanisms used to provide for this communication. Distributing systems over multiple processors also makes it possible for different subsystems to be active simultaneously or concurrently. This concurrency needs to be designed into the system explicitly rather than left to chance.

Many organizations have existing standards for their systems. These may involve interface design issues such as screen layouts, report layouts or how online help is provided. Decisions about the standards to be applied across the whole system are part of system design, whereas the design of individual screens and documents (to comply with these standards) is part of detailed design.

When a new system is introduced into an organization, it will have an impact on people and their existing working practices. Job design is often included in system design and addresses concerns about how people's work will change, how their interest and motivation can be maintained and what training they will require in order to carry out their new jobs. How people use particular use cases will be included in the detailed design of the human–computer interface.

12.4.2 Detailed design

Traditionally, detailed design has been about designing inputs, outputs, processes and file or database structures; these same aspects of the system also have to be designed in an object-oriented system, but they will be organized in terms of classes. During the analysis phase of a project, concepts in the business will have been identified and elaborated in terms of classes, and use cases will have been identified and described. The classes that have been included in the class diagram will reflect the business requirements but they will only include a very simplistic view of the classes to handle the interface with the user, the interface with other systems, the storage of data and the overall co-ordination of the other classes into programs. These classes will be added in design with greater or lesser degrees of detail depending on the hardware and software platform that is being used for the new system.

12.5 Qualities and Objectives of Design

There are a number of criteria for a good design and these are discussed in Section 12.5.1. Perhaps the most obvious measure of design quality is whether the finished application is of high quality. This assumes that the analysis that preceded the design work was itself of high quality. (Analysis quality was discussed in Chapter 7.) However, this is a rather vague and circular way of assessing quality. There are some criteria that can be applied to determine whether a design is fit for purpose. Some of the criteria given below for a good design will bring benefits to the developers, while some will provide benefits for the eventual users of the system. In Section 12.5.2 we discuss how it is often necessary to make trade-offs between different design criteria, as it may not be possible to achieve all of them in a single design. In Section 12.5.3 the ways in which we can measure whether the business objectives have been met are explored.

12.5.1 Objectives and constraints

The designers of a system seek to achieve many objectives that have been identified as the characteristics of a good design since the early days of information systems development. Yourdon and Constantine (1979) cite efficiency, flexibility, generality, maintainability and reliability; DeMarco (1979) proposes efficiency, maintainability and buildability; and Page-Jones (1988) suggests that a good design is efficient, flexible, maintainable, manageable, satisfying and productive. These latter two points highlight issues concerned with human–computer interaction and remind us of the need for the design to produce a usable system. Other characteristics of a good design are that it should be functional, portable, secure and economical; in the context of object-oriented systems, reusability is a priority objective. The characteristics of good design that will influence the design of the Agate sysem are shown in Figure 12.3 and listed below.

Functional
When we use a computer system, we expect it to perform correctly and completely those functions that it is claimed to perform; when an information system is developed

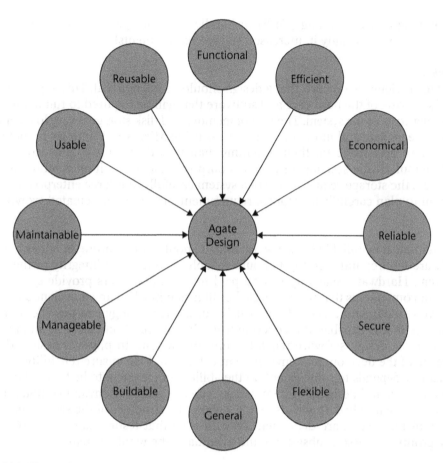

Figure 12.3 The qualities of good design.

for an organization, the staff of that organization will expect it to meet their documented requirements fully and according to specification. So, for example, the staff of Agate will expect their system to provide them with the functionality required to document advertising campaigns, record notes about campaigns and store information about the advertisements to be used in those campaigns. If it does not perform these functions, it is not fully functional. Referring back to Rumbaugh's definition of design as 'how the system will be constructed without actually building it', a functional design should show how every element of the required system will work.

Efficient
It is not enough that a system performs the required functionality; it should also do so efficiently, in terms both of time and resources. Those resources can include disk storage, processor time and network capacity. This is why design is not just about producing any solution, but about producing the optimal solution. This objective may apply to Agate's requirement to store textual notes about ideas for campaigns and advertisements. A sample two lines of text containing twenty words takes up about 100 bytes in text format, but stored in the format of a well-known word-processor can take as much as 13,800 bytes (this is without the use of any special fonts or styles). A poor design might use

object linking and embedding (OLE) to handle the word-processing of the notes but would pay a severe penalty in increased storage requirements!

Economical

Linked to efficiency is the idea that a design should be economical. This applies not only to the fixed costs of the hardware and software that will be required to run it, but also to the running costs of the system. The cost of memory and disk storage is very low compared to twenty years ago, and most small businesses using Microsoft Windows probably now require more disk space for their programs than they do for their data. However, the growth of multimedia systems for business purposes may make it once more important to calculate the storage requirements of a system carefully. For large enterprises, it is still important to plan carefully for storage requirements and their anticipated growth.

Reliable

The system must be reliable in two ways: first, it should not be prone to either hardware or software failure; and second, it should reliably maintain the integrity of the data in the system. Hardware reliability can be paid for: manufacturers provide systems with redundant components that run in parallel or that step in when an equivalent component fails; RAID (redundant arrays of inexpensive disks) technology can provide users with disk storage that is capable of recovering from the failure of one drive in an array. The designers must design software reliability into the system. In physical design, detailed knowledge of the development environment is likely to help ensure reliability.

Reliability depends to some extent on the ability of the system to be tested thoroughly. A well-analysed and designed system will specify the valid and invalid combinations of data that can be handled. It will also show clearly the structure of the system and which elements of the system are dependent on others so that testing can work up through classes, groups of classes, subsystems and eventually the whole system.

Secure

Systems should be designed to be secure against malicious attack by outsiders and against unauthorized use by insiders. System design should include considerations of how people are authorized to use the system and policies on passwords. It should also cover protection of the system from outsiders, including firewalls in either hardware or software to protect the system from access via public networks, such as the Internet. In European countries that are members of the European Union, there are data protection laws that are designed to protect the interests of individuals about whom data is held in information systems, such as the Data Protection Acts (1984 and 1998) and the Computer Misuse Act (1990) in the UK. Where such legislation exists, the designer should ensure that the design of the system will comply with its requirements.

Flexible

Some authors treat flexibility as the ability of the system to adapt to changing business requirements as time passes. Yourdon and Constantine (1979) call this feature *modifiability*. By flexibility they mean the ability to configure the system to handle different circumstances based on control values that are not compiled into the system but are available for the user to set at run-time. In the Agate system, this could be reflected in the choice of Open Database Connectivity (ODBC) as the means to access the database. This provides a standard mechanism for accessing databases, and changing the ODBC driver used would allow either the system to access a local or a remote version of the database or for the system to be migrated to a different database management system at a later date. Another possibility would be to ensure that all the prompts and error messages used by the system are held in an external data file that can be loaded up when the program runs or in response to a menu option. This allows for the creation of multiple files of messages and would enable users to set the language that they wish to use. The use of Unicode, which provides a character set that includes ideographic characters (for example, Chinese, Japanese and Korean) as well as all the world's alphabets, would enable a system to be developed for Agate that could be localized for each location in which it is used.

General

Generality describes the extent to which a system is general-purpose. It is more applicable to utility programs than to large information systems. However, it includes the issue of *portability*, which applies to the Agate system that is to be developed in Java so that it can run on different hardware (PCs and Apple Macs). The system may also exhibit generality from the point of view of the developers, who may wish to use the same system for other clients in the advertising industry. Reuse is discussed below.

Buildable

From the perspective of the programmer who has to write the program code to build the system, it is important that the design is clear and not unnecessarily complex. In particular, the physical design should relate closely to the features that are available in the development language. Not all object-oriented languages offer the same features: for example, in the visibility of attributes and operations (public, private, protected, friend etc.); in the ability to handle multiple inheritance; or in the availability of utility classes such as collections or linked lists in the base language. Designs that rely on features such as these will force the programmer to work around them if a different language is being used from the one that the designer had in mind.

Manageable

A good design should allow the project manager to estimate the amount of work involved in implementing the various subsystems. It should also provide for subsystems that are relatively self-contained and can be marked off as completed and passed on for testing without fear that changes to other parts of the system still in development will have unforeseen consequences on them.

Maintainable

Maintenance is cited as taking up as much as 60% of the data-processing budget of organizations. Maintenance activities include fixing bugs, modifying reports and screen layouts, enhancing programs to deal with new business requirements, migrating systems to new hardware and fixing the new bugs that are introduced by all of the above. A well-designed and documented system is easier to maintain than one that is poorly designed and documented. If maintenance is easy then it is less costly. It is particularly important that there is a close match between the developed program code and the design. This makes it easier for the maintenance programmer to understand the intention of the designer and to ensure that it is not subverted by the introduction of new code. Maintenance programmers can spend up to 50% of their working time just trying to understand the code that they are maintaining.

Usable

Usability covers a range of aspects including the idea, mentioned above, that a system should be both satisfying and productive. It may seem odd to suggest that people should enjoy using their computer systems and find it a satisfying experience. However, if you think about the times that you have used a computer system and have found it a source of dissatisfaction, then you can perhaps imagine a satisfying system as one with an absence of dissatisfying features. Many of the features that contribute to user satisfaction are characteristic of good human–computer interface (HCI) design. For example, the concept of *affordance* (meaning that objects on the interface suggest their function) can reduce the number of errors made by users. Reducing error rates and ensuring that if users do make an error it is clear both where they went wrong and how to recover from the error can contribute to the satisfaction of users. Productivity can be enhanced by ensuring that the tasks that users wish to carry out using the system are straightforward to carry out and do not introduce an overhead of keystrokes or mouse-clicks to achieve. If usability requirements have been captured (see Section 6.2.2), then the design should take these into account. Usability is considered in more detail in Chapter 16.

Reusable

Reusability is the Holy Grail of object-oriented development. Many of the features of object-oriented systems are geared to improve the possibility of reuse. Reuse affects the designer in three ways: first, he or she will consider how economies can be made by designing reuse into the system through the use of inheritance; second, he or she will look for opportunities to use design patterns, which provide templates for the design of reusable elements; and third, he or she will seek to reuse existing classes or components either directly or by subclassing them. Design patterns are described in detail in Chapter 15. Existing classes could be classes that have been developed for other projects, classes in class libraries that are associated with the development language (such as the Java AWT) or classes that are bought in from outside vendors. To date, object-oriented development has not achieved the levels of reuse that were expected. In order to reuse a software class, a designer must be aware of the existence of the class, and be able to determine both that its interface matches the interface for the class that he or she requires and that the methods of the class match those required. It is arguable that in order to determine whether an available class matches requirements, the required class must already have been designed. The economies from reuse thus appear during the construction of the software and require a change to a culture of project management that supports reuse; this means that project managers must be able to recognize the effort that is saved by **not** writing and testing lines of code (because a class is being reused). The development of strategies to parcel up classes as components and the provision of component management software are discussed in Chapter 20.

There is clearly some overlap between the categories that have been listed here. Aspects of maintainability overlap with flexibility, generality with reuse, efficiency with economy. What is often the case, however, is that some design objectives will conflict with one another. This happens more often at the level of specific objectives rather than general ones such as those described above. However, it should be possible to see that functionality, reliability and security could all conflict with economy. Many of the conflicts result from constraints that are imposed on the system by the users' non-functional requirements.

12.5.2 Design trade-offs

Design frequently involves choosing the most appropriate compromise. The designer is often faced with design objectives or constraints that are mutually incompatible and he or she must then decide which objective is the more important.

Design constraints arise from the context of the project as well as from the users' requirements. The clients' budget for the project, the timescale within which they expect the system to be delivered, the skills of staff working on the project, the need to integrate the new system with existing hardware or systems and standards set as part of the overall systems design process can all constrain what can be achieved. Resolving conflicts between requirements and constraints results in the need for compromises or trade-offs in design. A couple of examples should illustrate how these can occur.

■ If the users of Agate's new system require the ability to change fonts in the notes that they write about campaigns and adverts, then they will want to be able to edit notes with the same kind of functionality that would be found in a word-processor. As pointed out earlier in Section 12.5.1 when we discussed efficiency, this will seriously impact the storage requirements for notes. It will also have an effect on network traffic, as larger volumes of data will need to be transferred across the network when users browse through the notes. The designers will have to consider the impact of this requirement. It may be that the users will have to accept reduced functionality or the management of Agate will have to recognize that their system will have higher costs for storage than first envisaged. Compromise solutions may involve transferring only the text of a note (without the overhead of all the formatting information) when users are browsing a note and transferring the full file only when it needs to be viewed or edited. However, this will increase the processing load on the server. Another compromise solution might be to use a different file format such as RTF (rich text format) rather than the word-processor format. For the short text file discussed above this reduces the byte count to 1,770 while retaining formatting information.

■ Agate would like the system to be configurable so that prompts, help and error messages are displayed in the language of the user. This means that each prompt and error message must be read into the programs from data files or the database. While this is good software design practice and makes the system more flexible, it will increase the workload of the designers when they design elements of the interface. Without this requirement, it is enough for each designer to specify that messages such as 'Campaign' or 'Not on file' appear on screen; there is a minimal need for liaison between designers. With this requirement, the designers will need to draw up a list of prompts, labels and error messages that can be referred to by number or by some other key so that the same message is used consistently wherever it is applicable. This means that the programmers will not hard code messages into the system, but will refer to them as elements in an array of messages, for example. While this increases the flexibility and to some extent the maintainability of the system, it is likely to increase the cost of the design phase.

It is important that these design decisions are clearly documented, and the reasoning behind compromises and trade-offs is recorded. Keeping the client informed of these decisions is always important to ensure that the decisions are consistent with the client's needs.

The requirements model may indicate the relative priorities of the different objectives or constraints but, if it does not, then it is useful to prepare general guidelines. These guidelines must be agreed with clients since they determine the nature of the system and what functionality will be delivered. Guidelines for design trade-offs ensure consistency between the decisions that are made at different stages of development. They also ensure consistency between different subsystems. However, no guidelines can legislate for every case. Design experience and further discussions with the client will remain necessary to resolve those situations that cannot be anticipated—at least some of these occur on almost every project.

12.5.3 Measurable objectives in design

In the last but one section, we discussed some of the general objectives of the designers in a systems development project. Some objectives are specific to a particular project, and it is important to be able to assess whether these objectives have been achieved. One way of doing this is to ensure that these objectives are expressed in measurable terms so that they can be tested by simulation during the design phase, in prototypes that are built for this purpose or in the final system.

Measurable objectives often represent the requirements that we referred to as non-functional requirements in Chapter 6. They also reflect the fact that information systems are not built for their own sake, but are developed to meet the business needs of some organization. The system should contribute to the strategic aims of the business, and so should help to achieve aims such as:

- provide better response to customers;
- increase market share.

However, such aims are vague and difficult to assess. If they are expressed in measurable terms, then it is possible to evaluate whether they can be achieved by the design or whether they have been achieved by the finished system. Ideally, they should be phrased in a way that shows how these objectives are attributable to the system. If a company expects to increase its market share as a result of introducing a new computer system but does not achieve this, it should be possible to tell whether this is a failure of the new system or the outcome of other factors outside the control of the system developers, such as economic recession. The system may contribute to business objectives such as those above by providing better information or more efficient procedures, but for the objectives to be measurable they need to be phrased as operational objectives that can be quantified, such as:

- to reduce invoice errors by one-third within a year;
- to process 50% more orders during peak periods.

These set clear targets for the designers and a way of checking whether these objectives can be achieved (within the constraints on the system) and whether they have been achieved once the system is up and running.

12.6   Summary

While analysis looks to the business in order to establish requirements, design looks to the technology that will be used to implement those requirements. An effective design will meet general objectives that will make the system both easier to build and maintain and more usable and functional for the end-users. The design of a system should also meet specific objectives relating to the business needs of the users, and these specific objectives should be phrased in quantifiable, operational terms that allow them to be tested. This process of design takes place in the context of constraints that are imposed by the users, their budget and existing systems, the available technology and the skills and knowledge of the design and development team.

System design focuses on determining a suitable architectural structure (discussed in Chapter 13) for the system and defines the context within which the remaining design activity is performed.

In Chapter 14 we describe detailed design of the classes in the required system. Chapter 15 explains how patterns can be used to assist the design process. Chapters 16 and 17 look specifically at the design of the human–computer interface and Chapter 18 discusses the design of data storage.

Review Questions

12.1 What are the advantages of separating the analysis and design phases of a project?

12.2 What are the advantages of separating the analysis and design activities of a project?

12.3 Users at Agate require a report of unpaid campaigns. Which of the following aspects of the report represents analysis, logical design and physical design?

The size of the paper and the position of each field in the report.

The fact that the user wants a report of completed campaigns that have not yet been paid for by the client.

The selection of the business objects and their attributes used by the report.

12.4 Which of the following sentences describing an element of the FoodCo system represents analysis, logical design and physical design?

The reason for stopping a run will be selected from one of the values displayed in a listbox (Java `Choice`) in the Record Line Stop dialogue window.

When a production line stops during a run, the reason for stopping will be recorded.

The reason for stopping a run will be entered into the system by selecting from a list of valid reasons.

12.5 What is meant by *seamlessness* in object-oriented systems development?

12.6 What are the differences between system design and detailed design?

12.7 List twelve quality criteria for good design.

12.8 Reread the description of the FoodCo case study in Case Study B1. Identify any constraints that you think might be imposed on the design of the new system.

12.9 Based on the same information try to identify possible measurable objectives for the new FoodCo system.

12.10 Agate wants the new system to provide access to the same data from every office around the world. Maintaining a network that is constantly connected between all the offices is considered too expensive, while using a network that dials up remote offices as required would provide response times that are too slow. What kind of compromise solution can you come up with to this problem?

Case Study Work, Exercises and Projects

12.A FoodCo requires a data entry screen for entering details of staff holidays. Without knowing what software or hardware is going to be used to develop this data entry screen, list as many features of the design as you can that are not dependent on the implementation platform.

12.B Design applies to a wide range of artefacts, for example cars, buildings, books and packaging. Choose an artefact that you use and try to identify what makes for a good design in this context. Are there aspects that do not apply to systems design? Are there aspects of systems design that should perhaps apply to the design of artefacts that you use?

12.C Find out what laws (if any) exist in your country to protect computer systems against malicious attack from hackers. What implications does the law have for the design of systems?

12.D In the introduction to Section 12.5. We pointed out that some criteria for good quality in design will bring benefits to the designers, while others will bring benefits to the eventual users of the system. Try to decide which of the characteristics discussed in Section 12.5.1 bring benefits to the designers as well as the end-users.

Further Reading

For those with an interest in the historical development of systems design, the classics of structured design are Jackson (1975) and Yourdon and Constantine (1979). The classics of object-oriented design would include Meyer (1997), Booch (1994) and Jacobson et al. (1995). Sommerville (2007) and Pressman (2009) both provide detailed discussions of design issues.

If you are interested in an approach to the analysis and design of requirements that is completely different from object-oriented approaches, SSADM (Structured Systems Analysis and Design Method) makes a very clear distinction between requirements analysis, logical design and physical design. A separate stage in SSADM is used to carry out the choice of development environment (Technical System Options), and the physical design is then prepared for this environment. Skidmore et al. (1994), Goodland and Slater (1995) or any other book on SSADM explains the way in which these stages are handled.

Chapter 13

System Design and Architecture

LEARNING OBJECTIVES

In this chapter you will learn
- ☑ the major concerns of system design
- ☑ what is meant by architecture in information systems development
- ☑ the factors that influence the architecture of a system
- ☑ the range of architectural styles that can be used, including layers and partitions
- ☑ how to apply the Model–View–Controller architecture
- ☑ which architectures are suitable for distributed systems.

13.1 Introduction

The system design activity defines the context in which detailed design will occur. In Chapter 5 we described the Unified Software Development Process (USDP) (Jacobson et al., 1999) as 'architecture-centric'. A major part of system design is defining the architecture of the system. However, up to this point we have not stated what we mean by architecture in the context of information systems; nor have we explained how to design the architecture of a system.

Every system has an architecture of some sort. If the designers and developers do not take the time or have the skills to produce explicit architectural models of the system, the system will still have an architecture. However, that architecture will be implicit and will be influenced by factors such as the choice of programming language, database and platform, and the skills and experience of the development team. Any such implicit architecture is likely to result in a system that does not meet the non-functional requirements and is difficult to maintain or enhance. Producing an explicit architecture means that the architect has to consider the non-functional requirements, the context of the system and how it and its components may be used and further developed in the future.

In this chapter, we explain what is meant by system architecture, what are the factors that influence the development of an architecture and the kind of issues that are addressed by an architecture. The architecture is part of the design framework that sets the context for the detailed design of the system. During system design, the following activities will be undertaken.

- Priorities are set for design trade-offs. (Chapter 12)
- Subsystems and major components are identified. (Chapter 13)
- Any inherent concurrency is identified. (Chapter 13)
- Subsystems are allocated to processors. (Chapter 13)
- Design patterns that can be used will be identified (Chapter 15)
- A strategy and standards for human–computer interaction are chosen. (Chapters 16 and 17)
- A data management strategy is selected. (Chapter 18)
- Code development standards are specified. (Chapter 19)
- System test plans are produced. (Chapter 19)
- Implementation requirements are identified (for example, data conversion). (Chapter 19)

13.2 What Do We Mean by Architecture?

The use of the term 'architecture' in the development of information systems obviously derives from the practice of architecture in the built environment. The Royal Institute of British Architects (RIBA) describes 'What Architects Do' as follows:

> Architects are trained to take your brief and can see the big picture–they look beyond your immediate requirements to design flexible buildings that will adapt with the changing needs of your business.

> Architects solve problems creatively–when they are involved at the earliest planning stage, they gain more opportunities to understand your business, develop creative solutions, and propose ways to reduce costs.

If we replaced the word 'buildings' with 'information systems' many systems architects and software architects would happily sign up to this definition of what they do. There are certain key features in these two sentences that apply as much to systems architecture as to the architecture of buildings.

- Systems architects act on behalf of the client. Part of their role is to understand the client's business and how that business can best be supported by an information system. However, the client may make conflicting demands on the new information system, and part of the systems architect's role is to resolve those conflicts.
- Systems architecture addresses the big picture. The architecture of an information system is a high-level view of the system: it is modelled in terms of the major components and the way they are interconnected; it does not normally address the detailed design of the system, though it may set standards to be applied.
- If flexibility is important, then systems architects will produce an architecture that is intended to deliver this quality. In the current climate of rapid change in the business environment, flexibility is often cited as a reason for adopting certain types of systems architecture. However, there are other qualities of information systems that may be more important for a particular client, in which case those qualities will be addressed by the architecture.
- Systems architects are concerned with solving problems. In information systems development, problems manifest themselves in terms of risks to the success of the project. The reason that the Unified Process is architecture-centric is that by

concentrating on the architecture and making architectural decisions early in the project lifecycle, the risks can be reduced or mitigated.

- Reducing costs is not a primary objective of systems architects. However, proposing unnecessarily expensive solutions never wins anyone any friends, and producing an explicit architecture for a new system means that the specific needs of that system are addressed and unnecessary features eliminated. It also means that risks are tackled early in the project lifecycle and that the chance is minimized of discovering late in the project that the new system will not meet some requirement, with the need for costly design changes or reworking.

Of these, probably the most important is that architecture is about the big picture. Analysis is inevitably about detail: the business analyst needs to understand and document every requirement in a clear and unambiguous way; the systems analyst must consider use cases and other requirements and translate them into a complete model of the classes necessary to support those use cases, their attributes and responsibilities or operations and a first-cut view of how instances of those classes will interact. Design is about translating every aspect of the analysis model into a design model that will effectively implement the requirements: the designer must consider the type of every attribute and design each operation to take the necessary parameters, return the right value and be efficient in its working. Architecture, on the other hand, looks at the large-scale features of the system and how those features work together as a whole: the architect groups classes together into packages, models the system as a set of interacting components and considers what platforms to deploy those components on in order to deliver the required qualities of the system.

There are a number of different views of architecture in the development of information systems. Our focus here is on systems architecture and software architecture. In Section 13.4 we discuss enterprise architecture and technical architecture and their relationship with systems and software architectures.

In their book on large-scale software architecture, Garland and Anthony (2003) use the definition of architecture from the Institute of Electrical and Electronics Engineers (IEEE) standard IEEE 1471–2000 (IEEE, 2000). This provides the following definitions of key terms.

- *System* is a set of components that accomplishes a specific function or set of functions.
- *Architecture* is the fundamental organization of a system embodied in its components, their relationships to each other and to the environment, and the principles guiding its design and evolution.[1]
- *Architectural description* is a set of products that document the architecture.
- *Architectural view* is a representation of a particular system or part of a system from a particular perspective.
- *Architectural viewpoint* is a template that describes how to create and use an architectural view. A viewpoint includes a name, stakeholders, concerns addressed by the viewpoint, and the modelling and analytic conventions.

Given this definition of architecture, then *software architecture* is the organization of a system in terms of its software components, including subsystems and the relationships

---

1   From IEEE *Standard 1471–2000*, Copyright 2000 IEEE.

Type of architecture	Examples of elements	Examples of relationships
Conceptual	Components	Connectors
Module	Subsystems, modules	Exports, imports
Code	Files, directories, libraries	Includes, contains
Execution	Tasks, threads, object interactions	Uses, calls

Figure 13.1 Four aspects of software architecture according to Soni et al. (adapted from Weir and Daniels, 1998).

and interactions among them, and the principles that guide the design of that software system.

The IEEE definition is important because it stresses the fact that the same system can be shown in different views that emphasize different aspects of that system. Bass et al., (2003) point out that architecture is often defined as something like 'the overall structure of the system', but criticise this because it implies that a system has only a single structure. They suggest asking anyone who takes this position exactly which structure of the system the architecture represents.

Soni et al. (1995) identify four different aspects of software architecture, which are shown in Fig. 13.1.

In terms of object-oriented development, the conceptual architecture is concerned with the structure of the static class model and the connections between the components of the model. The module architecture describes the way the system is divided into subsystems or modules and how they communicate by exporting and importing data. The code architecture defines how the program code is organized into files and directories and grouped into libraries. The execution architecture focuses on the dynamic aspects of the system and the communication between components as tasks and operations execute.

The Rational Unified Process uses five views of the system, known as the '4 + 1 views' (Kruchten, 2004). The four views are the *logical view*, the *implementation view*, the *process view* and the *deployment view*. The one view that ties them all together is the *use case view*. These five views are explained in Fig. 13.2.

These five views conform to the IEEE 1471 definition of what constitutes a view. They provide a description of the system from a particular perspective. The static structural relationships between classes and packages in the logical view present a different aspect of the system from the dynamic relationships between runtime processes in the process view. A single diagram or model cannot easily combine both these perspectives, let alone all five.

Different views are like different maps of a country. It is possible to find maps that show the physical topography–mountains, hills, rivers and lakes; maps that show the human geography–towns, cities and the road and rail networks; maps that show the land use–farming, woodland, industry and human settlements; and maps that show schematically the volume of transport flow between major conurbations. However, trying to combine all these views of the country in a single map would make it confusing and difficult to understand.

Maps conform to particular conventions for how they represent the geography of a country. For example, the physical topography is shown using contour lines, colour or

View	Explanation
Use case view	The important use cases in the system and scenarios that describe architecturally significant behaviour
Logical view	Important design classes and interfaces in a package structure, with composite structure diagrams
Implementation view	Architectural decisions made for the implementation in terms of subsystems and components and relationships among them
Process view	A description of the processes (operating system processes and threads) and inter-process communications using stereotyped classes
Deployment view	Physical nodes for the likely deployment platform, components deployed on the nodes and the communication channels between them, using deployment diagrams

Figure 13.2 The 4 + 1 views.

shading, or some combination of these three, to represent the height of features and the location of water. Clearly, models that represent different views of a system must adopt some conventions for the different features that are shown in the model. The use of conventions makes it possible for the systems architect to communicate with stakeholders about the system and to provide guidance to designers and developers. A set of conventions for drawing architectural models is known as an *architecture description language* (ADL). Bass et al. (2003) use UML as an ADL. UML 2.0 has specific features that have been added and adapted in order to make it more suitable for modelling architectures as well as producing analysis and design models. The UML 2.0 Request for Proposals (OMG, 2000), which solicited proposals for the changes that should be made to the specification, had as one of its specific objectives the following:

> Enable the modeling of structural patterns, such as component-based development and the specification of run-time architectures.

This has resulted in the introduction of composite structure diagrams and changes to the component diagram notation.

13.3 Why Produce Architectural Models?

A software architect uses architectural models based on different views in order to reason about the proposed system and the way it will operate from different perspectives. In particular, this makes it possible to assess how well the system will deliver the non-functional requirements. Bass et al. (2003) do not like the term non-functional requirements. They argue that what they term *quality attributes* of a system, such as performance, security or fault tolerance, are intimately bound up with the behaviour of the system and the way that it responds to inputs. They believe that defining a set of non-functional requirements that are somehow separate from the functional behaviour of the system is dangerous, as it implies that the functionality of the system can be addressed first and then the non-functional requirements can be tacked onto the system towards the end of the development process. We have used the term 'non-functional requirements' because it is widely understood and because it focuses attention during requirements gathering on all those aspects of how well the system will deliver the functionality. However, we do not believe that this is a licence to ignore such requirements until the end of the development process.

Development processes based on the Unified Process are architecture-centric. This means that getting the architecture right is a priority, and this in turn means that from the start of the project the architects are trying to address the non-functional requirements of the system, because the architecture provides the framework for delivering these quality attributes of the system. Getting the architecture right early on is also about reducing the risks in the project. If one of the requirements of a new system is that it should be able to handle very large peak processing volumes (for example, in an online order processing system), then it is important to prove as soon as possible in the project that the architecture supports the achievement of these peak loads. If the early work addresses only the ability to process orders but does not ensure that the design can be scaled up to handle the peak loads, then there is always the risk that the fact that the system cannot handle the loads will not be discovered until late in the project, and that this will result in delays while the software is redesigned to cope with the peak volumes.

Using architectural models, the architect can assess the ability of the system architecture to deliver quality attributes such as high performance. The way that the different views in the 4 + 1 view of the system can contribute to assessing performance is shown in Fig. 13.3.

It is important to realize that some of the features shown in Fig. 13.3 to increase performance will not contribute to the achievement of other quality attributes. For example, adding lightweight versions of classes will mean that for every business class there are two versions, and any change to the attributes of the business class means an associated

View	Contribution to assessing performance
Use case view	The use cases that require high performance can be identified and the scenarios used to walkthrough how the other views will affect the performance requirement
Logical view	The logical view of classes will show whether techniques such as creating lightweight objects or value objects have been used to reduce the overheads associated with passing values around
Implementation view	The more components or subsystems involved, the more likely there are to be communication overheads, so the implementation view should show a small number of components used in the process
Process view	The process view can be used to assess how many running processes will exist, and whether there will be multiple instances of the same process so that the work can be shared out by a special process that handles load-balancing. The kind of interprocess communication that is used will affect how efficiently data can be passed between processes
Deployment view	The deployment view will show where different components are deployed, and whether data has to travel from machine to machine, or whether all the processes needed to deliver a high performance use case are located on the same machine

Figure 13.3 The contribution of the 4 + 1 views to assessing performance.

change to the attributes of the lightweight version; this makes the code more complex to maintain. Similarly, reducing the number of components involved in a process may mean that functionality that does not naturally belong together is grouped into the same component or subsystem, and this reduces the flexibility of the system.

13.4 Influences on System Architecture

The systems architect developing the architecture for a new system does not operate in isolation. In any organization there will be existing systems that will constrain and influence the architecture. Many large organizations are now developing or have developed an *enterprise architecture*, which provides a framework for all system development. An enterprise architecture links the design of the business to the information systems that are needed to support that business. Either as part of an enterprise architecture or as a separate framework, many organizations have technology standards or a *technical reference architecture* that lays down a set of technologies, often including specific products that are acceptable, and defines how they should be used.

In the following subsections, we explain each of these influences in turn and the effect that they have on the architecture. In Section 13.5 we explain the range of *architectural styles* that are typically applied within the organization's information systems and that the architect can choose to adopt in developing new systems.

13.4.1 Existing systems

In many cases, the architecture of a new system will be designed to conform to the existing systems in the organization. This applies to the technical aspects such as choice of operating system, database and programming language, and to the way in which the components of the new system will be chosen, designed and interconnected. An organization that has adopted Java 2 Enterprise Edition (J2EE) or Microsoft .NET for its systems will expect new systems to be developed to fit in with this framework. Frameworks such as J2EE and .NET are well documented in books and web resources, but any business that adopts them is also likely to maintain a set of technology standards or a technical reference architecture that explains how to use the framework in the particular company.

Where there are existing systems, any new system may be able to take advantage of reuse of components in those systems. This is particularly the case when the new system and the old share the same architecture. In Chapter 8 we introduced the idea of reusable components, and we develop it further in Chapter 20. Organizations that plan for software reuse will typically use some kind of searchable repository in which they store reusable assets. The OMG, the body that manages the UML standard, also maintains the standard for the *Reusable Asset Specification* (RAS), which provides a set of guidelines about the structure, content and description of reusable software assets. Products such as LogicLibrary's Logidex and Select Asset Manager from Select Business Solutions provide tools to help manage collections of components.

Heritage systems
Sometimes the existing systems may not provide a pattern for development of new systems. The technologies that were used to develop them may be out of date and difficult to support. The systems may still be doing a good job of supporting the business, but a

Figure 13.4 Wrapping a legacy system as a service.

decision has been made to adopt new technologies. The term *heritage system* is sometimes used in preference to legacy system to describe a system that uses out-of-date technology but is still delivering a clear benefit to the business or is key to its operations. If a heritage system is not being replaced, the new system may need to access data from it via some kind of interface. *Enterprise Application Integration* (EAI) tools are software tools that connect to systems in order to integrate them with one another. If the heritage system uses a well-known technology, there is likely to be an *adapter* available that will connect it to the EAI tool and enable the EAI tool to extract data from the old system and make it available to the new or pass data into it in order to use its functionality.

Services
A technique for connecting to heritage systems that is growing in popularity is to wrap them in a layer of software that exposes the required functionality as *services*. *Web services* are the most recent technique applied to this problem, but the idea of a *Service-Oriented Architecture* (SOA) has been around for longer than the Web.

The wrapper acts as a service proxy, so that it looks the same as other services to the client systems that invoke operations on the service, as shown in Fig. 13.4.

There may be many kinds of interface to legacy systems. Sometimes they have been written to provide an Application Programming Interface (API), in which case it may be possible to use this, although there may be a limited choice of programming languages to use. Often they do not have an API, but may provide some other kind of interface: they listen on a TCP/IP socket for connections, or they check for files placed in a certain directory and treat the file as input. Sometimes the only way to access a legacy system is for the wrapper to pretend to be a terminal (*terminal emulation*) and connect to it and send text and terminal codes as though a user were typing the data in, and then to read the data that comes back and extract what is required from the mix of prompts, actual data values and control sequences. This is known as *screen-scraping*.

Reverse-engineering and model-driven architecture
Model-Driven Architecture (MDA) is one of the reasons for some of the changes that were made to UML to produce Version 2.0. The idea of MDA is to separate the business and application logic of a system from the underlying platform technology. This abstract view of what the system must do is known as a *platform-independent model* (PIM). The PIM is then combined with a definition of the platform architecture in order to produce a *platform-specific model* (PSM) that can be built and executed on a particular platform. In order to produce a PIM, it is necessary to be able to specify actions that must be carried out within a system in a precise and verifiable way. Using this approach, it should be possible to build a platform-independent specification of a system and then, using different standard mappings, to transform it into a platform-specific model. The PSM is then further transformed to implementation code using automated tools that are already available for building software from models. A single PIM could thus be implemented in different ways: J2EE, .NET, CORBA.

The OMG also has an initiative to promote MDA. UML is central to the MDA initiative. Although earlier versions of UML provided ways of modelling structures (class diagrams), interaction (sequence diagrams) and lifecycles (state machine diagrams), the specification of actions in activity diagrams was not up to the task of precisely defining how classes should carry out operations. The developers of UML 2.0 have added a precise *action semantics* to the language. Combined with the notation of activity diagrams (which have also been defined more precisely in UML 2.0), this is intended to make UML the language of choice for producing PIMs.

As well as creating applications by transforming PIMs, the OMG also promotes the idea of reverse-engineering existing applications into PIMs. The idea is that if the business and application logic of a legacy system can be separated from the implementation details, and represented in an abstract specification language (UML with action semantics), then that PIM can then be used to re-implement the functionality of the system on a different, more modern platform. Products such as ArcStyler from InteractiveObjects not only provide a way of producing implementations from PIMs, but also of reverse-engineering existing application code into a PIM.

13.4.2 Enterprise architectures

In large, complex organizations, particularly those that operate in many countries and have different divisions of the business that address different markets, there is a risk that system development will be unco-ordinated. Indeed, there is a risk that nobody will have an overall understanding of the business, let alone the systems that support it. When a project for a new system is proposed, it is difficult to analyse the effect of that new system. Questions that might be asked include the following.

- How does the system overlap with other systems in the organization?
- How will the system need to interface with other systems?
- Will the system help the organization to achieve its goals?
- Is the cost of the system justified?

Enterprise architectures provide a way of modelling the enterprise and aspects of the way it conducts business and of driving these concepts down into the practical issues of how the information systems are intended to support the business. Various US federal government departments have created their own enterprise architecture frameworks. Outside government, the most widely known framework is the Zachman framework (Zachman, 1987), developed originally by John Zachman, and extended in collaboration with John Sowa (Sowa and Zachman, 1992). The framework has undergone a process of evolution since then, described by Zachman himself (2009), and a current concise definition is available on the Zachman International website (Zachman, 2008).

The Zachman framework seeks to build explicit models of the enterprise from two views. The first asks the questions: What? How? Where? Who? When? and Why? The second looks at the system at different levels, from the most conceptual, business view down to the view of the actual implemented system. The two dimensions are usually viewed as a matrix and the values that fill the thirty-six cells in the matrix are the actual models of aspects of the enterprise at different levels and from different perspectives.

The task of the *enterprise architect* is to build up a total picture of the enterprise using these categories. This total picture of the enterprise and its systems supports the process of ensuring that any IT investment is aligned to the goals of the business. Clearly this is a daunting task for a large organization, and one of the criticisms of the Zachman framework is that it is a heavyweight approach to enterprise architecture.

In an organization that has adopted any kind of enterprise architecture framework, that framework should be the starting point for identifying constraints on the architecture of new systems.

13.4.3 Technical reference architectures

Whereas enterprise architectures address the entire organization and its systems, *technical reference architectures* focus on the technology that is used within the enterprise, the standards for the technologies to apply and guidance on how to apply that technology. This may be in terms of a standards document, or a list of approved technologies or architectural models that show how different technologies should be applied in a typical system.

For organizations that do not have the time or resources to develop their own framework for technology standards, The Open Group produced The Open Group Architecture Framework (TOGAF) in 1995. The current version is 9.0 (The Open Group, 2009).

TOGAF consists of three main parts.

- The Architecture Development Method describes an approach for developing enterprise IT architectures.
- The Enterprise Continuum shows the continuum of architectures from a general foundation architecture to a specific architecture for the particular organization.
- The Resources section provides a range of useful information and examples of architectural patterns, principles and other guidance.

The Open Group also maintains an online Standards Information Base (SIB) that lists hundreds of IT standards categorized according to the building blocks in the Foundation Architectures model.

13.5　Architectural Styles

Architects designing buildings do not start from scratch every time they are given a new commission. They design buildings that are similar to others that they or other architects have built previously, and they learn what works and what does not. Systems architects are very similar: they design systems that conform to the prevailing standards, and fashions in systems architecture come and go, like flying buttresses on Gothic churches or lifts on the outside of buildings.

In systems architecture, the term *architectural styles* is used to apply to these ways of designing systems that conform to the prevailing fashion. Often these fashions are the result of changes in technology: for example, until the advent of the PC, it would not have been possible to implement client–server system architectures using PCs connected to mini-computers. Architectural styles also apply to software architecture. Bass et al. (2003) describe five main types: independent components, data flow, data centred, virtual machine, and call and return, each with subtypes. Each style has characteristics that make it more or less suitable for certain types of application. We will consider some of the major alternatives. It is worth noting that software architectures have been documented in the patterns form by Buschmann et al. (1996) and Schmidt et al. (2000) amongst others.

13.5.1 Subsystems

A subsystem typically groups together elements of the system that share some common properties. An object-oriented subsystem encapsulates a coherent set of responsibilities in order to ensure that it has integrity and can be maintained. For example, the elements of one subsystem might all deal with the human–computer interface, the elements of another might all deal with data management and the elements of a third may all focus on a particular functional requirement.

The subdivision of an information system into subsystems has the following advantages.

- It produces smaller units of development.
- It helps to maximize reuse at the component level.
- It helps the developers to cope with complexity.
- It improves maintainability.
- It aids portability.

Each subsystem should have a clearly specified boundary and fully defined interfaces with other subsystems. A specification for the interface of a subsystem defines the precise nature of the subsystem's interaction with the rest of the system but does not describe its internal structure (this is a high-level use of contracts, which are described in Chapter 10). A subsystem can be designed and constructed independently of other subsystems, simplifying the development process. Subsystems may correspond to increments of development that can be delivered individually as part of an incremental lifecycle (if the developers are using the spiral lifecycle model or an iterative and incremental approach such as the Unified Process).

Dividing a system into subsystems is an effective strategy for handling complexity. Sometimes it is only feasible to model a large complex system piece by piece, with the subdivision forced on the developers by the nature of the application. Splitting a system into subsystems can also aid reuse, as each subsystem may correspond to a component that is suitable for reuse in other applications. A judicious choice of subsystems during design can reduce the impact on the overall system of a change to its requirements. For example, consider an information system that contains a presentation subsystem that deals with the human–computer interface (HCI). A change to the data display format need not affect other subsystems. Of course there may still be some changes to the requirements that affect more than one subsystem. The aim is to localize the consequences of change, so that a change in one subsystem does not trigger changes in other subsystems (sometimes referred to as the ripple effect). Moving an application from one implementation platform to another can be much easier if the software architecture is appropriate. An example of this would be the conversion of a Windows application so that it could run in a Unix environment. This would require changes to the software that implements the human–computer interface. If this is dealt with by specialized subsystems then the overall software change is localized to these subsystems. As a result, the system as a whole is easier to port to a different operating environment.

Each subsystem provides services for other subsystems, and there are two different styles of communication that make this possible. These are known as *client–server* and *peer-to-peer* communication and are shown in Fig. 13.5. The circles represent the interfaces exposed by the subsystems, and the dashed arrows represent dependencies on those interfaces.

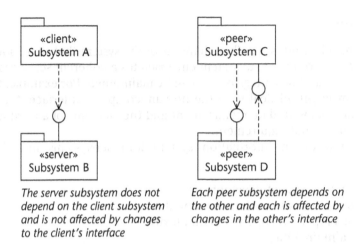

The server subsystem does not depend on the client subsystem and is not affected by changes to the client's interface

Each peer subsystem depends on the other and each is affected by changes in the other's interface

Figure 13.5 Styles of communication between subsystems.

Client–server communication requires the client to know the interface of the server subsystem, but the communication is only in one direction. The client subsystem requests services from the server subsystem and not vice versa. Peer-to-peer communication requires each subsystem to know the interface of the other, thus coupling them more tightly. The communication is two-way since either peer subsystem may request services from the other.

In general, client–server communication is simpler to implement and to maintain, as the subsystems are less tightly coupled than they are when peer-to-peer communication is used. In Fig. 13.5 the subsystems are represented using packages that have been stereotyped to indicate their role. Component diagrams can be used to model logical subsystems, and deployment diagrams can be used to model the implementation of subsystems (see Chapter 20).

13.5.2 Layering and partitioning

There are two general approaches to the division of a software system into subsystems. These are known as *layering*–so called because the different subsystems usually represent different levels of abstraction[2]–and *partitioning*, which usually means that each subsystem focuses on a different aspect of the functionality of the system as a whole. In practice both approaches are often used together on one system, so that some of its subsystems are divided by layering, while others are divided by partitioning.

Layered subsystems
Layered architectures are among the most frequently used high-level structures for a system. A schematic of the general structure is shown in Fig. 13.6.

Each layer corresponds to one or more subsystems, which may be differentiated from each other by differing levels of abstraction or by a different focus of their functionality. It works like this: the top layer uses services provided by the layer immediately below it. This in turn may require the services of the next layer down. Layered architectures can

---

2 Or layers of service.

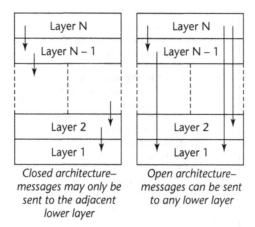

Closed architecture–
messages may only be
sent to the adjacent
lower layer

Open architecture–
messages can be sent
to any lower layer

Figure 13.6 Schematic of a layered architecture.

be either open or closed, and each style has its particular advantages. In a closed layered architecture a certain layer (say layer N) can only use the services of the layer immediately below it (layer N – 1). In an open layered architecture layer N may directly use the services of any of the layers that lie below it.

A closed architecture minimizes dependencies between the layers and reduces the impact of a change to the interface of any one layer. An open layered architecture produces more compact code since the services of all lower-level layers can be accessed directly by any layer above them without the need for extra program code to pass messages through each intervening layer. However, this breaks the encapsulation of the layers, increases the dependencies between layers and increases the difficulty caused when a layer needs to be changed.

Networking protocols provide some of the best-known examples of layered architectures. A network protocol defines how computer programs executing on different computers communicate with each other. Protocols can be defined at various levels of abstraction and each level can be mapped onto a layer. The OSI (Open Systems Interconnection) Seven Layer Model was defined by the International Organization for Standardization (ISO) as a standard architectural model for network protocols (Tanenbaum et al., 2002). The structure provides flexibility for change since a layer may be changed internally without affecting other layers, and it enables the reuse of layer components. The OSI Seven Layer Model is illustrated in Fig. 13.7.

Buschmann et al. (1996) suggest that a series of issues need to be addressed when applying a layered architecture in an application. These include:

- maintaining the stability of the interfaces of each layer
- the construction of other systems using some of the lower layers
- variations in the appropriate level of granularity for subsystems[3]
- the further subdivision of complex layers
- performance reductions due to a closed layered architecture.

---

3 The context determines an appropriate size for the subsystems. Granularity refers to the size of the elements of a larger whole, fine-grained being small elements and coarse-grained being large.

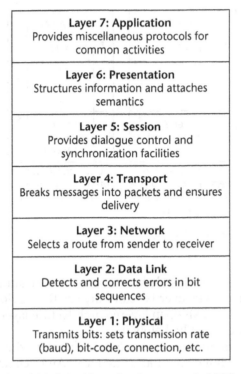

Figure 13.7 OSI Seven Layer Model (adapted from Buschmann et al., 1996).

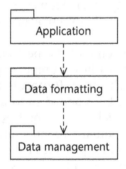

Figure 13.8 Simple layered architecture.

The OSI model has seven layers only because it covers every aspect of the communication between two applications, ranging from application-oriented processes to drivers and protocols that directly control network hardware devices. Many layered architectures are much simpler than this. Figure 13.8 shows a simple example of a three layer architecture.

The lowest layer of the architecture in Fig. 13.8 consists of data management library classes. The layer immediately above this, the data formatting layer, uses services that are provided by the data management library classes in order to get data from a database management system. This data is formatted before it is passed upwards to the application layer. Supposing this system were to be modified to allow it to use a different database management system, the layered architecture limits major changes to the data management library class layer with some possible changes to the data formatting layer.

The following steps are adapted from Buschmann et al. (1996) and provide an outline process for the development of a layered architecture for an application. Note that this does not suggest that the specification of a system's architecture is a rule-based procedure. The steps offer guidelines on the issues that need to be addressed during the development of a layered architecture.

1. Define the criteria by which the application will be grouped into layers. A commonly used criterion is the level of abstraction from the hardware. The lowest layer provides primitive services for direct access to the hardware while the layers above provide more complex services that are based upon these primitives. Higher layers in the architecture carry out tasks that are more complex and correspond to concepts that occur in the application domain.
2. Determine the number of layers. Too many layers will introduce unnecessary overheads while too few will result in a poor structure.
3. Name the layers and assign functionality to them. The top layer should be concerned with the main system functions as perceived by the user. The layers below should provide services and infrastructure that enable the delivery of the functional requirements.
4. Specify the services for each layer. In general it is better in the lower layers to have a small number of low-level services that are used by a larger number of services in higher layers.
5. Refine the layering by iterating through steps 1 to 4.
6. Specify interfaces for each layer.
7. Specify the structure of each layer. This may involve partitioning within the layer.
8. Specify the communication between adjacent layers (this assumes that a closed layer architecture is intended).
9. Reduce the coupling between adjacent layers.[4] This effectively means that each layer should be strongly encapsulated. Where a client–server communication protocol will be used, each layer should have knowledge only of the layer immediately below it.

One of the simplest application architectures has only two layers—the application layer and a database layer. Tight coupling between the user interface and the data representation would make it more difficult to modify either independently, so a middle layer is often introduced in order to separate the conceptual structure of the problem domain. This gives the architecture shown in Fig. 13.9, which is commonly used for business-oriented information systems.

A common four-layer architecture separates the business logic layer into application logic and domain layers, and this is illustrated in Fig. 13.10. The approach that has been adopted during the analysis activity of use case realization results in the identification of boundary, control and entity classes. It is easy to see that it is possible to map the boundary classes onto a presentation layer, the control classes onto an application logic layer and the entity classes on a domain layer. Thus from an early stage in the development of an information system some element of layering is being introduced into the software architecture. However, it is important to appreciate that as we move through design, the allocation of responsibility amongst these types of class may be adjusted to accommodate non-functional requirements.

---

4 For more details of what we mean by coupling, see Section 14.4.3.

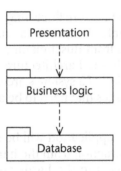

Figure 13.9 Three layer architecture.

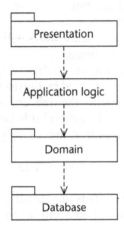

Figure 13.10 Four layer architecture.

Separation of the application logic layer from the domain layer may be further justified because several applications share (or are likely to share) one domain layer, or because the complexity of the business objects forces a separation into two layers. It can also be used when the objects are physically distributed (see Chapter 19). However, it must be emphasized that there is no perfect solution to this kind of design problem. There are only solutions that have different characteristics (perhaps different levels of efficiency or maintainability). A good design solution is one that balances competing requirements effectively.

Layered architectures are used quite widely. J2EE (Sun Java Centre, 2005) adopts a multi-tiered[5] approach and an associated patterns catalogue has been developed. The architecture has five layers (client, presentation, business, integration and resource tiers) and the patterns catalogue addresses the presentation, business and integration tiers.

Partitioned subsystems

As suggested earlier, some layers within a layered architecture may have to be decomposed because of their intrinsic complexity. Figure 13.11 shows a four-layer architecture for part of Agate's campaign management system that also has some partitioning in the upper layers.

---

5   These use the term tier as broadly equivalent to layer.

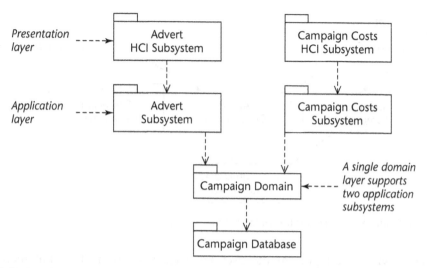

Figure 13.11 Four-layer architecture applied to part of the Agate campaign management system.

In this example the application layer corresponds to the analysis class model for a single application, and is partitioned into a series of subsystems. These subsystems are loosely coupled and each should deliver a single service or coherent group of services. The Campaign Database layer provides access to a database that contains all the details of the campaigns, their adverts and the campaign teams. The Campaign Domain layer uses the lower layer to retrieve and store data in the database and provides common domain functionality for the layers above. For example, the Advert subsystem might support individual advert costing while the Campaign Costs subsystem uses some of the same common domain functionality when costing a complete campaign. Each application subsystem has its own presentation layer to cater for the differing interface needs of different user roles.[6]

A system may be split into subsystems during analysis because of the system's size and complexity. However, the analysis subsystems should be reviewed during design for coherence and compatibility with the overall system architecture.

The subsystems that result from partitioning should have clearly defined boundaries and well-specified interfaces, thus providing high levels of encapsulation so that the implementation of an individual subsystem may be varied without causing dependent changes in the other subsystems. The process of identifying subsystems within a particular layer can be detailed in much the same way as for subsystem layers.

13.5.3 Model–View–Controller

Many interactive systems use the Model–View–Controller (MVC) architecture. This structure was first used with Smalltalk but has since become widely used with many other object-oriented development environments. The MVC architecture separates an application into three major types of component: models that comprise the main

---

6 This example is for illustrative purposes only. Our analysis class model for Agate is too small to justify this kind of partitioning in practice.

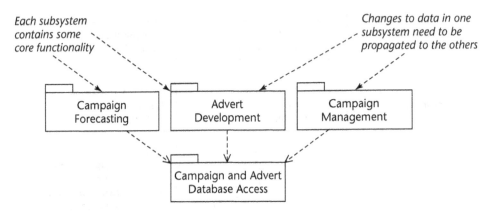

Figure 13.12 Multiple interfaces for the same core functionality.

functionality, views that present the user interface and controllers that manage the updates to models and views. This structure is capable of supporting user requirements that are presented through differing interface styles, and it aids maintainability and portability.

It is common for the view of an information system that is required for each user to differ according to their role. This means that the data and functionality available to any user should be tailored to his or her needs. The needs of different types of user can also change at varying rates. For both these reasons it makes sense to give each user access to only the relevant part of the functionality of the system as a whole. For example, in the Agate case study many users need access to information about campaigns, but their perspectives vary. The campaign manager needs to know about the current progress of a campaign. She is concerned with the current state of each advertisement and how this impacts on the campaign as a whole–is it prepared and ready to run, or is it still in the preparation stage? If an advert is behind schedule, does this affect other aspects of the campaign? The graphic designer also needs access to adverts but he is likely to need access to the contents of the advert (its components and any notes that have been attached to it) as well as some scheduling information. A director may wish to know about the state of all live campaigns and their projected income over the next six months. This gives at least three different perspectives on campaigns and adverts, each of which might use different styles of display. The director may require charts and graphs that summarize the current position at quite a high level. The campaign manager may require lower level summaries that are both textual and graphical in form. The graphic designer may require detailed textual displays of notes with a capability to display graphical images of an advert's content. Ideally, if any information about a campaign or an advert is updated in one view then the changes should also be immediately reflected in all other views. Figure 13.12 shows a possible architecture, but some problems remain.

The design of such varied and flexible user interfaces that still incorporate the same core functionality is likely to be expensive because elements of functionality may have been duplicated for different interfaces. This makes the software more complex and thus also more error prone. There is an impact on maintainability too, since any change to core functionality will necessitate changes to each interface subsystem.

We repeat below some of the difficulties that need to be resolved for this type of application.

- The same information should be capable of presentation in different formats in different windows.
- Changes made within one view should be reflected immediately in the other views.
- Changes in the user interface should be easy to make.
- Core functionality should be independent of the interface to enable multiple interface styles to co-exist.

While the four-layer architecture in Fig. 13.11 resolves some of these problems it does not handle the need to ensure that all view components are kept up to date. The MVC architecture solves this through its separation of core functionality (model) from the interface and through its incorporation of a mechanism for propagating updates to other views. The interface itself is split into two elements: the output presentation (view) and the input controller (controller).

Figure 13.13 shows the basic structure of the MVC architecture.

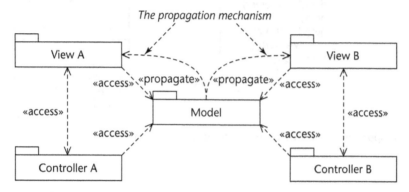

Figure 13.13 General structure of Model–View–Controller (adapted from Hopkins and Horan, 1995).

The responsibilities of the components of an MVC architecture are listed below.

- *Model.* The model provides the central functionality of the application and is aware of each of its dependent view and controller components.
- *View.* Each view corresponds to a particular style and format of presentation of information to the user. The view retrieves data from the model and updates its presentations when data has been changed in one of the other views. The view creates its associated controller.
- *Controller.* The controller accepts user input in the form of events that trigger the execution of operations within the model. These may cause changes to the information and in turn trigger updates in all the views ensuring that they are all up to date.
- *Propagation mechanism.* This enables the model to inform each view that the model data has changed and as a result the view must update itself. It is also often called the dependency mechanism.

Figure 13.14 represents the capabilities offered by the different MVC components as they might be applied to part of the campaign management system at Agate.

The operation update() in the AdvertView and AdvertController components triggers these components to request data from the CampaignModel component.[7] This

---

7 In this example the CampaignModel will hold details of campaigns and their adverts.

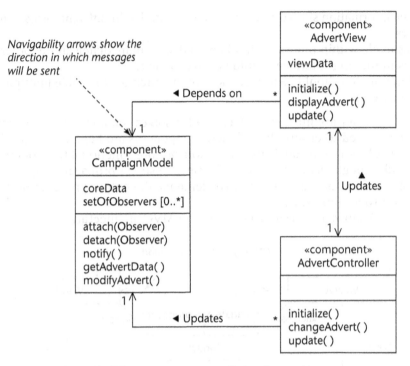

Figure 13.14 Responsibilities of MVC components, as applied to Agate.

model component has no knowledge of the way that each view and controller component will use its services. It need only know that all view and controller components must be informed whenever there is a change of state (a modification either of object attributes or of their links).

The attach() and detach() operations in the CampaignModel component enable views and controllers to be added to the setOfObservers. This contains a list of all components that must be informed of any change to the model core data. In practice there would be separate views, each potentially with its own controller, to support the requirements of the campaign manager and the director.

The interaction sequence diagram in Fig. 13.15 illustrates the communication that is involved in the operation of an MVC architecture. (The choice of message type–synchronous or asynchronous–shown in this diagram is only one of the possibilities that could be appropriate; the features of the implementation environment would influence the actual design decision.) An AdvertController component receives the interface event changeAdvert. In response to this event the controller invokes the modifyAdvert operation in the CampaignModel object. The execution of this operation causes a change to the model.

For example, the target completion date for an advertisement is altered. This change of state must now be propagated to all controllers and views that are currently registered with the model as active. To do this the modifyAdvert operation invokes the notify operation in the model, which sends an update message to the view. The view responds to the update message by executing the displayAdvert operation which

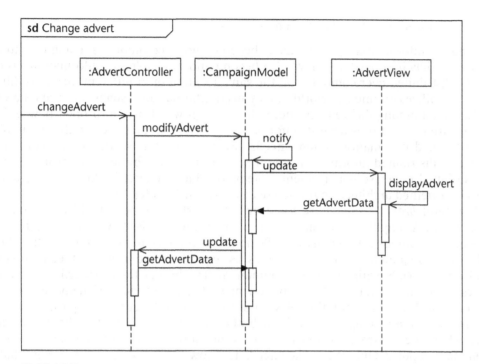

Figure 13.15 MVC component interaction.

requests the appropriate data from the model via the `getAdvertData` operation. The model also sends an `update` message to the `AdvertController`, which then requests the data it needs from the model.

One of the most important aspects of the MVC architecture is that each model knows only which views and controllers are registered with it, but not what they do. The `notify` operation causes an update message to all the views and controllers (for clarity, only one view and one controller are shown in the diagram, but interaction with the others would be similar). The `update` message from the model is in effect saying to the views and controllers: 'I have been updated and you must now ensure that your data is consistent.' Thus the model, which should be the most stable part of the application, is unaffected by changes in the presentation requirements of any view or controller. The change propagation mechanism can be structured so that further views and controllers can be added without causing a change to the model. Each of these may support different interface requirements but require the same model functionality. However, since views and controllers need to know how to access the model in order to get the information they require, some changes in the model will inevitably still cause changes in other components.

Other kinds of communication may take place between the MVC components during the operation of the application. The controller may receive events from the interface that require a change in the way that some data is presented to the user but do not cause a change of state. The controller's response to such an event would be to send an appropriate message to the view. There would be no need for any communication with the model.

13.5.4 Architectures for distributed systems

Distributed information systems have become more common as communications technology has improved and have also become more reliable. An information system may be distributed over computers at the same location or at different locations. Since Agate has offices around the world, it may need information systems that use data that is distributed among different locations. If Agate grows, it may also open new offices and require new features from its information systems. An architecture that is suitable for distributed information systems needs also to be flexible so that it can cope with change. A distributed information system may be supported by software products such as distributed database management systems or object request brokers or may adopt a service-oriented architecture (these are discussed in Chapter 19).

A general *broker* architecture for distributed systems is described by Buschmann et al. (1996). A simplified version of the broker architecture is shown in Fig. 13.16.

A broker component increases the flexibility of the system by decoupling the client and server components. Each client sends its requests to the broker rather than communicating directly with the server component. The broker then forwards the service request to an appropriate server. A broker may offer the services of many servers and part of its task is to identify the relevant server to which a service request should be forwarded. The advantage offered by a broker architecture is that a client need not know where the service is located, and it may therefore be deployed on either a local or a remote computer. Only the broker needs to know the location of the servers that it handles.

Figure 13.17 shows a sequence diagram for client–server communication using the broker architecture. In this example the server subsystem is on a local computer. In addition to the broker itself, two additional *proxy* components have been introduced to insulate the client and server from direct access with the broker. On the client side a `ClientSideProxy` receives the initial request from the client and packs the data in a format suitable for transmission. The request is then forwarded to the `Broker` which finds an appropriate server and invokes the required service via the `ServerSideProxy`.

The `ServerSideProxy` then unpacks the data and issues the service request sending the `service` message to the `Server` object. The `service` operation then executes and on completion responds to the `ServerSideProxy`. The response is then sent to the `Broker` which forwards it to the originating `ClientSideProxy`. Note that these are both new messages and not returns. The reason for this is that a broker does not wait for

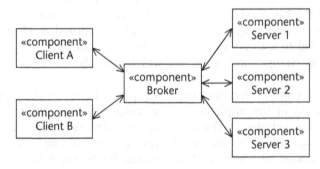

Figure 13.16 Schematic of simplified broker architecture.

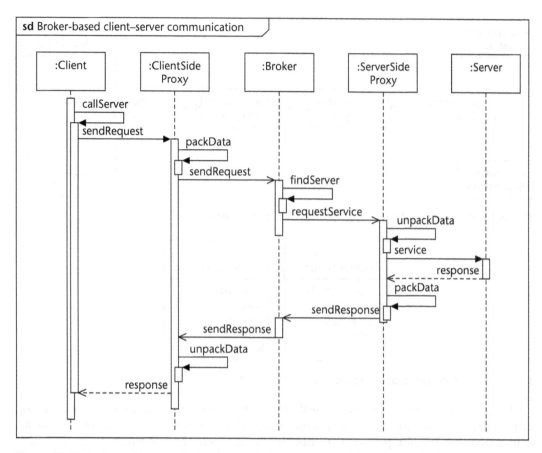

Figure 13.17 Broker architecture for local server (adapted from Buschmann et al., 1996).

each response before handling another request. Once its `sendRequest` activation has been completed, the broker will in all probability deal with many other requests and thus requires a new message from the `ServerSideProxy` object to cause it to enter a new activation. Unlike the broker, the `ClientSideProxy` has remained active; this then unpacks the message and the response becomes available to the `Client` as control returns.

Figure 13.18 shows how the participants in this interaction can be allocated to different processes, with the client and its proxy running in one process thread, the broker in another and the server and its proxy in a third.

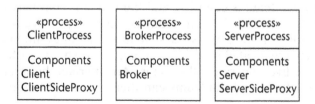

Figure 13.18 Process allocation of components in Figure 13.17.

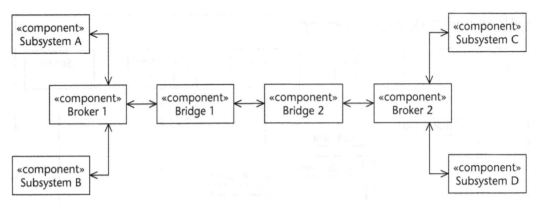

Figure 13.19 Schematic of broker architecture using bridge components.

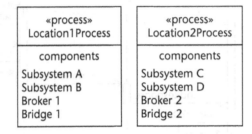

Figure 13.20 Process allocation of components in Figure 13.19.

Figure 13.19 shows a schematic broker architecture that uses *bridge* components to communicate between two remote processors. Each bridge converts service requests into a network specific protocol so that the message can be transmitted. Figure 13.20 shows a possible allocation of these components to processes.

13.5.5 Organization structures for architecture and development

Dividing a system into subsystems has benefits for project management. Each subsystem can be allocated to a single development team, which can operate independently of other teams, provided that they adhere to the interface requirements for their subsystem. Where a subsystem must be split between two development teams, there is a heavy communications overhead that is incurred in ensuring that the different parts of the subsystem are constructed to consistent standards. In such cases the structure of either the organization or of the software tends to change so that they become more closely aligned with each other; this helps to minimize the communications overhead and is sometimes known as Conway's Law[8] (Coplien, 1995). If a subsystem that is being developed by more than one team is cohesive, and the way it is split between teams has no apparent functional basis, then the teams may coalesce in practice and operate as one. Teams that are working on the same subsystem are sometimes inhibited from merging, perhaps because they are located on different continents. The subsystem should then be treated as if it were two separate subsystems. An interface between these two new subsystems can be defined and the teams can then operate autonomously. Where the

---

8 This is an example of an organizational pattern.

allocation of one subsystem to two teams is such that one team deals with one set of requirements and the other deals with a different set of requirements, the subsystem can also be treated as if it were actually two subsystems, with a defined interface between them.

13.6 Concurrency

In most systems there are many objects that do not need to operate concurrently but some may need to be active simultaneously. Object-oriented modelling captures any inherent concurrency in the application principally through the development of interaction diagrams and state machines. The examination of use cases also helps with the identification of concurrency. There are several ways of using these models to identify circumstances where concurrent processing may be necessary. First, a use case may indicate a requirement that the system should be able to respond simultaneously to different events, each of which triggers a different thread of control. Second, if a state machine reveals that a class has complex nested states which themselves have concurrent substates, then the design must be able to handle this concurrency. The state machine for the class Campaign has nested concurrent states within the Active state (see Fig. 11.20) and there may be the possibility of concurrent activity. In this particular example, the concurrent activity that occurs in the real world need not necessarily be represented as concurrent processing in the computerized information system.

In cases where an object is required to exhibit concurrent behaviour it is sometimes necessary to split the object into separate objects in order to avoid the need for concurrent activity within any one object. Concurrent processing may also be indicated if interaction diagrams reveal that a single thread of control requires that operations in two different objects should execute simultaneously, perhaps because of asynchronous invocation. This essentially means that one thread of control is split into two or more active threads. An example of this is shown in Fig. 13.21.

Different objects that are not active at the same time can be implemented on the same logical processor (and thus also on the same physical processor—this distinction is

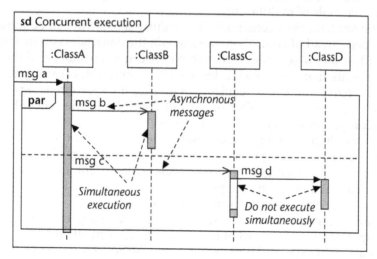

Figure 13.21 Concurrent activity in an interaction diagram.

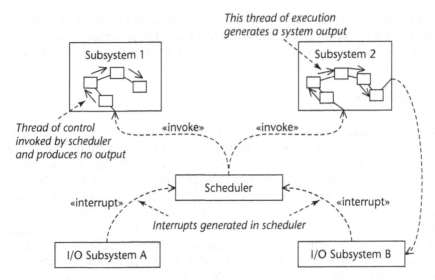

Figure 13.22 Scheduler handling concurrency.

explained below). Objects that must operate concurrently must be implemented on different logical processors (though perhaps still on the same physical processor).

The distinction between logical and physical concurrency is as follows. There are a number of ways of simulating the existence of multiple processors using only a single physical processor. For example, some operating systems (Unix and Windows XP) allow more one than one task to appear to execute at the same time, and are thus called multi-tasking operating systems. In fact, only one task really takes place at any one time, but the operating system shares the processor between different tasks so quickly that the tasks appear to execute simultaneously. Where there are no tight time constraints a multi-tasking operating system can provide a satisfactory implementation of concurrency. But it is important to ensure that the hardware configuration of the computer can cope with the demands of multitasking.

When there are tight time constraints a scheduler subsystem can be introduced that ensures that each thread of control operates within the constraints on its response time. Figure 13.22 illustrates a possible relationship between a scheduler and the other parts of a system. Events that are detected by the I/O (input/output) subsystems generate interrupts in the scheduler. The scheduler then invokes the appropriate thread of control. Further interrupts may invoke other threads of control and the scheduler allocates a share of physical processor time to each thread.

Another way of implementing concurrency is to use a multi-threaded programming language (such as Java). These permit the direct implementation of concurrency within a single processor task. Finally, a multi-processor environment allows each concurrent task to be implemented on a separate processor.

Most concurrent activity in a business information system can be supported by a multi-user environment. These are designed to allow many users to perform tasks simultaneously. Multi-user concurrent access to data is normally handled by a separate database management system (DBMS)—these are introduced briefly in Section 13.8.1 and are discussed in more detail in Chapter 18.

13.7 | Processor Allocation

In the case of a simple, single-user system it is almost always appropriate for the complete system to operate on a single computer. The software for a multi-user information system (all or part of it) may be installed on many computers that use a shared database server. More complex applications sometimes require the use of more than one type of computer, where each provides a specialized kind of processing capability for a specific subsystem. An information system may also be partitioned over several computers, because subsystems must operate concurrently, because some parts of the application need to operate in different locations (in other words, it is a distributed system), or because the processing load is greater than one processor can handle (in other words, the load must be balanced across multiple machines). Information systems that use the Internet or company intranets for their communications are now widespread. Such distributed information systems operate on diverse computers and operating systems.

The allocation of a system to multiple processors on different platforms involves the following steps.

- The application should be divided into subsystems.
- Processing requirements for each subsystem should be estimated.
- Access criteria and location requirements should be determined.
- Concurrency requirements for the subsystems should be identified.
- Each subsystem should be allocated to an operating platform–either general purpose (PC or workstation) or specialized (embedded micro-controller or specialist server).
- Communication requirements between subsystems should be determined.
- The communications infrastructure should be specified.

The estimation of processing requirements requires careful consideration of such factors as event response times, the data throughput that is needed, the nature of the I/O that is required and any special algorithmic requirements. Access and location factors include the difficulties that may arise when a computer will be installed in a harsh operating environment such as a factory shop floor.

13.8 | System Design Standards

System design sets standards that will be applied in later design and development activities. In particular, these include standards that will apply to the design of the database, the design of the user interface and the construction standards that will apply to the program code that is written to implement the system.

13.8.1 Database design

Suitable data management approaches for an information system can vary from simple file storage and retrieval to sophisticated database management systems of various types. In some applications where data has to be accessed very rapidly, the data may be kept in main memory while the system executes. However, most data management is concerned with storing data, often large volumes, so that it may be accessed at a later stage either by the same system or by another.

Database management systems (DBMS) provide various facilities that are useful in many applications and that make a DBMS the obvious choice for many applications. Once a decision has been made to use a DBMS, the most appropriate type must be selected. A relational DBMS is likely to be appropriate if there are large volumes of data with varying (perhaps ad hoc) access requirements. An object-oriented DBMS is more likely to be suitable if specific transactions require fast access or if there is a need to store complex data structures and there is not a need to support a wide range of transaction types. A third type of DBMS is emerging–the object-relational DBMS–that is similar to an object-oriented DBMS in its support for complex data structures, but that also provides effective querying facilities. These issues and the detailed design consequences of the choice of DBMS are explored further in Chapter 18.

13.8.2 User interface design standards

Standards for the human–computer interface are an important aspect of the design activity, since it is with the interface that users actually interact. There are standard style guides for applications written to run on Windows PCs or on Apple Macs. Organizations may also have their own style guides that define the conventions to be used in designing windows and dialogues so that users will experience the same style of user interface in every system they use and can easily transfer their knowledge of how to use one system to another. Some characteristics of good dialogues and the subject of style guides for HCI are discussed in Chapter 16.

13.8.3 Construction guidelines

Construction guidelines may not appear relevant at this stage in a systems development project. However, they are pertinent to system design because there is a growing tendency for developers to use CASE environments that have code generation capabilities. It is also the case that when a rapid development approach or an iterative approach is followed, application development will have begun while analysis and design on other parts of the system are still progressing.

Construction guidelines will normally include advice on the naming of classes, of operations and of attributes, and where this is the case these guidelines are also applicable during the analysis activity. Wherever possible, consistent naming conventions should be enforced throughout the project since this makes it easier to trace an analysis class directly through to its implementation. Other guidelines for construction might relate to the use of particular software features (for example, using only standard language constructs in order to aid portability) and the layout of the code. These issues are addressed in more detail in Chapter 19.

13.9 Agate Software Architecture

In the case study chapters, A2, A3 and A4, we have developed the models for the Agate system. The initial package architecture was shown in Fig. A2.8. However, this does not reflect a proper layering or partitioning of the software architecture. We may begin with a four-layer architecture that separates responsibility for the user interface, the application logic, the domain classes and the database. A simple view of this is shown in Fig. 13.23.

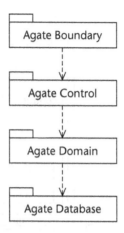

Figure 13.23 Four-layer architecture for Agate.

However, we know that Agate requires the system to be capable of distribution. One option would be to adopt a thin-client architecture. In this approach, all four of the layers shown in Fig. 13.23 would be located on one or more servers, and the user interface would be generated as HTML and displayed in a browser. However, this would not give us the kind of interactivity that we have been modelling in our prototype user interfaces, which rely on a client program running on the users' PCs. (Adding a rich Internet application (RIA) as the user interface in a browser would provide a similar separation of client and server to the one we have planned for.) So we need to decide where to split the system between the client side and the server side. The Agate Control package could be split into a client-side package that co-ordinates the user interface, playing the role of Controller, and a server-side package that orchestrates the business logic of the use cases and interacts with the domain classes. If we adopt this approach, we will break the closed layering of the architecture of Fig. 13.23. Both the client-side and the server-side classes will need to understand the structure of the entity objects in the domain package (Advert, Campaign, Client etc.). If we develop in Java, the jar file containing these classes will need to be located on the client as well as the server, even if their operations are not invoked on the client. One way to reduce this dependency is to use lightweight versions of the entity classes in the Agate Domain package. These are classes that have the attributes of the entity classes, but do not have any operations apart from constructors and those operations necessary to get and set attribute values. This is an established pattern in J2EE systems, and is shown in Fig. 13.24. Note that as we move into design, the human readable package names that we have been using so far are replaced with package names that will map to Java packages or C# namespaces.

Note that the dependency between the Agate Control Client package and the Agate Value Objects package is no more than that, a dependency. It does not imply that there is some kind of communication across the network between the two. In fact if we implement the packages as Java packages, and deploy them, the value object package (com.agate.domain.vo) will exist in both the client process and the server process. This is shown in Figure 13.25.

We shall revisit this architecture in the case study chapter A5, once we have considered in more detail the design of classes, the user interface and the database.

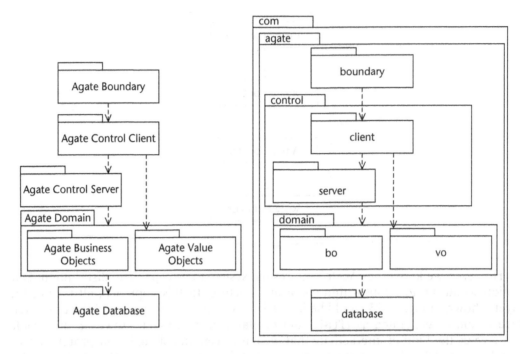

Figure 13.24 Possible package architecture for Agate, showing how it will be implemented as Java packages or C# namespaces.

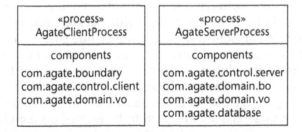

Figure 13.25 Process allocation for Agate.

13.10 Summary

Systems and software architecture have aspects in common with the architecture of buildings, and architectural models are typically produced using different views, which address different aspects of the architecture. In information systems, 'architecture is the fundamental organization of a system embodied in its components, their relationships to each other, and to the environment, and the principles guiding its design and evolution' (IEEE, 2000). Many architects now use UML in order to produce architectural models of systems.

One of the key concerns of architects is to ensure that the architecture of the system will enable it to meet the quality attributes (non-functional requirements) that are expected of it. The models allow them to reason about how well the proposed structures and relationships will support demands on performance, reliability, reusability and other quality attributes.

The architecture of new systems is often constrained by existing systems, because they define either explicitly or implicitly the way in which systems are built within the organization, or because the new systems will have to interoperate with the old. There is a growing interest in wrapping up existing systems as services to support a service-oriented architecture, or in extracting the business logic from heritage systems using reverse-engineering to produce platform-independent models, and then deriving new implementations in more modern technologies from the models. The Model-Driven Architecture movement places UML at the centre of its work and many of the features that have been improved or added in UML 2.0 are there to support MDA.

Large organizations may mandate approaches to architecture development based on enterprise architecture or technical reference architectures that lay down models of the business and how it operates (in the former case) or of standard technologies to be applied (in the latter case). Experienced architects also draw on architectural styles, which act as architectural patterns and provide well understood ways of constructing the high-level architecture of new systems.

Review Questions

13.1 Give a definition of architecture in an information systems context.

13.2 What is the difference between an architectural view and an architectural viewpoint?

13.3 What are the 4 + 1 views of architecture in the Unified Process?

13.4 What are the benefits of adopting an architecture-centric approach?

13.5 How do existing systems influence the architecture of new systems in the same organization?

13.6 Explain the difference between a PIM and a PSM.

13.7 What is meant by enterprise architecture?

13.8 What are the advantages of dividing a system into a collection of subsystems?

13.9 What is the difference between client–server and peer-to-peer communication between subsystems?

13.10 Why is an open layered architecture more difficult to maintain?

13.11 What are the disadvantages of the closed layered architecture?

13.12 What advantages would there be if the `Advert HCI subsystem` in Fig. 13.11 were designed to have direct access to the `Campaign Database` layer?

13.13 What are the main differences between the MVC architecture and the layered and partitioned architecture?

13.14 In what sense does a broker decouple two subsystems that need to communicate with each other? How does this work?

13.15 How do architectural divisions of systems help with project management?

13.16 Why is it sometimes necessary to design information systems that have explicitly concurrent behaviour?

13.17 How should you go about allocating system tasks to processors?

Case Study Work, Exercises and Projects

13.A Compare Soni's four aspects with the UP 4 + 1 views. What do they have in common and how do they differ?

13.B Consider a system that you use regularly. What, if anything, can you tell about the architecture of the system from the user's perspective?

13.C Develop a series of steps for the identification of partitioned subsystems within a layer in a layered architecture. Use the process for the identification of layers described in Section 13.5.2 as a starting point. Highlight any significant differences that you feel exist between the two processes.

13.D Investigate a framework for enterprise architecture. What support is there for it in modelling tools?

13.E Suggest a suitable layered architecture with any necessary partitioning for the FoodCo case study by following the procedures defined above.

Further Reading

Bass et al. (2003) is an updated version of their 1998 book, in which they have adopted UML as their architecture description language. The book mixes case studies from different kinds of projects with theory and practical guidance.

Garland and Anthony (2003) provide an excellent and practical approach to developing software architectures using UML.

Buschmann et al. (1996) and Schmidt et al. (2000) provide further details of the architectures discussed in this chapter and describe other interesting alternatives.

Details of the OMG's MDA initiative can be found at www.omg.org/mda/. Zachman International (www.zachmaninternational.com) provides information about the Zachman framework.

Detailed Design

14.1 | Introduction

The design activity is concerned with turning an analysis model into a specification of a system that can be given to a programmer to build, or that can be used in a modelling tool to generate code in a programming language like Java or C#. System design provides a framework for this. Detailed design is about examining the classes and the associations between them, deciding how well they will perform in a live system and making changes to improve the analysis class model in a way that meets the criteria for good design discussed in Chapter 12.

Design adds detail to the analysis model: the type and visibility of each attribute must be decided, and the visibility and signature of each operation must be determined. Design can also result in changes to the classes and associations that emerge from analysis: classes may be merged or split, new associations may be added, the direction in which associations can be navigated must be decided, and the location of operations may be changed in order that classes can meet their responsibilities effectively. Design will add new classes: these classes will support human–computer interaction and allow the data in attributes to be stored in a database.

The guiding principle in all of this is how well the chosen design allows classes to interact with one another to deliver the functionality of the system. However, there are also some other principles that can be applied to help in producing a good design, notably those associated with coupling and cohesion. There is also a view that changes to the analysis model should be kept to a minimum, as the analysis model represents a coherent and consistent description of the classes necessary to meet the requirements.

Integrity constraints that were identified in analysis must be adhered to if the system is to maintain its consistency and integrity. So there is a balance to be struck between retaining the structures that were discovered in analysis and making sure that they will support a working system.

14.2 What Do We Add in Object-Oriented Detailed Design?

In detailed design, we add to the analysis model at two levels. At the level of the class model, we add new classes to support inputs, outputs, processes and file or database structures. At the level of individual classes, we add new attributes, operations and associations to support the interaction between them and to meet criteria for good design. In this short section we briefly explain what we add to the class model. This is then dealt with in more detail in the following chapters. The rest of this chapter then addresses what we add to the analysis class model.

The analysis activities of a project will have identified concepts in the business and elaborated them in terms of classes; use cases will have been identified and described. The classes that have been included in the class model will reflect the business requirements but they will include only a very simplistic view of the other classes that are required to handle the interface with the user, the interface with other systems, the storage of data and the overall co-ordination of the classes into programs. These other classes will be added in design with greater or lesser degrees of detail depending on the hardware and software platform that is being used for the new system.

Coad et al. (1997) suggested that in addition to the problem domain or business classes, developing a detailed design involves three further elements. These are:

- human interface
- data management
- system interaction.

Chapter 16 discusses the principles of how to design good human–computer interaction, while Chapter 17 deals with the design of interface classes. Chapter 18 addresses the design of data management. As we add the additional classes to handle these aspects of the system, we also add control classes that manage the interaction between other classes in the system. We also use design patterns, which are explained in Chapter 15, in order to make best use of other designers' experience and good practice in the design of the way our classes interact.

14.3 Attribute and Operation Specification

As we stated above, one of the tasks in detailed design is to add more detail to the specification of attributes and operations in the classes that analysis has identified. This includes the following:

- deciding the data type of each attribute;
- deciding how to handle derived attributes;
- adding primary operations;
- defining the signature of operations including the types of parameters;
- deciding the visibility of attributes and operations.

14.3.1 Attribute data types

During analysis we have not considered in detail the data types of the attributes, although on occasions it may be useful to record data type information in analysis. For example, an attribute `temperature` may be a floating-point data type if it holds the temperature in Centigrade or it may be an enumerated data type if it holds one of the values 'hot', 'warm' or 'cold'. The attribute has a different meaning and would be manipulated differently for each of these data types and it is important to determine during analysis which meaning is appropriate and meets the users' needs. Most CASE tools require the user to choose a data type for each attribute as it is added to the model or will use a default type such as int or string.

Common primitive data types include Boolean (true or false), character (any alphanumeric or special character), integer (whole numbers) and floating-point (decimal numbers).[1] In most object-oriented languages more complex data types such as string and date are available, and others such as money or name can be constructed from the primitive data types or may be available in standard libraries. An attribute's data type is declared in a UML class diagram using the following syntax:

```
<property> ::= [<visibility>] ['/'] <name> [':' <prop-type>]
['[' <multiplicity> ']'] ['=' <default>]
['{' <property-string > [',' <property-string >]* '}']
```

The `visibility` is an indicator of whether other classes can access the value, and is explained in more detail in Section 14.3.5. The value `'/'` is a literal that denotes a derived attribute (see Section 14.3.2). The `name` is the attribute name, the `prop-type` is its data type, the `default` is the default value that the attribute is set to when an instance of the class is first created, and the `property-string` describes a property of the attribute, such as `constant` or fixed. The characters in single quotes are literals. The attribute name is the only feature of its declaration that is compulsory.

Figure 14.1 shows the class `BankAccount` with attribute data types declared. The attribute `balance` in a `BankAccount` class might be declared with an initial value of zero using the syntax:

```
balance: Money = 0.00
```

The attribute `accountName` might be declared with the property string indicating that it must have a value and may not be null using the syntax:

```
accountName: String {not null}
```

Attribute declarations can also specify the multiplicity of the attribute in much the same way as the multiplicity of an association may be specified. For example, an `Employee` class might include an attribute to hold a list of qualifications that would be declared using the syntax:

```
qualification: String[0..10]
```

This declaration states that the attribute qualification may hold from zero to 10 qualifications.

---

1 A list of Java primitive data types can be found in Deitel and Deitel (2007).

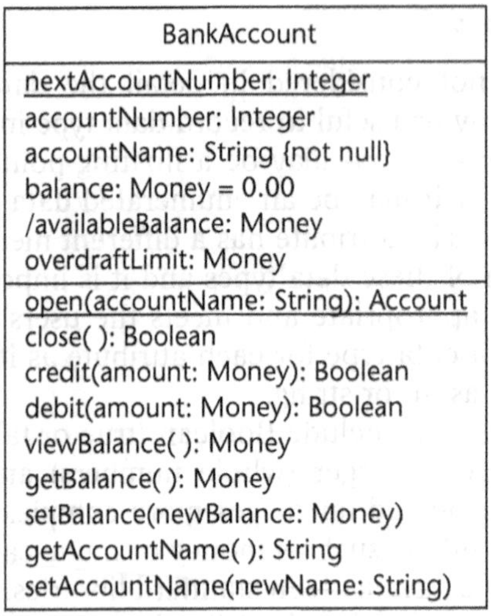

BankAccount
nextAccountNumber: Integer accountNumber: Integer accountName: String {not null} balance: Money = 0.00 /availableBalance: Money overdraftLimit: Money
open(accountName: String): Account close( ): Boolean credit(amount: Money): Boolean debit(amount: Money): Boolean viewBalance( ): Money getBalance( ): Money setBalance(newBalance: Money) getAccountName( ): String setAccountName(newName: String)

Figure 14.1 BankAccount class.

14.3.2 Derived attributes

The values of some attributes can be derived from other attributes in the same class or other classes. They may have been identified in analysis, but will not be implemented as attributes in design. They will have an operation to get the value, but not to set it (see Section 14.3.3). It is necessary to decide how these values will be calculated. There are two choices: to calculate them when they are needed; or to calculate them whenever one of the values on which they depend changes.

In Fig. 14.1, the attribute `availableBalance` is a *derived attribute* indicated in UML by the symbol '/' before the name of the attribute. The value of this attribute might be defined as the sum of the `balance` and the `overdraftLimit` attributes.

When we need the value of the `availableBalance` attribute, the operation `getAvailableBalance()` might include a line of code to add `balance` and `overdraftLimit` and return the result. Alternatively, every time that we update the `balance` or `overdraftLimit` attribute values, we could include a line of code to update the `availableBalance` value at the same time.

Typically the choice will depend on two factors, firstly how many operations may affect the value of the derived attribute and whether they are likely to change, and secondly how difficult it is to calculate the derived attribute from scratch compared to calculating it when the attributes it depends on change.

In our example, it is only necessary to change the `availableBalance` value when the `balance` or the `overdraftLimit` values change. However, the bank may change the way it calculates the `availableBalance` value to include any debit transactions that have been recorded during the day but not processed against the account balance: for example, cash withdrawals from automated teller machines (ATMs) or payments by debit card. (Banks typically process all such transactions overnight in a batch process and update the account balance, but don't want customers to withdraw more money than they have funds available.) So operations that record unprocessed transactions need to be updated to change the `availableBalance` value. Now when we process a debit transaction overnight, we also have to check whether it is one of the types (ATM and debit card) that have already been deducted from the `availableBalance` value or not. This is making the system more complicated, and we have to remember (document) what operations affect `availableBalance`. In this case, it is almost certainly simpler to calculate `availableBalance` when we need it.

However, if a customer has hundreds of unprocessed debit transactions in a day, and the only way to work out the `availableBalance` value is to get the current balance of the account and then deduct all the unprocessed debit transactions and add the overdraft limit, it would require a lot of processing each time the value is required. If the alternative is to take the existing `availableBalance` value and deduct the value of a debit transaction when it occurs, then we might choose the second approach, as it is simpler and quicker, though it adds a slight overhead to each transaction. However, it makes the system more complicated. We might want to add a new attribute called `committedAmount` that holds the value of all unprocessed debit transactions, and is updated each time a customer withdraws cash or uses their debit card. Calculating `availableBalance` then becomes a matter of adding the `balance` and the `overdraftLimit` and deducting the `committedAmount`. When the unprocessed debit transactions are processed in the overnight batch run, they can be deducted from the `committedAmount`, which will normally be zero at the end of the overnight process.

We have explained this example in some detail to show that there are trade-offs to be made between complexity and processing requirements, and that there are often several ways of designing classes that the designer must choose between.

14.3.3 Primary operations

In analysis we identify those operations that are necessary to support the use cases that we analyse. However, we are designing classes for reuse, so we need to provide them with a set of operations that can be used in use cases that we haven't anticipated yet.

There are certain standard operations that are normally included in all classes. These are operations to create instances of objects, to retrieve the attribute values of instances, to modify the attribute values of instances, to select instances based on some kind of key or identifier, and to delete instances. Yourdon (1994) calls these implicit services. These are also known as *primary operations* and include constructor, destructor, get and set operations.

- *Constructor*–operation to create an instance of a class. Usually has the same name as the class. There may be multiple versions with different signatures (see Section 14.3.4).
- *Destructor*–operation to delete an instance of a class from memory. C# and C++ have explicit destructors named the same as the class with a tilde at the beginning, e.g. ~BankAccount. In Java you can override the `finalize()` method of `Object`, which is the superclass of all other classes, if you need to carry out any processing before an object is removed from memory by the garbage collector. The C# destructor is similar to the Java `finalize()` method and is called by the garbage collector, whereas the C++ destructor must be called explicitly.
- *Get operation*–operation to get the value of an attribute, also known as an *accessor*.
- *Set operation*–operation to set the value of an attribute, also known as a *mutator*.

Some authors say that these usually need not be shown on diagrams, as they clutter up the diagrams and make them difficult to read. However, all operations have to be specified somewhere, and it is important to recognize that a class may have several different constructors for instances of that class. Sometimes it is important to be able to see these services in the diagrams. However, this is an issue about the functionality offered by modelling tools rather than methodologies. Ideally, it should be possible to switch off the display of any operation that the analyst or designer does not wish to have displayed in the operations compartment in a class. If you use a modelling tool that can generate set and get operations for every attribute, you do not need to include them in your class diagram.

We have shown primary operations on some class diagrams to emphasize their presence and have taken a pragmatic approach. In most parts of the book, we have shown those operations that were useful to show. We have usually included the operations that are not primary operations. We have included some primary operations, usually because they are referred to in the text or some related diagram.

One commonly held approach is normally not to show primary operations on analysis class diagrams as it can be assumed that such functionality is available. During analysis, issues such as the visibility of operations or the precise data types of attributes may not have been finally decided. However, when a design class model is completed it may be important to indicate that certain primary operations have public or protected visibility (see Section 14.3.5) and, as such, these may justifiably be shown on the diagram. Those that are private may be omitted as they do not constitute part of the class's public interface.

Exceptionally, primary operations may usefully be included on analysis class diagrams either if they reflect particular functionality that has to be publicly visible or if it is important to indicate, for example, that more than one constructor is required. A class may need more than one constructor if objects could be instantiated in one of several initial states that require different input parameters. Each constructor would have a different signature.

There are clearly alternative approaches and it is important that appropriate documentation standards are clearly defined at the outset of a project so that the absence of primary operations on a class diagram is not misinterpreted.

14.3.4 Operation signatures

Each operation also has to be specified in terms of the parameters that it passes and returns. The syntax used for an operation is:

```
[<visibility>] <name> '(' [<parameter-list>] ')'
[':' [<return-type>]
['[' <multiplicity> ']'] ['{' <property-string>
[',' < property-string >]* '}']]
```

The part that is mandatory is the name of the operation followed by a pair of brackets. The parameter-list is optional. If included, it is a list of parameter names and types separated by commas:

```
<parameter-list> ::= <parameter> [',' <parameter>]*
<parameter> ::= [<direction>] <parameter-name> ':'
<type-expression> ['['<multiplicity>']']
['=' <default>] ['{' < property-string >
[',' < property-string >]* '}']
```

An operation's *signature* is determined primarily by the operation's name, the number and types of its parameters and the type of the return value if any. The `BankAccount` class might have a `credit()` operation that passes the amount being credited to the receiving object and has a Boolean return value. The operation would be shown in the diagram as:

```
credit(amount: Money): Boolean
```

A `credit()` message sent to a `BankAccount` object could be written in a program as:

```
creditOK = accObject.credit(500.00)
```

where `creditOK` holds the Boolean return value that is available to the sending object when the `credit()` operation has completed executing. This Boolean value may be tested to determine whether the `credit()` operation performed successfully. Alternatively, in an object–oriented language like Java the operation would be designed to throw an exception if it failed rather than returning a Boolean, as in the following snippet of code:

```
try{
   accObject.credit(500.00);
} catch (UpdateException){
//some error handling; }
```

This uses Java syntax for handling exceptions. An exception is a way of handling errors in a programming language. Exceptions are not shown as part of the operation syntax in UML class diagrams, but can be held in the model.

The UML is a modelling language and does not determine what operations should be shown in a class diagram. It provides the notation to use and suggestions about presentation, but it does not tell the analyst or designer what to include and what not to include.

14.3.5 Visibility

The concept of encapsulation was discussed in Chapter 4 and is one of the fundamental principles of object-orientation. During analysis various assumptions have been made regarding the encapsulation boundary for an object and the way that objects interact with each other. For example, it is assumed that the attributes (or more precisely the values of the attributes) of an object cannot be accessed directly by other objects but only via get and set operations (primary operations) that are assumed to be available for each attribute. Moving to design involves making decisions regarding which operations (and possibly attributes) are publicly accessible. In other words we must define the encapsulation boundary.

Figure 14.1 shows the class `BankAccount` with the types of the attributes specified and the operation parameters defined. The class has the attribute `balance`, which, we might assume during analysis, can be accessed directly by the simple primary operations `getBalance()` and `setBalance()`. However, the designer may decide that the balance should be updated only through the operations `credit()` and `debit()` that contain special processing to check whether these transactions should be permitted, to maintain the `availableBalance` attribute value and to ensure that the transactions are logged in an audit trail. In these circumstances, it is important that changes to the value of the

Visibility symbol	Visibility	Meaning
+	Public	The feature (an operation or an attribute) is directly accessible by an instance of any class
–	Private	The feature may only be used by an instance of the class that includes it
#	Protected	The feature may be used either by instances of the class that includes it or of a subclass or descendant of that class
~	Package	The feature is directly accessible only by instances of a class in the same package

Figure 14.2 Visibility.

balance attribute can only occur through the debit() and credit() operations. The operation setBalance() should not be publicly available for use by other classes.

Meyer (1997) introduces the term 'secret' to describe those features that are not available in the public interface. Programming languages designate the non-public parts of a class, which may include attributes and operations, in various ways. The four commonly accepted terms[2] used to describe *visibility* are listed in Fig. 14.2 with their UML symbols. An example would be:

```
- balance: Money
```

Visibility may also be shown as a property string, for example:

```
balance: Money {visibility = private}
```

To enforce encapsulation the attributes of a class are normally designated private (Fig. 14.3 (a)). The operation setBalance() and others are also designated private to ensure that objects from other classes cannot access them directly and make changes that are not recorded in the audit trail. Private operations can, of course, be invoked from operations in the same class such as debit(). Commonly, complex operations are simplified by factoring out procedures into private operations.

In Fig. 14.3 (b) the private operations are assigned protected visibility so that subclasses of BankAccount can examine and set the value of the balance and accountName attributes. For example, the debit() operation might be redefined in a JuniorBankAccount subclass. The redefined operation would use getBalance() to access the balance and check that a debit would not result in a negative balance before setting it using setBalance().

The attribute nextAccountNumber in Fig. 14.3 is an example of a class-scope attribute (indicated by underlining). A class-scope attribute occurs only once and is attached to the class, not to any individual object. In this example nextAccountNumber holds the account number for the next new BankAccount object created. When a new BankAccount is created using the class-scope operation open(), nextAccountNumber is incremented by one. The attribute accountNumber is an example of an instance-scope

---

2   The precise meaning of the non-public categories of visibility depends on the programming language being used. When a designer is determining the visibility of parts of a model, he or she must be aware of the visibility (or scoping) offered by the implementation environment.

(a)   (b)

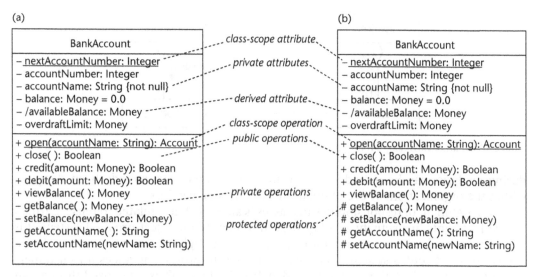

Figure 14.3 BankAccount class with visibility specified.

attribute (hence no underlining). Each `BankAccount` object has an instance-scope `accountNumber` attribute, which holds its unique account number.

14.4 Grouping Attributes and Operations in Classes

As well as adding information to the specification of attributes and operations, the designer may decide to change the allocation of attributes and operations to classes that were determined during the analysis activities. This may be done to create more reusable classes, to define standard behaviours that can be reused as interfaces, or to apply design principles that will produce a cleaner design that will require less refactoring later. The techniques the designer might use include the following:

- checking that responsibilities have been assigned to the right class;
- defining or using interfaces to group together well-defined standard behaviours;
- applying the concepts of coupling and cohesion;
- applying the Liskov Substitution Principle.

14.4.1 Assigning responsibilities

Certain aspects of the detailed design require special attention in the development of object-oriented systems. These include reuse and assignment of responsibilities to classes.

One of the arguments for the use of object-oriented languages is that they promote reuse through encapsulation of functionality and data together in classes and through the use of inheritance. This is not just a programming issue, but one that also affects analysis and design. There is a growing recognition of the need to reuse analysis results in object-oriented systems development. Design reuse already takes place at two levels: first through the use of design patterns, which are discussed in detail in Chapter 15; and second by recognizing during design that business classes that have been identified

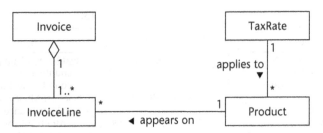

Figure 14.4 Partial class diagram for FoodCo.

during analysis may be provided by reusing classes that have already been designed within the organization, or even bought in from outside vendors.

The assignment of responsibilities to classes is an issue that is related to reuse. Larman (2005) highlights this activity as a key task in design. In an object-oriented system, it is important to assign responsibility for operations to the right classes and there is often a choice. In the FoodCo system, there will be a need to produce invoices for customers that include the calculation of Value Added Tax (VAT). (VAT is a tax used throughout Europe that is applied at each stage of the supply chain and not just as a purchase tax paid by the final end-user or consumer.) The calculation of VAT could be carried out by one of a number of classes in the model (Fig. 14.4):

- `Invoice`–which organizes the total information for the whole sale;
- `InvoiceLine`–which contains the detail of each item sold and to which the tax applies;
- `Product`–to which different VAT rates may apply;
- `TaxRate`–which carries the details of the percentage that applies for each valid rate.

If the designer makes the wrong decision, the resulting class will be less reusable and may constrain the design of other classes. For example, if the responsibility for tax calculation is allocated to `Invoice` or `InvoiceLine`, then this has implications for `CreditNote` and `CreditNoteLine`, which may also need to calculate tax. The same code may be copied and pasted from one class to the other, and then if it is changed in one, the programmer may forget to change it in the other. If it is assigned to `Product`, then it cannot be reused in the Agate project where VAT applies to services as well as products. In this case, it needs to be assigned to `TaxRate` in order to maximize the reuse that can be made of the classes in this design.

14.4.2 Interfaces

We have talked about the public interface of a class being the set of operations (and possibly attributes) that are visible to instances of other classes. Sometimes it is useful to be able to define a set of operations that must be implemented by different classes if they are to provide a particular standard behaviour. We can model this in UML as an *interface*.

An interface is a group of related methods with no implementations. Sometimes a designer will want to specify a set of operations that belong together and define a particular behaviour in what is called an interface. The purpose of this is so that classes that implement the interface can be guaranteed to implement that behaviour. An example from Java is the `java.lang.Runnable` interface, which is used for classes whose instances are intended to be executed by a `Thread`.

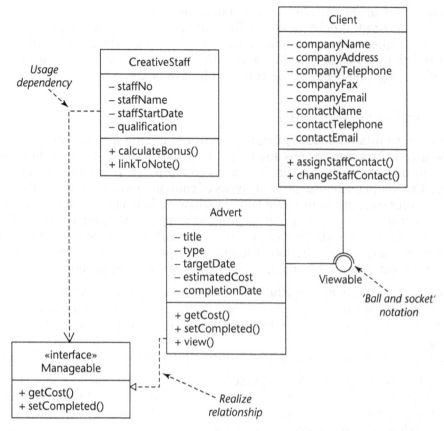

Figure 14.5 Interfaces for the Advert class.

An interface in UML is a group of externally visible (i.e. public) operations. The interface contains no internal structure, it has no attributes, no associations and the implementation of the operations is not defined. Formally, an interface is equivalent to an abstract class that has no attributes, no associations and only abstract operations. Figure 14.5 illustrates two alternative notations for an interface. The simpler of the two UML interface notations is a circle. This is attached by a solid line to the class that realizes the interface. For example, in Fig. 14.5 the Advert class realizes the interface Viewable using this notation, that is, it provides all of the operations specified by the interface (and maybe more).

Some modelling tools show a list of the operations under the circle, though this can usually be suppressed. The line with an open semicircle connecting the Client class to the Viewable interface circle icon indicates that it uses or needs at least one of the operations provided by the interface.

The alternative notation uses a stereotyped class icon. As an interface only specifies the operations and has no internal structure, the attributes compartment is omitted. This notation lists the operations on the diagram. The *realize* relationship, represented by the dashed line with a triangular arrowhead, indicates that the client class (e.g. Advert) provides implementations of at least the operations listed in the interface (e.g. Manageable). The dashed arrow from CreativeStaff means that the class uses the operations listed in the interface. The notation used for the realize relationship (the triangular arrowhead) is deliberately reminiscent of the notation for inheritance, as in a sense `Advert` inherits the operations in the `Manageable` interface. (Normally only one of these notations would be used in a diagram.) This concept can be implemented using the interface programming language construct in Java or C#.

14.4.3 Coupling and cohesion

Yourdon and Constantine (1979) defined a series of criteria for structured design that could be used in breaking systems and programs down into modules to ensure that they are easy to develop and maintain. These criteria concern two issues: *cohesion* and *coupling*. Criteria to maximize desirable types of cohesion have as their aim the production of modules—sections of program code in whatever language is used—that carry out a clearly defined process or a group of processes that are functionally related to one another. This means that all the elements of the module contribute to the performance of a single function. Poor cohesion is found when processes are grouped together in modules for other reasons. Examples of poor types of cohesion include:

- processes that are grouped together for no obvious reason (*coincidental cohesion*);
- logically similar processes that are handled together, such as inputs (*logical cohesion*);
- processes that happen at the same time, for example when the system initializes (*temporal cohesion*);
- the outputs of one process being used as inputs by the next (*sequential cohesion*).

By aiming to produce modules that are functionally cohesive, the designer should produce modules that are straightforward to develop, easy to maintain and have the maximum potential to be reused in different parts of the system. This will be assisted if coupling between modules is also reduced to the minimum.

Criteria to minimize the coupling between modules have as their aim the production of modules that are independent of one another and that can be amended without resulting in knock-on effects to other parts of the system. Good coupling is achieved if a module can perform its function using only the data that is passed to it by another module and using the minimum necessary amount of data.

The concepts of coupling and cohesion can be applied to object-oriented systems development to help enforce encapsulation. Coad and Yourdon (1991) suggested several ways in which coupling and cohesion can be applied within an object-oriented approach. Larman (2005) also considers the application of these criteria. The criteria can be used within object-orientation during both analysis and design as described below (adapted from Coad and Yourdon, 1991).

Coupling

Coupling describes the degree of interconnectedness between design components and is reflected by the number of links an object has and by the degree of interaction the object has with other objects.

Interaction coupling is a measure of the number of message types an object sends to other objects and the number of parameters passed with these message types. Interaction coupling should be kept to a minimum to reduce the possibility of changes rippling through the interfaces and to make reuse easier. When an object is reused in another application it will still need to send these messages (unless the object is modified before

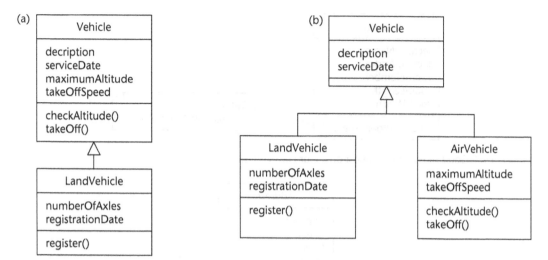

Figure 14.6 Inheritance coupling.

it is reused) and hence needs objects in the new application that provide these services. This affects the reuse process as it requires groups of classes to be reused rather than individual classes. (In Chapter 8 we introduced the idea of the *component* as the unit of reuse and discuss it further in Chapter 20. Components are groups of objects that together provide a clearly defined service.)

Inheritance coupling describes the degree to which a subclass actually needs the features it inherits from its base class. For example, in Fig. 14.6(a) the inheritance hierarchy exhibits low inheritance coupling and is poorly designed. The subclass LandVehicle needs neither of the attributes maximumAltitude and takeOffSpeed nor the operations checkAltitude() and takeOff(). They have been inherited unnecessarily. In this example it would appear that the base class, Vehicle, would perhaps be better named FlyingVehicle and the inheritance relationship is somewhat suspect. A land vehicle is not a kind of flying vehicle (not normally anyway). A better design is shown in Fig. 14.6(b). However, many systems developers view designs with a small degree of unnecessary inheritance as being acceptable if the hierarchy is providing valuable reuse and is meaningful. It can be argued that if attributes and operations are inherited unnecessarily it is merely a matter of not using these features in the subclass. However, a subclass with unnecessary attributes or operations is more complex than it needs to be and objects of the subclass may take more memory than they actually need. The real problems may come when the system needs maintenance. The system's maintainer may not realize that some of the inherited attributes and operations are unused and may modify the system incorrectly as a result. Alternatively the system's maintainer may use these unneeded features to provide a fix for a new user requirement, making the system even more difficult to maintain in the future. For these reasons, unnecessary inheritance should be kept as low as possible.

Cohesion

Cohesion is a measure of the degree to which an element contributes to a single purpose. The concepts of coupling and cohesion are not mutually exclusive but actually support each other.

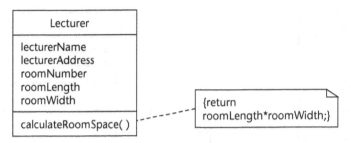

Figure 14.7 Good operation cohesion but poor class cohesion.

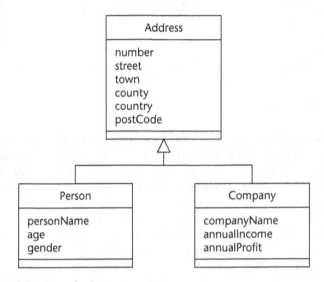

Figure 14.8 Poor specialization cohesion.

Operation cohesion measures the degree to which an operation focuses on a single functional requirement. Good design produces highly cohesive operations, each of which deals with a single functional requirement. For example in Fig. 14.7 the operation `calculateRoomSpace()` is highly cohesive.

Class cohesion reflects the degree to which a class is focused on a single requirement. The class `Lecturer` in Fig. 14.7 exhibits low levels of this type of cohesion as it has three attributes (`roomNumber`, `roomLength` and `roomWidth`) and one operation (`calculateRoomSpace()`) that would be more appropriate in a class `Room`. The class `Lecturer` should only have attributes that describe a `Lecturer` object (e.g. `lecturer-Name` and `lecturerAddress`) and operations that use them.

Specialization cohesion addresses the semantic cohesion of inheritance hierarchies. For example in Fig. 14.8 all the attributes and operations of the `Address` base class are used by the derived classes: the hierarchy has high inheritance coupling. However, it is true neither that a person is a kind of address nor that a company is a kind of address. The example is only using inheritance as a syntactic structure for sharing attributes and operations. This structure has low specialization cohesion and shows poor design. It does not reflect meaningful inheritance in the problem domain. A better design is shown in Fig. 14.9, in which a common class `Address` is being used by both the `Person` and `Company` classes. All the design criteria explained above may be applied at the same time to good effect.

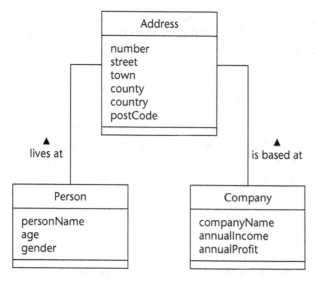

Figure 14.9 Improved structure using `Address` class.

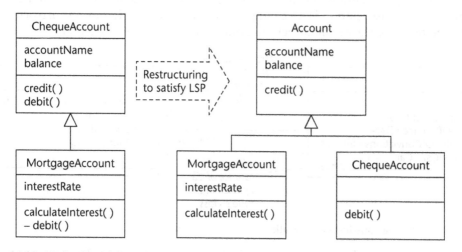

Figure 14.10 Application of the Liskov Substitution Principle.

14.4.4 Liskov Substitution Principle

The *Liskov Substitution Principle (LSP)* is another design criterion that is applicable to inheritance hierarchies. Essentially the principle states that, in object interactions, it should be possible to treat a derived object as if it were a base object. If the principle is not applied, then it may be possible to violate the integrity of the derived object. In Fig. 14.10 objects of the class `MortgageAccount` cannot be treated as if they are objects of the class `ChequeAccount` because `MortgageAccount` objects do not have a debit operation whereas `ChequeAccount` objects do. The `debit` operation is declared private in `MortgageAccount` and hence cannot be used by any other object. Figure 14.10

shows an alternative structure that satisfies LSP. Interestingly, this inheritance hierarchy has maximal inheritance coupling, and enforcing the LSP normally produces structures with high inheritance coupling.

14.5 | Designing Associations

An association between two classes indicates the possibility that links will exist between instances of the classes. The links provide the connections necessary for message passing to occur. When deciding how to implement an association it is important to analyse the message passing between the objects tied by the link.

14.5.1 One-to-one associations

In Fig. 14.11 objects of the class Owner need to send messages to objects of the class Car but not vice versa. This particular association may be implemented by placing an attribute to hold the object identifier (some authors prefer to use the term object reference) for the Car class in the Owner class. Thus Owner objects have the Car object identifier and hence can send messages to the linked Car object. As a Car object does not have the object identifier for the Owner object, it cannot send messages to the Owner object. The owns association is an example of a one-way association: the arrowhead on the association line shows the direction along which it may be navigated.

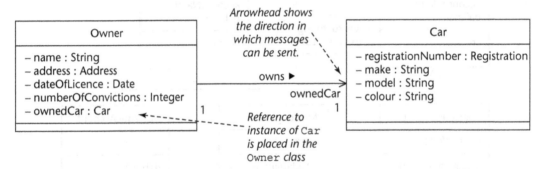

Figure 14.11 One-way one-to-one association.

The association end ownedCar is converted to an attribute of the same name that will hold a reference to the particular instance of Car that is owned by the instance of Owner. The ownedCar reference to the Car object is a reference to the Car in memory. It is not a database key (see Chapter 18) or a natural identifier like registrationNumber. With some CASE tools, it is not necessary to place the reference explicitly in the class like this; when the designer generates code from the model, it will automatically add the references for the association ends of all navigable associations.

So before an association can be designed it is important to decide in which direction or directions messages may be sent. (If messages are not sent in either direction along an association, then the need for its existence should be questioned.) Essentially we are determining the navigability of the association.

In general an association between two classes A and B should be considered with the following questions:

1. Do objects of class A have to send messages to objects of class B?
2. Does an A object have to provide some other object with B object identifiers?

If either of these questions is answered yes, then A objects need B object identifiers. However, if A objects get the required B object identifiers as parameters in incoming messages, A objects need not remember the B object identifiers. Essentially, if an object needs to send a message to a destination object, it must have the destination object's identifier either passed as a parameter in an incoming message just when it is required, or the destination object's identifier must be stored in the sending object. An association that has to support message passing in both directions is a two-way association. A two-way association is indicated with arrowheads at both ends.[3] As discussed earlier, it is important to minimize the coupling between objects. Minimizing the number of two-way associations keeps the coupling between objects as low as possible.

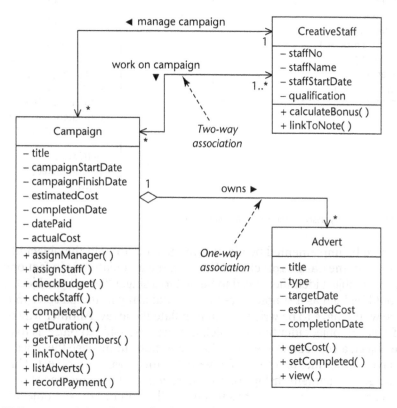

Figure 14.12 Fragment of class diagram for the Agate case study.

14.5.2 One-to-many associations

In Fig. 14.12, objects of the class `Campaign` need to send messages to objects of the class `Advert` but not vice versa. If the association between the classes was one-to-one, the

---

3 In UML a two-way association may be represented by drawing the association without the navigability arrowheads. However, an association without arrowheads may also represent an undefined association, that is, an association for which navigability is not yet decided.

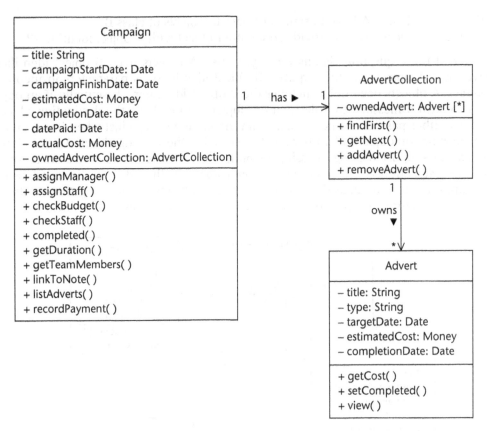

Figure 14.13 One-to-many association using a collection class.

association could be implemented by placing an attribute to hold the object identifier for the Advert class in the Campaign class. However, the association is in fact one-to-many and many Advert object identifiers need to be tied to a single Campaign object. The object identifiers could be held as a simple one-dimensional array in the Campaign object, but program code would have to be written to manipulate the array. Another way of handling the group of Advert object identifiers, which is more amenable to reuse, is to place them in a separate object, a collection object that has operations to manage the object identifiers and that behaves rather like an index of adverts for the Campaign object. This is shown in the class diagram fragment in Fig. 14.13. There will be many instances of the collection class, as each Campaign object has its own collection of Advert object identifiers. Notice that the AdvertCollection class has operations that are specifically concerned with the management of the collection. The findFirst() operation returns the first object identifier in the list and the getNext() gets the next object identifier in the list.

When a Campaign object wants to send a message to each of its Advert objects the Campaign object first sends a findFirst() message to the class to get the first object identifier. The Campaign object can now send a message to its first Advert object. The Campaign then uses getNext() to get the next object identifier from the collection class and sends the message to the next Advert object. The Campaign object can then iterate through the collection of object identifiers and send the message to each of the Advert objects in turn.

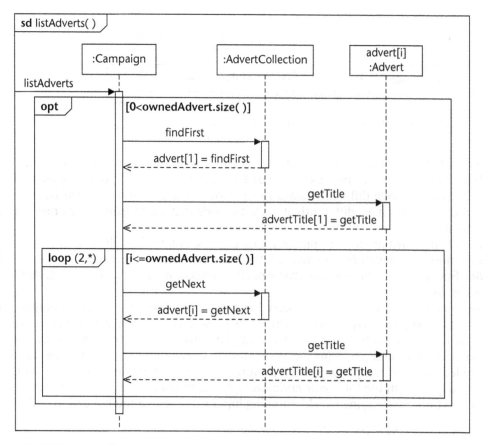

Figure 14.14 Sequence diagram for listAdverts().

Figure 14.14 shows the sequence diagram for the interaction that would enable the Campaign object to prepare a list of its adverts with their titles. The Campaign object holds the object identifier of the collection class so that it can send messages to it. As an Advert object does not have the object identifier for the Campaign object to which it belongs, it cannot send messages to the Campaign object. The interaction constraints in listAdverts() use the term ownedAdvert.size(), where ownedAdvert is the name of the attribute (in AdvertCollection) that holds the collection of object identifiers and size() is an OCL function that gives the number of elements in a collection. The opt interaction operator specifies that the interaction fragment will only execute if the constraint is satisfied–in this example, if there is at least one advert associated with the Campaign.

The designer may choose to use specific classes like AdvertCollection or may choose to use generic collection classes. The choice may depend on whether a decision has been made about the language in which the application will be developed. For example, both Java and C# have collection classes–in the java.utils package in Java, and the System.Collections namespace in C#–and both have a suitable class in the form of ArrayList. However, the Java class implements the Collection and List interfaces (among others), while the C# class implements the ICollection and IList interfaces (among others). Both ArrayList classes have add(), indexOf() and remove()

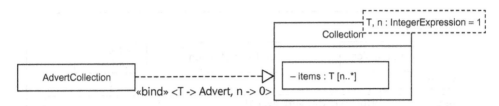

Figure 14.15 Template class used for `AdvertCollection`.

methods, but each has methods that are missing in the other, and some key methods, such as the one to return an `Iterator` or `Enumerator` to iterate over the elements of the `ArrayList`, have different names in the two languages, and the Java Iterator and the C# Enumerator have differently named methods to iterate through the objects in the collection.

In Java it is also possible to use *template classes*. A template class is one which has one or more *parameterable elements*, which can be bound to particular values in the model. Sticking with our non-language-specific collection classes, we could define them as in Fig. 14.15.

The template class `Collection` here has two parameters: T, which is unconstrained and could be any class type, and n, which must evaluate to an integer and has a default value of 1. The class `AdvertCollection` implements `Collection`, and binds T to the `Advert` class type and n to 0 (as the association between `Campaign` and `Advert`, which this collection class is replacing, has a multiplicity of 0..*). In Java, binding a template class to a type, as in the following code excerpt, which uses `ArrayList`, creates a type-safe collection class. Trying to add anything but an `Advert` to the collection will fail.

```
private ArrayList<Advert> items;
```

If the designer is intending to use a persistence framework such as Hibernate or NHibernate to store objects in the database (see Chapter 18), the choice of how collection classes are implemented when objects are brought into memory from the database may be determined by the framework. We continue to use non-language-specific collection classes in the rest of the examples in this chapter.

14.5.3 Many-to-many associations

The design of the many-to-many association work on campaign between `CreativeStaff` and `Campaign` (see Fig. 14.12) follows the principles described above. Assuming this is a two-way association, each `Campaign` object will need a collection of `CreativeStaff` object identifiers and each `CreativeStaff` object will need a collection of `Campaign` object identifiers. The designed association with the collection classes is shown in Fig. 14.16. Both the `CreativeStaff` and `Campaign` classes contain an attribute to hold the object identifiers of their respective collection classes.

Collection classes can be designed to provide additional support for object navigation. For example, if there is a requirement to find out if an employee works on a campaign with a particular title, a message may be sent from the `Creative Staff` object to each `Campaign` object the employee works on to get its title until either a match is found or the end of the collection is reached. Two separate messages are required to access each `Campaign` object. So, if an employee works on four campaigns, a maximum of eight

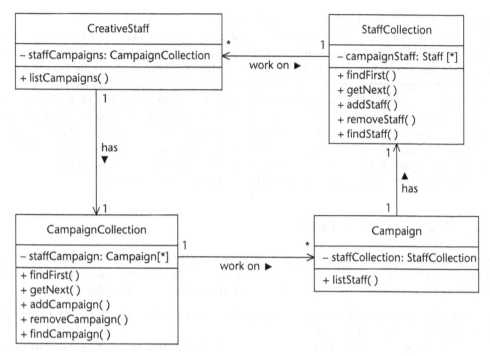

Figure 14.16 Two-way many-to-many association.

messages must be sent to find the campaign. In general, if the employee works on N campaigns a maximum of $2N$ messages must be sent.

An alternative search approach uses a findCampaign() operation in the collection class. This operation may be designed either to access an index in the collection object itself or to take responsibility to cycle through the Campaign objects searching for a title match. In the first case only the findCampaign() message is needed to find the campaign as the collection class indexes the campaigns by title. In the second case the collection object may have to send a maximum of N messages (one for each campaign on which the employee works). So in either case the inclusion of the findCampaign() operation in the collection class reduces the message passing required.

The management of object identifiers using collection classes may appear to increase appreciably the development effort required. In fact, the opposite is generally the case, as object-oriented languages normally provide collection classes of various types with standard collection management operations. The standard collection classes may offer various forms of indexing. They may also be subclassed to add additional application functionality. For example, Java provides, among others, standard LinkedList, Stack, Hashtable and Dictionary collection classes that may be subclassed to add application-specific behaviour or bound to specific class types to make them type-safe (Deitel and Deitel, 2007).

14.5.4 Keeping classes to a minimum

The association between Campaign and AdvertCollection is one-to-one (commonly the case with collection classes), and this suggests that one implementation strategy is to place the collection class inside the Campaign object. This approach generally produces more complex classes and limits extensibility. However, in this case it is likely that collection class behaviour will largely be provided by a library class as we have described in Section 14.5.2 or by a feature of the development language being used, so the issue of increased complexity may not be so significant. The problem of any reduction in extensibility is also less significant in this case: as only a Campaign object would want to know which Advert objects are tied to it, and any request to access a Campaign's Adverts would be directed to the Campaign first. So, on balance, placing the collection class inside the Campaign class is a sensible design decision, and using library collection classes where possible maximizes reuse and reduces development effort. Clearly, if another class, apart from Campaign, needs to use the list independently of the Campaign class then it is more appropriate to keep the collection class separate.

14.6 Integrity Constraints

Systems analysis will have identified a series of integrity constraints that have to be enforced to ensure that the application holds data that is mutually consistent and manipulates it correctly. These integrity constraints come in various forms:

- *referential integrity*, which ensures that an object identifier in an object is actually referring to an object that exists;
- *dependency constraints*, which ensure that attribute dependencies, where one attribute may be calculated from other attributes, are maintained consistently;
- *domain integrity*, which ensures that attributes only hold permissible values.

14.6.1 Referential integrity

The concept of referential integrity as applied to a relational database management system (see Chapter 18) is discussed by Howe (2001). Essentially the same principles apply when considering references between objects. In Fig. 14.12 the association manage campaign between CreativeStaff and Campaign is two-way, and an object identifier called campaignManagerId, which refers to the particular CreativeStaff object that represents the campaign manager, is needed in Campaign. (CreativeStaff needs a collection of Campaign object identifiers to manage its end of the association.) To maintain referential integrity the system must ensure that the attribute campaignManagerId either is null (not referencing any object) or contains the object identifier of a CreativeStaff object that exists. In this particular case the association states that a Campaign must have a CreativeStaff instance as its manager, and it is not correct to have a Campaign with a null campaignManagerId attribute. In order to enforce this constraint, the constructor for Campaign needs as one of its parameters the object identifier of the CreativeStaff object that represents the campaign manager, so that the campaignManagerId attribute can be instantiated with a valid object identifier.

Problems in maintaining the referential integrity of a Campaign may occur during its lifetime. For instance, the campaign manager, Nita Rosen, may leave the company to move to another job and Nita's CreativeStaff object will then be deleted.[4] Referential

---

4 This is a somewhat simplistic view. When an employee leaves the company the CreativeStaff object would be set to the state Ex-employee. In this case, although the object still exists, it is not appropriate for it to be referenced as a campaign manager.

integrity is maintained by ensuring that the deletion of a `CreativeStaff` object that is a campaign manager always involves allocating a new campaign manager. The task of invoking the operation `assignManager()` is included in the operation to delete a `CreativeStaff` object, and it will request the object identifier of the new campaign manager. Similarly, any attempt to remove the current campaign manager from a `Campaign` must always involve allocating the replacement. The multiplicity of exactly one represents a strong integrity constraint for the system. In the example just discussed, it seems to be appropriate that a campaign should always have a manager, even when it has just been created. However, great care should be taken when assigning a multiplicity of exactly one (or in general a minimum of one) to an association, as the consequences in the implemented system can be quite dramatic. Let us imagine that the campaign manager, Nita Rosen, does leave Agate but that there is no replacement campaign manager available. The strict application of the integrity constraint implied by the `manage campaign` association means that integrity can only be enforced if all the campaigns that Nita managed are deleted. Of course, because each `Advert` must be linked to a `Campaign`, all the `Advert` objects for each of the `Campaigns` must also be deleted in order to maintain referential integrity. This is an example of a cascade delete: deleting one object results in the deletion of many objects as referential integrity is applied. In the case of Agate, deleting the information about Nita's campaigns and their adverts would be disastrous. There are two solutions: either the constraint on the association is weakened by changing the cardinality to zero or one, or when Nita leaves a dummy `CreativeStaff` object is created and allocated as campaign manager to Nita's campaigns. Although the second solution is a fix, it has the advantage of providing an obvious place-holder, highlighting the problem of unmanaged campaigns but maintaining the integrity constraint. Of course, the minimum of one multiplicity was assigned to the association to reflect company policy that a campaign must always have a manager, so the dummy may not be a viable solution from a business perspective.

14.6.2 Dependency constraints

Attributes are dependent upon each other in various ways. These dependencies may have been identified during analysis and must now be dealt with during design. A common form of dependency occurs when the value of one attribute may be calculated from other attributes, as we have explained in Section 14.3.2. For instance, a requirement to display the total advertising cost may be satisfied either by storing the value in the attribute `totalAdvertCost` in the `Campaign` class or by calculating the value every time it is required. The attribute `totalAdvertCost` is a derived attribute and its value is calculated by summing the individual advert costs. Placing the derived attribute in the class reduces the processing required to display the total advertising cost as it does not require calculation. On the other hand, whenever the cost of an advert changes, or an advert is either added to or removed from the campaign, then the attribute `total-AdvertCost` has to be adjusted so that it remains consistent with the attributes upon which it depends. An example of the UML symbol ('/') used to indicate that a modelling element (attribute or association) is derived is shown in Fig. 14.3.

In order to maintain the consistency between the attributes, any operation that changes the value of an `Advert`'s cost must trigger an appropriate change in the value of `totalAdvertCost` by sending the message `adjustCost()` to the `Campaign` object. The operation `adjustCost()` is an example of a *synchronizing operation*. The operations that have to maintain the consistency are setAdvertCost() and the Advert destructor. When a new advert is created, the constructor would use setAdvertCost() to set the advert cost. This would invoke adjustCost() and hence ensure that the total-AdvertCost is adjusted. So any change to an Advert's cost takes more processing if the derived attribute totalAdvertCost is used. Thus one part of the system executes more quickly while another part executes more slowly. Generally, it is easier to construct systems without derived attributes, as this obviates the need for complex synchronizing operations. Derived attributes should only be introduced if performance constraints cannot be satisfied without them. If performance is an issue, then one of the skills needed in design is how to optimize the critical parts of the system without making the other parts of the system inoperable.

Another form of dependency occurs where the value of one attribute is constrained by the values of other attributes. For example, let us assume that the sum of the total advertising cost, the staff costs, the management costs and the ancillary costs must not exceed the campaign's authorized budget. Any changes to these values must check that the authorized budget is not exceeded by the sum of the costs. If a change to any of these dependent values would cause this constraint to be broken, then some action should be taken. There are two possibilities. Either the system prohibits any change that violates the constraint and an exception is raised, or it permits the change and an exception is raised. It is most likely that the violation of the constraint would occur as a result of an attempt interactively to change one of the constrained values and the exception raised would be a warning message to the user. If it is considered permissible for the constraint to be broken, then all access to or reporting about these values should produce a warning message to the user.

Dependency constraints can also exist between or among associations. One of the simplest cases is shown in Fig. 14.17 where the chairs association is a subset of the is a member of association.

This constraint is stating that the chair of a committee must be a member of the committee, and it can be enforced by placing a check in the assignChair() operation in Committee to confirm that the Employee object identifier passed as a parameter is already in the collection class of committee members. More complex constraints, which require several associations, may also exist. Derived associations may also be introduced to improve performance if absolutely necessary and, as in the case of derived attributes, synchronizing operations are needed to ensure that the derived links are consistent with the links on which they depend.

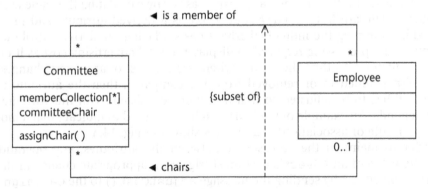

Figure 14.17 Constraints between associations.

14.6.3 Domain integrity

Domain integrity is concerned with ensuring that the values an attribute takes are from the appropriate underlying domain. For instance, the attributes from the `Cost` domain might reasonably be non-negative decimal values with two decimal places. These constraints may be viewed as an extended form of those implied by data types. The necessary integrity checking code is normally placed in the set operations or in any interactive interface that permits the entry of values. Such constraints may have been documented as business rules or in OCL.

14.7 Designing Operation Algorithms

The design of operations involves determining the best algorithm to perform the required function. In the simplest case, primary operations require little design apart from the inclusion of code to enforce integrity checks. For more complex operations, algorithm design can be an involved process. Various factors constrain algorithm design:

- the cost of implementation
- performance constraints
- requirements for accuracy
- the capabilities of the implementation platform.

Generally it is best to choose the simplest algorithm that satisfies these constraints, as this makes the operation easier to implement and easier to maintain. Rumbaugh et al. (1991) suggest that the following factors should be considered when choosing among alternative algorithm designs.

- *Computational complexity*. This is concerned with the performance characteristics of the algorithm as it operates on increasing numbers of input values. For example, the bubble sort algorithm has an execution time that is proportional to $N \times N$ where N is the number of items being sorted.
- *Ease of implementation and understandability*. It is generally better to sacrifice some performance to simplify implementation.
- *Flexibility*. Most software systems are subject to change and an algorithm should be designed with this in mind.
- *Fine-tuning the object model*. Some adjustment to the object model may simplify the algorithm and should be considered.

Designing the main operations in a class is likely to highlight the need for lower-level private operations to decompose complex operations. This process is much the same as traditional program design. Techniques such as step-wise refinement (Budgen, 1994) or structure charts (Yourdon and Constantine, 1979) may well be used to good effect. UML offers activity diagrams (see Chapters 5 and 10) as a technique both to document and to design operations. In circumstances where high levels of formality are required in operation design, formal specification techniques such as Z or VDM may be used.[5]

---

5   Z and VDM are formal languages that can be used to specify a system using mathematical entities such as sets, relations and sequences.

Responsibilities identified during analysis may map onto one or more operations. The new operations that are identified need to be assigned to classes. In general, if an operation operates on some attribute value then it should be placed in the same class as the attribute. On occasions, a particular operation may modify attributes in more than one class and could sensibly be placed in one of several classes. In choosing where to locate the operation, one view is that minimizing the amount of object interaction should be a major criterion, while another significant criterion is simplicity. However, in some cases it is not a clear-cut decision.

During analysis use case realization, control classes are introduced to control the execution of use cases. Typically these control classes may be the best place for operations that are particular to the use case or that have no obvious owning entity class. Some designers may choose to allocate control class responsibility to boundary or entity classes during design to achieve performance or other implementation requirements. However, this results in boundary or entity classes that have less well focused functionality (lower class cohesion) and can make maintenance more difficult. This yet again reflects the trade-offs that have to be made during design.

14.8   Summary

Class design is concerned with the detailed design of the system and is conducted within the architectural framework and design guidelines specified during system design. The detailed design process involves determining the data types of the attributes, deciding how to implement derived attributes, adding primary operations and defining operation signatures. The designer will decide how best to group attributes and operations in classes, assigning operations appropriately, guided by a series of criteria that incorporate the fundamental principles of coupling and cohesion. Interfaces may be specified. Associations have to be designed to support the message passing requirements of the operations. This involves determining how best to place object references in the classes. The application of integrity constraints is included in the design of operations. Operations have to be designed to enforce these integrity constraints. If derived attributes are included in any of the classes then synchronizing operations are required to maintain their consistency.

Review Questions

14.1   What aspects of the system are added to the class diagram(s) in object-oriented detailed design?

14.2   What levels of visibility may be assigned to an attribute or an operation?

14.3   Why should attributes be private?

14.4   What are primary operations?

14.5   What is a class-scope attribute?

14.6   What does the term 'interface' mean in UML?

14.7   How can collection classes be used when designing associations?

14.8 Under what circumstances should a collection of object references be included in a class?

14.9 How can referential integrity be enforced in an object-oriented system?

14.10 Under what circumstances should derived attributes be used?

14.11 Under what circumstances should derived associations be used?

Case Study Work, Exercises and Projects

14.A Specify the attribute types and the operation signatures for the class `ProductionLine` in the FoodCo case study.

14.B For each association in which `ProductionLine` participates allocate object identifiers to design the association.

14.C Show how referential integrity can be enforced for the associations designed in Exercise 14.B.

14.D For an object-oriented programming language of your choice investigate the language features available to support the use of collection classes.

Further Reading

Rumbaugh et al. (1991) and Booch (1994) provide good advice on object design. Budgen (1994) offers descriptions of various design techniques. Meyer (1997) contains a comprehensive discussion of object-oriented software design and provides many interesting insights. Sommerville (2007) and Pressman (2009) both provide detailed discussions of design issues.

Chapter 15

Design Patterns

In this chapter you will learn
- ☑ what types of patterns have been identified in software development
- ☑ how to apply design patterns during software development
- ☑ the benefits and difficulties that may arise when using patterns.

15.1 Introduction

Design patterns provide a means for capturing knowledge about problems and successful solutions in systems design. Experience that has been gained in the past can be reused in similar situations, reducing the effort required to produce systems that are more resilient, more effective and more flexible.

Successful software development relies on the knowledge and expertise of the developer, among other factors. These are built up and refined during the developer's working life. A systems analyst or software engineer applies potential solutions to development problems, monitors their success or failure and produces more effective solutions on the next occasion. It is in the nature of software development that the same problems tend to recur, though in different contexts. Individual developers may expend a great deal of development time and effort on solving these recurring problems from first principles each time they occur, and the solution that each individual produces may not be the most appropriate that could be achieved. This can result in information systems that are inflexible, difficult to maintain or inefficient or that possess some other undesirable features. This cycle of reinventing the wheel continued partly because there were no effective mechanisms for communicating successful solutions to recurring problems.

Patterns have been introduced in Section 8.5 where we considered analysis patterns in particular, and in Chapter 13 we discussed architectural patterns. We consider further detailed aspects of patterns in this chapter and we focus our attention on some better-known design patterns to illustrate their application. We introduce guidelines for using patterns and explore the advantages and disadvantages of using patterns.

15.2 Software Development Patterns

15.2.1 Frameworks

Patterns have the potential to be an important aspect of the reuse strategy within an organization. *Frameworks* also offer opportunities for reuse. There can be confusion between patterns and frameworks but there are important differences. Frameworks are partially completed software systems that may be targeted at a specified type of application: for example, sales order processing. An application system tailored to a particular organization may be developed from a framework by completing the unfinished elements and adding application- and organization-specific elements. This may involve the specialization of classes, the implementation of operations and perhaps the addition of new classes. Essentially a framework is a reusable mini-architecture that provides structure and behaviour common to all applications of this type.

The major differences between patterns and frameworks can be summarized as follows:

- Patterns are more abstract and general than frameworks. A pattern is a description of the way that a type of problem can be solved, but the pattern is not itself a solution.
- Unlike a framework, a pattern cannot be directly implemented in a particular software environment. A successful implementation is only an example of a design pattern.
- Patterns are more primitive than frameworks. A framework can employ several patterns but a pattern cannot incorporate a framework.

15.2.2 Pattern catalogues and languages

Patterns are grouped into catalogues and languages. A *pattern catalogue* is a group of patterns that are related to some extent and may be used together or independently of each other. The patterns in a *pattern language* are more closely related, and work together to solve problems in a specific domain. For example, Cunningham (1995) documented the 'Check Pattern Language of Information Integrity', which consists of eleven patterns that address issues of data validation. All were developed from his experience of developing interactive financial systems in Smalltalk.

One of these patterns, Echo, describes how data input should be echoed back to the user after it has been modified and validated by the information system (since Cunningham uses the Model–View–Controller structure he talks about this in terms of changes made by the model). Typically, users enter small batches of values and then look at the screen to check that they have been correctly entered. The sequence in which a user can enter data into fields may not be fixed and so validation feedback should be given one field at a time. For example, a user enters a value as 5.236. This might be echoed back by the system as 5.24 (correctly rounded to two decimal places). The user receives direct visual feedback that the value has been accepted and how it has been modified.

15.2.3 Software development principles and patterns

Patterns are intended to embody good design practice and hence are based upon sound software development principles, many of which have been identified since the early days of software development and applied within development approaches that are not object-orientated. Buschmann et al. (1996) suggest that the following are the key principles that underlie patterns:

- abstraction
- encapsulation
- information hiding
- modularization
- separation of concerns
- coupling and cohesion
- sufficiency, completeness and primitiveness
- separation of policy and implementation
- separation of interface and implementation
- single point of reference
- divide and conquer (this means breaking a complex problem into smaller, more manageable ones).

We have discussed these principles in earlier chapters.

15.2.4 Patterns and non-functional requirements

Patterns address the issues that are raised by non-functional requirements (Chapters 6 and 13). Buschmann et al. (1996) identify these as the important non-functional properties of a software architecture:

- changeability
- interoperability
- efficiency
- reliability
- testability
- reusability.

These properties may be required for a complete system or a part of a system. For example, a particular set of functional requirements may be seen as volatile and subject to change. The design based on these functional requirements will need to be able to cope with change and to minimize side effects. Another requirement could be that a part of an application must be highly reliable. Again, this requirement must be met by the design.

15.3　Documenting Patterns—Pattern Templates

15.3.1 Template contents

Patterns may be documented using one of several templates. The *pattern template* determines the style and structure of the pattern description, and these vary in the emphasis they place on different aspects of patterns. The differences between pattern templates may mirror variations in the problem domain but there is no consensus as to the most appropriate template even within a particular problem domain. Nonetheless it is generally agreed that a pattern description should include the following elements (at least implicitly).

- *Name*. A pattern should be given a meaningful name that reflects the knowledge embodied by the pattern. This may be a single word or a short phrase. These names become the vocabulary for discussing conceptual constructs in the domain of expertise. For instance, the names of three of the Gamma design patterns (Gamma et al., 1995), Bridge, Mediator and Flyweight, give an indication of how they are intended to work.

- *Problem.* This is a description of the problem that the pattern addresses (the intent of the pattern). It should identify and describe the objectives to be achieved, within a specified context and constraining forces. For example, one problem might be concerned with producing a flexible design, another with the validation of data. The problem can frequently be written as a question: for example, 'How can a class be constructed that has only one instance and be accessed globally within the application?' This question expresses the problem addressed by the Singleton pattern (discussed in Section 15.4.2).
- *Context.* The context of the pattern represents the circumstances or preconditions under which it can occur. The context should provide sufficient detail to allow the applicability of the pattern to be determined.
- *Forces.* The forces of a pattern are the constraints or issues that must be addressed by the solution. These forces may interact with and conflict with each other, and possibly also with the objectives described in the problem. They reflect the intricacies of the pattern.
- *Solution.* The solution is a description of the static and dynamic relationships among the parts of the pattern. The structure, the participants and their collaborations are all described. A solution should resolve all the forces in the given context. A solution that does not resolve all the forces fails.

15.3.2 Other aspects of templates

A pattern template may be more extensive than the elements described above. Some other features that have figured in pattern templates are:

- an example of the use of a pattern that serves as a guide to its application;
- the context that results from the use of the pattern;
- the rationale that justifies the chosen solution;
- related patterns;
- known uses of the pattern that validate it (some authors suggest that until the problem and its solution have been used successfully at least three times–the *rule of three*– they should not be considered as a pattern);
- a list of aliases for the pattern ('also known as' or AKA);
- sample program code and implementation details (commonly used languages include C++, Java and Smalltalk).

Gamma et al. (1995) use a template that differs from that described above. Although very detailed, this does not explicitly identify the forces. Cunningham's (1995) 'Check Pattern Language of Information Integrity' is described in the Portland Form.[1] These variations in template style and structure make it difficult to compare patterns. It can also limit their reusability since it is more difficult to use a pattern that is documented in an unfamiliar template.

---

1 Named after Portland, Oregon where it originated, this is essentially free-format text.

15.4   Design Patterns

15.4.1 Types of design pattern

Gamma et al. (1995) present a catalogue of 23 design patterns that are still widely used today. (The four authors are known as the 'Gang of Four' and the patterns they describe are sometimes referred to as the GOF patterns or the Gamma patterns.) The GOF patterns are categorized as *creational, structural* or *behavioural* to reflect their different purposes. An example of each of these categories is described in the following sections. The scope of a pattern may be primarily at either the class level or at the object level. Patterns that are principally concerned with objects describe relationships that may change at run-time and hence are more dynamic. Patterns that relate primarily to classes tend to be static and identify relationships between classes and their subclasses that are defined at compile-time. The GOF patterns are generally concerned with increasing the ease with which an application can be changed, by reducing the coupling among its elements and maximizing their cohesion. The patterns are based on principles of good design, which include maximizing encapsulation and the substitution of composition for inheritance wherever possible. Using composition as a design tactic produces composite objects whose component parts can be changed, perhaps dynamically under program control, hence resulting in a highly flexible system. Nonetheless, patterns will frequently use both inheritance and composition to achieve the desired result.

Changeability involves several different aspects (Buschmann et al., 1996): maintainability, extensibility, restructuring and portability. Definitions of these terms vary but we use the following.

- *Maintainability* is concerned with the ease with which errors in the information system can be corrected.
- *Extensibility* addresses the inclusion of new features and the replacement of existing components with new improved versions. It also involves the removal of unwanted features.
- *Restructuring* focuses on the reorganization of software components and their relationships to provide increased flexibility.
- *Portability* deals with modifying the system so that it may execute in different operating environments, such as different operating systems or different hardware.

15.4.2 Creational patterns

A creational design pattern is concerned with the construction of object instances. In general, creational patterns separate the operation of an application from how its objects are created. This decoupling of object creation from the operation of the application gives the designer considerable flexibility in configuring all aspects of object creation. This configuration may be dynamic (at run-time) or static (at compile-time). For example, when dynamic configuration is appropriate, an object-oriented system may use composition to make a complex object by aggregating simpler component objects. Depending upon circumstances different component objects may be used to construct the composite object and, irrespective of its components, the composite object will fulfil the same purpose in the application. A simple analogy illustrates this. A systems development department in an organization will vary in its composition from time to time. When permanent staff are on holiday contract staff may be employed to perform their roles. This enables the department to offer the same service to the organization at all times.

Creating composite objects is not simply a matter of creating a single entity but also involves creating all the component objects. The separation of the creation of a composite object from its use within the application provides design flexibility. By changing the method of construction of a composite object, alternative implementations may be introduced without affecting the current use.

Singleton pattern

As an example we consider the creational pattern, Singleton, which can be used to ensure that only one instance of a class is created. In order to understand the use of the pattern we need to consider the circumstances under which a single instance may be required. The Agate campaign management system needs to hold information regarding the company. For example, its name, its head office address and the company registration details need to be stored so that they can be displayed in all application interfaces and printed on reports. This information should be held in only one place within the application but will be used by many different objects. One design approach would be to create a global data area that can be accessed by all objects, but this violates the principle of information hiding. Any change to the structure of the elements of global data would require a change to all objects that access them. The creation of a Company class overcomes this problem by encapsulating the company attributes (Fig. 15.1) and ensuring that they are not public. These attributes are then only accessible to other objects through the operations of the Company object. But there is still a problem with this proposal. An object that wants to use the Company object needs to know the Company object's identifier so that it can send messages to it. This suggests that the Company object identifier should be globally accessible—but again this is undesirable since it violates information hiding.

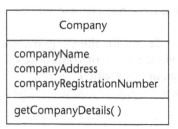

Figure 15.1 Company class for the Agate case study.

Some object-oriented programming languages (including Java and C++) provide a mechanism that enables certain types of operations to be accessed without reference to a specified object instance. These are called *class* (or *static*) *operations*. This mechanism offers a solution to the problem of providing global access without the need to globally define the object identifier. For example, a static operation getCompanyInstance() can be defined in such a way that it will provide any client object with the identifier for the Company instance. This operation can be invoked by referencing the class name as:

```
Company.getCompanyInstance()
```

When a client object needs to access the Company object it can send this message to the Company class and receive the object identifier in reply. The client object can now send a getCompanyDetails() message to the Company object.

There is one further aspect to this design problem. It is important that there should be only one instance of this object. To ensure system integrity the application should be constructed so that it is impossible to create more than one. This aspect of the problem can be solved by giving the Company class sole responsibility for creating a Company object. This is achieved by making the class constructor private so that it is not accessible by another object. The next issue that needs to be addressed is the choice of an event that causes the creation of the company object. Perhaps the simplest approach is to create the Company object at the moment when it is first needed. When the Company class first receives the message getCompanyInstance() this can invoke the Company class constructor. Once the Company object has been created, the object identifier is stored in the class (or static) attribute companyInstance so that it can be passed to any future client objects. When the Company object is first created its attribute values may, for example, be read in from a database or a file.

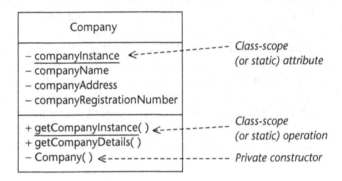

Figure 15.2 Company class with class-scope operation and attribute.

So far we have produced a design for the Company class (Fig. 15.2) that provides a single global point of access via the class operation getCompanyInstance() and that also ensures that only one instance is created.

A simple version of the logic for the getCompanyInstance() operation is:

```
If (companyInstance == null)
    {
    companyInstance = new Company()
    } return companyInstance
```

The sequence diagram in Fig. 15.3 shows the interaction Get company name for display. In this it can be seen that the :RequestingObject receives the object identifer (held in companyInstance) for the Company object in the same way whether the object has just been created or is already in existence.

The design may need to accommodate further requirements. Since Agate operates as a separate company in each country (each owned by the same multinational), variations in company law from country to country may necessitate different company registration details to be recorded for each country. This suggests a requirement for different types of Company class each with its own variation of the registration details. The creation of a

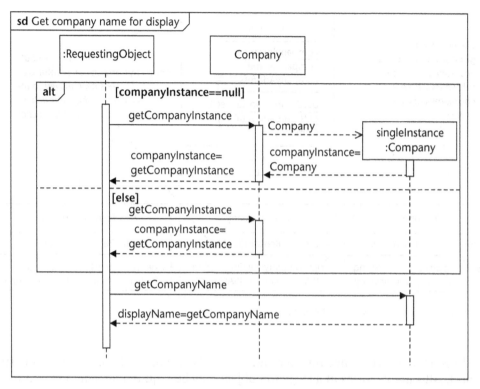

Figure 15.3 Sequence diagram for the interaction `Get company name for display`.

separate subclass for each style of company registration details provides a solution to this aspect of the problem (Fig. 15.4). When the `getCompanyInstance()` operation is first called, the appropriate subclass is instantiated. If the `Company` object has not yet been instantiated, its constructor operation can access details of the country (say, held in a `CurrentCountry` object) to determine which subclass should be instantiated. This could use the Factory Method pattern (Gamma et al., 1995) to create the appropriate subclass.

This part of the design for the campaign management system now has:

- a class `Company`, which is only instantiated once;
- an instance of this class, which is globally accessible;
- different subclasses of `Company`, which are instantiated as needed, depending on run-time circumstances.

We have described above an application of the Singleton pattern. The pattern is described below in more general language using the key elements of the pattern template that we discussed in Section 15.3.

- *Name.* **Singleton**.
- *Problem.* How can a class be constructed that should have only one instance and that can be accessed globally within the application?
- *Context.* In some applications it is important that a class has exactly one instance. A sales order processing application may be dealing with sales for one company. It is necessary to have a `Company` object that holds details of the company's name,

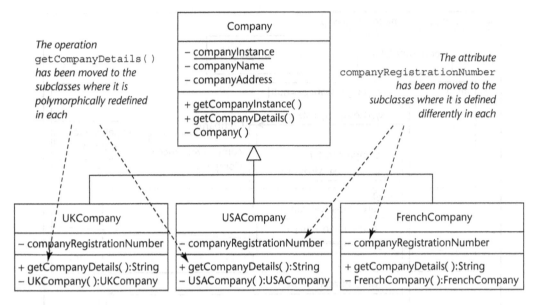

The operation
`getCompanyDetails()`
*has been moved to the
subclasses where it is
polymorphically redefined
in each*

The attribute
`companyRegistrationNumber`
*has been moved to the
subclasses where it is defined
differently in each*

Figure 15.4 Company class with subclasses.

address, taxation reference number and so on. Clearly there should be only one such object. Alternative forms of a singleton object may be required depending upon initial circumstances.

- *Forces.* One approach to making an object globally accessible is to make it a global variable, but in general this is not a good design solution as it violates information hiding. Another approach is not to create an object instance at all but to use class operations and attributes (called 'static' in C++ and Java). However, this limits the extensibility of the model since polymorphic redefinition of class operations is not possible in all development environments (for example C++).

- *Solution.* Create a class with a class operation `getInstance()`, which, when the class is first accessed, creates the relevant object instance and returns the object identity to the requesting object. On subsequent accesses of the `getInstance()` operation no additional instance is created but the object identity of the existing object is returned. A class diagram fragment for the singleton pattern is shown in Fig. 15.5.

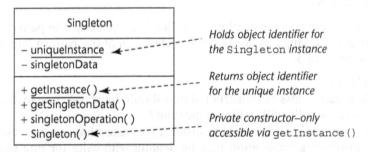

*Holds object identifier for
the* Singleton *instance*

*Returns object identifier
for the unique instance*

*Private constructor–only
accessible via* getInstance()

Figure 15.5 Creational patterns—Singleton.

The Singleton pattern offers several advantages but also has some disadvantages.

+ It provides controlled access to the sole object instance as the `Singleton` class encapsulates the instance.
+ The namespace is not unnecessarily extended with global variables.
+ The `Singleton` class may be subclassed. At system start-up, user-selected options may determine which of the subclasses is instantiated when the `Singleton` class is first accessed.
+ A variation of this pattern can be used to create a specified number of instances if required.
− Using the pattern introduces some additional message passing. To access the singleton instance the class scope operation `getInstance()` has to be accessed first rather than accessing the instance directly.
− The pattern limits the flexibility of the application. If requirements change, and many instances of the `Singleton` class are needed, then accommodating this new requirement necessitates significant modification to the system.
− The Singleton pattern is quite well known and developers are tempted to use it in circumstances that are inappropriate.

In UML terms a pattern describes a collaboration and the interaction of the participating elements that provide the required functionality. A pattern may be documented as a template collaboration, as shown in Fig. 15.6. In essence a template collaboration is a parameterized collaboration that may be implemented (that is, instantiated) with different classes or objects. The notation describes the pattern in terms of the roles that the participants occupy. In the case of the Singleton pattern there is only one role, `Singleton` class, and this is occupied by the `Company` class as in Fig. 15.6.

15.4.3 Structural patterns

Structural patterns address issues concerned with the way in which classes and objects are organized. Structural patterns offer effective ways of using object-oriented constructs such as inheritance, aggregation and composition to satisfy particular requirements. For

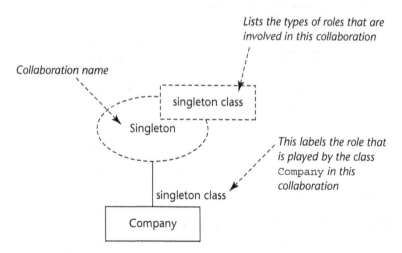

Figure 15.6 Template collaboration for `Singleton` pattern implemented with the class `Company`.

instance, there may be a requirement for a particular aspect of the application to be extensible. In order to achieve this, the application should be designed with constructs that minimize the side-effects of future change. Alternatively, it may be necessary to provide the same interface for a series of objects of different classes.

Composite pattern

It may be appropriate to apply the Composite structural pattern in a design for the Agate case study. In the following example we assume that further work is required to design a multimedia application that can store and play components of an advert.

Here an advert is made up of sound clips and video clips, each of which may be played individually or as part of an advert. The classes SoundClip and VideoClip have attributes and operations in common and it is appropriate that these classes are subclassed from MediaClip (Fig. 15.7). However, not all advert clips are primitive (that is, made up of only a single MediaClip). Some consist of one or more sequences of clips, such that each sequence is in turn an aggregation of SoundClip and VideoClip objects (Fig. 15.8).

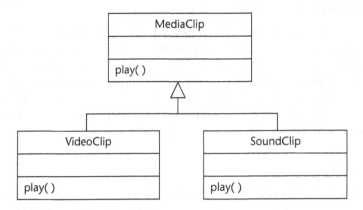

Figure 15.7 MediaClip inheritance hierarchy.

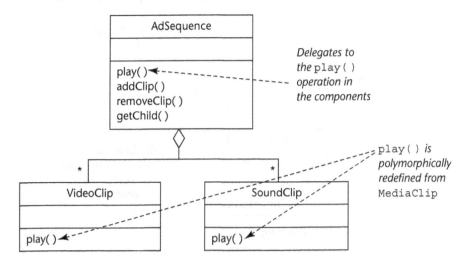

Figure 15.8 AdSequence aggregation hierarchy.

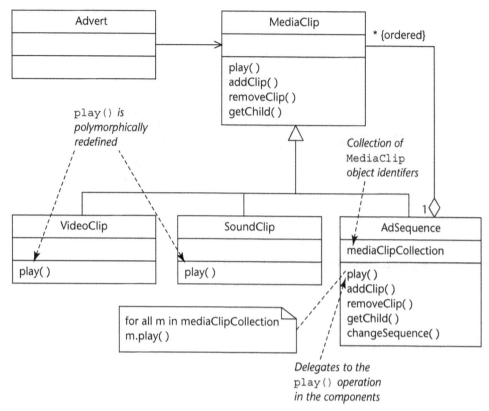

Figure 15.9 Integrating the two hierarchies for `MediaClip`.

These two orthogonal[2] hierarchies can be integrated by treating `AdSequence` both as a subclass of `MediaClip` and as an aggregation of `MediaClip` objects (see Fig. 15.9).

All the subclasses in Fig. 15.9 include the polymorphically redefined operation `play()`. For the subclasses `VideoClip` and `SoundClip` this operation actually plays the object. But for an `AdSequence` object, an invocation of the `play()` operation results in it sending a `play()` message to each of its components in turn. This structure is a straightforward application of the Composite pattern where a `MediaClip` object and an `AdSequence` object provide a common interface in part.

Figure 15.10 shows the template collaboration diagram for the `Composite pattern` with its roles and types and Fig. 15.11 shows the allocation of particular classes to the roles. Figure 15.12 contains another type of UML diagram, a composite structure diagram. The top compartment of the diagram references an interaction diagram that describes the interaction and the lower compartment shows the key relationships between the participating elements. A sequence diagram describing the interaction for the operation `play()` in an `AdSequence` object is shown in Fig. 15.13. The interaction constraint uses the OCL `size()` operation to get the size of the collection `mediaClipCollection`. The Composite pattern is described more generally below:

---

2 The term literally means 'at right angles to each other'. It is more loosely used here to describe hierarchies that cannot be directly mapped onto each other.

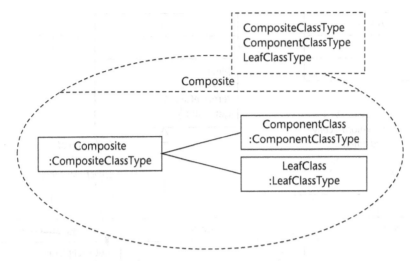

Figure 15.10 Template collaboration for `Composite Pattern`.

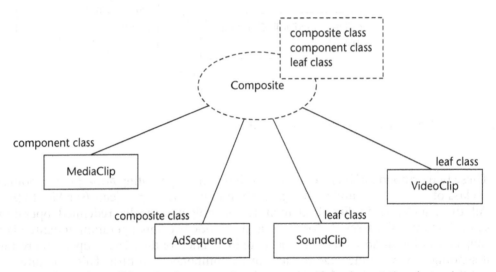

Figure 15.11 Template collaboration for `Composite Pattern` with implementation classes shown.

- *Name*. **Composite**.
- *Problem*. There is a requirement to represent whole–part hierarchies so that both whole and part objects offer the same interface to client objects.
- *Context*. In an application both composite and component objects exist and are required to offer the same behaviour. Client objects should be able to treat composite or component objects in the same way. A commonly used example for the composite pattern is a graphical drawing package. Using this software package a user can create (from the perspective of the software package) atomic objects like circle or square and can also group a series of atomic objects or composite objects together to make a new composite object. It should be possible to move or copy this composite object in exactly the same

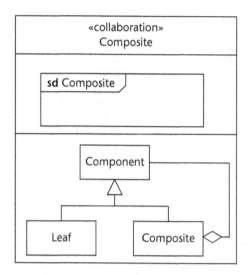

Figure 15.12 Composite structure diagram for the Composite Pattern.

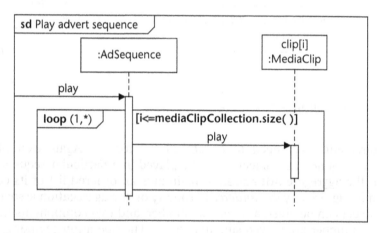

Figure 15.13 Sequence diagram for the interaction Play advert sequence.

way as it is possible to move or copy an individual square or a circle. See Figs 8.5 and 8.6 which illustrate a straightforward composition without using the Composite pattern.

■ *Forces.* The requirement that the objects, whether composite or component, offer the same interface suggests that they belong to the same inheritance hierarchy. This enables operations to be inherited and to be polymorphically redefined with the same signature. The need to represent whole–part hierarchies indicates the need for an aggregation structure.

■ *Solution.* The solution resolves the issues by combining inheritance and aggregation hierarchies. Both subclasses, Leaf and Composite, have a polymorphically redefined operation anOperation(). In Composite this redefined operation invokes the relevant operation from its components using a simple loop construct (Fig. 15.14). The Composite subclass also has additional operations to manage the aggregation hierarchy so that components may be added or removed.

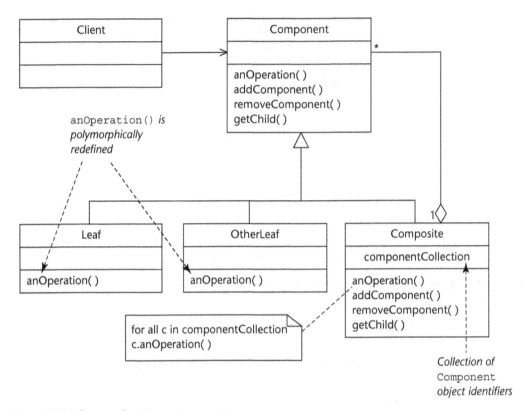

Figure 15.14 Structural patterns—Composite.

Further requirements may need to be considered for the Agate example. Perhaps VideoClip and SoundClip objects must be played in a particular sequence. This can be handled if the aggregate AdSequence maintains an ordered list of its components. This is shown in Fig. 15.9 by the {*ordered*} property on the aggregation association. Each component object can be given a sequence number, and two components that have the same sequence number are played simultaneously. The operation changeSequence() allows a component MediaClip object to be moved up or down within the sequence of clips in the advertisement (Fig. 15.9).

15.4.4 Behavioural patterns

Behavioural patterns address the problems that arise when responsibilities are assigned to classes and in designing algorithms. Behavioural patterns not only suggest particular static relationships between objects and classes but also describe how the objects communicate. Behavioural patterns may use inheritance structures to spread behaviour across the subclasses or they may use aggregation and composition to build complex behaviour from simpler components. The State pattern, which is considered below, uses both of these techniques.

State pattern
Let us examine the Agate case study to determine whether it has features that may justify the application of the State pattern. First, are there any objects with significant

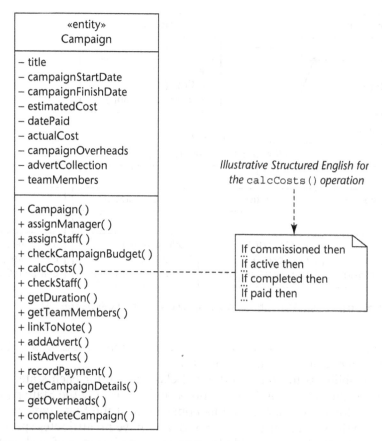

Figure 15.15 The Campaign class.

state-dependent behaviour? Campaign objects have behaviour that varies according to state; a Campaign object may be in one of four main states, as shown in Fig. 11.20 (for simplicity we ignore the substates of the Active state). Clearly a Campaign object's state changes dynamically as the campaign progresses, thus necessitating changes in the behaviour of the object.

For example, when the FoodCo campaign is planned a Campaign object is created in the Commissioned state. It remains in this state until a campaign budget has been agreed and only then does it become possible to run advertisements, although some preparatory work may be done for the campaign in the meantime. Once a Campaign object enters the Active state, all advert preparation and any other work that is done is subject to an agreed billing schedule. Several operations, for example addAdvert() and calcCosts(), will behave differently depending upon the state of the Campaign object. It would be possible to construct a working version of the software using the design for the Campaign class that is shown in Fig. 15.15. However, this would be a complex class that is further complicated by state-dependent operations such as calcCosts(), which would need to be specified with a series of case or if–then–else statements to test the state of the object. It would be simpler to subdivide the operations that have state-dependent behaviour, which in this case would result in four separate calcCosts() operations, one for each state. The inclusion of calcCostsCommissioned(), calcCostsActive()

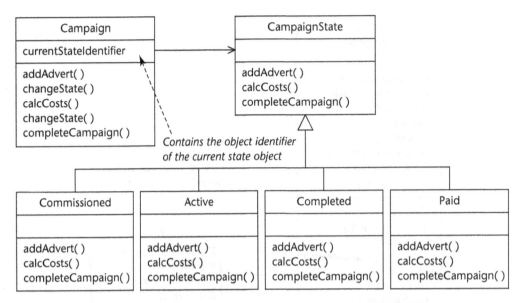

Figure 15.16 State pattern for Agate showing a simplified version of `Campaign` class.

and so on within `Campaign` would simplify the operation `calcCosts()`, but the class as a whole would become even more complex.

Another possibility is to create additional classes, one for each state, so that each holds a state-specific version of the operations, and this is how the State pattern works. A class diagram fragment illustrating this application of the State pattern is shown in Fig. 15.16. Since the subclasses of `CampaignState` have no attributes specific to a particular `Campaign` object, it is possible to have only one instance of each in the system. Thus there will be a maximum of four `CampaignState` objects, one for each state, and the additional overhead of manipulating the objects is unlikely to be significant (Fig. 15.16). These are examples of *pure state classes* as they contain no attributes. They could be implemented using a variation of the Singleton pattern that ensures one and only one instance of each subclass will exist (this differs from its more usual application of ensuring that there is at most one object for a whole hierarchy).

Figure 15.17 shows some sample `Campaign` objects linked to their state objects. The object c:Campaign and e:Campaign both have links to the :Active state object. This is a pure state object and has no attributes for any particular campaign and can be used by more than one `Campaign` object at a time. Any state dependent messages that are received by c:Campaign, for example `calcCosts()`, will essentially be passed on to the object whose identifier is held in the `currentState` attribute. In this case, for c:Campaign a `calcCosts()` message will be sent to the :Active object. If d:Campaign receives a `calcCosts()` message, this will result in a `calcCosts()` message being sent to :Completed. The state object that receives the `calcCosts()` message is determined by the value of `currentState` without the need for any conditional statements.

The State pattern is described more generally below.

■ *Name*. **State**.
■ *Problem*. An object exhibits different behaviour when its internal state changes making the object appear to change class at run-time.

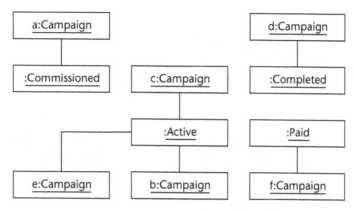

Figure 15.17 Some State pattern objects for Agate.

- *Context.* In some applications an object may have complex behaviour that is dependent upon its state. In other words, the response to a particular message varies according to the object's state. One example is the `calcCosts()` operation in the `Campaign` class.
- *Forces.* The object has complex behaviour, which should be factored into less complex elements. One or more operations have behaviour that varies according to the state of the object. Typically the operation would have large, multi-part conditional statements depending on the state. One approach is to have separate public operations for each state but client objects would need to know the state of the object so that they could invoke the appropriate operation. For example, four operations `calcCostsCommissioned()`, `calcCostsActive()`, `calcCostsCompleted()` and `calcCostsPaid()` would be required for the `Campaign` object. The client object would need to know the state of the `Campaign` object in order to invoke the relevant `calcCosts()` operation. This would result in undesirably tight coupling between the client object and the `Campaign` object. An alternative approach is to have a single public `calcCosts()` operation that invokes the relevant private operation (`calcCostsCommissioned()` would be private). However, the inclusion of a separate private operation for each state may result in a large complex object that is difficult to construct, test and maintain.
- *Solution.* The State pattern separates the state-dependent behaviour from the original object and allocates this behaviour to a series of other objects, one for each state. These state objects then have sole responsibility for that state's behaviour. The original object, shown as `Context` in Fig. 15.18, delegates responsibility to the appropriate state object. The original object becomes an aggregate of its states, only one of which is active at one time. The state objects form an inheritance hierarchy.

The responsibility for transitions from one state to another may either be taken by the `Context` class or it may be shared among the `State` subclasses. If the rules for state changes are volatile and subject to change, it may be better for the current `State` object to be responsible for the next transition. In this way the current state object always knows all the states into which the object may move next. However, this has the disadvantage of producing dependencies between state subclasses.

For example, in Fig. 15.19 the `:Campaign` object (the `Context` object) receives the `completeCampaign()` message. This results in a `completeCampaign()` message being sent to the current state object, in this case represented by the `:Active` object.

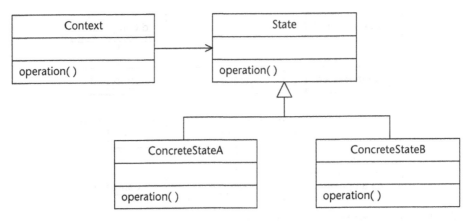

Figure 15.18 Behavioural patterns—State.

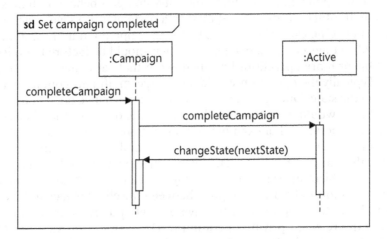

Figure 15.19 Sequence diagram for the interaction Set campaign completed.

The completeCampaign operation in the Active class then sends the changeState(nextState) message back to the :Campaign object and places the object identifier for the next state object (:Completed) in the currentState attribute. When the :Campaign object next receives a state dependent message, it will be passed on to the :Completed object. In Fig. 15.19 it is assumed that the Active state object already exists. As it is a pure state object, it could be created using the Singleton pattern the first time it is accessed.

Figure 15.20 shows the template collaboration for the State pattern and the classes allocated to the roles shown in Fig. 15.18.

If the Campaign class was taking responsibility for managing the state, there would a be a nextState() message from the :Campaign object to itself when it received the completeCampaign() message.

If it is not appropriate to use pure state classes, then a new state object may have to be created whenever a Context object changes state and the old state object may have

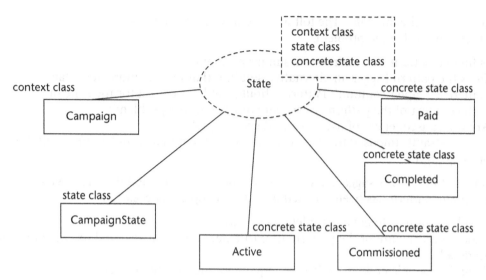

Figure 15.20 Template collaboration for `State Pattern`.

to be deleted. This increases processing load for various transactions and may affect performance.

Use of the State pattern has both advantages and disadvantages, the latter particularly in terms of its possible side-effects on system performance.

+ State behaviour is localized and the behaviour for different states is separated. This eases any enhancement of the state behaviour, in particular the addition of extra states.
+ State transitions are made explicit. The state object that is currently active indicates the current state of the `Context` object.
+ Where a state object has no attributes relevant to a specific `Context` object it may be shared among the `Context` objects. This State object is a Singleton!
− If the State objects cannot be shared among the `Context` objects, each `Context` object will have to have its own State object thus increasing the number of objects and the storage requirements for the system.
− State objects may have to be created and deleted as the `Context` object changes state, thus introducing a processing overhead.
− Use of the State pattern introduces at least one extra message, the message from the `Context` class to the State class, thus adding a further processing overhead.

15.5 How to Use Design Patterns

When using a pattern the problem that is being addressed and its context must be carefully analysed. Before contemplating the application of patterns within a software development environment it is important to ensure that all members of the team are trained in the use of patterns.

When a developer identifies a part of the application that may be subject to high coupling, a large, complex class or any other undesirable feature, there may be a pattern that addresses the difficulty. The following issues should be considered before employing a pattern to resolve the problem.

- Is there a pattern that addresses a similar problem?
- Does the pattern trigger an alternative solution that may be more acceptable?
- Is there a simpler solution? Patterns should not be used just for the sake of it.
- Is the context of the pattern consistent with that of the problem?
- Are the consequences of using the pattern acceptable?
- Are constraints imposed by the software environment that would conflict with the use of the pattern?

Gamma et al. (1995) suggest a seven-part procedure that should be followed after an appropriate pattern has been selected in order to apply it successfully.

1. Read the pattern to get a complete overview.
2. Study the structure of the pattern, its participants (e.g. classes) and its collaborations in detail.
3. Examine sample code to review an implementation of the pattern.
4. Choose names for the classes that relate to the application context.
5. Define the classes.
6. Give the operations application-specific names.
7. Implement operations that perform the necessary responsibilities and collaboration.

A pattern should not be viewed as a prescriptive solution but rather as guidance on how to find a suitable solution. It is quite likely (in fact almost certainly the case) that a pattern will be used differently in each particular set of circumstances. At a simple level the classes involved will have attributes and operations that are determined by application requirements. Often a pattern is modified to accommodate contextual differences. For example, the inclusion of the changeSequence() operation shown in Fig. 15.9 represents a variation on the Composite pattern to allow the sequence of MediaClip objects in AdSequence to be changed. When a developer is considering using a pattern to address a problem this may suggest to the developer some other design solution that is better than using the pattern itself.

If patterns are going to be used by a developer, then relevant pattern catalogues and languages should be made available and easily accessible. Many patterns are documented on the Internet or on company intranets. It is important to consider the way a pattern is documented so that it is easy for the developer to determine its applicability. The minimum information we suggest to document a pattern is described earlier in Section 15.3. Modelling tool support for patterns has developed and is provided by some vendors. Some tools allow the user to select classes and apply a pattern to them, or to import a pattern template set of classes into a model and rename the classes to fit the application domain.

Software developers may wish to capture their experience in a pattern format and build their own pattern catalogue or language. The process of identifying patterns is known as *pattern mining* and requires careful validation and management to ensure that the patterns that are captured suggest good solutions to recurring problems. Again, the pattern elements described earlier provide a checklist against which any candidate pattern can be compared.

If a pattern satisfies these criteria, then its quality should be assured via a walk-through. The most commonly used form of walkthrough for a pattern is known as a pattern writer's workshop. This involves a small of group of pattern authors who constructively comment upon each other's patterns. The focus of a workshop helps the participants describe useful patterns effectively.

15.6 Benefits and Dangers of Using Patterns

One of the most sought-after benefits of object-orientation is reuse. Reuse at the object and class levels has proved more elusive than was expected in the early days of object-orientation. Patterns provide a mechanism for the reuse of generic solutions for object-oriented and other approaches. They embody a strong reuse culture. Within the design context, patterns suggest reusable elements of design and, most significantly, reusable elements of demonstrably successful designs. This reuse permits the transfer of expertise to less experienced developers so that a pattern can be applied again and again.

Another benefit gained from patterns is that they offer a vocabulary for discussing the problem domain (whether it be analysis, design or some other aspect of information systems development) at a higher level of abstraction than the class and object, making it easier to consider micro-architectural issues and systems architecture as well. Pattern catalogues and pattern languages offer a rich source of experience that can be explored and provide patterns that can be used together to generate effective systems.

Some people believe that the use of patterns can limit creativity. Since a pattern provides a standard solution, the developer may be tempted not to spend time on considering alternatives. The use of patterns in an uncontrolled manner may lead to over-design. Developers may be tempted to use many patterns irrespective of their benefits, thus rendering the software system more difficult to develop, maintain and enhance. When a pattern is used in an inappropriate context, the side-effects may be disastrous. For example, the use of the State pattern may significantly increase the number of objects in the application with a consequent reduction in performance. If the concrete state classes are not pure state classes (i.e. they hold attributes), then it will not be possible to share state classes, as is shown in Fig. 15.17. Each context class may need its own state class and the total number of objects could be doubled, resulting in an additional procession load for object creation and deletion as states change.

The introduction of any new approach to software development has costs for the organization. Developers need to spend time understanding the relevant pattern catalogues, they need to be provided with easy access to the relevant catalogues and they need to be trained in the use of patterns. Another aspect of the introduction of patterns is the necessary cultural change. Patterns can only be used effectively in the context of an organizational culture of reuse. Ironically, the introduction of a patterns approach may arouse less opposition to the encouragement of a reuse culture than an attempt to introduce procedures for code reuse. Developers need to think about how to apply a pattern to their current context, and thus there are greater opportunities for individual creativity.

These issues emphasize that the use of patterns in software development requires care and planning. In this respect patterns are no different from any other form of problem solving: they must be used with intelligence and an awareness of any side-effects. It is also important to appreciate that patterns address only some of the issues that occur during systems development. In no way should patterns be viewed as a 'silver bullet' that conquers all problems in systems development.

15.7 Summary

This chapter has considered how patterns can be used in software development. Patterns have been identified in many different application domains and are applicable at many different stages of the software development process. A significant aspect of the growth of interest in patterns is the increased awareness of design issues that follows as a consequence. Patterns represent a important change in the reuse culture in software development. Reuse need no longer be focused solely on elements of code, whether these are individual classes or complex frameworks, but realistically can also include the reuse of analysis or design ideas as described by patterns.

Related patterns are grouped together in catalogues. A pattern language is a group of patterns focused on a particular aspect of a problem domain so that when used together they provide solutions to the problems that arise.

Review Questions

15.1 What is the difference between a pattern and a framework and how is each used?

15.2 What are the main aspects of changeability?

15.3 Why is the class constructor private in the Singleton pattern?

15.4 What are the advantages of using the Singleton pattern?

15.5 What are the disadvantages of using the Singleton pattern?

15.6 What implementation problems may occur when using the State pattern?

15.7 What are the differences between a pattern language and a pattern catalogue?

15.8 List two general dangers and two general benefits of the use of patterns.

15.9 What seven steps are suggested by Gamma et al. for the effective use of patterns?

15.10 What are the advantages of using the Composite pattern?

Case Study Work, Exercises and Projects

15.A Read the design patterns Bridge and Decorator in Gamma et al. (1995) and rewrite their description using the structure of the template given in Section 15.3.

15.B In the FoodCo case study the ProductionLine class might be a candidate for design using the State pattern. Show how a variation of the State pattern could handle this requirement. What benefits and disadvantages are there in applying this solution?

15.C Where and how could the Singleton pattern be used in the FoodCo case study? Prepare a design class specification for a suitable Singleton class.

Further Reading

Gamma et al. (1995) and Buschmann et al. (1996) are two excellent texts that give important advice concerning software construction and should be on the essential reading list of any software developer. Schmidt et al. (2000) provide a further set of architectural patterns. Even where the patterns they discuss are not directly relevant, there is much to learn from their approach to solving design problems.

The 'Pattern Languages of Program Design' (known as the PLOP) books (Coplien and Schmidt, 1995; Vlissides et al., 1996; Martin et al., 1998; Harrison et al., 2000; Manolescu, 2006) catalogue a wide range of patterns for all aspects of software development.

The Hillside Group maintains a large body of information about patterns on its website at http://hillside.net/. This site hosts an online catalogue of patterns at http://hillside.net/patterns/onlinepatterncatalog.htm.

Further useful patterns are available in the Portland Pattern Repository at http://c2.com/ppr/. IBM Patterns for e-Business can be found at the website http://www-128.ibm.com/developerworks/patterns/.

A series of Java related patterns (some architectural and some design) are available at http://developer.java.sun.com/developer/technicalArticles/J2EE/patterns/. Two other more recent texts are *Core J2EE Patterns* (Alur et al., 2003) and Metsker's (2002) *Design Patterns Java Workbook*.

Chapter 16

Human–Computer Interaction

16.1 Introduction

Human–computer interaction (HCI) is the discipline of designing effective interaction between people and the information systems that they use; it combines the techniques of psychology and ergonomics with those of computer science. Designing the user interface can be critical in the development of an information system. The interface is what the users see. To them it *is* the system. Their attitude towards the entire system can be coloured by their experience of the user interface. Before we move on to the design of the classes that make up the user interface in Chapter 17, we will address some of the HCI issues that influence the design of the user interface.

This chapter is about the human factors aspects of designing the inputs into and outputs from information systems. The inputs and outputs can be in the conventional form of data entry and enquiry screens and printed reports, or they can take the form of speech recognition, scanners, touch screens, gestures and movements of handheld remote devices. We shall be concentrating on the conventional inputs and outputs used in information systems, although we recognize that the growth in the use of multimedia systems means that even quite conventional business information systems may incorporate multiple media as inputs and outputs.

There are two metaphors that are widely used to represent the user interface: first, the idea that the user is conducting a dialogue with the system, and, second, the idea that the user is directly manipulating objects on screen. Much HCI work in the past has concentrated on producing guidelines for dialogue design, and we include a section on the characteristics of a good dialogue.

It is possible to adopt an informal approach to designing the human–computer interaction for a system in which the designer considers the nature of the task that the user is carrying out, the type of user, the amount of training that the user will have undertaken, the frequency of use and the hardware and software architecture of the system. There are more formal approaches available, using structured, ethnographic or scenario-based approaches to HCI design. The scenario-based method is closest to the object-oriented approach that uses use cases to document the requirements for the system.

There are a number of international standards for the ergonomics of workstation design and, for European readers, legal obligations for HCI design that are imposed by the European Union's directive on health and safety requirements for work with display screens. With the growth of the Internet and the use of World Wide Web (WWW) technologies for intranets and access to information systems within organizations, accessibility of user interfaces for people with disabilities has become an important HCI issue. We highlight the legal requirements for accessibility and some of the initiatives that set guidelines to improve the accessibility of browser-based user interfaces.

16.2 | User Interface

16.2.1 What is the user interface?

Users of an information system need to interact with it in some way. Whether they are users of FoodCo's telesales system entering orders made over the telephone by customers, or members of the public using a touch-screen system to find tourist information, they will need to carry out the following tasks:

- read and interpret information that instructs them how to use the system;
- issue commands to the system to indicate what they want to do;
- enter words and numbers into the system to provide it with data to work with;
- read and interpret the results that are produced by the system, either on screen or as a printed report;
- respond to and correct errors.

It is important to note that these are mostly secondary tasks: they are concerned with using the system, not with the users' primary objectives. In the examples above, the primary tasks are to take a customer order and to find tourist information. If the system has been designed well, the secondary, system-related tasks will be easy to carry out; if it has not been designed well, the secondary tasks will intrude into the process and will make it more difficult for the users to achieve their primary tasks.

16.2.2 Dialogue metaphor

In the design of many computer systems, interaction between the user and the system takes the form of a *dialogue*. The idea that the user is carrying on a dialogue with the system is a *metaphor*. (A metaphor is a term that is used figuratively to describe something but is not applied literally.) There is no real dialogue in the sense of a conversation

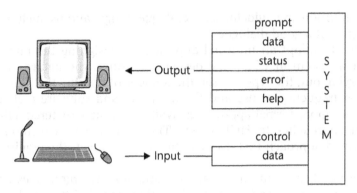

Figure 16.1 Schematic form of human–computer dialogue.

Output	prompt	Request for user input
	data	Data from application following user request
	status	Acknowledgement that something has happened
	error	Processing cannot continue
	help	Additional information to user
Input	control	User directs which way dialogue will proceed
	data	Data supplied by user

Figure 16.2 Types of messages in human–computer dialogue.

between people going on between the user and the computer,[1] but as in dialogues between people, messages are passed from one participant to the other. Figure 16.1 shows the human–computer dialogue in schematic form. Figure 16.2 describes what is meant by each of the types of message that can be found in this dialogue.

Figure 16.3 shows a sample screen layout from FoodCo's existing system, which runs on a mini-computer with displays on dumb terminals. Although this shows only one screen, you can describe it in terms of the dialogue between the user and the system.

- The user may enter a command by selecting an option from a menu (not shown).
- The system responds with this data entry screen and automatically displays the Order Date and next Order No.
- The user enters a Customer Code.
- The system responds with the name and brief address of the customer as a confirmation that the correct number has been entered.

And so on. Such screens may be unfamiliar to many readers, who have only ever experienced windowing interfaces, but used to be the only way of entering data into computer systems and are still widely used in older business systems.

The dialogue may not take exactly the same form each time that a user enters data into this screen. Sometimes the user may not know the Customer Code and may have to

---

1 Although speech recognition and text to speech systems now make voice input and output possible, even if it is not yet a true dialogue.

```
┌─────────────────────────────────────────────────────────────────────────┐
│  CUSTORD1              Customer Order Entry              25/04/2010       │
│                                                                           │
│  Order Date 25/04/2010              Order No.      37291                 │
│  Customer Code CE102_ Central Stores, Lytham St Annes                    │
│  Customer Order Ref. R20716__                                            │
│                                                                           │
│       Prod.     Product                              Unit     Line       │
│       Code      Description                 Qty      Price    Price      │
│    01 12-75__   Sandwich spread 24 × 250g    _3      18.00    54.00      │
│    02 09-103_   Brown sauce 30 × 500g       _10      24.60   246.00      │
│    03 _____                              ____                         │
│    04 _____                              ____                         │
│    05 _____                              ____                         │
│    06 _____                              ____                         │
│    07 _____                              ____                         │
│    08 _____                              ____                         │
│                                             ____                         │
│                                             Total            300.00      │
│                                             Tax               52.50      │
│                                             Order            _____     │
│                                             Total            352.50      │
│                                                                           │
│  F1-Help    F2-Save   F3-Cancel   F4-New   F5-Cust.   F6-Prod.           │
│  F10-Exit                          Cust.   Lookup     Lookup            │
└─────────────────────────────────────────────────────────────────────────┘
```

Figure 16.3 FoodCo customer order entry screen layout with sample data.

use some kind of index look-up facility, perhaps entering the first few characters of the customer name in order to view a display of customers that start with those characters. Sometimes an order may consist of one line, usually it will consist of more and, if it consists of more than eight, it will be necessary to clear those that have been entered from the screen and display space for a further eight lines to be entered. It also illustrates elements of the interface that support some of the message types listed in Fig. 16.2. These are described in Fig. 16.4.

In the requirements model of the new system for FoodCo, there will be a use case for Enter customer order, as in Fig. 16.5. This will be supported by a use case description, which may be quite brief early in the project. As the project progresses through further iterations, the use case description will be filled out in more detail. Not all the use cases will be for interactive dialogues: some will be for enquiries and some will be for printed reports. Figure 16.6 shows some of the use cases that the FoodCo sales clerks use. For each of these use cases there may be a sequence diagram to show the interaction between the collaborating objects. However, these sequence diagrams will not yet show the details of the interaction between the user and the system at the interface. This will be covered in Section 17.5.

16.2.3 Direct manipulation metaphor

The other metaphor for the design of the user interface, which has become more widespread in the last few years, is the *direct manipulation* metaphor. Most people are now familiar with this through the use of GUIs. When you use a software package with this

Output	prompt	Request for user input and labels for automatically generated data, shown in bold, for example Customer Code
	data	Automatic display of Order Date and next Order No., automatic calculation of totals and tax (shown in italics to distinguish it from input data)
	status	Screen heading; could include display to confirm that a new order has been saved
	error	Messages to warn of incorrect data entered, for example if a Customer Code is entered that does not exist or if a negative Quantity is entered
	help	Additional information to user in response to the user pressing F1; may be general about the order entry screen or context-sensitive—specific to a particular type of data entry
Input	control	Use of function keys to control dialogue
	data	Numbers, codes and quantities typed in by user

Figure 16.4 Examples of types of messages in human–computer dialogue.

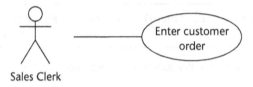

Sales Clerk

Enter customer order

Enter Customer Code or look up customer in index. For each line of the order, enter Product No. and Quantity. Calculate Line Price, Tax and totals automatically.

Figure 16.5 Use case diagram and description for `Enter customer order`.

kind of interface you are given the impression that you are using the mouse to manipulate objects on the screen. This metaphor is reflected in the concrete nature of the terms used. You can:

- drag and drop an icon
- shrink or expand a window
- push a button
- pull down a menu.

(Though many of the metaphors break down if examined too closely. Why would you put an open window on your desktop?) Such interfaces are *event-driven*. Graphical objects are displayed on the screen and the window management part of the operating system responds to events. Most such events are the result of the user's actions. The user can click on a button, type a character, press a function key, click on a menu item or hold down a mouse button and move the mouse. The design of user interfaces to support this kind of interaction is more complicated than for text-based interfaces using the dialogue metaphor, and is becoming more complicated still with the advent of user interface devices such as the WiiMote for the Nintendo Wii, which the user wields as though it were a tennis racket, golf club, sword or whatever.

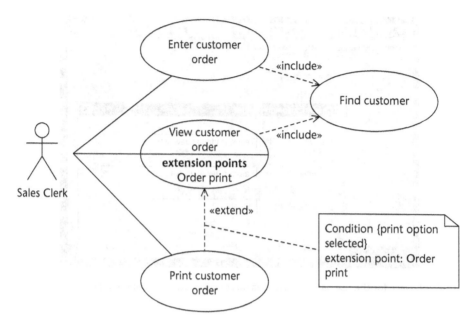

Figure 16.6 Use case diagram showing use cases used by sales clerks at FoodCo.

Figure 16.7 shows the interface of a Java program to implement the use case Check campaign budget for the Agate case study. In this use case, the user first selects the name of a client from a list box labelled **Client**. Having selected the client, a list of all active campaigns for that client is placed in the list box labelled **Campaign**. At this point, no campaign is selected, and the user can click on the arrow at the end of the list box to view the list and select a campaign. When a campaign has been selected, the user can click on the button labelled **Check**. The program then totals up the cost of adverts in that campaign, subtracts it from the budget and displays the balance as a money value (negative if the campaign is over budget). In this interface design, there is no point in the user selecting a campaign until a client has been selected or clicking the **Check** button until a client and a campaign have been selected. The designer may choose to disable the **Campaign** list box until the client has been selected, and disable the button until both client and campaign have been selected. Having checked one campaign, the user may choose a different client, in which case the contents of the **Campaign** list box have to be changed and the button disabled again until a different campaign has been selected. In Section 17.8 we use state machine diagrams to model the state of elements of a user interface like this in order to ensure that we have correctly specified the behaviour of the interface.

Windows like the one in Fig. 16.7 are usually called *dialogue boxes* in GUI environments. In terms of the metaphors that we have discussed, they combine elements of a dialogue with the user with direct manipulation of buttons and lists.

16.2.4 Characteristics of good dialogues

Many authors of books and reports on HCI have produced sets of guidelines to help designers to produce good designs for the user interface. Some such guidelines are

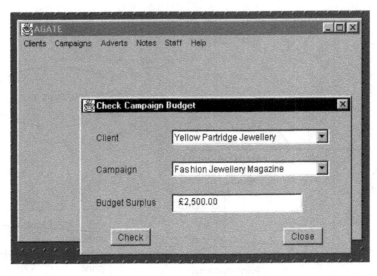

Figure 16.7 Interface for the use case Check Campaign Budget developed in Java.

specific to certain types of interface. Shneiderman et al. (2009) propose five high-level objectives for data entry dialogue design that date back to the original edition in 1986 when most interfaces were text-based. Other authors such as Gaines and Shaw (1983), also writing at a time when text-based interfaces were predominant, have proposed as many as seventeen.

Regardless of whether a system is being developed for a text-based environment or for a GUI environment, there are a number of important general characteristics of good dialogue design. These include:

- consistency
- appropriate user support
- adequate feedback from the system
- minimal user input.

These are considered in turn below.

Consistency

A consistent user interface design helps users to learn an application and to apply what they know across different parts of that application. This applies to commands, the format for the entry of data such as dates, the layout of screens and the way that information is coded by the use of colour or highlighting. As an example of a command, if the user has to press function key F2 to save data in one part of the system, then they will expect the key to have the same effect elsewhere in the system. If it does not result in data being saved then they will have made an error. The outcome of this could be that pressing F2 does something else that the user did not expect, or that it does nothing, but the user thinks that they have saved the data and then exits without saving it. Whichever is the case, the user is likely to become annoyed or frustrated at the response of the system. Guidelines in corporate style guides or in those from Microsoft and Apple help to prevent this kind of user frustration. Style guides are discussed in Section 16.2.5.

Appropriate user support
When the user does not know what action to take or has made an error, it is important that the system provides appropriate support at the interface. This support can be informative and prevent errors by providing help messages, or it can assist the user in diagnosing what has gone wrong and in recovering from their error. Help messages should be context-sensitive. This means that the help system should be able to detect where the user has got to in a dialogue and provide relevant information. In a GUI environment, this means being able to detect which component of the interface is active (or has the *focus*) and providing help that is appropriate to that part of the interface. The help provided may be general, explaining the overall function of a particular screen or window, or it may be specific, explaining the purpose of a particular field or graphical component and listing the options available to the user. It may be necessary to provide a link between different levels of help so that the user can move between them to find the information they require. The hypertext style of help in Microsoft Windows provides this facility. Help information may be displayed in separate screens or windows, it may be displayed simultaneously in a status line as the user moves through the dialogue or it may be displayed using *tooltips* that appear as the user positions the cursor over an item. Many web page designers provide help about elements of their pages by displaying messages in the status line at the bottom of the browser window or by displaying a tooltip-style message in a box as the cursor moves over an item on the page.

Error messages serve a different purpose and require careful design to ensure that they inform rather than irritate the user. An error message that tells the user that he or she has just deleted an essential file and then expects the user to click on a button marked OK when it is anything but OK is likely to annoy the user. Error messages should explain what has gone wrong and they should also clearly explain what the user can or should do to recover the situation. This information should be in language that the user can understand. This may mean using jargon from the user's business that they will recognize and understand rather than using computer jargon. Figure 16.8 shows three different error message boxes for the same situation. Only one is really of any help to the user.

Warning messages can prevent the user from making serious errors by providing a warning or caution message before the system carries out a command from the user that is likely to result in an irreversible action. Warning messages should allow the user to cancel the action that is about to take place. Figure 16.9 shows an example of a warning message.

Adequate feedback from the system
Users expect the system to respond when they make some action. If they press a key during data entry, they expect to see the character appear on the screen (unless it is a control command or a function key); if they click on something with the mouse, they expect that item to be highlighted and some action from the system. Users who are uncertain whether the system has noticed their action keep on pressing keys or clicking with the mouse, with the possible result that these further keypresses and clicks are taken by the system to be the response to a later part of the dialogue, with unpredictable results. It is important that users know where they are in a dialogue or direct manipulation interface: in a text-based interface there should be a visible cursor in the current active field; in a GUI environment the active object in the interface should be highlighted. The

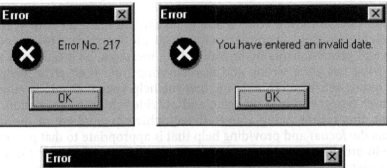

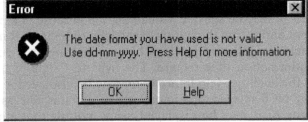

Figure 16.8 Example error messages for the same error.

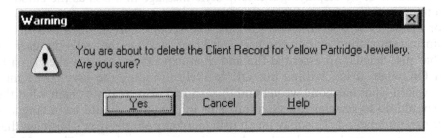

Figure 16.9 Example warning message.

Yes button in Fig. 16.9 is highlighted in this way, and this means that it will respond to the user pressing <Return> on the keyboard.

The system's response time should be appropriate to the type of user action: responses to data entry keypresses should be instantaneous, while responses to commands in menus or by means of buttons may take longer. If a system response is going to take some time, the system should respond first with some kind of feedback indicating that it is busy. This can be changing the cursor to a different form, or it can be displaying a progress monitor that shows what proportion of the task has been completed. If possible, the user should be given the option of cancelling the command. The purpose of this kind of feedback is to reduce the user's uncertainty about whether the system has received the input and is doing something about it or is waiting for the next input.

Minimal user input
Users resent making what they see as unnecessary keypresses and mouse clicks. Reducing unnecessary input also reduces the risk of errors and speeds data entry. The interface should be designed to minimize the amount of input from the user. The user can be helped in this way by:

- using codes and abbreviations;
- selecting from a list rather than having to enter a value;
- editing incorrect values or commands rather than having to type them in again;
- not having to enter or re-enter information that can be derived automatically;
- using default values.

Some of these have a basis in the psychological aspects of the discipline of HCI. For example, being able to select values from a list rather than having to enter them from memory allows the user to work by recognizing information rather than having to recall it.

It is also possible to reduce the amount of input as users become more familiar with a system by providing shortcuts or accelerators, key combinations that the user can use instead of selecting a command from a menu. However, these require the user to remember the key combinations and are less useful for new users, who will find menus easier to use.

16.2.5 Style guides

In Section 16.2.4 consistency of the interface has been highlighted as one of the characteristics of good dialogue design. Some organizations provide standard guidelines for the design of user interfaces. One way in which standardization of user interface design has come about is through the domination of the PC market by Microsoft. Microsoft produces a book of guidelines *The Windows Interface Guidelines for Software Design* (Microsoft, 1997) that lays down the standards to which developers must adhere if they are to be granted Windows certification. A more recent book is *Developing User Interfaces Microsoft for Windows* (McKay, 1999). Similar guidelines are available from Apple for the Apple Macintosh operating system—*Macintosh Human Interface Guidelines* (Apple, 1996). The effect of such guidelines is apparent in the similarity of many applications from different sources that make use of toolbars, status bars and dialogue boxes with buttons and other graphical components placed in similar positions. The benefit of this similarity for users is that different applications will look similar and behave in similar ways. This means that users can transfer their knowledge of existing applications to a new one and make inferences about the way that the new one will respond to certain types of user interaction.

Guidelines for user interface design are usually referred to as *style guides*, and large organizations with many different information systems produce their own style guides for the design of systems to ensure that all their applications, whether they are produced in-house or by outside software companies, conform to a standard set of rules that will enable users quickly to become familiar with a new application. Figure 16.3 reflects the use of an existing style guide in FoodCo. The layout of the screen with standard heading information at the top, the use of bold text to highlight prompts and labels, the position of the information about function keys and the use of specific function keys for particular commands are all standards within FoodCo for the design of text-based screens. This is important, as it means that a user can be confident that pressing function key F2 in any data entry screen will save the data on the screen.

The use of style guides and the characteristics of a good dialogue relate to dialogue and interface design in general. In the next part of this chapter, we consider how to ensure that the user interface is appropriate to the specific application for which it is being designed.

16.3 Approaches to User Interface Design

16.3.1 Informal and formal approaches

There are many different ways of designing and implementing the elements of the user interface that support the interaction with users. The choices that the designer makes will be influenced by a number of factors. These include:

- the nature of the task that the user is carrying out;
- the type of user;
- the amount of training that the user will have undertaken;
- the frequency of use;
- the hardware and software architecture of the system.

These factors may be very different for different systems. They are listed in Figure 16.10 for the FoodCo telesales system and a tourist information system for mobile PDAs and smartphones. Systems that are used by members of the public are very different from information systems used by staff. The Internet and Mobile Internet have made information systems available to people who are unlikely to receive training in using these systems, and who may have no experience of information systems in business settings.

This way of comparing the two systems and identifying factors that affect their design is very informal. More formal and methodical approaches to the analysis of usability requirements have been developed by researchers in the discipline of HCI. These approaches can be categorized under three headings:

	Telesales system	Tourist information system for mobile PDAs and smartphones
The nature of the task that the user is carrying out	Routine task; closed solution; limited options	Open-ended task; may be looking for information that is not available
The type of user	Clerical user of the system; no discretion about use (must use it to do their job)	Could be anyone; discretion about use of system; novice in relation to this system
The amount of training that the user will have undertaken	Training provided as part of job	No training provided
The frequency of use	Very frequent; taking an order every few minutes	Very occasional; may never use it again
The hardware and software architecture of the system	Mini-computer, dumb terminals with text screens, keyboard data entry. All software runs on the mini-computer. Structured programs with subroutines for data access and screen-painting	Mobile telephone screen with keypad and scroll buttons to move through menus. Browser runs on mobile PDA or smartphone HTML may be tailored to the screen size using XML and stylesheets

Figure 16.10 User interface design factors for two systems.

- structured approaches
- ethnographic approaches
- scenario-based approaches.

These approaches are very different from one another. However, they all carry out three main steps in HCI design:

- requirements gathering
- design of the interface
- interface evaluation.

Each of these approaches has similar objectives in each of these main steps. Typical objectives are shown in Fig. 16.11. However, they differ in the ways that they set out to achieve these objectives. This is described below.

Structured approaches

Structured approaches to user interface design were developed in response to the growth in the use of structured approaches to systems analysis and design during the 1980s. Structured analysis and design methodologies have a number of characteristics. They are based on a model of the systems development lifecycle, which is broken down into stages, each of which is further broken down: for example, into steps that are broken down into tasks. Specific analysis and design techniques are used, and the methodology specifies which techniques should be used in which step. Each step is described in terms of its inputs (from earlier steps), the techniques applied and the deliverables that are produced as outputs (diagrams and documentation). These approaches are more structured than the simple waterfall model of the lifecycle, as they provide for activities being carried out in parallel where possible rather than being dependent on the completion of the previous step or stage. Typically such structured approaches use data flow diagrams to model processes in the system and take a view of the system that involves decomposing

Step	Objectives
Requirements gathering	Determine characteristics of the user population: types of user, frequency of use, discretion about use, experience of the task, level of training, experience of computer systems
	Determine characteristics of the task: complexity of task, breakdown of task, context environment of task
	Determine constraints and objectives: choice of hardware and software, desired throughput, acceptable error rate
Design of the interface	Allocate elements of task to user or system; determine communication requirements between users and system
	Design elements of the interface to support the communication between users and system in the light of characteristics of the users, characteristics of the task and constraints on design
Interface evaluation	Develop prototypes of interface designs
	Test prototypes with users to determine if objectives are met

Figure 16.11 Steps in HCI design and objectives in each step.

it in a top-down way. Structure charts or structure diagrams are used to design the programs that will implement the system.

Proponents of structured approaches argue that they have a number of benefits.

- They make management of projects easier. The breakdown of the project into stages and steps makes planning and estimating easier, and thus assists management control of the project.
- They provide for standards in diagrams and documentation that improve understanding between the project staff in different roles (analyst, designer and programmer).
- They improve the quality of delivered systems. Because the specification of the system is comprehensive, it is more likely to lead to a system that functions correctly.

Advocates of structured approaches to HCI believe that similar benefits can be brought to HCI by adopting structured approaches. These approaches assume that a structured approach to analysis and design of a system is being used and that a structured approach to the HCI design can take place at the same time and be integrated to some extent into the project lifecycle. Two examples of such approaches are discussed briefly below.

- STUDIO (STructured User-interface Design for Interface Optimization) developed with KPMG Management Consulting in the UK (Browne, 1994)
- The RESPECT User Requirements Framework developed for the European Union Telematics Applications Programme by a consortium of Usability Support Centres (Maguire, 1997)

Structured approaches make use of diagrams to show the structure of tasks and the allocation of tasks between users and the system. They also make extensive use of checklists in order to categorize the users, the tasks and the task environments. Evaluation is typically carried out by assessing the performance of the users against measurable usability criteria. STUDIO is used here as an example of a structured approach.

STUDIO is divided into Stages, and each Stage is broken down into Steps. The activities undertaken in each of the Stages are shown in Figure 16.12. STUDIO uses a number of techniques such as:

- task hierarchy diagrams
- knowledge representation grammars
- task allocation charts
- state machines.

It is not possible to provide examples of all of these here. Statecharts in STUDIO are similar to UML state machines and based on the work of Harel (1988). Examples of UML state machines applied to user interface design are included in Section 17.7. A sample task hierarchy diagram for Take an Order is shown in Fig. 16.13. This diagram applies to the order entry screen of Fig. 16.3. The diagram is read from top to bottom and left to right. In it, the boxes with a small circle in the top right-hand corner are selections, only one of which will take place each time an order is taken; the box with an asterisk in the top right-hand corner is an iteration, which will take place usually more than once.

Structured approaches may involve evaluation of the user interface designs in a laboratory situation. This reflects the need to have operational measures of usability that can be tested and used to assess the effectiveness of the design. These operational measures are derived from objectives that were gathered during the requirements analysis phase

Stage	Summary of activities
Project Proposal and Planning	Decide whether user interface design expenditure can be justified. Produce quality plan
User Requirements Analysis	Similar to systems analysis, with focus on gathering information relating to user interface design rather than general functionality
Task Synthesis	Synthesize results of requirements analysis to produce initial user interface design. Produce user support documentation
Usability Engineering	Prototyping combined with impact analysis to provide an approach to iterative development that is easy to manage
User Interface Development	Handover of the user interface specification to developers to ensure that usability requirements are understood

Figure 16.12 Summary of activities in each Stage of STUDIO.

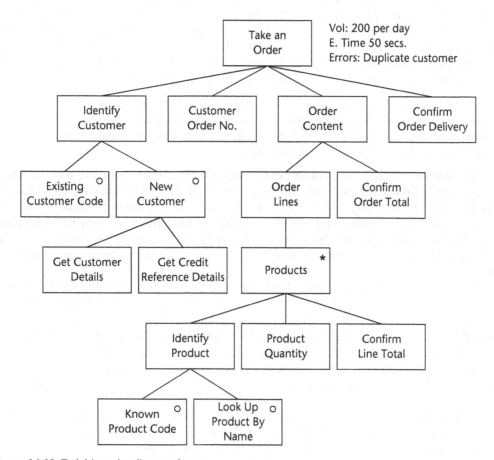

Figure 16.13 Task hierarchy diagram for Take an Order.

of the project described in Chapter 6. Examples include measures of how quickly users learn to use the system, error rates and time taken to complete tasks.

Serco Usability Services, which emerged out of the National Physical Laboratory in the UK, one of the partners in the consortium that produced the RESPECT methodology, has a usability laboratory in which interface designs are tested with users under laboratory conditions. One criticism of this approach is that people do not use systems under laboratory conditions, they use them in busy offices, noisy factories or crowded public spaces. Usability tests conducted in laboratories lack *ecological validity*. This means that they do not reflect the real conditions in the environment in which the systems will be used. As an alternative to laboratory-based usability studies, ethnographic approaches to the establishment of usability requirements, and to the testing of those requirements, have been proposed.

Ethnographic approaches

The term 'ethnography' is applied to a range of techniques used in sociology and anthropology and reflects a particular philosophy about how scientific enquiry should be carried out in these disciplines. Researchers who employ an ethnographic method seek to involve themselves in whatever situation they are studying. They believe that only by doing this and becoming part of that situation can they truly understand and interpret what is happening. Ethnographic methods belong to a wide range of *qualitative* research methods. (Qualitative means 'concerned with the quality of something' and is usually taken to be the opposite of *quantitative*, which means 'concerned about the quantity of something'. Quantitative methods typically rely on statistics to draw conclusions.) Hammersley and Atkinson (1995) provide a definition of ethnography:

> In its most characteristic form it involves the ethnographer participating, overtly or covertly, in people's daily lives for an extended period of time, watching what happens, listening to what is said, asking questions–in fact, collecting whatever data are available to throw light on the issues that are the focus of the research.

In HCI this means that the professional charged with carrying out the user interface design spends time with the users immersed in their everyday working life. Only by spending time in this way can the real requirements of the users be understood and documented. Ethnographic methods also emphasize that different users interpret their experience of using systems subjectively, and it is this subjective interpretation that the HCI professional must understand rather than assuming that the system can be assessed objectively.

Some HCI methods are criticised for failing to capture information about the context in which people are using systems, by focusing on the user and their tasks. Ethnographic approaches attempt to answer this criticism by the professional experiencing the daily working life of the people who will be the users of the system so that it can be better designed to meet their needs. Some structured approaches have also attempted to respond to the criticism about failing to take context into account, typically by adding some kind of contextual analysis questionnaire to the battery of checklists that they use.

There is no one ethnographic approach that covers the three steps in user interface development: requirements gathering, design of the interface and interface evaluation. There are a number of approaches that can be classed as ethnographic, although their originators may use particular terms to describe their approaches.

Contextual enquiry is an approach developed by John Whiteside and others at Digital Equipment Corporation (Whiteside et al., 1988). It is used to carry out evaluation of the usability of a system in the users' normal working environment. The aim of contextual enquiry is to get as close to the users as possible and to encourage them to develop their interpretation of the system.

Participative or co-operative design and evaluation involve users actively in the design and evaluation of the user interface of systems (Greenbaum and Kyng, 1991). The social and political issues in the workplace that affect the use of systems are part of the material that is captured by these approaches.

Ethnographic approaches use a range of techniques to capture data: interviews, discussions, prototyping sessions and videos of users at work or using new systems. These data are analysed from different perspectives to gain insights into the behaviour of the users. Video is also used in other approaches, particularly in laboratory-based usability studies. Analysis of video can be particularly time-consuming.

Scenario-based approaches

Scenario-based design has been developed by John Carroll and others (Carroll, 1995). It is less formal than the structured approaches but more clearly defined than most ethnographic approaches. Scenarios are step-by-step descriptions of a user's actions that can be used as a tool in requirements gathering, interface design and evaluation. Use cases are similar to scenarios, and Carroll's book includes chapters by Ivar Jacobson and Rebecca Wirfs-Brock, who have developed use cases and responsibility-based approaches to modelling interaction in object-oriented analysis and design. Of the three approaches discussed here, scenario-based design fits best with use case modelling.

Scenarios can be textual narrative describing a user's actions or they can be in the form of storyboards (a series of pictures that depict those actions), video mockups or even prototypes. Figure 16.14 shows a scenario that describes the actions of Peter Bywater from Agate when he demonstrates how he creates notes following the interview used as a case study example at the end of Chapter 6.

Pete starts up the word-processor.

He types in a title for the note and changes its style to *Title*.

He types in two paragraphs describing his idea for an advertisement for the Yellow Partridge campaign to be used in fashion magazines in Europe during the summer of 2010.

He types his initials and the date and time.

He uses the short-cut keys to save the file.

The save-as dialogue box appears and, using the mouse, he changes to the *Summer 2010 Campaign* folder in the *Yellow Partridge* folder on the server.

He scrolls to the bottom of the list of files already in the folder and reads the title of the last note to be added, *Note 17*. He calls the new note *Note 18* and clicks on Save.

He exits from the word-processor.

Figure 16.14 Scenario describing Pete Bywater of Agate adding a new note.

Scenarios can be used like this in requirements gathering to document the actions that a user carries out in their current system. They can also be used to document ideas about how the user would see themselves using the new system. This is called envisioning the design. Alternative scenarios describing different approaches to the design can be compared by the designers and the users. Figure 16.15 shows a scenario describing how a staff member at Agate might use the new system to create a new note about an advert.

The user selects Add a Note from the menu. A new window appears.

From the list box at the top of the window she selects the name of the client.

A list of campaigns appears in the list box below, and she selects a particular campaign.

A list of adverts appears in the next list box, and she selects a specific advert.

She types a few paragraphs into a text box to describe her idea for the advert. She fills the space on screen and a vertical scrollbar appears and the text in the text box scrolls up.

She enters her initials into a text box, and the system checks that she is allocated to work on that campaign.

The date and time are displayed by the system, and the Save button is enabled.

She clicks on the Save button and the word Saved appears in the status bar.

The text box, the text field for initials and the date and time are cleared.

Figure 16.15 Scenario describing how a user might add a note in the new system.

For evaluation of the system, more detailed scenarios are prepared so that the actual system can be compared against the expectations that the designer has of how the user will interact with it. Carroll (1995) claims that scenarios can be used in more than just these three ways. He lists the following roles for scenarios:

- requirements analysis
- user–designer communication
- design rationale
- envisionment
- software design
- implementation
- documentation and training
- evaluation
- abstraction
- team building.

Two of these are worth further comment: user–designer communication and design rationale.

In Chapter 6 we pointed out that the diagrams used by systems analysts and designers are used to communicate ideas, among other things. Information systems professionals need to communicate with the end-users of the systems that they are developing. Scenarios provide a means of communication that can be used by professionals and end-users to communicate about the design of the users' interaction with the system. They are simple enough that users can produce them without the need for the kind of

> The Save button is disabled until the user has selected a client and a campaign, entered some text and entered his or her initials. This prevents the user attempting to save the note before all data has been entered and getting an error message.
>
> The initials of the user could be entered automatically from their network login, but observation shows that the creative staff often work together as a group and different people will come up with ideas that they record as notes. It would be inconvenient for them to be logging in and out of the system each time a different person wants to enter a new note. For this reason, they are required to enter their initials.
>
> The initials, date, time and text fields are cleared after a note is saved, but the client, campaign and advert list boxes are left untouched so that the user can enter another note for the same advert or campaign without having to reselect these items.

Figure 16.16 Claims for the design scenario in Fig. 16.15.

training that they would need to understand class diagrams, for example. Scenarios can be used with use cases. The use cases can provide a description of the typical interaction; scenarios can be used to document different versions of the use case: for example, to document what happens when a user is adding a new note but is not authorized to work on the project they try to add it to. Use cases are concerned with the functionality offered by the system, while scenarios focus on the interaction between the user and the system.

Scenarios can be supported by additional documentation to justify design decisions that have been taken. Carroll (1995) calls these design justifications *claims*. The designer can document the reasoning behind alternative designs, explaining the advantages and disadvantages of each. Figure 16.16 shows some claims for the scenario in Fig. 16.15. These usability claims from design can be checked during evaluation of the software or of prototypes.

Scenario-based design can result in large volumes of textual information that must be organized and managed so that it is easily accessible. There is a document management task to be undertaken that requires a rigorous approach to control different versions of scenarios and to cross-reference them to claims and feedback from users. Developers run the risk of delaying implementation while they work through and document alternative scenarios for different parts of the system. Rosson and Carroll (1995) present one way to try to prevent this happening. They use a computer-based tool to develop and document their scenarios and to develop working models of the scenarios in Smalltalk as they go along. This allows them to document software implementation decisions at the same time, and they propose that there are benefits to recording design decisions and software implementation decisions together in this way.

These three types of approach have been presented as though they were very separate. However, there are elements that they have in common. Some structured approaches have attempted to take on board the criticisms that they fail to address the context in which people work and use computer systems. Ethnographic methods may use the same data-gathering techniques as other approaches, and may be used to provide information that can be used as the basis for drawing up scenarios. What they all share is a concern to enhance the usability of information systems and a recognition that usability issues must be integral to the design of computerized information systems.

16.3.2 Achieving usability

People often talk about how *user-friendly* a piece of software is, but it is often very difficult to tell what it is they mean by this. As a concept it is very vague. Usability may seem like a similar concept, but the HCI community has developed definitions of usability that can be used to test a piece of software. Shackel (1990) produced definitions of four criteria that were originally developed in the 1980s.

- *Learnability*–how much time and effort is needed to achieve a particular level of performance.
- *Throughput*–the speed with which experienced users can accomplish tasks and the number of errors made.
- *Flexibility*–the ability of the system to handle changes to the tasks that users carry out and the environment in which they operate.
- *Attitude*–how positive an attitude is produced in users of the system.

In Chapter 6 we mentioned the International Organization for Standardization (ISO) definition of usability as 'the extent to which specified users can achieve specified goals with effectiveness, efficiency and satisfaction in a specified context of use'. These criteria can be used in conjunction with the users' acceptance criteria documented during requirements gathering to assess how easy a software product is to use. Some of these can be quantified: for example, we can count the number of errors made by staff at FoodCo using the new system and compare that with the number of errors made with the old system and the objectives that they have set for the new system.

Sometimes conflicts will exist between different criteria and between usability criteria and other design objectives, and the designers will have to make compromises or trade-offs between different objectives. In particular, increasing flexibility is likely to conflict with the objective of developing the system at a reasonable cost.

Whatever approach is taken to engineering usability into the design of a software system, it is important to evaluate whether the objectives have been achieved. All three of the approaches mentioned above apply some form of evaluation to test the usability of prototypes or the final system.

16.4   Standards and Legal Requirements

In Section 16.2.5 we discussed style guides, which set standards for the design of user interfaces. Style guides like these determine the use of standard layouts, colour and function keys and the overall appearance of the system. The International Organization for Standardization has produced standards that have a broader impact on the use of computer systems. ISO 9241 is an international standard for the ergonomic requirements for work with visual display terminals, including both hardware and software, which has been updated in 2008 and 2009 to include guidance on areas such as accessibility and tactile and haptic interfaces. The standard covers physical aspects of the user's workstation (including positioning of equipment and furniture), the design of the computer equipment and the design of the software systems. ISO 14915-2002 is a further standard, entitled 'Software ergonomics for multimedia user interfaces', which gives recommendations for and guidance on the design, selection and combination of interactive user interfaces that integrate and synchronize different media. These standards are intended to ensure the quality of systems and to prevent local standards becoming barriers to free trade.

In the European Union (EU), this has been taken one step further and the EU Council issued a directive on 29 May 1990 that has the force of law for member states. In the UK, for example, this directive has been implemented in the Health and Safety (Display Screen Equipment) Regulations 1992. Under these regulations all workstations must now comply with certain minimum requirements, and employers have a duty in law to ensure the health and safety of employees using display screen equipment.

The regulations provide a number of definitions:

- display screen equipment–any alphanumeric or graphic display screen;
- user–an employee who habitually uses display screen equipment as a significant part of his or her normal work (see table of criteria in Health and Safety Executive, 2003);
- operator–self-employed person as above;
- workstation–display screen equipment, software providing the interface, keyboard, optional accessories, disk drive, telephone, modem, printer, document holder, work chair, work desk, work surface or other peripheral item and the immediate work environment around the display screen equipment.

The definition of display screen equipment excludes certain types of equipment, such as equipment in the cab of a vehicle, cash registers and some portable equipment.

As well as covering the physical equipment that is used by the user, the regulations cover environmental factors such as position of equipment, lighting, noise, heat and humidity in the workplace. Employers are required to:

- analyse workstations to assess and reduce risks;
- take action to reduce risks identified;
- ensure workstations meet the requirements of the regulations;
- plan the work activities of users to provide breaks;
- provide eyesight tests for users;
- provide corrective appliances for eyes if required;
- provide training relevant to health and safety issues and workstations;
- provide information to employees about health and safety risks and measures taken to reduce them.

The analysis of workstations in order to reduce risks includes analysis of the software, and the guidelines published to assist employers to meet their responsibilities state the following requirements.

Employers must take into account the following principles in designing, choosing, commissioning and modifying software and in designing tasks for people that require them to use display screen equipment.

- The software that is used must be suitable for the task.
- The software must be easy to use and able to be adapted to the level of knowledge or experience of the operator or user.
- The employer is not allowed to use any kind of quantitative or qualitative checking facility without the knowledge of the operators or users.
- Systems must give feedback to operators or users about the performance of the systems that they are using.

- Systems must display information for users both in a format and at a pace that are adapted to the operators or users.
- The principles of software ergonomics must be applied, particularly to the way that people process data.

Clearly the effect of this is to require employers, and so also software developers, to demonstrate that they are applying good HCI practice in the way that they design software.

Many countries in the world have regulations in place to promote good practice in workstation use. The USA is a significant exception to this. The Occupational Safety and Health Administration (OSHA) has proposed rules designed to prevent musculo-skeletal disorders caused by poor work design, bad posture and repetitive activities and covering workstation design and layout. These were rejected by Congress, backed by industry lobbyists. However, this is the exception rather than the rule in developed countries and there is plenty of online material on the subject, including the OSHA's own website, http://www.osha.gov, which provides advice on good workstation design.

One area where the United States does have some strong legislation is in the area of access to information technology by people with disabilities. The Americans with Disabilities Act (1990) ensures equal opportunity for persons with disabilities in employment, State and local government services, public accommodations, commercial facilities and transportation. Because so many services are now delivered, booked or accessed electronically, and so much work involves the use of IT, this has had an impact on the design of information systems, and US businesses have improved the accessibility of their systems.

In the UK, the Disability Discrimination Acts (1995 and 2005) have, since 1999, required that service providers take reasonable steps to change practices that make it unreasonably difficult for disabled people to make use of their services. This requirement is defined in the Code of Practice (Disability Rights Commission, 2006).

Access to information systems by people with disabilities has improved in many countries, driven by the expansion of the Internet and by legislation. The World Wide Web Consortium runs the Web Accessibility Initiative to develop guidelines and techniques for improving the accessibility of material on the Internet.

16.5 Summary

System designers must take account of the requirements of the people who will use their software if they are to reduce errors and maximize the satisfaction of the users with the system. The user interface can be viewed as part of a dialogue between the user and the system and there are a number of characteristics of good dialogue design that can be used to ensure that the user is supported by the interface and assisted in carrying out their primary task.

It is possible to apply an informal approach to determining characteristics of the users, the task and the situation that will affect the interface design, or to apply a more formal approach using structured, ethnographic or scenario-based techniques or some combination of these. The main aim of this is to produce software that can be demonstrated to meet the usability requirements of the people who will use it. This may be done in order to ensure compliance with international standards or it may be to meet legal requirements in some countries.

Review Questions

16.1 Think of a computerized information system that you use regularly. This could be a library system, an automated teller machine (ATM) that you use to get cash, a database that you use in your work or any other system that you are familiar with. Write down which elements of the interface support the five tasks listed at the start of Section 16.2.1.

16.2 For each of the elements of the interface that you have listed in Question 16.1, write down your ideas about how they could be improved.

16.3 What is the difference between the dialogue and direct manipulation metaphors?

16.4 Make a list of direct manipulation metaphors that are used in a GUI that you are familiar with. Are there any metaphors that do not work as you might expect?

16.5 What are the four characteristics of good dialogues described in Section 16.2.4?

16.6 Figure 16.9 shows the **Yes** button in a dialogue highlighted. What do you think is the risk associated with making this the active button by default?

16.7 For the system that you wrote about in Question 16.1, note down information relevant to the design factors in Fig. 16.10.

16.8 List as many differences as you can think of between structured, ethnographic and scenario-based approaches.

16.9 Make your own list of what you think the advantages and disadvantages could be of structured, ethnographic and scenario-based approaches.

Case Study Work, Exercises and Projects

16.A Using a user interface that you are familiar with as an example, try to identify features that you think might be part of the style guidelines for that user interface. This could be a GUI, a website or even a mobile phone.

16.B Using the four criteria for good dialogues discussed in Section 16.2.4, evaluate an application that you use regularly. Identify the ways in which it meets these criteria and the ways in which it does not meet the criteria. Suggest ways in which it could be improved.

16.C Write a scenario to describe what is done when Rik Sharma of FoodCo starts to plan staff allocation, based on the interview transcript in Exercise 6.B (Chapter 6). (Make sure that you concentrate on what he does and not on what is done by other staff at other times.)

16.D For the system that you wrote about in Question 16.1, identify measurable objectives that could be used to measure how usable that system is. (You may like to start by thinking about how long it takes you to use it and how many errors you make.)

16.E　Find out whether there are any legal requirements on software designers to comply with legislation that covers ergonomics or HCI in your country. Write a short report to summarize these requirements as though you were an analyst reporting to your manager on this legislation.

16.F　Look at the World Wide Web Consortium's website on access for users with disabilities at http://www.w3.org/WAI/. Identify some of the practical recommendations. Choose a website (perhaps one you have developed yourself) and evaluate it against these criteria. Write a short report summarizing what improvements need to be made.

Further Reading

Many computer science and information systems courses include HCI as a subject. If you have not come across HCI before and want to find out more, there are a number of suitable textbooks, such as Booth (1989), Sharp et al. (2007), Stone et al. (2005) and Dix et al. (2003). A classic text in this area is Shneiderman et al. (2009), which has been updated to cover graphical user interfaces in more detail since its first publication.

Style guidelines are available from some of the largest companies in the industry. Links are available to the online versions of these in the book's website.

For a structured method for user interface design Dermot Browne's book (Browne, 1994) provides a step-by-step approach to user requirements analysis, task analysis, usability and interface design. Browne also uses Harel state machines to model the behaviour of the interface in a more thorough way than many authors. Horrocks (1999) provides another view of how to use state machines in interface design. Carroll (1995) provides a good coverage of scenario-based methods and is very practical in approach, while Rosson and Carroll (2002) provide a more comprehensive view.

In the UK, The Stationery Office (TSO) publishes a booklet that explains the requirements of the Display Screen Regulations. This book's website includes links to other resources on health and safety and workstation ergonomics. Australian and Canadian government organizations provide a good starting point for investigating standards and legislation. The US OSHA also has a good website, http://www.osha.gov, with guidelines and checklists for ergonomic workstation design.

One of the best overview sites on access to information systems for people with disabilities is the World Wide Web Consortium's Web Accessibility Initiative (http://www.w3.org/WAI/), which has links to information on legislation in a number of countries.

Chapter 17

Designing Boundary Classes

LEARNING OBJECTIVES

In this chapter you will learn

☑ what we mean by the presentation layer

☑ how prototyping can be applied to user interface design

☑ how to add boundary classes to the class model

☑ how to model boundary classes in sequence diagrams

☑ how design patterns can be applied to the design of the user interface

☑ how to model the control of the user interface using state machine diagrams.

17.1 | Introduction

In Chapter 12 we introduced the three-tier system architecture. The presentation layer in this architecture contains the boundary classes that handle the interface with the user–usually windows and reports–or with other systems. We shall be concentrating here on interaction with the human user. We can use the techniques and diagrams of UML to model the user interface by adding detail to the boundary classes in the class model. These classes handle the user interface and allow us to design business (or entity) classes that do not contain details of how they will be presented. This enables the reuse of the business classes.

Prototyping can be used to try out different interface designs by producing sample window layouts, which can be evaluated with users as we described in Chapter 16. Prototypes and the eventual finished design of the user interface will use classes from reusable class libraries such as the Java Abstract Windowing Toolkit (AWT). The UML notation for packages and for package dependency can be used to show how class diagrams can reference classes from such libraries and how boundary classes can be placed in separate packages. The window layouts can be modelled as classes if required, but this is not always necessary unless the behaviour of the interface or of graphical objects in the user interface is the subject of the application being developed.

The sequence diagrams developed in Chapter 9 can be extended to include the detail of interaction with the boundary classes, and the model of the boundary classes is developed iteratively as we increase our understanding of the interaction.

469

Patterns can be used to provide generic models for the way that the interaction will work. Many systems written in Smalltalk use the Model–View–Controller (MVC) architecture, which separates the model (domain or business classes) from classes that handle the interaction between user and system.

The dynamic behaviour of the user interface is modelled with state machine diagrams. UML state machines were used in Chapter 11 to model the response of objects to events that take place during their lifetimes and to show how they change state as time passes. The same notation can be used to show the state of the user interface and how it responds to events such as mouse clicks on buttons or the entry of text into data entry screens. A state machine for the control class that manages the user interface for one use case is developed and alternative versions are presented.

17.2 Architecture of the Presentation Layer

In Chapter 7 the idea of boundary classes was introduced, and in Chapter 13 a layered model of the system was presented. The three-tier architecture is a common way to separate out user interface classes from the business and application logic classes and from mechanisms for data storage. There are a number of reasons for doing this, and these are shown in Fig. 17.1.

This is not to say that classes should contain no means of displaying their contents to the outside world. It is common practice to include in each class a print() (or a toString()) method that can be used to test the classes before the presentation layer has been developed. Such methods typically take an output stream (a file or a terminal window) as a parameter and produce a string representation of their attributes on that stream. This enables the programmer to check the results of operations carried out by classes without needing the full system in place. (See Chapter 19 for more on testing.)

Logical design	The project team may be producing analysis and design models that are independent of the hardware and software environment in which they are to be implemented. For this reason, the entity classes, which provide the functionality of the application, will not include details of how they will be displayed.
Interface independence	Even if display methods could be added to classes in the application, it would not make sense to do so. Object instances of any one class will be used in many different use cases: sometimes their attributes will be displayed on screen, sometimes printed by a printer. There will not necessarily be any standard layout of the attributes that can be built into the class definition, so presentation of the attributes is usually handled by another class.
Reuse	One of the aims is to produce classes that can be reused in different applications. For this to be possible, the classes should not be tied to a particular implementation environment or to a particular way of displaying the attribute values of instances.

Figure 17.1 Reasons for separating business and user interface classes.

The three-tier architecture was discussed in Section 13.5.2. Different approaches to object-oriented development use different names for the layers of the three-tier architecture. The Unified Process uses the terms boundary, control and entity classes for the three types of classes and these are the terms that we have used. Developers using Smalltalk to implement systems have for many years adopted a similar approach using the MVC approach that was described in Chapter 13. In the MVC approach a system is divided into three components:

- *Model*–the classes that provide the functionality of the system
- *View*–the classes that provide the display to the user
- *Controller*–the classes that handle the input from the user and send messages to the other two components to tell them what operations to carry out.

Whatever approach is chosen in a particular project, all these approaches share the objective of keeping the behaviour of the interface separate from the behaviour of the classes that provide the main functionality of the system. To use the anthropomorphic style of some authors about object-oriented systems, the entity classes 'know' nothing about how they will be displayed.

Taking a three-tier architectural approach does not necessarily mean that the different types of classes will end up running on different machines or even that they will be completely separate. It is useful to distinguish between the logical architecture of the system and the physical architecture. The physical architecture may combine layers of the logical architecture on a single physical platform or it may split logical layers across physical systems. If you are designing an AJAX application, some of the responsibilities for control will be located in the JavaScript classes, together with the boundary classes, while other control responsibilities may be located in classes on a server together with entity classes. In a distributed system, the entity classes may exist on different servers and the control classes would pull the data together from these different sources in order to deliver it to the boundary classes.

For the Agate system, we are going to keep the boundary, control and entity classes separate. The boundary classes will run on the users' machines, while the control classes will be located on servers, and the entity classes will initially be on local servers but may later be distributed in different offices. (We shall discuss mechanisms for achieving this in Chapters 18 and 19.)

In the next four sections, we shall develop the boundary classes by:

1. prototyping the user interface
2. designing the user interface classes
3. modelling the interaction involved in the interface
4. modelling the control of the interface using state machines.

17.3   Prototyping the User Interface

Prototyping was discussed in Chapter 3 as an approach to the development lifecycle and in Chapter 6 as a way of helping to establish what the requirements for a system are. In Chapter 6 we used it to produce models of the user interface. The UML models we have produced so far have been analysis and design diagrams; they are rather like an architect's drawings–they represent what the finished product will be capable of but they do not really show how it will look. A prototype is a model that looks, and to some extent behaves, like the finished product, but is lacking in certain features; it is more like an architect's scale model of a new building.

There are different kinds of prototype that can be built. A prototype that only provides a model of the user interface is one example of a *horizontal prototype*. It is horizontal because it deals with one layer of the layered architecture of the system. A *vertical prototype* takes one subsystem of the whole system and develops it through each layer: user interface, business classes, application logic and data storage. A horizontal prototype need not only deal with the user interface; there may be circumstances where it is more important to prototype the middle tier in order to test whether an innovative aspect of the system functionality works correctly.

Another distinction is made between those prototypes that are developed further and eventually, by an iterative process, become part of the finished system, and those prototypes that are simply used to test out design ideas and are then thrown away after they have served their purpose. This second kind of prototype is known as a *throwaway prototype*. A throwaway prototype can be built using any programming language that is suitable for the purpose. Figure 17.2 shows a prototype of the user interface for Agate that was created in a matter of minutes using Microsoft Visual Basic. Although this application will be developed in Java, a visual programming environment such as Visual Basic or Delphi can be used to produce prototypes of the user interface. In fact, the Java prototype examples used in the book took no more time than the Visual Basic examples, as they were produced in a Java visual programming environment.

Visual programming environments can be used to develop prototypes of the user interface to applications. These can be shown to the users and used, for example, in conjunction with techniques from scenario-based design (described in Chapter 16) to agree with users how they will interact with the user interface. In this way, prototypes can be used to design the interaction between the system and the user and establish a set of guidelines for how this interaction will take place.

Because visual programming environments are so easy to use, developers are often tempted to develop applications from the outside in: starting with the interface and

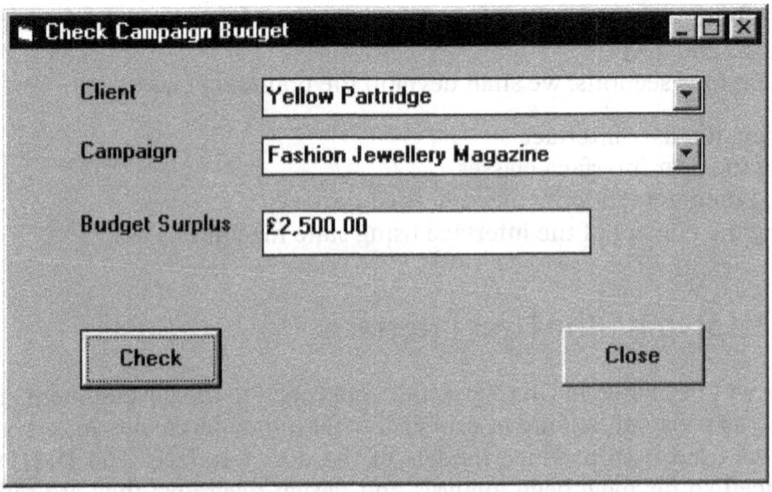

Figure 17.2 Visual Basic prototype of the Check Campaign Budget interface.

linking the functionality to the visual components that appear on the screen. Without thorough analysis of the business requirements for the system, this can lead to a blurring of the distinction between the presentation layer and the business classes and application logic. Applications developed in this way often have a large amount of program code associated with interface objects such as buttons. This program code should be an operation of a control class or of one or more entity classes. If it is linked to a button it cannot be reused in the same way as if it is carefully encapsulated in a class. Typically, the programmer then needs to reuse the code in another window and copies and pastes the code to another button in the new window; then when a change is made to the code linked to one button it may not be copied to the code linked to the second button and discrepancies creep into the system. This is not to say that it is not possible to develop good applications in visual environments; the important thing is that a thorough analysis should have been carried out first and the business objects and application logic should be kept separate from the visual components.

Prototyping can be used to try out alternative approaches to the same use case. In the example screen layout shown in Fig. 17.2 we have assumed that the users will select first a client and then a campaign from dropdown lists. There are many possible alternatives to this. Three of these are:

- to use a separate look-up window for each class;
- to allow the user to enter part of a name (for example, of a client) and for a list of close matches to be returned;
- to use a tree structure which shows the instances of clients and campaigns in a tree-like hierarchy.

Prototyping allows us to experiment with these approaches and build models which the users can try out for themselves. Figures 17.3 and 17.4 show screenshots of prototypes based on two of these different ways of handling the look-up process.

The choice of how the look-up in this use case is handled on screen will be determined by the style guidelines that were discussed in Chapter 16. It is important that style guidelines are agreed before development starts; prototyping can be used during design to try out various different interface styles and to get the users' agreement on which style will be followed.

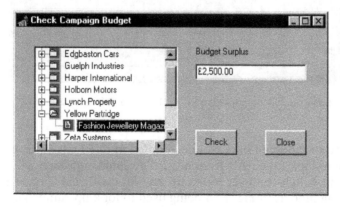

Figure 17.3 Prototype developed in Delphi using TreeView control.

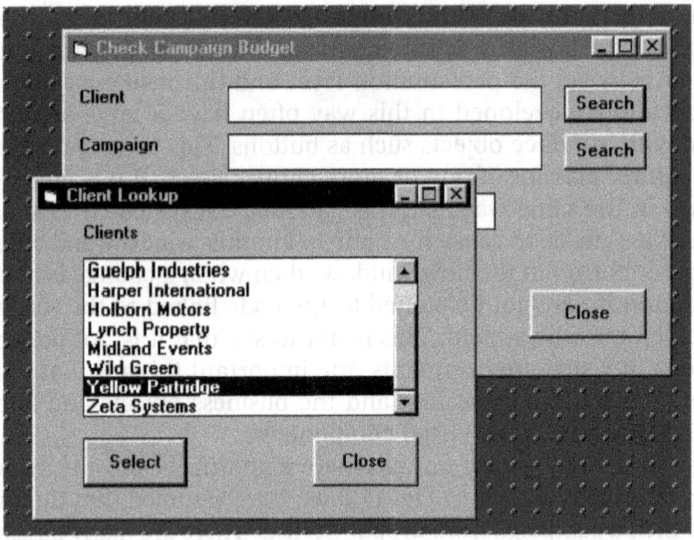

Figure 17.4 Prototype developed in Visual Basic showing separate look-up window.

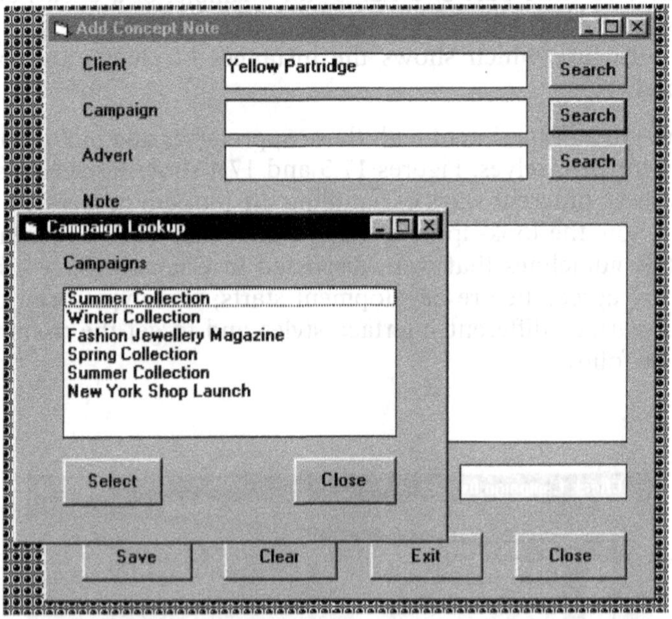

Figure 17.5 Use of the same style of look-up as in Fig. 17.4 in a different use case.

Whichever style is adopted here will be adopted in other use cases in which the user needs to be able to look up clients from a list. The same approach will also be adopted in all use cases in which the user looks up any kind of class. For example, Fig. 17.5 shows the same method as in Fig. 17.4 being used to look up campaigns for a particular client in the use case for Add a concept note.

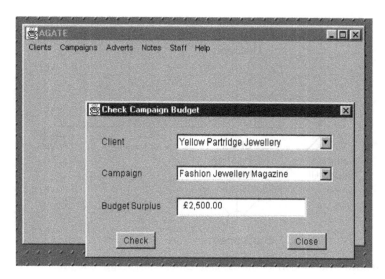

Figure 17.6 Dialogue window for the use case Check Campaign Budget.

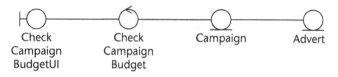

Figure 17.7 Collaboration for the use case Check campaign budget.

17.4 Designing Classes

The next step is to design the classes that will provide the user interface. The use case for Check Campaign Budget is used as an example. At the simplest level, there will be an object that provides an interface onto the functionality of this use case. This could be a dialogue window like the one shown in Fig. 17.6 (in the foreground). The analysis collaboration for this use case is shown in Fig. 17.7.

In the simple analysis collaboration in Fig. 17.7 we have not shown the class Client because it does not participate in the main functionality of the use case. In order to calculate what is left in the budget for a campaign we do not need the client object. However, in order to find the right campaign we do need the client: we home in on the right campaign in the context of the particular client. We need to be able to list all the clients and display them in the first dropdown. Once the client has been selected, we then need to list all the campaigns for that client in the second dropdown. In the approach that we have taken in this user interface design, using dropdowns rather than separate dialogue windows, we may want to add further control classes to the collaboration: one to list the clients and the other to list the campaigns. This is shown in Fig. 17.8.

If we had adopted the user interface style of Figs 17.4 and 17.5, then we should have separate user interface classes for each of these, and the collaboration would look like Fig. 17.9.

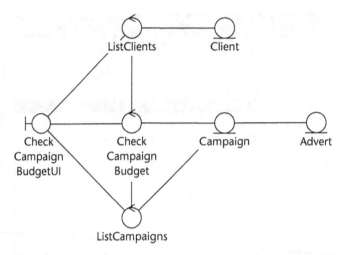

Figure 17.8 Extended collaboration for the use case Check campaign budget.

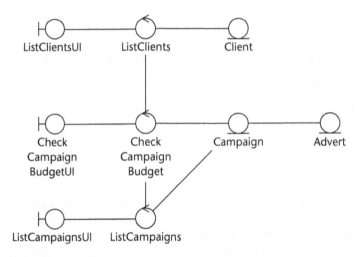

Figure 17.9 Revised collaboration for the use case Check campaign budget.

We will work with the collaboration of Fig. 17.8. We shall treat instances of the boundary class CheckCampaignBudgetUI as single objects. We may not want to be concerned about the objects that make it up. In reality, this window may well be an instance of a subclass of a class such as JDialog that is available in a library of user interface classes, and it may contain a number of components: buttons, labels, dropdowns and a textbox. This can be shown in a class diagram, as in Fig. 17.10 (JComboBox is the Java Foundation Classes (JFC) Swing term for a dropdown list). The composition associations represent the fact that the CheckCampaignBudgetUI is made up of instances of the other classes. (Alternatively, this can be represented as a class with attributes for each of the components. This is shown in Fig. 17.11 and makes it easier to draw a class diagram for the boundary classes.) The component classes that are used here all come from the

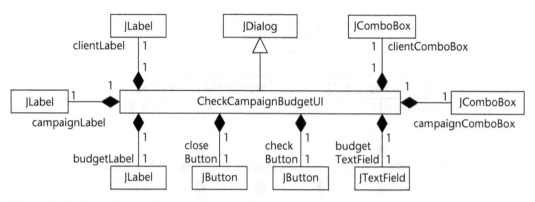

Figure 17.10 Class diagram showing dialogue components.

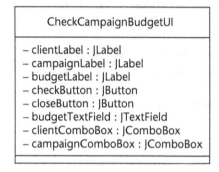

Figure 17.11 Class for dialogue window showing dialogue components as attributes.

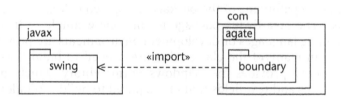

Figure 17.12 Class diagram to show dependency between classes in different packages.

Java Swing GUI classes. The `CheckCampaignBudgetUI` class is dependent on the classes in Swing, and this can be shown using packages in a class diagram, as in Fig. 17.12.

The «import» stereotype on the dependency shows that it will be necessary to import the classes from this Swing package in order to make them available to be used with the classes in the Application Windows package. How this is done will depend on the language that is used for implementation. In Java it is done simply with a line of code:

```
import javax.swing.*;
```

In C# this is done with a `using` statement, for example:

```
using System.WinForms;
```

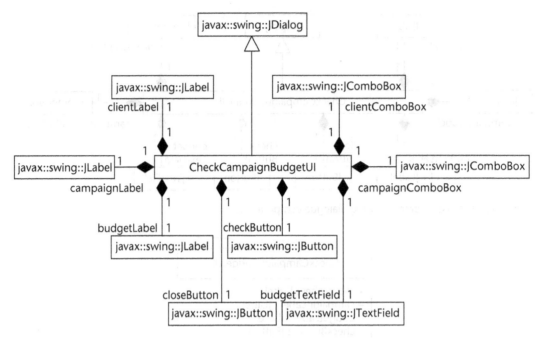

Figure 17.13 Class diagram showing Swing components with their package name.

We have used the «import» stereotype as it is now part of the UML Infrastructure Specification (OMG, 2009a).

Figure 17.13 illustrates how classes from other packages can be shown in the class diagram by adding the pathname of the package, using two colons as a separator, to the name of the class. The Java Swing package is only one example of this. Most object-oriented programming languages or development environments are provided with *class libraries* that contain many of the classes that are needed to build a working system. Microsoft, for example, provides the Windows Forms library, which includes all the classes such as buttons and text fields that are required to build a Windows interface to an application. These classes are grouped together and provided in what UML terms 'packages'. This is an example of the reuse that is claimed as a benefit of object-oriented systems. These user interface classes, whether in Java or C# or another language, have been implemented by other developers and can be reused in many new applications.

If the application being designed is mainly concerned with the behaviour of the objects in the interface itself–for example a drawing package, a modelling tool or an application with a strong visual element–then it may be advisable to model the user interface using a class diagram as shown in Fig. 17.13. In most applications in which the user interface will display text and numbers, it is not necessary to produce a model of the classes that make up the interface. It may be useful to show them in the style of Fig. 17.11 in a class diagram in a separate package. Note that there are not normally associations among the classes in the interface package in the way that there are associations between entity classes in the domain model. However, there may be transient links between instances of these classes.

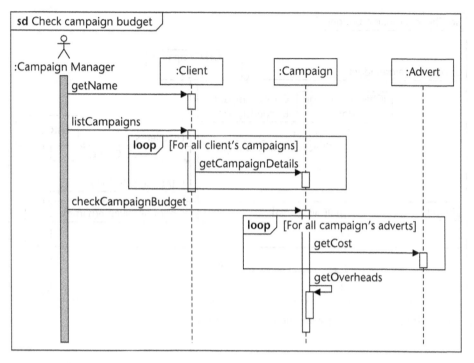

Figure 17.14 Sequence diagram for use case Check campaign budget.

17.5 Designing Interaction with Sequence Diagrams

The sequence diagram for the use case Check campaign budget in Fig. 10.4 did not show the boundary or control classes, but concentrated on the operations of the entity classes. We have shown it again in Fig. 17.14. The communication diagram of Fig. A3.8 showed the boundary and control classes, and we shall now elaborate the interaction in more detail.

We need to add the boundary and control classes of the collaboration in Fig. 17.8 to this sequence diagram. (If we had adopted the design from Fig. 17.9, then we would need to add three boundary classes rather than one.) Rather than trying to draw the entire sequence diagram in one go, we shall build up the interaction step by step. We are assuming here that it is an instance of the control class CheckCampaignBudget that is created first and that this creates a new instance of the CheckCampaignBudgetUI class to handle the user interface. As soon as it has created the boundary class, the control class needs to have the first dropdown populated with the names of all the clients, so it creates an instance of the control class ListClients and requests it to pass back the client names to the boundary class, passing it a reference to the boundary class in the message (ccbUI). The instance of ListClients sends the message addClientName(name) repeatedly to the boundary class until it has finished. It then returns control to the CheckCampaignBudget instance and destroys itself. The main control class can now enable the boundary class, allowing the user to select a particular client. This is shown in Fig. 17.15.

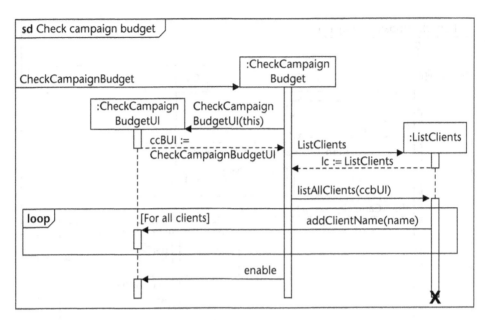

Figure 17.15 First part of detailed interaction for use case Check campaign budget.

We have shown the names of return values and parameters in this diagram to illustrate what is happening. For example, the instance of CheckCampaignBudget needs to have a reference to the instance of CheckCampaignBudgetUI (ccbUI) so that it can pass it to the instance of ListClients. This enables :ListClients to send the addClientName message directly to :CheckCampaignBudgetUI. When :CheckCampaignBudgetUI is created, it is passed a reference to the control class instance :CheckCampaignBudget (this). In this way, it will be able to send messages back to the main control class when it needs to notify it of events.

Instances of :CheckCampaignBudgetUI need to be able to respond to the message addClientName(name). Many other boundary classes will need to allow the user to select a client from a dropdown, for example AddConceptNoteUI. We shall want to reuse ListClients in all the use cases where a list of clients has to be displayed in a boundary class, but cannot expect ListClients to know about all the different boundary classes to which it could send the message addClientName(name). We can use an interface to specify the operations that all these boundary classes must respond to. (See Section 14.4.2 for an explanation of interfaces.) We could define the interface ClientLister, and all the boundary classes that need to display a list of clients will realize it, as CheckCampaignBudgetUI does in Fig. 17.16.

Design of other use cases may identify other operations that must be part of this interface: for example, clearAllClientNames() or removeClientName(name). The operation addClientName(name) must be implemented by program code in the class definition for CheckCampaignBudgetUI. For example, in Java it may be as in Fig. 17.17 (with much code not shown).

One of the important features of this design is that any object that wants to manipulate the list of clients in the boundary object must do so through operations. We could change the design of the boundary class so that it displayed the list of clients in a scrolling list

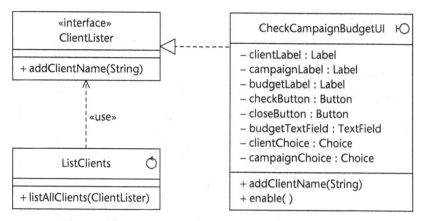

Figure 17.16 `ClientLister` interface.

```
import javax.swing.*;
public class CheckCampaignBudgetUI extends Frame
                              implements ClientLister {
    private JComboBox clientComboBox;
    ...
    public void addClientName(String name) {
        clientComboBox.addItem(name);
    }
    ...
}
```

Figure 17.17 Possible Java definition of `addClientName(name)`.

(a `JList` in Java Swing). We would then have to change the Java program that implements `CheckCampaignBudgetUI`, but we would not have to change the classes that use it, because the interface remains the same. (Other object-oriented languages use slightly different ways of achieving the same thing, but the principle is the same.)

Note that in Fig. 17.15 we have not shown what the `ListClients` control class instance does to get the names of all the clients. This level of detail can be hidden in this diagram. UML 2.0 introduces the notation of interaction uses to allow fragments of sequence diagrams to be reused in other diagrams. Figure 17.18 shows what happens when an instance of `ListClients` receives a `listAllClients` message. At this stage of the design we have not addressed how clients are to be stored in a database, so this is left vague. Design of the data storage is covered in Chapter 18.

Rosenberg and Scott (1999) use control classes as placeholders for operations that may later be assigned to other classes. This technique could be used in this example, where the `ListClients` control class may become part of some other class that handles the database access for the `Client` class. This approach can help in preventing an object-oriented system from ending up with a lot of classes like `ListClients` that are little more than wrappers for one or two operations, and more like programs than objects. On the other hand, this can break the architectural layering of the system, as the classes in the data storage layer will need to know about classes in the presentation layer.

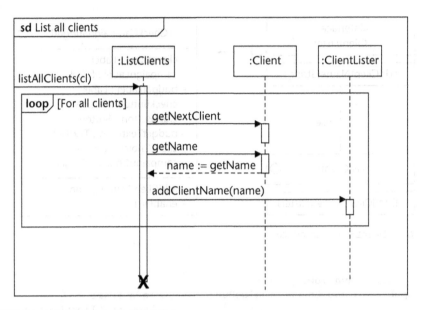

Figure 17.18 `listAllClients()` operation.

Returning to the sequence diagram for this collaboration, the next event that will take place is that the user will select a client from the dropdown that has been populated with clients by the processes that we have just described. When a particular client has been selected, then the list of campaigns in the boundary class must be populated with only those campaigns in the database that belong to that client. This is shown in Fig. 17.19.

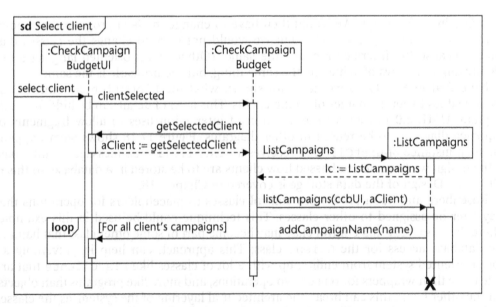

Figure 17.19 Second part of interaction for use case `Check campaign budget`.

Part of this sequence diagram is similar to the one in Fig. 17.15. We would apply the same design principles to this, with a `CampaignLister` interface, which must also be implemented by `CheckCampaignBudgetUI`. The interaction is slightly different, as we need to pass the client to `ListCampaigns` so that it knows which client's campaigns to display. We can model the interaction within the boundary class in more detail if we wish.

When the instance of `CheckCampaignBudgetUI` is created it will add the instance of `JComboBox`, `clientComboBox`, to itself and register an interest in events from the user that affect `clientComboBox`. (A `JComboBox` is a dropdown list.) In Java, for example, this means that `CheckCampaignBudgetUI` must implement the `ItemListener` interface. When an event takes place, such as the user selecting a client in the dropdown, `:CheckCampaignBudgetUI` will be sent a message `itemStateChanged(evt)`, with the data associated with the event passed in the parameter `evt`. If the source of the event is `clientComboBox`, then it should notify the control class by sending it the `clientSelected` message. Figure 17.20 shows this interaction.

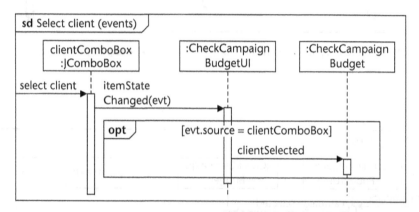

Figure 17.20 Detail of Swing component interaction for use case `Check campaign budget`.

At this point in the interaction, the user could either select a campaign from the list of campaigns or could select another client from the client list. In the latter case, then the interaction of Fig. 17.19 could take place again. With the design as it is at present, this would result in the campaigns for the newly selected client being added onto the list of campaigns already in the dropdown. This is clearly incorrect, and this is where the interface needs an operation to clear the list: `clearAllClientNames()` was suggested for the `ClientLister` interface. The equivalent `clearAllCampaignNames()` is shown in Fig. 17.21.

If the user does select a campaign, then the button `checkButton` should be enabled, and if the user clicks that, then the budget for the selected campaign should be calculated and displayed in the textfield. This is shown in Fig. 17.22. We have not shown all the parameters and return values in this diagram, as it is very easy to clutter up such a diagram with additional text.

In the same way as we did not show the detail of the interaction within the boundary class on the earlier diagrams, we have left the detail of how `:CheckCampaignBudgetUI` will get the values from the dropdowns and set the value of the textfield out of this diagram. This provides us with a clean interface, and `:CheckCampaignBudget` need know

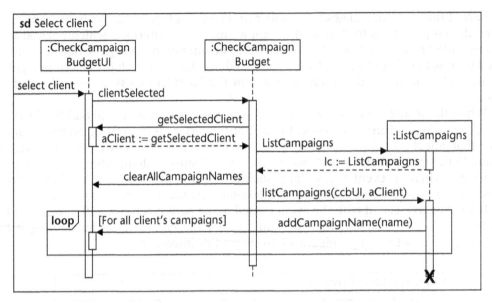

Figure 17.21 Revised second part of interaction for use case `Check campaign budget`.

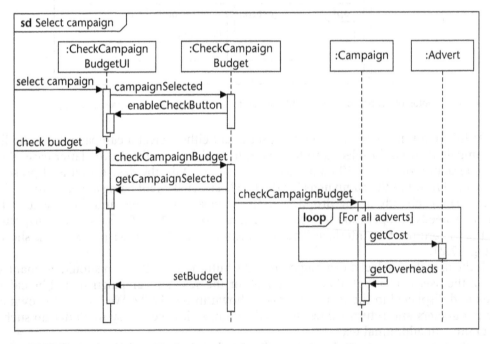

Figure 17.22 Final part of interaction for use case `Check campaign budget`.

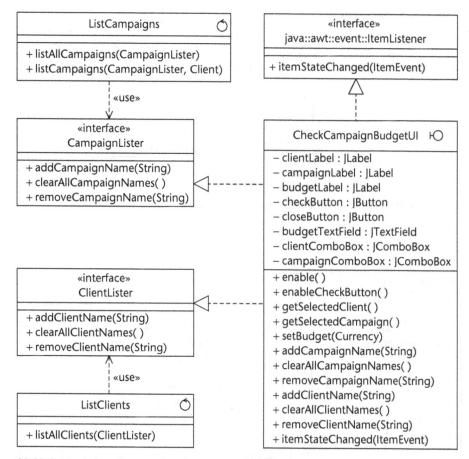

Figure 17.23 Revised class diagram showing CheckCampaignBudgetUI.

nothing of the internal workings of the boundary class. The display of the budget amount could be changed from a textfield to a label, or even digital speech, but the control class only needs to know that the boundary class will respond appropriately to the setBudget message.

There may be many places in the system where the same patterns of interaction as in Figs 17.18 and 17.20 take place. Rather than producing separate interaction sequence diagrams for all of these, we may choose to produce some generic sequence diagrams that show the pattern of interaction that is expected to take place when objects are listed in a dropdown or when an item is selected from a list.

We can further extend the class diagram with the operations that have been identified for our boundary class. Figure 17.23 shows this for the CheckCampaignBudgetUI class. The code that manages the interface is the implementation of an operation of CheckCampaignBudgetUI that is invoked by the control class. It also shows the interfaces that it must realize, both some that are specific to this application and one that is part of the Java Abstract Window Toolkit (AWT) event handling model, which is used by Java Swing.

Boundary classes include reports as well as screen displays, and reports can be shown in interaction diagrams as well. The simplest form of report is produced by opening an

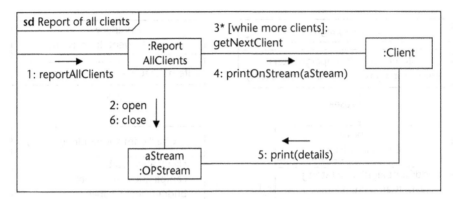

Figure 17.24 Report design in which the Client formats its own data.

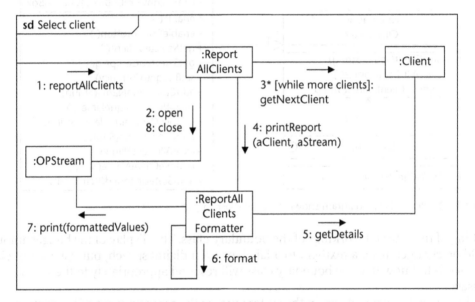

Figure 17.25 Report design in which a boundary class formats the data.

output stream to a device such as a printer. In this case each object that is to be printed out can be sent the message to print itself with a reference to the output stream as a parameter. This is shown in Fig. 17.24 for a simple report of all clients, where a control class co-ordinates the printing of the report. (We have used communication diagrams for the following diagrams to show how they can be used for this kind of design as well.) If the user is required to enter parameters, for example selecting a client in order to print a report of all campaigns for that client, then a dialogue of some sort will also be required.

In the simple solution of Fig. 17.24, the instances of Client are responsible for formatting themselves for output to the printed report. An alternative solution is to design a boundary class to handle the formatting of the attributes of one or more instances of one or more classes. This solution is shown in Fig. 17.25.

The decision as to which of these approaches is best will depend on the development environment being used.

Control classes to manage the user interface like this are not always necessary. In Java applets, the Applet class can handle both the presentation and the control. In some applications, for example real-time applications where the attributes of objects are changing and those changes need to be reflected in different views of the data, it may be better to use a design based on the MVC style of developing applications, which is discussed in Section 17.7.

17.6 Class Diagram Revisited

The boundary classes can be added to the class diagram. They can be shown in a single diagram for the Agate Boundary package (com::agate::boundary) (see Fig. 17.12) or in separate diagrams, grouped by type or subsystem. The buttons and other classes that are used to make these interface classes need not be shown in the diagrams. However, all the boundary classes in the application will have a package dependency to the package where the buttons and other classes are held.

There may be some commonality among boundary classes that can be abstracted out into an inheritance hierarchy. For example, all dialogue boxes that are concerned with printed reports may have a standard set of buttons, **Print**, **Cancel** and **Select Printer**, and radio buttons for **Portrait** and **Landscape**. These buttons and the associated event-handling mechanisms could be placed in a generic PrintDialog superclass, from which all other report dialogue boxes could inherit this functionality. If we had chosen the design for the lists of clients and campaigns that required a separate dialogue box for each, as in Figs 17.4, 17.5 and 17.9, then we would need to add a LookupDialog class which would be the parent of all look-up dialogues in the system. This is in turn a subclass of the JDialog class from the Java Swing package. The JDialog class is also the superclass of PrintDialog, the parent of all dialogues used to run reports. Figure 17.26 shows the beginnings of a possible inheritance hierarchy based on this approach. Note that LookupDialog and PrintDialog are both abstract classes: there will never be instances of either.

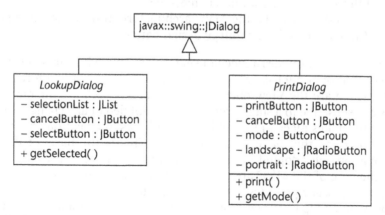

Figure 17.26 Beginnings of an inheritance hierarchy for possible dialogue classes.

17.7 | User Interface Design Patterns

We have suggested that in an application of this sort generic patterns of interaction can be documented for the design of the user interface and the boundary classes. It is also possible to use standard design patterns as we discussed in Chapter 15.

The MVC architecture is the classic object-oriented pattern for designing the user interface. It has been mentioned more than once in this chapter and was described in Chapter 12. The Model class is the business object, the View is its presentation to the user and the Controller defines how the user interface responds to the user's actions.

Java uses MVC in the user interface by means of the `EventListener` subinterfaces and `EventObject` subclasses. There are a number of subclasses of `EventObject` for different types of event, such as `MouseEvent` for mouse events and `ItemEvent` for checkboxes and lists, and different subinterfaces of `EventListener` to handle them (such as `MouseListener`, `ItemListener` and `ActionListener`). We used this mechanism to handle the event when the user selects a client in Fig. 17.20. Because it involves a dropdown list (a `JComboBox`), we use `ItemEvent` and `ItemListener`.

Any class that implements the `ItemListener` interface must implement the method `itemStateChanged()`; this means that it must include code so that its instances can respond appropriately to the message `itemStateChanged(ItemEvent)` whenever they receive it. Any class that implements `ItemListener` can register its interest in the events that affect an instance of certain user interface components, such as the `Choice` and the `Menu` classes. This is done by sending the message: `AddItemListener(ItemListener)` to an instance of one of these classes. It adds the new instance of `ItemListener` to a list it keeps of all the `ItemListeners` it must notify of any events. Then when the `Menu` is selected or the `Choice` is changed, it sends the message `itemStateChanged()` to each of the objects in its list and passes them an `ItemEvent` object as a parameter.

Each of the objects that receives the message can then inspect the `ItemEvent` object and decide whether it is interested in that particular event and whether it needs to take some action in response. The action could be to notify other classes of the event, particularly if the class that is implementing the `ItemListener` interface is a control class. This is shown in Fig. 17.27. The use of the interface mechanism in Java means that the user interface component does not need to know the actual class of the class that implements `ItemListener`; as long as it implements the interface it will know what to do when it is sent the `itemStateChanged()` message.

Gamma et al. (1995) describe the MVC architecture in terms of three patterns: the Observer, the Composite and the Strategy design patterns.

- The *Observer pattern* provides a mechanism for decoupling business objects from their views. It is based on a publish–subscribe model. There are two main types of objects: Observers, which are the View objects, and Subjects, which are the business objects. Observers can subscribe to a subject and ask to be notified of any changes to the subject. When a change takes place in the subject, it publishes information about the changes to all the observers that have subscribed to it. This is the basis of the Observer–Observable approach adopted in Java 1.1 (and later versions of Java). The Observer pattern is the core of the MVC architecture, but two other patterns also apply.
- The *Composite pattern* provides a means to structure objects into whole–part hierarchies. Most windowing interfaces use this approach to form composite views made up of smaller components. The class diagram of Fig. 17.10 shows this kind of composite

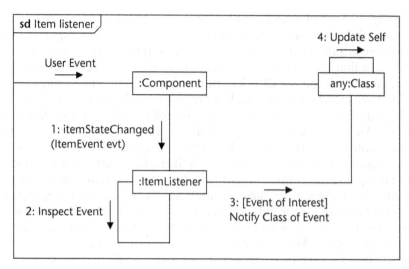

Figure 17.27 Java `ItemListener` response to an external event.

structure. The Composite pattern is a way of structuring views to include nested views. For example, a graphical display may represent the same model in two different views, a graph and a table of numbers that may be nested within another view.

■ The *Strategy pattern* offers a way of defining a family of algorithms, encapsulating each one and making them interchangeable. This allows the strategy to vary independently of client objects that use it. In MVC one controller can be replaced by another. For example, an on-screen calculator could be designed and built initially to respond to mouse clicks on the buttons on the screen. The controller for the calculator detects mouse clicks and notifies the internal application objects and the view objects about these mouse events. Later the calculator could be modified to respond instead to keypresses on the computer numeric keypad, or to both mouse clicks and keypresses. The controller object can be replaced without having any impact on the application objects.

Design patterns provide a way of reusing design experience and best practice. Separating the concerns of the user interface and the control of interaction from the business application objects is a proven technique to produce good designs and maximize the opportunities for reuse of the classes that are designed and developed.

17.8 Modelling the Interface Using State Machines

State machines can be used to model the rules that control how the user interface responds to events. In Fig. 17.10 we showed the classes that make up the user interface for the use case `Check campaign budget` in the Agate project. That diagram shows the static structure of the interface, but it provides no information about how it will behave in response to the user. The sequence diagrams developed in Section 17.5 and the prototype in Fig. 17.6 provide additional information, but they tell us nothing about the permitted states of the interface. The sequence diagrams show the sequential view of the user working through the fields on the screen from top to bottom, but it is in the nature of GUI interfaces that the user can click on interface objects out of sequence. So what happens if the user clicks on the **Check** button before a client and a campaign have been selected? The user may choose to check more than one budget. What happens if they select a different client—how does that affect the other fields where data has already been selected? All these issues can be modelled using a state machine diagram. State machines were introduced in Chapter 11, and were used there to model the way that events affect instances of a class over its lifetime. They are used to model shorter timescales in designing the control of real-time systems. They can also be used to model the short-term effects of events in the user interface. Browne (1994) uses state machines in this way to model the user interface as part of the STUDIO methodology. Horrocks (1999) uses state machines in a more rigorous way than Browne in his user interface–control–model (UCM) architecture and relates the use of state machines to coding and testing of the user interface. Browne's approach leads to a bottom-up design of the interface, assembling state machines for components into a complete model of an interface; Horrocks develops his state machines in a top-down way, successively introducing nested substates where they are necessary. We are using Horrocks's approach in what follows.

For the example that follows, we are using the original design for the user interface with dropdowns for `Client` and `Campaign`, as in the prototype of Fig. 17.6.

As a design principle in our user interfaces, we want to prevent users from making errors wherever possible rather than having to carry out a lot of validation of data entry in order to pick up errors that have been made. One way of doing this is to constrain what users can do when they are interacting with the interface. For example, in the `Check campaign budget` user interface it makes no sense to click the **Check** button until both a client and a campaign have been selected. Rather than check whether a client and campaign have been selected every time the button is clicked, we can choose only to enable the button when we know that both have been selected. To do this we need to model the state of the user interface and it is this that we model using state machines. This process involves five tasks.

1. Describe the high-level requirements and main user tasks.
2. Describe the user interface behaviour.
3. Define user interface rules.
4. Draw the state machine (and successively refine it).
5. Prepare an event–action table.

We have simplified Horrocks's approach here. His book (Horrocks, 1999) provides a full and clear exposition of this approach.

1. Describe the high-level requirements and main user tasks
The requirement here is that the users must be able to check whether the budget for an advertising campaign has been exceeded or not. This is calculated by summing the cost of all the adverts in a campaign, adding a percentage for overheads and subtracting the result from the planned budget. A negative value indicates that the budget has been overspent. This information is used by a campaign manager.

2. Describe the user interface behaviour

There are five active elements of the user interface: the **Client** dropdown, the **Campaign** dropdown, the **Budget** textfield, the **Check** button and the **Close** button. These are shown in Fig. 17.6.

The **Client** dropdown displays a list of clients. When a client is selected, their campaigns will be displayed in the **Campaign** dropdown.

The **Campaign** dropdown displays a list of campaigns belonging to the client selected in the **Client** dropdown. When a campaign is selected the **Check** button is enabled.

The **Budget** textfield displays the result of the calculation to check the budget.

The **Check** button causes the calculation of the budget balance to take place.

The **Close** button closes the window and exits the use case.

3. Define user interface rules

User interface objects with constant behaviour

- The **Client** dropdown has constant behaviour. Whenever a client is selected, a list of campaigns is loaded into the **Campaign** dropdown.
- The **Budget** textfield is initially empty. It is cleared whenever a new client is selected or a new campaign is selected. It is not editable.
- The **Close** button may be pressed at any time to close the window.

User interface objects with varying behaviour

- The **Campaign** dropdown is initially disabled. No campaign can be selected until a client has been selected. Once it has been loaded with a list of campaigns it is enabled.
- The **Check** button is initially disabled. It is enabled when a campaign is selected. It is disabled whenever a new client is selected.

Entry and exit events

- The window is entered from the main window when the Check Campaign Budget menu item is selected.
- When the **Close** button is clicked, an alert dialogue is displayed. This asks 'Close window? Are you sure?' and displays two buttons labelled **OK** and **Cancel**. If **OK** is clicked the window is exited; if **Cancel** is clicked then it carries on in the state it was in before the close button was clicked.

4. Draw the state machine

At the top level, there are three states the application can be in. It can be in the Main Window (and we are assuming that this is modelled in detail elsewhere), in the Check Budget Window or in the Alert Dialogue. Figure 17.28 shows these top-level states.

Horrocks uses the convention of names of buttons in single quotes to represent button press events. We have used that notation here for the values that will be returned from the alert dialogue, but have used operation signatures for the other events, as we want to be able to check them against the sequence diagrams.

Within the Check Budget Window state, there are different substates of the user interface that must be modelled. Initially, no client is selected; then the user can select a client. Figure 17.29 shows the resulting two states. Because there will be actions associated with the user selecting a different client, we have shown the clientSelected() event returning to the Client Selected state if it occurs again.

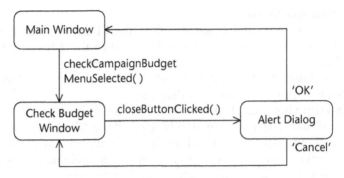

Figure 17.28 Top-level states.

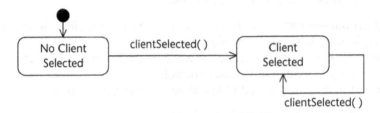

Figure 17.29 Client selection states within the state Check Budget Window.

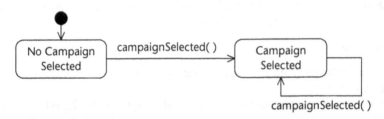

Figure 17.30 Campaign selection states within the state Client Selected.

Similarly, once the interface is in the Client Selected state, it can be in either the substate where a campaign has not yet been selected or the substate where a campaign has been selected. These two states are shown in Fig. 17.30.

If the user interface is in the Campaign Selected state, then if the **Check** button is pressed, the result will be displayed in the textfield, which will initially be blank. This is shown in Fig. 17.31.

These various state machines can be combined and nested within the top-level state for the Check Budget Window. This is shown in Fig. 17.32.

Note the use of the *deep history indicator* where the 'Cancel' event returns control from the Alert Dialogue to the Check Budget Window. The H* in a circle shows that when that transition takes place, it will return to the exact same state that it was in before the transition to the Alert Dialogue state, however far down in the nested hierarchy of states it was. This works like a memory. The state of the user interface

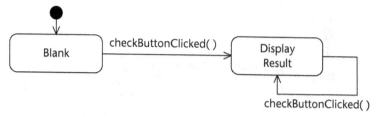

Figure 17.31 Display of result states within the state Campaign Selected.

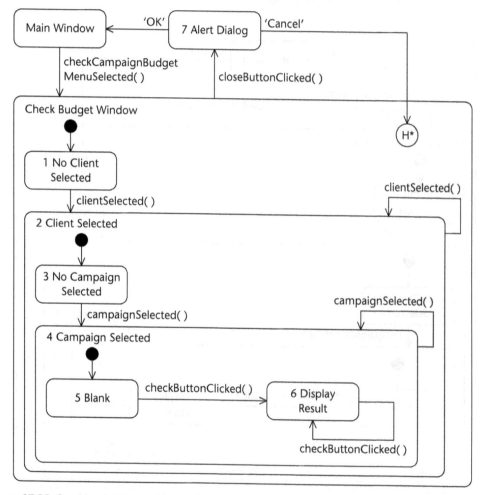

Figure 17.32 Combined state machine with nested states.

before the `closeButtonClicked()` event is recorded, and the 'Cancel' event returns it back to that recorded state.

Horrocks's approach has some notational differences from the UML standard. He numbers his states (as in Fig. 17.32), because the numbers of the states can be stored as the values of the state variables that hold the information about the current state of the

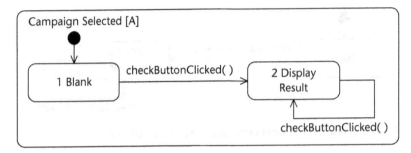

Figure 17.33 State variable and numbered states.

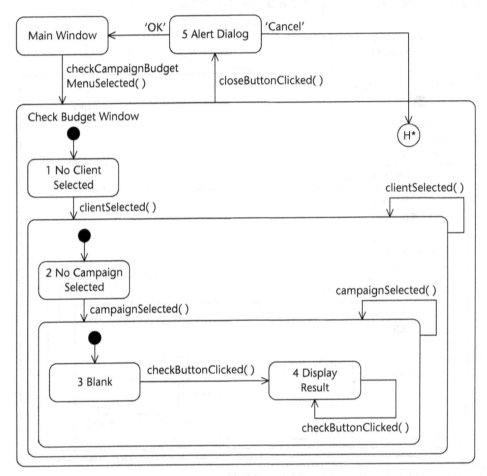

Figure 17.34 Simplified version of state machine in Fig. 17.32.

system. He also explicitly names the state variables in square brackets. Figure 17.33 shows an example of this notation. Using explicit state variables and numbers for states will help in coding the implementation of this design, and the numbered states make the production of the event–action table simpler. Figure 17.32 is slightly more complicated

Current State	Event	Action	Next State
–	Check Campaign Budget menu item selected	Display CheckCampaignBudgetUI. Load **Client** dropdown. Disable **Campaign** dropdown. Disable **Check** button. Enable window	1
1	Client selected	Clear **Campaign** dropdown. Load **Campaign** dropdown. Enable **Campaign** dropdown	2
2, 3, 4	Client selected	Clear **Campaign** dropdown. Load **Campaign** dropdown. Clear **Budget** textfield. Disable **Check** button	2
2	Campaign selected	Clear **Budget** textfield. Enable **Check** button	3
3	**Check** button clicked	Calculate budget. Display result	4
3, 4	Campaign selected	Clear **Budget** textfield	3
4	**Check** button clicked	Calculate budget. Display result	4
1, 2, 3, 4	**Close** button clicked	Display alert dialogue	5
5	**OK** button clicked	Close alert dialogue. Close window	–
5	**Cancel** button clicked	Close alert dialogue	H*

Figure 17.35 Event–action table for Fig. 17.34.

than it needs to be. States 2 and 4 have no real meaning; they can be treated as no more than a grouping of the enclosed substates to keep the number of states and transitions down. Figure 17.34 is a simplification. The simplified state machine has been used to prepare the event–action table in Fig. 17.35.

5. Prepare an event–action table

UML state machine notation allows you to label transitions and states with actions. On a transition the action can be an action of the object itself or it can involve a message being sent to another object. Within states, *entry* and *exit actions* can be documented, as well as *do actions* that are carried out continuously while the object is in that state and *event actions* that are carried out if a particular event occurs while the object is in that state (as explained in Section 11.3).

The use of these actions on state machine diagrams can make them very cluttered and difficult to read, especially if there are also guard conditions on the transitions as well as actions. UML allows you to put actions both on transitions and on states, although some authors on the subject suggest that you use either actions on transitions or actions on states, but not both.

For complex state machines, rather than displaying the actions in the state machine as in Chapter 11, an alternative is to list the actions in a table. This is an event–action table. From the point of view of the programmer, this table will be easier to use than a state machine labelled with actions. It should also make it easier to validate the state machine and to test the code once it has been implemented.

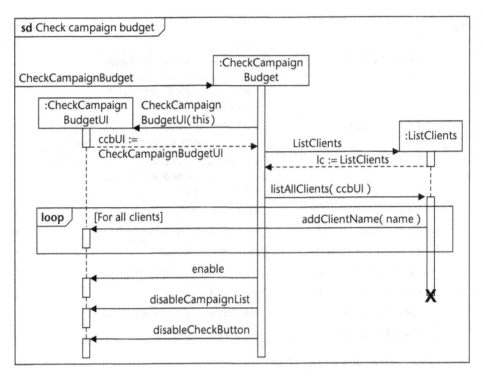

Figure 17.36 Revised sequence diagram for first part of interaction.

The event–action table lists the following values in columns:

- the current state of the object being modelled
- the event that can take place
- the actions associated with the combination of state and event
- the next state of the object after the event has taken place; if more than one state variable is used, these are shown in separate columns.

Figure 17.35 shows an event–action table for the state machine of Fig. 17.34.

We can now use this information to revisit the sequence diagrams. Indeed, if we know what the names of the messages or operations in the sequence diagrams are, we can use them in the event–action table instead of the natural language descriptions of the actions.

If we examine the first sequence diagram from Fig. 17.15, we can see that we need some additional operations to be shown in the sequence diagram. The sequence diagram shows the boundary class being created, the **Client** dropdown being loaded and the window being enabled, but we have not explicitly disabled the **Campaign** dropdown and the **Check** button. Figure 17.36 shows these additional operations.

We can apply the same approach to the sequence diagram of Fig. 17.18, which shows what happens when the client is selected, and thus the transition from State 1 to State 2. This is shown in Fig. 17.37.

If the names of the events and operations have already been decided, because the sequence diagrams have been produced and the operations of classes have been designed, then the event–action table can list them using these names. For example, in the transition

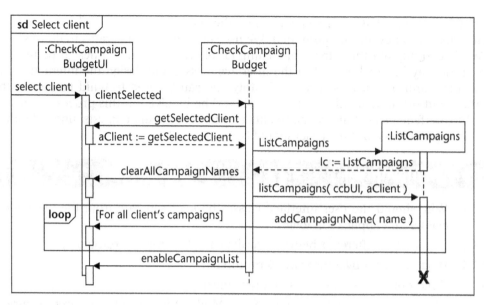

Figure 17.37 Revised sequence diagram for second part of interaction.

from State 1 to State 2 in Fig. 17.35, the event would be called `clientSelected()`, and the actions would be:

```
ListCampaigns();
CheckCampaignBudgetUI.clearAllCampaignNames();
ListCampaigns.listCampaigns();
CheckCampaignBudgetUI.enableCampaignList();
```

Working through the design of the interface in this way will lead to the addition of more operations to the class diagram in Fig. 17.22. For example, the operation `disable-CheckButton()` needs to be added to `CheckCampaignBudgetUI`, and the operations `enableCampaignList()` and `disableCampaignList()` need to be added to the interface `CampaignLister` and to `CheckCampaignBudgetUI`.

17.9 | Summary

Designing the interface objects requires us to model three important aspects of the interface. First, we need to determine the classes of the objects that will participate in the interaction with the user and decide on how we will reuse interface classes that are available in class libraries. The choice of interface objects will depend on the style guidelines that have been adopted for the system. These classes are shown in class and package diagrams. Second, we need to model the interaction with the user in sequence or collaboration diagrams. The way that the interaction is modelled will depend on the architecture that has been chosen for the system. The three-tier architecture and the Model–View–Controller architecture separate the boundary objects from the entity and control objects using well-defined methods. Third, we need to model the state of the interface to ensure that we understand how the interface will respond to events and what sequences of events are permitted. We use state machine diagrams to do this.

While carrying out these three modelling tasks, we can draw on design patterns to inform the way in which we select the interface classes and design the interaction between them and the business classes. Prototyping can be used to build models of the interface and test how it will work. Users should be involved in this process to ensure that the interface meets their requirements and to validate the analysts' understanding of their requirements for how tasks should be carried out.

Review Questions

17.1 Why should the user interface classes be kept separate from the business classes and application logic?

17.2 Explain the difference between vertical and horizontal prototyping.

17.3 What is meant by a throwaway prototype?

17.4 What does the «import» stereotype mean?

17.5 What role does each element of the Model–View–Controller architecture play?

17.6 What else do we use state machine diagrams for, apart from modelling the state of interface objects?

17.7 What are the five steps in preparing a state machine to model a user interface?

17.8 What information is held in an event–action table?

17.9 Convert the communication diagram of Fig. 17.25 into a sequence diagram.

17.10 Convert the communication diagram of Fig. 17.27 into a sequence diagram.

17.11 What are the differences between the MVC and Java EventListener approaches?

17.12 Convert the sequence diagram of Fig. 17.36 into a communication diagram.

17.13 Convert the sequence diagram of Fig. 17.37 into a communication diagram.

Case Study Work, Exercises and Projects

17.A Decide how you will handle the interaction between the user and the system for the use case Record problem on line for FoodCo. Draw a prototype user interface design.

17.B Draw a sequence diagram to include the interface objects that are needed for your prototype in Exercise 17.A.

17.C Draw a class diagram to show the classes that are used in the prototype from Exercise 17.A.

17.D Extend your class diagram from Exercise 17.C to show the superclasses of the interface classes.

17.E If you are familiar with a class library, such as the Java AWT, Java Swing, Microsoft Windows Forms or Ruby, then try to determine how your interface classes relate to classes in that class library.

17.F Produce a prototype for the use case `Record problem on line` using a language or visual programming environment with which you are familiar.

17.G Draw a state machine diagram for the interface to the use case `Record problem on line` to model the behaviour of your prototype developed in Exercise 17.F.

17.H Update your sequence diagram from Exercise 17.B to make sure that it reflects the state machine diagram of Exercise 17.G.

Further Reading

The MVC architecture is explained in a number of books, particularly books that use Smalltalk as a programming language. Gamma et al. (1995) specifically explain it in terms of patterns.

The Java `EventListener` event model was introduced into Java in Version 1.1. (Version 1.0 used a less efficient model.) There are a number of these `EventListener` interfaces for different kinds of events. Most introductory Java programming books explain them. The Swing classes can also use the MVC approach.

Few books on object-oriented analysis and design provide much detail on state machines, and those that do often provide simple models of telephone systems as examples rather than user interfaces. Browne (1994) is one of the few authors who seriously applies state machine diagrams to user interface design. Although he does not use the UML notation, his diagrams in Chapter 3 are similar enough to provide a clear idea of how they can be used to model the detail of user interface interaction. Horrocks (1999) applies a more rigorous software engineering approach to the use of state machines to design interfaces. Browne's approach is bottom-up, while Horrocks's is top-down. Both use the state machine notation that was originally developed by Harel (1987). For a more recent view of state machines from Harel, see Harel and Politi (1998), which presents the STATEMATE approach.

Chapter **18**

Data Management Design

18.1 Introduction

Real information systems require *persistent* data: data that continues to exist even when the system is not active, and data that is stored so that it can be shared between many users in different places and at different times. If you have to design the storage of data, one of the first decisions is whether to store it in files or in a database. A database is a more likely solution, as it provides a set of tools for storing data, but there are some things that simple files of various types are good at: holding configuration data is one example.

Using a database management system (DBMS) offers a number of advantages over files, and there is a further decision to make: whether to use an *object* DBMS, which should require minimum effort to take objects in programs and store them in the database; or whether to use a *relational* database, in which case the objects will have to be mapped to tables in the database. Many organizations already have relational DBMSs, so the designer of an object-oriented system can be constrained by the organization's existing investments in hardware and software and have to use a relational database management system (RDBMS) to store data. *Normalization* can be used to design tables for a relational database. Alternatively there are rules of thumb that can be applied to convert a class diagram to a suitable set of tables.

Designing for an object DBMS will have a minimal impact on the design model. Commercial and open-source products exist that can take plain objects in Java or C#

and store them in the database. With some extra work, usually in configuration, such databases can be set up to minimize the work required of the programmer.

It is possible to build your own framework for storing objects in a relational database, but few designers or programmers would do this, as there are standards such as the Java Persistence API and Java Data Objects and many products that implement these standards, that mean that you should never have to design your own persistence framework.

Databases don't necessarily run on a single computer or in a single location, and there are different ways of distributing data across multiple machines, although designing for distributed databases is an advanced topic beyond the scope of this book.

18.2 Persistence

18.2.1 Requirement for persistence

For some applications the data that is created or used while the application is running is not required after the application terminates. This applies mainly to simple applications: an example would be the on-screen calculators provided with GUI operating systems. Such data is called *transient data*.

Most applications, however, need to store data between one execution of the program and the next. In some cases, the data that is stored is secondary to the operation of the application. When you use a browser, one of the first things that happens as it loads is that it reads data from files that describe the user's preferences and record the last websites visited. The ability to store user settings and to configure applications in this way is an important factor in their usability, but it is not their primary purpose: a browser still works if the user's preferences and history are not available.

In the case of information systems, storing data is a primary requirement. Businesses and other organizations rely on their information systems to record data about other organizations, people, physical objects and business events and transactions. The data entered into such a system today will be required in the future; operations being carried out on data today rely on data that was stored in the past. Computerized information systems have replaced systems based on paper in files and ledgers, and must provide the same relatively permanent storage that is provided by paper-based systems. In most organizations, it is also important that data can be shared between different users. Data in the memory of a particular computer is not normally accessible to multiple users. It must be written away to some kind of shared data storage system so that other users can retrieve it when they require access to it.

This is what we mean by *persistent data*. It is data that must be stored in a secondary data storage system, not just in computer memory, that must be stored after the program that creates or amends it stops running and that usually must be available to other users. Information systems also use transient data: for example, the results of calculations or lists of objects that are required for a particular purpose such as printing a report, but that are not required permanently and can be destroyed after they have been used.

In an object-oriented system, we are concerned with both *persistent objects* and *transient objects*. Persistent objects are those that must be stored using some kind of storage mechanism, while transient objects will be erased from memory after they have been used.

18.2.2 Overview of storage mechanisms

Ultimately all data in computer systems is stored in files of some sort. In Section 18.3, we explain the different kinds of file organizations and access methods that are available, and the purposes that files are used for. However, most information systems use a database management system of some sort in which to store their data. Database management systems provide a layer of abstraction that hides from the programmer the fact that the data is stored in files. If the database is a relational database, then the user of the database sees tables containing data. Each table may relate to part of a file, to a single file or to many files, but that is not important to the user of a relational database (who may be a designer or programmer). The way that the database stores tables in files is important to the database administrator, who has to be concerned with where the data is stored, taking backups and so on. If the database is an object database, then the programmer sees objects and links between them. Again these objects will be stored in files of some sort, but the designer or programmer does not need to know the details.

In an object-oriented system, a database of some sort is the most likely way of providing persistent storage for objects. However, it is possible to store objects in files. Most object-oriented languages provide mechanisms for converting objects into a form that can be written out to a file–*serializing* them–and for reading them back into memory from a file. This is unlikely to provide an efficient mechanism for a business information system. However, files can be used for many other storage purposes in object-oriented systems. They can be used to hold data that is transferred in from other systems, and in Section 19.6 we discuss the conversion of data from a system that is being replaced. Files can also hold configuration information, and in Section 18.3.5 we provide an example of how files can be used to localize the Agate system so that text items such as labels, button captions and menu entries are displayed in the language of the country where the application is being used.

The choice of database management system will have a significant impact on the work that is required of the systems designers. If an object database is used, then there should be little work involved in designing the way that objects are stored. If a relational database is used, then more work is involved. In Section 18.5 we describe two approaches to converting classes to tables and, in Section 18.8, we describe some ways of designing persistence frameworks. In Section 18.8.4 we explain the tools and frameworks that are available to automate the process of mapping classes to tables.

18.2.3 Architecture for persistence

Part of the process of system architecture design is to determine how the requirements for the storage of persistent data will be met by the system. There may be trade-offs to be made between the requirements for a new system and the existing hardware and software that is available. Many organizations also have corporate standards for the database management systems that they use, and these will influence the architecture of a new system and the design of data storage.

Existing systems may have a different architecture from the one proposed for a new system, but there may be parts of the existing system that can be reused. This is often the case with databases, as organizations often have existing business systems and wish to use the data from those existing systems in new ways. If the new system is to be developed in an object-oriented language, it may be necessary to create a layer in the

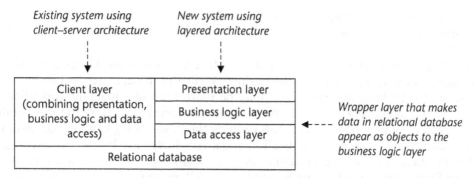

Figure 18.1 Layered architecture for existing and new systems sharing an existing relational database.

architecture that wraps the existing data so that it looks like objects even if it is stored in a relational database. This is shown in Fig. 18.1. An example of an existing system like this might use SQL-Server as its database and Visual Basic for the existing client programs. The Visual Basic client programs access the data in the database using ODBC (Open Database Connectivity) and SQL (Structured Query Language). The new system might use Java applications for the presentation layer, and Java components for the business logic layer and for the data access layer. The Java components would provide a wrapper around the rows of data in the relational database, so that they appeared as objects to the business logic layer. The data access layer would probably still use ODBC—or in this case JDBC (Java Database Connectivity)—and SQL to connect to the database, but the objects used to access the data could be reused in other applications. If the data access layer is well designed, it may be possible later to replace the old client–server application by adding to the presentation and business logic layers and reusing the data access layer.

For the architect designing the persistent storage of a system there are a number of questions to be answered.

- Are there parts of the system where storage in files is appropriate?
- Is the system truly an object-oriented system or a simple database system with a GUI user interface? For simple systems, it is possible to write programs in an object-oriented language such as C# or Java, which provide a front-end to a database. The front-end could connect to the database using ODBC or JDBC and treat the data purely as rows of data in tables, without using any entity objects. We are not taking this approach here, as it is not appropriate for our case studies.
- Will the system use an existing DBMS or is there freedom to choose an appropriate DBMS? If an existing system is to be used, it will constrain the system design in some ways, but, as we have shown above, it is possible to use a more flexible layered architecture to replace a client–server system while retaining the same DBMS.
- Will the system use a relational DBMS? If a relational DBMS is to be used then classes must be mapped to tables. This can be done using tools that automate this process, or by designing the tables and a suitable mechanism to fetch data from the database and assemble it into objects, and to save the objects back into the database when required.
- Will the system use an object DBMS? If an object DBMS is to be used, then work on designing the persistence mechanisms is likely to be much simpler.

- What is the logical layering of the system? A layered architecture is likely to be more flexible, separating the user interface, the business logic and the access to and storage of data.
- What is the physical layering of the system? More than one logical layer can reside on the same machine: for example, the business logic and the data access can be on the same server. In large systems, there may be more than one machine providing the services of a single layer, for example several web-servers handling the presentation layer, which connect to two machines running the business logic, which connect to a single database server. If an application is delivered over the Internet or a company intranet, then much of the presentation layer will reside on the web server, where Active Server Pages (ASP), Java Server Pages (JSP) or some other related technology will be used to construct the web pages dynamically and deliver them to the client's browser.
- What is the distribution of the system? It is conventional for the presentation layer to be located on many client machines, but, if the entity objects and the business logic are located on multiple machines, then the system must be designed to use a distributed DBMS to make it possible for clients to transparently access the objects they need to connect to in order to provide the functionality of the system.
- What protocols will be used to connect between layers of the system, particularly in a distributed architecture? Language- or operating system-specific protocols such as Java's Remote Method Invocation (RMI) or Microsoft's .NET Framework can be used but restrict the design to implementation on certain platforms. Open standards such as CORBA or web services which use XML (Extensible Markup Language) make it possible to build component-based systems that are not tied to particular platforms.

Building large, distributed systems is beyond the scope of this book, but in the rest of this chapter we explain some of the mechanisms that can be used to design persistence into an object-oriented system, and we start with the simplest–files.

18.3 File Systems

The simplest means of persistent storage available for computerized information systems uses files. Most users of personal computers are familiar with the idea of files. Word-processors and spreadsheets store their data in files; browsers download them from websites where they are stored. At the simplest level, a file is a stream of bytes of data stored on some physical medium. In most cases, files are stored magnetically by adjusting the magnetic properties of the surface layer of a disk or tape. Files can also be stored optically on CD-ROMs and other optical storage systems or electronically in special kinds of memory, such as the flash memory used in palmtops and USB memory devices. However, the user is normally shielded from the physical implementation of the file system by the operating system of the computer or by a programming language, which provides high-level functions to create files, store data in them and retrieve that data.

18.3.1 File and record structures

Programming languages, and in some cases operating systems, also impose a structure on files. This structure breaks a file up into individual records, each of which groups together a number of fields representing the data that is to be held in the file. In the same way as each object contains a number of attributes, each one of which holds a particular kind of data about the object, each field in a record holds a particular kind of data about whatever it is that the record describes. For example, each record in a simple address book file would have fields to contain a name, lines of the address, city, postcode and telephone number. Records in files can take different forms, described below.

- *Fixed length*–Each record is made up of a number of fields, each of which has a fixed length in bytes. If the data in a particular field does not fill it, the field is padded out with special characters (often spaces). Each record is of the same, fixed length and it is possible to skip from the beginning of one record to the beginning of the next by jumping that fixed number of bytes ahead.
- *Variable length*–Each record is made up of a number of fields, each of which may have a maximum length but has a minimum length of zero bytes. Fields are usually separated or delimited by a special character that would not appear in the data. Records may also be delimited by a special character. The length of each record may also be stored at the start of the record, making it possible to skip to the beginning of the next record by jumping that variable number of bytes ahead.
- *Header and detail*–Records may be of two types: each transaction recorded consists of a header record, followed by a variable number of detail records. This approach can be used with many business documents, such as orders, invoices and delivery notes that have a variable number of lines on them. Each record will contain a `record type` field. The number of detail records may be held in the header so that it is possible to tell where the next header record starts.
- *Tagged data*–The data may have a complex structure, as in object-oriented systems, and it may even be necessary to hold objects of different classes in the same file. Every object and attribute may be tagged with some kind of description that tells a program reading the file what the type of each item is. This approach is used for data in files that use Hypertext Markup Language (HTML) and Extensible Markup Language (XML).

Some systems store information about the structure of the file in a data dictionary and this may be held in a separate file or at the start of the data file itself. This makes it possible to write programs which can read the data out of any file that uses this format: the program first reads the data dictionary information and configures itself to read the appropriate data structures from the rest of the file.

As well as having alternative ways in which the data can be structured within files, files can have different types of organization, can be accessed in different ways and can serve different purposes in a system.

18.3.2 File organization

There are three ways in which files can be organized: serial, sequential and random.

- *Serial organization*–Each record in the file is written onto the end of the existing records in the file. If a record is to be deleted, the file must be copied from the start up to the deleted record, which is skipped, and then the rest of the file is copied back to the disk.

- *Sequential organization*—In the basic form of sequential organization, each record is written to the file in some pre-determined order, usually based on the value of one of the fields in each record, such as an invoice number. Records must be deleted in the same way as for serial files. Each record must be added to the file in its appropriate place and, if it is necessary to insert a record into a file, the file is copied up to the point where the record is to be inserted, the new record is written to the file and then the rest of the file is copied.
- *Random organization*—The term random is a poor way of describing the organization of random files, as the organization is really anything but random. The records are added to the file by means of precise algorithms that allow records to be written and read directly without having to read through the rest of the file. What this means is that if you choose any record *at random*, it should be possible to access it more or less straightaway without searching through the file. The algorithm usually converts a key field of each record into an address in the file that can be reached directly.

18.3.3 File access

Depending on the file organization chosen, different ways of accessing the data in the files are available to the designer. The main ones are serial, index-sequential and direct.

Serial access
Serial and basic sequential files can only be accessed serially. To find a particular record, it is necessary to read through the file, record by record, until the required record is located.

Index-sequential access
Access to sequential files can be improved by maintaining an index on the field that is used to order the data in the file (the key). Index-sequential files are used where it is necessary to read the file sequentially, record by record, and to be able to go straight to a particular record using its key. The indexing mechanism used for index-sequential files dates back to the time when mainframe operating systems made it possible to allocate the particular disks, cylinders and tracks where a file would be stored.

Records are stored sequentially within blocks (areas of the disk that have a defined size). Enough blocks are allocated to the file for the total anticipated number of records. Records are written into blocks in key order, but the blocks are not filled up from the start of the file; rather, records are distributed evenly across the blocks, leaving space for new records in each block.

The index on the file can be dense or sparse. In a dense index, there is an entry for every key with a pointer to the first record in the file with that key (there may be more than one). In a sparse index, there is an entry for the last record in each data block. To find a record, a program reads through the index until it finds a key value greater than the value of the key it is searching for. It then jumps to the block pointed to by that index entry and reads through it until it finds the required record.

To support large files, there may be two or more levels of index. For example, there may be a master index and a series of block indexes. The master index holds the value of the key field of the last record in each block index. Each block index holds the value of the key field of the last record of each block in a set of blocks. To find a record by its key, the master index is read until a key value is found that is greater than or equal to

Master Index	
Record key	Block index address
Feng	1
Patel	2
Zarzycki	3

Block Index (Index block 2)	
Record key	Block address
Finlayson	55
Gomez	56
Hanson	57
Jacobson	58
. . .	. . .
Patel	84

Data records in blocks (for simplicity only the keys are shown)				
Block address	Records			
55	Fern	Finch	Finlayson	
56	Finn	Firmin	Ford	Gangar	Gomez
57	Gordon	Govan	Hamer	Hanson
58	Ho	Ibrahim	Jacobson	
. . .	. . .			

Figure 18.2 Schematic of indexes and data in an index-sequential file ordered by surname.

the key of the record being sought. This makes it possible to go to the block index for that record. The block index is then read until a key value is found that is greater than or equal to the key of the record being sought. This makes it possible to go to the block in which the record is held. The records in the block are then read sequentially until the desired record is found. A similar approach is taken in order to add records to an index-sequential file. The block in which the record is located is identified using the index, then the records in the block are read into memory and copied to the disk up to the point that the new record is to be inserted, the new record is written into the block, and then the rest of the records in the block are copied back to the block. The index may also need to be updated. Eventually some blocks will fill up, and it will be necessary to write some records into special overflow blocks. The addresses of the overflow blocks will be held in the blocks that have overflowed. Performance tuning of such files involves resizing them so that there are more blocks in the file and no records have to be stored in overflow blocks. Figure 18.2 shows the organization of data and indexes in an index-sequential file.

Index-sequential files have the advantage over sequential files that records can be read and written more quickly, although there is a storage overhead associated with maintaining the indexes. Compared to direct access, which is described next, there is also the overhead of the time taken to access the indexes before the data is reached.

Direct access

Direct access methods rely on the use of algorithms to convert the values of key fields in the records to addresses in the file. (The term random access is sometimes used.) The first and simplest of these is *relative addressing*. This access method requires the use of fixed length records and successive positive integers as keys. If each record is 200 bytes long, then record 1 will start at byte 1 of the file, record 2 at byte 201, record 3 at byte 401 and so on. It is possible to calculate the position of any record in the file by subtracting 1 from its key, multiplying the result by the size of the records and adding 1. Each record can be read directly by reading from that point in the file.

Hashed addressing is the second approach. This can use keys of any form. As with indexed sequential files, a fixed number of blocks is initially allocated to the file. This is usually a prime number of blocks, as this helps to achieve a more even spread of records into blocks. The key is then hashed to determine to which block a particular record will be allocated. The hashing function is an algorithm that takes an ASCII string and converts it to an integer. There are many approaches. A simple approach is to take the characters in the string and convert them to their ASCII values (for example, 'A' is 65). These ASCII values are summed together. The sum is divided by the number of blocks in the file and the remainder or modulo gives the number of the block in the file into which that record will be placed, starting at block 0. If a block fills up, then an additional block will be used as overflow, and its address will be held in the block that the record would have been stored in. Figure 18.3 shows the organization of a hashed direct access file and the calculation of a simplified version of the hashing algorithm based on just three characters of the key.

Improving access

There are a number of ways of improving access to data in files. Files with a random organization can normally only be accessed directly or serially (for example, to copy the file), so it is not possible to read through them sequentially in an order based on key fields. However, it is possible to add two extra fields to each record containing the key

Records hashed on first three characters of key field
Khan → Kha ASCII Values = 75, 104, 97 75 + 104 + 97 = 276 276 divided by 7 leaves a modulo of 3 So Khan will be added in Block 3.

Data records in blocks (for simplicity only the keys are shown)

Block no. in file	Records			
0	Hao			
1	Ford	Farmer		
2	Firmin	Firth		
3	Harris			
4	Hastings	Gomez	Jacobson	
5	Ibrahim	Finch	Fern	Gangar
6	Hanson			

Figure 18.3 Organization of a sample hashed direct access file.

values of the next record and the previous record in sequence (a linked list). This makes it possible to read through the records sequentially, but adds a considerable overhead when a record is added or deleted.

A common way of improving access to a file is to add a secondary index. This is a similar approach to that used in adding an index to an index-sequential file. It is used when there is a requirement either to access records in a file based on the values in some field other than the key field (for example, to find address records by postal code or zipcode) or to provide sequential access to a random file, by building an index of sequential keys. A separate file is created in which the keys are the values from the indexed field (for example, the postal code) in all the records in the main file. Each record also contains either the keys or the block addresses of each of the records that contain that indexed field. This kind of index is known as an *inverted file*. There are various structures that can be used for indexes, such as B-trees, which have different benefits–in terms of speeding up retrieving records–and different disadvantages–in terms of adding an overhead to updates to the file.

18.3.4 File types

We have seen that as well as files that hold data, there can also be files that hold indexes to the data in the main files. Other types of files may be required in a file-based system.

- *Master files*–hold the essential, persistent data records for the system. In transaction-processing systems the master files are updated with details of transactions that are recorded in transaction files. Master files usually require some kind of direct access so that records can be updated quickly.
- *Transaction files*–record business transactions or events that are of interest to the organization and that are used to update records in master files. In a banking system, transactions that take place when customers withdraw cash from an automatic teller machine (ATM) may be recorded in a transaction file. At the end of the day, the transaction file is processed in order to update all the accounts of customers who have withdrawn cash.
- *Index files*–used to speed up access to records in master files, as described above. There are many index file structures that can be used, and the choice of index structure will depend on the nature of the data and the type of access required.
- *Temporary files or work files*–During the course of processing data, it may be necessary to create a temporary file that is used to hold the results of one process before it is used in another process. For example, it may be necessary to sort records into a particular order so that a report can be produced; a work file containing the records in the correct order would be produced and then deleted once the report had been created. When you use applications that print your work in the background (while you get on with another task), then they are using spool files to hold the printed output that is sent to the printer. These spool files are deleted when they have been printed.
- *Backup files*–may be direct copies of master files or transaction files that are held on the system and that allow the data to be restored if the originals are destroyed or corrupted. Alternatively, they may be files with a special structure that can be used to reconstruct the data in the system.
- *Parameter files*–Many programs need to store information about items of data of which there is only one record. These are typically system settings, such as the name

and address of the company using the software, and configuration information, such as the currency format to be used to print out money values or the format to be used for printing the date. Parameter files hold this kind of information.

In a project that uses files to store data, part of the role of the designer is to choose the appropriate file organization and access method for the storage of all the objects in the system. In most cases, objects will need to be stored and retrieved using some kind of object identifier and direct access files will be required. However, there may be requirements for all the objects of a particular type to be retrieved from the file in sequence, which may indicate the need for an organization that supports sequential access, or for the addition of an index. Some object-oriented languages provide mechanisms for streaming objects out to a serial file. This is the case with both Smalltalk and Java. Java, for example, contains two classes called `ObjectOutputStream` and `ObjectInput-Stream` that can be used to write objects together with information about their class to a disk file and read them back again.

Many organizations use DBMSs to hold data. In their systems, there will be no need for designers to make decisions about the physical file structures used to provide persistent storage for objects. However, there are still situations where files are the appropriate mechanism for storing data in an application. In the next section we present one example.

18.3.5 Example of using files

In the Agate system, one of the non-functional requirements is that the application can be customized for use in different countries with different languages. This means that all the prompts that are displayed in windows, labels on buttons and menus, and error and warning messages cannot be written into the classes in the presentation layer as string literals. For example, if a user interface class was implemented in Java using string literals, the line of code to create a cancel button would look like this:

```
Button cancelButton = new Button ("Cancel");
```

To use the program in French, someone would have to go through finding all the strings like this and translating them. Then there would be two versions of the program, and any changes would have to be made in both. This is unmanageable with just two languages, let alone several. In Java, it is possible to use the class `java.util.Locale` to hold information about the current locale in which an application is running. This includes information about the language, the country and a variant value, for example 'fr' for French, 'FR' for France. When France changed to the Euro as its currency in January 2002, the variant value could have used the string 'EURO', but that is no longer necessary, as there is no longer an alternative currency. For an application running in French in Canada, the language code 'fr' and the country code 'CA' would be required.

Another Java class, `java.util.ResourceBundle`, uses the locale information to hold objects in memory, each of which is associated with a key value. It can load these objects from a file, and the name of the file is made up of the name of the resource and the language, country and variant codes. So for a resource called `UIResources`, designed to hold the values for all the prompts and labels, there could be different versions called `UIResources_fr_FR`, `UIResources_en_UK`, and `UIResources_en_US`, for France, the United Kingdom and the USA, respectively.

When the user interface class is instantiated, it needs to find out its locale and then load the correct resources into memory with a line of Java like this:

```
resources = ResourceBundle.getBundle
                ("UIResources",currentLocale);
```

Then the code to set up the cancel button becomes the following:

```
Button cancelButton = new Button
                        (resources.getString("Cancel"));
```

The resource file is made up of records, each of which is on a separate line, with an equals sign to separate the key from the associated string, for example:

```
Cancel = Annuler
OK = OK
File = Fichier
```

for the French version. When the application is deployed, either the installation routine must install the correct resource files on the machines that will be running the user interface classes, or a full set of files must be deployed, and the appropriate one will be chosen at runtime. (See Chapter 19 for more detail about implementation and deployment.)

18.4 Database Management Systems

18.4.1 Files and databases

Files are appropriate for simple programs and for storing data that does not need to be shared and updated by many users. During the 1960s systems were built using files to store data; since the 1970s most large commercial systems have used databases of some sort to hold their data and, more importantly, DBMSs to organize and manage the tasks associated with storing and providing effective access to large volumes of data.

Using files to store data can result in a number of problems.

- As the number of applications grows, the number of different files grows. Some of these files may hold the same data for different applications in different formats and so data is duplicated, taking up unnecessary storage space. This is known as redundancy.
- There is the risk that the updates to data in different applications will not be synchronized: for example, a customer address may be changed in one file but not in another, leaving the data inconsistent.
- Each application must contain its own mechanisms for storing the data in its set of files. If the data changes or the way that it is stored has to be changed, then each program within an application that accesses that data must be amended. This makes it difficult to add new programs to an application that use some of the same data but also need to store additional data.
- As business requirements change, users may want to access the data in new ways: for example, to produce a report combining data from different applications. This cannot be implemented without considerable programming effort.

The first step towards resolving these problems is to analyse the storage requirements of different applications across the organization and to build an enterprise database that contains all the data from different applications. Each application then uses a subset of

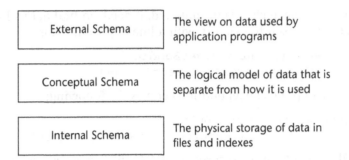

Figure 18.4 The Three-schema Architecture.

this database for its own requirements. The second step is to use a DBMS to organize and manage the data and to decouple the storage mechanisms from the application programs. The aim of using a DBMS is to separate the details of the way that data is stored physically from the way that it is used in application programs. This is achieved by producing a logical model of the data that is independent of the demands of applications and that could be stored in different ways in the database. This is known as the Three-schema Architecture. Figure 18.4 shows the Three-schema Architecture. The external schema represents the ways in which data is used in application programs. The conceptual schema is a logical model of the data and is independent both of the external schema and of the details of how the data will be stored. The physical organization of the data is to be found in the internal schema, which defines the files used to store the data. The aim of this approach is to isolate the application programs from the details of how any particular item of data is stored. This is central to the way that relational DBMS work. Design for relational DBMSs is described in more detail in Section 18.5.

Note that just using a DBMS does not necessarily eliminate the problems of redundancy and inconsistency described above. Many organizations end up with different databases for different applications with redundant and inconsistent data in some databases, and many large organizations find that Microsoft Access databases proliferate as end-users develop their own mini-applications.

DBMSs provide more than just a means of storing data that can be shared across many applications. They provide tools and features that can be used to manage the data.

- *Data definition language (DDL)*. The DDL is used to specify the data that is held in a database management system and the structures that are used to hold it.
- *Data manipulation language (DML)*. The DML is used to specify updates and retrievals of the data in the DBMS. Structured Query Language (SQL) is the de facto standard for both DDL and DML in relational databases.
- *Integrity constraints*. Constraints can be specified to ensure that the integrity of the data is maintained.
- *Transaction management*. Updates to the database can be specified as *transactions* in which all of the updates to different objects must succeed. If one update cannot be successfully made to the database, all the updates must be stopped, so that the database returns to a consistent state. The entire transaction is *rolled back*, which means that it is not committed to the database, and updates that had already been processed are cancelled. Transactions depend on a process called *two-phase commit*, in which each update is prepared and checked to see that it will succeed. Only when it is

known that all updates will succeed is the data finally committed to the database. A simple example would be if you have a current account and a savings account with the same bank and you make an online transfer between your two accounts. You would be unhappy if the update to reduce the balance of the source account was successful, but the addition to the balance of the target account failed! Both must be successful or the whole transaction must be stopped.

- *Concurrency.* Many users can simultaneously use the database and update its contents.
- *Security.* Access to the data in the database can be controlled, and permissions granted to different users for different levels of access (for example in SQL, select, insert, update and delete).
- *Tuning of storage.* Tools can be used to monitor the way that data is accessed and to improve the structures in the internal schema in order to make the access more efficient. These changes can then be made without having any impact on the application programs.

As mentioned above, these structures in the internal schema will be files. An important feature of a DBMS is that the kind of file used, the access methods and the indexes that are held on the file are hidden from users of the DBMS (typically application programmers) and can be changed without affecting the programs that use that data.

These changes to the database do not happen automatically. For large systems a database administrator (DBA) must be employed to manage the database and to ensure that it is running efficiently. The DBA will be responsible for controlling the data dictionary that defines the conceptual schema of the database, for controlling access to data and for tuning the performance of the database. For smaller systems a DBA will not be needed, but someone will need to be responsible for managing the database.

In summary, the use of a DBMS based on the Three-schema Architecture has a number of advantages over the use of files to store data for an information system.

- The use of a conceptual schema can eliminate unnecessary duplication of data.
- Data integrity can be ensured by the use of integrity constraints and transaction management techniques.
- Changes to the conceptual schema, the logical model, should not affect the application programs, provided the external schema used by the application programs does not have to be changed.
- Changes to the internal schema, the physical storage of the data, have no impact on the conceptual schema and should not affect the application programs, except perhaps positively in enabling them to access data more efficiently. Compromises may have to be made between the needs of different application programs.
- Tools are available for tuning the performance of the database, for the back-up and recovery of data and to control security and access to data by multiple simultaneous users.

However, the use of DBMS may also have disadvantages for organizations that decide to go down this route.

- There is a cost associated with investing in a large DBMS package.
- There is a running cost involved in employing staff to manage the DBMS.
- There will be a processing overhead in converting data from the database to the format required by the application programs.

The most widely used type of DBMS is the relational DBMS. For object-oriented systems one might hope to be able to use an object DBMS. However, in many situations, organizations have an existing relational DBMS and new object-oriented applications must share that enterprise database. A relational database with C++, C# or Java as the application development language is still more common than an object DBMS.

18.4.2 Types of DBMS

The three main types of database that we are concerned with here are relational, object and hybrid object-relational.

Relational databases

The idea of relational databases was first suggested by Codd (1970). His proposal was followed by considerable research effort that led to the development of commercial relational database management systems (RDBMS) during the 1970s. However, it was not until 1986 that the American National Standards Institute published the first SQL standard based on this work (ANSI, 1986). SQL (Structured Query Language) is now the standard language for relational databases and provides both DDL and DML capabilities.

Relational databases have a theoretical foundation in set theory and their operations are defined in terms of the *relational algebra*, a mathematical specification of the operations that can be carried out on *relations*. The essence of the relational model is to eliminate redundancy from data and to provide the simplest possible logical representation of that data. This is achieved by means of a series of steps that can be applied in analysing the data and that result in normalized data. This normalized data is held in relations or tables. This process simplifies a complex data structure until it can be held in a series of tables. Each table is made up of *rows* of data. Each row contains attribute values that are organized in *columns*. Each column contains data values of the same attribute type. The data in each row must be distinct and can be uniquely identified by some combination of attribute values in that row. Each attribute value in the table must be *atomic*, that is, it may not contain multiple values or be capable of being broken down further. Figure 18.5 shows the conventional form for representing tables on paper. In existing RDBMSs, all data structures must be decomposed into this kind of two-dimensional table.[1]

The weakness of current implementations of RDBMSs lies in the fact that objects in object-oriented systems do not fit easily into this model. They can be broken down into tables, as is shown in Section 18.4, but there is a processing overhead associated with breaking them down and reconstructing them. References to other objects (represented by associations in the class diagram) must also be maintained when an object is stored in a relational database, and restored when it is retrieved. And, even if the associated object is not itself in memory, some mechanism must be created to allow it to be referenced and to be sent messages. Tables in RDBMSs are linked to one another by common attribute values (foreign keys), whereas objects are linked to one another by references or pointers. Data in relational DBMSs is processed in sets, while data in object DBMSs must be navigated through, following links from object to object.

---

1   Date and Darwen (1998) argue that the relational model can handle complex data types, but it is the way that relational DBMSs have been implemented that leads to their inability to handle these data types.

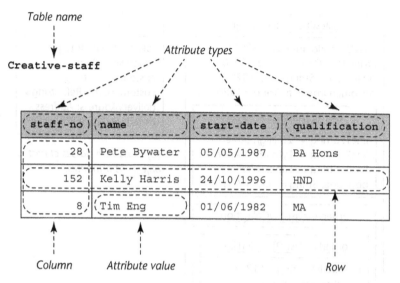

Figure 18.5 Conventional representation of a table.

Relational DBMSs are currently the most widely used type of DBMS. They are based on a sound mathematical theory, they have been developed over a number of years, they are robust and they are efficient and flexible for the kind of data that they are designed to handle. The best known is probably Access; others include Oracle, SQL-Server, DB2, Informix, Ingres, Progress and Sybase. The growth of Linux has also led to the availability of free and open source databases such as MySQL and PostgreSQL.

Object databases

In contrast, objects in an object-oriented system are not flat, two-dimensional structures. Each object may contain other objects nested within it. For example, a SalesOrder object could contain an Address object that contains its own attributes, and a Collection of OrderLine objects, each of which is made up of two attributes. An example of this is shown in Fig. 18.6 with a SalesOrder object with its class definition in UML notation. Object database management systems (ODBMSs) have been developed to handle complex objects of this sort. Part of the motivation for the development of ODBMSs has been the growth in the number of applications that use complex data structures. These include multimedia applications, in which objects such as sounds, images and video clips are not easily represented in tables, and applications such as computer aided design packages in which the designer may want to deal with different levels of abstraction: for example, treating a subassembly in terms of its behaviour as a subassembly, in terms of the individual chips or in terms of the components such as logic gates that make up those chips. ODBMSs provide services that make it possible to store complex objects of this type. Examples of ODBMSs include Versant Object Database, db4objects, JADE and ObjectStore. Section 18.6 includes an example using db4objects.

Object-relational databases

Object-relational databases combine the simplicity and efficiency of relational databases with the ability of object databases to store complex objects and to navigate through the associations between classes. The SQL standard is being updated to allow the relational

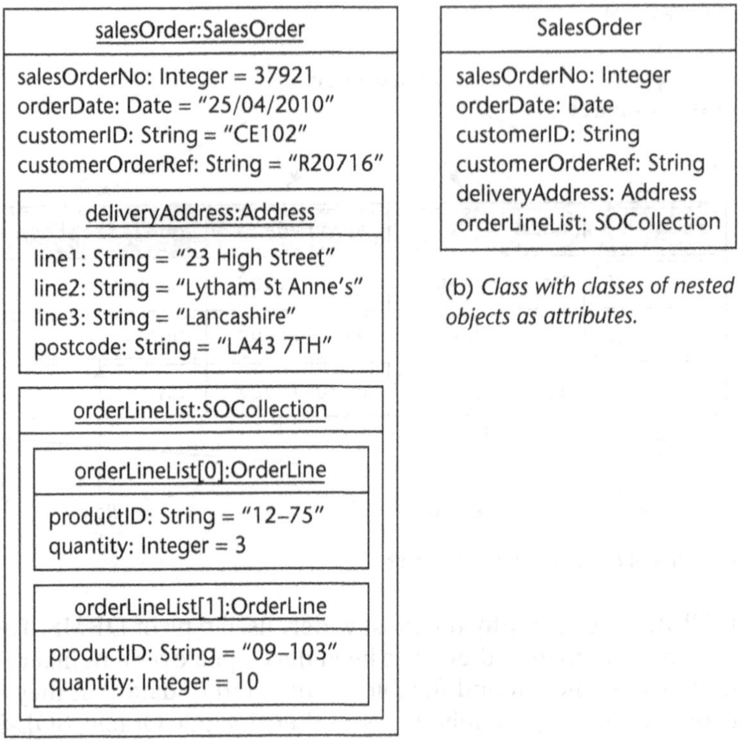

salesOrder:SalesOrder
salesOrderNo: Integer = 37921
orderDate: Date = "25/04/2010"
customerID: String = "CE102"
customerOrderRef: String = "R20716"

deliveryAddress:Address
line1: String = "23 High Street"
line2: String = "Lytham St Anne's"
line3: String = "Lancashire"
postcode: String = "LA43 7TH"

orderLineList:SOCollection

orderLineList[0]:OrderLine
productID: String = "12–75"
quantity: Integer = 3

orderLineList[1]:OrderLine
productID: String = "09–103"
quantity: Integer = 10

(a) *Complex object.*

SalesOrder
salesOrderNo: Integer
orderDate: Date
customerID: String
customerOrderRef: String
deliveryAddress: Address
orderLineList: SOCollection

(b) *Class with classes of nested objects as attributes.*

Figure 18.6 Composite `SalesOrder` object with equivalent UML class.

model to incorporate many features of object-oriented systems such as user-definable abstract data types, inheritance and operations. The open source product PostgreSQL is probably the most well-known hybrid DBMS. Oracle now includes some hybrid features. In what follows we shall focus on relational and object databases.

18.5 Designing for Relational Database Management Systems

18.5.1 Relational databases

RDBMSs have been in use since the 1970s. They use mature technology and are robust. It is common for an object-oriented system to be built to use a relational DBMS. Relational databases hold data in flat two-dimensional tables, whereas classes may have complex nested structures with objects embedded within other objects. If it is necessary to use an RDBMS to provide the storage for a system built using an object-oriented programming language, then it will be necessary to flatten the classes into tables in order to design the storage structures. When the system requires an instance of a class from the database, it will have to retrieve the data from all the tables that hold parts of that object instance and reconstruct it into an object. When a complex object instance has to be stored, it will have to be taken apart and parts of it will be stored in different tables. The designer of such a system has to decide on the structure of the tables to use to represent classes in the database. It should be emphasized that it is only the attribute values of object instances that are stored in an RDBMS; operations are implemented in the programming language used.

There are two ways in which classes can be converted to tables in a relational database. The first, normalization, is suitable for decomposing complex objects into tables. It is used in systems that are not object-oriented to design the structure of tables in databases. It can also be used during object design to simplify large complex objects that are not cohesive. The second approach is based on a series of rules of thumb that can be applied to classes in a class diagram to produce a set of table structures. In this section, we describe these two approaches and, in Section 18.6, we discuss the impact that this will have on the design of classes in the system.

18.5.2 Data modelling and normalization

In order to store the objects from an object-oriented system in a relational database, the objects must be flattened out. *Normalization* is an approach that is also used to convert the complex structures in business documents into tables to be stored in a relational database. A typical example of its use would be to design a set of tables to hold the data in a sales order like the FoodCo example in Fig. 16.3. How then do we apply normalization? Normalization is based on the idea of *functional dependency*.

For two attributes, A and B, A is functionally dependent on B if for every value of B there is exactly one value of A associated with it at any given time.

Attributes may be grouped around functional dependencies according to the rules of normalization to produce normalized data structures that are largely free of redundancy. There are five normal forms of normalized data. The data is free of redundancy in fifth normal form. For practical purposes it is usually adequate to normalize data into third normal form. Normalization is carried out in a number of steps, and we shall apply these to an example from the Agate case study.

Analysis activity during a further iteration has identified a class called `InternationalCampaign`, which is a kind of campaign that runs in more than one country, and the attribute values of two instances of this class are shown in Fig. 18.7. As stated earlier, we may wish to decompose this class into simpler classes because it is not cohesive or we may need to decompose it into table structures for storage using an RDBMS. The same approach is used in both cases. Here we are applying normalization as part of the design for a relational database.

The first step is to remove any calculated values (derived attributes). The attribute `locationCount` is a derived attribute. It is the number of locations associated with any one international campaign and can be calculated when an instance of `InternationalCampaign` is instantiated.

We now create a relation that is said to be in unnormalized form. Each `InternationalCampaign` is uniquely identified in this system by its `campaignCode`. This is the *primary key* attribute. Figure 18.8 shows the data from these instances in a table. Each `InternationalCampaign` is represented in a single row. Note that there are multiple values in some of the columns in each row. These relate to the locations where the campaign will run and the manager in each location.

A table is in *first normal form* (1NF) if and only if all row/column intersections contain atomic values. The table in Fig. 18.8 does not conform to this criterion and must be redrawn as in Fig. 18.9. These multiple values are often known as *repeating groups*.

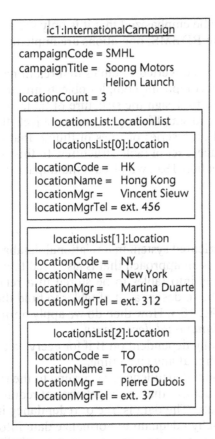
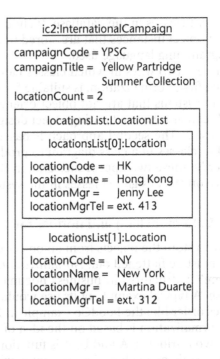

Figure 18.7 Example `InternationalCampaign` objects.

InternationalCampaign					
campaign Code	campaign Title	location Code	location Name	locationMgr	location MgrTel
SMHL	Soong Motors Helion Launch	HK NY TO	Hong Kong New York Toronto	Vincent Sieuw Martina Duarte Pierre Dubois	456 312 37
YPSC	Yellow Partridge Summer Collection	HK NY	Hong Kong New York	Jenny Lee Martina Duarte	413 312

Figure 18.8 Table for sample International Campaigns.

The `campaignCode` no longer uniquely identifies each row in the table. Each row is identified by a combination of `campaignCode` and `locationCode`. These attributes form a candidate *primary key* for the table.

The data values have been flattened out into a two-dimensional table and could now be stored in a relational database as they are. However, there is redundancy that we want to eliminate from the data. If redundant data is held in the database, there is the risk that values will not be updated correctly. For example, if Martina Duarte's telephone extension number changes, the system must ensure that it is correctly updated in every row in which it appears. This is inefficient and prone to error.

InternationalCampaign-1

campaign Code	campaign Title	location Code	location Name	locationMgr	location MgrTel
SMHL	Soong Motors Helion Launch	HK	Hong Kong	Vincent Sieuw	456
SMHL	Soong Motors Helion Launch	NY	New York	Martina Duarte	312
SMHL	Soong Motors Helion Launch	TO	Toronto	Pierre Dubois	37
YPSC	Yellow Partridge Summer Collection	HK	Hong Kong	Jenny Lee	413
YPSC	Yellow Partridge Summer Collection	NY	New York	Martina Duarte	312

Figure 18.9 Revised table for International Campaigns without repeating groups.

InternationalCampaign-2

campaignCode	locationCode	locationMgr	locationMgrTel
SMHL	HK	Vincent Sieuw	456
SMHL	NY	Martina Duarte	312
SMHL	TO	Pierre Dubois	37
YPSC	HK	Jenny Lee	413
YPSC	NY	Martina Duarte	312

Campaign

campaignCode	campaignTitle
SMHL	Soong Motors Helion Launch
YPSC	Yellow Partridge Summer Collection

Location

locationCode	locationName
HK	Hong Kong
NY	New York
TO	Toronto

Figure 18.10 2NF tables.

The next step is to convert these relations to *second normal form* (2NF). A relation is in 2NF if and only if it is in 1NF and every non-key attribute is fully dependent on the primary key. Here the attribute `campaignTitle` is only dependent on `campaignCode`, and `locationName` is only dependent on `locationCode`. (These are sometimes called 'part-key dependencies'.) The other attributes are dependent on the whole primary key. (Remember A is dependent on B if for every value of B there is exactly one value of A associated with it at a given time.) Figure 18.10 shows the creation of two new relations `Campaign` and `Location`.

The next step is to convert the tables to *third normal form* (3NF). A relation is in 3NF if and only if it is in 2NF and every attribute is dependent on the primary key and not on another non-key attribute. `Campaign` and `Location` are in 3NF, but in

InternationalCampaign-3		
campaignCode	locationCode	locationMgr
SMHL	HK	Vincent Sieuw
SMHL	NY	Martina Duarte
SMHL	TO	Pierre Dubois
YPSC	HK	Jenny Lee
YPSC	NY	Martina Duarte

LocationManager	
locationMgr	locationMgrTel
Vincent Sieuw	456
Martina Duarte	312
Pierre Dubois	37
Jenny Lee	413

Campaign	
campaignCode	campaignTitle
SMHL	Soong Motors Helion Launch
YPSC	Yellow Partridge Summer Collection

Location	
locationCode	locationName
HK	Hong Kong
NY	New York
TO	Toronto

Figure 18.11 3NF tables.

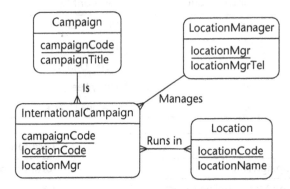

Figure 18.12 Entity–relationship diagram for tables of Fig. 18.11.

`InternationalCampaign-2`, `locationMgrTel` is dependent on `locationMgr` and not on the primary key. Figure 18.11 shows the tables in 3NF with the addition of a new table called `LocationManager`.

These relations can be shown in a diagram using the notation of entity–relationship diagrams, which are often used to represent the logical structure (conceptual schema) of relational databases. Note that this is not part of the UML notation. Figure 18.12 shows the relations of Fig. 18.11 as an entity–relationship diagram. Some UML CASE tools can also produce entity–relationship diagrams, and some can generate the SQL statements to create the tables.

If we examine the attributes of these relations, we may come to the conclusion that `InternationalCampaign` was not a very well analysed class in the first place. It should perhaps be a subclass of `Campaign`. `LocationManager` appears to be nothing more than `CreativeStaff` with an association to `International Campaign`. We also require a new class called `Location` with an association to

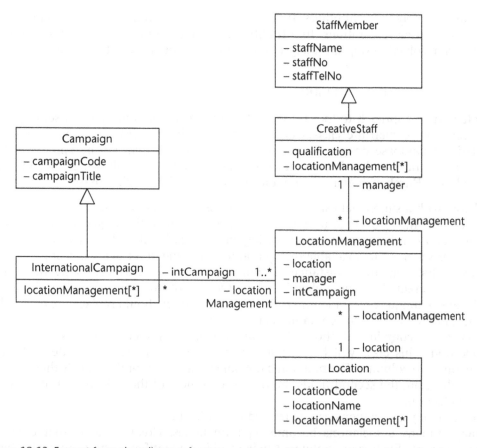

Figure 18.13 Excerpt from class diagram for InternationalCampaign.

InternationalCampaign. However, if we simply create associations between CreativeStaff and InternationalCampaign and between Location and InternationalCampaign, it will not be possible to tell which manager is managing the campaign in which location. There is presumably also an association between StaffMember (the superclass of CreativeStaff) and Location, but we should not rely on that to find out which Location an InternationalCampaign is running in, as the member of staff who is LocationManager could move offices. In Figure 18.13, we have added a new class LocationManagement, to relate a particular instance of CreativeStaff to a particular instance of Location and a particular instance of InternationalCampaign. Association ends are shown as attributes, but collection classes have not been added.

The classes in Fig. 18.13 raise a number of questions that should have been addressed during the analysis of requirements. Some of these are listed below.

- Does each campaign have a location? Is this the main location for an international campaign?
- Does each member of staff work in a location?
- Are there different versions of adverts for different locations?
- How are international campaigns costed? What currencies are used?

You can probably think of others. In an iterative lifecycle, it is acceptable to be raising these issues in early iterations. In a traditional Waterfall Lifecycle, these issues should have been resolved during the analysis stage, but in reality may not have been.

18.5.3 Mapping classes to tables

An alternative approach to that provided by normalization is to follow a set of guidelines for how to map the classes and multiplicities in the class diagram to tables in a relational database design. A summary of the patterns that can be applied to this mapping can be found in Brown and Whitenack (1996). The following guidelines are derived from Rumbaugh et al. (1991) and Brown and Whitenack (1996).

- Classes with a simple data structure. These classes become tables.
- Object identifiers become primary keys. A unique identifier is generated for every object and can be used as a primary key in the relational table in which it is held. (Various schemes are available that guarantee a unique id for every object.)
- Classes that contain an instance of another class as an attribute. A separate table should be created for the embedded class. Objects of the embedded class should be allocated a unique object identifier. The object identifier should replace the embedded object in the table for the container class as a foreign key.
- Classes that contain collections. Allocate an object identifier to the class held in the collection. This class will be represented by a table. Create a separate table that contains two columns. The first holds the object identifiers of the objects that contain the collection; the second holds the object identifiers of the objects that are held in the collection.
- One-to-many associations can be treated like collections.
- Many-to-many associations become separate tables. Create a table that contains two columns. Each row contains a pair of object identifiers, one from each object participating in the association. (These are like two collections.)
- One-to-one associations are implemented as foreign key attributes. Each class gains an extra attribute in which to hold the object identifier of the associated object.

(A *foreign key* is used in relational databases to create the relationships between tables. In the `InternationalCampaign-3` table in Fig. 18.11, `locationCode` is an example of a foreign key. Objects do not have keys, and this is why object identifiers are allocated to them. It may be possible to use an attribute that will have a unique value in each instance of a class as a foreign key.)

When a relational database is used, collection classes that exist only to provide access to a set of objects of the same class need not be part of the data that is stored in tables. If it is necessary to iterate through every instance of a particular class, this can be done by selecting every row from the table.

Inheritance poses more of a problem. There are three alternative ways of mapping an inheritance hierarchy to relational database tables.

- Only implement the superclass as a table. Attributes of subclasses become attributes of the superclass table and hold null values where they are not used. This approach is most appropriate where subclasses differ from their superclass more in behaviour than in attributes. A `type` attribute is required to indicate which subclass each row represents.

```
CREATE TABLE Campaign (
        campaignCode VARCHAR(4) NOT NULL,
        campaignTitle VARCHAR(50) NULL,
        PRIMARY KEY (campaignCode)
        );
CREATE TABLE InternationalCampaign (
        campaignCode VARCHAR(4) NOT NULL,
        locationCode VARCHAR(2) NOT NULL,
        locationMgr VARCHAR(30) NULL,
        PRIMARY KEY (campaignCode, locationCode)
        );
CREATE TABLE Location (
        locationCode VARCHAR(2) NOT NULL,
        locationName VARCHAR(20) NULL,
        PRIMARY KEY (locationCode)
        );
CREATE TABLE LocationManager (
        locationMgr VARCHAR(30) NOT NULL,
        locationMgrTel INT NULL,
        PRIMARY KEY (locationMgr)
        );
```

Figure 18.14 SQL statements to create tables of Figs 18.11 and 18.12.

- Only implement the subclasses as tables. The attributes of the superclass are held in all the subclass tables. This only works if the superclass is abstract and there will be no instances of it.
- Implement all the classes (both superclass and subclasses) as separate tables. To retrieve the data for a subclass, both its own table and the table of its superclass must be accessed. Again, a `type` attribute may be required in the superclass table.

The solution that is chosen may depend on the requirements of the particular application or may be constrained by the use that will be made of the data in the database by other applications.

This brings us to a further aspect of relational databases: data is added to and retrieved from them using SQL statements. SQL provides both the DDL and DML for relational databases. Figure 18.14 shows the SQL statements necessary to create the tables of Figs 18.11 and 18.12 in Oracle generated by the CASE tool from the storage class diagram.

Figure 18.15 shows an SQL statement that finds all the international campaigns with the `locationName` 'Hong Kong'. Typically this kind of query would be written as a procedure with a variable in place of the string `'Hong Kong'`, and the variable would be replaced with a parameter value when the procedure was invoked, allowing the same query procedure to be reused to find campaigns in any location.

There is a design decision to be made in deciding where to place the responsibility for this kind of requirement.

- This SQL statement could be executed and only data for those objects that are required would be returned from the database. This replaces the interaction to select the relevant objects modelled in a sequence diagram with functionality provided by the DBMS.

```
SELECT campaignTitle FROM Campaign c, InternationalCampaign ic,
Location l
        WHERE c.campaignCode = ic.campaignCode
        AND ic.locationCode = l.locationCode
        AND l.locationName = 'Hong Kong'
```

Figure 18.15 SQL statement to find campaigns running in Hong Kong.

- Alternatively, the data from all these tables could be retrieved from the database and used to instantiate the objects in the system. Each `International Campaign` object could then be sent a message to check whether it includes the `Location` 'Hong Kong'. This will involve it sending a message to each associated `Location` object. This is more object-oriented, but will take a longer time to execute.
- The third alternative is to retrieve data from each table in turn, as though navigating through the structure of the class diagram, first the `International Campaign` then each of the `Locations` for that `InternationalCampaign`. This approach requires use of indexes on the tables to make access possible in a reasonable time.

This kind of design decision trades off the pure object-oriented approach against the efficiency of the relational database. In order to retrieve this data into objects in a programming language such as Java, the SQL statements must be embedded in the program. In Chapter 19, we present examples of how this can be done using JDBC (Java Database Connectivity). During design, we have to decide which classes have the responsibility for accessing the database. In Section 18.8 we describe two different approaches to this design decision and show how they can be modelled in UML. However, before we address how we can model the database management responsibilities of the system, we need to consider object DBMSs and what they have to offer the designer as an alternative to relational DBMSs.

18.6 Designing for Object Database Management Systems

18.6.1 Object databases

Object DBMSs differ from current relational DBMSs in that they are capable of storing objects with all their complex structure. It is not necessary to transform the classes in the design model of the system in order to map them to storage objects. As you might expect, using an object database maintains the seamlessness that is claimed for object-oriented systems right through to the storage of objects in the database. Designing for an object database will have a minimal impact on the design of the system.

The standard for object databases was originally set by the Object Data Management Group (ODMG) and is currently available in Version 3.0 (Cattell et al., 2000). The standard defines both the Object Definition Language (ODL) and the Object Manipulation Language (OML) for object databases. The ODL is similar to the DDL elements of SQL for relational databases but allows objects to maintain their complex structure: objects can contain other objects, including collections, as attributes. Figure 18.16 shows the ODL definition of the `InternationalCampaign`, `StaffMember` and `CreativeStaff` classes based on Fig. 18.12 but with the `StaffIntCampaignList` as an embedded

```
interface InternationalCampaign
(extent    international_campaigns
  key      (campaignCode, locationCode))
{
         attribute    String campaignCode;
         attribute    String locationCode;
}
interface StaffMember
(extent    staff_members
  key      staffNo)
{
         attribute    Short staffNo;
         attribute    String staffName;
         attribute    Date staffStartDate;
}
interface CreativeStaff: StaffMember
(extent    creative_staff
  key      staffNo)
{
         attribute    String qualification;
         attribute    List<InternationalCampaign>
                                    staffIntCampaignList;
         relationship Client isContact;
         inverse Client::hasContact;
}
```

Figure 18.16 ODL for `InternationalCampaign`, `StaffMember` and `CreativeStaff`.

attribute of `CreativeStaff`. Note also that the client contact association with `Client` is shown as a one-to-one association to illustrate the syntax.

However, in 2001 the ODMG was disbanded and the work that had been done on the standard was submitted to the Java Community Process (JCP) in response to Java Specification Request (JSR) 12, the Java Data Objects (JDO) Specification Version 1.0. This has subsequently been replaced by JDO 2.0 in response to JSR 243; JDO provides an abstract API for Java programs to access databases that is independent of the underlying database technology. The mapping between the Java classes and the structures in the database is set up in an XML configuration file. Mapping tools are explained in Section 18.8.4.

Individual ODBMSs do not necessarily conform to the ODMG standard, although some may provide a JDO-compliant API. Not all object databases require the developer to use ODL, and there are a number of ways of querying the database, most of which are extensions to the programming language. As an example here, we use db4o (Database For Objects) by Versant, which is available for Java and .NET under the GPL (General Public Licence).

At its simplest, db4o will work with existing Java classes: they do not require any special code adding to them, although, for more sophisticated uses of the database, classes do require either to implement the `com.db4o.ta.Activatable` interface or the compiled classes must be run through an enhancer that changes the byte code.

Figure 18.17 shows the class `Client` with `Address` and `StaffMember` linked to it by the association roles `address` and `staffContact`, and with Java constructors and get and set methods. Note that only primary operations (see Section 14.3.3) are shown here.

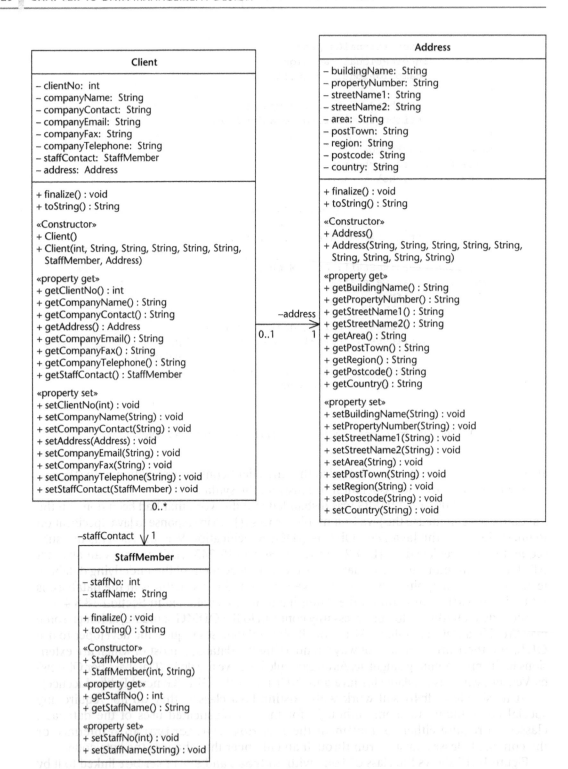

Figure 18.17 Class diagram excerpt showing primary operations for `Client`, `Address` and `StaffMember`.

It is possible to store objects like this in a way that stores associated objects simply by opening a connection to the database, for example,

```
String filename = new String("AgateDB.db4o");
ObjectContainer db = Db4o.openFile(filename);
```

and calling

```
db.store(Object);
```

where `Object` is an object instance in the program.

Figure 18.18 shows some example code in Java that creates a Client, an Address and a StaffMember, links them together and stores them in the database. For the developer, this is about as seamless as it gets. There is no creating a database, no creating tables with appropriate columns, no mapping attributes in the classes to columns in the database, no special database manipulation language to learn.

The method `retrieveClientsByContact()` illustrates three important points. First, it is possible to use Query By Example (QBE) to retrieve objects: an object of the class `StaffMember` is populated with the values that are to be looked up in the database, and used to retrieve data. This query works just as well if the `staffNo` is set to zero, or if the `staffName` is set to null, though one of the attributes must have a value, otherwise all instances of `StaffMember` and the `Client` they are linked to will be retrieved. Second, no special coding is necessary to retrieve the `Client` linked to the `StaffMember`: there is no attribute in `StaffMember` to link it through a collection class to `Client`, so if the `StaffMember` is the `staffContact` for more than one `Client`, all those clients will be retrieved. Third, in storing the `Client` in the database, the associated `StaffMember` and `Address` are stored transparently.

This is clearly a simple example, and for a commercial system, an architect or system designer would want to be confident that the database is capable of handling the volumes of data required and performing as fast as specified by the non-functional requirements. However, db4o provides support for a number of features, which can be switched on relatively easily by configuring the database before connecting to it: transparent activation, transparent persistence and transactions. These are explained briefly here.

- *Transparent activation*. When a group of objects are joined together by links, and are retrieved for the database, the DBMS needs to know how far down the chain of links it should go. This can be configured in db4o, or transparent activation can be used. Transparent activation means that if the DBMS finds an object that is activatable, it does not retrieve it from the database, but waits to see if it is needed. If an operation references an operation or attribute of that object, it transparently retrieves it from the database and brings it into memory. This is effectively the same as the proxy pattern described in Section 18.8.3.
- *Transparent persistence*. When a complex group of interrelated objects is in memory, and some are updated and some are not, it can be difficult to keep track of which ones must be saved to the database, and which ones haven't changed and don't need to be saved. Transparent persistence manages this for the developer.
- *Transactions*. A transaction is a group of updates to multiple objects that must be persisted to the database on an all or nothing basis. If one of the updates fails, all the others must be rolled back.

```
package com.agate.dbtest;

import com.agate.entity.domain.*;
import java.io.File;
import com.db4o.Db4o;
import com.db4o.ObjectContainer;
import com.db4o.ObjectSet;

public class DBTest {
  public static void main(String[] args) {
    String filename = new String("AgateTest.db4o");
    new File(filename).delete();
    ObjectContainer db = Db4o.openFile(filename);
    try {
      createClients(db);
      retrieveClientByContact(db, 1, "Amarjeet Grewal");
    }
    finally {
      db.close();
    }
  }

  public static void createClients(ObjectContainer db) {
    StaffMember staff1 = new StaffMember(1,"Amarjeet Grewal");
    Address address1 = new Address("Holborn House", "", "High
    Street", "", "Holborn", "London", "", "SW1 8YH", "United
    Kingdom");
    Client client1 = new Client(45, "Holborn Motors", "Dave
    Richards", "company@holborn.co.uk", "02079996780",
    "02079996790", staff1, address1);
    db.store(client1);
    System.out.println("Stored \n" + client1);
  }

  public static void retrieveClientsByContact(ObjectContainer db,
                                    int staffNo,
                                    String staffName) {
    StaffMember staffProto = new StaffMember(staffNo, staffName);
    Client clientProto = new Client();
    clientProto.setStaffContact(staffProto);
    ObjectSet result = db.queryByExample(clientProto);
    listResult(result);
  }

  public static void listResult(ObjectSet result) {
    System.out.println("Retrieved: " + result.size());
    while(result.hasNext()) {
        System.out.println(result.next());
    }
  }
}
```

Figure 18.18 Example Java code to store objects in db4o.

The structure of the class diagram will require minimal changes to be used with an object database.

Although object DBMSs make it easier to map an object-oriented design straight to a database, there is one area where the seamlessness breaks down. Apart from very simple operations, such as those to insert new values or to do simple arithmetic, ODL and hence object databases do not support the storage of operations in the database. Operations must still be implemented in an object-oriented programming language such as Java or C++.

18.7 Distributed Databases

Before we consider how to design the classes that handle data management for a database that is not object-oriented, it is worth briefly considering the issue of distributed databases.

In a simple system, objects can be stored on the local machine in a database, brought into the memory of the machine and sent messages to invoke their operations before being saved back to the database and removed from memory. Alternatively, in an n-tier architecture, objects are stored on a database server, and the client sends data or requests to an application server, the objects are brought into the memory of the application server, sent messages to invoke processing, and saved back to the database. Data is sent back to the client machine to display to the user.

However, there are some situations where either by design or for historic reasons, data is held in a number of databases in different locations and processed by multiple processors. There are a number of possible architectures that may have to be taken into account when designing the database. Four of them are discussed here to different levels of detail:

- parallel database systems
- multi-database systems
- distributed database systems
- replicated or mobile database systems.

Parallel database systems

Parallel databases are designed to handle large volumes of transactions–more than a single processor can handle–and are distributed across multiple processors or computers. Typically these processors are located in the same multi-processor machine, or the computers are located together in a cluster linked by a high-speed network. The data may be held in disks that are local to each processor or on a storage area network (SAN). The transaction processing load may be spread across the different processors by a load-balancer. Oracle Real Application Clusters (RAC) is an example of a clustered system.

Organizations usually adopt parallel database systems to provide scalability (the ability to create a database system that is larger than a single machine could handle, and that can grow as volumes of data and transactions grow), fault tolerance (individual processors in the cluster can fail, but processing will continue) and load balancing (the ability to spread the load evenly across the cluster of processors). High transaction volume applications, such as on-line stores, or high data volume applications, such as data warehouses, are the kind of application that uses database clusters.

Multi-database systems

Multi-database systems usually reflect a situation where, for historical reasons, the data that an organization needs to operate is held in multiple different databases in different locations, and possibly from different vendors. While some applications may need to access data from several of these databases, there are still applications that are local to each database and are updating data in their own database without regard for the other databases. Often there is data duplication with, for example, customer data being held in a customer relationship management system and the sales ledger.

In this situation, an additional layer of database management software is installed over these databases. This software creates a conceptual schema for the data that cuts across multiple databases, and a mapping is created between this schema and the conceptual schemas of the underlying databases. So a table in this conceptual schema may contain columns that are held in different physical databases in different locations. The mapping software presents a consolidated conceptual schema on which external schemas can be built for different applications, and handles the transactional updates to the underlying databases. Sybase Enterprise Connect Data Access is an example of a package that performs this role.

Organizations adopt a multi-database system where there are many existing databases, possibly at different sites, and new applications need to access the data in these underlying databases as though it were in a single database.

Distributed database systems

Distributed database systems are designed to create a database that is distributed across multiple locations. Each part of a distributed database in a different location is called a *fragment*. In order to give each location in the organization rapid access to data that it needs, the data is split across multiple sites. If an application in one location needs data that is managed elsewhere, either that data may be replicated on the application's local database, or the distributed database management system (DDBMS) will transparently fetch the data from a remote site.

The data may be fragmented horizontally, with all data for each location held in that location (for example, all UK customers held in the UK database while all US customers are held in the US database); or it can be fragmented vertically, with data for different business functions held in different locations (for example, all customer data held in the sales office, while stock data is held in the warehouse database); or it can be fragmented by a combination of these techniques.

A DDBMS holds local information about the data that it holds in a data dictionary or data catalogue, and a global catalogue holds information about the location of other data in other databases. To the application that requires the data, the location of data is irrelevant. The application makes requests to the local instance of the DDBMS, and if it doesn't have the data, it will transparently fetch it from another database.

The Open Group has developed and maintains the Distributed Relational Database Architecture (DRDA) as an interoperability standard for distributed databases. IBM's DB2 DBMS is an example of a DRDA-compliant DDBMS.

Organizations adopt distributed database systems where there is a case for data to be held locally for performance reasons, but some functions within the organization require access to data from other business functions or geographical locations.

Replicated or mobile database systems

The growth of mobile applications and other applications that must run on a client, that need to share data, but that connect to the central DBMS over unreliable or intermittent network connections, has led to the associated growth in database software that replicates data between databases, typically between one central database and many smaller client databases.

Mobile applications that run on mobile phones or personal digital assistants (PDAs) are typical users of replicated databases. Web-based applications are fine where connectivity over the Mobile Internet is good, but in remote areas, or those where reception of mobile signals is poor, the user is cut off from their application. If the connection is lost, the user can't record a delivery, place an order, or do whatever the application was designed to do. One solution to this is to write an application that runs on the PDA or mobile device with its own local database. The application reads from and updates the local database, and whenever there is a good connection to the central system, the data is replicated: data that is needed on the PDA, such as latest prices, stock availability or the next job, is transferred to the PDA, and data that has been updated on the PDA, such as new orders or delivery confirmations, is transferred to the central database.

Sybase SQL Anywhere is an example of a product that replicates data between mobile devices and a central database or between databases. Most large DBMSs provide replication capabilities between instances of the same DBMS for disaster recovery.

Organizations adopt replication for mobile applications when it is critical that the application always has access to the data that it needs and the web-based style of application is therefore unsuitable. Database replication is also used as part of a distributed DBMS–to make some data that is managed on remote sites available locally–and to provide back-up databases hosted on a disaster recovery system, that enable an organization to continue operating if the primary data centre is damaged or disconnected from power or the network.

Figure 18.19 shows schematic views of the architecture of each of these four types of database system.

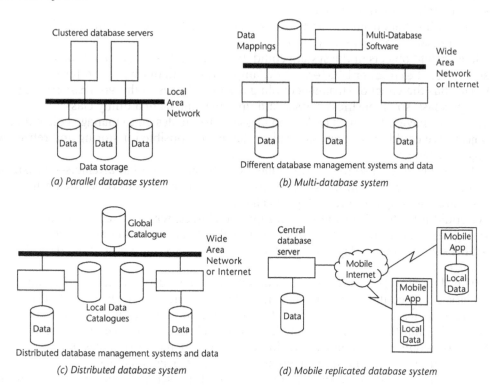

Figure 18.19 Schematic views of different types of distributed database.

18.8 | Designing Data Management Classes

18.8.1 Layered architecture

In designing the boundary classes, one of our aims has been to keep them separate from the control and entity classes. In designing the presentation layer we isolated the entity classes in the system from the way that they are presented on screen and in reports and documents. We did this in order to maximize the reusability of the classes. Our aim is to do the same with the data storage layer. Classes are less reusable if they are tightly coupled to the mechanisms for storing instances in a file system or database. We also want to decouple the entity classes from the business logic.

What are the options for locating the operations that handle the tasks of storing and retrieving objects?

1. We could add operations to each class to enable objects to save and store themselves.
   - This reduces reusability. Each class must now contain code to implement the operations that couple the class to the particular data storage mechanism used.
   - This breaches the idea of cohesion. Each business class should contain operations that are relevant to the behaviour of instances of that class. Data storage methods belong in a data storage class.
   - If an object is not currently instantiated, how can we send it a message to invoke an operation to load itself?
2. We can get around this last problem by making the storage and retrieval operations class-scope methods rather than instance-scope methods (static methods in Java or static member functions in C++).
   - This still suffers from the first two problems listed above for option 1. The class is less reusable and lacks cohesion.
3. All persistent objects in the system could inherit methods for storage from an abstract superclass—`PersistentObject` for example, rather than `Object` in Java.
   - This has the effect of strongly coupling existing classes to the `PersistentObject` superclass, so all business classes end up inheriting from a utility class.
4. Where we have introduced collection classes into the design to manage collections of objects, we could make these collection classes responsible for storing and retrieving object instances.
   - This is closer to a solution. The collection classes are design artefacts—not part of the business classes in the system. However, we may wish to reuse the design, and we are coupling it to the storage mechanisms.
5. We could introduce into the system separate classes, whose role is to deal with the storage and retrieval of other classes. This is the database broker approach.
   - This solution fits the layered architecture. These classes are part of the data storage layer.
   - The data storage classes are decoupled from the business classes. The business classes will contain nothing that indicates how they are to be stored. The same business classes can be reused unchanged with different storage mechanisms.
6. We could limit the number of new data storage classes to one. Different instances of this class would be created with attributes to hold the names of tables or files that are to be used to store and retrieve instances of their associated classes.
   - This parameterized version is more difficult to set up and more difficult to implement.

- It requires some part of the system outside the database broker class to know what parameters to set for each instance that is created.

Option 5 is the approach that is favoured by most developers of object-oriented systems. It involves the use of a number of patterns. Larman (2005) describes it in some detail as a *persistence framework*, the main feature of which is the use of *database brokers* or *database mappers*, which mediate between the business classes and the persistent storage and which are responsible for storing and retrieving objects. However, we shall first describe the use of option 3–inheritance from a persistent superclass–before looking at option 5.

18.8.2 `PersistentObject` superclass

A simple approach to the design of data storage classes is to design an abstract superclass `PersistentObject` that encapsulates the mechanisms for an object of any class to store itself in and retrieve itself from a database. Eriksson and Penker (1998) use this approach in order to keep their example case study application simple and independent of any vendor's DBMS. The `PersistentObject` superclass implements operations to get an object by object identifier, to store, delete and update objects, and to iterate through a set of objects. These operations are implemented in terms of two abstract operations, to write and read objects, that must be implemented by each subclass that inherits from the `PersistentObject` superclass. This is shown in Fig. 18.20 (adapted from Eriksson and Penker, 1998).

This approach also uses an aspect of option 2, as the `getObject()` operation is a class-scope method rather than an instance-scope method (as are the others underlined in the class diagram of Fig. 18.20).

The `PersistentObject` hides some of the detail of the implementation of the data storage from the business objects in the application. However, they must implement the `write()` and `read()` operations and this will limit their reusability.

This approach does have the benefit of limiting the changes that will be made to sequence diagrams. Messages that have been shown being sent to object instances to select an instance or to iterate through a set of instances can be shown as being sent to the class rather than the instances. Figure 18.21 shows an example of this for the use case `Get number of campaigns for location`. We have shown the class `Location` using a constructor `Location()` to make the particular instance `:Location` available. While the object instance is being created in memory for this instance of the collaboration, strictly speaking it already exists as an object and is just being *materialized* from the database.

However, the use of a persistent superclass is unlikely to be robust enough for business applications and a more sophisticated approach, such as the database broker, must be used.

18.8.3 Database broker framework

The database broker framework separates the business objects from the data storage implementation. The classes that provide the data storage services will be held in a separate package.

Our objective here is to separate the data storage mechanisms completely from the business classes. For each business class that needs to be persistent, there will be an

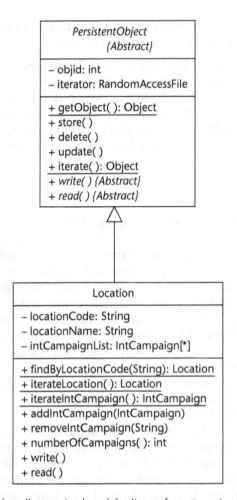

Figure 18.20 Excerpt from class diagram to show inheritance from `PersistentObject`.

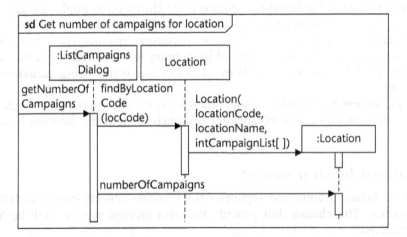

Figure 18.21 Sequence diagram for `Get number of campaigns for location` showing `Location` retrieving (or materializing) an instance.

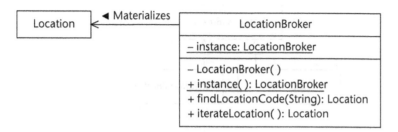

Figure 18.22 `Location` and `LocationBroker` classes.

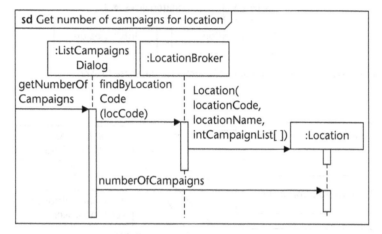

Figure 18.23 Sequence diagram for `Get number of campaigns for location` showing `LocationBroker` retrieving an instance of `Location`.

associated database broker class that provides the mechanisms to materialize objects from the database and dematerialize them back to the database. A simple form of this is shown in Fig. 18.22 for the `Location` class. The `LocationBroker` is responsible for the storage and retrieval of `Location` object instances. In order to ensure that there is only ever one `LocationBroker` instance, we can use the Singleton pattern (see Chapter 15). This means that we use a class-scope operation, but only to obtain an instance of the `LocationBroker` that can be used subsequently to access the database. The sequence diagram involving the `LocationBroker` is very similar to that of Fig. 18.21, and is shown in Fig. 18.23. (Note that this diagram does not show the creation of the instance of `LocationBroker`.)

Each persistent class in the system will require a broker class, so it makes sense to create a superclass that provides the services required by all these broker classes. Larman (2005) suggests two levels of generalization. At the top of his hierarchy is an abstract `Broker` class that provides the operation to materialize an object using its object identifier. This is then subclassed to produce different abstract classes of brokers for different kinds of storage: for example, one for a relational database and one for a file system. Finally, the appropriate broker is subclassed into the concrete classes for each persistent class in the system. A simplified version of this inheritance hierarchy is shown in Fig. 18.24.

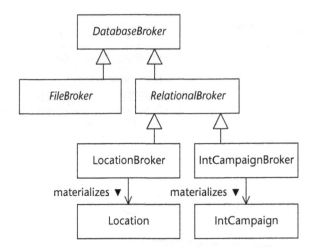

Figure 18.24 Simplified version of inheritance hierarchy for database brokers.

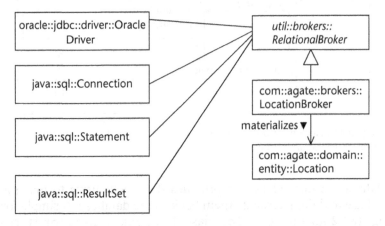

Figure 18.25 `RelationalBroker` class and classes from other packages.

In the Agate case study, we could use JDBC to link the Java programs to a relational database. This will require the use of classes from the `java.sql` package, in particular: `Connection`, which is used to make a connection to the database; `Statement`, which is used to execute SQL statements; and `ResultSet`, into which the results of SQL Select statements are placed (we can then iterate through the `ResultSet` retrieving each row in turn and extracting the values from each column). An appropriate driver will also be required. Figure 18.25 shows the associations between the `RelationalBroker` abstract class and these other classes. The figure shows the Oracle JDBC driver; to access a database such as Access via a link from JDBC to ODBC, the appropriate driver would be `sun::jdbc::odbc::JdbcOdbcDriver`.

The dependencies between the application classes and those in other packages can be shown using packages in a package diagram, as for the classes in the presentation layer in Chapter 17, Fig. 17.12. This is shown in Fig. 18.26.

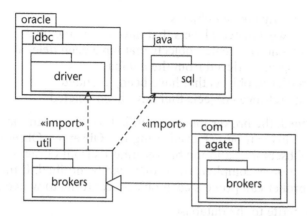

Figure 18.26 Class diagram showing packages for database brokers package.

This simple framework using database broker classes can be extended to deal with some of the problems that remain.

- The most important problem concerns the way in which persistent objects maintain references to other objects. If the LocationBroker retrieves an instance of Location, what happens when an operation of the Location requires it to send a message to one of its IntCampaigns? The IntCampaign will not necessarily have been retrieved from the database. The same applies to the many other operations that involve collaboration between objects.
- The second problem concerns the ability to manage transactions in which a number of objects are created, retrieved from the database, updated and deleted.

Two extensions to the database broker framework can be used to resolve these problems. The first uses the Proxy pattern to provide proxy objects for those objects that have not yet been retrieved from the database. The second uses caches to hold objects in memory and keep track of which have been created, updated or deleted.

The Proxy pattern (Gamma et al., 1995) provides a proxy object as a placeholder for another object until it is required. In this case, we can use proxies for each business class to link to where there is an association with another object or objects. If no message is sent to the associated objects, then the proxy does nothing. If a message is sent then the proxy asks the relevant database broker to retrieve the object from the database and, once it has been materialized, the proxy can pass the message directly to it. Subsequently, messages can be sent directly to the object by the proxy, or the proxy can replace the reference to itself in the object that sent the message with a reference to the real object. For this to work, the proxy must hold the object identifier of the object that it is a placeholder for. When the object itself is retrieved from the database, the object identifier is effectively transformed into a reference to the object itself. The proxy class must also implement the same interface as the real class so that it appears to other objects as if it is the real thing.

Caches can be combined with this approach. The database broker can maintain one or more caches of objects that have been retrieved from the database. Each cache can be implemented as a hashtable, using the object identifier as the key. Either a single cache is maintained and some mechanism is used to keep track of the state of each object, or six caches can be maintained:

- new clean cache–newly created objects
- new dirty cache–newly created objects that have been amended
- new deleted objects–newly created objects that have been deleted
- old clean cache–objects retrieved from the database
- old dirty cache–retrieved objects that have been amended
- old deleted objects–retrieved objects that have been deleted.

As objects are changed, the broker must be notified so that it can move them from one cache to the other. This can be achieved using the Observer–Observable pattern: the object implements Observable, and the broker inherits from Observer.

When the transaction is complete, the broker can be notified. If the transaction is to be committed, the broker can process each object according to which cache it is in:

- new clean cache–write to the database
- new dirty cache–write to the database
- new deleted objects–delete from the cache
- old clean cache–delete from the cache
- old dirty cache–write to the database
- old deleted objects–delete from the database.

The cache or caches can be used by the proxy object to check whether an object is already available in memory. When it receives a message, the proxy can ask the broker for the object. If it is in a cache, the broker will return a reference to it directly; if it is not in the cache, the broker will retrieve it. Figure 18.27 shows the associations between the broker class, the caches and the proxy.

The collaboration between these classes can be seen in the communication diagram in Fig. 18.28, which represents the following interaction.

A Location object is in memory with an IntCampaignProxy object as a place-holder for the real IntCampaign object that runs in that Location. In order to print a list of campaigns, the title of the IntCampaign object is required.

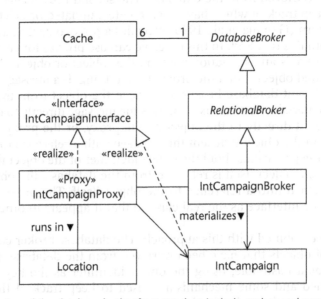

Figure 18.27 Extension of the database broker framework to include caches and proxies.

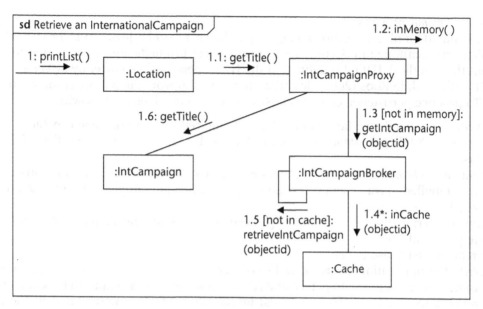

Figure 18.28 Communication diagram showing proxy, broker and cache objects collaborating to retrieve an object instance.

1.1 The :Location sends the message getTitle to the :IntCampaignProxy.

1.2 The :IntCampaignProxy checks whether the :IntCampaign is in memory.

1.3 It is not, so it then requests the object by object identifier from the broker :IntCampaignBroker.

1.4 The :IntCampaignBroker checks if the object is in a :Cache.

1.5 It is not, so the :IntCampaignBroker retrieves the object from the database and returns it to the :IntCampaignProxy.

1.6 The :IntCampaignProxy sends the getTitle message to the :IntCampaign object and returns the result to the Location.

This may appear to be overkill, but it enables us to maintain our objective of decoupling the business classes from the data storage mechanisms that are provided by the classes in the persistence framework. This should make it possible to migrate the data storage to a different platform without having an impact on the business classes or the application logic, simply by replacing the database broker class with the broker for a different database.

18.8.4 Using a data management product or framework

In the previous two sections, we have considered ways of designing a persistence mechanism yourself. However, this is not necessary, as there are a number of products and frameworks available that provide a persistence mechanism for you. We have included the previous section in order to give an idea of what is involved in developing a persistence framework. We shall consider two standards-based approaches that will handle the mapping of objects to relational database tables, and the frameworks in the Java 2 Enterprise Edition (J2EE) that handle persistent objects.

Object–relational mappings

The standard for object–relational mapping in the Java world is Java Data Objects (JDO), which was mentioned in Section 18.6. A number of products are available that implement this standard. JDO 2 is defined in the JDO Specification, currently at Version 2.2 (JCP, 2008), while Roos (2003) describes how JDO 1.0 works in a more readable form.

To produce persistence-capable classes using JDO involves the following steps.

- Write and compile the Java classes that are required to be persistence-capable.
- Write an XML *persistence descriptor* file to describe various properties of these classes.
- Run an *enhancer* program that reads the persistence descriptor and processes the compiled Java classes to add operations that implement the interface `PersistenceCapable`.
- Run a program that generates the SQL necessary to create the database tables to hold the persistent classes.
- Create the database tables.
- Write the application to use a JDO `PersistenceManagerFactory` to provide a `PersistenceManager` to persist and retrieve instances of the enhanced classes. (The `PersistenceManagerFactory` must be passed a set of properties that define the connection to the database that will be used.)

Different JDO implementations work in slightly different ways but all conform to the standard API. The persistence descriptor for a class can be very simple, essentially just defining the class as persistent, or can contain a number of elements that define properties of the way the class is persisted such as the primary key to be used.

JDO handles transactions, cacheing and queries using JDO Query Language (JDOQL). It can also be used to provide persistence for EJBs in a Java Enterprise Edition (JEE) application server.

Java Persistence API

Enterprise Java Beans (EJBs) have provided a mechanism for creating enterprise Java applications that run in an application server. In EJB2, container managed persistence (CMP) provided a persistence mechanism for EJBs. However, the EJB framework in Java 2 Enterprise Edition (J2EE) was considered by many people to be too heavyweight and complicated a framework. The latest version, EJB3, incorporated a new mechanism for persisting Java classes to a relational database by mapping the structure of the classes to the tables in the database, as described earlier in this chapter. This framework is the Java Persistence API (JPA), and although it is documented in the JEE standard, it has effectively been broken out of the JEE environment and can be used as a generic persistence mechanism for Java programs using the standard edition. As such it works with plain Java objects.

There are two ways of using JPA. The first uses an XML file that defines the mappings between classes and their attributes and tables and columns in the database. The second uses Java annotations–special tags that can be added to Java code since Java 5, which are processed when the class is compiled and used to add behaviours to classes.

The minimum that is required to create persistent classes is that they should be annotated or included in the mapping file, and the attribute that is to be used as the primary key to retrieve data from the table is also marked. A simple Java annotations example for the `Client` class of Figure 18.17 would be as follows:

```
import javax.persistence.*;
...
@Entity
public class Client {
  @Id
  private int clientNo;
```

Implementations of JPA provide default values for mappings, so would typically map the `Client` class to a table called `CLIENT`, and the `clientNo` attribute to a primary key column called `CLIENTNO`. To change these default mappings, the programmer simply adds additional annotations, such as `@Table` and `@Column`.

Using JPA is simpler than JDO, as it is not necessary to use an XML persistence descriptor file if the classes are annotated, and it is not necessary to enhance the compiled classes, unless certain functionality is required. To produce persistence-capable classes using JPA involves the following steps.

- Write and compile the Java classes that are required to be persistence-capable.
- Run a program that generates the SQL necessary to create the database tables to hold the persistent classes, or create the SQL manually.
- Create the database tables.
- Write the application to use a JPA `EntityManagerFactory` to provide an `EntityManager` to persist and retrieve instances of the enhanced classes. (The `EntityManagerFactory` must be configured with a set of properties that define the connection to the database that will be used.)

18.9 Summary

The design of persistent storage for object-oriented systems is not straightforward. For simple systems, it is possible to use files to store the objects. However, commercial systems require a more robust and sophisticated approach so that objects can be shared between applications and users. Database management systems provide the facilities to build robust, commercial-strength information systems and offer a number of advantages. Object DBMS can be used and will have a less significant impact on the design of the classes in the system than if a relational DBMS is used. However, many organizations have an existing investment in a relational DBMS and it may be necessary to build the system to use this database. In this case it is necessary to design tables, either by normalizing object instances or by following a set of guidelines for mapping classes and associations to tables. To decouple the business objects from the persistent storage mechanism, a persistence framework can be designed that can be extended to handle the resolution of object identifiers into references to real objects and that can use caches to manage transactions involving multiple objects.

The design of the persistent data storage mechanisms should ideally be carried out in conjunction with the object design activities of Chapter 14. If an object DBMS is being used, it will probably have little impact on the design of classes. If a relational DBMS is being used, the simplest approach is to use a mapping framework based on either JDO or JPA. It should not be necessary to build your own persistence framework.

Review Questions

18.1 Give one example each of a persistent and a transient object.

18.2 Explain the difference between different types of file organization and file access.

18.3 Of the different kinds of record type listed in Section 18.3.1 suggest which would be most appropriate for storing complex nested objects. Explain the reasons for your choice.

18.4 Outline the advantages and disadvantages of using a DBMS over developing an application using files.

18.5 What is the key difference between a relational DBMS and an object DBMS?

18.6 List in your own words the three steps used in going from an unnormalized relation to a relation in third normal form.

18.7 What are the three ways of mapping the classes in an inheritance hierarchy to tables?

18.8 What is meant by OML and ODL?

18.9 What is the difference between a multi-database and a distributed database?

18.10 Explain what is meant by (i) a broker and (ii) a proxy.

Case Study Work, Exercises and Projects

18.A Find out what you can about localization mechanisms in a programming language or environment such as Java or .NET. What use do they make of files?

18.B Normalize the data in the Agate invoice in Fig. 6.1. (Remember to remove the calculated values first.)

18.C Normalize the data in the FoodCo sales order entry screen of Fig. 16.3. (Remember to remove the calculated values first.)

18.D Use the guidelines in Section 18.5.3 to decide on the tables necessary to hold the classes of Fig. 14.12.

18.E Find information about a relational DBMS and an object DBMS and write a short report comparing the features they offer.

18.F Extend the sequence diagram of Fig. 17.18 to show the use of a proxy class and database broker.

18.G Redraw your answer to Exercise 18.F as a communication diagram.

18.H Draw communication diagrams similar to Fig. 18.28 to show what happens (i) when the `IntCampaign` is already in memory, and (ii) when it is in one of the caches.

Further Reading

Codd's (1970) paper on relational databases was reprinted in the 25th Anniversary issue of the *Communications of the ACM*, which is more likely to be available in a library (1983, 26(1) pp. 64–69). This 25th Anniversary issue is well worth looking at for other papers by some of the greats of computer science.

Silberschatz, Korth and Sudarshan (2005) provide a good overview of database theory. Howe (2001) explains normalization in detail. Connolly and Begg (2010) provide a good overview with strong sections on distributed and object databases.

Loomis (1995) deals with background to object databases and the functionality they offer, whereas Eaglestone and Ridley (1998) present the ODMG standard and provide a worked example case study using O_2.

db4o is available from http://www.db4o.com/.

Roos (2003) explains Java Data Objects. The JDO 2.0 standard is being developed under the auspices of JSR 243 and information is available on the Sun Microsystems website (http://java.sun.com/jdo/index.jsp).

There are links to the web pages of the standards bodies–ANSI, ISO, ODMG and OMG–and to the web pages of various database providers in the website for this book.

Agate Ltd Case Study—Design

Agate Ltd

A5.1 | Introduction

In this chapter we show how part of the analysis model presented in Chapter A4 has been modified by the activities of design. The design activities have been concerned with finalizing the software architecture, designing the entity classes, their attributes, operations and associations, designing the boundary classes and the human–computer interaction, designing the mechanisms used for data storage, and designing the control classes. These activities have been explained in Chapters 12 to 18.

The following sections include:

- package diagrams to illustrate the overall software architecture
- class diagrams to illustrate the classes in the design model
- sequence diagrams to illustrate the interaction between instances of classes
- a state machine for the control of the user interface.

A5.2 | Architecture

The architecture of the system (shown in Fig. A5.1) has been designed to use Java Remote Method Invocation (RMI) for communication between the client machines and the server.[1] Control classes have been split into two layers. First, there are the control classes that reside on the client machines (in the package `Agate Control Client`) and manage the interaction between users and the boundary classes. These control classes are essentially those that were designed in Chapter 17. Second, there are control

---

1 To meet the non-functional requirements relating to the distribution of the system, we will need a more complex architecture than this. The eventual solution will probably involve Java 2 Enterprise Edition (J2EE) and Enterprise Java Beans (EJB), and will require the use of application server software. For now we are presenting a design that is not so dependent on an application server, the design for which is beyond the scope of this book.

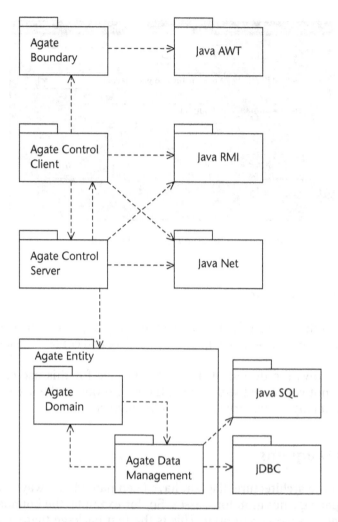

Figure A5.1 Package diagram for software architecture.

classes that reside on the server. These control classes handle the interaction between the business logic of the application and the entity classes (and the associated data management classes). This helps to decouple the layers: the only communication between the clients and the server will be the communication between the client and server control classes, using RMI.

Not all control classes will have versions on both the clients and the server. For example, the ListClients and ListCampaigns classes in Figs 17.36 and 17.37 could just exist on the server, where they will have more immediate access to the entity and data management classes. One consequence of this will be visible in the sequence diagrams, where these two classes will no longer be passed references to the boundary class as a parameter, but will return their results to the control class on the client machine, which will set the values in the boundary class. This is shown in Figs A5.11 and A5.12.

On the server, we are using JDBC, and we will map the classes to relational database tables. A design based on the Broker pattern will be used to handle this.

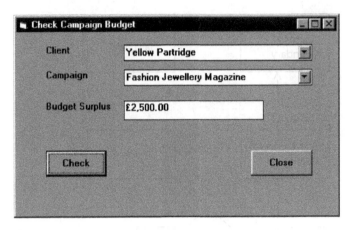

Figure A5.2 Prototype user interface for Check campaign budget.

A5.3 Sample Use Case

For the purpose of this case study chapter we are going to present the design of one use case Check campaign budget, for which the boundary and control classes were designed in Chapter 17.

Figure A5.2 shows the design of the user interface for this use case. In the first iteration, we are not concerned with adding the extensions to the use case that handle printing of the campaign summary and campaign invoice.

A5.4 Class Diagrams

The packages on the architecture diagram have been named in a way that will allow us to use the Java package notation for classes. So, for example, the boundary classes will be in the package Agate::Boundary. This is the first package that we are illustrating here, and the classes we are concerned with are shown in Fig. A5.3.

The boundary class CheckCampaignBudgetUI will implement the two interfaces CampaignLister and ClientLister. Note that some of the operations that were included in the class CheckCampaignBudgetUI, such as getSelectedClient(), have been moved into the interfaces, as it is thought that they will apply to any class that implements these interfaces.

Because the control class CheckCampaignBudget will now be split, the version that resides on the client machines (now called CheckCampaignBudgetClient) must be able to respond to the messages addCampaignName() and addClientname(). We have used interfaces for this, because they have to be sent messages remotely by the control classes on the server. This is shown in Fig. A5.4. Note also that this class will need to hold a reference to the version of itself that exists on the server. We have not shown the full package name in the class diagram, but the attribute ccbRemote will in fact be an instance of Agate::Control::Server::CheckCampaignBudgetRemote. In fact, there will be an instance of Agate::Control::Server::CheckCampaign-BudgetServer on the server, and for the object on the client to communicate with it

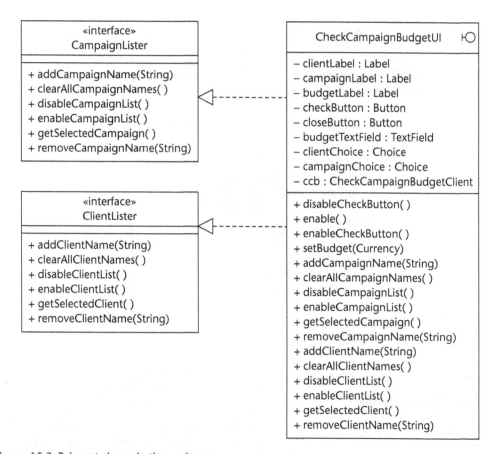

Figure A5.3 Relevant classes in the package `Agate::Boundary`.

via RMI it will have to implement the interface `Agate::Control::Server::Check-CampaignBudgetRemote`. If `ListCampaigns` and `ListClients` only exist on the server, then they will also be in the same package and will implement the interfaces `ListCampaignsRemote` and `ListClientsRemote`.

All the classes that communicate via RMI will need to inherit from the Java RMI package. Rather than being subclasses of the default Java class `Object`, they will need to be subclasses of `java.rmi.server.UnicastRemoteObject`.

In Fig. A5.5 we have shown the control classes that reside on the server and the remote interfaces that they must implement. Although we have not shown the full package names, the references to `ClientListerRemote` and `CampaignListerRemote` are to the interfaces in the package `Agate::Control::Client`, shown in Fig. A5.4.

The entity classes that collaborate in this use case are `Client`, `Campaign` and `Advert`. They are shown in a first draft design in Fig. A5.6. However, this design will only work for the kind of application where all the objects are in memory. We need to be able to deal with the process of materializing instances of these classes from the database and, when required, materializing their links with other object instances or collections of object instances. For example, when a particular `Client` is materialized, we do not necessarily want to re-establish its links with all its `Campaigns` and

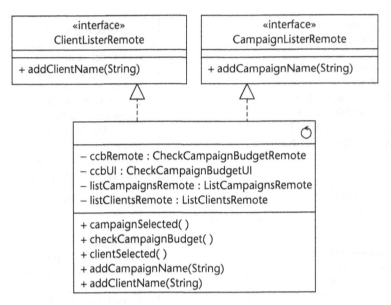

Figure A5.4 The class `Agate::Control::Client::CheckCampaignBudgetClient`.

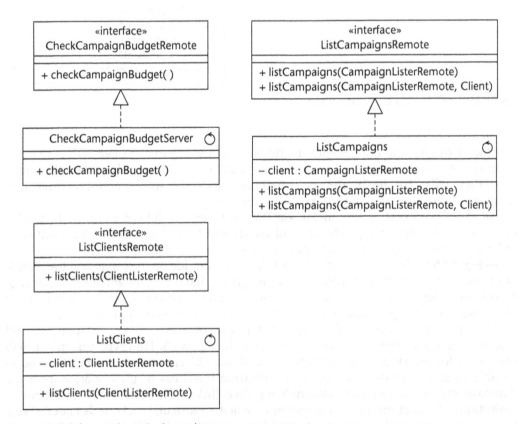

Figure A5.5 Relevant classes in the package `Agate::Control::Server`.

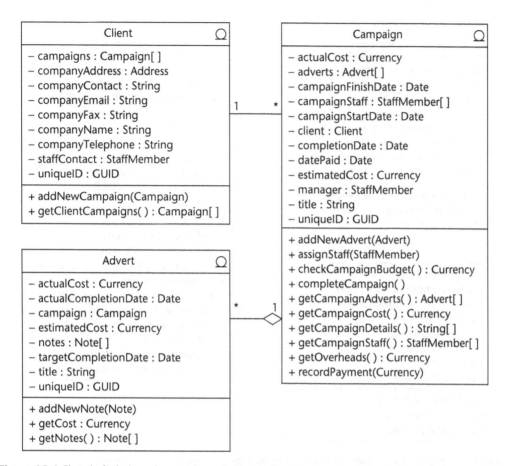

Figure A5.6 First draft design of some classes in the package `Agate::Entity::Domain`.

the instance of `StaffMember` that is its `staffContact`. The Broker pattern, which we discussed in Chapter 18, is a way of making it possible to materialize the objects that are linked to other objects only when they are required.

In order to achieve this, we can replace the references to the arrays of linked objects with references to the various subclasses of `Broker`, for example `ClientBroker`, `CampaignBroker` and `AdvertBroker`. Since these are still private attributes, they cannot be referred to directly by other objects and their values can only be obtained by calling one of the operations of the object in which they are contained. The result of this is shown in Fig. A5.7.

The broker subclasses could use the Singleton pattern (see Chapter 15). If this is done, then the design of the operations to return sets of whatever objects they are acting as brokers for will have to be carefully designed to handle concurrent requests from different clients. Alternatively, there could be multiple instances of brokers, and they could be created and destroyed as required, or there could be a pool of brokers available in the server, and when an object needs a broker of a certain type, it would request one from the pool. Figure A5.8 shows the brokers that we are interested in for this use case. We have not used the Singleton pattern in this design.

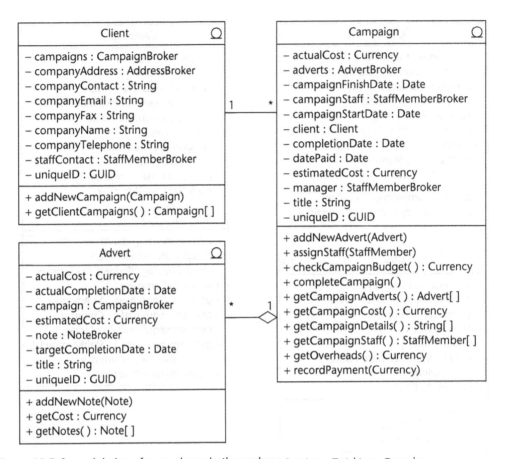

Figure A5.7 Second design of some classes in the package `Agate::Entity::Domain`.

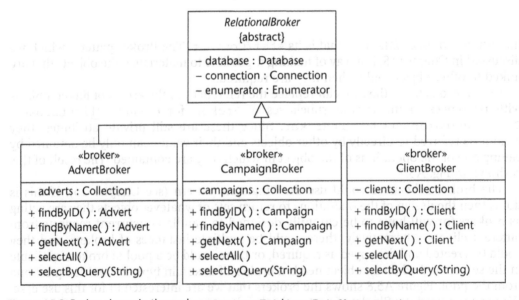

Figure A5.8 Broker classes in the package `Agate::Entity::DataManagement`.

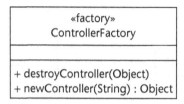

Figure A5.9 Factory class in the package `Agate::Control::Server`.

These brokers will also be used directly by the control classes, for example, when they need to obtain a list of all the objects of a particular class in the system. The brokers have been shown with attributes in which to hold references to the objects necessary for connecting to the database and issuing queries. We have also assumed that having obtained a list of results, a broker may store it internally in a collection class and allow client objects to iterate through the list of results using an enumerator.[2]

The brokers will be in the package `Agate::Entity::DataManagement`, together with any other necessary classes to handle the connection to the database. (In this design we are not using proxies or caches, in order to keep it relatively simple.)

The final piece of design necessary to enable the interaction of this use case realization to take place concerns how the control objects on the client machine will obtain references to control objects on the server. For this, we shall use the Factory pattern. A Factory class creates instances of other classes and returns a reference to the new instance to the object that requested it. This is shown in Fig. A5.9.

So an instance of the control class `CheckCampaignBudgetClient` on the client machine will request a Factory on the server to provide it with a reference to an instance of `CheckCampaignBudgetServer`. The Factory will create this instance and pass back a reference to it via the RMI connection with the client. From that point onwards, the client object can make direct requests to the control object on the server. When it is finished with it, it can destroy it, or ask the Factory to destroy it.

In a more sophisticated design, the Factory could hold a pool of already instantiated control classes ready for use. When a client requests an instance of a particular control class, the Factory will take one from the pool if it is available. When the client is finished with the instance, the Factory can put it back into the pool. We are not using pooling in this design, but it is an approach that is commonly used to improve the performance of servers to prevent delays while instances are created and destroyed on demand.

In this design the control class on the server has only one method. This class `Agate::Control::Server::CheckCampaignBudgetServer` could be designed to hold the business logic for checking the budget of a campaign, but we have taken the decision to leave the responsibility for calculating whether or not the budget is over-spent in the `Campaign` class. There is a case for giving this responsibility to the control class; then, if the business logic changes, it only has to be updated in the control class. However, this makes the entity objects little more than data stores.

Figure A5.10 shows the package diagram with the classes (but not the interfaces) from Figs A5.3 to A5.9. Note that we have not used value objects, which we discussed in Chapter 13 and showed in Fig. 13.24.

---

2 A mechanism for working through a collection dealing with each object in turn.

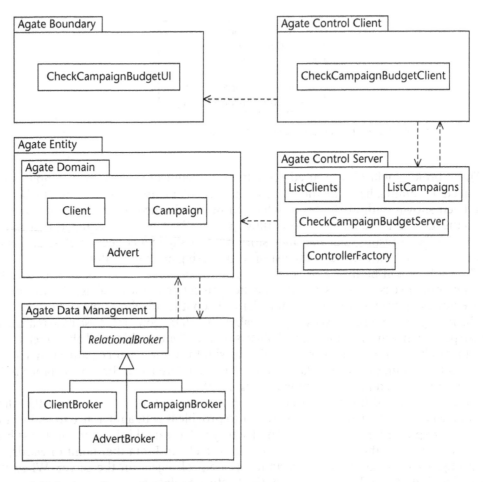

Figure A5.10 Package diagram showing classes.

A5.5 Sequence Diagrams

Figures A5.11 to A5.13 show the sequence diagrams from Chapter 17 revised to take account of the splitting of the control objects and the addition of the Factory class. The package names of objects are also shown.

Although we show the control class on the client as able to directly connect to the instance of `ControllerFactory` on the server, in reality it would have to request a reference to this object from a naming service or registry on the server: for example, a running instance of the Java `rmiregistry`.

In Fig. A5.14 we show the interaction between the control class, the brokers and the entity classes. Note how the broker classes perform the tasks involved in retrieving instances or sets of instances from the database.

We have used a simple approach for obtaining the adverts linked to a particular campaign, by having the broker return an array of `Adverts`. As mentioned above, this could return an enumerator so that the control class could iterate through the collection of `Adverts`.

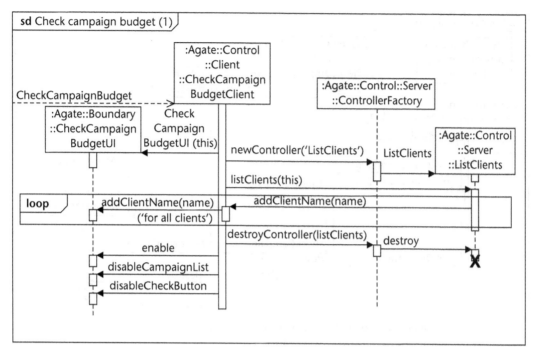

Figure A5.11 First sequence diagram for Check campaign budget.

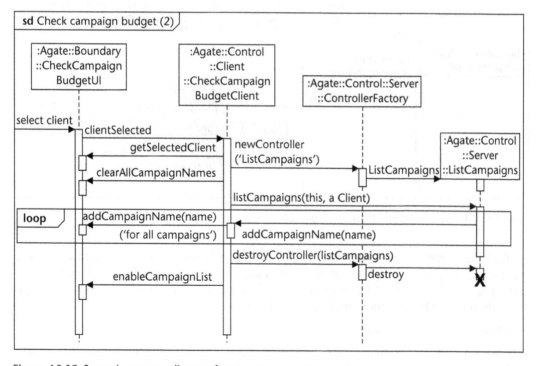

Figure A5.12 Second sequence diagram for Check campaign budget.

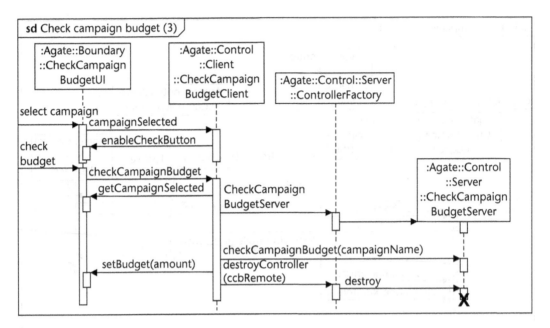

Figure A5.13 Third sequence diagram for Check campaign budget.

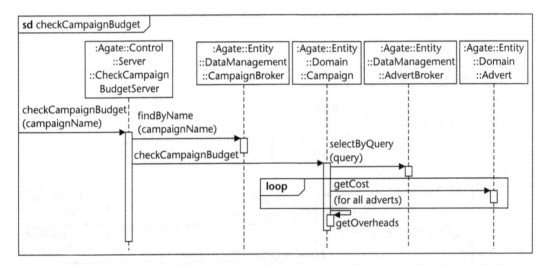

Figure A5.14 Sequence diagram for the operation checkCampaignBudget().

A string named query has been passed to the selectByQuery() operation of the AdvertBroker. The exact format of this will depend on how the object-relational database mapping is set up. If the uniqueID attributes are used in the database as foreign keys, then the SQL statement will be something like:

```
SELECT * FROM adverts WHERE adverts.campaignID = '123456789';
```

and the ID of the particular campaign is added into the query string before it is passed to the broker.

A5.6 Database Design

Figure A5.15 shows the SQL to create the tables to map to the classes in Fig. A5.7. The indexes are required to ensure that it is possible quickly to retrieve all the campaigns linked to a client or all the adverts linked to a campaign. A character field has been used to hold the unique ID for each object. We are assuming that some mechanism will be used to generate these, but have not detailed it here. An alternative would be to use long integer values.

A5.7 State Machines

Figure A5.16 shows the event–action table for the state machine of Fig. A5.17. This state machine is the same as the one shown in Chapter 17.

```
CREATE TABLE Clients
   (VARCHAR(30) uniqueID PRIMARY KEY NOT NULL,
   VARCHAR(30) companyAddress,
   VARCHAR(40) companyContact,
   VARCHAR(30) companyEmail
   VARCHAR(30) companyFax,
   VARCHAR(50) companyName NOT NULL,
   VARCHAR(30) companyTelephone,
   VARCHAR(30) staffContactID);
CREATE INDEX client_idx ON Clients (staffContactID, companyName);
CREATE TABLE Campaigns
   (VARCHAR(30) uniqueID PRIMARY KEY NOT NULL,
   FLOAT actualCost,
   DATE campaignFinishDate,
   DATE campaignStartDate,
   VARCHAR(30) clientID NOT NULL,
   DATE completionDate,
   DATE datePaid,
   FLOAT estimatedCost,
   VARCHAR(30) managerID,
   VARCHAR(50) title);
CREATE INDEX campaign_idx ON Campaigns (clientID, managerID, title);
CREATE TABLE Adverts
   (VARCHAR(30) uniqueID PRIMARY KEY NOT NULL,
   FLOAT actualCost,
   DATE actualCompletionDate,
   VARCHAR(30) campaignID NOT NULL,
   FLOAT estimatedCost,
   DATE targetCompletionDate,
   VARCHAR(50) title);
CREATE INDEX advert_idx ON Adverts (campaignID, title);
```

Figure A5.15 SQL to create tables for the classes `Client`, `Campaign` and `Advert`.

Current State	Event	Action	Next State
–	Check Campaign Budget menu item selected	Display CheckCampaignBudgetUI. Load **Client** dropdown. Disable **Campaign** dropdown. Disable **Check** button. Enable window	1
1	Client selected	Clear **Campaign** dropdown. Load **Campaign** dropdown. Enable **Campaign** dropdown	2
2, 3, 4	Client selected	Clear **Campaign** dropdown. Load **Campaign** dropdown. Clear **Budget** textfield. Disable **Check** button	2
2	Campaign selected	Clear **Budget** textfield. Enable **Check** button	3
3	**Check** button clicked	Calculate budget. Display result	4
3, 4	Campaign selected	Clear **Budget** textfield	3
4	**Check** button clicked	Calculate budget. Display result	4
1, 2, 3, 4	**Close** button clicked	Display alert dialogue	5
5	**OK** button clicked	Close alert dialogue. Close window	–
5	**Cancel** button clicked	Close alert dialogue	H*

Figure A5.16 Event–action table for Fig. A5.17.

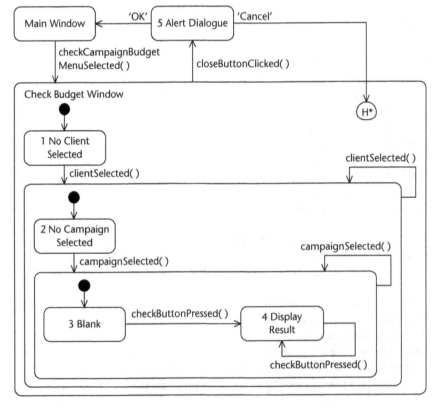

Figure A5.17 State machine for control of the user interface in Check campaign budget.

A5.8 Activities of Design

The activities in the design workflow are shown in the activity diagrams of Figs A5.18 and A5.19.

In order to keep the diagram simple, we have shown the flow of activities in Fig. A5.19 without dependencies on the products that are used and created. Although we have shown a flow through the activities from top to bottom, there will inevitably be some iteration through this workflow even within a major iteration.

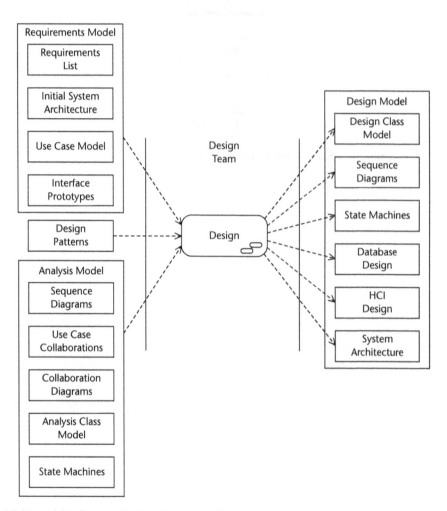

Figure A5.18 Activity diagram for the design workflow.

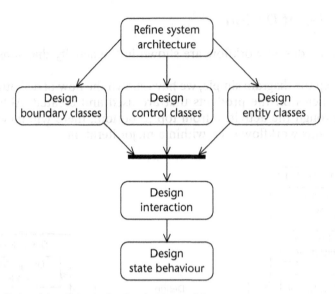

Figure A5.19 Detailed activity diagram for the design workflow.

Implementation

19.1 Introduction

Implementation is concerned with the process of building the new system. This involves writing program code, developing database tables, testing the new system, setting it up with data, possibly transferred from an old system, training users and eventually switching over to the new system.

Implementation might be considered outside the scope of analysis and design. However, in projects that use rapid application development techniques, the distinction between different roles tends to break down. Analysts in particular may have a role during implementation in dealing with system testing, data conversion and user training. In other organizations staff may be employed in specialist roles to carry out these tasks. UML diagrams can be used to plan and document the implementation of the software.

A range of different software packages are required for implementation: for example, languages and database management systems. It is important to keep track of the relationship between different elements of the system such as source code files, object code files and software libraries. It is also important to maintain standards in the software development process: classes, objects and variables should be named in ways that make their purpose clear to others and make it possible to trace from analysis through design to code; programs should be self-documenting and well-structured.

UML provides two diagrams that can be used to document the implementation of a system. *Component diagrams* are used to document dependencies between the different elements of the system. They can also be combined with *deployment diagrams* to show how the software components relate to the physical architecture of the system. For a large system these diagrams may be an unwieldy way of documenting the implementation and it may be simpler to use tables of information using a spreadsheet.

The testing of a new system is an essential part of implementation and includes testing of individual components, subsystems and the complete system. A major task when a new system is introduced is to take data from an existing system or systems and transfer it into the new system. The existing data may be held on paper or in a computerized information system that is being replaced. Temporary staff may have to be employed during the changeover to the new system. They and the existing staff will require training in how to use the system, and user documentation will have to be produced. There are four different strategies for the introduction of a new system into an organization. These different approaches are appropriate to different circumstances, and each has its own advantages and disadvantage. Even after a system has been implemented there is work to be done in maintaining it and updating it as requirements change.

19.2 Software Implementation

19.2.1 Software tools

The implementation of a system will require a range of tools. Ensuring that these are available in compatible versions and with sufficient licences for the number of developers who will be using them is part of the project management role. The Rational Unified Process (Kruchten, 2004) adds an Environment Discipline to those of the generic Unified Process. The purpose of the Environment Discipline is to support the development organization with appropriate processes and tools. Many such tools have been designed and developed to make the work of the system developer easier. In this section we describe each in turn.

Modelling tools

Modelling tools (sometimes known as computer-aided software engineering (CASE) tools) allow the analysts and designers to produce the diagrams that make up their models of the system. Modelling tools were discussed in detail in Section 3.8 There are now many modelling tools that support UML notation. If they have been implemented to use the UML XML Metadata Interchange format (XMI), it is possible to exchange models between different vendors' tools. The repository for the project should also be maintained using the modelling tool to link the textual and structured descriptions of every class, attribute, operation, state and so on to its diagrammatic representation.

To ensure that the implementation accurately reflects the design diagrams, it may be possible to generate code in one or more programming languages from the models in the modelling tool. Modelling tools exist that generate code for languages such as Visual Basic, C++, C# and Java. Some support the generation of SQL statements to create relational database tables to implement data storage, and the generation of Enterprise Java Beans (EJB) and XML schemas. Some modelling tools provide support for reverse engineering from existing code to design models. When this is combined with code generation it is known as round-trip engineering.

Compilers, interpreters, debuggers and run-time support

Whatever the language being used, some kind of compiler or interpreter will be required to translate the source code into executable code. C++ must be compiled into object code that can be run on the target machine. Smalltalk is interpreted, each command is translated as the program executes. Java is compiled into an intermediate bytecode format and requires a run-time program to enable it to execute. For applets, this run-time program is provided in the web browser, otherwise it is provided by the program called simply java or java.exe. C# can be compiled into bytecode in Microsoft Intermediate Language (MSIL) format for .NET applications. Developers also require the use of debugging tools that allow them to analyse problems in the code by stopping execution at breakpoints and examining the contents of variables.

Visual editors

Graphical user interfaces can be extremely difficult to program manually. Since the advent of Visual Basic, visual development environments have been produced for a wide range of languages. These enable the programmer to develop a user interface by dragging and dropping visual components onto forms and setting the parameters that control their appearance in a properties window. All the user interface examples in Chapters 6, 16 and 17 were produced in this way.

Integrated development environment

Large projects involve many files containing source code and other information such as the resource files for prompts in different human languages discussed in Chapter 18. Keeping track of all these files and the dependencies between them, and recompiling all those that have changed as a project is being built is a task best performed by software designed for that purpose. Integrated development environments (IDEs) incorporate a multi-window editor, mechanisms for managing the files that make up a project, links to the compiler so that code can be compiled from within the IDE and a debugger to help the programmer step through the code to find errors. An IDE may also include a visual editor to help build the user interface and a version control system to keep track of different versions of the software. Some also include modelling tools that either allow the developer to model in UML or provide UML visualizations of the code.

Configuration management

Configuration management tools keep track of the dependencies between components and the versions of source code and resource files that are used to produce a particular release of a software package. Each time a file is to be changed, it must be checked out of a repository. When it has been changed it is checked in again as a new version. The tool keeps track of the versions and the changes from one version to the next. When a software release is built, the tool keeps track of the versions of all the files that were used in the build. To ensure that an identical version can be rebuilt, other tools such as compilers and linkers should also be under version control.

Some such tools are simple and easily available such as CVS and RCS, while others are for large-scale distributed projects and require full-time administrators. Web interfaces are available for some, and these make it possible to check items in and out over the Internet for work on Open Source software or distributed development.

There are standard protocols for version control software, which make it possible for users of editors, IDEs and CASE tools to check items out and in from within the tool.

Class browsers

In an object-oriented system, a browser provides a visual way of navigating the class hierarchy of the application and the supporting classes to find their attributes and operations. Smalltalk-80 was the first language to provide this kind of browsing capability. Some IDEs now provide it. The Java Application Programming Interface (API) is documented in HTML and can be browsed with a web browser.

Component managers

Chapter 20 discusses how software reuse can be achieved through the development of reusable components. Component managers provide the user with the ability to search for suitable components, to browse them and to maintain different versions of components.

Database management system

A large-scale DBMS will consist of a considerable amount of software. If it supports a client–server mode of operation, there will be separate client and server components as well as all the tools discussed in Section 18.2.6. To use ODBC or JDBC will require software installed on the client. For any database, special class libraries or Java packages may be required on the client either during compilation or at run-time or both. The object database db4o includes an enhancer that can be used to process Java class files to make them Activatable. Using object–relational mapping tools such as those based on JDO (see Chapter 18) also requires the use of post-processors that change compiled classes.

Application containers

With the growth of web-based applications, much software now runs in *containers* of some sort. For web applications that are not part of larger enterprise applications, this may be a web container such as Tomcat, while large-scale enterprise applications are now often developed to run in application servers such as IBM's WebSphere or Red Hat's JBoss. These provide a framework within which classes can be implemented as EJBs and deliver the business logic of the system. Lightweight containers such as Spring provide a framework for applications built of plain Java objects that can be 'wired together' using configuration files.

Testing tools

Automated testing tools are available for some environments. What is more likely is that programmers will develop their own tools to provide harnesses within which to test classes and subsystems according to company standards. Section 19.3 covers testing in more detail.

Installation tools

Anyone who has installed commercial software on a Windows PC or a Mac or used a package manager on Linux will have experienced one of these tools, which automate the creation of directories, the extraction of files from archives and the setting up of parameters or registry entries. To do this they maintain the kind of information that can be modelled using component and deployment diagrams (see Sections 19.3 and 19.4). In our experience, uninstallation tools do not work as well!

Conversion tools

In most cases data for the new system will have to be transferred from an existing system. Whereas once the existing system was usually a manual system, most projects nowadays replace an existing computerized system, and data will have to be extracted from files or a database in the existing system and reformatted so that it can be used to set up the database for the new system. There are packages that provide automated tools to extract data from a wide range of systems and format it for a new system.

Documentation generators

In the same way that code can be generated from the diagrams and documents in a CASE tool, it may be possible to generate technical and user documentation. In Windows there are packages that can be used to produce files in Windows Help format. Java includes a program called javadoc that processes Java source files and builds HTML documentation in the style of the API documentation from special comments with embedded tags in the source code. C# uses special XML tags embedded in comments to generate documentation.

19.2.2 Coding and documentation standards

Even one person developing software on his or her own is likely to find at some point that they cannot remember the purpose of a class, an attribute or an operation in a program. On any project in which people collaborate to develop software, agreed standards for the naming of classes, attributes, operations and other elements of the system are essential if the project is not to descend into chaos. (See also Chapter 5 and Section 13.8.)

Naming standards should have been agreed before the analysis began. In this book we have tried to conform to a typical object-oriented standard.

- Classes are named with an initial capital letter. Words are concatenated together when the class name is longer than one word. Capital letters within the name show where these words have been joined together: for example `SalesOrderProxy`.
- Attributes are named with an initial lower case letter. The same approach is taken as for classes by concatenating words together: for example `customerOrderRef`.
- Operations are named in the same way as attributes: for example `getOrderTotal()`.

There are other standards. In C++ one convention is to use *Hungarian* notation: all member variable (attribute) names are prefixed by an abbreviation that indicates the type of the member variable: for example, `b` for a Boolean, `i` for an integer, `f` for a float, `btn` for a button and `hWnd` for a handle to a window object. This can be particularly useful in languages that are not strongly typed, like Smalltalk, as it helps to enforce the consistent use of the same variable for the same purpose by different developers.

Consistent naming standards also make it easier to trace requirements through from analysis through design to implementation. This is particularly important for class, attribute and operation names.

Not everything in a program can be deduced by reading the names of classes, attributes and operations. Beveridge (1996) in a book on Java programming gives five reasons for documenting code.

- Think of the next person. Someone else may be maintaining the code you have written.
- Your code can be an educational tool. Good code can help others, but without comments complicated code can be difficult to understand.

- No language is self-documenting. However good your naming conventions, you can always provide extra help to someone reading your code.
- You can comply with the Java coding standards. Your documentation will be in the same hypertext format as the Java API documentation.
- You can automate its production. The javadoc program is discussed below. It generates HTML from your comments.

(The comments about Java apply just as well to other languages.) Standards should be enforced for the way that comments are added to a program. This should include a block at the start of each class source file (or header file in C++) that describes the purpose of the class and includes details of its author and the date on which it was written. The amendment history of the source file can be included in this block. Every operation should begin with a comment that describes its purpose. Any obscure aspect of the code should be documented with a comment. If you are developing in Java, you can use the javadoc conventions to generate HTML documentation for your classes. You can embed HTML tags and javadoc tags in the comments, and javadoc will also use its own special tags to add information about the author and version to the HTML. The javadoc tags include:

- `@see classname`–'See also' hypertext link to the specified class
- `@version text`–'Version' entry
- `@author name`–'Author' entry.

C# uses XML tags embedded in comments in the code to generate documentation. The recommended tags include:

- `<see cref="classname" />`–Link to the specified class
- `<seealso cref="classname" />`–Cross-reference to a `<see>` link
- `<summary>text</summary>`–Summary description.

As well as technical documentation, there will be a need for user documentation that will be required for training users and for them to refer to once the system is in use. Standards need to be agreed with the users for the format of this documentation, which may be produced by analysts or by specialist technical authors.

19.3 Component Diagrams

Component diagrams are used to show the logical or physical software components that make up a system. We have already introduced component diagrams in Chapter 8. The notation and use of component diagrams has changed in UML 2.0. A distinction has been made between components and *artefacts*. Artefacts are new in UML 2.0 and are used in deployment diagrams (see Section 19.4). They are used to represent development artefacts that were previously represented by components. In UML 2.0 components are specifically used to represent modular software units with a well-defined interface. They can be logical or physical components, so component diagrams can be used to model either the abstract, logical view of the components in a system or subsystem or the actual physical components that are deployed. Cheesman and Daniels (2001) make a clear distinction between different forms of component.

- *Component Specification*–specification of a modular software unit in terms of its behaviour (interfaces)
- *Component Implementation*–deployable implementation of a component specification
- *Installed Component*–a copy of an implementation in a runtime environment
- *Component Object*–an instance of an installed component that actually carries out the specified behaviour.

They also define a *Component Interface* as the set of behaviours that can be offered by a component object.

Dependencies between components can be shown in a component diagram, as in Fig. 19.1. However, they are more commonly shown using the notation used in Fig. 8.10, in which the required interface of one component is 'wired up' to the provided interface of another component. An example of this is shown in Fig. 19.2, where the Production scheduler provides a Scheduling interface and requires a Planning interface, which is provided by the Staff planner component. These wiring connections can also be shown as dependency arrows between the required and provided interfaces, but the ball and socket view is clearer.

The interfaces of components can be shown connected to ports. Ports are small rectangles drawn on the edge of the component. Where an interface is connected to a port, it means that the component delegates responsibility for the behaviour associated with that interface to a subcomponent or object within it. This is shown in Fig. 19.3, and Fig. 19.4 illustrates the internal structure of a component with the delegation dependencies and the connections between the internal subcomponents.

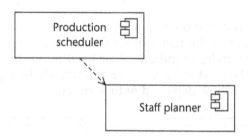

Figure 19.1 Dependency between high-level components.

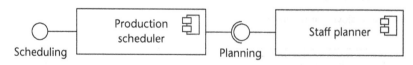

Figure 19.2 Wiring connection between required and provided interfaces.

Figure 19.3 Component with ports.

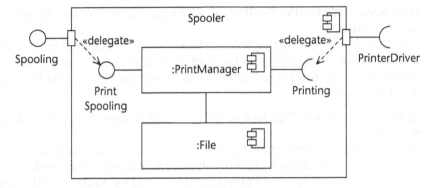

Figure 19.4 Delegation of interfaces to subcomponents within a component.

19.4 Deployment Diagrams

The main implementation diagram provided by UML is the *deployment diagram*. Deployment diagrams are used to show the configuration of run-time processing elements and the software artefacts and processes that are located on them. They are made up of *nodes* and *communication paths*. Nodes are typically used to show computers, and the communication paths show the network and protocols that are used to communicate between nodes. Nodes can be used to show other processing resources such as people or mechanical resources. Nodes are drawn as 3D views of cubes or rectangular prisms, and the simplest deployment diagrams show just the nodes connected by communication paths as in Fig. 19.5.

Deployment diagrams can show either types of machine or particular instances as in Fig. 19.5, where *swift* is the name of a PC. Deployment diagrams can be shown with artefacts within the nodes to indicate their location in the run-time environment. Figure 19.6 shows that the AgateClient.jar artefact will be deployed onto PC Client and AgateServer.jar will be deployed onto a server.

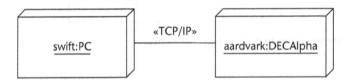

Figure 19.5 Simple deployment diagram.

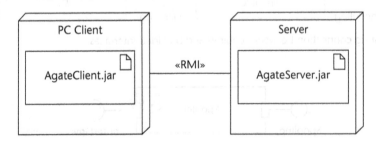

Figure 19.6 Deployment diagram with artefacts.

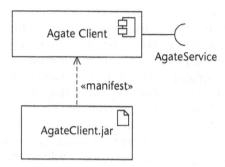

Figure 19.7 Relationship between a component and an artefact.

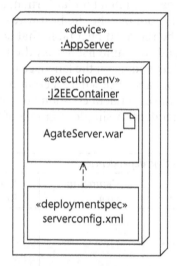

Figure 19.8 Device containing an execution environment with an artefact and a deployment specification.

The relationship between components and artefacts can be shown using a «manifest» dependency. Figure 19.7 shows this for the `Agate Client` component and the `AgateClient.jar` artefact.

Nodes can represent *execution environments* as well as processing *devices*, and can be stereotyped as either in order to distinguish between them. A device is a kind of composite node that consists of other devices or nodes. An execution environment is an environment into which executable components can be deployed as artefacts. A typical example would be a J2EE application server. Artefacts can have *deployment specifications* associated with them. A deployment specification is a set of properties that define the parameters necessary for the execution of an artefact on a node. A *deployment descriptor* is an artefact that represents a deployment specification. Figure 19.8 illustrates these diagram elements. Note that in Figs 19.5 and 19.6 the nodes shown are node types, whereas in Fig. 19.8, an instance of a node is shown. The same conventions are used as for classes and objects, with a colon and underlining to indicate the instance.

If you try to show all the artefacts of a system in deployment diagrams, the diagrams are likely to become very large or difficult to read. They can serve the purpose of communicating information about the location of key components to other members of the team or to users. Indeed, most computer professionals will have drawn an informal diagram like this at some time in their working lives to show where different parts of a system are to be located. Deployment diagrams show the physical architecture of the system.

If you intend to use component and deployment diagrams to illustrate general principles about the way that the new system will be structured, then they are fine as a diagramming technique. However, if the aim of drawing these diagrams is to provide a complete specification of the dependencies between components at compile-time and run-time and the location of all software components as artefacts in the implemented system, then this may be one of those cases where a picture is not worth a thousand words. Even for a relatively simple system that involves multiple nodes, keeping track of all these dependencies and documenting which components have to be on which machines is not a trivial task. For large systems, it is next to impossible. For most systems, this information may be easier to maintain in a tabular format, and a spreadsheet, a database or a configuration management tool may be the best way of doing this.

Component diagrams can be replaced by a table that shows a list of all the software components down the rows and the same list across the top of the columns. It may be best to keep up to three tables (depending on the language used) for compile-time, link-time and run-time dependencies. For each case where a component is dependent on another, place a mark where the row of the dependent component intersects with the column of the component on which it is dependent. A simple example of this is shown in Fig. 19.9.

Campaign database – compilation time dependencies				
	JDBC sun.jdbc.*	Campaign. java	Campaign Broker.java	Campaign Proxy.java
JDBC sun.jdbc.*				
Campaign. java				
Campaign Broker.java	✓	✓		
Campaign Proxy.java		✓	✓	

Figure 19.9 Excerpt from example table to show artefact dependencies.

Campaign database – run-time locations		
	Client PC	Database server
jdbc-odbc.jar	c:\jdbc	
agateclient.jar	c:\agate\client\lib	
SQL*Net		✓
OCI Listener		✓
...		

Figure 19.10 Excerpt from example table to replace deployment diagram.

In the same way, deployment diagrams can be replaced by a table that lists components down the rows and either types of machines or particular instances across the top of the columns. A mark is entered in the row–column intersection for every component that has to be on a particular machine or type of machine. If the exact location of components in a directory structure is important, then that location can be entered into the table. This is shown in Fig. 19.10. Later this will form the basis of the information required for installing software onto users' machines for testing and eventual deployment.

Some configuration management and software build tools also make it possible to store this kind of information and use it to automate the building and deployment of software.

19.5 Software Testing

Testing of software is necessary to ensure that it meets the requirements, both to check that the software complies with the requirements (verification), and to check that it has been written correctly and effectively (validation). The distinction between verification and validation is described as: verification checks that the right software has been written; validation checks that the software has been written right. In an iterative project, testing takes place throughout the phases of the project, and is supported by quality assurance processes to review analysis and design models and documents as they are produced. Testing should always be carried out in a test system–a copy of the system used for testing–and never in the live system!

19.5.1 Who carries out the testing?

One view of testing is that it is too important to be left to the programmers who have developed the software for the system. This is not meant as a criticism of programmers but reflects the fact that it is important that testing is carried out by someone whose assessment of the software will be objective and impartial. It is often difficult for programmers to see the faults in the program code that they have written. An alternative view is provided by Extreme Programming (XP) (Beck, 2004). XP is an approach to rapid application development in which programmers are expected to write test harnesses for their programs before they write any code. Every piece of code can then be tested against its expected behaviour and if a change is made it can easily be retested. XP is explained in Section 21.6.

Some organizations employ specialist software testers. The following paragraph is an excerpt from an advertisement in the British computer press for a post as a tester:

> A leading financial institution has an opportunity for a systems tester to work on a business critical project. Testing throughout the project lifecycle, you will liaise closely with developers and team leaders to implement test cases and organize automated testing scripts. All testing is organized within a fully automated environment. With a background in testing you will have strong business acumen ...

However, not all organizations can afford the luxury of specialist testers. Often the analysts who carried out the initial requirements analysis will be involved in testing the system as it is developed. The analysts will have an understanding of the business requirements for the system and will be able to measure the performance of the system against functional and non-functional requirements.

The people responsible for testing will use their knowledge of the system to draw up a test plan. This will specify what is to be tested, how it is to be tested, the criteria by which it is possible to decide whether a particular test has been passed or failed and the order in which tests are to take place. Based on their knowledge of the requirements, they will also draw up sets of test data values that are to be used.

The other key players in the process of testing new software are the eventual users of the system or their representatives. Users may be involved in testing the system against its specification, and will almost certainly take part in final user acceptance tests before the system is signed off and accepted by the clients. If a use-case-driven approach to testing is used, the use cases are used to provide scenarios to form the basis of test scripts.

19.5.2 What is tested?

In testing any component of the system, the aim is to find out if its requirements have been met. One kind of testing seeks to answer the following questions:

Does it do what it's meant to do?
Does it do it as fast as it's meant to do it?

This is equivalent to asking 'Never mind how it works, what does it produce?' and is known as *black box* testing because the software is treated as a black box. Test data is put into it and it produces some output, but the testing does not investigate how the processing is carried out. Black box testing tests the quality of performance of the software. It is also necessary to check how well the software has been designed internally. This second kind of testing seeks to answer the following question:

Is it not just a solution to the problem, but a *good* solution?

This is equivalent to asking 'Never mind what it's for, how well does it work?' and is known as *white box* testing because it tests the internal workings of the software and whether the software works as specified. White box testing tests the quality of construction of the software. In a project where reusable components are bought in, it may not be possible to apply white box testing to these components, as they may be provided as compiled object code. However, some suppliers will supply source code as well as compiled code, and there is a growing Open Source movement that makes this possible. As an aside, some organizations require, as part of their software contracts, that source code is placed in *escrow*. This means that a copy of the source code is lodged with a third party, usually a lawyer or a trade association, so that it is available to the client if the software company goes out of business. By this means the client ensures that they will be able to maintain and enhance the software even if its original developers are no longer able to.

Ideally, testers will use both white box and black box testing methods together to ensure:

- completeness (black box and white box)
- correctness (black box and white box)
- reliability (white box)
- maintainability (white box).

However, the aim of any kind of testing is always to try to get the software to fail–to find errors–rather than to confirm that the software is correct. For this reason the test data should be designed to test the software at its limits, not merely to show that it copes acceptably with routine data.

Testing can take place at as many as five levels:

- unit testing
- integration testing
- subsystem testing
- system testing
- acceptance testing.

In an object-oriented system, the units are likely to be individual classes. Testing of classes should include an initial *desk check,* in which the tester manually walks through the source code of the class before compilation. The class should then be compiled, and the compilation should be clean with no errors or warnings. To test the running of a class the tester will require some kind of test program (the term *harness* is often used) that will create one or more instances of a class, populate them with data and invoke both instance operations and class operations. If pre-conditions and post-conditions have been specified for operations, as suggested in Chapter 10, then the operations that have been implemented will be tested to ensure that they comply with the pre-conditions and that the post-conditions are met when they have completed. State machine diagrams can be used to check that classes are conforming to the behaviour in their specification.

It may be difficult to test classes in isolation. For the reasons that are discussed in Chapter 20 on reuse, most classes are coupled in some way to other classes in the system. Unit testing merges into integration testing when groups of classes are tested together. The obvious test unit at this point is either the use case to test the system from the user's perspective or the component to test the correct working of components and the interaction between components. The interaction between classes or components can be tested against the specification of the sequence diagrams, timing diagrams and communication diagrams. User interface classes and data management classes will also have to be tested in conjunction with the classes in the application logic layer. If scenario-based design has been used (see Chapter 16), then the scenarios can form the basis for testing scenarios in which a use case can be tested against a typical business situation.

Use cases that share the same persistent data should be tested together. This kind of testing should check that applications work correctly when multiple clients are accessing the database and that transactional database updates are carried out correctly. This is one form of subsystem testing in which the subsystems are built around different business functions that make use of the same stored data.

If significant changes are made to a system, then some of the tests must be run again to ensure that the changes have not broken existing functionality. This is *regression testing.*

Testing is sometimes described as taking place at three levels.

Level 1
- Tests individual modules (e.g. classes or components).
- Then tests whole programs (e.g. use cases).
- Then tests whole suites of programs (e.g. the Agate application).

Level 2
- Also known as alpha testing or verification.
- Executes programs in a simulated environment.
- Particularly tests inputs that are:
  - negative values when positive ones are expected (and vice versa)
  - out of range or close to range limits
  - invalid combinations.

Level 3
- Also known as beta testing or validation.
- Tests programs in live user environment:
  - for response and execution times
  - with large volumes of data
  - for recovery from error or failure.

A final stage of testing is *user acceptance testing*, during which the system is evaluated by the users against the original requirements before the client signs the project off. Document-ation produced during requirements capture and analysis will be used to check the finished product, in particular use case scenarios and non-functional requirements.

19.5.3 Test documentation

Thorough testing requires careful documentation of what is planned and what is achieved. This includes the expected outcomes for each test, the actual outcomes and, for any test that is failed, details of the retesting. Figure 19.11 shows part of a test plan for the Agate case study. It shows details of each test and its expected outcomes. The results of the actual tests will be documented in a separate, but similar, format, with columns to show the actual result of each instance of each test and the date when each test was passed, and to document problems. Many organizations have standard forms for these documents or may use spreadsheets or databases to keep this information. The advantage of using a spreadsheet or database is the ability to produce reports that show what percentage of tests are complete. If requirements are held in a database, it is possible to link requirements

Test no.	23		
Purpose	Test correct addition of campaign and adverts.		
Step no.	Test description	Test data	Expected result
23.1	Create a new Campaign		Campaign added to database. Campaign Estimated Cost is set to £0.00
23.2	Add Advert 1 to Campaign	Advert Estimated Cost = £500.00	Advert added to database. Campaign Estimated Cost is set to £500.00
23.3	Add Advert 2 to Campaign	Advert Estimated Cost = –£500.00	Advert not added to database. Negative value rejected. No change to Campaign Estimated Cost. Error message displayed
23.4	Add Advert 2 to Campaign	Advert Estimated Cost = £300.00	Advert added to database. Campaign Estimated Cost is set to £800.00
23.5	Set Advert 1 Completed	Advert Actual Cost = £400.00	Campaign Estimated Cost is set to £700.00. Actual Cost is set to £400.00

Figure 19.11 Excerpt from test plan for Agate.

to the tests that show whether they have been met and thus to provide a mechanism for tracing through from the original requirements to functionality in the finished system.

Testers should also watch out for unexpected results. Interaction between different operating systems can often cause unanticipated problems with different conventions for newline characters or case sensitivity of filenames. Problems such as these should be reported as bugs and recorded in a fault reporting package for action by the developers.

19.6 Data Conversion

Data from existing systems will have to be entered into a new system when it is introduced. The organization may have a mixture of existing manual and computerized systems that will be replaced by the new system. The data from these systems must be collated and converted into the necessary format for the new system. The timing of this will depend on the implementation strategy that is used (see next section), but it is likely to be a costly task, involving the use of staff time, the employment of temporary staff or the use of software to convert data from existing computer systems. These costs should have been identified in any cost–benefit analysis that was carried out at the inception of the project.

If data is being collated from existing manual systems, it may be necessary to gather it from different sources. Data may be stored in different files, on index cards, in published documents, such as catalogues, or in other paper-based systems. If this data is going to be entered manually into the new system by users keying it in, then the designers should draw up paper forms that can be used to collate the information so that it is all in one place when it is keyed in. Some data will only ever be entered when the system is started up: for example, codes that are used in the system and will not be altered. Special data maintenance windows may be required for this kind of one-off activity.

Data from existing computer systems will have to be extracted from existing files and databases and reformatted to be usable with the new system. This provides an opportunity to clean up the data: removing out-of-date records and tidying up the values that are stored. Address and telephone number fields of existing systems are likely to have been abused or misused by users. The work of converting the data may be done by using special programs written by the developers of the system, by employing consultants who specialize in this kind of work or by using commercial software that is capable of reading and writing data in a variety of formats; some packages are capable of working out the format of an unknown file.

The tasks involved in data conversion can be summarized as follows:

- creating and validating the new files, tables or database
- checking for and correcting any format errors
- preparing the existing data for conversion:
  - verifying the existing data for correctness
  - resolving discrepancies between data items from different sources
  - collating data in special forms for input
  - obtaining specially written programs to convert and enter the data
- importing or inputting the data
- verifying the data after it has been imported or input.

All the converted data may have to be ready for entry into the new system to meet a tight deadline, or it may be possible to enter it over a period of time. It is best to convert relatively static data such as product information and customer details first and leave dynamically changing files of information such as orders or other business transactions until last. It may be that only open orders should be taken over into the new system. If historic data is kept in the old system, then this system may have to be maintained for a period of time after the start of the new system in order to answer queries about past transactions. The implementation strategy will determine the timescale for conversion.

Always carry out a trial data conversion exercise with the test system before doing it for real. One of the authors was involved in converting data from one stock and manufacturing system to another. In both packages (from the same supplier) the Part ID field was case-sensitive. However, in that same supplier's data conversion software all alphabetic characters in Part IDs were converted to upper case. Because upper and lower case letters were used to distinguish major and minor subassemblies of the same product, this caused problems that would have delayed the implementation if the error in the data conversion program had not been identified well before the planned implementation date.

19.7 User Documentation and Training

19.7.1 User manuals

As well as preparing the technical documentation for the system, analysts or specialist staff in the role of technical authors will be involved in producing manuals for end-users. The technical documentation will be required by the system manager and other staff responsible for running the system and by staff who have to maintain the system. Ordinary users of the system, who will be using it to carry out their daily work tasks, require a different kind of documentation.

Users will require two kinds of manual. During training they will need training materials that are organized around the tasks that they have to carry out with the new system. Online computer-based training materials can be developed so that users learn the tasks in a staged way. These may be in the form of self-study tutorials that users can work through independently of any formal training that is provided.

The users will also need a reference manual that they can refer to while they are using the system. The reference manual should be a complete description of the system in non-technical language. Many software companies employ technical authors to write manuals in language that users can understand. The manual should be organized for ease of use. This involves the author understanding how the user will carry out their tasks and the kind of problem that they will face. The manual should be organized around the users' tasks, and should be supplemented with a comprehensive index based on the terms that the users will be familiar with, rather than the technical terms used by the system developers. Particular attention should be paid to exceptional circumstances and not just routine tasks.

The reference manual may be replicated in the online help so that the users can refer to it while they are using the system. However, it should also be available as a paper manual that the users can refer to if there is a problem with the system, or on a CD-ROM that can be loaded onto a separate machine.

19.7.2 **User training**

Temporary staff and existing staff will have to be trained in the tasks that they will carry out on the new system. Specialist trainers or analysts are likely to be involved in the design of the training programme, the development of training materials, the planning of the training sessions and the delivery of the training itself.

Training programmes should be designed with clear learning objectives for the trainees. They will be using the system and it is important that the training is practical and geared to the tasks that they will be performing. If it is too theoretical or technical, they will not find it useful. Training should be delivered 'just in time'—when the users need it—as they will forget much of what they are told within a short space of time, so training delivered even a few weeks before it is required is likely to be wasted. Online computer-based training using video and audio materials that users can refer to when they need it is likely to be of most use. If formal training sessions are used, then trainees should be given learning tasks to take away and carry out in their workplace. This implies that they will be allocated adequate time for training—skimping on training in order to save money is likely to be counter-productive. Staff will not get the best out of the system and are likely to become frustrated if they do not understand how to work the system. It is often worth following up after users have started using a new system to check that they are using it correctly and identify needs for refresher training.

19.8 ▌ Implementation Strategies

There are four main strategies for switching over to the new system:

- direct changeover
- parallel running
- phased changeover
- pilot project.

Figure 19.12 shows three of these changeover strategies in diagram form. Each of them has its advantages and disadvantages.

Direct changeover

Direct changeover means that on an agreed date users stop using the old system and start using the new system. Direct changeover is usually timed to happen over a weekend to allow some time for data conversion and implementation of the new system. This does not mean that everything happens in a couple of days, as preparatory work will have been carried out in advance. The advantages and disadvantages of this approach are:

+ The new system will bring immediate business benefits to the organization, so should start paying for itself straight away.
+ It forces users to start working with the new system, so they will not be able to undermine it by using the old system.
+ It is simple to plan.
− There is no fallback if problems occur with the new system.
− Contingency plans are required to cope with unexpected problems.
− The plan must work without difficulties for it to be a success.

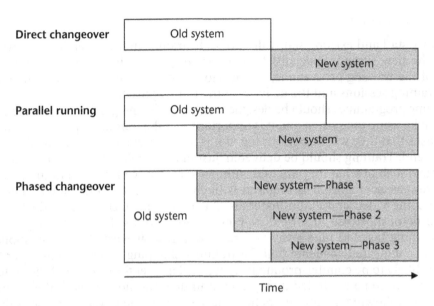

Figure 19.12 Changeover strategies.

Direct changeover is suitable for small-scale systems and other systems where there is a low risk of failure, such as the implementation of established package software.

Parallel running
Parallel running allows the existing system to continue to run alongside the new system. The advantages and disadvantages of this approach are:

+ There is a fallback if there are problems with the new system.
+ The outputs of the old and new systems can be compared–so testing can continue.
– There is a high cost as the client must pay for two systems during the overlap period, and this includes the staffing necessary to enter information into the old system as well as the new.
– There is a cost associated with comparing the outputs of the two systems.
– Users may not be committed to the new system as it is easier to stick with the familiar system.

Parallel running should be used in situations where there is a high level of risk associated with the project and the system is central to the business operations of the organization.

Phased changeover
In a *phased changeover*, the system is introduced in stages. The nature of the stages depends on the subsystems within the software, but introduction into one department at a time may be appropriate. The advantages and disadvantages are:

+ Attention can be paid to each individual subsystem as it is introduced.
+ If the right subsystems can be chosen for the first stages, then a fast return on investment can be obtained from those subsystems.
+ Thorough testing of each stage can be carried out as it is introduced.

- Disaffection and rumour can spread through the organization ahead of the implementation if there are problems with the early phases.
- There can be a long wait before the business benefits of later stages are achieved.

Phased changeover is suitable for large systems in which the subsystems are not heavily dependent on one another. The different phases can be introduced on a geographical basis or by department. Phased changeover works well with an iterative and incremental development approach.

Pilot project

A variation on phased changeover is the use of a *pilot project* approach. This involves trialling the complete system in one department or on one site. The decision on extending the system to the rest of the organization depends on the success of the pilot scheme. The pilot project can be used as a learning experience, and the system can be modified on the basis of the practical experience in the pilot project. As such, pilots are suitable for smaller systems, or packaged software, as it is unlikely that a large-scale system will be developed and then introduced in a way that makes its full-scale implementation dependent on the success of a pilot.

Although we have included information about implementation strategies at this late stage in the book, it is important to stress that liaison with operational staff about a new system and planning for its implementation should begin early in the development life-cycle. Adopting an iterative approach, in which incremental deliveries of software may occur from the start of the construction phase, means that the necessary infrastructure to run and support the new system has to be in place before the transition phase. It also means that planning for implementation of the new system must be based on a gradual migration from existing manual processes or an existing system.

New systems often mean new or changed business processes, and changing business processes may mean changes to organizational structures in the functional business departments within the organization. Staff may be assigned to change management roles in order to ensure that process and organizational changes are planned and that they deliver the benefits that were claimed for them when the project was justified in cost–benefit terms.

19.9 Review and Maintenance

19.9.1 The next steps

The work of analysts, designers and programmers does not stop after a system has been implemented. There is a continuing requirement for staff to work on the new system. First, it is important that the organization reviews both the 'finished' product and the process that was undertaken to achieve it. This may be for contractual reasons, in order to check that the product meets requirements. However, there is a growing recognition of the need for organizations to learn from experience and to record and manage the organizational knowledge that results from this learning. If there were any problems during the lifetime of the project, then these should be reviewed and conclusions drawn about how they might be avoided in the future. The amount of time spent on different tasks during the project can be used as the basis for metrics to estimate the amount of time that will be required for similar tasks in future projects. Second, it is unlikely that the system will be working perfectly according to the users' requirements, and further work will have to be done. Third, in an object-oriented project, the design should be reviewed to identify candidate components for future reuse, although as we suggest later in this chapter, planning for reuse should begin in the early stages of a project. Identifying reusable software components is not an activity to be left until the completion of the project. This subject is covered in Chapter 20.

19.9.2 The review process and evaluation report

The review process will normally be carried out by the systems analysts who have been involved in the project from the start, although it is possible to involve outside consultants in the process for an impartial view. They will normally be supported by representatives of users and user management. The various stakeholders who have invested time, money and commitment in the project will all have an interest in the content of the evaluation report. The report can be very detailed or can provide an overview evaluation–like every- thing else in the project, there will be a cost associated with producing it. The report's authors should consider the following areas.

- *Cost–benefit analysis*. The evaluation should refer back to criteria that were set for the project at its inception. It may not be possible to determine whether all the benefits projected in the cost–benefit analysis have been achieved, but most of the costs of development, installation, data conversion and training will have been incurred and can be compared with the projections.
- *Functional requirements*. It is important to check that the functional requirements of the system have been met. Clearly, this is something that should have been taking place throughout the lifetime of the project, but a summary can now be produced. Any actions that were taken to reduce the functional requirements, perhaps to keep the project within budget or on schedule, should be documented for future action under the heading of maintenance. If large areas of functionality were removed to bring the project in on schedule or within budget, a new project should be considered. Major bugs should similarly be documented if they have emerged since the implementation of the new system.
- *Non-functional requirements*. The system should be reviewed to ensure that it meets the targets for non-functional requirements that were documented during requirements analysis. It is now possible to assess whether quantitative objectives for learnability, throughput, response times or reduction of errors have been achieved.
- *User satisfaction*. Both quantitative and qualitative evaluations of the users' satisfaction with the new system can be undertaken, using questionnaires or interviews or both. The results should be treated carefully, as users can pick on quite minor problems or be influenced in their views of the finished product by experiences during the project.
- *Problems and issues*. As stated above, this is an important part of the evaluation pro- cess. Problems that occurred during the project should be recorded. These problems may have been technical or political, and it is important to handle the political issues with tact. Including a section criticizing unco-operative users or obstructive user management will mean that some readers take no notice of the rest of the report.

Solutions to problems should also be included in the report, as should an indication of who should be acting on the learning from this part of the process.

- *Positive experiences*. It is all too easy to focus on the negative aspects of a completed project. It is worth recording what parts of the project went well and to give credit to those responsible.
- *Quantitative data for future planning*. The evaluation report provides a place in which to record information about the amount of time spent on different tasks in the project, and this information can be used as the basis for drawing up future project plans. The quantitative data should be viewed in the light of the problems and issues that arose during the project, as the amount of time spent on a difficult task that was being tackled for the first time will not necessarily be an accurate predictor of how much time will be required for the same task in the future.
- *Candidate components for reuse*. If these have not already been identified during the project itself, then they should be identified at this stage. There will be different issues to be addressed, depending on whether the project has been carried out by in-house development staff or external consultants. For in-house projects, the reuse of software components should be viewed as a process of recouping some of the investment made and being able to apply those reusable elements of the system in future projects. For projects undertaken by external consultants, it may highlight legal issues about who owns the finished software that should have been addressed in the contract at the start of the project.
- *Future developments*. Any requirements for enhancements to the system or for bugs to be fixed should be documented. If possible, a cost should be associated with each item. Technical innovations that are likely to become mature technologies in the near future and that could be incorporated into the system in an upgrade should also be identified.
- *Actions*. The report should include a summary list of any actions that need to be undertaken as a result of carrying out the review process, with an indication of who is responsible for carrying out each such action and proposed timescales.

The end of a project provides a good opportunity for managers of the development staff to review performance on the project as part of a separate review process, the results of which are not necessarily in the public domain. This may feed into staff appraisal procedures and can affect the payment of bonuses, promotion prospects and staff development issues. The latter can include the choice of the next project for a member of staff to work on, their training needs, or opportunities to manage or act as a mentor to less experienced staff.

19.9.3 Maintenance activities

Very few systems are completely finished at the time that they are delivered and implemented, and there is a continuing role for staff in ensuring that the system meets the users' requirements. As well as maintenance of the system, there will be a need for support of users: providing initial and on-going training, particularly for new staff; improving documentation; solving simple problems; implementing simple reports that can be achieved using SQL or OQL without the need for changes to the system software; documenting bugs that are reported; and recording requests for enhancements that will be dealt with by maintenance staff. In large organizations these tasks are often handled by a helpdesk that supports all the organization's systems, and it may be appropriate for a member of the development team to join the helpdesk staff either temporarily or permanently. Whether or not this happens, helpdesk or support staff will need to be provided with training so that they can support the new system.

Maintenance involves more significant amendments to a system once it is up and running. Maintenance may be required for a number of reasons.

- There will almost certainly be bugs in the software that will require fixing. The use of object-oriented encapsulation should mean that it is easier to fix bugs without creating knock-on problems in the rest of the system. It is sometimes suggested that bug-fixing involves spending as much time fixing bugs that were introduced by the previous round of maintenance as it does in fixing bugs in the original system.
- In an iterative lifecycle, parts of the system may be in use while further development is undertaken. Subsequent iterations may involve maintaining what has already been developed.
- Users request enhancements to systems virtually from day one after implementation. Some of these will be relatively simple, such as additional reports, and may be dealt with by support staff, while others will involve significant changes to the software and will require the involvement of a maintenance team. Often these user requests will reflect the fact that until the system is running and users have a chance to see what it can do, it is difficult for them to have a clear idea of what their requirements are.
- In some cases, changes in the way that the business operates or in its environment, for example new legislation, will result in the need for changes to the system.
- There is a growing expectation that systems will be built as a collection of loosely coupled services (service-oriented architecture), and that business processes will be assembled by linking these services together with a business process management tool. The reason for this is to allow the business users to change their processes and link the services together in new ways. Such changes may result in the need to make changes to the implementation of services.
- Similarly, changes in the technology that is available to implement a system may result in the need for changes in that system.
- Disasters such as fires that result in catastrophic system failure or loss of data may result in the need for maintenance staff to be involved in restoring the system from data back-ups. Procedures for handling disastrous system failure should be put in place before disasters take place.

In each of these cases, it is necessary to document the changes that are required. In the same way as it is necessary to have a system in place during a project for handling users' requests for changes to the requirements (a change control system), it is necessary to have a system for documenting requests for changes and the response of the maintenance team. This should include the following elements.

- *Bug reporting database*. Bugs should be reported and stored in a database. The screen forms should encourage users to describe the bug in as much detail as possible. In particular, it is necessary to document the circumstances in which the bug occurs so that the maintenance team can try to replicate it in order to work out the cause.
- *Requests for enhancements*. These should describe the new requirement in a similar amount of detail. Users should rate enhancements on a scale of priorities so that the maintenance team can decide how important they are.

- *Feedback to users.* There should be a mechanism for the maintenance team to feed back to users on bug reports and requests for enhancements. Assuming that bugs affect the agreed functionality of the system, users will expect them to be fixed as part of the original contract or under an agreed maintenance contract. The maintenance team should provide an indication of how soon each bug will be fixed. Enhancements are a different matter. Depending on the contractual situation, enhancements may be carried out under a maintenance contract or they may be subject to some kind of costing procedure. Significant enhancements may cost large amounts of money to implement. They will require the same kind of assessment as the original requirements. They should not be left to maintenance programmers to implement as they see fit, but should involve managers to authorize the expenditure and analysts and designers to ensure that the changes fit into the existing system and do not have repercussions on performance or result in changes to subsystems that affect others. This process itself may incur significant costs just in order to work out how much an enhancement will cost to implement. Significant enhancements should therefore be regarded as mini projects in their own right and involve the professional skills of project managers, analysts and designers.

- *Implementation plans.* The maintenance team will decide how best to implement changes to the system, and this should be carried out in a planned way. For example, significant additions to a class that affect what persistent data is stored in the database will require changes to the database structure and may also require all existing instances of that class to be processed in order to put a value into the new attribute. This will probably have to take place when the system is not being used: for example, over a weekend. Enhancements to the system may fall into one of four categories: those to be made at no cost; those that will be made at a cost to be agreed with the client; those that will be held over until a major upgrade to the software is made and that will be part of a future version; and those that cannot or will not be made in the foreseeable future.

- *Technical and user documentation.* Amendments to a system must be documented in exactly the same way as the original system. Diagrams and repository entries must be updated to reflect the changes to the system. If this is not done, then there will be a growing divergence between the system and its technical documentation; this will make future amendments all the more difficult, as the documentation that maintenance analysts consult will not describe the actual system. Clearly, user documentation, training and help manuals as well as online help must all be updated.

In large organizations with many systems, staff in the information systems department may spend more time on maintenance of existing systems than they do on development of new systems. There is a growing movement for organizations to *outsource* their maintenance. This means handing over the responsibility for maintenance of a system to an external software development company under a contractual agreement that may also involve the provision of support. Some companies now specialize entirely in maintaining other people's software.

The other impact of the growth of the maintenance task is that the time will come when a system is such a burden in terms of maintenance that a decision must be made about its replacement. The review process that takes place at this stage may lead to the inception of a new project and to the systems development lifecycle starting again.

19.10 Summary

The implementation of a new system involves a large number of different types of software package that are used to produce and to support the finished system. Component diagrams and deployment diagrams are the two UML implementation diagrams that can be used to document the software components and their location on different machines in the system. For large, complex installations, these diagrams may become unwieldy, and a table format in a spreadsheet or database may be easier to maintain.

Analysts and designers may have a role during the implementation stage in maintaining system and user documentation and in providing user training. They may also plan and carry out testing, plan for data conversion from existing systems and assist the project management in planning the appropriate implementation strategy for the system. In larger organizations, these tasks may be carried out by staff in specialist roles.

After a new system has been implemented, it is customary and advisable to carry out a post-implementation review. This will result in the production of an evaluation report to stakeholders that will measure the success of the project and identify issues and problems from which the organization should learn. Typically the evaluation report will include the following sections:

- Cost–benefit analysis
- Functional requirements
- Non-functional requirements
- User satisfaction
- Problems and issues
- Quantitative data for future planning
- Opportunities for reuse
- Future developments
- Actions.

New systems rarely work exactly as expected, and maintenance must be carried out in order to ensure that the system is bug-free and meets users' requirements. Procedures must be put in place for the maintenance team (project manager, analysts, designers and programmers) to document the process and the changes that are made.

Review Questions

19.1 List the different categories of software packages that may be used in developing a system.

19.2 What development packages have you used and which categories do they fall into?

19.3 What is the difference between an artefact and a component?

19.4 Draw a component diagram to show two components wired together with required and provided interfaces.

19.5 Draw a deployment diagram with artefacts to show the run-time dependency between a Java class file, the java.exe run-time program and the Java classes in a class library stored in a zip file.

19.6 Draw a deployment diagram to show how a web browser and web server are located on different machines and the communication protocol they use.

19.7 List five tests that you would carry out on the FoodCo use case `Start Line Run`.

19.8 List the sections that you would include in a post-implementation evaluation report and explain the content of each section.

19.9 What is the difference between maintenance work carried out to fix bugs and work carried out to add requested enhancements to a system?

19.10 Why should decisions about enhancements not be left to maintenance programmers?

19.11 What tasks do maintenance staff undertake?

Case Study Work, Exercises and Projects

19.A Draw a component diagram for a program that you have written.

19.B Find out about the library system in your school, college, university or local library. Draw a deployment diagram to show the physical hardware architecture.

19.C The FoodCo system will have a database on a central server and PCs in different offices that access that server. Draw a deployment diagram to show this architecture.

19.D There are commercial packages to automate the installation of software such as InstallShield for Windows and RPM for Red Hat Linux. Investigate how these packages maintain information about what artefacts must be installed on a machine.

19.E Read the user manual or online help for a software package that you use. What examples can you find of good practice and bad practice in what has been written? How would you improve it?

19.F What would you include in the screen layouts for users to fill out for bug reports and enhancement requests? Produce a draft design for each of these two layouts.

Further Reading

Implementation takes us on into areas that are outside the scope of this book. There are a number of excellent books on Java implementation, for example Deitel and Deitel (2007). Wutka's book on Java 2 Enterprise Edition (2001) gives a clear idea of the techniques involved in building J2EE systems. There are now many books available on .NET, for example Fedorov (2002) or the various books by Deitel and Deitel.

Many modelling tools now offer a wide range of functionality, including integration with configuration management tools, built-in IDEs for programming, code generation and reverse engineering, object-relational mapping tools, software metrics and deployment tools. Vendor websites are the best starting point for understanding what is on offer.

Chapter 20

Software Reuse

LEARNING OBJECTIVES

In this chapter you will learn
- ☑ why reuse is regarded as important
- ☑ some of the problems with reuse
- ☑ how to plan systems development to achieve reuse of components
- ☑ the different techniques for obtaining and managing reuse
- ☑ how to design a reusable component.

20.1 Introduction

Reusable software has been one of the objectives of developers for many years. In Chapter 4 reusability was discussed as one of the reasons for adopting object-oriented development techniques and programming languages, in Chapter 8 inheritance and composition were discussed as two techniques that facilitate the development of reusable components and in Chapter 13 we highlighted reusability as one of the characteristics of a good object-oriented design. In this chapter we focus on how object-oriented software can be reused. In particular we look at the idea of *componentware*–software packaged into components that can be reused as part of other systems.

We discuss approaches to developing component-based software: we raise issues concerning planning for reuse during the project and consider how to package software to make it reusable. We discuss an example of industrial strength componentware and present an example from the case studies used in this book which demonstrates how software can be designed and packaged for reuse. The use of web services as a way of achieving reuse is growing and we discuss the development of web services and service-oriented architecture. Chapter 22 on the book's website addresses the project management issues associated with planning for reuse.

584

20.2 Why Reuse?

Early moves to produce reusable software include the development of reusable libraries of functions in languages such as Fortran or C making it possible for programmers to save time and effort by reusing others' work. The growth of Visual Basic as a programming language was aided by the availability of controls that could be bought off the shelf and incorporated into applications to provide functionality that would be difficult for the less experienced programmer to develop–and in any case, why reinvent the wheel? Object-oriented languages have always been promoted as significantly enabling the reuse of software and, when Java was released in the mid 1990s, part of the hype surrounding the language was the ability to download and reuse services as Applets over the Internet. Why then is reuse regarded as so important?

The arguments for reuse are partly economic, partly concerned with quality and partly about business flexibility.

- If some of the requirements of a project can be met by models or software components that have been developed on a previous project or are bought in from an outside supplier, then the time and money spent producing those models or code is saved, although the saving will be partly offset by the cost of managing a catalogue of reusable models or code or of paying to buy them from elsewhere. In 2005 Standard Life, a British mutual insurance company, claimed to have achieved savings of £2m by creating a culture of reuse and the supporting tools. From a collection of 246 reusable services, 123 had been reused in 253 separate instances of reuse.

- If a developer can reuse a design or a component that has been tested and proved to work in another application, then there is a saving in the time spent to test and quality assure the component. Jacobson et al. (1997) cite IBM as an example of a company that has invested in software reuse and that has reuse support centres that maintain a library of 500 zero-defect components in Ada, PL/X and C++. In 2004, IBM adopted Logidex from LogicLibrary as its component repository.

- From the point of view of business users of information systems, reuse is not such a critical issue (although it has an impact on cost). In a dynamic business world, organizations need to be able to respond to a changing environment by changing business processes. The ability to recombine information system components or services in new ways to create new business processes or adapt existing ones is important to business stakeholders.

Developers of object-oriented systems are often end-users of reusable components, when they use packages, libraries, classes or controls in their chosen development environment. However, object-oriented systems have not achieved the level of reuse that was expected of them in terms of generating reusable components that can be applied again within the same organization. There are a number of reasons for this; some are technical and some are concerned with organizational culture.

- *Inappropriate choice of projects for reuse.* Not all organizations or projects within those organizations are necessarily suitable to take advantage of or act as sources of reusable components.

- *Planning for reuse too late.* If reuse is appropriate, it is something that needs to be planned for even before a project starts, not an afterthought. By the time a project has been completed, it is likely that anything that might have been reusable will have been designed in such a way that it cannot easily be extracted from the rest of the system.

To achieve reuse, the organization needs to be structured to support it, with the people and tools in place to make it possible.

- *The level of coupling between different classes in an object-oriented design.* Many people have thought of classes as the unit of reuse in object-oriented developments. However, when we come to design classes for different systems, it may be possible to identify similar classes that could be developed in a way that makes them of use in more than one system, but, more often than not, the implementations of these classes will include attributes and associations that tie them into other classes in the particular application of which they are a part. This means that reuse needs to be at a more coarse-grained level than classes, typically components or services.
- *The platform dependence of reusable components.* Most components are built to run on a particular platform. Although Java provides a measure of platform independence at run-time and CORBA makes it possible to connect together components on different platforms, interoperability can still be an issue. One of the attractions of the web services standards is that they allow services on different platforms to be connected together using a standard protocol.
- *The lack of standards for reusable components.* This has changed with developments in the technology of repositories in which to store components and services and with the introduction of standards such as the Object Management Group's Reusable Asset Specification (RAS) for managing software and metadata assets and the W3C's SOAP (Simple Object Access Protocol) for web services. In the following sections, we will address each of these issues.

20.2.1 Choice of project

Not all projects are necessarily suitable for the development of reusable components. The two main factors that influence this are the nature of the business within which the software development is taking place and the maturity of the organization's object-oriented development.

Jacobson et al. (1997) identify four kinds of software business, which they suggest are suitable candidates for developing reusable components. In all of these they talk of the organization developing a Reuse-driven Software Engineering Business (RSEB).

- Organizations where creating an RSEB improves the business processes within the organization: large organizations with a considerable information systems infrastructure and a portfolio of projects to support business activities.
- Organizations producing hardware products that contain embedded software: they cite Hewlett-Packard and Ericsson as examples of this type of organization.
- Consultancy companies and software houses that develop software for external clients that have outsourced their information systems development: particularly those which target particular vertical markets (companies in the same kind of business).
- Developers of software products, such as Microsoft, where reusable components can be applied across a large product range and where end-users can also benefit from the interoperability of software through mechanisms such as the .Net framework.

Small, one-off projects in small organizations are unlikely to bring significant benefits from building reuse into the software development lifecycle. Large organizations with a significant portfolio of systems are beginning to see benefits from reuse through the adoption of a service-oriented architecture. By wrapping existing systems behind a service façade and building new applications as a set of loosely coupled services with a Business Process Management (BPM) layer above them that combines the services to support business processes, they are achieving both reuse and flexibility.

If we consider our two case study companies, we have to ask whether they would fall into any of the categories listed. Although both of them are developing systems to support their business activities, are they large enough and with enough potential projects to justify taking a reuse-driven approach to these projects? Building the organizational structures to support reuse costs money, and that expense is only justified if it can be recouped by savings on other projects. In both cases, they do not have a developed information systems department and we would probably have to say that they are not going to benefit from developing an RSEB.

If, however, an outside consultancy company is doing the development for both Agate and FoodCo, then there are a number of areas where reuse may be applicable. A software company looking at the two systems would identify areas such as managing information about staff that are common to both. If the software company specializes in a vertical market—media and advertising or food manufacturing—then there are going to be parts of the software systems that can be reused elsewhere. Indeed, if the software company has already introduced a reuse-driven approach to its business, the systems for Agate and FoodCo could be developed from a range of existing components tailored to the specific requirements of these companies.

20.2.2 Organizational structure

Jacobson et al. (1997), based on experience at Hewlett-Packard, describe organizations as typically going through six stages of development of a reuse culture. At each stage some benefit is to be gained, but it is unlikely that an organization can leap from a situation in which there is no reuse of design models or software taking place to one in which there is a complete organizational culture of reuse and the structures and tools are in place to support the consistent reuse of components in a way that brings the kind of business benefits that were mentioned earlier. The six stages are shown in Fig. 20.1.

Allen and Frost (1998) argue that, despite moves to client–server and three-tier architectures, most software development organizations still have an application mind-set, and software is developed for individual applications, even within the same organization, without regard for reuse. (Many professional developers would counter this with the argument that they have always developed reusable libraries of code.) This may even be a step backwards from the developments of the 1970s and 1980s when the growth of corporate databases under the central control of database administrators meant that at least the data model was likely to be consistent across the whole organization. The development of web services and interest in Service Oriented Architecture is rekindling the interest in software reuse in large organizations.

To gain the benefits of an RSEB requires an incremental process of change within the organization, involving: technical champions to argue the technical case and develop the software architecture; management champions who believe in the business benefit and will provide the support and investment to allow the change to take place; pilot projects to kick-start the process; education and training of developers to enable them to understand the process; and the development of support structures within the organization. Of these, the first is the most critical: to achieve effective reuse, the elements of the software architecture must be common across different systems.

Stage of Reuse	Description
None	No code reuse takes place; everything is developed from scratch
Informal code reuse	Developers trust each other enough to begin to reuse each other's code in order to save time on development
Black-box code reuse	Particular pieces of code are engineered for reuse, and all developers are encouraged or required to use them to ensure a consistent approach and reduce maintenance costs
Managed workproduct reuse	An organizational structure is developed to manage reusable code, to maintain versions, to document functionality and to train developers
Architected reuse	In order to ensure that components work together, a common architecture is designed and applied to all development processes
Domain-specific reuse-driven organization	The organization's software development is geared to the production of reusable components for the business domain, and the culture and structure of the organization supports this approach

Figure 20.1 Jacobson's six stages of reuse.

One of the most significant requirements for support structures is that if developers are to use reusable components in their code they need some way of finding out what components are available and what their specifications are. This requires software tools to manage a repository of components and staff to maintain the components in the repository and to document them.

Allen and Frost (1998) place a repository at the centre of their model of the development process for reusable components. Figure 20.2 shows this with the two complementary processes: sowing reusable components during development and harvesting reusable components for reuse in other projects. The Select Perspective has evolved since then into three workflows concerned with supplying, managing and consuming components and is described in more detail in Section 20.3.1.

20.2.3 Appropriate unit of reuse

In Chapter 8 we talked about components as the unit of reuse, and we have used the term throughout this chapter so far. However, we have not yet defined what we mean by a component in this context.

If we again consider the case studies, there is a need for a `Client` or `Customer` class both in the Agate system and in the FoodCo system. During analysis, these two classes may look very similar, but, as we move into design, the associations between these classes and others in their system will be resolved into specific attributes. The Agate `Client` class will have attributes to link it to `Campaigns` while the FoodCo `Customer` class will be linked to `SalesOrders`. If the development of both systems is being carried out by the same software company, then it requires a novel style of project management and organization to recognize this commonality in two different projects. If the

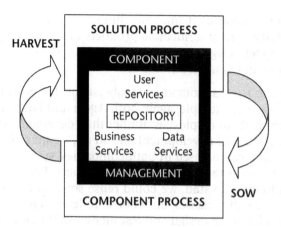

Figure 20.2 The SELECT Perspective service-based process (adapted from Allen and Frost, 1998).

commonality is recognized, then there is no guarantee of successful reuse unless a suitable architecture is developed that will support the reuse of the common elements of the Client class and allow them to be tailored to the requirements of the individual systems.

For example, either a Client class can be obtained from elsewhere and subclassed differently for each project, or a Client class can be written that is domain-neutral and then subclassed for each different project. This inheritance-based approach also helps to solve a problem that is common with software that is tailored to the needs of different customers of the software house: it clearly separates those parts of the class that are common to all users from those that have been tailored to specific needs. This helps with the installation of upgrades and prevents the changes made for one customer being implemented for all customers.

However, even if we can reuse the Client class in both applications by extending its functionality through inheritance, there are going to be other aspects of the Client class that we may or may not want to take through into another system. These include control classes and the business logic associated with the management of clients, related boundary classes and the mechanisms that manage the persistent storage of instances of Client in some kind of database. So can we reuse the class on its own?

Allen and Frost (1998) argue that the class is the wrong level of granularity at which to apply reuse. They argue that reuse should take place at the level of components rather than classes. Their definition of a component states that:

- a component should be executable code;
- component functionality should only be accessible through a consistent published interface;
- the interface should include an interaction standard and the component should be connectable to other components.

However, this view of a component as executable code limits the types of reuse that can be made of a component. Jacobson et al. (1997) have a much less restrictive definition:

- a component is any artefact produced during systems development constructed to be reusable.

This definition is more useful, as it does not limit the developer to only considering executable code for reuse. The intermediate products of the development lifecycle–use case model, analysis model, design model, test model–can all be considered as candidates for reuse. There are two outcomes from this view.

- First, we may choose to reuse as components subsystems that provide more functionality than just a single class. For example, again both Agate and FoodCo have requirements to manage information about employees. Rather than developing two separate systems that handle staff, grades, staff development and so on, we may aim to produce a single reusable subsystem that can be used in both companies' systems.
- Second, we may choose to reuse intermediate products. For example, if we have an existing subsystem to manage staff, we could reuse some of the use cases and related boundary, control and entity classes, but choose to leave out others. Tracing through from the analysis model to the design and test models of the system, we should also be able to reuse elements of these models.

Essentially, we are dealing here with the difference between black-box and white-box reuse. Allen and Frost are suggesting a black-box model in which the contents of the components are not visible to the consumer; Jacobson et al. are suggesting a white-box model in which the internals of the component are visible, giving more flexibility to the consumer about how they make use of the component.

Jacobson et al. also make the point that there are different mechanisms for reusing components. In Chapter 8 we discussed the use of inheritance and composition as mechanisms for reuse. However, using inheritance to subclass existing classes is not the only mechanism for reuse and, if the class is not the unit of reuse, then other mechanisms must be used. Jacobson et al. suggest the following:

- inheritance
- the «include» relationship between use cases
- extensions and extension points in use cases and classes
- parameterization, including the use of template classes
- building applications by configuring optional components into systems
- generation of code from models and templates.

The last two are development processes rather than specific design structures and make reuse easier to achieve. To this list we must add the use of loosely coupled services along the lines of web services, which are the basis of service-oriented architectures.

20.2.4 Component standards

If we are talking about black-box reuse, then the potential for reuse depends on the software mechanisms for reusable components. If we want to consider white-box reuse, then the potential depends on the mechanisms for exchanging software models. In the latter case, UML is clearly a candidate for exchangeable, reusable software models, especially if modelling tool vendors implement the XMI (XML Metadata Interchange). In the former case, then we are dependent on the developers of programming languages and software development infrastructure to deliver appropriate tools to the development community to enable them to develop reusable components.

A number of programming languages and development environments provide mechanisms by which developers can package software into components. Figure 20.3 lists

Language or development environment	Mechanism for component reuse
Microsoft Visual Basic	.vbx files—Visual Basic Extensions .ocx files
Microsoft Windows	.ole files—Object Linking and Embedding DDE—Dynamic Data Exchange .dll files—Dynamic Link Libraries COM—Common Object Model DCOM—Distributed Common Object Model
CORBA	.idl files—Interface Definition Language IOP—Inter-ORB Protocol
Java	.jar files—Java Archive packages JavaBeans
Microsoft .NET	MSIL—Microsoft Intermediate Language CLR—Common Language Runtime
Web Services	SOAP—Simple Object Access Protocol WSDL—Web Service Description Language UDDI—Universal Description, Discovery and Integration

Figure 20.3 A sample of languages and development environments with mechanisms for reuse.

some of these. This table shows that the search for ways of promoting reuse through some kind of modular architecture is not new in the software development industry. Reuse has been an objective that has driven the design of programming languages and has informed the development of programming styles. However, the potential for developing reusable components has been increased by five factors:

- the development of CORBA as a standard for interoperability of components written in different languages and running on different platforms;
- the promotion of Java as an object-oriented language with relatively straightforward mechanisms for producing software in packages to deliver different services;
- the growth of the Internet and the World Wide Web, which has made it possible for people to make their software components easily available to a wide marketplace of potential consumers;
- the spread of web services accessed using the SOAP protocol over networks, which may be private within an organization or public for business-to-business exchanges;
- the availability of the Reusable Asset Specification (RAS), which provides a standard format for packaging up the artefacts associated with a reusable component, including specification, design, code, executables and metadata that makes it possible to search for components in a catalogue.

The platform independence of Java and CORBA makes them different from the other languages and environments shown in Fig. 20.3.

However, web services provide even greater interoperability between components running on different platforms. The Universal Description, Discovery and Integration (UDDI) standard provides a way for potential clients of services to search for services in a registry and connect to them dynamically at run-time. The descriptions of the services are provided in Web Services Description Language (WSDL), an XML language, which defines the input and output parameters of the services and their location on the network. The use of web services makes it possible to create components in different languages that can interoperate and do not require the use of a CORBA Object Request Broker (ORB) in order to do this. Many businesses are also wrapping functionality of legacy systems in web services to make it possible to reuse their functionality in conjunction with new systems.

Microsoft .NET also defines extensions to Microsoft's Portable Executable (PE) format so that metadata is stored with the bytecode in Microsoft Intermediate Language (MSIL) executables, allowing them to provide information about the services they offer in response to requests in the correct format. However, this does not provide the same degree of interoperability as languages such as Java, which are platform-independent. However, the MONO project, which is porting the Microsoft run-time environment to other platforms such as Linux, is increasingly successful. The Reusable Asset Specification (RAS) from OMG promises to make it easier to support reuse within an organization by standardizing the way in which information about reusable components and the executables for the components can be stored in a repository by producers and located in a catalogue by potential consumers. There are an increasing number of products that support this standard.

However, the existence of CORBA, Java, web services, .NET and RAS does not guarantee that effective reuse of components will take place. A strategy needs to be put in place within the organization to ensure that reuse is built into the systems development lifecycle.

20.3 Planning a Strategy for Reuse

In some organizations, reuse may just be about making use of reusable components from elsewhere, using the kinds of mechanisms that are listed in Fig. 20.3. In others, reuse will be about the kind of organizational change that we discussed in Section 20.2.2. In the rest of this section we describe two approaches to the introduction of a reuse strategy and then in Section 20.4 give an example of a commercially available reusable component package.

20.3.1 The SELECT Perspective

Allen and Frost (1998) first described the SELECT Perspective approach to the development of reusable components. At the level of practical techniques, this includes guidelines for the modelling of business-oriented components and for wrapping legacy software in component wrappers. They distinguish between reuse at the level of component packages, which consist of executable components grouped together, and service packages, which are abstractions of components that group together business services. The focus of this approach is to identify the services that belong together and the classes that implement them. Service classes in a single package should have a high level of internal interdependency and minimal coupling to classes in other packages.

The SELECT Perspective has been updated by Apperly et al. (2003), who define the process in terms of three workflows.

- *Supply*–delivers and maintains components. Participants negotiate requirements with consumers, and design, construct and test the components. This may entail the wrapping of legacy systems as services.

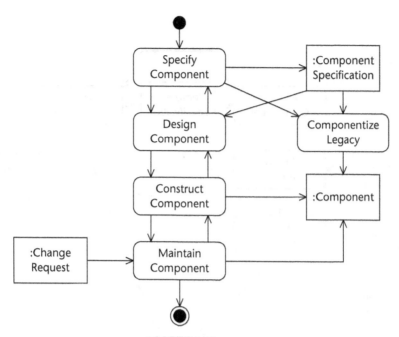

Figure 20.4 SELECT Perspective Supply workflow (adapted from Apperly et al., 2003).

- *Manage*–deals on the one hand with acquiring, certifying and publishing components and on the other with locating and retrieving components for reuse.
- *Consume*–delivers solutions to stakeholders based on components produced by the suppliers. Ensures component specifications are aligned to business needs.

These three workflows are shown in Figs 20.4, 20.5 and 20.6.

20.3.2 Reuse-driven Software Engineering Business (RSEB)

Jacobson et al. (1997) describe an approach to developing reusable software components that is rooted in Jacobson's OOSE and Objectory (Jacobson et al., 1992) and that uses the notation of UML Version 1.0. The approach is based on practical experience within Ericsson and Hewlett-Packard.

Unlike Allen and Frost, who consider components as executables or as packages of executables designed to deliver a particular service, Jacobson et al. consider reuse in terms of any of the work products of systems development. This means that models that are produced before the finished program code are candidates for reuse, and that artefacts other than classes, for example use cases, can be reused. However, the key point of this approach is that the design of systems to make use of reusable components requires an architectural process right from the start. And that means changing the way the business operates.

In order to transform the business into a reuse business, Jacobson et al. also draw on another book from the same stable. Jacobson et al. (1995) explain an approach to business process re-engineering that is based on OOSE and Objectory. The task of developing a reuse business is a re-engineering task that can be modelled using object-oriented

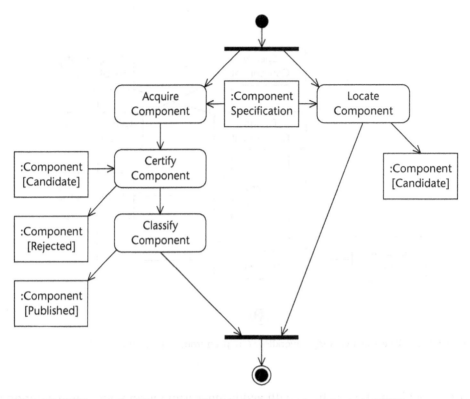

Figure 20.5 SELECT Perspective Manage workflow (adapted from Apperly et al., 2003).

business engineering and that leads to the development of systems to support the RSEB. Jacobson et al. suggest that the end result is a business consisting of the following competence units: requirements capture unit, design unit, testing unit, component engineering unit, architecture unit and component support unit. These competence units are groupings of staff with particular skill-sets and the business data and documents for which they are responsible.

The emphasis in RSEB is to design an architecture for systems that supports reuse from the start. This is done through three engineering processes.

- *Application Family Engineering* (AFE) is an architectural process that captures the requirements for a family of systems and turns them into a layered architecture, consisting of an application system and a supporting component system.
- *Component System Engineering* (CSE) is the process of focusing on the requirements for the component system and developing the use cases, analysis models and design for reusable components to support application development.
- *Application System Engineering* (ASE) is the process of developing the requirements for applications and developing the use cases, analysis models and design to produce application software that makes use of the reusable component systems developed by CSE.

The lifecycle for this kind of project is an iterative one. The engineering processes can run concurrently, with the emphasis changing as the project progresses. Model elements

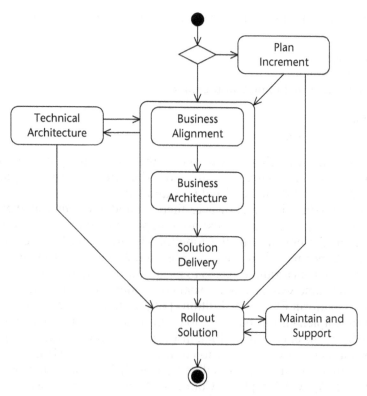

Figure 20.6 SELECT Perspective Consume workflow (adapted from Apperly et al., 2003).

in the component systems are exposed to those in the application systems through façades. The Façade pattern is explained in Section 20.5. Jacobson et al. use the Façade pattern to organize components in packages and then expose those components to other packages. (We take a slightly different approach in Section 20.5.)

20.4 Commercially Available Componentware

Until recently, most commercially available components took the form of utilities or graphical user interface components. The best example of this is the wide variety of controls that are available for use with Microsoft Visual Basic. Originally these were supplied as add-ins in the form of .vbx files, which could be included in the Visual Basic toolbar in the same way as the built-in controls, or in the form of OLE (Object Linking and Embedding) objects, which allowed the functionality of other software packages such as word-processors to be embedded in applications. With the introduction of ActiveX, based on the Microsoft COM architecture, these add-ins are now available as .ocx files. If you look through the catalogue of a good software supplier that sells development tools, you will find pages of ActiveX controls that can be used in your applications and that provide the developer with the possibility of building a wide range of different functions into their software without having to reinvent the wheel. Examples include:

- serial communications
- computer-aided design
- project management including Gantt charts
- spreadsheets
- scientific charts
- barcode reading and printing.

The use of standardized mechanisms to access the functionality of these controls has meant that other software companies can also write interfaces to them, although they are mainly used in Visual Basic or Visual C++ and C#.

For applications written in Java, however, there is another mechanism that can be used: the JavaBean. JavaBeans (or just Beans) are components written in Java that typically combine a graphical element with the functionality to support it. Beans support the Component–Container model in the Java Abstract Windowing Toolkit (AWT), which means that Beans that encapsulate access to particular domain objects can be added into applications in the same way as other visual components can be added to the applications. In the Java Platform Enterprise Edition (JEE), Enterprise Java Beans (EJBs) are the standard way of implementing business logic in a Java-based application server, and provide entity beans to encapsulate domain objects and their business logic as well as session beans that act in a way similar to control objects in the MVC model. Persistent storage of data in Java has been simplified since EJB 3.0 with the use of the Java Persistence API (JPA), which replaces Container Managed Persistence (CMP).

Most of these add-in controls provide generic capabilities rather than reusable components for particular types of business operations. However, commercial componentware to deliver business functionality has not developed in the same way as components for user interface functions such as producing charts. There are examples of suppliers producing reusable components for business functions such as through IBM's WebSphere range of products for e-business development .

IBM's SanFrancisco project originally provided distributed, server-based components for different types of business processes. SanFrancisco used a layered architecture (shown in Fig. 20.7). The Foundation layer provided a programming model to support distributed transactions, and used a set of distributed object services and utilities written entirely in Java. It also provided an optional GUI framework written using JavaBeans. The Common Business Objects layer implemented general purpose business objects, together with the facts and rules required for any business application. This included business objects such as company, business partner, address and calendar. Four components were originally provided in the Core Business Processes layer. These were:

- general ledger
- accounts receivable and accounts payable
- warehouse management
- order management.

These were built using design patterns, many of which were discovered as the project developed, and provided support for electronic commerce. IBM now makes them available to business partners as Business Components for WebSphere Application Server.

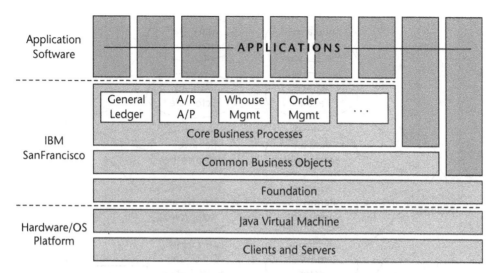

Figure 20.7 Layered architecture of the SanFrancisco project (adapted from IBM, 1998).

20.5 | Case Study Example

A common feature of many applications is the need to control the access of members of staff to the different programs that make up a system. A non-functional requirement both for Agate and for FoodCo is to restrict access of staff to the use cases that they are permitted to use. This requirement can be summarized as follows.

> *Each program in the system will be represented by a use case in the use case diagram. One or more actors will be associated with each use case, and each actor may be associated with more than one use case. A member of staff will fill the role of one or more actors, and each actor will be represented by one or more members of staff. Each actor will be given access rights to use specific use cases (programs). A member of staff may only use those use cases (programs) for which one of the actor roles they fill has been given an access right.*

This non-functional requirement in the context of the main systems can be viewed as the basis for functional requirements in a security subsystem. This subsystem is a potential candidate for the development of a reusable component. Figure 20.8 shows the use cases for this subsystem. It can be modelled in a class diagram in the same way as the business classes that meet the functional requirements of the system. Figure 20.9 shows the initial domain class diagram for this requirement. Two association classes, `ActorRole` and `AccessRight,` have been included in the class diagram, as it was initially thought that there might be some data associated with the creation of links between instances, for example the date that an access right was given, or the type of access right (read/write/ update). However, further discussion with users and analysis of the requirements indicates that this is likely to make the subsystem more complicated than it needs to be, so they have been removed from Fig. 20.10, which shows the analysis class diagram.

There are many design alternatives for this part of the system. The particular design alternative that we choose will affect the detailed design of this subsystem. If we look at it as though we are the software company developing software for both Agate and FoodCo, some of the alternatives are as follows.

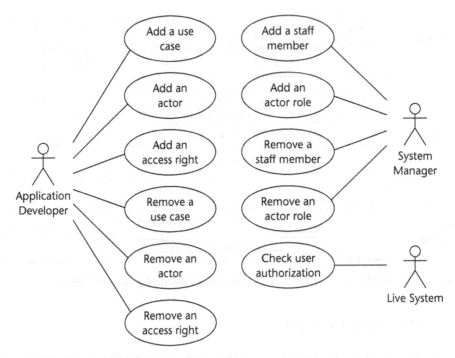

Figure 20.8 Use case diagram for security requirement.

- Do we design this subsystem with a set of boundary and control classes to support the use cases in Fig. 20.8?
- Can we reuse the existing StaffMember class in the business domains of Agate and FoodCo (and any other companies with similar systems)? We do not really want to have to set up data about staff members in two places.
- What happens if we do reuse the StaffMember class in the business domain and then want to use this security subsystem to support a system that does not have StaffMember as an entity class?
- If this security subsystem is to be implemented for all the application software we develop, then we are going to have to make some classes in the software (presumably the control classes) aware of the interface to this subsystem. How do we extend these control classes: rewrite them, extend them or subclass them?
- How do we provide persistent data storage for this subsystem? Does it have its own storage mechanisms or will it use the same storage mechanisms as whatever application it is supporting?
- What parts of this subsystem are we going to make visible to other applications? Are we going to make all the classes visible or are we going to provide a single interface?

We might choose to design the system so that when a user starts running the application, they are prompted for their name or login and a password. Alternatively, if they are required to log into a network anyway, the software could obtain the user's login from the network operating system. Each time a user starts a new use case in the main application, the application will need to check with the security classes whether that user is authorized to use that particular use case.

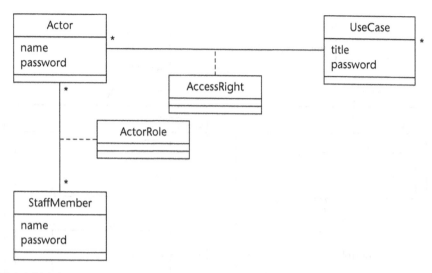

Figure 20.9 Initial domain class diagram for security requirement.

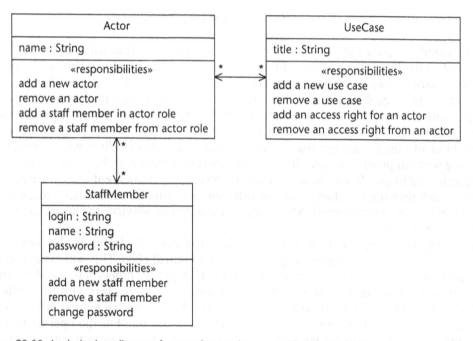

Figure 20.10 Analysis class diagram for security requirement with responsibilities.

The security requirement is not part of the business requirements of the domain applications, and we want to reuse the security software in other applications, so it makes sense to separate these classes from the rest of the software and put them in a package of their own. The security classes will require their own boundary classes, to allow the actors shown in Fig. 20.8 to carry out the use cases. These will run on client computers and will be in a separate package within the overall security package. They will have dependencies on other packages that provide these services, such as the Java AWT. We

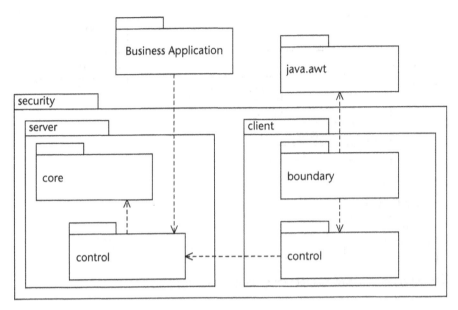

Figure 20.11 Package diagram showing security classes and dependencies.

have created two packages for control classes, one for classes that will run on the clients and control the boundary classes and one for control classes that will run on the server. These control classes will have a dependency on the core security classes. Figure 20.11 shows these package dependencies. We have also shown a package to represent a business application that will be using the services of the security package to authenticate users. It is arguable whether this should have a dependency on the server control classes or on some kind of client package that hides the implementation. Whatever approach we take, we want to provide a clean interface to the functionality of the security subsystem for developers to use. It should be possible to design and implement a separate security client, which uses the interface to the security server control classes. Also, programmers should have a straightforward API to the authorization service–the use case Check user authorization.

One way of doing this would be to replace the control classes in the Security Server Control Classes package with a single control class. This will make it easier for developers to reuse the package, and application programmers only need to know the API of this one class. However, that would lead to a single class with no attributes and a large number of operation implementations. An alternative approach is to leave the control classes as they are and to create a Façade class that has the operations from the control classes within the subsystem but does not contain their implementation.

This approach is based on a design pattern, called the Façade pattern. (See Chapter 15 for more on design patterns.) The Façade pattern is a Gang of Four structural pattern (Gamma et al., 1995) and using the format from Chapter 15 is described as:

- *Name*. **Façade**.
- *Problem*. How can a simple interface be constructed for a complex subsystem?
- *Context*. A subsystem may provide different elements of functionality using several classes or objects. These classes or objects may each have dependencies with the rest of the system. Each may be accessed directly resulting in a complex set of interfaces

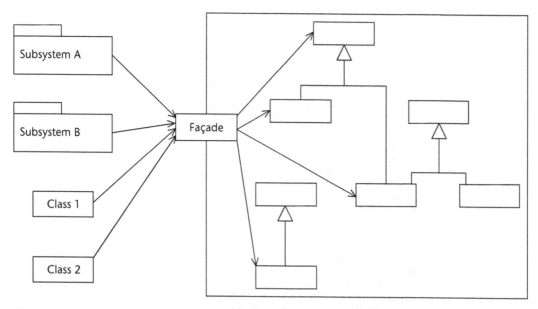

Figure 20.12 Structure of Façade pattern (adapted from Gamma et al., 1995, p.187).

between the subsystem and the rest of the system. This complexity reflects high levels of coupling with the rest of the system and makes development, maintenance and reuse more difficult.

- *Forces*. It is desirable to decouple the subsystem from the rest of the system. This can be achieved by introducing an intermediate class to handle the interactions with the rest of the system. However, this interface management class introduces additional message passing which, for real-time systems, might cause performance issues.
- *Solution*. Create a separate class to act as gatekeeper for the subsystem, the Façade class. All access to the subsystem is via the Façade which sends messages on to the appropriate objects in the subsystem. This decouples the subsystem by exposing a single interface class. The Façade hides the complexity and the implementation of the sub-system and is essentially applying Parnas' (1972) information hiding dictum at the subsystem level.

The structure of the Façade pattern is shown in Fig. 20.12. We could use this structure to add a single class, called `SecurityManager`, which provides the API to the func-tionality in the security package. Or we could add two separate Façade classes, one for the management of the security subsystem (adding staff members etc.), and one for the authorization service used by business applications. This is shown in the class diagram in Fig. 20.13. We have added other operations that will be required in order to support the use cases for maintaining the information in the subsystem: for example, to list all the actors for a particular use case.

The control classes in the `Security Server Control Classes` package can probably be designed to be Singletons (see Section 15.4.2). Figure 20.14 shows the con-trol classes in this package.

The security package, either needs to make use of whatever data storage mechanisms are used in the application with which it is supplied or it needs to have its own mechanism

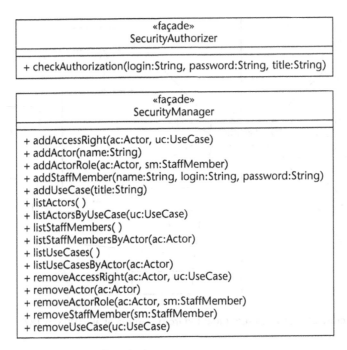

Figure 20.13 Class diagram showing Façade classes.

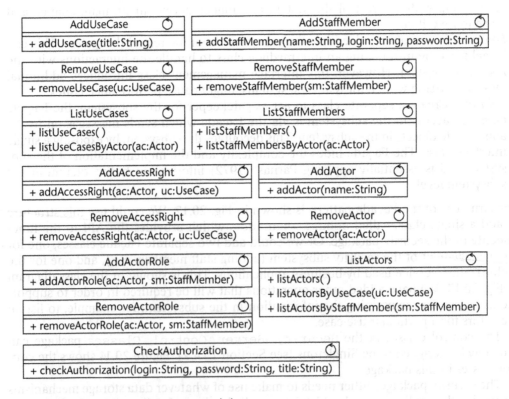

Figure 20.14 Class diagram showing control classes.

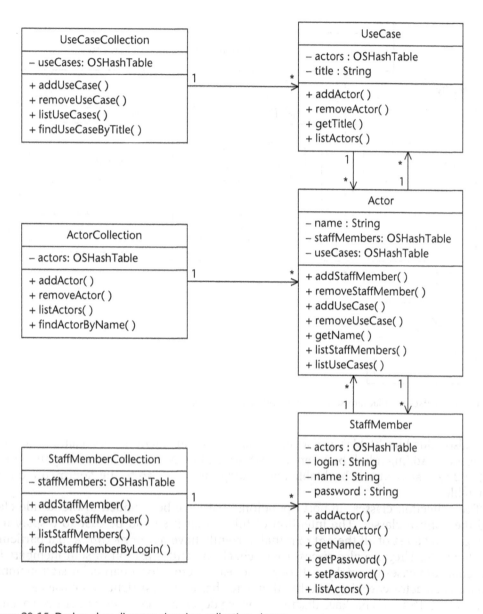

Figure 20.15 Design class diagram showing collection classes.

for persistent storage. The simplest approach, that makes the package as reusable as possible, is to provide the security package with its own persistence mechanism. We can use an object-oriented database management system such as db4o to provide a persistence mechanism without having to worry about brokers and proxies. (Alternatively, given the relatively small volumes of data that are involved, it is possible for the persistence to be provided by using a system of files. If the data is to be stored in simple files, then it should be encrypted before storage. An encryption package could be added.)

In the design in Fig. 20.15 we have added collection classes to provide entry points from the control classes to the lists of Actors, UseCases and Staff Members. We

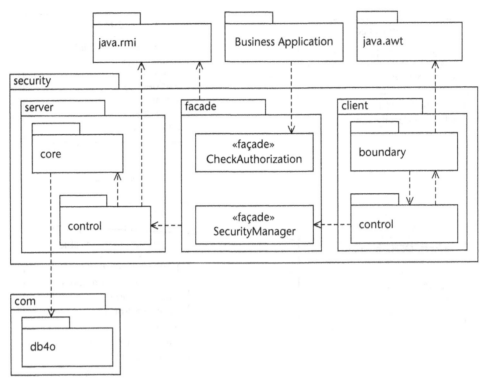

Figure 20.16 Package diagram showing dependencies of the `security` package.

have also added hashtables as collection classes to implement the associations between the classes. Adding a link between a `UseCase` and an `Actor` means adding the `Actor` to the `UseCase.actors` hashtable and adding the `UseCase` to the `Actor.usecases` hashtable.

The collection classes support operations that have been added to the façade class and the control classes. The intention of this is that it should be easy to display in a dialogue box a list of all the `Actors` that currently have `AccessRights` to a particular `UseCase` etc. They are also necessary to check the authorization of staff members for particular use cases by working through the list of actors for a particular staff member, and for each actor checking whether that actor has an access right to the use case.

Figure 20.16 shows package diagram showing dependencies of the `security` package. For persistent storage of the objects in the `security` package, we can use db4o (introduced in Chapter 18), which requires minimal changes to the classes in order to enable them to be stored in an object-oriented database.

All the operations that update the database will require a reference to a db4o database and must take place in the context of a transaction. The dependencies on db4o `Database` and `Transaction` classes are also reflected in the dependencies of Fig. 20.16.

If we use Java Remote Method Invocation (RMI) to allow client packages to connect to the `security` package, then we also require the dependency on the Java RMI package, which is also shown in Fig. 20.16. We have also shown the façade packages in a separate façade package.

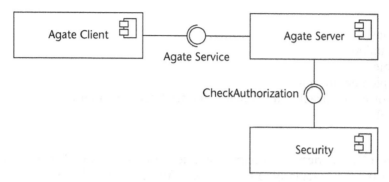

Figure 20.17 Component diagram showing dependency on the `Security` component.

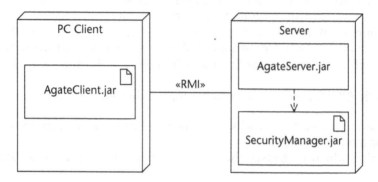

Figure 20.18 Deployment diagram showing the `SecurityManager.jar` artefact.

Clearly, the security package itself should not be accessible to unauthorized users, so there will be a requirement for the security package to use its own services to restrict access to the developers of the system, who will set up the associations between use cases and actors, and to the system manager who will authorize staff within the company to use particular use cases by linking them to specific actor roles.

The `Security` component will provide an interface to the `Agate Server` component that allows it to check security authorizations, as shown in Fig. 20.17.

The security package could be implemented in Java, compiled and stored in Java Archive (.jar) files. This can be shown in a deployment diagram, as in Fig. 20.18, which shows the dependency of the Agate server classes (also stored in a .jar file) on the `SecurityManager.jar`. This component can be used in both the Agate and FoodCo projects and in other future projects.

20.6 Web Services

As discussed earlier the use of web services is an increasingly important way of achieving software reuse. Web services need to exhibit some properties that are different from components not implemented as web services. Erl (2004) suggests that they should adhere to the following principles:

- reusable
- autonomous
- loosely coupled
- composable
- hiding implementation logic
- having a formal contract that explicitly defines how they interact
- discoverable
- stateless.

The first five of these design principles should be followed by all components, while the last three relate particularly to web services. We have already described how WSDL provides a way to define the way that web services interact and how the UDDI is one mechanism for discovering available web services. For components that are not implemented as web services, interfaces would not be defined using WSDL and discoverability is not normally an issue that needs to be addressed. The key difference, and one that is important when deciding how to implement a service, is that wherever possible web services should be stateless. A web service should maintain the minimum amount of information regarding the activity it is performing and should operate consistently.

Sommerville (2007) suggests three stages for the development of web services:

- *candidate service identification* which is concerned with selecting the most appropriate services for implementation;
- *service design* which addresses the design of both the logical and WSDL service interfaces;
- *service implementation and deployment* where the service is constructed, tested and deployed.

When identifying the most appropriate web services it is helpful to consider the three main categories that Erl (2005) identifies:

- utility services that provide a general service such as currency conversion;
- business services that provide specific business functionality, like reserving a book at a university library;
- process services that provide a more general business service, such as on-line enrolment at university which involves registering for a programme of study, choosing classes to attend and paying fees.

Erl also categorizes web services as entity or task oriented. An entity-oriented service relates to a business entity such as a bank account. A task-oriented service deals with a business activity such as applying for a bank loan. To select suitable web services for implementation Sommerville (2007) suggests a series of questions that developers should ask themselves. The issues that need to be considered include the following.

- *How independent is the service?* If the service is dependent on the availability of other services then its availability to be used by other systems may be constrained.
- *Does the service need to maintain state?* If the service has to remember its state then it may have to maintain persistent data. A service that maintains an internal state may be more difficult to use as its operation will depend upon its current state.

- *How widely could the service be used within the organization?* If a service can be used widely then its mode of operation may impose a standard approach to this service across its users. This standard approach must be acceptable to all users.
- *Could the service be used outside the organization?* If the service can be used outside the organization then the range of potential client systems and users must be determined. In some cases there may be no constraints and in other cases the service may be restricted to a particular user group. For example, an order processing service may be available only to certain customers who maintain accounts with the company.
- *Will users' non-functional requirements vary?* If these do vary then it may be necessary to offer multiple versions of the same service. For example, a service may be offered with different interfaces.

Detailed discussion concerning the use of appropriate technologies to develop web services is beyond the scope of this book. However, it is worth noting that during web service design the developer should make the minimum assumptions about how a service is going to be used. The interface has to be carefully designed and potential exceptions clearly identified so that they can be reported to the client user. For example, input messages may be in the wrong format, no matter how clearly the required format is defined in WSDL, and this error has to be reported to the client user.

20.7 Summary

Adopting object-oriented software development is not on its own a sufficient cause for a business to benefit from the reusability that is claimed as one of the benefits of object-orientedness. Businesses thinking of taking advantage of reusability in object-oriented software need to take into account a number of factors.

- Is the organization the right kind to be able to develop reusable components as well as use them?
- How will the organization systematically move from a situation of little or no reuse to one in which reuse is built into the design of systems from the start?
- What organizational support systems and software tools are required to enable reuse?

Given a commitment to the introduction of a reuse business, an organization needs to re-engineer its software development operations to provide the structures and support for a reuse culture and to train developers in this approach. For reuse to be effective, it should not be left until the maintenance stage but should be planned into the project from the outset. The architecture of the systems should be designed from the start to support reuse.

The SELECT Perspective is one methodology that focuses on techniques and project planning to achieve reuse. The RSEB of Jacobson et al. is another approach, and one that advocates an approach based on re-engineering the business and designing architectures for reuse. This approach is based on three processes, which produce a layered architecture: separating the component layer from the application layer, engineering the component layer and building the application layer on top of the component layer.

CORBA, Java and web services make it easier for developers to produce and distribute reusable software components. The Reusable Asset Specification provides a standard for packaging up the artefacts that comprise a reusable component. Commercially available components include the products of IBM's SanFrancisco project, which provides business components for general ledger, for accounts receivable and payable and for warehouse and order management. The Façade pattern provides a means for hiding the complexity of components from application programmers by means of classes that handle the API to the classes in the component.

Review Questions

20.1 What are the benefits of reusable components?

20.2 What are some of the obstacles to reuse?

20.3 Give Jacobson et al.'s definition of a 'component'.

20.4 Name three mechanisms for creating reusable components in different programming languages.

20.5 What are the three workflows in the revised SELECT Perspective (Apperly et al., 2003)?

20.6 How does Allen and Frost's definition of a component differ from that of Jacobson et al.?

20.7 What are the three processes in Jacobson et al.'s approach to reuse, and what is meant by each?

20.8 What is the purpose of the Façade pattern?

Case Study Work, Exercises and Projects

20.A Describe the mechanisms that are available in an object-oriented language with which you are familiar for creating reusable components.

20.B A data encryption package is required to be added to the security package to provide services to encrypt different data types, such as the `Integer`, `String` and `Date` classes. Draw a class diagram (with packages and classes) to show new classes `CryptInteger`, `CryptString` and `CryptDate`. Access to `Encryption` and `Decryption` control classes is to be provided by a single Façade class called `EncryptionManager`. Include these in your diagram in suitable packages.

20.C Redraw the package diagram in Fig. 20.11 to include the encryption package and add any new dependencies necessary.

20.D Draw a deployment diagram for FoodCo showing the security packages as artefacts, some of which will be on client machines and some of which will be on a server.

20.E Complete the design of the security package and implement it in an object-oriented language such as Java, Smalltalk, C# or C++. (This is suitable for a coursework assignment or small project.)

Further Reading

Allen and Frost (1998) introduced the SELECT Perspective, while Apperly et al. (2003) have brought it up to date. Jacobson et al. (1997) present a different view of developing a reuse-driven software development process, which builds on the Objectory and object-oriented business re-engineering approaches of Jacobson's other books. It also uses UML as a notation.

Cheesman and Daniels (2001) also provide a straightforward process for specifying component-based systems.

For a comparison of the mechanisms involved in CORBA and DCOM (and some other approaches to distributed systems), Orfali and Harkey (1998) provide a clear and readable coverage, which includes detailed instructions on how to implement systems which use these techniques.

Daniels et al. (2004) provide an introduction to building web services using Java and explain the related specifications such as UDDI and WSDL.

Sommerville (2007) provides a clear introduction to service-oriented architecture and the development of services. Erl (2004, 2005) provides detailed guidance on service development. Erl (2009) also catalogues a range of design patterns for service-oriented architecture.

To find the wide range of software add-ins that are available as ActiveX controls, look at the website of a supplier such as www.devdirect.com.

Software Development Processes

LEARNING OBJECTIVES

In this chapter you will learn

- ☑ what a software development 'process' is, and how this relates to 'method' and 'methodology'
- ☑ why methodologies are used
- ☑ some characteristics of different methodologies
- ☑ the difference between hard and soft methodologies
- ☑ some of the issues in choosing an appropriate methodology.

21.1 Introduction

The process or method of a software development project refers to the particular tasks carried out and how they are structured over the project lifecycle. Many of these tasks involve the application of the UML techniques described in the earlier parts of this book. The use of a set of modelling or documentation standards such as that provided by UML has a very important part to play, but this is not enough on its own. The techniques must be organized into an appropriate development process if they are to work together. For example, once an analyst has constructed communication diagrams for the main use cases, should the next steps be to convert these into sequence diagrams and write operation specifications, or should he or she now concentrate on preparing a class diagram and developing inheritance and composition structures? All of these tasks need to be completed at some point, but how is the analyst to know which one is appropriate at a specific point in the project? UML itself contains nothing that helps to make this decision, but developers need practical guidance on the many questions that arise when the techniques are applied in a real-life situation.

In this chapter we describe what is meant by 'process', 'method' and 'methodology', and explain why methodologies are so widely used and why they continue to evolve.

Next, some representative methodologies are described, including the USDP, on which we based the development process followed in this book, Atern (the latest version of the Dynamic Systems Development Method, or DSDM) and the agile methodologies Scrum and eXtreme Programming (XP). We then consider the issues in selecting a methodology that is suited both to the context and to the kind of project to be carried out. Finally, we explain the distinction between the so-called soft and hard views of systems development.

21.2 | Process, Method and Methodology

The terms 'process', 'method' and 'methodology' are used interchangeably by many authors, but there are significant differences in their meanings. A method is a step-by-step description of the steps involved in doing a job. Since no two projects are exactly alike, any method is specific to one project. A methodology is a set of general principles that guide a practitioner or manager to the choice of the particular method suited to a specific task or project. In object-oriented terms, we could say that a methodology is a type while a method is its instantiation on a particular project.

To complicate the picture further, 'process' has come to be used as a synonym for both methodology and method. For example, in both USDP and the IBM Rational Unified Process (RUP), the term 'process' has an all-embracing meaning that includes both the particular development activities and techniques used on a given project, and also the overall framework that describes what the tasks are, how they are carried out and how they are organized. In this book, wherever possible, we stick to using method and methodology for greater clarity.

Software developers, project managers and their bosses all need to be able to think at different levels of abstraction, depending on the task in hand. In order to run a current project plan, a manager must think at the level of method. In order to plan and organize for the next project, he or she must also be able to think at a higher level, that of methodology. Figure 21.1 summarizes some of the different levels of abstraction involved in software development.

Increasing level of abstraction	Example of application	Typical product
Task	Developing a first-cut class diagram for FoodCo	A specific iteration of the FoodCo class diagram
Technique	Description of how to carry out the technique of UML class modelling	Any UML class diagram
Method	Specific techniques used on the FoodCo project (use cases, class model, communication diagrams, etc.) that lead to a specific software application product	FoodCo's product costing system
Methodology	General selection and sequence of techniques capable of producing a range of software products	A range of object-oriented business applications

Figure 21.1 Increasing levels of abstraction in software development.

21.2.1 Methodology

A methodology in the IS domain is, then, a generalized approach to developing information systems. It must cover a number of aspects of the project, although coverage varies from one to another. Avison and Fitzgerald (2006) describe a methodology as a collection of many components. Typically, each methodology has procedures, techniques, tools and documentation aids that are intended to help the system developer in his or her efforts to develop an information system. There is usually also a lifecycle or structure that contains and organizes the procedures. Finally, there is some kind of underlying philosophy that captures a particular view of the meaning and purpose of information systems development. (Note that, according to this view, process is merely one aspect of a methodology.)

Checkland (1997), in a conference address that discussed the potential contribution of the wider systems movement to information systems development, gave a more general definition that captures well the notion of methodology as a guide to method. In his view, a methodology is a set of principles that in any particular situation has to be reduced to a method uniquely suited to that situation.

The following examples illustrate these aspects.

- The UML class diagram is a technique, and so is operation specification.
- Sparx Systems' Enterprise Architect software is a tool.
- The IBM Rational Unified Process software, which provides information and guidance about how to follow RUP, is a documentation aid.
- The activity represented by 'find classes by inspecting the use case descriptions' is an aspect of procedure. So is the advice that an analyst is usually the best person to write test plans.
- The advice that 'operation specifications should not be written until the class model is reasonably stable' is an aspect of structure, as it identifies a constraint on the sequence in which two steps should be performed.
- Analysis and design can (reasonably) be viewed as distinct procedures.
- The statement 'object-oriented development promotes the construction of software which is robust and resilient to change' is an element of a systems development philosophy.

A package that contains enough information about each of these aspects of the overall development process is fit to be named a methodology. Many attempts have been made to capture the essence of methodology for software development, and the resulting methodologies are almost as varied as are the projects themselves. In practice, methodologies vary widely in philosophy, in completeness of definition or documentation, in coverage of the lifecycle and even in the type of application to which they are best suited.

One example of an attempt to define a metamodel for software development is the OMG's Software Process Engineering Metamodel (SPEM). This uses UML notation for entities that include *roles, activities, products* and *phases*. The software process followed on a specific project is modelled at the least abstract level and could be represented by instances of real workers, activities and actual modelling products. At the next more abstract level come specific methodologies such as RUP (in SPEM they are called processes). The abstract features of methodologies are themselves modelled by SPEM in UML, as a process metamodel, and these in turn are derived from the still more abstract Meta Object Facility (MOF). The assumptions behind SPEM are in close agreement with the definitions given earlier in this section, although the concerns of the authors of SPEM differ in at least one respect. Part of the underlying rationale of SPEM, as also of

MDA, is to move towards automating the process of software development. In order to achieve this, it is necessary to define activities, products and so on with rather more rigour than has usually been needed in the past.

Some authors believe that the idea of a published methodology is misleading, if it is taken to mean that following a methodology leads inevitably to a good product. For example, Daniels (an early and influential contributor to UML) argued in a conference presentation (1995) that an IS methodology is more a means for learning the process of systems development than a recipe for practising it. He compared a methodology to a ladder that, once used, can be thrown away (the metaphor is borrowed from Wittgenstein). We are safe to 'throw the ladder away', not because we do not need one, but because, having once climbed it, we know how to build one of our own that is better suited to our needs. In Daniels's view, the skill and judgement of an experienced developer count for much more than the prescriptive steps of a methodology, however comprehensive the latter may be.

Note that Daniels's position expresses two key principles of the Agile Manifesto: *'Individuals and interactions* over processes and tools' and *'Responding to change* over following a plan' (the Agile Manifesto was introduced in Chapter 3). As we shall see in the following sections, the recent Agile movement has much in common with earlier efforts to build software in a way that is responsive to changing circumstances and to individuals.

Beginning with Section 21.3, we will describe some alternative methodologies with different historical antecedents, and some real differences in approach. But they have many common features and these could be summarized as follows.

- Avoid getting bogged down in documentation.
- Be flexible in approach when circumstances change.
- Devolve control to project team level as far as possible.
- Maintain creativity; do not just follow a rigid, dogmatic process.
- Involve users in a way that shares ownership of both the problem and the solution.
- Maximize the productivity of the team.

This seems like such obvious common sense that it may be hard to understand why common sense on its own is not enough for software development to be successful. However, as we saw in Chapter 2, most reasons for a project to run into difficulty lie in the human aspects, and managing these will always require great skill and care.

21.2.2 Why use a methodology?

Over many decades, IS methodologies have been developed and introduced specifically to overcome those problems of software development projects that were perceived to be important at the time. However, to date, no methodology has been wholly successful in fulfilling its objectives, partly because computing is a highly dynamic field, and the nature of both projects and their problems is constantly changing. In a changing world, it is unlikely that yesterday's solution will ever completely solve today's problems.

Nevertheless, many advantages have been claimed for the use of a methodology, including the following.

- The use of a methodology helps to produce a better quality product, in terms of documentation standards, acceptability to the user, maintainability and consistency of software. We believe this to be generally true, even if only the minimum necessary set of documentation is maintained—as is recommended by DSDM, for example.

- A methodology can help to ensure that user requirements are met completely. This does not necessarily imply that all requirements must be captured, documented and agreed in advance of any development work.
- Use of a methodology helps the project manager, by giving better control of project execution and a reduction in overall development costs.
- Methodologies promote communication between project participants, by defining essential participants and interactions and by giving a structure to the whole process.
- Through the standardization of process and documentation, a methodology can also encourage the transmission of know-how throughout an organization.

If all these claims could be fulfilled in practice, the benefits would be clear. However, the evidence is mixed. This is mainly because organizations differ so widely in their characteristics, and so do the types of project that they conduct. On both counts, it is very difficult indeed to make a rigorous comparison that would demonstrate the contribution of the methodology to the success or failure of any given project. The picture in the UK at present is that approximately two-thirds of businesses use some form of IS methodology. Even where this actually means little more in practice than an in-house set of standards for documentation and procedures (as it certainly is in at least some cases), this still shows a consistent level of faith in the utility of a methodology of some kind.

21.3 Unified Software Development Process

We have already briefly introduced the main principles that underlie USDP (often now just called UP) in Chapters 3 and 5. In this section, we present a more detailed picture of the methodology.

Philosophy and principles

This part of UP should be familiar to anyone who has read much of the rest of this book, since the development process that we have followed is partly based upon and broadly consistent with UP. In particular, UP is a use-case driven, architecture-centric, iterative and incremental process. These terms can be explained briefly as follows.

The starting point for all modelling is some sort of interaction, called a use case, between a user and the software system under consideration. This interaction is the beginning of the modelling activity and also the fundamental unit from which later models are derived. Use cases are thus important in several different ways. Each use case is a thread that links a series of models from requirements to implementation; it is also a unit of delivery that has practical significance to users; it is a constant reminder to the systems developers that only the users' requirements really matter.

In UP, the resulting software architecture is an essential theme in modelling from the earliest stages of a project. This is reflected in the stereotyping of the classes that contribute to realizing a use case as boundary, control and entity classes.

Phases and workflows

Figure 21.2 repeats a diagram shown earlier in Chapter 5. This illustrates the relationship between the phases, iterations and workflows of UP. We do not need to dwell on workflows (requirements, analysis, design and so on) here, beyond noting that they are made up of activities, since these are the main subject of the greater part of this book. We explain the UP view of activities a little later in this section. In the paragraphs that

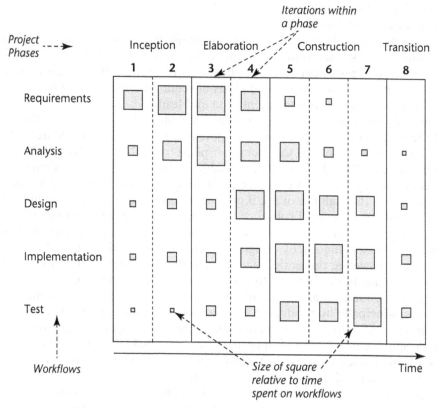

Figure 21.2 Phases, iterations and workflows in the Unified Process.

immediately follow, we explain the phases of UP and relate these to the activities that are carried out within each phase.

While an activity is something that has particular meaning for the developers who carry it out, a *phase* is considered primarily from the perspective of the project manager. He or she must necessarily think in terms of milestones that mark the progress of the project along its way to completion. In UP, for example, two key milestones are Initial Operational Capability (which marks the close of the Construction phase) and Product Release (which marks the close of the Transition phase).

Phases are sequential. A project passes through each phase in turn and then (usually) moves on to the next. The end of a phase is a decision point for the project manager. When each phase is complete, those in charge must decide whether to begin the next phase or to halt development at that point. The focus of the project manager's attention shifts as the project progresses from one phase to the next.

Within each phase, the activities are carried out in an iterative manner that could be summed up in a very simplistic way as follows:

Do some investigation, model the requirements, analyse them, do some design, do some coding, test the code, then repeat the process.

There is no set rule that states how many iterations should be conducted within a phase; this is a matter for the project management team to judge, depending on the project characteristics and the available resources. (There is more information about managing object-oriented projects on the book website.)

Within each phase, the workflows are essentially the same. All four phases include the full range of workflows from requirements to testing, but the emphasis that is given to each workflow changes between the phases. In the earlier phases, the emphasis lies more on the capture, modelling and analysis of requirements, while in the later phases the emphasis moves towards implementation and testing.

During the inception phase, the essential decision is that of assessing the potential risks of the project in comparison with its potential benefits. This judgement of project viability (or otherwise) during the inception phase resembles the feasibility stage of a Waterfall Lifecycle. The decision will probably be based partly on a similar financial assessment (typically some sort of cost–benefit analysis). One principal difference at this early stage is that the viability of a UP project is much more likely to be judged partly also on the delivery of a small subset of the requirements as working software. During the inception phase, the main activities are thus requirements capture and analysis, followed by a small amount of design, implementation and testing. Another major difference is that, even at this early stage, there is the likelihood of iteration. That this is even possible is due to the fact that the development approach is object-oriented.

During the elaboration phase, attention shifts to the reduction of cost uncertainties. This is done principally by producing a design for a suitable system that demonstrates how it can be built within an acceptable timescale and budget. As the emphasis shifts towards design, the proportion of time spent on design activities increases significantly. There is a further small increase in the time spent on implementation and testing, but this is still small in relation to the analysis and design activity.

The construction phase concentrates on building, through a series of iterations, a system that is capable of satisfactory operation within its target environment.

Implementation and testing rapidly become core activities in this phase, with a move further away from design and towards testing as each iteration gives way to the next.

Finally, the transition phase concentrates on achieving the intended full capability of the system. This deals with any defects or problems that have emerged late in the project. It could also include system conversion, if an older system is being replaced (see Chapter 19).

Workers and activities

UP differentiates between the real people who are involved with any project, such as users, analysts, managers and customers, and the more abstract *worker*. This term denotes someone who plays a specified part in carrying out an activity. Some examples of workers are: use-case specifier, system architect, component engineer and integration tester. There need not be a direct one-to-one mapping between people and workers. An employee may play the part of different workers at different times, and, conversely, a group of people could represent a single worker engaged on an activity.

Most UP activities can be partially defined in terms of the workers who carry them out, and the artefacts that either serve as inputs or are produced as outputs. Figure 21.3 illustrates this for the activity `Analyse a use case` (this can be compared with the process that we follow in Chapter 7).

As we mentioned above, a workflow can be seen as a flow of activities. Since each activity can be related to a worker who will carry it out, we can identify which workers

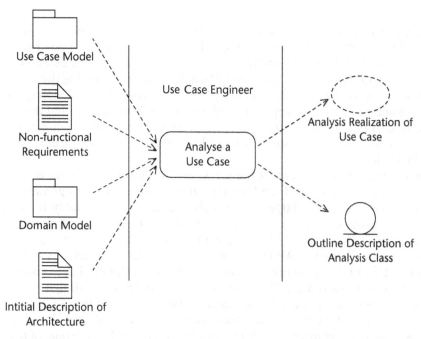

Figure 21.3 Inputs and outputs of the activity Analyse a use case (adapted from Jacobson et al., 1999).

will need to participate in the project. Figure 21.4 shows the analysis workflow broken down into its constituent activities.

Artefacts

By now, it should be reasonably clear what the main artefacts are in UP. These clearly include models, such as the use case model or the design class model, and products, such as an implementation package or subsystem.

However, Jacobson et al. (1999) define an artefact very broadly as almost any kind of information that is created, used or amended by those who are involved in developing the system. This means that the term also covers small-scale things, such as a class specification or an operation signature, and transient things, such as notes and prototypes.

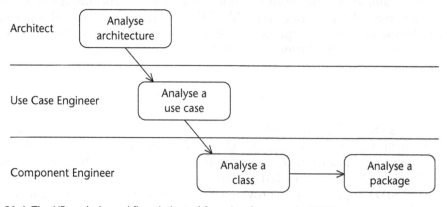

Figure 21.4 The UP analysis workflow (adapted from Jacobson et al., 1999).

Summary
At the time of its release, UP represented the most mature object-oriented methodology that had yet been released. In large part, this is due to its ancestry. Rosenberg and Scott (1999) comment that the Booch method provided good methods for detailed design and implementation, OMT had particular strengths in its tools for exploring the problem space and Objectory was particularly strong in its approach to defining the solution space, but that all three ingredients are necessary for overall success. UP strove to bring these together.

Many aspects of UP follow almost inevitably from its basis in object-orientation. For example, no object-oriented approach would be taken seriously if it did not follow an iterative lifecycle.

However, in at least one respect the UP is distinct from most other object-oriented methodologies that preceded it, and we regard this as probably its greatest weakness. As methodologies go, UP is large and complex. There will inevitably be a significant learning curve involved wherever UP is adopted within an organization. One recent attempt to address this is the Agile Unified Process or AUP (Ambler, 2009), which we first mentioned in Chapter 3. Although the four-phase lifecycle remains the same, AUP differs from UP in a number of other respects. First, the workflows have changed. Four of UP's workflows—business modelling, requirements, analysis and design—are combined in AUP into a single discipline called modelling. The purpose of this discipline is to produce models and documents that are 'just barely good enough' for the task (Ambler, 2009). AUP also includes three new disciplines that increase the coverage of the lifecycle: configuration management, project management and environment.

The same point about size and complexity is also true for UP's proprietary sibling, IBM RUP. However, IBM RUP differs significantly in the level of documentation, tool support and other guidance available to the adopter. These make the latter an industrial-strength methodology, which continues to evolve today.

Our experience suggests that complex methodologies tend to be fully adopted only in organizations with sufficient resources to provide thorough training, and with the culture to impose relatively strict discipline. Many software development organizations take from a methodology only what is easiest to implement. The complexity of UP undoubtedly derived from a natural desire to retain the best features of the three contributing methodologies. But this is unlikely to encourage its adoption in any complete form. In some cases, there may be little more than the use of UML and some form of iterative lifecycle. The development approach that we have advocated in this book provides one example of a subset of UP, but many other approaches are possible that adhere to the spirit of UP without slavishly following its every detail. But perhaps in time, with the increasingly widespread adoption of agile approaches, this whole debate may become no more than a historical footnote.

21.4   Dynamic Systems Development Method

The Dynamic Systems Development Method (DSDM) is a management and control framework for agile project delivery. The DSDM Consortium was originally formed in 1994 to produce an industry standard definition of what at the time was known as Rapid Application Development (RAD). Over the next decade, the same concerns that produced the RAD approach also provided the initial impetus for the agile software development movement.

The first version of DSDM was released in January 1995. This defined the structure and controls to be used in a RAD project but did not specify a particular development methodology. As a result, DSDM came to be used comfortably alongside object-oriented development techniques, although it did not require them.

The current version of DSDM was released in 2007 and is known as DSDM Atern (or just Atern). Although there has been a change of name, many distinctive features of previous versions of DSDM remain prominent. In particular, this includes its innovative perspective on project requirements. Instead of seeing the requirements as fixed and then attempting to match resources to the project, as most methodologies had done in the past, Atern fixes the resources for the project (including the time available for completion) and then sets out to deliver only what can be achieved within these constraints. Atern is designed, like earlier DSDM versions, so that it can be used in conjunction with other project management methodologies such as PRINCE2™ and also with development methodologies such as RUP. (PRINCE™ is an acronym for PRojects IN Controlled Environments, and is a UK government standard approach to project management. There is more information about PRINCE2™ in the online chapter on Project Management on the book website.) Atern is based upon eight underlying principles (DSDM Consortium, 2007).

- *Focus on the business need.* The essential criterion for acceptance of a deliverable is fitness for business purpose. Atern is entirely focused on delivering the essential functionality at the specified time.
- *Deliver on time.* In an Atern project, the main variable is the extent to which requirements are met. Delivery deadlines are never sacrificed in order to meet lower priority requirements. This relates to the techniques of timeboxing and MoSCoW prioritization, which are both explained below.
- *Collaborate.* A collaborative and co-operative approach between all stakeholders is essential. The emphasis here is on the inclusion of all stakeholders in a collaborative development process. Stakeholders not only include team members–who are expected to include end-users–but also others such as resource managers and the quality assurance team. In addition, Atern teams are empowered to make decisions that refine the requirements and possibly even change them without the direct involvement of higher management.
- *Never compromise quality.* Product quality is not seen as a variable that can be sacrificed in favour of meeting lower priority requirements. Like the delivery deadlines, this too relates to the techniques of timeboxing and MoSCoW prioritization. It also requires that testing should be integrated throughout the lifecycle. Each software component is tested by the developers for technical compliance and by user team members for functional appropriateness.
- *Develop iteratively.* Iterative development, just as we have described it throughout this book, is seen as necessary to converge on an accurate business solution.
- *Build incrementally from firm foundations.* Incremental development allows user feedback to inform the development of later increments. The delivery of partial solutions is considered acceptable if they satisfy an immediate and urgent user need. These solutions can be refined and further developed later.
- *Communicate continuously and clearly.* A failure to communicate effectively is seen as one of the main reasons why some projects fail to meet their users' and sponsors' expectations. The DSDM Atern solution includes the key technique of facilitated workshops (explained below) together with modelling and prototyping.

- *Demonstrate control.* This principle is partly about transparency: all appropriate stakeholders must be kept informed of progress and plans at all times. It is also partly about the philosophy and techniques of project management. Timeboxing is important among the techniques, while the philosophy emphasizes the delivery of products rather than the mere completion of activities.

It is easy to see common ground between Atern and the UP-based development process that we have followed through this book. In particular, we have shared Atern's emphasis on iterative and incremental development and its focus on fitness for business purpose. One other useful aspect of the DSDM Atern approach that is not highlighted in the eight principles is the stress on frequent delivery of products. Team meetings in organizations that have adopted DSDM are often characterized by a rule that team members are not permitted to talk about tasks that they are working on now, only about products that they have completed since the last meeting. This helps to maintain the team's focus on completion and also minimizes the time spent away from productive work in meetings.

21.4.1 The Atern lifecycle

The lifecycle has a total of seven phases, although strictly speaking two of these (Pre- and Post-Project) are outside the bounds of the current project:

- Pre-project
- Feasibility
- Foundations
- Exploration
- Engineering
- Deployment
- Post-project.

The phases and their relationships are shown graphically in Fig. 21.5 and each phase is described in more detail below. Note that the diagram highlights the iteration between phases and within Exploration and Engineering, as it is most to be expected here. However, iteration is possible within all phases.

It is interesting to note that both the names and the emphasis of the four main development phases in Atern (Foundations, Exploration, Engineering and Deployment) correspond quite closely to the four phases of UP (see Section 21.3 to make the comparison for yourself).

- *Pre-project.* This phase relates the project to the organization's wider strategic planning process, and places it within the context of other projects currently being undertaken or planned.
- *Feasibility.* This phase determines whether the project is suitable for an Atern approach. It typically lasts only weeks, whereas the feasibility stage may last months on a traditionally run project. The study should also answer traditional feasibility questions such as the following:
  - Is the computerized information system technically possible?
  - Will the benefit of the system be outweighed by its costs?
  - Will the information system operate acceptably within the organization?

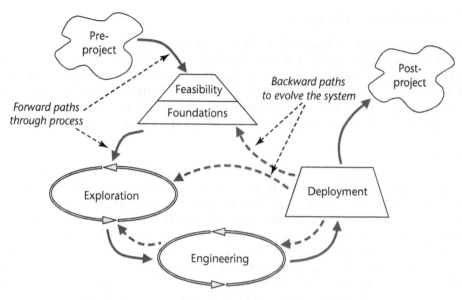

Figure 21.5 Simplified DSDM lifecycle (adapted from DSDM Consortium, 2007).

- *Foundations*. This phase identifies the overall scope of the project and results in agreed high-level functional and non-functional requirements. Although detail is deliberately limited, the outcome of this phase must show how an identified business need will be met by the proposed application.
- *Exploration*. This phase is concerned with the iterative and incremental development of models and prototypes that elicit the detailed requirements and demonstrate a viable solution. The intention of Atern is to develop prototypes that can ultimately be delivered as operational systems, so these must be built from the start to be sufficiently robust for operational use and also to satisfy any non-functional requirements such as performance.
- *Engineering*. During this phase, the prototypes produced during the Exploration phase are developed further to the point where they can be used operationally. The distinction between the two phases is not clear-cut and is more a matter of focus than of sequence. Both phases can even run concurrently. It is not uncommon for a project to move to and fro between Exploration and Engineering on successive increments.
- *Deployment*. This phase deals with the installation of the latest increment into its operational environment. For a commercial product, this means making it ready for market. For internal development projects it will include user training. There may be a number of passes through Deployment, partly depending on the extent to which the initial requirements have been met. If they have been fully satisfied the project is complete. If some non-functional requirements have yet to be addressed, the project may return to the Engineering phase. If some element of functionality was omitted due to time constraints, the project may return to the Exploration phase. If a new functional area is identified, the project may return to the Foundations phase. The return flows of control are shown with dashed arrows in Fig. 21.5.
- *Post-Project*. It is important following a deployment to review the extent to which the business needs have been met. This gives a link to the strategic planning process, and also means that lessons can be learned by the business as a whole, not just by the current project team (which, in any case, has probably now been disbanded).

21.4.2 DSDM Atern techniques

Atern stipulates a number of key techniques, including timeboxing, MoSCoW prioritization, facilitated workshops, iterative development and modelling. We will not say more here about iterative development, which should by now need no further explanation. Nor will we discuss modelling techniques, about which Atern has little to say beyond an insistence that they should be used in preference to purely textual specifications. We will concentrate on the first three techniques, which are explained below.

Timeboxing
This is an approach to project planning and control that fixes the resource allocation for a project, or for a part of a project. It limits the time available for the refinement of a product. Overall, an Atern project has a fixed completion date and this defines a timebox for the project as a whole. Smaller timeboxes are identified within this, each with a set of prioritized objectives. Each timebox produces one or more deliverables that allow progress and quality to be assessed. Examples of deliverables include requirements and design artefacts, software increments, documentation and so on. The idea is to deliver, within the agreed time, a product that satisfies the *minimum usable subset* of all requirements for the product. (This subset of requirements is identified through MoSCoW prioritization, which we discuss below.) Within a timebox, the team members have three major concerns:

- They must carry out any investigation needed to determine the direction they should take for that part of the project.
- They must develop and refine the specified deliverables.
- They must consolidate their work prior to the final deadline.

This is illustrated in Fig. 21.6.

MoSCoW prioritization
This is a way of prioritizing requirements, without which timeboxing could not work. 'MoSCoW' is a mnemonic that stands for 'Must...Should...Could...Won't...'.

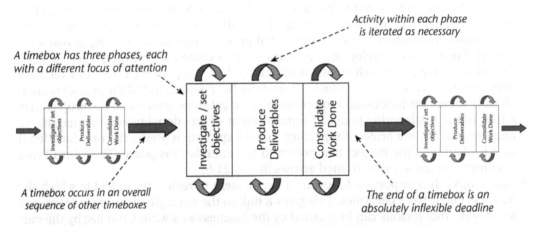

Figure 21.6 The internal structure of a timebox (adapted from DSDM/Stapleton, 2003).

- 'Must (have)' requirements are crucial. If these are omitted the system will not operate. In DSDM the set of Must have requirements is known as the minimum usable subset.
- 'Should (have)' requirements are important but if necessary the system can still operate without them.
- 'Could (have)' requirements are desirable but provide less benefit to the user.
- 'Won't (have this time around)' requirements are expected to be left for development in a later increment or a later project.

All requirements matter, by definition, but not to the same extent. If the full set cannot be addressed within the scope of a timebox, the MoSCoW categorization helps to focus the development work on those that matter the most from a business perspective.

Facilitated workshops

A facilitated workshop consists of a group of people working together under the guidance of a trained facilitator (who is typically external to the organization), in a controlled environment designed to be free of everyday work distractions, usually under time-constrained conditions. The concept has a venerable history that can be traced back to the Joint Application Development (JAD) workshops pioneered at IBM in Canada in the late 1970s. JAD workshops were innovative for their time in that they specifically involved a range of participants, including the project sponsor (so that the workshop could arrive at binding decisions), users, developers and other experts as necessary—hence the name 'joint.' The success of the technique depends to a large extent on the commitment and shared sense of ownership that can be achieved when a diverse group of people work together to solve a problem.

21.4.3 Project selection in DSDM

Some earlier publications on DSDM (for example, DSDM Consortium/Stapleton, 2003) include advice on how to choose projects that are suitable for a DSDM approach. This advice can be distilled down to two simple rules, which appear to be still relevant to the selection of projects in Atern.

- The system should not be too algorithmically complex, and its main functionality should be visible at the user interface. This is understandable if we consider the key Atern attitude that the system should be focused on the direct provision of useful functionality to business users. Without that, user involvement would be much less relevant.
- There should be a real business need for early delivery of the software. This is also understandable if we consider the Atern emphasis on delivery of products on time. It is hard to see how the team could continue to take this seriously if there were no pressure to complete.

One other condition applies more to the managers of the organization as a whole than to the individual project or to the team. It is a prerequisite that senior managers should give their unequivocal support to the use of Atern, since it relies on project teams having a great deal of freedom about how to interpret the requirements for the system on which they are working. The team's energy and enthusiasm will soon be stifled if their independence turns out to be an illusion.

21.5 Scrum

Scrum is described by its founder (Schwaber, 2009) as 'a framework within which complex products can be developed' rather than either a process or a technique. In the terminology we have used in this chapter, this makes it a methodology rather than a method. It has a philosophy, techniques, tools (a number of software tools are now available), procedures and so on, but above all–not surprisingly for an agile methodology–it is designed to be versatile and flexible in use. Scrum has been in use since the early 1990s, but has recently gained momentum and has emerged as one of the most popular agile methods.

Probably the first thing to strike the novice is the peculiarity of the language used in Scrum. The following are some examples.

- The name of the methodology itself is derived (very indirectly) from rugby football.
- People are assigned to roles named *pigs* and *chickens*.
- The team leader is called a *ScrumMaster*.
- Work is done in timeboxed cycles of activity known as *Sprints*, punctuated by daily *ceremonies*.
- There are artefacts called *Backlogs* and *Burndowns*.

Once the vocabulary is mastered, the methodology will begin to make much more sense. In essence, the aim of Scrum is to develop teams that are creative, enthusiastic, empowered and that that work well together. The Scrum approach is designed to leave a great deal of the day-to-day functioning of the team under the control of its members, while ensuring that they remain responsive to their clients and customers. Hence the division of people into *pigs*–full members of a Scrum team–and *chickens*–all other stakeholders. The distinction comes from an old joke, one version of which talks about the respective roles of a pig and a chicken in a ham-and-egg breakfast: the pig is committed while the chicken is merely involved (vegetarians, Muslims and Jews may be forgiven for not thinking the joke very funny). One of the rules of a Scrum project (rules are important in Scrum) is that chickens can't tell pigs how they should do their work, although a particular chicken may have the right to specify the result.

The most important aspects of the Scrum framework are the roles that make up a Scrum team, the way that timeboxes work, the artefacts that are produced, and the rules that govern the behaviour of participants in a Scrum project. These are briefly explained below.

- *Roles*. Three key roles are involved in implementing the Scrum framework. First, team members do all the development work, and are expected to be completely self-organizing in their approach. Second, the *ScrumMaster* is in a sense the team leader, but his or her role is not to direct the work of the team members, but instead to coach and motivate them, and to ensure that the Scrum process is followed. A ScrumMaster may also be a team member, but this is not essential. Third, the *Product Owner* represents the business perspective in relation to the product that is being developed. These three roles count among the pigs (the committed ones) while everyone else is a chicken in relation to this project (involved but not committed).
- *Timeboxes*. The most important of the timeboxed elements is the *Sprint*, which is where most of the work gets done. A Sprint is a 2–4 week iteration devoted to the production of an increment that is capable of release to the customer. A project consists of a number of consecutive Sprints, most of which result in an increment of

completed software. A number of other elements are timeboxed in Scrum, including all meetings. These include the Sprint Planning Meeting, the *Daily Scrums* that punctuate the progress of each Sprint and the Sprint Review Meeting. These three meetings are collectively known as Scrum's *ceremonies*. Daily Scrums resemble team meetings in DSDM Atern, in that they focus on the completion of products rather than ongoing progress with activities.

- *Artefacts*. Project documentation in Scrum centres on four key artefacts. The *Product Backlog* documents in priority order all requirements for the current product, typically in the form of 'user stories' (see the next section on XP) or use cases. The Product Owner has responsibility for the contents of the Product Backlog and for determining their priority. It is closely related to the *Release Burndown*, which shows in graphic form an estimate of the total remaining work needed to complete the current project. Both documents are constantly updated during the progress of the project. The *Sprint Backlog* and *Sprint Burndown* fulfil a similar purpose at the level of an individual Sprint.

- *Rules*. These describe the relationships between the various roles, timeboxes and artefacts, and also how people are permitted to behave in certain contexts. One example of a rule is that only team members can talk during a Daily Scrum, although others may be invited to attend. Another rule relates to the completion of work during a Sprint. The purpose of each Sprint is to take one item from the Product Backlog and to turn it into a 'done' increment. A done increment is only regarded as such if it meets a definition of 'done' that is understood and agreed by the Product Owner. In some cases, an increment may be accepted as done only when all analysis, design and other documentation is complete, together with the fully tested software. In other cases, a done increment may not include documentation, or unit testing, or acceptance testing, or indeed anything other than completed code. Perhaps the most important rule of all in Scrum is that teams are self-organizing and do not have a formal leader imposed on them. Nor is anyone outside the team permitted to tell a team member how to do his or her work.

Beyond an insistence on iterative development, Scrum does not stipulate a particular lifecycle. This distinguishes it from other methodologies, most of which have a clear view of the phases of a project. However, since a Scrum team is expected to be flexible and has a great deal of freedom to decide its sequence of activities, this creates the possibility for Scrum to be adopted in conjunction with a methodology such as UP or DSDM. Scrum also avoids being prescriptive about techniques, but this too leaves a team with freedom to adopt those techniques that they feel are most appropriate to the project. In practice, most Scrum software projects follow an object-oriented development approach with UML as the preferred documentation standard.

21.6 eXtreme Programming

The approach known as eXtreme Programming (XP) is a combination of elements of best practice in systems development. It was first publicized by Beck (2004) and incorporates a highly iterative approach to development. It became well known in a relatively short period of time for its use of *pair programming*, though it has other important contributions to make. Pair programming involves writing the program code in pairs and not individually. At first sight it might appear that this approach would significantly increase the staffing level and hence the cost of developing an information system. Advocates of XP claim the reverse. Beck identifies the four underlying principles of XP as communication, simplicity, feedback and courage.

- *Communication*. Poor communication is a significant factor in failing projects. XP highlights the importance of good communication among developers and between developers and users.
- *Simplicity*. Software developers are sometimes tempted to use technology for technology's sake rather than seeking the simplest effective solution. Developers justify complex solutions as a way of meeting possible future requirements. XP focuses on the simplest solution for the immediate known requirements.
- *Feedback*. Unjustified optimism is common in systems development. Developers tend to underestimate the time required to complete any particular programming task. This results in poor estimates of project completion, constant chasing of unrealistic deadlines, stressed developers and poor product quality. Feedback in XP is geared to giving the developers frequent and timely feedback from users and from test results. Work estimates are based on the work actually completed in the previous iteration.
- *Courage*. The exhortation to be courageous urges the developer to throw away code that is not quite correct and start again, rather than trying to fix the unfixable. Essentially the developer has to abandon unproductive lines of development, despite the personal emotional investment in work done.

XP argues that embracing change is an important key to systems development and that development staff are motivated by the production of quality work.

Requirements capture in XP is based on *user stories* that describe the requirements. These are written by the user and form the basis of project planning and the development of test harnesses. A user story is very similar to a use case, though some proponents of XP suggest that there are key differences in granularity. A typical user story is about three sentences long and does not include any detail of technology. When the developers are ready to start work they get detailed descriptions of the requirements by sitting face to face with their customer. Beck describes the systems development process as being driven by the user stories in much the same way that the UP is use case driven.

XP involves the following activities.

- The *planning game* involves quickly defining the scope of the next release from user priorities and technical estimates. The plan is updated regularly as the iteration progresses.
- The information system should be delivered in small releases that incrementally build up functionality through rapid iteration.
- A unifying *metaphor* or high-level *shared story* focuses the development.
- The system should be based on a *simple design*.
- Programmers prepare unit tests in advance of software construction and customers define acceptance tests.
- The program code should be restructured to remove duplication, simplify the code and improve flexibility–this is known as *refactoring*, and is discussed in detail by Fowler (1999).
- Pair programming means two programmers write code together on one workstation.
- The code is owned collectively and anyone can change any code.
- The system is integrated and built frequently each day. This gives the opportunity for regular testing and feedback.

- Normally staff should work no more than forty hours a week.
- A user should be a full-time member of the team.
- All programmers should write code according to agreed standards that emphasize good communication through the code.

The XP approach is best suited to relatively small projects—say with no more than ten programmers. It relies on clear communicative code and rapid feedback. If circumstances preclude either of these, then XP is not the most appropriate approach.

One key feature of XP is that the code itself is its own design documentation. This runs counter to many aspects of the approach suggested in this book. We have suggested that requirements are best analysed and suitable designs produced through the use of visual models using UML. Nonetheless, XP offers an interesting insight into a different way of organizing and managing a software development project.

21.7 | Issues in Choosing a Methodology

The introduction of any methodology to an organization is not a trivial matter. There are many costs, some quite difficult to estimate. Staff must be trained in the techniques, structure and management of the new methodology, documentation must be purchased and software licences must be obtained for CASE tools that support the methodology. The indirect, hidden costs are often underestimated. Productive time is lost during training, and for some time after the change there may be a reduction in productivity and an ongoing need for support from external consultants. This is true whether or not the organization already uses a methodology. Even with careful evaluation before a decision is made, followed by careful planning of the change, it is often still prudent to conduct a full-scale trial of a new methodology on a pilot project, which must also be chosen carefully. It would be unwise to risk the failure of a critical system, yet a pilot project must be sufficiently complex to put the new methodology to a thorough test.

The choice of the 'right' methodology is also fraught with difficulties, as there are now many hundreds to choose from, and these differ radically in their philosophies, their coverage of the lifecycle and their suitability to particular application domains. Many factors affect the appropriateness of a methodology, including type of project (large, small, routine or mission-critical), application domain (e.g. realtime, safety-critical, user-centred, highly interactive, distributed or batch-mode) and nature of the IS development organization.

One very influential thinker on the management of software development is Humphrey (1989), whose 'process maturity framework' has now evolved into the Software Engineering Institute's Capability Maturity Model Integration (Ahern et al., 2001). This model suggests that organizations evolve through stages of maturity, which necessarily follow each other in a pre-defined sequence. By analogy, a butterfly must first pass through the stages of egg, then caterpillar, then chrysalis, and it would simply make no sense for one to attempt to fly before it emerged as an adult. The logic for software development is that there is little point in introducing practices too far beyond the organization's current level of maturity.

Humphrey originally described five stages. First comes an 'initial' level, where development activities are chaotic, and each developer uses ad hoc procedures that they have probably devised themselves. There are no common standards and no dissemination of good practice through the organization, so the success of any project depends solely on

Box 21.1 Methodology and Student Projects

We include here some remarks about the role of methodology in student projects. Supervisors of projects at undergraduate and postgraduate levels usually require students to follow some explicit methodology. It is also often a condition for professional accreditation of a degree that students should show that they can choose and apply an appropriate methodology.

The requirement is not trivial. The driving force that led to the existence of so many methodologies is the constant struggle by software developers to learn how to avoid past errors, and how to repeat past successes. But what does this mean in practice? What must a student do in order to claim that he or she has 'followed an appropriate methodology'? Most of the methodologies described in this chapter simply do not fit the context of an assessed student project without at least some adaptation. This is for several reasons:

- There is typically only one developer, and he or she is usually quite inexperienced.
- There is often no real client, and no real business need for the product.
- Even if there is a real client, access may be limited when compared to a commercial project.
- Access to the project supervisor may also be limited when compared to a project manager in a commercial setting.
- The student must usually substitute self-study for formal training and mentoring in processes and tools.

It is hardly surprising that students are sometimes confused about how to cope with this set of challenges. Our suggestions for resolving this confusion are threefold.

First, we take the general view that methodologies, like software systems, should be fit for purpose. In other words, the methodology chosen for a project should be one that at least appears likely to be helpful in achieving the project aims. For example, a project expected to use software components in its implementation should make use of techniques fit for specifying components.

Second, all methodologies are capable of some adaptation, and very few need be adopted in their entirety. For example, students working alone may benefit from following some aspects of XP, but they will certainly find pair programming to be an irrelevance. Furthermore, there are more marks to be gained by producing explicit analysis and design models that document decisions made along the way, than by slavishly following the principle that the code can serve as its own documentation.

Finally, a methodology is as much a means for learning how to do systems development as it is a recipe. This is particularly true for a student project, where it is taken for granted at the outset that the developer has only limited experience. Every student project is intended partly as a learning experience, and this applies as much to the methodology as to any other aspect of the project. For this reason, it is not really important whether the 'right' methodology is chosen at the outset. Instead, the student should reflect on his or her chosen methodology during the course of the project, and, at the end, should write up the lessons learned from this reflective evaluation.

the skill and experience of the development team. At this level there is no point in introducing any methodology, since management have neither the skill nor the structures required to control it. Instead, the focus should be on moving to the next 'repeatable' level, where an organization has adopted simple development standards and project management procedures. These allow successes to be repeated on later projects and the organization can benefit from a methodology, since management procedures are capable of enforcing its application. However, while individual managers may repeat their successes, there is no clear understanding of which specific factors led to each success.

It is unlikely that success can be generalized to different kinds of project or application, and the flexibility of the organization is still limited. A prescriptive methodology that defines all steps in some detail is more likely to be successful.

An organization at the next, 'defined' level has its own definition of the software process and is able to standardize activities throughout the organization. A methodology can now be introduced more readily and is likely to produce greater benefits, since the organization already has a culture of working to defined procedures. But staff still adapt much more readily to a methodology that is in harmony with their current ways of working. The next step is typically to introduce a metrics programme (see the book website for more information about metrics). If successful, this can lift the organization to the 'managed' level–but few organizations are yet at this level. Only a tiny handful have reached the final 'optimizing' level, where there is a capability for continuous improvement in all activities (corresponding to the general management approach called 'Total Quality Management').

21.8 | Hard v. Soft Methodologies

This chapter would not be complete without some mention of the long-running critical debate that turns on the distinction between *hard* and *soft* methodologies, and that sometimes divides both the profession and the academic community into two opposing camps. The distinction emerged principally from the broad systems movement. While there is no single precise definition of the difference, it is summarized in Fig. 21.7.

'Hard' is usually taken to mean objective, quantifiable or based on rational scientific and engineering principles. In contrast, 'soft' involves people issues and is ambiguous and subjective. UP can be seen as deriving mainly from the hard tradition. However, influence of a softer approach can be discerned in DSDM Atern, in Scrum, and also to a lesser extent in techniques such as the user stories in XP and the use case

Hard systems view	Soft systems view
The activity of IS development is all about building a technical system that is made only of software and hardware	An IS also comprises the social context in which the technical system (software and hardware) will be used
Human factors are chiefly important from the perspective of the software's usability and acceptability. Politics and group behaviour are only an issue for project managers	A new IS impacts on interpersonal communication, social organization, working practices and much more, so human and social factors are paramount
Organizations exist only to meet rational objectives, through the application of rational principles of business management. It is possible to be both rational and objective about the requirements for a new system	Organizations are made up of individuals with distinct views and motivations, so any picture of requirements is subjective. It is not always possible even to reach a consensus. In practice, this means that the powerful decide, not the wise
When requirements are uncertain or unclear, it is up to management to decide. Setting objectives is a principal role of management, and others should follow their lead	If management has not accommodated the full range of views in the organization, encouraging managers to decide on the requirements may be completely counter-productive

Figure 21.7 Some underlying assumptions of hard and soft systems approaches.

technique, since these aim at eliciting the practical, context-based requirements of individual users.

On the whole, those methodologies that might be characterized as principally soft in their orientation tend to focus more on making sure that the 'right' system is developed, than on how to actually develop the system. Their intellectual antecedents are diverse. For example, Checkland's influential Soft Systems Methodology (SSM) (Checkland, 1981; Checkland and Scholes, 1990; Checkland and Holwell, 1998) originally grew out of an attempt to apply hard systems engineering techniques that failed because the problem situations were messy and ill-defined. SSM is grounded in a set of philosophical ideas about the nature of systems at a conceptual level. Its techniques, such as the conceptual model and the rich picture, provide ways of exploring and agreeing the characteristics of the problem situation, before any attempt is made to define a specific system that will help users to meet their goals.

This is very different from the approach taken by 'hard' methodologies. These tend to assume that the purpose and nature of the organization can, to a large extent, be taken for granted, and that every project begins with an identified need for an information system to solve some recognized problem.

One way of reconciling the contradiction is to argue that soft and hard methodologies cover different parts of the lifecycle. In this view, a soft methodology is more useful in the earlier stages of the lifecycle, particularly when there is uncertainty about the goals or strategy of the organization as a whole. A hard approach will be more appropriate once any initial uncertainties and ambiguities have been resolved (insofar as this is possible), since the emphasis then shifts to a specific project with relatively clear goals and boundaries. This has led to the suggestion that, in certain situations, hard and soft methodologies can complement each other and can be used together to help overcome some of the perennial difficulties in systems development. Flynn (1998) proposes a 'contingency framework', shown in Figure 21.8, which aims at helping to select an appropriate methodology for a specific organizational context.

A project is rated along both dimensions, and this helps to indicate an appropriate development approach. 'Requirements uncertainty' is the extent to which requirements are unknown or subject to debate or disagreement, and also whether they are expected

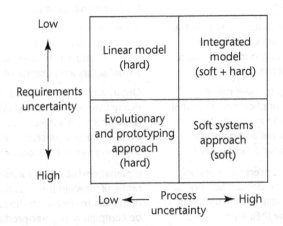

Figure 21.8 The contingency framework can be used to help select an appropriate methodology for a given organizational context (adapted from Flynn, 1998).

to change during development. For example, a new system intended primarily to automate an existing manual system may have relatively low requirements uncertainty. Agate's Campaign Management system might fall into this category. 'Process uncertainty' refers to the degree of doubt about the best way to build the proposed system. On this count, too, we would probably categorize the Agate system as 'low uncertainty.' There is not likely to be much doubt about the best way to build such a relatively straightforward business system. Applying Flynn's framework thus leads to the conclusion that we should adopt a 'linear model' or hard methodology. 'Linear' refers to a sequential lifecycle model like the Waterfall model, which indicates that in some respects this framework is now very dated. As we saw in Chapter 3, few people today would recommend a linear waterfall approach in any but a very few unusual situations. In practice today this would be interpreted as meaning a fully featured methodology with clear tasks and phases, such as UP. Alternatively, it might indicate the procurement of a ready-made solution, in which case much of the lifecycle would indeed be linear.

On the other hand, it may be more difficult to decide on the best process for a new system that will use untried technology, with unpredictable effects on the organization's employees. A project to introduce electronic commerce to an organization with no previous experience of it might fall in this category. Here, the framework recommends an integrated approach. However, in a contemporary context we would probably interpret this as indicating an agile approach, since this would accommodate uncertainty regarding both the requirements and the process.

Where the process uncertainty is low but the requirements are highly uncertain, an agile approach such as DSDM or Scrum would also be recommended. Finally, where everything is unclear, a soft systems approach is recommended. Effectively, this means that the character of the problem must be clarified before any commitment can be made to development work.

In seeking to merge together a soft and a hard methodology, the development team is really trying to devise a unique method suited to the project. This implicitly recognizes the complementary nature of their strengths and weaknesses.

21.9 Summary

We began this chapter by considering how the concept of methodology differs from method and how both relate to process. These are important distinctions, since the development approach is an important factor in the success or failure of a project, and selection of an appropriate methodology is a necessary precursor to choosing the specific method or process to be followed. Many methodologies have been developed over the years, stemming from different traditions, and each in some way attempting to counter a perceived shortcoming in contemporary rivals. The 1990s were a prolific time for the spread of object-oriented methodologies, which have comprehensively replaced the older structured methods in many organizations today. Among the object-oriented methodologies, UP and its derivatives look set to be the survivors. Over the same period, there was also much research into the possible merging of hard and soft methodologies. This was aimed at meeting a wider range of demands, and thus improving the overall success rate of IS development projects. However, the concerns of the soft systems community have to a large extent been subsumed into those of the much more recent Agile movement. Agile development differs in some important respects from earlier methodological approaches, in particular its flexible approach and its emphasis on keeping the quantity of documentation to the absolute minimum that is necessary. Agile methodologies and frameworks such as DSDM, Scrum and XP aim to complement object-oriented development rather than to replace it. As a result, it appears likely that they will continue to evolve alongside UML for the foreseeable future.

Review Questions

21.1 What is the difference between 'methodology' and 'method'?

21.2 Distinguish between 'task' and 'technique', and give some examples of each.

21.3 What does it mean to say that XP is 'agile'?

21.4 Explain the key elements in the philosophy of DSDM Atern.

21.5 In what respects does Scrum agree with UP?

21.6 How does Scrum differ from UP?

21.7 How does the full UP approach differ from the simplified approach followed in this book?

21.8 Name the five levels of the Capability Maturity Model.

21.9 Distinguish between the hard systems view and the soft systems view.

21.10 Why might a methodology based on a hard systems approach be unsuccessful in a situation where the goals of the organization are unclear?

21.11 What general advantages are claimed for using a methodology?

21.12 What might be the disadvantages of using an inappropriate methodology?

Case Study Work, Exercises and Projects

Do some research in your library or on the Internet, and collect material that describes four or more different systems development methodologies. Try to make these as different from each other as possible, for example by choosing one that is agile (e.g. Scrum), one that is object-oriented (e.g. UP), one based on a soft systems view (e.g. SSM) and one from a completely different tradition (e.g. Participatory Design, which we have not covered in this chapter). Then use the following questions as a basis for comparison.

21.A What techniques are used by each methodology? In particular, what aspects of the system do they represent and what techniques do they use to do this?

21.B To what extent does each methodology cover the full project lifecycle, from project selection through to implementation and maintenance?

21.C How far do you think each methodology can be adapted to suit differing projects or circumstances?

21.D Can you find a statement that gives an underlying philosophy for each methodology? If not, is it possible to identify the intellectual tradition from which the methodology has been derived?

Further Reading

The DSDM Atern Pocketbook (DSDM Consortium, 2007) is a brief but readable introduction to this methodology.

Ambler (2004) is a very useful resource on agile methods, and Ambler's website www.ambysoft.com also includes a number of articles and a comprehensive description of AUP.

Larman (2003) is another readable introduction to agile development, with chapters devoted to XP, the Unified Process and other agile methodologies.

Fitzgerald et al. (2002) is a comparative review of some traditional methodologies (not discussed in this chapter) and some not-so-traditional methodologies that include RUP, DSDM, XP, SSM. There is also some coverage of the role of the CMMI and a helpful discussion of the theoretical background to methodologies and their use.

Avison and Fitzgerald (2006), now in its fourth edition, remains a key text for issues in understanding and selecting software development methodologies.

Vidgen et al. (2002)–though mainly devoted to the development of web information systems, which is beyond the scope of this book–include a useful summary of systems thinking and SSM, and there is also some coverage of PD.

Flynn (1998), although older than other texts mentioned here, remains a good introduction to the many traditions behind today's methodologies, and is also still worthwhile reading for its treatment of the issues that cause difficulty in choosing the 'right' way to do systems development.

For more detailed information about SSM, readers should ideally consult the primary sources: Checkland (1981), Checkland and Scholes (1990) and Checkland and Holwell (1998).

Jacobson et al. (1999) remains the definitive work on UP, while Kruchten (2004) and Kroll and Kruchten (2003) are both good sources on RUP.

APPENDIX A Notation Summary

Use Case Diagram

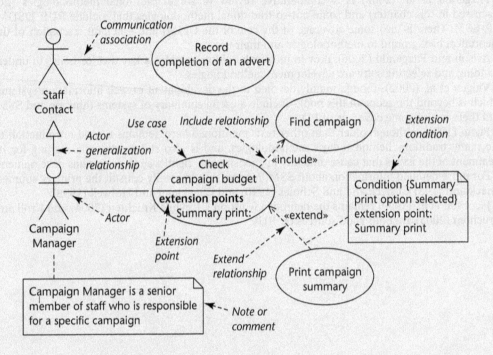

Static Structure Diagrams

Object instance notation

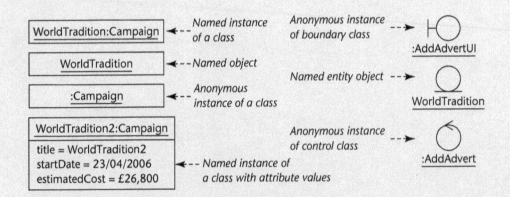

Class notation

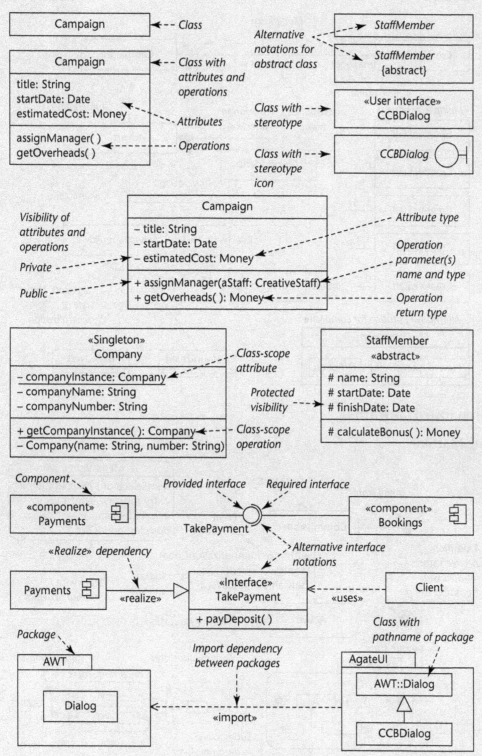

Associations

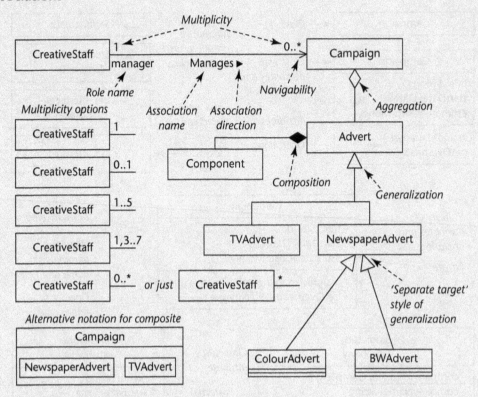

Behaviour Diagrams

State Machine

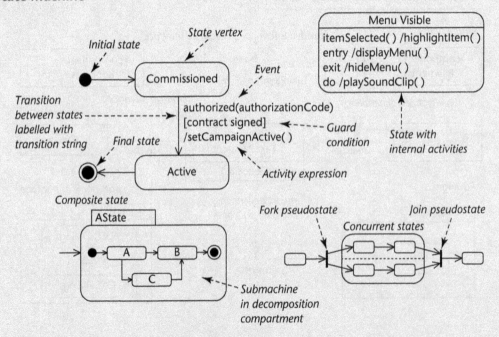

Activity diagram

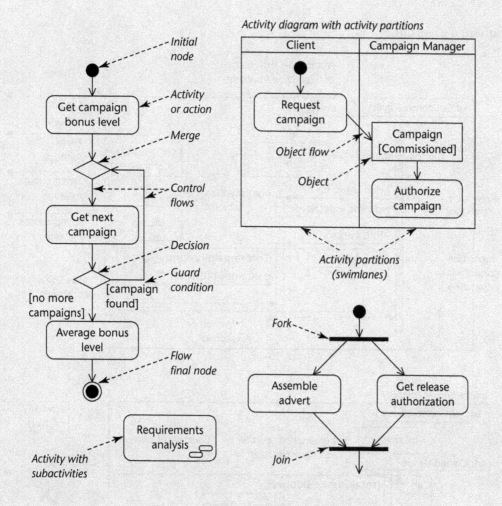

Interaction Diagrams

Sequence diagram

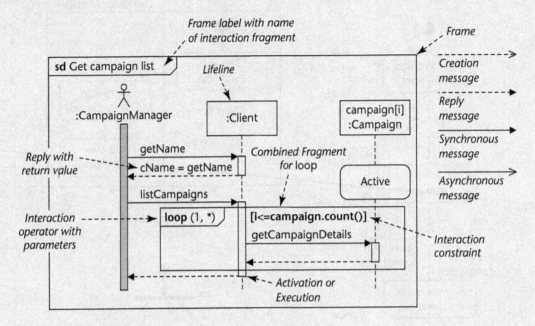

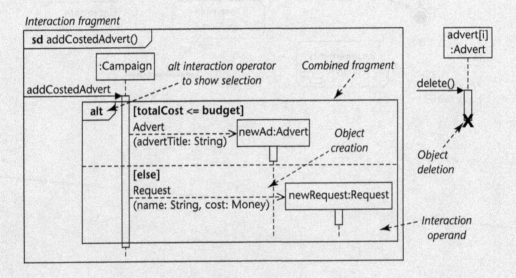

Interaction sequence diagram with duration and time constraints

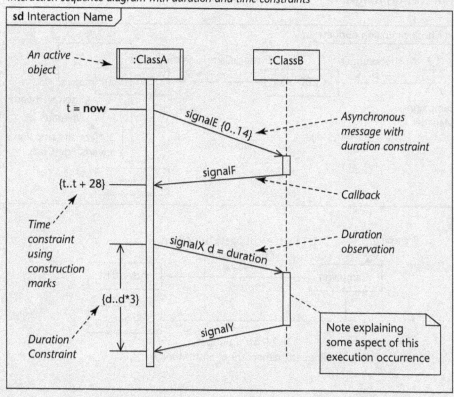

Continuations betwen two interaction fragments

Interaction occurrence transfers execution to Calculate costs

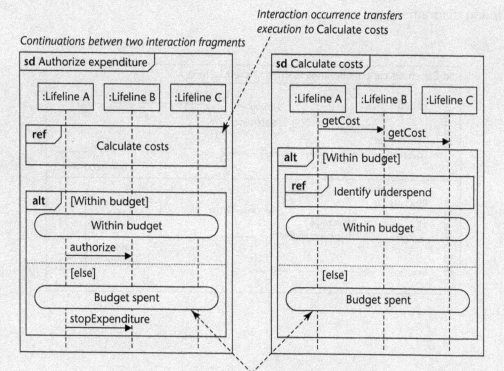

Continuation from Calculate costs back to Authorize expenditure

Communication diagram

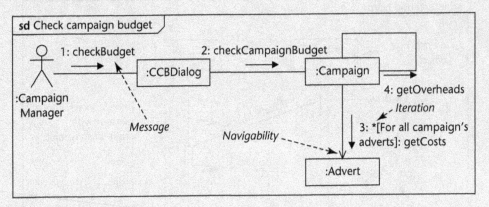

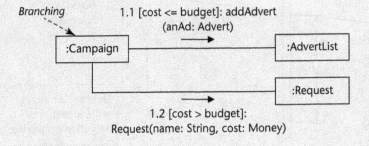

Timing diagram

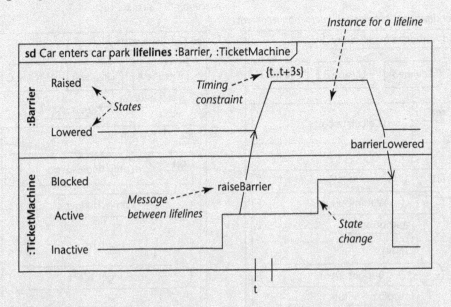

Interaction overview diagram

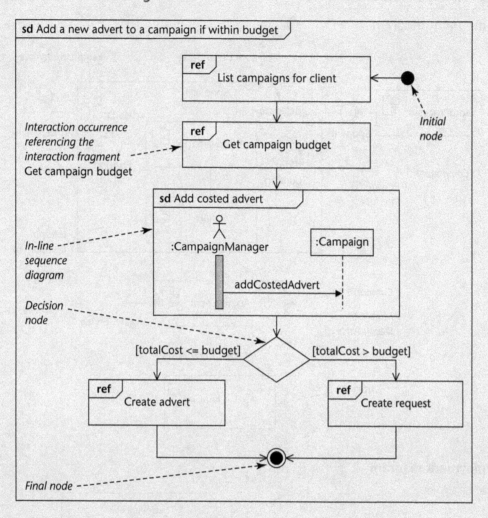

Implementation Diagrams

Component diagram

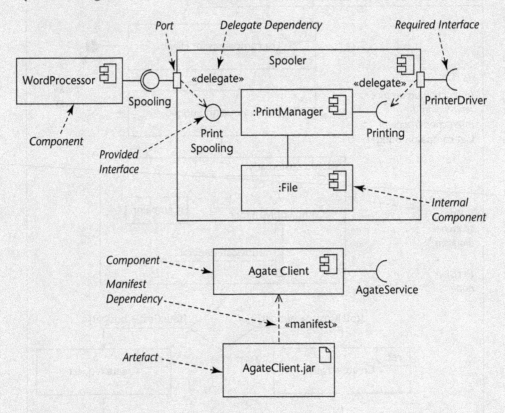

Deployment diagram

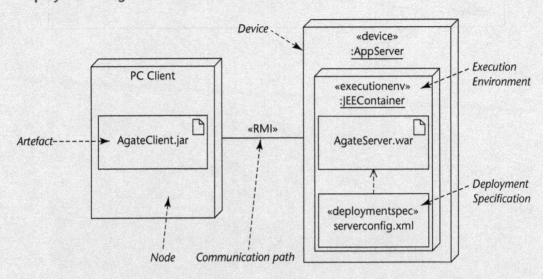

APPENDIX B Selected Solutions and Answer Pointers

In this section we give solutions to a selection of the review questions in the chapters, and also pointers on possible approaches to some of the end-of-chapter case study work, exercises and projects.

Answers to Selected Review Questions

1.3 Even if something isn't a system (or might not be one), thinking of it as one still gives useful insights.

1.5 Feedback is sampling one or more outputs of a system for comparison with a control value. Feed-forward is sampling a system input, usually before it enters the system. The control value may be an output, input or an internal measure of system performance.

1.6 Because each participant in the system may have a different view of its purpose. It is not always possible to reach complete agreement on a shared, single purpose.

1.7 A management support system provides information that helps managers to make decisions. Most use feedback or feed-forward to monitor the performance of that part of the organization for which the manager is responsible.

1.9 Business goals and strategy are typically defined first, as they provide the context. An IS strategy identifies applications that can help to meet business goals, and an IT strategy identifies IT needed to develop and run the applications. Each informs its predecessor about what can realistically be achieved. The process is iterative.

1.10 One of the simplest definitions says that information is data with a structure and a meaning derived from the context in which it is used.

2.1 They differ in their view of the problems because their view of the meaning and purpose of IS development also differs (see also Review Question 1.6).

2.3 The simplest definition is 'fitness for purpose'. But it can be hard to identify and define the purpose unambiguously. A more practical alternative is 'meeting all user requirements, both stated and implied'.

2.6 The system may address irrelevant problems. It may not fit the way that people work. It may be unsuitable for its environment. It may be out of date before delivery. Political difficulties may lead to delay or cancellation.

2.7 A stakeholder has an interest in a project because they are (or will be) affected by its progress or by its results.

3.1 Key approaches include using a systematic approach to development (e.g. RUP, AUP, etc), ensuring effective user involvement, using incremental development, applying effective project management, and giving appropriate consideration to installation and operational issues.

3.2 Some disadvantages of the Waterfall Lifecycle:
- Real projects rarely follow a simple sequential lifecycle.
- Iterations are almost inevitable.
- The lapsed time between inception and delivery is frequently too long.
- It is unresponsive to changes in the technology or requirements.

3.5 Prototyping is not necessarily concerned with the delivery of a working system, whereas an incremental approach delivers a working system in successive increments. Note that in the Unified Software Development Process an increment can produce any lifecycle product.

3.7 Syntactic correctness is concerned with using the notation (e.g. UML) correctly, consistency relates to producing a set of models or diagrams that are consistent with each other and completeness refers to producing models that are completely defined.

3.8 The term requirements traceability refers to the capability of tracking each requirement to all the systems development deliverables (from requirements models to program code) that relate to it.

3.9 A diagram may be syntactically correct and complete and consistent with other diagrams and models, but it may not relate accurately or completely to the user requirements, the most important criterion for any diagram or model.

4.2 Semantics is the study of meaning. In object-oriented development it is generally used to denote the meaning that an element has for the user. (User may include the modeller or developer, not just the end-user of the software.) An object's semantics include its purpose, description, relationships and behaviour seen from a user perspective.

4.3 Other parts of a system only see an object's interface (services it can perform and operation signatures). Internal details including data and the implementation of operations are hidden and can only be accessed by a message that contains a valid signature.

4.4 Polymorphism means that when one message is sent to objects of different types, each has an appropriate, but different, implementation for its response. The object that sends the message need not know which type of object is addressed, since the operation signature is the same. One way of implementing polymorphism is through inheritance and overriding.

4.6 A subclass inherits all characteristics of its superclass and other ancestors (some may be overridden, but are still technically inherited). Each subclass is different from its ancestors in at least one way.

5.2 Structural and behavioural diagrams.

5.4 To promote communication between team members in a project. To communicate over time to other people who will work on the system. To communicate good practice and experience.

5.7 A rectangle with rounded corners.

5.8 Control flows.

5.10 The start node (a filled black circle) and the final node (a filled black circle within another circle).

5.13 An arrow between an object and an action.

6.1 Examples of functional requirements are: the need for a process to be run that allocates staff to lines based on their skills and experience, and on holidays and sick leave; printing out an allocation list; amending the allocation list. Examples of non-functional requirements include: printing the allocation list by 12.00 noon; the need to handle 200 operatives' details.

6.4 Use cases are produced to model the functionality of the system from the users' point of view and to show which users will communicate with the system. They show the scope of the system.

6.6 An essential use case documents the interaction between user and system in a way that is free of technological and implementation details, and a real use case describes the concrete detail of a use case in terms of its design.

6.10 The use cases represent the functions of the business rather than functions of the computer system, and the actors represent people and organizations outside the business interacting with those functions.

7.2 An attribute is a characteristic of a class (every person has a height). An attribute value is a characteristic of an instance (this author is 1.75m tall).

7.3 An element's stability is the relative infrequency of change in its description. Instances may be created, destroyed or updated frequently, but it is unlikely that the class description will change as often.

7.6 Multiplicity denotes the range of values for the number of objects that can be linked to a single object by a specific association. It is a constraint because it limits the behaviour of a system. If a client can have only one staff contact, it should not be possible to link a second.

7.10 A link is a connection between two objects. 'Changing' a link (say by substituting another object at one end) is equivalent to destroying the link and creating a new one. (Think about two objects tied with a single length of string. In a substitution, there is a moment when neither one nor the other is connected—unless you tie on the second before untying the first, but an object link cannot do this).

7.12 A communication diagram shows only those objects that collaborate to provide the functionality of a particular use case (or operation), although they are usually identified as anonymous instances of their class. The links that are shown are only those required for that purpose. A class diagram typically shows all the classes in a particular package and all the associations between them.

8.1 Use of a component saves time and work. A friend of one of the authors once said: 'Have you ever wondered how much it would cost to make your own light bulb?'

8.3 Objects are well encapsulated, and object structures can be designed this way. The hierarchic nature of generalization abstracts out the more general features of a class. Hierarchic organization of models helps the developer to find components easily when they are needed. Composition hides whole structures within a composite object.

8.4 A component of a composition cannot be shared with another composition. The component has a coincident lifetime with the composition (although a component can be explicitly detached before the composition is destroyed).

8.5   This is a basis for polymorphism. The superclass operation defines the signature, but each subclass has a different method that implements the behaviour (see Chapter 10).

8.6   An abstract class has no instances and exists only as a superclass in a hierarchy. It provides a generalized basis for concrete subclasses that do have instances.

8.12 An antipattern documents unsuccessful attempts at solving problems and suggests how the failed solution may be adapted to solve the problem successfully.

9.1   Communication diagrams discourage both using a large number of messages between two objects and having too many parameters for each message as these are clumsy to represent on the diagram.

9.2   Small self-contained classes are easier to develop, test and maintain.

9.3   Sequence diagrams have a time dimension (normally vertically down the page) while communication diagrams do not. Communication diagrams show the links between objects, which are not shown on sequence diagrams.

9.5   A lifeline represents the existence of the entity being modelled (e.g. an object) during the interaction represented in an interaction diagram. It may be used in sequence diagrams, communication diagrams, timing diagrams or interaction overview diagrams (within interaction fragments).

9.6   An execution occurrence indicates which operation is executing at a particular stage in an interaction represented in a sequence diagram.

9.9   Sequence numbers are written in a nested style in a communication diagram to represent nested procedural calls.

9.11 Complex interactions may be represented using UML by:
  ■ hiding some of the detail of the interaction using interaction uses referencing other interaction fragments. Common interaction fragments may be referenced from several other sequence diagrams.
  ■ using lifelines to represent groups of objects and their interaction or to represent subsystems. These lifelines refer to another interaction fragment, which contains the hidden detail.
  ■ using interaction overview diagrams to show the overall flow of control with in-line interaction fragments and interaction use to hide the detail of the interaction.

9.15 Timing diagrams are used to show how state changes occur over time. They are of particular value when specifying how time constraints affect the interaction between lifelines.

10.1 Operation specifications confirm the user's view of the logical behaviour of a model. They also specify what the designer and programmer must produce to meet the users' requirements.

10.2 Decision tables are particularly suited to representing decisions with complex multiple input conditions and complex multiple outcomes, where the precise sequence of steps is either not significant or is not known.

10.4 An algorithm defines the step-by-step behaviour of an operation. A non-algorithmic approach defines only pre-conditions and results.

10.5 Non-algorithmic methods of operation specification emphasize encapsulation.

10.9 OCL expressions have:

- a context within which the expression is valid (for example, a specified class);
- a property within the context to which the expression applies (for example, an attribute of the specified class);
- an operation that is applied to the property (for example, a mathematical expression that tests the value of the attribute).

11.2 A guard condition is evaluated when a particular event occurs and only if the condition is true does the associated transition fire.

11.3 All the guard conditions from a state should be mutually exclusive so that for each set of circumstances there is only one valid transition from a state. If they are not mutually exclusive more than one transition may be valid and the behaviour of the state machine is indeterminate.

11.4 A composite state contains substates and is used to represent complex state behaviour in a hierarchical fashion. A composite state may contain a single decomposition compartment with a single submachine or it may contain several decomposition compartments, each with a submachine. In the latter case the composite state has concurrent substates.

11.5 If an object is occupying a composite state that has more than one submachine then it will occupy a substate in each of the submachines in the composite state. Consequently it will occupy more than one substate at any one time while it is in the composite state.

11.6 The substates in a composite state are nested and may be nested to any arbitrary depth. In most cases nesting substates to one or two levels down will model the state behaviour adequately. Only if the composite state contains orthogonal submachines will these nested substates be concurrent.

11.11 The typical symptoms that a state machine has not been drawn to model state changes include the following.

- Most transitions are fired by state completion.
- Many messages are sent to 'self', reflecting code reuse rather than actions triggered by events.
- States do not capture state-dependent behaviour associated with the class.

12.3 User wants report etc.–analysis. Selection of business objects etc.–logical design. Size of paper etc.–physical design.

12.5 Seamlessness means that the same model (class diagram) is used and successively refined throughout the project.

12.7 Functional, efficient, economical, reliable, secure, flexible, general, buildable, manageable, maintainable, usable, reusable.

13.2 An architectural view is a representation of a particular system or part of a system from a particular perspective. An architectural viewpoint is a template that describes how to create and use an architectural view.

13.3 The four views are the *logical view*, the *implementation view*, the *process view* and the *deployment view*. The additional view is the *use case view*.

13.7 An enterprise architecture links the design of the business to the information systems that are needed to support that business.

13.10 Open layered architectures are more difficult to maintain because each layer may communicate with all lower layers, hence increasing the degree of coupling in the architecture. A change to one layer may ripple to many layers.

13.11 A closed layered architecture may require more processing as messages have to be passed through intervening layers.

13.13 The main differences between the MVC and the layered architecture include the update propagation mechanism and the separation of the presentation layer into the View and Controller components in the MVC.

13.14 A broker decouples subsystems by acting as an intermediate messaging-passing component through which all messages are passed. As a result a subsystem is aware of the broker and not directly in communication with the other subsystems. This makes it easier to move the subsystems to distributed computers.

14

14.1 We elaborate user interface and application control classes; we add mechanisms to support data management. The class diagram is also updated with the types and visibility of attributes and operations and to show how associations are designed.

14.2 Private, public, protected or package visibility.

14.3 Attributes should be designated private to enforce encapsulation.

14.7 Collection classes can be used to hold the object identifiers of the linked objects at the many end of an association. Collection classes provide collection-specific behaviour for manipulating the collection.

14.8 A collection class of object identifiers should be included in a class if it is not used by another class and it does not increase the complexity of the class unduly.

14.10 A derived attribute should be used to reduce the processing time for one or more transactions so that user response times are appropriate. However, it should be noted that this may increase the processing time of other transactions in order to ensure that the data integrity is maintained.

15

15.2 The main aspects of changeability are maintainability, extensibility, restructuring and portability.

15.3 The class constructor in the Singleton pattern is private so that it can only be accessed by the class-scope `instance()` method. This ensures that the Singleton class has total control over its own instantiation.

15.4 The Singleton pattern ensures that only one instance of a class exists and provides system-wide access to that instance.

15.7 A pattern catalogue is a group of largely unrelated patterns, which may be used together or independently. A pattern language is a group of related patterns that relate to a particular problem domain.

16

16.3 Dialogue metaphor describes interaction in terms of conversation between user and system involving different kinds of communication. Direct manipulation metaphor represents objects of interest to the user as objects on the screen that they can manipulate through the use of the mouse. Dialogue follows sequence determined by system. Direct manipulation is event-driven, and user can determine sequence of events.

16.6 User may hit Return key without thinking and delete the Client in error.

16.9 Possible advantages: structured–aids management of projects, applies standards that aid communication, forces consideration of all aspects of HCI design; ethnographic–analyst gets detailed understanding of context of system, active user involvement, social and political factors taken into account; scenario-based–helps to think through possible alternative routes in use cases, can be used to justify design decisions, valuable for testing programs. Possible disadvantages: structured–can be bureaucratic; ethnographic–can be time-consuming; scenario-based–generates large volume of documentation.

17.2 A horizontal prototype deals with only one layer of the system architecture, usually the user interface. A vertical prototype takes one subsystem and develops it through each layer.

17.6 We use state machine diagrams to model the lifetime of instances of business classes.

17.8 A list of states, for each state the valid events that can cause a transition from that state, the state that each transition leads to, and any operations associated with the transition into the new state.

17.11 Java `EventListener` only handles changes to interface objects. MVC deals with changes to Model objects. The Java `Observer` and `Observable` interfaces provide MVC mechanisms.

18.3 Tagged data, with a tag for the class of each object and the attribute of each value within each object. This way, it is possible to reconstruct any object from the data in the file without having to hard code the structure of every possible complex object. (This is the approach used by the Java `ObjectOutputStream` and `ObjectInputStream` classes, and by XML and SOAP.)

18.6 1. Remove repeating groups. Ensure all row–column intersections contain only atomic values.
2. Make sure every attribute is dependent on the whole primary key. Create a separate table for part-key dependencies.
3. Ensure every attribute is dependent on the primary key and not on another non-key attribute. Create a separate table for non-key dependencies.

18.8 Object Manipulation Language and Object Definition Language.

19.3 Artefact represents development artefacts, typically physical files that are deployed on a system, whereas a component represents modular software units with a well-defined interface and can be a logical or physical component of the system.

19.7 Possible tests would be to test validation of date, test validation of start time, check validation of job number, line number, product etc. More detailed validation of time could be to check that it is within a certain amount of time of current time–if not, then a warning should be displayed.

19.8 Review of cost–benefit analysis. Summary of functional requirements met and amended. Review of achievement of non-functional requirements. Assessment of user satisfaction. Problems and issues with the system. Extract of quantitative data for future planning. Identification of candidate components for reuse. Possible future developments. Actions required. (See Section 19.9.2 for the detail.)

19.10 Because analysts or designers will have the wider view of the system and can ensure that changes fit in and do not have a detrimental impact on other subsystems.

20.1 Saving time and money in developing the components, saving time and money in testing the components, and creating components that can be recombined to create flexible business processes.

20.3 Jacobson et al. define a component as any artefact produced during systems development constructed to be reusable.

20.6 It considers a component to be an executable unit of code rather than a type or class. It specifies that a component should have an interface, and that it should be capable of being connected together with other components via its interface.

21.1 A methodology is essentially a set of principles. A method is an instantiation of the principles in a given situation.

21.2 A task is something you do in a particular project. Tasks have products. A technique specifies how to carry out a task. A task might be 'Analyse the requirements for a use case'. One technique for doing this would be the UML collaboration diagram.

21.4 A full statement of DSDM Atern would repeat the eight principles—focus on the business need, deliver on time, collaborate, and so on. But perhaps the key feature is the use of time boxing combined with the MoSCoW approach to prioritizing requirements.

21.5 Scrum doesn't agree with UP on much apart from its emphasis on an iterative approach and its implicit acceptance of object-orientation.

Answer Pointers for Selected Case Study Work, Exercises and Projects

1.B Some main subsystems are: online sales, retail shops, supplies, deliveries, systems support and accounts, and more. Some of the control mechanisms involve supplier re-orders, the product catalogue, network performance and security. Most have some human activities and automated support. One example of feedback includes online shoppers, watching the progress of their orders. The market researcher uses feed-forward (what attracts customers to web pages).

1.C Main business aim: say, 'To establish FoodCo as an independent branded name supplying a range of high quality food products to consumers'. Subsidiary aims: diversification of customer base; achievement of international recognition and sales. Each will be translated into measurable objectives: for example, as a basis for the selection of information systems development projects.

2.C Stakeholders should include many of the following. Very good if you listed them all; excellent if you thought of some not shown below (provided you can justify their inclusion). Patients and potential patients, patients' relatives, ambulance drivers, paramedics, control room operators, accident and emergency staff, supervisors of professional stakeholders, managers who control affected budgets, policy level managers, taxpayers (or purchasers of medical insurance policies if this is how the system is funded), general medical practice staff, politicians (particularly if the service is publicly funded), members of the general public (who make the emergency calls), other road users.

3.A An incremental development can be justified for the following reasons:

- Useful increments can be delivered quite quickly. For example, staff management and material tracking could be implemented initially.
- Users can gain experience with the systems.
- Risk is minimized.
- Requirements can be refined in light of the initial increments.

4.A The human activity system referred to is the application domain for the proposed IS. Other human activity systems include the project team, the analyst's department, the business planning system and the wider (political and cultural) system of the organization. The project team probably use various information systems, including CASE tools. Formal and informal structures of communication and relationships are the main interfaces. Other installed software and hardware systems may be important (consider the discussion in Box B1.2).

4.D You should have equivalents for most of the following. The names are not significant at this stage, nor is an exact match in the way that you have grouped concepts together.

```
Factory, Product, ProductRange, PackedProduct, SaladPack, VegetablePack,
CookedProduct, Sauce, Pickle, SandwichTopping, Ingredient, Customer,
Supermarket, Brand, Farm, Supplier, Employee, Consumer.
```

5.A Some kinds of information systems can be used to model the real world in order to try out ideas. For example, decision support systems typically model some aspect of a business and allow staff and managers to ask 'What if?' questions: 'What would happen to demand for a product if the price was increased by 10%?' or 'If we targeted a particular area with a mailshot, what kind of response to our product could we expect, based on what we know about the population of that area?' However, a customer in an information system is not a model of the customer, it is a set of data values that describe attributes of the customer. Also, some things in information systems are the real-world objects. An invoice in a sales order processing system is the real invoice; it is not a model. In object-oriented systems, there is sometimes a belief that the operations of objects are things that those objects do to themselves. (Rumbaugh et al. (1991) suggest operations for a `Bicycle` class, like `move` and `repair`.) Typically the operations of objects are actually operations that we want the system to carry out on those objects, and we package them in the class as a way of organizing the design of the software system.

5.B Designing cars, designing aircraft (models to use in wind tunnels), architecture and town planning, packaging design for products.

6.B Here are some of the use cases that should be in the diagram with the actor in brackets. `Check Staff Availability (Production Planner)`, `Enter Details of Staff Illness (Production Planner)`, `Print Availability Lists (Production Planner)`. There is a need for some means of entering details of staff holidays. The decision about who does this will affect the scope of the system. It could be done by the staff themselves and authorized online by the factory manager, or this process could be done on paper and only authorized holidays entered by the production planners.

7.A The following are sample descriptions for two of the use cases.
Record employee leaving the line

Normally employees are recorded as leaving the line when they clock off at the end of a working shift. Although there are breaks in the operation of the line during a shift these are not normally recorded as employees leaving the line. Date, time and location are recorded.

Stop run

When the production line stops for a routine reason, e.g. for a break, to restock or to reload equipment, the time the run stopped is recorded and a reason is recorded. The line supervisor or chargehand can do this.

7.B For the use case realization for `Record employee leaving the line`, you should have a collaboration involving `Employee`, `Supervisor`, `ProductionLine`, `ProductionLineRun` and `EmployeeAbsence`, as well as a boundary class and a control class.

8.C Possible subclasses include `TelevisionAdvert`, `RadioAdvert`, `MagazineAdvert`, `PosterAdvert`, `LeafletAdvert`. We could introduce another layer of hierarchy by grouping `NewspaperAdvert` and `MagazineAdvert` under `PrintMediaAdvert`, and `TelevisionAdvert` and `RadioAdvert` under `BroadcastMediaAdvert`. (You may have chosen equally valid alternative names.)

8.E Some generalization and composition can be justified by the inclusion of the following classes: `Operative`, `RoutineBreak`, `AbsenceRecord`.

9.A The sequence diagrams should be derivable and consistent with the communication diagrams produced during use case realization when you answered Exercise 7.B. However, you will be adding more detail in terms of message signatures and message types.

9.B Variations in allocations of responsibility will depend upon how much responsibility the control class has and how much is devolved to the entity classes or the boundary classes. At one extreme the control class orchestrates all the functionality of the use case, at the other the control class delegates the complete control of the use case to one of the entity classes. A good design will lie between these extremes.

10.A One of the more complex (and therefore one that is well worth trying) would be `ProductionLineRun.start()`. Preconditions for this operation should be suggested by your use case description.

10.D Most decision tables can be converted easily into Structured English with either case or nested-if. For very simple tables (two outcomes) if-then-else may be enough.

11.A The events that affect `ProductionLine` include `start run`, `end run`, `detect problem`, `pause run`. The possible states for `ProductionLine` include `Idle`, `Running`, `ProblemInterrupted` and `Paused`.

12.A Examples include sequence of entry, branching points (where the user has a choice), repetition of entries (can the user enter more than one holiday at the same time?), commands that the user might need to use while entering data (but not whether they use a menu, function keys or control keys).

12.D In Windows there are many standards, for example: the use of function keys, particularly in combination with Alt and Ctrl keys; the standards for the appearance of menus, for example, menu entries followed by dots ('…') when the menu entry leads to a dialogue box; the positioning of certain buttons in dialogue boxes ('OK' and 'Cancel').

13.D An example would be support for the Zachman Framework in Enterprise Architect from Sparx Systems. There is a plug-in that allows the user to create a six by six matrix, and clicking on the cells in the matrix takes the user to a diagram of the appropriate type.

13.E The FoodCo Production Control System could contain the subsystems Employee Management, Product and Production Line Management.

14.A All attributes should be designated private and operations public. Choose data types that reflect the domains from which the attribute values are selected.

14.B The one-way associations are Line-LineFault. The two-way associations are Supervisor-ProductionLine and Line-LineRun.

15.B The ProductionLine class could use the state pattern with the state subclasses Idle, Running, ProblemInterrupted, Waiting. This use of the state pattern reduces the complexity of the ProductionLine class but may increase the storage and processing requirements for the application as a whole.

16.A See answer pointer to 12.D.

16.C Something along these lines...

First, Rik runs off the three availability lists to show who is available for work the following week. He then starts with operatives who are available all week. For each operative, he views their record on screen, looking at their skills and experience, the line they are currently working on, and how long they have been on that line. He allocates each operative in turn to a line and a session in one of the factories.

This does not provide any detail of actual interaction with the system.

17.A If you are expecting to develop for a windowing environment, you will need a dialogue window as a minimum. Depending on how you handle looking up information, for example a list of valid reasons for stopping the line, you may need separate windows in which to display these look-ups. However, in the factory environment you may want to use a simpler device with an LCD screen for display and a sealed keyboard with dedicated keys. A PC with a mouse may be unnecessary and unsuitable in a messy environment. However, we are assuming a windowing environment for the other exercises in this chapter.

18.B You should end up with the following tables (or similar names): SalesOrder, OrderLine, Customer and Product.

18.F This will be similar to Figure 18.23, with a ClientBroker class to handle the operation to find each Client.

19.B Many libraries now use a web browser to access catalogue services. If this is the case, then your deployment diagram will include the client machines (PCs, Apple Macs or workstations), the web server and probably another machine running the library software. Library staff may access the system from simple terminals for use cases to issue and return books. They will connect directly to the machine running the software, not via the web server. (The actual configuration will depend on your particular system.)

19.E Issues to consider are as follows. Is the manual organized around the tasks a user carries out? Has it got an index? Can you find the terms in the index that you, the user, know, or does it use computer jargon? Does it show screenshots? Are they the same as actual screens or windows in the version you are using? (You should be able to think of other criteria.)

19.F Possible inclusions for bug reports: user name, telephone no., building, room, address etc. Date and time bug occurred. Type of machine on which bug occurred. Operating system of machine. Software in which bug occurred. Other software running at the same time. Program/window/function being used at time of bug. Any error messages displayed for the user. What the user expected to happen. What actually happened. What the user did (key strokes, mouse clicks on buttons or menus etc.) immediately beforehand.

20

20.C You could either include the encryption package within the security package or have it as a separate package. The `core` security classes will need its services and will have a dependency on it. Will it need any kind of user interface classes, for example, if it requires setting up with some kind of parameters? If it does, it will presumably need somewhere to store these parameters, in which case it will also need data storage services.

Glossary

Abstract class a class that can have no instances; a superclass that acts only as a generalized template for its instantiated subclasses.

Abstract data type (ADT) a set of data values and operations that act on them. An ADT is specified formally using mathematical notation. The concept of an ADT is a precursor to object-orientation as it associates operations with a data structure; it is also the essence of encapsulation (*q.v.*). Stack and queue are commonly used examples of ADTs.

Abstract operation an operation that is not implemented in the class in which it appears (usually an abstract superclass), but that will be implemented in a subclass.

Abstraction a simplified representation that contains only those features that are relevant for a particular task; the act of separating out the general or reusable parts of an element of a system from its particular implementation.

Action a step in an activity, used to represent where work is taking place; an executable statement, commonly associated with a state or transition in a state machine.

Activation the execution of an operation, represented in interaction sequence diagrams as a long thin rectangle.

Activity an activity is a group of one or more actions that may execute as a result of a triggering event.

Activity diagram a diagram that shows activities and actions to describe workflows.

Activity edge a flow between elements in an activity.

Activity final node the final node in an activity that terminates the actions in that activity.

Activity partition a column or row in an activity diagram used to show an area of responsibility for the actions in it. Sometimes referred to as a swimlane.

Actor an external entity of any form that interacts with the system. Actors may be physical devices, human roles (rather than individual persons) or information systems.

Adornment an element attached to another model element: for example, a stereotype icon or a constraint.

Aggregation a whole–part association between two or more objects or components, where one represents the whole and the others parts of that whole.

Algorithm a description of the internal logic of a process or decision in terms of a structure of smaller steps. The structure may consist of steps in sequence, selection between alternatives and iteration.

Analysis class stereotype one of three specialized kinds of class (boundary, control and entity classes (*q.v.*)) that feature in analysis class diagrams. These represent a separation of concerns that forms the basis of the architecture recommended for most models developed following UP guidelines (*cf* stereotype).

Antipattern documents unsuccessful attempts at providing solutions to certain recurring problems but includes reworked solutions that are effective.

Artefact a model element used in deployment diagrams representing a file or collection of files containing source code or an executable. (Artifact in US spelling.)

Association a logical connection between two instances. Associations are commonly found between classes, although in some circumstances a class can have an association with itself. An association describes possible links between instances, and may correspond either to logical relationships in the application domain or to message paths in software.

Association class a class that is modelled in order to provide a location for attributes or operations that properly belong to an association between other classes.

Association instance another name for a link (*q.v.*).

Asynchronous message a message that does not cause the invoking operation to halt execution while it awaits the return of control.

Attribute an element of a class where a data item is stored as a value; together with operations, attributes define a class. Describes some property of instances of the class.

Attribute value the value of an attribute that is held by a particular object at a particular time.

Behavioural classifier a UML classifier (*q.v.*) that models a behavioural aspect of a system; for example, a collaboration (*q.v.*).

Behavioural model a UML model that focuses on the behaviour of the elements of an application as opposed to their structure: for example, a use case model.

Behavioural state machine (see *state machine*).

Boundary class a stereotyped class that provides an interface to users or to other systems (see *stereotype*).

Business rule see *enterprise rule*.

Capta data that has been selected for processing because of its relevance to a particular purpose.

Cardinality the number of elements in a set; contrast with *multiplicity* (*q.v.*).

Choice pseudostate allows the splitting of a transition into multiple exit transitions and is a dynamic conditional branch. The guard conditions are evaluated when the transition reaches the choice pseudostate.

Class a descriptor for a collection of objects that are logically similar in terms of their possible behaviour (operations) and the structure of their data (attributes).

Class diagram a UML structure diagram that shows classes with their attributes and operations, together with the associations between classes.

Class Responsibility Collaboration (CRC) CRC cards provide a technique for exploring the possible ways of allocating responsibilities to classes and the collaborations that are necessary to fulfil the responsibilities

Class-scope an element that occurs only once and is attached to the class, not to any individual object. A class-scope attribute or operation is accessed through the class (i.e. prefixed with the class name) not through an object. Model elements that are of class scope are underlined in class diagrams.

Classifier a classifier is a group of abstract model elements that have similar structure. The classifiers in UML are Actors, Artefacts, Classes, Collaborations, Components, Enumerations, Data types, Interfaces, Nodes, Roles, Signals and Use cases.

Cohesion a measure of the degree to which the elements of a component (e.g. a model or class) contribute to a single purpose for the component; regarded as a desirable feature.

Collaboration the structure and links between a group of instances that participate in a behaviour. The behaviour can be that of an operation, a use case or any other behavioural classifier.

Collaboration diagram a UML 1.X term for a communication diagram (see *communication diagram*).

Collection class provides collection-specific behaviour to maintain a collection. Used when designing associations with a many multiplicity to hold collections of object identifiers.

Combined fragment a combined fragment contains one or more interaction operands (or compartments) and is enclosed in a frame; each operand contains an interaction fragment; the meaning of a combined fragment is determined by its interaction operator.

Common Object Request Broker Architecture (CORBA) a mechanism to support the construction of systems in which objects, possibly written in different languages, reside on different machines and are able to interact by message passing.

Communication diagram type of interaction diagram (*q.v.*) that shows an interaction between lifelines (e.g. objects) and the context of the interaction in terms of the links between the lifelines.

Communication path a path between nodes in a deployment diagram that allows communication between the nodes, usually stereotyped with the protocol for the communication.

Component a replaceable part of a system defined primarily in terms of the interfaces that it provides and the interfaces that it requires in order to operate. Components may be executable software modules that have a well-defined interface and identity; they may also be complex model elements that will be realized as free-standing software modules.

Component-Based Development (CBD) an approach to software development that focuses on the use of replaceable components. CBD differs from other development approaches, in particular, through its emphasis on the assembly of software systems from pre-existing components.

Component diagram a diagram that shows the organization of and dependencies among components.

Composite structure diagram a diagram that shows the internal structure of a composite. For instance, a composite structure diagram may be used to show the elements of a collaboration and how the collaboration as a whole interacts with the rest of the system.

Composition a strong form of aggregation with a lifetime dependency between each part and the whole. No part can belong to more than one composition at a time and, if the composite whole is deleted, its parts are deleted with it.

Concrete class a class that may have instances.

Concurrent states if an object may be in two or more states at the same time, then these states are said to be concurrent.

Constructor operation an operation that creates a new instance of a class.

Context (of a pattern) the circumstances in which a particular problem occurs.

Contract a black box description of a service (of a class or subsystem) that specifies the results of the service and the conditions under which it will be provided.

Control class a stereotyped class that controls the interaction between boundary classes and entity classes (see *stereotype*).

Control flow a flow between actions in an activity diagram that indicates the flow from one to another.

Coupling relates to the degree of interconnectedness between design components and is reflected by the number of links and the degree of interaction an object has with other objects.

Critical path analysis (CPA) a diagrammatic technique for analysing the dependencies between project tasks and determining those tasks that must be completed on time if the project itself is to be completed on time.

Data raw facts, not yet identified as relevant to any particular purpose.

Decision node a node in an activity diagram where a flow branches into multiple alternative flows.

Deep history pseudostate shows that a region in a composite state will resume at the last active substate in each of the nested submachines within that region, no matter how deeply nested they are.

Degree another word for *multiplicity (q.v.)*.

Dependency a relationship between two model elements, such that a change in one element may require a change in the dependent element.

Dependency constraint (see *integrity constraint*)

Deployment diagram A diagram that shows the run-time configuration of processing nodes *(q.v.)* and the artefacts that are located on them.

Deployment specification an artefact deployed to a node in a deployment diagram in order to configure other artefacts deployed to the same node.

Design constraint a constraint that limits the design options that may be used. Common design constraints include cost and data storage requirements.

Destructor operation an operation that destroys an instance of a class.

Device a node representing a processor in a deployment diagram.

Diagram a graphical illustration that documents some aspect of a system, not necessarily complete or consistent.

Domain integrity (see *integrity constraint*)

Domain model an analysis class model that is independent of any particular use cases or applications, and that typically contains only entity objects. A domain model may serve as a basis for the analysis and design of components that can be reused in more than one software system.

Encapsulation the practice of locating operations together with the data on which they operate, typically within the same class or component (see also *information hiding* and *abstract data type*).

Enterprise (or business) rule a statement that expresses an association between domain concepts together with any business constraints on its multiplicity: for example, each order is placed by exactly one customer while a customer may place one or more orders.

Entity class a stereotyped class that represents objects in the business domain model (see *stereotype*).

Entry pseudostate shows an exceptional entry point into a submachine state.

Event an occurrence that is of significance to the information system and in some way affects its

operation: for example, by causing a transition in state; may be included in a state machine (*q.v.*).

Exception a mechanism in object-oriented languages for handling errors or unexpected inputs.

Execution or Execution occurrence (see *activation*).

Execution environment a type of node in a deployment diagram representing an implementation environment, container or platform in which an artefact is deployed.

Exit pseudostate an exceptional exit point from a submachine state.

Extend relationship a relationship between use cases where one use case extends or adds optional new actions to another. Written as a stereotype «extend».

Extension point the point in a use case where an extension occurs, based on satisfying some condition.

eXtreme Programming (XP) an approach to systems development that focuses on producing the simplest coding solution for application requirements. One characteristic is the use of pair programming, with code being written by two developers working at a single workstation.

Final node the exit point from an activity diagram.

Final pseudostate a notational convenience used to indicate the final state in a state machine.

Flow final node the node in an activity diagram that

terminates a flow but leaves other flows unaffected.

Forces (of a pattern) the particular issues that must be addressed in resolving a problem.

Fork a node in an activity diagram where a flow is split into multiple parallel flows.

Frame a labelled rectangle that represents the boundary of a diagram; frames may be used for all diagram types but may be omitted where the boundary of the diagram is clear (except for interaction diagrams where a frame must always be used).

Functional requirement a requirement that specifies a part of the functionality required by the user.

Generalization the abstraction of common features among elements (for example, classes) by the creation of a hierarchy of more general elements (for example, superclasses) that contain the common features.

Guard condition a Boolean expression associated with a transition so that the transition only occurs if the condition evaluates as true at the time the event fires. May involve parameters of the triggering event and also attributes and links of the object that owns the state machine.

Implementation diagram a generic term for the UML diagrams used in modelling the implementation of a system.

Include relationship a relationship between use cases where one use case includes the actions described in another use case. Written as a stereotype «include».

Incremental development development and delivery of software in incremental stages, where each increment provides some useful functionality. Some initial analysis scopes the problem and identifies major requirements. These are then reviewed and those that deliver most benefit to the client become the focus of the first increment. The installation of the first increment provides feedback to the team, which informs the second increment and so on.

Information facts that have been selected as relevant to a purpose and then organized or processed in such a way that they have meaning for that purpose.

Information hiding the practice of designing a component (e.g. a module, class or subsystem) so that its internal implementation details are not exposed to other components and its data can be accessed only through its own operations.

Inheritance the mechanism by which object-oriented programming languages implement a relationship of generalization and specialization between classes. A subclass instance automatically acquires features of its superclasses.

Initial node the entry point to an activity diagram.

Initial pseudostate a notational convenience used to indicate the starting state in a state machine. A state machine may not

remain in its initial pseudostate.

Instance usually a single object (also object instance), although the term instance can also be applied to other elements: for example, an association instance is a link. Instances are generally only called such in the context of their membership of a particular class or type.

Instance diagram a UML diagram similar in form to a class diagram, but which contains object instances instead of classes, links instead of associations and may show attribute values (also known as an object diagram).

Integrity constraint ensures that an information system holds data that is mutually consistent and is manipulated correctly. Referential integrity ensures that object identifiers in one object refer only to objects that exist. Dependency constraints ensure that attribute dependencies, where one attribute may be calculated from other attributes, are maintained consistently. Domain integrity ensures that attributes hold only permissible values.

Interaction defines the message passing between lifelines (e.g. objects) within the context of a collaboration to achieve a particular behaviour.

Interaction constraint a Boolean expression that must be true before the interaction fragment in the combined fragment region it guards can execute.

Interaction diagram an umbrella term for sequence, communication, timing and interaction overview diagrams.

Interaction fragment a part of an interaction shown on a separate sequence diagram.

Interaction occurrence is replaced by the term InteractionUse (*q.v.*) in UML 2.2.

Interaction operand a compartment in a combined fragment; contains an interaction fragment.

Interaction operator determines the meaning of a combined fragment: for example, the interaction operator 'loop' indicates that the combined fragment specifies an iteration.

Interaction overview diagram a variant of an activity diagram that incorporates interaction diagrams. An interaction overview diagram focuses on the flow of control in an interaction where the nodes in the diagram are interactions or interaction occurrences.

Interaction sequence diagram (see *sequence diagram*)

Interaction use a frame that does not show the detail of an interaction fragment, but refers to another sequence diagram (an interaction fragment) that does show this detail. A mechanism to hide complex detail that may be included in a sequence diagram or an interaction overview diagram.

Interface that part of the boundary between two interacting systems through which they communicate; the set of all signatures for the public operations of a class, package or component.

Interface class a class via which a system can interact with its actors (see also *boundary class*).

Invariant an aspect of a UML model expressed as a formal statement that must always remain true. For example, the value of a derived attribute totalCost must always be equal to the total of all cost attribute values. Usually expressed in OCL (*q.v.*).

Join a node in an activity diagram where multiple parallel flows are merged into a single flow.

Junction pseudostate a junction between transitions in a state machine diagram that allows the merging or splitting of transitions.

Knowledge a complex structure of information that allows its possessor to decide how to behave in particular situations.

Legacy system a computerized information system, probably in use for a long time and built with technologies that are now outmoded (perhaps also using different technologies and/or development approaches at different times)–but that continues to deliver benefit to the organization.

Lifecycle (of a project) the phases through which a development project passes from the inception of the idea through to the completion and use of the product and its eventual decommissioning.

Lifeline represents the period of existence of a modelling element (e.g. object, subsystem) in an interaction diagram.

Link a connection between objects; an instance of an association.

Merge a node in an activity diagram where alternative flows created at a decision node merge back to a single flow.

Message a request to an object for it to provide some specified service, either an action that it can carry out or information that it can provide. A message invokes an operation or service.

Message passing a metaphor for the way that objects interact in an object-oriented system by sending each other messages that request services, or request or supply information. Since objects interact only through the messages they exchange, their internal details need not be exposed (see *information hiding*).

Method the implementation of an operation; the instantiation of a methodology (*q.v.*) on a specific project.

Methodology a framework that describes an overall approach to software development; typically comprises a programming paradigm (e.g. object-orientation), a set of techniques and notations (e.g. UML) that support the approach, a lifecycle model (e.g. spiral and incremental) with phases that structure the development process, and a unifying set of procedures and philosophy. Examples include UP and Scrum.

Model a complete view of a system at a particular stage of development and from a particular perspective: for example, an analysis model shows the logical specification for a system, while an implementation model shows the detailed allocation of software components to processors and network nodes.

Model Driven Architecture (MDA) an OMG initiative and an approach to developing systems in which a platform-independent architectural model (*q.v.*) is produced and transformed into a platform-specific model (*q.v.*) from which code can be generated.

Modular construction an approach that aims to build component-based systems that are easy to maintain, modify or extend. Relies on software modules that are essentially decoupled (see *coupling*) subsystems, with their internal details hidden from other modules.

Multiplicity a constraint that specifies the range of permitted *cardinalities* (*q.v.*), for example, in an association role or in a composite class. For example, an association may have a multiplicity of between 1 and 5 (written as 1..5), and a particular instance of that association may have a cardinality of 3.

Node (in activity diagram) a diagram element that typically represents an action, a decision, or the start or end of the overall activity. Nodes are connected to each other by paths called object flows and control flows (*q.v.*)

Node (in deployment diagram) a physical computational resource used by a system at run-time, typically having processing capability and memory in a deployment diagram.

Non-functional requirement a requirement that relates to system features that cannot be expressed in the form of specific functions, such as performance, maintainability and portability.

Normalization a technique that groups attributes based upon functional dependencies according to several rules to produce normalized data structures that are largely redundancy free.

Object a single thing or concept, either in a model of an application domain or in a software system, that can be represented as an encapsulation (*q.v.*) of state, behaviour and identity; a member of a class that defines a set of similar objects.

Object constraint language (OCL) a specification language designed to accompany UML and that can be used to define elements of a model, their behaviour (such as operations), constraints (such as guard conditions), etc. with greater rigour than is possible in the purely graphical language of UML itself.

Object diagram (see *instance diagram*).

Object flow flow between an object and an action or activity in an activity diagram, that indicates that the object is used or its state is changed by the action or activity.

Operation an aspect of the behaviour that defines a class; an element of the services that are provided by a class; a specification (often written in OCL, *q.v.*) of an element of system functionality that will be implemented as a method.

Operation signature the interface to an operation, defined by the operation's name, the number and type of its parameters and the type of the return value, if any. Polymorphically redefined operations have the same signature.

Package a mechanism for grouping UML elements, usually classes, into groups. Packages can be nested within other packages.

Pattern an abstract solution to a commonly occurring problem in a given context.

Phase a distinct period of time in the lifecycle of a development project, marked by a particular focus of activity and often also by deliverables that are characteristic of that phase. For example, during the elaboration phase in UP, activity concentrates on producing a design for a suitable system that demonstrates how it can be built within an acceptable timescale and budget.

Platform-independent model (PIM) a model produced in model-driven architecture (*q.v.*) that is independent of a development or deployment environment.

Platform-specific model (PSM) a model produced in model-driven architecture (*q.v.*) that is generated from a platform-independent model (*q.v.*) for a particular deployment environment.

Polymorphism the ability of different methods to implement the same operation, and thus to respond to the same message in different ways that are appropriate to their class. For example, objects of different subclasses in an inheritance hierarchy may respond differently to the same message, yet with a common meaning to their responses.

Post-condition part of an operation specification or used in a protocol state machine; those conditions that must be true after the operation has executed or a transition has fired—in other words, the valid results of the operation or the completion of the transition.

Pre-condition part of an operation specification or used in a protocol state machine; those conditions that must be true before the operation can execute in an operation specification or before a transition may fire in a protocol state machine.

Primary operation an operation to create or destroy an instance of a class, or to get or set the value of an attribute.

Procedural call (see *synchronous message*).

Processing node a node in a deployment diagram.

Property a feature or characteristic of a UML element, usually one for which there is no specific UML notation.

Protocol state machine (see *state machine*).

Prototype a system or partially complete system that is built quickly to explore some aspect of the system requirements. Usually not intended as the final working system, but in some development approaches a prototype may be iteratively refined to become the final working system.

Query operation an operation that returns data or information but causes no change of state within a model or a software system.

Realize relationship a relationship between two elements where one is in some sense an implementation of the other, although it may not necessarily have the same structure. Commonly used to show that a class supports an interface or that a collaboration implements a use case. Written as a stereotype «realize».

Refactoring to restructure and simplify program code so that duplication is removed and flexibility is enhanced.

Referential integrity (see *integrity constraint*).

Relation a group of related data items organized in columns and rows, also known as a table.

Reply a return of control to the object that originated the message that began the activation.

Repository that part of a CASE or modelling tool environment that handles the storage of models, including diagrams, specifications and definitions.

Responsibility a high-level description of the behaviour of a class or component. Primarily reflects the services that it can offer to other elements, and also the knowledge or information that is available to it, either stored internally or requested via collaboration with other elements.

Reuse the assembly of all or part of a new software system from elements, components or abstractions that already exist. Reuse can refer to binary software, designs or specifications, or to more abstract features such as elements in a generalization hierarchy.

Semantics the meaning of an element, diagram, model or expression, as distinct from the syntactic rules that determine whether it is valid UML. Semantics can apply at a relatively abstract level: for example, an association between two classes signifies that there can be links between their instances. Semantics can also apply at an application- or domain-related level: for example, in a typical bank

application it is not meaningful for an account to be associated with more than one customer.

Sequence diagram (or **interaction sequence diagram**) shows an interaction between objects arranged in a time sequence. Sequence diagrams can be drawn at different levels of detail and also to meet different purposes at several stages in the development lifecycle.

Service a useful function (or set of functionality) that is carried out by an object, component or subsystem when requested to do so by another object or component.

Service oriented architecture (SOA) an approach to systems architecture that relies on defining loosely-coupled components that can interact by exchanging requests for services over a network.

Shallow history pseudostate shows that a region in a composite state in a state machine will resume at the last active substate at the level of the shallow history pseudostate.

Signal (see *asynchronous message*).

SOAP (formerly Simple Object Access Protocol) a protocol used in the provision of web services to define message format and other aspects of the exchange between the client application and the server.

Software architecture describes the subsystems and components of a software system and the relationships between the components.

Specialization the other face of generalization; an element (for example, a class) is said to be specialized when it has a set of characteristics that uniquely distinguish it from other elements. Distinguishes subclasses from their superclass.

Stakeholders anyone who is affected by the information system. Stakeholders include not only users and development team members, but also resource managers and the quality assurance team, for example.

State the state of an object is determined by values of some of its attributes and the presence or absence of certain links with other objects. It reflects a particular condition for the object and normally persists for a period of time until a transition to another state is triggered by an event.

State machine a model of states and state-dependent behaviour for a modelling element (e.g. object, subsystem, port, interface) and for interactions. There is a distinction between protocol and behavioural state machines. Protocol state machines only show all the legal transitions with their pre- and post-conditions. Behavioural state machines include activity expressions to show the actions that result from triggering events.

Static conditional branch (see *junction pseudostate*).

Stereotype a specialized UML modelling element. The stereotype name is contained within matched guillemets «. . .». For example, an interface package is a stereotype of a package and an entity class is a stereotype of a class.

Structural model a UML model that focuses on the structure of the elements of an application as opposed to their behaviour: for example, a class or component model.

Subclass a specialized class that acquires general features from its ancestor superclasses in a generalization hierarchy, but that also adds one or more specialized characteristics of its own.

Subsystem a part of a system that can be regarded as a system in its own right.

Superclass a generalized class that is an abstraction of the common characteristics of its subclasses in a generalization hierarchy.

Swimlane (see *activity partition*).

Synchronizing operation an operation that ensures that those attribute values which are dependent upon each other (e.g. may be calculated from each other) have consistent values.

Synchronous message or **procedural call** causes the invoking operation to suspend execution until control has been returned to it.

Syntax the rules that determine whether an element, diagram, model or expression is valid UML. For example, an association must connect two typed instances, and must have at least two ends, each of which must be connected to the type at that end. Syntax differs from semantics (*q.v.*) in that it is concerned only with the formal rules for a technically valid model, and not for whether the model actually means what it should mean.

System an abstraction of a complex interacting set of elements, for which it is possible to identify a boundary, an environment, inputs and outputs, a control mechanism and some process or transformation that the system achieves.

Table group of related data items organized in columns and rows. Used to store data in relational databases.

Task a specific activity or step in a project.

Technique a method for carrying out a project task.

Template collaboration a parameterized collaboration which may be implemented (that is, instantiated) with different classes or objects.

Timing diagram type of interaction diagram that shows the state changes for one or more lifelines, typically those with important time-dependent behaviour; messages between lifelines may be shown.

Transaction an elementary exchange, say of an item of capta (*q.v.*) or of a unit of value; a complex database function involving updates to several objects, such that if any single update were to fail the entire function must be rolled back, with all involved objects being restored to their initial state to ensure that the database is left in a consistent state overall.

Transition the movement from one state or activity to another, triggered by an event. A transition may start and end at the same state.

Trigger an event that is capable of causing a transition to fire.

Type a stereotype of class that is distinct from an implementation class; a type is defined by attributes and operations but, since it is a pure specification, may not have methods. Classes that represent application domain concepts are in fact types. An object may change type dynamically during system execution, and may thus appear at different times to belong to different classes.

Usability requirement user requirement that describes criteria by which the ease of use of the system can be judged.

Use case describes, from a user's perspective, a behaviourally related set of transactions that are normally performed together to produce some value for the user. Use cases can be represented graphically in a use case diagram, each use case being described in the repository. Use cases may be modelled at varying degrees of abstraction: essential use cases, the most abstract, are technologically and implementation independent, whereas real use cases describe how the use case actually operates in a particular environment.

Use case realization a set of model elements that show the structure and behaviour of the software that corresponds to the use case—usually a collaboration or class diagram.

User requirement something that users require a software system to do (functional requirement); alternatively, a standard for the performance of a system (nonfunctional requirement).

User story in eXtreme Programming requirements are captured as user stories. A user story is similar to a use case.

Value (see *attribute value*).

Vertex (plural vertices) a node in a state machine diagram.

Visibility UML modelling elements (e.g. attributes or operations) may be designated with different levels of accessibility or visibility. Public visibility means that the element is directly accessible by any class; private visibility means that the element may only be used by the class that it belongs to; protected visibility means that the element may only be used by either the class that includes it or a subclass of that class; and package visibility means that an element is visible to objects in the package.

Web service a mechanism that allows one application to provide a service to other applications over the web, involving messages that are transmitted using a protocol such as SOAP (*q.v.*). Many web services present an interface that includes a machine-readable definition of the services that they provide.

Web Service Definition Language (WSDL) a language based on XML that has been specialised for use in defining web services; a client application can read the WSDL definition of a web service to discover the operations that are available together with their signatures.

Workflow in UP, a set of activities carried out by members of the development team aimed at creating models with a particular focus, for example requirements or implementation.

Wrapper or object wrapper, used to integrate object-oriented and non-object-oriented systems by encapsulating the non-object-oriented system with an object-oriented style of interface.

Bibliography

Adams, D., *The Restaurant At The End Of The Universe*, London: Pan Books, 1980.

AgileAlliance, 'The Agile Manifesto', 2002, at www.agilemanifesto.org/.

Ahern, D. M., Clouse, A. and Turner, R., *CMMI Distilled: A Practical Introduction to Integrated Process Improvement*, Reading, MA: Addison-Wesley Professional, 2001.

Alexander, C., Ishikawa, S., Silverstein, M., Jacobson, M., Fiksdahl-King, I. and Angel, S., *A Pattern Language: Towns, Buildings, Construction*, New York: Oxford University Press, 1977.

Allen, P. and Frost, S., *Component-Based Development for Enterprise Systems: Applying the SELECT Perspective™*, Cambridge: Cambridge University Press; SIGS Books, 1998.

Allison, B., O'Sullivan, T., Owen, A., Rice, J., Rothwell, A. and Saunders, C., *Research Skills for Students*, London: Kogan Page, 1996.

Alur, D., Crupi, J. and Malks, D., *Core J2EE Patterns: Best Practices and Design Strategies* (2nd edn), Upper Saddle River, NJ: Prentice Hall and Sun Microsystems Press, 2003.

Ambler, S. W., *The Object Primer: Agile Model-Driven Development with UML 2.0*, Cambridge: Cambridge University Press, 2004.

Ambler S. W., *Agile Unified Process (AUP)*, 2009, at www.ambysoft.com/unifiedprocess/agileUP.html

Ambler S. W., John Nalbone J. and Vizdos M., *The Enterprise Unified Process: Extending the Rational Unified Process*, Upper Saddle River, NJ: Prentice Hall, 2005.

ANSI, *American National Standard for Information Systems: Database Language SQL*, ANSI X3,135-1986. New York: ANSI, 1986.

Apperly, H., Hofman, R., Latchem, S., Maybank, B., McGibbon, B., Piper, D. and Simons, C., *Service- And Component-Based Development: Using the Select Perspective and UML*, Harlow: Addison-Wesley / Pearson Education, 2003.

Apple Computer Inc., *Macintosh Human Interface Guidelines*, Reading, MA: Addison-Wesley, 1996.

Avison, D. and Fitzgerald, G., *Information Systems Development: Methodologies, Techniques and Tools* (4th edn), Maidenhead: McGraw-Hill, 2006.

Barker, C., 'London Ambulance Service gets IT right', *Computing*, 25 June 1998.

Bass, L., Clements, P. and Kazman, R., *Software Architecture in Practice* (2nd edn), Upper Saddle River, NJ: Software Engineering Institute; Addison-Wesley, 2003.

BBC, 'Barclays re-opens online banking site', 31 July 2000 at news.bbc.co.uk/1/hi/business/860104.stm

BBC, 'Greece puts brakes on Street View', 12 May 2009 at news.bbc.co.uk/1/hi/technology/8045517.stm

BCS, 'Code of Conduct', 2009, at www.bcs.org/server.php?show=nav.6030

Beck, K., *Extreme Programming Explained: Embracing Change*, Reading, MA: Addison-Wesley, 2004.

Beck, K. and Cunningham, W., 'A laboratory for teaching object-oriented thinking', *Proceedings of OOPSLA '89*, pp. 1–6, 1989.

Bell, D., *The Coming Of Post-Industrial Society*, New York: Basic Books, 1973. Cited in Webster (1995).

Bellin, D. and Simone, S. S., *The CRC Card Book*, Reading, MA: Addison-Wesley, 1997.

Bennett, S., Skelton, J. and Lunn, K., *Schaum's Outline of UML* (2nd edn), Maidenhead: McGraw-Hill, 2005.

Beveridge, T., 'Java Documentation', in *Java Unleashed*, Indianapolis: Sams.net Publishing, 1996.

Boehm, B. W., *Software Engineering Economics*, Englewood Cliffs, NJ: Prentice-Hall, 1981.

Boehm, B. W., 'A Spiral Model of Software Development and Enhancement', in Thayer, R. H. (ed.), *Tutorial: Software Engineering Project Management*, Los Alamitos, CA: IEEE Computer Society Press, 1988.

Boehm, B. W., 'Get Ready for Agile Methods, with Care', *IEEE Computer*, **35** (1), pp. 64–69, 2002.

Booch, G., *Object-Oriented Analysis and Design with Applications* (2nd edn), Menlo Park, CA: Benjamin/Cummings, 1994.

Booch, G., Rumbaugh, J. and Jacobson, I., *The Unified Modeling Language User Guide*, Reading, MA: Addison-Wesley; ACM Press, 1999.

Booth, P., *An Introduction to Human-Computer Interaction*, Hove: Lawrence Erlbaum Associates, 1989.

Brown, K. and Whitenack, B. G., 'Crossing Chasms: A Pattern Language for Object-RDBMS Integration', in Vlissides, J. M., Coplien, J. O. and Kerth, N. L. (eds) *Pattern Languages of Programme Design 2*, pp. 227–238, Reading, MA: Addison-Wesley, 1996.

Brown, W. J., Malveau, R. C., McCormick, H. W. and Mowbray, T. J., *AntiPatterns: Refactoring Software, Architectures and Projects in Crisis*, New York, NY: John Wiley, 1998.

Browne, D., *STUDIO: Structured User-interface Design for Interaction Optimization*, Hemel Hempstead: Prentice-Hall, 1994.

Budgen, D., *Software Design*, Reading, MA: Addison-Wesley, 1994.

Buschmann, F., Meunier, R., Rohnert, H., Sommerlad, P. and Stal, M., *Pattern Oriented Software Architecture Volume 1*, Chichester: John Wiley, 1996.

Carroll, J. M. (ed.), *Scenario-Based Design: Envisioning Work and Technology in System Development*, New York: John Wiley, 1995.

Cattell, R. G. G., Barry, D. K., Berler, M., Eastman, J., Jordan, D., Russell, C., Schadow, O., Stanienda, T. and Velez, F. (eds) *The Object Data Standard: ODMG 3.0*, San Francisco: Morgan Kaufmann, 2000.

Checkland, P., *Systems Thinking, Systems Practice*, Chichester: John Wiley, 1981.

Checkland, P., unpublished presentation given at *Systems for Sustainability: People, Organisations and Environments*, 5th International Conference of the United Kingdom Systems Society, Milton Keynes: The Open University, July 1997.

Checkland, P. and Holwell, S., *Information, Systems and Information Systems: Making Sense Of The Field*, Chichester: John Wiley, 1998.

Checkland, P. and Scholes, J., *Soft Systems Methodology In Action*, Chichester: John Wiley, 1990.

Cheesman, J. and Daniels, J., *UML Components: A Simple Process for Specifying Component-Based Software*, Upper Saddle River, NJ: Addison-Wesley, 2001.

Claret J., 'Why Numbers Are Not Enough', *Accounting Technician: The Journal of the Association of Accounting Technicians*, pp. 24–25, October 1990.

Coad, P. with North, D. and Mayfield, M., *Object Models: Strategies, Patterns and Applications* (2nd edn), Upper Saddle River, NJ: Yourdon Press; Prentice-Hall, 1997.

Coad, P. and Yourdon, E., *Object-Oriented Analysis* (2nd edn), Englewood Cliffs, NJ: Yourdon Press; Prentice-Hall, 1990.

Coad, P. and Yourdon, E., *Object-Oriented Design*, Englewood Cliffs, NJ: Yourdon Press; Prentice-Hall, 1991.

Cockburn, A., *Writing Effective Use Cases*, Reading, MA: Addison-Wesley, 2000.

Codd, E. J., 'A Relational Model for Large Shared Data Banks', *Communications of the ACM*, **13** (6), pp. 377–387, 1970. (Also **26** (1), pp. 64–69, 1983)

Coleman, D., Arnold, P., Bodoff, S., Dollin, C., Gilchrist, H., Hayes, F. and Jeremaes, P., *Object-Oriented Development: The Fusion Method*, Englewood Cliffs, New Jersey: Prentice-Hall International, 1994.

Collins, T., 'Banking's Big Brother option', *Computer Weekly*, 19 November 1998a.

Collins, T., 'MPs lambast NHS for double project fiasco', *Computer Weekly*, 12 December 1998b.

Collins, T., 'Lords inquiry to follow up Chinook campaign', *Computer Weekly*, 8 March 2001.

Collins, T., 'New disclosures will be made shortly on Chinook crash on the Mull of Kintyre in 1994', *Computer Weekly*, 2 June 2007 at www.computerweekly.com/cgi-bin/mt/mt-tb.cgi/7131.

Connolly, T. and Begg, C., *Database Systems: A Practical Approach to Design, Implementation, and Management* (5th edn), Boston, MA: Pearson Education Inc., 2010.

Connor, D., *Information System Specification And Design Road Map*, Englewood Cliffs, NJ: Prentice-Hall, 1985.

Constantine, L., 'The Case for Essential Use Cases', *Object Magazine*, May 1997.

Cook, S. and Daniels, J., *Designing Object Systems: Object-Oriented Modelling With Syntropy*, Hemel Hempstead: Prentice-Hall, 1994.

Coplien J. O., *Advanced C++: Programming Styles and Idioms*, Reading, MA: Addison-Wesley, 1992.

Coplien, J. O., 'A Generative Development Process Pattern Language', in Coplien, J. O. and Schmidt, D. C. (eds), *Pattern Languages of Program Design*, Reading, MA: Addison-Wesley, 1995.

Coplien, J. O., *Software Patterns*, New York: SIGS Books, 1996.

Coplien, J. O. and Schmidt, D. C. (eds), *Pattern Languages of Program Design*, Reading, MA: Addison-Wesley, 1995.

Cunningham, W., 'The CHECKS Pattern Language of Information Integrity', in Coplien, J. O. and Schmidt, D. C. (eds), *Pattern Languages of Program Design*, Reading, MA: Addison-Wesley, 1995.

Daniels, G., Davis, D., Nakamura, Y., Simeonov, S., Boubez, T., Graham, S. and Brittenham, P., *Building Web Services with Java: Making Sense of XML, Soap, WSDL and UDDI*, Que, 2004.

Daniels, J., unpublished presentation given at *Migrating to Object Technology*, TattOO '95, Leicester: De Montfort University, January 1995.

Date, C. J. and Darwen, H., *Foundation for Object/Relational Databases: The Third Manifesto*, Reading, MA: Addison-Wesley, 1998.

de Champeaux, D., *Object-Oriented Development Process and Metrics*, Upper Saddle River, NJ: Prentice Hall, 1997.

Deitel, H. M. and Deitel, P. J., *Java: How to Program* (7th edn), Upper Saddle River, NJ: Prentice-Hall, 2007.

DeMarco, T., *Structured Analysis and System Specification*, Upper Saddle River, NJ: Yourdon Press; Prentice-Hall, 1979.

DeMarco, T., *Controlling Software Projects*, Englewood Cliffs, NJ: Yourdon Press, 1982.

DeMarco, T. and Boehm, B., 'The Agile Methods Fray', *Software Technologies*, June 2002.

Disability Rights Commission, *Code of Practice Rights of Access: services to the public, public authority functions, private clubs and premises*, London: The Stationery Office, 2006.

Dix, A., Finlay, J., Abowd, G. and Beale, R., *Human–Computer Interaction* (3rd edn), Hemel Hempstead: Prentice-Hall, 2003.

Douglass B. P., *Real-Time UML: Advances in the UML for Real-time Systems* (3rd edn), Reading, MA: Addison-Wesley, 2004.

Drummond, H., 'The politics of risk: trials and tribulations of the Taurus project', *Journal of Information Technology*, **11**, pp. 347–357, 1996.

DSDM Consortium, *DSDM Atern Pocketbook*, Ashford: DSDM Consortium, 2007.

DSDM Consortium / Stapleton, J. (ed.), *DSDM: Business Focused Development* (2nd edn), Harlow: Addison Wesley/Pearson Education, 2003.

Eaglestone, B. and Ridley, M., *Object Databases: An Introduction*, Maidenhead: McGraw-Hill, 1998.

e-GIF, *e-Government Interoperability Framework* (Version 6.0), Office of the e-Envoy, 2004.

Eriksson, H.-E. and Penker, M., *UML Toolkit*, New York: John Wiley, 1998.

Erl, T., *Service-Oriented Architecture: Concepts, A Field Guide to Integrating XML and Web Services*, Upper Saddle River, NJ: Prentice Hall, 2004.

Erl, T., *Service-Oriented Architecture: Concepts, Technology and Design*, Upper Saddle River, NJ: Prentice Hall, 2005.

Erl, T., *SOA Design Patterns*, Upper Saddle River, NJ: Prentice Hall, 2009.

Fedorov, A., *A Programmer's Guide to .Net*, London: Addison-Wesley, 2002.

Ferry, G. 'A Computer Called LEO: Lyons Tea Shops and the World's First Office Computer', HarperPerennial, 2004.

Fitzgerald, B., Russo, N. L. and Stolterman, E., *Information Systems Development: Methods in Action*, Maidenhead: McGraw-Hill, 2002.

Flowers, S., 'IS Project Risk–The Role of Management in Project Failure', *Proceedings of BIT '97*, Manchester Metropolitan University, November 1997.

Flynn, D., *Information Systems Requirements: Determination And Analysis* (2nd edn), Maidenhead: McGraw-Hill, 1998.

Fowler, M., *Analysis Patterns: Reusable Object Models*, Reading, MA: Addison-Wesley, 1997.

Fowler, M., *Refactoring: Improving the Design of Existing Code*, Boston: Addison Wesley Professional, 1999.

Fowler, M., *UML Distilled: A Brief Guide To The Standard Object Modeling Language* (3rd edn), Reading, MA: Addison-Wesley, 2003.

Fowler, M., 'The New Methodology', 2004, at www.martinfowler.com/articles/newMethodology.html.

Gabriel, R., *Patterns of Software: Tales from the Software Community*, New York: Oxford University Press, 1996.

Gaines, B. R. and Shaw, M. L. G., 'Dialogue engineering', in Sime, M. E. and Coombs, M. J. (eds), *Designing for Human-Computer Communication*, London: Academic Press, 1983.

Galin, D., *Software Quality Assurance: From Theory to Implementation*, Harlow: Addison Wesley/Pearson Education, 2003.

Gamma, E., Helm, R., Johnson, R. and Vlissides, J. M., *Design Patterns: Elements of Reusable Object-Oriented Software*, Reading, MA: Addison-Wesley, 1995.

Garland, J. and Anthony, R., *Large-Scale Software Architecture: A Practical Guide Using UML*, Chichester: John Wiley, 2003.

Gilb, T., *Principles of Software Engineering Management*, Wokingham: Addison-Wesley, 1988.

Goodland, M. with Slater, C., *SSADM Version 4: A Practical Approach*, Maidenhead: McGraw-Hill, 1995.

Google, 'Street View, Privacy & You', *GoogleChannelUK*, 9 March 2009, at www.youtube.com/watch?v=zVvtii5j_d4

Goss, E. P., Buelow, V. and Ramchandani, H., 'The Real Impact of a Point-of-Care Computer System on ICU Nurses', *Journal of Systems Management*, pp. 43–47, January/February 1995.

Greenbaum, J. and Kyng, M., *Design at Work: Cooperative Design of Computer Systems*, Hillsdale, NJ: Lawrence Erlbaum Associates, 1991.

Hammersley, M. and Atkinson, P., *Ethnography: Principles in Practice* (2nd edn), London: Routledge, 1995.

Harel, D., 'Statecharts: a visual formalism for complex systems', *Science of Computer Programming*, **8**, pp. 231–274, 1987.

Harel, D., 'On visual formalisms', *Communications of the ACM*, **31** (5), pp. 514–530, 1988.

Harel, D. and Politi, M., *Modeling Reactive Systems with Statecharts: The Statemate Approach*, New York, NY: McGraw-Hill, 1998.

Harrison, N., Foote, B. and Rohnert, H., *Pattern Languages of Program Design 4*, Addison Wesley, 2000.

Hart, A., *Knowledge Acquisition for Expert Systems*, London: Kogan Page, 1989. (New edition 1997 published by Chapman & Hall.)

Hatley, D. J. and Pirbhai, I. A., *Strategies for Real-Time Systems Design*, New York: Dorset House, 1987.

Hay, D., *Data Model Patterns Conventions of Thought*, New York: Dorset House, 1996.

Health and Safety Executive, *Work with Display Screen Equipment*, Publication No. L26, Sudbury: HSE Books, 2003.

Heineman, G. T. and Councill, W. T., *Component-Based Software Engineering: Putting the Pieces Together*, Reading, MA: Addison-Wesley Professional, 2001.

Hicks, M. J., *Problem Solving in Business and Management*, London: Chapman & Hall, 1991.

Hoffer, J. A., George, J. F. and Valacich, J. S., *Modern Systems Analysis and Design* (4th edn), Upper Saddle River, NJ: Prentice Hall, 2005.

Hopkins, T. and Horan, B., *Smalltalk: an introduction to application development using VisualWorks*, Hemel Hempstead: Prentice-Hall, 1995.

Horrocks, I., *Constructing the User Interface with Statecharts*, Harlow: Addison-Wesley, 1999.

Howe, D. R., *Data Analysis for Data Base Design* (3rd edn), Oxford: Butterworth-Heinemann, 2001.

Humphrey, W. S., *Managing the Software Process*, Wokingham: Addison-Wesley, 1989.

Hyde, M., 'Boo rises from the ashes', *Guardian*, 3 November 2000.

IBM, *IBM San Francisco Base*, Rochester, MN: IBM, 1998.

IBM, *IBM-Rational Unified Process*, 2009, at www-306.ibm.com/software/rational/index.html or www-130.ibm.com/developerworks/rational/products/rup/.

ICO, 'Common sense on Street View must prevail', 23 April 2009, at www.ico.gov.uk/upload/documents/pressreleases/2009/google_streetview_220409_v2.pdf.

IEEE, 'IEEE Recommended Practice for Architectural Description of Software-Intensive Systems', in *Standard 1471–2000*, IEEE, 2000.

Jackson, M., *Principles of Program Design*, London: Academic Press, 1975.

Jacobson, I., Booch, G. and Rumbaugh, J., *The Unified Software Development Process*, Reading, MA: Addison-Wesley; ACM Press, 1999.

Jacobson, I., Christerson, M., Jonsson, P. and Övergaard, G., *Object-Oriented Software Engineering: A Use Case Driven Approach*, Wokingham: Addison-Wesley, 1992.

Jacobson, I., Ericsson, M. and Jacobson, A., *The Object Advantage: Business Process Reengineering with Object Technology*, New York, NY: ACM Press, 1995.

Jacobson, I., Griss, M. and Jonsson, P., *Software Reuse: Architecture, Process and Organization for Business Success*, Harlow: Addison-Wesley, 1997.

JCP (Java Community Process), *JSR-000243 Java Data Objects 2.2 Maintenance Release 2*, Sun Microsystems, 2008.

Jeffries, R., *Essential XP: Documentation*, XProgramming.com, 2001, at http://www.xprogramming. com/xpmag/expDocumentationInXP.htm.

Johnston, S., *Rational UML Profile for business modeling*, IBM, 2004 at www.ibm.com/developerworks/rational/library/5167.html.

Kelly, N., 'High failure rate hits IT projects', *Computing*, 20 August 2007.

Kendall, K. E. and Kendall, J. E., *Systems Analysis and Design* (6th edn), Upper Saddle River, NJ: Prentice Hall, 2005.

Knapton, S., 'Pilots were responsible for Mull of Kintyre helicopter crash', *Daily Telegraph*, 8 December 2008, at http://www.telegraph.co.uk/news/newstopics/politics/scotland/3686316/Pilots-were-responsible-for-Mull-of-Kintyre-helicopter-crash.html.

Koestler, A., *The Ghost in the Machine*, London: Hutchinson, 1967.

Kroll, P. and Kruchten, P., *The Rational Unified Process Made Easy: A Practitioner's Guide to the RUP*, Boston: Addison-Wesley, 2003.

Kruchten, P., *The Rational Unified Process: An Introduction*, Reading, MA: Addison-Wesley, 2004.

Larman, C., *Agile and Iterative Development: A Manager's Guide*, Boston, MA: Addison Wesley/Pearson Education, 2003.

Larman, C., *Applying UML and Patterns: An Introduction to Object-Oriented Analysis and Design and Iterative Development* (3rd edn), Upper Saddle River, NJ: Prentice-Hall, 2005.

Lethbridge, T. and Laganiere, R., *Object-Oriented Software Engineering* (2nd edn), Maidenhead: McGraw Hill Education, 2003.

Loomis, M. E. S., *Object Databases: The Essentials*, Reading, MA: Addison-Wesley, 1995.

Lorenz, M. and Kidd, J., *Object-Oriented Software Metrics: A Practical Guide*, Englewood Cliffs, NJ: Prentice-Hall, 1994.

Maciaszek, L. A., *Requirements Analysis and Design* (2nd edn), Harlow: Addison Wesley/Pearson Education, 2005.

Maguire, M., *RESPECT User Requirements Framework Handbook*, European Usability Support Centres, 1997.

Manolescu, D., Voelter, M., Noble, J., *Pattern Languages of Program Design 5*, Reading, MA: Addison-Wesley, 2006.

Martin, D., Riehle, D. and Buschmann, F. (eds), *Pattern Languages of Program Design 3*, Reading, MA: Addison-Wesley, 1998.

McBride, N., 'Business Use of the Internet: Strategic Decision or Another Bandwagon?', *European Management Journal*, **15**, pp. 58–67, 1997.

McGrath, M., *Java in Easy Steps* (3rd edn), Computer Step, 2007.

McKay, E. N., *Developing User Interfaces Microsoft for Windows*, Redmond, WA: Microsoft Press, 1999.

McLaughlin, B., Pollice, G. and West, D., *Head First Object-Oriented Analysis and Design: A Brain Friendly Guide to OOA&D*, O'Reilly, 2006.

Mellor, S. J. and Balcer, M. J., *Executable UML: A Foundation for Model Driven Architecture*, Boston, MA: Addison-Wesley, 2002.

Melton, A. (ed.), *Software Measurement*, London: Thompson Computer Press, 1995.

Metsker, S., *The Design Patterns Java Workbook*, Indianapolis, IN: Addison Wesley Professional, 2002.

Meyer, B., *Object-Oriented Software Construction*, Hemel Hempstead: Prentice-Hall International, 1988.

Meyer, B., 'Design by Contract', in *Advances in Object-Oriented Software Engineering*, Mandrioli, D. and Meyer, B. (eds), London: Prentice-Hall, 1991.

Meyer, B., *Object Success: A Manager's Guide to Object Orientation, its Impact on the Corporation, and its Use for Reengineering the Software Process*, Hemel Hempstead: Prentice-Hall, 1995.

Meyer, B., *Object-Oriented Software Construction* (2nd edn), Upper Saddle River, NJ: Prentice-Hall PTR, 1997.

Microsoft Corporation, *The Windows Interface Guidelines for Software Design*, Redmond, WA: Microsoft Press, 1997.

Moore, 'Google Street View: Residents block street to prevent filming over crime fears', Daily Telegraph, 2 April 2009, at http://www.telegraph.co.uk/scienceandtechnology/technology/google/5095241/Google-Street-View-Residents-block-street-to-prevent-filming-over-crime-fears.html.

Newkirk, J. and Martin, R., *Extreme Programming in Practice*, Upper Saddle River, NJ: Addison-Wesley, 2001.

OGC, *Common Causes of Project Failure: OGC Best Practice Guide*, Office of Government Commerce, 2005, at www.ogc.gov.uk/sdtkdev/new_content/OGCCommonCausesProjectFailure.pdf.

OMG, *UML 2.0 Superstructure RFP* (ad/00-09-02), OMG, 2000.

OMG, *Object Constraint Language Version 2.0*, OMG, 2006.

OMG, *Unified Modeling Language: Version 2.2*, OMG, 2009.

OMG, *Unified Modeling Language: Infrastructure Version 2.2*, OMG, 2009a.

OMG, *Unified Modeling Language: Superstructure Version 2.2*, OMG, 2009b.

Oppenheim, A. N., *Questionnaire Design, Interviewing and Attitude Measurement*, Continuum International, 2000.

Orfali, R. and Harkey, D., *Client/Server Programming with JAVA and CORBA* (2nd edn), New York, NY: John Wiley, 1998.

Page-Jones, M., *The Practical Guide to Structured Systems Design* (2nd edn), Englewood Cliffs, NJ: Prentice-Hall, 1988.

Parnas, D. L., 'On the Criteria to be Used in Decomposing Systems into Modules', *Communications of the ACM*, **5** (12), pp. 1053–1058, 1972.

Peters, T., *Thriving on Chaos: Handbook for a Management Revolution*, London: Macmillan, 1988.

Philips, T., 'A Slicker System for the City', *The Guardian On-Line*, 3 April 1997.

Pollice G., *Using the Rational Unified Process for Small Projects: Expanding Upon eXtreme Programming*, Rational Software Corporation, 2001.

Porter, M., *Competitive Strategy*, New York: Free Press, 1985.

Pressman, R., *Software Engineering: A Practitioner's Approach* (7th edn), McGraw-Hill, 2009.

Reuters, 'Google reshoots Japan views after privacy complaints', 13 May 2009, at http://www.reuters.com/article/internetNews/idUSTRE54C22R20090513.

Riehle, D. and Zullighoven, H., 'Understanding and Using Patterns in Software Development', *Theory and Practice of Object Systems*, **2** (1), pp. 3–13, 1996.

Rifkin, J., *The End of Work*, New York: Putnam Publishers, 1995. Cited in Ellwood, W., 'Seduced by Technology', *New Internationalist*, December 1996.

Roberts, G., *The Users' Role in Systems Development*, Chichester: John Wiley; Central Computer and Telecommunications Agency, 1989.

Rogerson, S. and Gotterbarn, D., 'The Ethics of Software Project Management', in *Ethics and Information Technology*, Collste G. (ed.), Delhi: New Academic Publisher, 1998.

Roos, R., *Java Data Objects*, London: Addison-Wesley, 2003.

Rosenberg, D., with Scott, K., *Use Case Driven Object Modeling with UML: a Practical Approach*, Upper Saddle River, NJ: Addison-Wesley, 1999.

Rosenberg, D. and Scott, K., *Applying Use Case Driven Object Modeling with UML: an Annotated E-Commerce Example*, Upper Saddle River, NJ: Addison-Wesley, 2001.

Rosson, M. B. and Carroll, J. M., 'Narrowing the Specification-Implementation Gap in Scenario-Based Design', in Carroll, J. M. (ed.), *Scenario-Based Design: Envisioning Work and Technology in System Development*, New York: John Wiley, 1995.

Rosson, M. B. and Carroll, J. M., *Usability Engineering: Scenario-Based Development of Human–Computer Interaction*, San Francisco, CA: Morgan Kaufmann Publishers, 2002.

Rumbaugh, J., 'Models through the development process', *Journal of Object-Oriented Programming*, May 1997.

Rumbaugh, J., Blaha M., Premerlani, W., Eddy, F. and Lorensen, W., *Object-Oriented Modeling and Design*, Englewood Cliffs, NJ: Prentice-Hall International, 1991.

Sachs, P., 'Transforming Work: Collaboration, Learning and Design', *Communications of the ACM*, **38** (9), pp. 36–44, 1995.

SAGA, *Standards and Architectures for e-Government Applications* (Version 2.0), Federal Ministry of the Interior, 2003.

Sanders, J. and Curran, E., *Software quality: a framework for success in software development and support*, Wokingham: Addison-Wesley, 1994.

Sauer, C., *Why Information Systems Fail: A Case Study Approach*, Maidenhead: McGraw-Hill, 1993.

Schmidt, D., Stal, M., Rohnert, H. and Buschmann, F., *Pattern Oriented Software Architecture: Patterns for Concurrent and Networked Objects: Volume 2*, Chichester: John Wiley, 2000.

Schneider, G. P., *Electronic Commerce* (6th edn), Boston, MA: Course Technology, 2009.

Schwaber, K., *SCRUMGUIDE*, Scrum Alliance Inc, 2009, at http://www.scrumalliance.org/resource_download/598.

Selic, B., Gullekson, G. and Ward, P. T., *Real-Time Object-Oriented Modeling*, New York, NY: John Wiley, 1994.

Shackel, B., 'Human factors and usability', in Preece, J. and Keller, L. (eds), *Human–Computer Interaction: Selected Readings*, Hemel Hempstead: Prentice-Hall, 1990.

Sharp, H., Rogers, Y. and Preece, J., *Interaction Design: Beyond Human-Computer Interaction*, John Wiley, 2007.

Shneiderman, B., Plaisant, C., Cohen, M. and Jacobs, S., *Designing the User Interface* (5th edn), Reading, MA: Addison-Wesley, 2009.

Silberschatz, A., Korth, H. F. and Sudarshan, S., *Database System Concepts* (5th edn), New York: McGraw-Hill, 2005.

Skidmore, S., Mills, G. and Farmer, R., *SSADM Models & Methods*, Manchester: NCC Blackwell, 1994.

Sommerville, I., *Software Engineering* (4th edn), Reading, MA: Addison-Wesley, 1992.

Sommerville, I., *Software Engineering* (8th edn), Reading, MA: Addison-Wesley, 2007.

Soni, D., Nord, R. and Hofmeister, C., 'Software Architecture in Industrial Applications', in *Proceedings of the 17th International Conference on Software Engineering*, pp. 196–207, Seattle, WA: ACM Press, 1995.

Sowa, J. F. and Zachman, J. A., 'Extending and Formalizing the Framework for Information Systems Architecture', *IBM Systems Journal*, **31** (3), 1992.

Standish Group, 'CHAOS Summary 2009', Standish Consulting Group, 2009, at https://secure.standishgroup.com/reports/reports.php.

Stone, B., 'Amazon Posts Profit Gains as Offline Rivals Struggle', *New York Times*, 23 April 2009, at http://www.nytimes.com/2009/04/24/technology/companies/24amazon.html

Stone, D., Jarrett, C., Woodroffe, M. and Minocha, S., *User Interface Design and Evaluation*, San Francisco, CA: Morgan Kaufmann Publishers, 2005.

Sun JavaCentre, 2005, at http://java.sun.com.

Symons, V., 'Evaluation of information systems: IS development in the processing company', *Journal of Information Technology*, **5**, pp. 194–204, 1990.

Szyperski, C., *Component Software: Beyond Object-Oriented Programming* (2nd edn), Boston, MA: Addison-Wesley Professional, 2002.

Tanenbaum, A. S., Day, W. and Waller, S., *Computer Networks* (4th edn), Englewood Cliffs, NJ: Prentice Hall, 2002.

Texel, P. P. and Williams, C. B., *Use Case Combined with Booch/OMT/UML: processes and products*, Upper Saddle River, NJ: Prentice Hall, 1997.

The Open Group, *TOGAF™ Version 9*, The Open Group, 2009.

Thurston, R., 'Large public-sector Linux project flops', ZDNet UK, 13 November 2006, at http://news.zdnet.co.uk/software/0,1000000121,39284683,00.htm.

TIOBE Software BV, 'TIOBE Programming Community Index for July 2009', at http://www.tiobe.com/index.php/content/paperinfo/tpci/index.html.

Turban, E., Aronson, J. E. and Liang, T. P., *Decision Support Systems and Intelligent Systems* (7th edn), Upper Saddle River, NJ: Prentice Hall, 2005.

Veitch, M., 'Over half of IT projects fall short of expectation', *Computing*, 2 July 2007.

Vidgen, R., Avison, D., Wood, B. and Wood-Harper, T., *Developing Web Information Systems: From Strategy to Implementation*, Oxford: Butterworth Heinemann, 2002.

Vlissides, J.M., Coplien, J. O. and Kerth, N., (eds), *Pattern Languages of Program Design 2*, Reading, MA: Addison-Wesley, 1996.

Ward, P. and Mellor, S., *Structured Development for Real-Time Systems Vol 1: Introduction & Tools*, Englewood Cliffs, NJ: Yourdon Computing Press, 1985.

Ward, P. and Mellor, S., *Structured Development for Real-Time Systems Vol 2: Essential Modeling Techniques*, Englewood Cliffs, NJ: Yourdon Computing Press, 1985.

Ward, P. and Mellor, S., *Structured Development for Real-Time Systems Vol 3: Implementation Modeling Techniques*, Englewood Cliffs, NJ: Yourdon Computing Press, 1986.

Warmer, J. and Kleppe, A., *The Object Constraint Language: Getting Your Models Ready for MDA* (2nd edn), Boston: Pearson Education, 2003.

Webster, F., *Theories of the Information Society*, London: Routledge, 1995.

Weir, C. and Daniels, J., 'Software Architecture Document', in *Proceedings of Object Technology 98*, Oxford, 1998.

Whiteside, J., Bennett, J. and Holtzblatt, K., 'Usability engineering: our experience and evolution', in Helander, M. (ed.), *Handbook of Human-Computer Interaction*, Amsterdam: North-Holland, 1988.

Wirfs-Brock, R., Wilkerson, B. and Wiener, L., *Designing Object-Oriented Software*, Englewood Cliffs, NJ: Prentice-Hall International, 1990.

Withal, S., *Software Requirement Patterns (Best Practices)*, Redmond, WA: Microsoft Press, 2007.

Wutka, M., *Special Edition Using Java 2 Enterprise Edition (J2EE): With JSP, Servlets, EJB 2.0, JNDI, JMS, JDBC, CORBA, XML and RMI*, Que, 2001.

Yourdon, E., *Structured Walkthroughs*, Englewood Cliffs, NJ: Yourdon Press, 1985.

Yourdon, E., *Modern Structured Analysis*, Englewood Cliffs, NJ: Prentice-Hall, 1989.

Yourdon, E., *Object-Oriented Systems Design: An Integrated Approach*, Englewood Cliffs, NJ: Prentice-Hall International, 1994.

Yourdon, E. and Constantine, L. L., *Structured Design: Fundamentals of a Discipline of Computer Program and Systems Design*, Englewood Cliffs, NJ: Yourdon Press; Prentice-Hall, 1979.

Zachman, J. A., 'Framework for Information Systems Architecture', *IBM Systems Journal*, **26** (3), 1987.

Zachman, J. A., *Concise Definition of the The Zachman Framework*, 2008, at http://www.zachmaninternational.com/concise definition.pdf.

Zachman, J. A., *The Zachman Framework Evolution*, 2009, at http://www.zachmaninternational.com/index.php/ea-articles/100#maincol.

Zuboff, S., *In the Age of the Smart Machine: The Future of Work and Power*, Oxford: Heinemann, 1988.

Index

abstraction
object-orientation origins
106
software development
processes 611
activities of design, Agate Ltd
557–8
activity diagrams
activity partitions 127–8
algorithmic approaches 304
control flow 123–5
decision node 124–5
drawing 122–8
frames 125–6
models/modelling 115–18,
122–8
notation 123–8, 637
object flows 127
purpose 122–3
swimlanes 127–8
activity partitions, activity
diagrams 127–8
actors, Agate Ltd 171–6
AFE (Application Family
Engineering), reusable
software 594
Agate Ltd
activities of design 557–8
activities, requirements
analysis 231, 344–6
activities, requirements
modelling 178–9
actors 171–6
analysis class diagram 231
analysis, further 338–46
architecture 390–2, 544–5
business activities 5–6
case study 4–7, 169–79,
225–32, 338–46, 544–58
class diagram 343–4,
546–52
database design 555
design 544–58
existing computer systems
5
glossary of terms 176–7

human activity system 32–3
initial architecture 177
operation specifications
342–3
requirements analysis
225–32, 344–6
requirements list 169–70
requirements model
169–79
requirements summary 6–7
sequence diagrams 339–41,
552–4
state machines 340–1,
555–6
subsystems 29
use case realization 225–30
use case sample 546
use cases 171–6, 546
aggregation
composition 244, 245
generalization 244, 245
Agile approaches
methodological approaches
79–80
XP 80
airline seat booking system
components 249–52
reusable software 249–52
algorithmic approaches
activity diagrams 304
control structures 299–300
operation logic 299–304
pseudo-code 303–4
Structured English 300–3
algorithms, operation,
detailed design 419–20
analysis, cf. design 347–50
analysis class diagram
Agate Ltd 343–4, 546–52
analysis class stereotypes
198–201
assembling 218–19, 231
associations 213–14
associations between
classes 187–9
attributes 184–6, 211–13

boundary classes 198–9,
487
case study 343–4
case study work/exercises/
projects 221–4
classes 184, 198–211
communication diagram
206–8
concepts 184–94
control classes 200–1
CRC cards 215–18
domain model 208–10
drawing 197–215
entity classes 199–200
identifying classes 201–6
linked instances 186–7
multiplicity 189–91, 214
notation 184–94
object state 186
objects 184, 208–11
operations 191–3, 214–15
requirements analysis
184–94
robustness analysis
197–8
stability 193–4
analysis class stereotypes,
analysis class diagram
198–201
analysis model, requirements
analysis 181–4
analysis, requirements see
requirements analysis
answer pointers, case study
work/exercises/projects
650–4
answers to selected review
questions 643–50
application containers,
software tools 562
Application Family
Engineering (AFE),
reusable software 594
Application System
Engineering (ASE),
reusable software 594

architecture 363–94
see also system design
Agate Ltd 390–2, 544–5
broker architecture 384–6
case study work/exercises/
projects 394
concurrency 387–8
Conway's Law 386–7
data management classes
532–3
defining 364–7
describing 364–7
design relationships 352–4
distributed systems 384–6
enterprise architectures
371–2
existing computer systems
369–71
heritage systems 369–70
influences 369–72
key terms 365–7
layered architecture 532–3
layering 374–9
MDA 370–1
models/modelling 367–9
MVC architecture 379–83
organization structures
386–7
OSI model 375–9
partitioning 374–9
persistence 502–4
presentation layer,
boundary classes 470–1
processor allocation 389
SOA 370
styles 372–87
subsystems 373–4
system architecture/design,
development process
133–4
technical reference
architectures 372
artefacts
Scrum 625
USDP 617
ASE *see* Application System
Engineering
associations
analysis class diagram
213–14
notation 636
object state 189

associations between classes,
analysis class diagram
187–9
associations, designing
410–16
classes, minimizing 415–16
many-to-many associations
414–15
one-to-many associations
411–14
one-to-one associations
410–11
asynchronous messages,
interaction sequence
diagrams 276–7
Atern *see* Dynamic Systems
Development Method
(DSDM)
attributes
analysis class diagram
184–6, 211–13
attribute specification,
detailed design 396–403
class 403–10
data types 397–8
derived 398–9
encapsulation 401–3
grouping 403–10
object state 186
visibility 401–3

background reading,
requirements capture 142
backup files 509
basic concepts
class 93–6
disjoint nature 100–1
encapsulation 101–3
generalization 96–101
information hiding 101–3
inheritance 99–100
message passing 101–3
object-orientation 91–106
object state 105–6
objects 91–3
polymorphism 103–4
specialization 96–101
taxonomic relationships
96–8
transitive operation 100
behaviour diagrams, notation
636–7

behavioural approach, state
machines 329–30
behavioural patterns, design
patterns 436–41
behavioural state machines,
control 333–4
boundary, systems thinking
23, 27–8
boundary classes 469–99
analysis class diagram
198–9
architecture of the
presentation layer 470–1
case study work/exercises/
projects 498–9
class design 475–9
class diagram 487
designing 469–99
interface modelling, state
machines 489–97
prototyping the user
interface 471–5
sequence diagrams 479–87
state machines, interface
modelling 489–97
user interface design
patterns 488–9
branching, interaction
sequence diagrams
274–6
broker architecture 384–6
business activities, Agate Ltd
5–6
business modelling, use cases
162–3
business needs changes,
information systems
50–1
business strategy
information systems
strategy 39–41
IT strategies 39–41

capta, smoke example 34
case study
activities, requirements
analysis 231, 344–6
Agate Ltd 4–7, 169–79,
225–32, 338–46,
544–58
analysis class diagram 231
class diagram 343–4

design 544–58
FoodCo Ltd 8–15
interaction sequence
 diagrams 339–41
operation specifications
 342–3
requirements analysis
 225–32, 344–6
requirements model
 169–79
state machines 340–1
use case realization 225–30
case study examples
requirements capture
 151–2, 164–6
reusable software 597–605
case study work/exercises/
 projects
analysis class diagram
 221–4
answer pointers 650–4
architecture 394
boundary classes 498–9
challenges 62, 88
control 336
data management design
 542
design 362
design patterns 444
detailed design 421
HCI 467–8
implementation 583
information systems 42
models/modelling 137
object interaction 291
object-orientation 112
operation specifications
 311
requirements capture
 167–8
requirements model 257–8
reusable software 608
state machines 336
system design 394
CASE tools see Computer
 Aided Software
 Engineering tools
CBD see component-based
 development
challenges
case study work/exercises/
 projects 62, 88

information systems
 development 43–63
meeting 64–89
CHAOS reports 44
characteristics of good design
 354–60
choice pseudostate, state
 machines 326
class
analysis class diagram 184,
 198–211
associations between
 classes 187–9
associations, designing
 415–16
attributes, grouping 403–10
basic concepts 93–6
boundary classes 198–9
class cohesion 408
cohesion 407–9
control classes 200–1
coupling 406–9
data management classes
 532–41
entity classes 199–200
grouping attributes 403–10
grouping operations
 403–10
identifying classes 201–6
interfaces 404–6
LSP 409–10
membership 94–6
objects 93–4
operation cohesion 407–8
operations, grouping
 403–10
responsibilities 403–4
specialization cohesion
 408–9
structure 94–6
tables, mapping classes to
 522–4
class browsers, software tools
 562
class cohesion, class 408
class design
boundary classes 475–9
development process 134
user interface 475–9
class diagram see analysis
 class diagram
class notation 635

Class Responsibility
 Collaboration (CRC)
 cards, analysis class
 diagram 215–18
client's perspective, information
 systems 47–50
coding standards, software
 implementation 563–4
cohesion
class 407–9
class cohesion 408
operation cohesion 407–8
specialization cohesion
 408–9
collaboration
object interaction 260–2
use case realization 195–6,
 230–5
communication, XP 626
communication diagram
analysis class diagram
 206–8
basic concepts 280–2
message labels 282–4
notation 280–2, 640
object interaction 280–4
use case realization 196–7
compilers, software tools 561
completeness, requirements
 analysis 183
component-based development
 (CBD) 248–9
component diagrams
implementation 564–6
notation 642
component managers,
 software tools 562
component standards,
 reusable software 590–2
Component System
 Engineering (CSE),
 reusable software 594
components
airline seat booking system
 249–52
CBD 248–9
example 249–52
notation 248
reusable software 246–52
componentware,
 commercially available,
 reusable software 595–7

Composite pattern
  design patterns 432–6
  user interface 488–9
composite states, state
  machines 321–3
composition
  aggregation 244, 245
  finding/modelling 242–4
  generalization 244, 245
  requirements model 242–4
Computer Aided Software
  Engineering (CASE)
  tools 83–4
  see also software tools
  software implementation
  560
  use cases 161–2
concurrency
  architecture 387–8
  database management
  systems 513
  interaction sequence
  diagrams 278, 279
concurrent states, state
  machines 323–4
configuration management,
  software tools 561
consistency
  consistency checking,
  control 334–5
  model consistency, object
  interaction 289
  requirements analysis
  184
  user interface 452
constraints, design 354–60
construction
  development process 135
  guidelines 390
content, requirements
  analysis 183–4
context, OCL 305–8
continuations, interaction
  sequence diagrams 276
contracts, operation
  specifications 294–5
control
  see also state machines
  behavioural state machines
  333–4
  case study work/exercises/
  projects 336

consistency checking
  334–5
  events 314–15
  notation 316–28
  protocol state machines
  333–4
  quality guidelines 335
  specifying 313–37
  state machines, preparing
  328–33
  states 314–15
  systems thinking 25, 28–31
control classes, analysis class
  diagram 200–1
control flow, activity
  diagrams 123–5
control structures, algorithmic
  approaches 299–300
conversion tools, software
  tools 562–3
Conway's Law, architecture
  386–7
costs of failure, information
  systems 60–1
coupling
  class 406–9
  inheritance coupling 406–7
  interaction coupling 406–7
courage, XP 626
CRC (Class Responsibility
  Collaboration) cards,
  analysis class diagram
  215–18
creational patterns, design
  patterns 426–31
CSE (Component System
  Engineering), reusable
  software 594
current system, requirements
  capture 139–40

data, smoke example 34
data conversion,
  implementation 573–4
data definition language
  (DDL), database
  management systems 512
data management classes
  data management design
  532–41
  data management product/
  framework 539–41

database broker framework
  533–9
  designing 532–41
  Java Persistence API 540–1
  layered architecture 532–3
  object-relational mappings
  540
  PersistentObject superclass
  533
data management design
  500–43
  case study work/exercises/
  projects 542
  data management classes
  532–41
  database management
  systems 511–16
  development process 135
  distributed databases 529–31
  file systems 504–11
  object database
  management systems
  524–9
  persistence 501–4
  relational database
  management systems
  516–24
data management product/
  framework, data
  management classes
  539–41
data manipulation language
  (DML), database
  management systems 512
data modelling
  normalization 517–22
  relational database
  management systems
  517–22
database broker framework,
  data management classes
  533–9
database design 389–90
  Agate Ltd 555
database management
  systems
  advantages 513
  concurrency 513
  data management design
  511–16
  databases and files 511–14
  DDL 512

disadvantages 513–14
DML 512
files and databases 511–14
integrity constraints 512
object databases 515
object-relational databases
    515–16
relational databases 514–15
security 513
software tools 562
storage tuning 513
Three-schema Architecture
    512, 513–14
transaction management
    512–13
tuning of storage 513
types 514–16
databases and files, database
    management systems
    511–14
DDL (data definition
    language), database
    management systems 512
debuggers, software tools 561
decision node, activity
    diagrams 124–5
decision tables, operation
    logic 296–7
dependency
  requirements capture
    244–6
  use case realization 195–6
dependency constraints,
    integrity constraints
    417–18
deployment diagrams
  implementation 566–9
  notation 642
derived attributes 398–9
design 347–62
  see also detailed design;
    system design; user
    interface design
  activities of design 557–8
  Agate Ltd 544–58
  cf. analysis 347–50
  architecture 544–5
  architecture relationships
    352–4
  case study 544–58
  case study work/exercises/
    projects 362

characteristics of good
    design 354–60
class diagram 546–52
constraints 354–60
database design 555
iterative lifecycle 350
logical 350–2
objectives 354–60
physical 350–2
platform influences 350–2
qualities 354–60
sequence diagrams 552–4
state machines 555–6
trade-offs 359–60
use case sample 546
design patterns 422–45
  behavioural patterns
    436–41
  benefits 443
  case study work/exercises/
    projects 444
  Composite pattern 432–6,
    488–9
  creational patterns 426–31
  dangers 443
  documenting patterns
    424–5
  how to use 441–3
  Observer pattern 488
  Singleton pattern 427–31
  software development
    patterns 423–4
  State pattern 436–41
  Strategy pattern 489
  structural patterns 431–6
  templates 424–5
  types 426–41
  user interface 488–9
  using 441–3
detailed design 352–4,
    395–421
  see also design; system
    design
  associations, designing
    410–16
  attribute specification
    396–403
  case study work/exercises/
    projects 421
  grouping attributes and
    operations in classes
    403–10

integrity constraints
    416–19
object-oriented 396
operation algorithms
    419–20
operation specifications
    396–403
developer's perspective,
    information systems
    50–2
development environments,
    reusable software 590–2
development process
  activities 130–5
  class design 134
  construction 135
  data management design
    135
  implementation 135
  methodological approaches
    77–9
  models/modelling 128–35
  principles 129–30
  Rational Unified Process
    128
  requirements analysis
    132–3
  requirements capture/
    modelling 132
  system architecture/design
    133–4
  testing 135
  USDP 128–35
  user interface design 134–5
  waterfall lifecycle 129–31
diagrams
  defining 115–18
  models/modelling 114–22
  models/modelling
    comparison 118–19
dialogue boxes, user interface
    451–5
dialogue metaphor, user
    interface 447–9
direct access, file access
    507–8
direct changeover,
    implementation strategy
    575–6
direct manipulation
    metaphor, user interface
    449–51

disjoint nature, basic concepts 100–1
distributed database systems, distributed databases 530
distributed databases 529–31
  data management design 529–31
  distributed database systems 530
  mobile database systems 530–1
  multi-database systems 529–30
  parallel database systems 529
  replicated database systems 530–1
distributed systems, architecture 384–6
DML (data manipulation language), database management systems 512
document sampling, requirements capture 146, 147
documentation, software testing 572–3
documentation generators, software tools 563
documentation standards, software implementation 563–4
documentation, user 574
documenting patterns, design patterns 424–5
documenting requirements, requirements capture 152–4
domain integrity, integrity constraints 419
domain model, analysis class diagram 208–10
Dynamic Systems Development Method (DSDM) 618–23
  Atern 618–23
  facilitated workshops 623
  lifecycle 620–1
  MoSCoW prioritization 622–3
  PRINCE2™ 619
  principles 619–20

project selection 623
techniques 622–3
timeboxing 622

emergent properties, systems thinking 26, 32
encapsulation
  attributes 401–3
  basic concepts 101–3
  object-orientation contributions 237
  reusable software 237
  visibility 401–3
end-user's perspective, information systems 45–7
enterprise architectures 371–2
entity classes, analysis class diagram 199–200
entry pseudostate, state machines 324–5
environment, systems thinking 22–3, 27–8
environments, development, reusable software 590–2
ethical dimension
  ethical issues within a project 58–9
  information systems 56–60
  stakeholders 57–8
  wider ethical issues 59–60
ethnographic approaches, user interface design 460–1
evaluation report, review 578–9
event-driven programming, object-orientation origins 106–7
events, control 314–15
existing computer systems
  Agate Ltd 5
  architecture 369–71
exit pseudostate, state machines 324–5
external events, information systems 55–6
eXtreme Programming (XP)
  activities 626–7
  Agile approaches 80
  communication 626
  courage 626
  feedback 626
  simplicity 626

software development processes 625–7
software testing 569

facilitated workshops, DSDM 623
fact-finding techniques, requirements capture 142–50
failure causes
  installation & operation 65
  productivity problems 65
  quality problems 65
failure costs, information systems 60–1
failure reasons, information systems 52–60
feed-forward, systems thinking 25–6
feedback
  systems thinking 25–6, 28–31
  user interface 453–4
  XP 626
fighter Command, information systems 18–19
file access, file systems 506–9
file organization, file systems 505–6
file structures, file systems 504–5
file systems
  data management design 504–11
  example of using files 510–11
  file access 506–9
  file organization 505–6
  file structures 504–5
  file types 509–10
  record structures 504–5
file types, file systems 509–10
files and databases, database management systems 511–14
fixed length record structure 505
FoodCo Ltd
  case study 8–15
  current thinking 11
  information systems 11–14
  proposal 15

formal approaches, user interface design 456–63
frames, activity diagrams 125–6
functional dependency, normalization 517–22
functional requirements, requirements capture 141

generalization
  aggregation 244, 245
  basic concepts 96–101
  composition 244, 245
  finding/modelling 237–42
  requirements model 236, 237–42
  reusable software 236
glossary 655–64
glossary of terms, Agate Ltd 176–7
grouping attributes, class 403–10
grouping operations, class 403–10
GUIs, object-orientation origins 107

hard v. soft methodologies 629–31
HCI see human-computer interaction
header and detail record structure 505
heritage systems, architecture 369–70
hierarchy, systems thinking 27–8
history, information systems in 17–20
history pseudostates, state machines 326–8
holistic view, systems thinking 32
human activity system
  Agate Ltd 32–3
  information systems 32–3
human-computer interaction (HCI) 446–68
  see also user...
  case study work/exercises/projects 467–8
  legal requirements 464–6

standards 464–6
user interface 447–55
user interface design approaches 456–64

identifying classes, analysis class diagram 201–6
implementation 559–83
  case study work/exercises/projects 583
  component diagrams 564–6
  data conversion 573–4
  deployment diagrams 566–9
  development process 135
  maintenance 577–81
  review 577–9
  software implementation 560–4
  software testing 569–73
  strategies 575–7
  user documentation 574
  user training 575
implementation diagrams, notation 642
implementation problems, information systems 56
improving access, file access 508–9
incremental development, project lifecycles 76–7
index files 509
index-sequential access, file access 506–7
informal approaches, user interface design 456–63
information
  and information systems 33–8
  smoke example 34
information hiding
  basic concepts 101–3
  object-orientation contributions 237
  reusable software 237
information systems 16–42
  business needs changes 50–1
  case study work/exercises/projects 42
  client's perspective 47–50

costs of failure 60–1
developer's perspective 50–2
development 32–3
development challenges 43–63
development, managing 81–2
end-user's perspective 45–7
ethical dimension 56–60
external events 55–6
failure costs 60–1
failure reasons 52–60
fighter Command 18–19
FoodCo Ltd 11–14
in history 17–20
human activity system 32–3
implementation problems 56
information and 33–8
IT strategies 39–41
iterative lifecycle 81–2
in organizations 34–6
productivity problems 53, 55–6
quality problems 52–5
RAF 18–19
railway signalling 17–18
reasons for failure 52–60
requirements analysis 54
requirements changes 50–1
requirements drift 55
systems 22–33
today 20–1
user's perspective 45–7
information systems strategy
  business strategy 39–41
  IT strategies 39–41
information technology (IT) 37–8
  strategies for success 39–41
inheritance, basic concepts 99–100
inheritance coupling 406–7
inputs/outputs, systems thinking 23, 28–31
installation & operation problems
  project failure cause 65
  responding to 68
installation tools, software tools 562

integrated development
  environment, software
  tools 561
integrity constraints 416–19
  database management
    systems 512
  dependency constraints
    417–18
  detailed design 416–19
  domain integrity 419
  referential integrity 416–17
interaction constraint,
  interaction sequence
  diagrams 264
interaction coupling 406–7
interaction diagrams,
  notation 638–41
interaction, object *see* object
  interaction
interaction overview
  diagrams
  notation 641
  object interaction 284–6,
  287
interaction sequence
  diagrams 262–80
  Agate Ltd 339–41, 552–4
  asynchronous messages
    276–7
  basic concepts 262–71
  boundary classes 479–87
  branching 274–6
  case study 339–41
  concurrency 278, 279
  continuations 276
  guidelines for preparing
    278–80
  interaction constraint 264
  managing 271–4
  notation 262–71, 638–9
  procedural call 265–71
  real-time systems 278, 279
  reflexive message 266–9
  synchronous message
    265–71
  time constraints 277–8
interface modelling, state
  machines, boundary
  classes 489–97
interfaces
  class 404–6
  systems thinking 24

interpreters, software tools
  561
interviewing
  guidelines 144
  requirements capture 143–4
IT strategies
  business strategy 39–41
  information systems 39–41
iterative lifecycle
  design 350
  information systems 81–2
  project lifecycles 76–7

Jacobson's six stages, reusable
  software 586–8
Java Persistence API, data
  management classes
  540–1
junction pseudostate, state
  machines 325–6

key terms, architecture 365–7
knowledge, smoke example 34

languages
  object-oriented languages
    today 109–11
  reusable software 590–2
  software development
    patterns 423
layered architecture, data
  management classes
  532–3
layering, architecture 374–9
legal requirements, HCI
  464–6
lifecycle approach, state
  machines 330–3
lifecycle problems, object-
  orientation origins 108
lifecycles
  see also project lifecycles
  DSDM 620–1
limitations, object-orientation
  110–11
linked instances, analysis
  class diagram 186–7
Liskov Substitution Principle
  (LSP), class 409–10
logical design 350–2
LSP *see* Liskov Substitution
  Principle

maintenance, implementation
  577–81
management support systems
  (MSS), organizations
  35–6
many-to-many associations
  414–15
map, systems development 44
master files 509
MDA (Model-Driven
  Architecture) 370–1
message labels, communication
  diagram 282–4
message passing, basic
  concepts 101–3
message types, user interface
  447–8
method, software
  development processes
  611–14
methodological approaches
  77–80
  Agile approaches 79–80
  USDP 77–9
methodology
  advantages 613–14
  choosing 627–9
  hard v. soft 629–31
  principles 612
  reasons for 613–14
  roles 628
  software development
    processes 611–14, 627–9
  SPEM 612–13
minimal user input, user
  interface 454–5
mobile database systems,
  distributed databases
  530–1
model and technique support,
  software development
  tools 84–6
model consistency, object
  interaction 289
Model-Driven Architecture
  (MDA) 370–1
model transitions, object-
  orientation origins 108
Model–View–Controller
  (MVC) architecture
  379–83
  responsibilities 381–3

modelling tools *see* Computer Aided Software Engineering (CASE) tools
models/modelling 113–37
  activity diagrams 115–18, 122–8
  architectural 367–9
  case study work/exercises/ projects 137
  defining 114–15, 119–20
  developing 120–2
  development process 128–35
  diagrams 114–22
  diagrams comparison 118–19
  requirements capture 163–4
  UML, models in 119–20
  use case model 120–2
modular software, object-orientation origins 107–8
MoSCoW prioritization, DSDM 622–3
MSS *see* management support systems
multi-database systems, distributed databases 529–30
multiple inheritance, requirements model 242
multiplicity, analysis class diagram 189–91, 214
MVC (Model–View–Controller) architecture 379–83

new requirements, requirements capture 140–2
non-algorithmic approaches, operation logic 296–9
non-functional requirements
  requirements capture 141
  software development patterns 424
normalization
  data modelling 517–22
  functional dependency 517–22
  relational database management systems 517–22

notation
  activity diagrams 123–8, 637
  analysis class diagram 184–94
  associations 636
  behaviour diagrams 636–7
  class notation 635
  communication diagram 280–2, 640
  component diagrams 642
  components 248
  control 316–28
  deployment diagrams 642
  implementation diagrams 642
  interaction diagrams 638–41
  interaction overview diagrams 641
  interaction sequence diagrams 262–71, 638–9
  object instance notation 634
  state machines 316–28, 636
  static structure diagrams 634–6
  summary 634–42
  timing diagrams 640
  use cases 155–9, 634

Object Constraint Language (OCL)
  context 305–8
  operation 305–8
  operation specifications 304–8
  property 305–8
object database management systems
  data management design 524–9
  designing for 524–9
  object databases 524–9
  transactions 527
  transparent activation 527
  transparent persistence 527
object databases
  database management systems 515
  object database management systems 524–9

object flows, activity diagrams 127
object instance notation, notation 634
object interaction 259–91
  case study work/exercises/ projects 291
  collaboration 260–2
  communication diagram 280–4
  interaction overview diagrams 284–6, 287
  interaction sequence diagrams 262–80
  model consistency 289
  timing diagrams 286–8
object-orientation 90–112
  basic concepts 91–106
  case study work/exercises/ projects 112
  limitations 110–11
  origins 106–9
  overview 90–1
object-orientation contributions
  encapsulation 237
  information hiding 237
  reusable software 236–7
object-oriented languages today 109–11
object-relational databases, database management systems 515–16
object-relational mappings, data management classes 540
object state
  analysis class diagram 186
  associations 189
  attributes 186
  basic concepts 105–6
  control 314–15
  operations 192–3
objectives, design 354–60
objects
  analysis class diagram 184
  basic concepts 91–3
  characteristics 91–3
  class 93–4
  defining 91
observation, requirements capture 145–6

Observer pattern, user interface 488
OCL (Object Constraint Language) 304–8
office systems, organizations 36
one-to-many associations 411–14
one-to-one associations 410–11
Open Systems Interconnection Seven Layer Model (OSI model), architecture 375–9
operation, OCL 305–8
operation algorithms, detailed design 419–20
operation cohesion, class 407–8
operation logic
  algorithmic approaches 299–304
  decision tables 296–7
  non-algorithmic approaches 296–9
  operation specifications 295–304
  pre- and post-conditions 297–9
operation signatures, operation specifications 400–1
operation specifications 292–312
  Agate Ltd 342–3
  case study 342–3
  case study work/exercises/projects 311
  contracts 294–5
  creating 308–10
  detailed design 396–403
  OCL 304–8
  ⸱ration logic 295–304
  tion signatures 400–1
  y operations
  400
  ⸱–4
  l systems,
  zations 34–5

  ass diagram
  14–15
  0

grouping 403–10
object state 192–3
preliminary allocation 215
organization structures, architecture 386–7
organizational structure, reusable software 587–8
organizations
  information systems in 34–6
  management support systems (MSS) 35–6
  office systems 36
  operational systems 34–5
  real-time control systems 36
origins, object-orientation 106–9
  abstraction 106
  event-driven programming 106–7
  GUIs 107
  lifecycle problems 108
  model transitions 108
  modular software 107–8
  reusable software 108–9
OSI model (Open Systems Interconnection Seven Layer Model), architecture 375–9
outputs see inputs/outputs
overview
  object-orientation 90–1
  UML 3

packages, requirements capture 244–6
parallel database systems, distributed databases 529
parallel running, implementation strategy 576
parameter files 509–10
partitioning, architecture 374–9
patterns see design patterns; software development patterns
persistence
  architecture 502–4
  data management design 501–4
  requirement for 501
  storage mechanisms 502

PersistentObject superclass, data management classes 533
phased changeover, implementation strategy 576–7
physical design 350–2
pilot project, implementation strategy 577
platform influences, design 350–2
polymorphism, basic concepts 103–4
pre- and post-conditions, operation logic 297–9
presentation layer, architecture, boundary classes 470–1
primary operations, operation specifications 399–400
PRINCE2™, DSDM 619
problem-solving model, project lifecycles 70–1
procedural call, interaction sequence diagrams 265–71
processes, development see development process; software development processes
processor allocation, architecture 389
productivity problems
  information systems 53, 55–6
  project failure cause 65
  responding to 69–70
project lifecycles 70–7
  incremental development 76–7
  iterative lifecycle 76–7
  problem-solving model 70–1
  prototyping 73–6
  waterfall lifecycle 71–3
project selection, DSDM 623
property, OCL 305–8
protocol state machines, control 333–4
prototyping
  project lifecycles 73–6
  use cases 159–61
  user interface, boundary classes 471–5

pseudo-code, algorithmic
approaches 303–4

qualities, design 354–60
quality guidelines, control 335
quality problems
information systems 52–5
project failure cause 65
requirements drift 67–8
responding to 66–8
questionnaires
guidelines 148–9
requirements capture
146–50

RAF, information systems
18–19
railway signalling,
information systems
17–18
RAM see responsibility
assignment matrix
random file organization 506
Rational Unified Process 128
real-time control systems,
organizations 36
real-time systems, interaction
sequence diagrams 278,
279
realization, use case see use
case realization
reasons for failure, information
systems 52–60
record structures, file systems
504–5
reductionism, systems
thinking 32
referential integrity, integrity
constraints 416–17
reflexive message, interaction
sequence diagrams 266–9
relational database
management systems
data management design
516–24
data modelling 517–22
designing for 516–24
mapping classes to tables
522–4
normalization 517–22
relational databases 516–17
tables, mapping classes to
522–4

relational databases
database management
systems 514–15
relational database
management systems
516–17
replicated database systems,
distributed databases
530–1
requirements analysis 180–224
activities 231
Agate Ltd 225–32, 344–6
analysis class diagram
184–94, 231
analysis model 181–4
case study 225–32, 344–6
completeness 183
consistency 184
content 183–4
criteria 182–4
development process 132–3
incorrect 54, 67
information systems 54
scope 183
use case realization 194–7,
225–30
requirements capture 138–68
background reading 142
case study examples 151–2,
164–6
case study work/exercises/
projects 167–8
current system 139–40
dependency 244–6
development process 132
document sampling 146, 147
documenting requirements
152–4
fact-finding techniques
142–50
functional requirements 141
interviewing 143–4
models/modelling 163–4
new requirements 140–2
non-functional
requirements 141
observation 145–6
other techniques 150
packages 244–6
questionnaires 146–50
usability requirements
141–2
use cases 154–63

user involvement 150–2
user requirements 138–42
requirements changes,
information systems 50–1
requirements drift
information systems 55
productivity problems 69
quality problems 67–8
requirements list, Agate Ltd
169–70
requirements model
activities 178–9
actors 171–6
Agate Ltd 169–79
case study 169–79
case study work/exercises/
projects 257–8
composition 242–4
generalization 236, 237–42
glossary of terms 176–7
initial architecture 177
multiple inheritance 242
refining 233–58
requirements list 169–70
reusable software 234–7,
246–52
software development
patterns 252–6
use cases 171–6
requirements summary,
Agate Ltd 6–7
responding
installation & operation
problems 68
productivity problems
69–70
quality problems 66–8
responsibility assignment
matrix (RAM), user
involvement 83
reusable software 584–609
achieving 235–6
AFE 594
airline seat booking system
249–52
ASE 594
case study example 597–605
case study work/exercises/
projects 608
choice of project 586–7
component standards
590–2
components 246–52

reusable software (*continued*)
componentware,
commercially available
595–7
CSE 594
development environments
590–2
generalization 236
Jacobson's six stages 586–8
languages 590–2
object-orientation
contributions 236–7
object-orientation origins
108–9
organizational structure
587–8
reasons for 234, 585–92
requirements model 234–7,
246–52
RSEB 586–8, 593–5
SELECT Perspective 592–3
software and specification
234–7
strategy 592–5
unit of reuse 588–90
web services 605–7
Reuse-driven Software
Engineering Business
(RSEB), reusable
software 586–8, 593–5
review
evaluation report 578–9
implementation 577–9
process 578–9
robustness analysis, analysis
class diagram 197–8
RSEB (Reuse-driven Software
Engineering Business),
reusable software 586–8,
593–5
rules, Scrum 625
-time support, software
ols 561

ased approaches,
terface design 461–3
irements analysis

see requirements

rules 625
software development
processes 624–5
timeboxing 624–5
security, database
management systems 513
SELECT Perspective,
reusable software 592–3
sequence diagrams see
interaction sequence
diagrams
sequential file organization
506
serial file organization 505
Service-Oriented
Architecture (SOA) 370
Singleton pattern, design
patterns 427–31
smoke example
capta 34
data 34
information 34
knowledge 34
SOA (Service-Oriented
Architecture) 370
soft v. hard methodologies
629–31
software construction,
software development
tools 86–7
software development
patterns
analysis patterns 254–6
catalogues 423
defining 252–4
describing 253–4
design patterns 423–4
frameworks 423
languages 423
non-functional
requirements 424
origins 252–3
requirements model
252–6
software development
principles 423–4
software development
processes 610–33
abstraction 611
case study work/exercises/
projects 632
DSDM 618–23
method 611–14

methodology 611–14,
627–9
process 611–14
Scrum 624–5
USDP 77–9, 128–35,
614–18
XP 625–7
software development tools
83–7
see also software tools
benefits 87
CASE tools 83–4, 161–2, 560
difficulties 87
model and technique
support 84–6
software construction 86–7
software implementation
560–3
software implementation
560–4
see also implementation
coding standards 563–4
documentation standards
563–4
software tools 560–3
standards 563–4
Software Process Engineering
Metamodel (SPEM),
methodology 612–13
software reuse see reusable
software
software testing
implementation 569–73
items tested 570–2
people responsible 569–70
test documentation 572–3
XP 569
software tools
see also software
development tools
application containers 562
class browsers 562
compilers 561
component managers 562
configuration management
561
conversion tools 562–3
database management
systems 562
debuggers 561
documentation generators
563
installation tools 562

integrated development environment 561
interpreters 561
run-time support 561
testing tools 562
visual editors 561
specialization, basic concepts 96–101
specialization cohesion, class 408–9
SPEM *see* Software Process Engineering Metamodel
spiral model, incremental development 76–7
stakeholders, ethical dimension 57–8
standards
  coding standards 563–4
  component standards, reusable software 590–2
  documentation standards 563–4
  HCI 464–6
  software implementation 563–4
  system design 389–90
state machines 314–34
  see also control
  Agate Ltd 340–1, 555–6
  behavioural approach 329–30
  behavioural state machines 333–4
  boundary classes 489–97
  case study 340–1
  case study work/exercises/ projects 336
  choice pseudostate 326
  composite states 321–3
  concurrent states 323–4
  control 328–33
  entry pseudostate 324–5
  exit pseudostate 324–5
  history pseudostates 326–8
  interface modelling 489–97
  junction pseudostate 325–6
  lifecycle approach 330–3
  notation 316–28, 636
  preparing 328–33
  protocol state machines 333–4
  specialization 328
state, object *see* object state

State pattern, design patterns 436–41
static structure diagrams, notation 634–6
storage mechanisms, persistence 502
storage tuning, database management systems 513
strategies
  business strategy 39–41
  implementation 575–7
  reusable software 592–5
strategies for success 38–41
  business strategy 38
  information systems contribution 38–9
  IT strategies 39–41
  SWOT analysis 38
  Value Chain Analysis (VCA) 38–9
Strategy pattern, user interface 489
structural patterns, design patterns 431–6
structured approaches, user interface design 457–60
Structured English, algorithmic approaches 300–3
style guides, user interface 455
subsystems
  Agate Ltd 29
  architecture 373–4
  systems thinking 26
success, strategies for 38–41
swimlanes, activity diagrams 127–8
SWOT analysis, strategies for success 38
synchronous message, interaction sequence diagrams 265–71
system architecture/design, development process 133–4
system design 352–4
  see also architecture; design; detailed design
  case study work/exercises/ projects 394
  construction guidelines 390
  database design 389–90
  standards 389–90

user interface design standards 390
systems 22–33
  see also information systems
  systems thinking 22–6
systems analysts, roles 1–2
systems designers, roles 2
systems thinking
  boundary 23, 27–8
  control 25, 28–31
  emergent properties 26, 32
  environment 22–3, 27–8
  feed-forward 25–6
  feedback 25–6, 28–31
  hierarchy 27–8
  inputs/outputs 23, 28–31
  interfaces 24
  reductionism 32
  subsystems 26
  transformation 24–5
  usefulness 26–32

tables
  mapping classes to 522–4
  relational database management systems 522–4
tagged data record structure 505
taxonomic relationships, basic concepts 96–8
technical reference architectures 372
templates, design patterns 424–5
temporary files 509
testing
  development process 135
  software testing 569–73
  use cases 163
testing tools, software tools 562
Three-schema Architecture, database management systems 512, 513–14
timeboxing
  DSDM 622
  Scrum 624–5
timing diagrams
  notation 640
  object interaction 286–8
tools, software development *see* software development tools

trade-offs, design 359–60
training, user 575
transaction files 509
transaction management,
      database management
      systems 512–13
transactions, object database
      management systems 527
transformation, systems
      thinking 24–5
transitive operation, basic
      concepts 100
transparent activation, object
      database management
      systems 527
transparent persistence,
      object database
      management systems 527
tuning of storage, database
      management systems 513

Unified Software
      Development Process
      (USDP) 128–35, 614–18
see also development
      process; software
      development processes
activities 616–17
artefacts 617
iterations 614–16
methodological approaches
      77–9
phases 614–16
philosophy 614
principles 614
summary 618
waterfall lifecycle 129–31
workers 616–17
workflows 614–16
unit of reuse, reusable
      software 588–90
usability, achieving, user
      interface design 464
bility requirements,
      uirements capture
      ?
            ified Software
            t Process
            dels/

            , 230–5

communication diagram
      196–7
dependency 195–6
requirements analysis
      194–7
use cases
      Agate Ltd 171–6, 546
      business modelling 162–3
      CASE tools 161–2
      example 155
      notation 155–9, 634
      prototyping 159–61
      purpose 154–5
      requirements capture
            154–63
      sample, Agate Ltd 546
      supporting 159–62
      testing 163
user documentation,
      implementation 574
user interface
      see also human-computer
            interaction (HCI)
      characteristics of good
            design 451–5
      class design 475–9
      Composite pattern 488–9
      consistency 452
      design patterns 488–9
      dialogue boxes 451–5
      dialogue metaphor 447–9
      direct manipulation
            metaphor 449–51
      feedback 453–4
      guidelines 451–5
      HCI 447–55
      message types 447–8
      minimal user input 454–5
      Observer pattern 488
      prototyping, boundary
            classes 471–5
      Strategy pattern 489
      style guides 455
      user support 453
user interface design
      approaches 456–64
      development process
            134–5
      ethnographic approaches
            460–1
      formal approaches
            456–63

informal approaches
      456–63
patterns, boundary classes
      488–9
scenario-based approaches
      461–3
standards 390
structured approaches
      457–60
usability, achieving 464
user involvement 82–3
      requirements capture
            150–2
user manuals 574
user requirements,
      requirements capture
      138–42
user support, user interface
      453
user training, implementation
      575
user…
      see also human-computer
            interaction (HCI)
user's perspective,
      information systems 45–7

Value Chain Analysis (VCA),
      strategies for success
      38–9
vapourware 45
variable length record
      structure 505
VCA (Value Chain Analysis),
      strategies for success
      38–9
visibility
      attributes 401–3
      encapsulation 401–3
visual editors, software tools
      561

waterfall lifecycle
      development process
            129–31
      project lifecycles 71–3
      USDP 129–31
web services, reusable
      software 605–7
work files 509

XP see eXtreme Programming